Confronting the Color Line

ALAN B. ANDERSON

GEORGE W. PICKERING

Confronting the Color Line

THE BROKEN PROMISE OF

THE CIVIL RIGHTS MOVEMENT

IN CHICAGO

THE UNIVERSITY OF GEORGIA PRESS

ATHENS AND LONDON

© 1986 by the University of Georgia Press
Athens, Georgia 30602

Designed by Sandra Strother Hudson
Set in Mergenthaler 10 on 12 Times Roman
by the Composing Room of Michigan
Printed and bound by Braun-Brumfield
The paper in this book meets the guidelines for
permanence and durability of the Committee on
Production Guidelines for Book Longevity of the
Council on Library Resources.

Printed in the United States of America

90 89 88 87 86   5 4 3 2 1

Library of Congress Cataloging in Publication Data

Anderson, Alan B., 1934–
    Confronting the color line.

    Bibliography: p.
    Includes index.
    1. Afro-Americans—Civil rights—Illinois—Chicago.
2. Chicago (Ill.)—Race relations.   3. Afro-Americans—
Civil rights.   I. Pickering, George W.   II. Title.
F548.9.N4A53 1986   305.8'96073'077311   86-4276
ISBN 0-8203-0842-0 (alk. paper)
ISBN 0-8203-0843-9 (pbk.: alk. paper)

The photograph by John Tweedle is from his *A Lasting
Impression: A Collection of Photographs of Martin Luther
King, Jr.,* edited by Hermene D. Hartman (Columbia:
University of South Carolina Press, 1984). Reproduced with
permission from the University of South Carolina Press.

The photographs from the *Chicago Sun-Times* and the
Chicago Daily News are © 1986 by News Group Chicago,
Inc., and are reproduced with permission from the Chicago
Sun-Times. The photographs were printed by Jim Mescall,
Joe Erhardt, and Vaughn Patterson.

To the delegates of CCCO
and the supporters of the
Chicago Freedom Movement,
whose vision of an open city
is still our best hope.

Contents

Acknowledgments

We gratefully acknowledge the assistance we received from Frank Steiner, Janet Dunton, Janice Millhouser, Laura Colston-Brooks, and Sonya Little who typed the manuscript for this book; from Gwyneth B. Davis, Alan Lewis, and Deana Sears who read the proofs and checked the footnotes; from Michael Soll of the *Chicago Sun-Times,* Marjorie Adkins of the *Chicago Defender,* and John Curry of Data Search who located and reproduced the photographs; from Malcolm Call, Trudie Calvert, Debbie Winter, Sandra Strother Hudson, and other members of the superb staff of the University of Georgia Press who helped us in countless ways; and from our colleagues in the Social Ethics Seminar with whom we discussed and developed the ideas presented here.

Maps

Abbreviations

ACT	Full name; not an acronym
AFL	American Federation of Labor
AFSC	American Friends Service Committee
AFSCME	American Federation of State, County and Municipal Employees
AMPC	Altgeld-Murray Parents Council
CAPCC	Chatham-Avalon Park Community Council
CCCO	Coordinating Council of Community Organizations
CCHR	Chicago Commission on Human Relations
CCRR	Chicago Conference on Religion and Race
CED	Committee to End Discrimination in Chicago Medical Institutions
CFM	Chicago Freedom Movement
CHA	Chicago Housing Authority
CHC	Citizens Housing Committee
CIC	Catholic Interracial Council
CIO	Congress of Industrial Organizations
CORE	Congress of Racial Equality
CREB	Chicago Real Estate Board
CUL	Chicago Urban League
DUR	Department of Urban Renewal (Chicago)
ESCRU	Episcopal Society for Cultural and Racial Unity
FOR	United Citizens Committee for Freedom of Residence in Illinois
HEW	Department of Health, Education, and Welfare (U.S.)
HUD	Department of Housing and Urban Development (U.S.)
IVI	Independent Voters of Illinois
IUD	Industrial Union Department of the AFL-CIO
KOCO	Kenwood-Oakland Community Organization
NAACP	National Association for the Advancement of Colored People
NALC	Negro American Labor Council
NAREB	National Association of Real Estate Boards
NEA	National Education Association
SDS	Students for a Democratic Society
SCLC	Southern Christian Leadership Conference
SNCC	Student Nonviolent Coordinating Committee

TAC	Tenants Action Council
TFIS	Teachers for Integrated Schools
TWO	The Woodlawn Organization
UAW	United Auto Workers
UPHW	United Packinghouse, Food, and Allied Workers (District 1)
UTC	Urban Training Center for Christian Mission
WCCIA	West Chatham Community Improvement Association
WSCP	West Side Christian Parish
WSF	West Side Federation
WSO	West Side Organization

Introduction

The civil rights movement of the 1950s and 1960s was a remarkable phenomenon in American life in that all across the country black citizens and their white allies came together to produce a tidal wave of protest against racial segregation and discrimination. The marches, boycotts, and sit-ins these people conducted gave new visibility to the American color line, and their protests eventually succeeded in eliminating Jim Crow laws and practices.

The story of the civil rights movement is, in part, a national one, which is well documented in studies of such organizations as the National Association for the Advancement of Colored People (NAACP), the Urban League, the Congress of Racial Equality (CORE), the Student Nonviolent Coordinating Committee (SNCC), and the Southern Christian Leadership Conference (SCLC), as well as in the writings and biographies of the leaders associated with these organizations—Roy Wilkins, Whitney Young, James Farmer, Martin Luther King, Jr., and others. The history of the civil rights movement includes countless local movements and campaigns addressing local issues. Some of these stories, too, are now part of the record, especially those that took on national significance, as, for example, the events in Montgomery, Greensboro, Birmingham, and Selma.[1]

This book is the first to tell the story of the civil rights movement in Chicago. It is a part of the history of the civil rights movement in America, and it adds much to our understanding of that larger movement. The movement in Chicago was most active from 1957 to 1967, the same years that the national movement was at its peak. The interplay of local and national civil rights activities can be traced from the Supreme Court's *Brown* decision in 1954 through the emergence of black power in 1966 and the increasingly problematic relationship between civil rights and peace issues in 1967.

The civil rights movement in Chicago is also significant because it was as inclusive in its membership as it was persistent over time. No single organization or personality dominated the Chicago movement as sometimes happened elsewhere. Even before its formal organization as the Coordinating Council of

1

Community Organizations (CCCO) in 1961, the Chicago coalition was composed of a variety of groups—local affiliates of established national organizations such as the NAACP and the Urban League, black professional associations, community organizations in black neighborhoods, and the Chicago chapter of CORE, a proponent of direct action. The Chicago affiliate of SNCC and various religious interracial councils joined in 1963, and by 1966 some fifty organizations were official participants. This book examines the interaction in Chicago among the diverse organizational goals and leadership styles that also characterized the civil rights movement nationally, and it does so in relationship to both local and national issues.

Most important, however, to this story and to the light it sheds on the civil rights movement nationally, is the setting in Chicago—a major northern city. At issue in the South were segregated public accommodations (buses, waiting rooms, lunch counters, rest rooms, drinking fountains, and so on), the disfranchisement of blacks, and racially separate schools—all practices established by law and enforced by the police and the courts. This form of the color line was addressed by the *Brown* decision; it was challenged by the freedom rides, the Montgomery bus boycott, the Greensboro sitins, and the Birmingham and Selma campaigns; and it was eliminated by the 1964 Civil Rights Act, the 1965 Voting Rights Act, and the judicial implementation of *Brown*.

In the North, however, the issues were different. Legally mandated segregation and discrimination had been mostly eliminated by midcentury, but the color line continued in the form of segregated and inferior schools and housing for blacks and in black poverty and unemployment. This de facto segregation was not legally mandated, but many of its major causes were legally sanctioned. The civil rights movement in Chicago tried to address these issues of de facto segregation, but failed repeatedly to secure meaningful change. At the same time that the civil rights movement nationally was increasingly victorious over de jure segregation in the South, the Chicago movement was increasingly frustrated in its attack on de facto segregation in that city.

In 1966 the national and local stories came together. When their campaigns in Birmingham and Selma led to the 1964 Civil Rights Act and the 1965 Voting Rights Act, Martin Luther King and his Southern Christian Leadership Conference turned to issues of de facto segregation in the North. They chose Chicago as their point of entry, and the SCLC joined with CCCO to form the Chicago Freedom Movement. The stakes were high, for King was pitting his international prestige against the well-entrenched political machine of Mayor Richard J. Daley. Throughout the summer of 1966, national attention focused on Chicago, the scene of open housing marches, black and white riots, and, finally, the summit meeting between King and the Chicago Freedom Movement, on the one hand, and Mayor Daley and Chicago's civic elite, on the other.

2

These events proved to be the movement's final unsuccessful attempt to secure significant social change in Chicago. The Chicago campaign was the second major failure of King's career, and, unlike the one in Albany, Georgia, in 1961 and 1962, he did not live to redeem it. But most important, King's Chicago campaign turned out to be the national civil rights movement's most dramatic, sustained, and finally unsuccessful encounter with the issues of de facto segregation.

Perhaps these events in Chicago would not be so definitive if the civil rights movement had continued to be the vital presence in American life which it was before 1966. But the movement came apart in the late 1960s, amid white backlash and cries of black power. The civil rights leaders of that generation have not been replaced, the aggressive coalition that sustained concerted efforts has not been renewed, and the civil rights organizations that have not disappeared persist now in only an attenuated form.

Perhaps the story of the civil rights movement in Chicago would have less significance if the issues it addressed were no longer prevalent in American society. But the problems of de facto school segregation, ghetto housing, massive black unemployment, and racially differentiated income levels are still preeminent characteristics of our social order.

Tragic as it may be, therefore, the issues of the civil rights movement in Chicago continue to shape our lives. The metropolitan color line is with us yet, and we have been no more successful than the movement in Chicago was in overcoming the distortion it inflicts on the body politic. The movement that addressed those issues is gone, and American public life, once infused with debatable purpose and vitality by its presence, is diminished by its absence.

The story of that movement can illuminate our lives. The struggle in Chicago gave new and sometimes detailed visibility to the color line in its metropolitan form, and its story can inform our understanding of racial issues today. Of course, the desirability, viability, and effectiveness of the goals of that movement—school desegregation and open housing—and of its strategies— boycotts and marches—are now questioned. But the principles and tactics of that movement were controversial in their own time, and any thoughtful judgment about their relevance—then or now—will take account of these events in Chicago.

The efforts of the Chicago movement to redefine the issues of de facto segregation and to reshape public perceptions of them are especially important. As we shall see, this movement explored the roles of public agencies in creating and maintaining the color line, and they set out to show that there was no important moral or legal distinction to be made between de facto and de jure segregation. In the eyes of the movement, at least, racial segregation in the North involved much less innocence, much more public complicity and, therefore, much more public responsibility than was generally thought. In this volume we will use the term "de facto segregation" because the Chicago

3

movement used it—and tried to strip it of its innocence. Because neither the Chicago movement nor any other movement succeeded in stripping the term of its innocence, it is still problematic and possibly morally bankrupt today. It is for this reason, among others, that we will propose the color line as a more fundamental concept for analyzing the issues at stake in the metropolitan areas.

Meanwhile, the innocence of de facto issues has continued because the views of the civil rights movement were not the only or even the dominant understandings of race relations in Chicago during that period. What we here call the civic credo, which promised equality in the long run while denying it in the short, and racist realism, which saw no possibility of equality at all, had both emerged with and, in the case of the latter, as part of the metropolitan color line before the appearance of the civil rights movement. Because the civil rights movement was eventually defeated by the civic credo interpretation, and its demise was marked by a resurgence of racist realism, these events provide the occasion to examine the moral claims and empirical accuracy of the two interpretations of the color line. Because both these interpretations and the prospects for racial social change have continued to dominate the public discussion of racial issues, the pursuit of racial justice today must take their measure—and perhaps nowhere is better than in the encounter with both by the civil rights movement in Chicago.

Fortunately, it has been possible to reconstruct the Chicago story in unusually rich detail. In addition to the usual newspaper records, organizational files, interviews with key informants, a survey of the background and opinions of CCCO delegates, and observations based on our own participation, this narrative is based on three remarkable documents. The first is the minutes of the CCCO, which, during the crucial years, were taken by Father William E. Hogan in his official capacity as CCCO recorder. These minutes record in lively detail the debate among CCCO delegates as they met regularly and at length, sometimes weekly or even daily, to analyze civil rights issues and to plan their next steps.[2]

The records of the summit meetings between civil rights and civic leaders in August 1966 are similarly detailed. John McKnight, a participant in those meetings as director of the Midwest Office of the U.S. Civil Rights Commission, shared Father Hogan's sense of drama and ear for dialogue. McKnight's account, which he transcribed from his notes shortly after the summit conference, reveals the characters of King, Daley, and other major participants even as it records the twisting path of their negotiations.

The records of the Agenda Committee, which served as the decision center of the Chicago Freedom Movement and became the primary locus of decision making and reflection during 1966 and 1967, are also extremely valuable. These minutes were kept by Alvin Pitcher, a key staff person of the Chicago

Freedom Movement, for his own use in a barely decipherable phonetic short-hand, and they vary from annotated meeting agendas to the most extensive contemporaneous records we have of reflections by civil rights leaders on the stalemate in Chicago and in the nation.

Because of the unusual quality of these sources, this narrative is based primarily on them—rather than on what the actors were able to recall in later interviews. Because these documents preserve what was said and done at that time, we have been able to cast the story of the civil rights movement as a dialogue in search of effective forms of action against de facto segregation. In this dialogue, the actors' speeches cross, join, and build in dramatic form as CCCO delegates sought some way to pierce the veil of innocence and euphe-mism drawn around Chicago's public schools, as King came together with Chicago civil rights leaders to create a civic crisis that would bring Mayor Daley to the bargaining table, and as movement leaders probed the meaning of their failure to secure change.

This narrative is based secondarily on reports and editorials from the five Chicago daily newspapers—one of which, the *Chicago Defender,* was black.[3] Although these sources frequently lack an adequate interpretive con-text, when correlated with our other sources they help provide an objective chronology of events. More important, these newspaper reports and editorials document what the contemporaneous general public might have known about civil rights aims and activities and how key members of the public—editorial writers, public officials, and group representatives—interpreted them. One of the purposes of this book is to examine and evaluate these public interpreta-tions as we examine and evaluate the perspectives of civil rights leaders.

Such evaluation is not our only purpose. Our initial goal is to tell the story of the civil rights movement in Chicago from within, largely on its own terms or at least from a point of view formed from within it. In this endeavor we stand apart from both the scholarly and popular critics who conclude from the failure of the civil rights movement in the North that its aims and activities were not important.

Of course, we now know that civil rights actions in the North were not finally effective. The color line remains a preeminent fact in our social order. The Chicago story, at best, tells of the discovery of that reality, which we shall try to measure in our concluding chapters. In our narrative chapters we focus on the dilemmas encountered by the actors. From this perspective, forms of action are still being discussed and even being invented, choices are in the process of being made, and the consequences and outcomes of these choices are uncertain.

We believe that this perspective is crucial. If, as we shall argue, the color line today involves the same issues faced by the civil rights movement in Chicago, and if, as a result, the dilemmas of action that we face in our present

5

efforts to deal with that color line are continuous with theirs, then the better we understand the issues and dilemmas of that time, the better we can understand our own.

Of course, current efforts to end the continuing rule of the color line may prove no more successful than those of the civil rights movement in Chicago. If so, we should find some way of discerning the significance of that movement, of affirming its worth in the face of its failure, lest the pages of our lives, like those of the civil rights movement in Chicago, be lost from the book of human memory. Such is the result of those who equate historical significance with historical success—a "might makes right" view if ever there was one. But theirs is not the only perspective, and it certainly is not ours.

What we find in this story of the civil rights movement in Chicago is something of the haunting greatness that from time to time ennobles human speech and deed. This quality is usually linked with achievement only in the narrow sense—with the winning speech or the accomplished aim. But just as persuasive speech may lack substance and successful results may be trivial, so, too, greatness of aim, nobility in purpose, and grandeur of spirit may be found in enterprises that are, for the moment or even finally, futile. We do not believe the story told here is finally futile, though it may well be—that, too, remains to be seen. We are sure that it is a story which illumines our own dark times. Thus our focus in the narrative chapters is on the story itself, told for its own sake and for its inherent value as a record of significant human endeavor.[4]

Beyond this intrinsic significance, however, this story of the civil rights movement in Chicago traces the developing dilemmas of action for racial justice, which in the end were crucial to the demise of that movement in Chicago and in the nation. These dilemmas did not arise for the first time in the civil rights movement of the 1960s, however, nor did they end with the demise of that movement. Indeed, it is a thesis of this book that they have persistently characterized the search for racial justice in a democratic society. Hence we call them the dilemmas of democratic social change.

To trace the transformation of these dilemmas in the civil rights movement, we will examine their emergence with the formulation of new perspectives on the color line by W. E. B. DuBois, Gunnar Myrdal, and the Warren Court. In the face of a prevailing racist realism that denied the possibility of racial equality, each of these perspectives sought to advance the prospects of meaningful change in American race relations by altering public assumptions about what was actual, what was possible, and what was desirable to do about the issues of race—that is, each addressed and recast the problematic relationship among facts, values, and race in American life.

6

FACTS, VALUES, AND RACE IN AMERICAN LIFE:
BEFORE, DURING, AND SINCE THE CIVIL RIGHTS MOVEMENT

When the United States of America came into being as a liberal democracy which nonetheless allowed the continued existence of black slavery, it entered history as a "house divided against itself." Liberal democracy is a promise of equality of civil and political rights to each and every citizen, regardless of any other consideration. Slavery and liberal democracy stood in complete moral opposition to each other; and although pathetic ingenuity was expended in the attempt to deny or smooth over that moral opposition, in the end a tragic civil war was required to abolish slavery.

The abolition of slavery, however, did not lead to equality of civil and political rights for blacks. The continuing subjection of blacks to considerations other than their rights and merits has created one of the deepest dilemmas of liberal democracy: if its promise is not for everyone, is it a good promise or is it an ideological mask for the accidental privileges and interests of class and color?

The adaptive persistence of a discriminatory color line in the American social order in spite of sweeping social changes in almost every other aspect of the national life has served only to deepen the question about the real promise of liberal democracy. There have, of course, always been those who, like Alexis de Tocqueville, did not share liberal democratic hopes and therefore had little difficulty in concluding that, however unfortunate it might be, the liberal democratic promise of equality stops at the color line.[5] Certainly the "facts" of our history have generally been in support of such persuasions. We shall, in the pages that follow, refer to this orientation as racist realism. The basic strategy of this persuasion is to reduce to a "fact" what is actually a wide-ranging moral problem. It is an assertion that whites just do not like blacks and there is nothing to be done about it.

This mixture of fact and value is everywhere in the historic discussions of race in American life. There is no separating them. Even the most rigorously descriptive accounts of what is at issue bear, at least implicitly, prescriptive implications about what can or should be done. This is to be expected if race poses genuinely moral problems. In the analysis of moral problems, therefore, the analytical task is not to separate the facts from the values. The first task is to identify the characteristic configurations of fact and value that keep recurring in the discussion.

In matters of race, these configurations crystallize around the shifting status of equality. We have already identified one such configuration—racist realism—which claims that equality stops at the color line because the antipathies of whites are too great to overcome. The implicit advice to blacks is that they

7

change themselves so that they are acceptable to whites or at least so that whites are not so antagonized by them. The implicit advice to whites, if they are so inclined, is to support efforts by blacks to change themselves. Futility and cynicism merge in racist realism and claim to justify each other.

A counterpersuasion to this racist realism was developed by W. E. B. Du-Bois in his 1903 book, *The Souls of Black Folk*. This persuasion held that blacks had to assert their equality even and especially in the face of its denial because the indignities of the color line were too great to suffer in silence and apparent acquiescence.[6] In the pages that follow we shall refer to this orientation as the "democratic dilemma of black dignity." The implicit advice to whites is to stop obstructing the legitimate claims of blacks to civil and political equality. The dilemma was that the very act of asserting this equality as human beings set blacks apart as citizens with a "special interest."

By 1944, yet another orientation had crystallized in the work of Gunnar Myrdal. *An American Dilemma: The Negro Problem and Modern Democracy* was the most comprehensive and one of the most important studies of race in America ever to appear.[7] Myrdal's analysis claimed to show that equality was not only possible but likely to develop across the color line because the value conflicts within the white conscience were too severe to be denied or to remain unresolved. "Though our study includes economic, social, and political race relations," he said, "at bottom our problem is the moral dilemma of the American—the conflict between his moral valuations on various levels of consciousness and generality." In Myrdal's view, the American creed of liberal democracy was so deeply embedded not only in American institutions but in the sentiments and convictions of individuals that the "Negro problem" had come to focus "in the heart of the American." The conflict between the American creed, on the one hand, and the petty jealousies, prejudices, and local interests directed against blacks, on the other, constituted Myrdal's "American dilemma." Viewed in this light, racial inequality was simply "a century-long lag of public morals," a lag he believed would be resolved in favor of the American creed. In the pages that follow, we shall refer to this as the "democratic dilemma of white culture." The implicit advice to whites was to trust their "better angels"; that to blacks was to trust liberal democracy as the best hope for interracial justice. The democratic dilemma of white culture lay in committing the good name of liberal democracy to the "better angels" of the whites. What if they did not prevail?

In 1954, the U.S. Supreme Court in *Brown* v. *Board of Education* ruled that equal protection of the laws required abolition of publicly enforced segregation in the schools of the South.[8] It held that the use of the law to enforce discrimination was contrary to the purpose of the law under our Constitution. Because the law had been used to enforce discrimination in public institutions under a system that had come to be called "Jim Crow," the Court began in

Brown to formulate a position which in the pages that follow we shall call the "democratic dilemma of constitutional duties." The advice stemming from this orientation was explicit in certain respects: public bodies from the local to the national levels could not use their legitimate powers to enforce racial discrimination and, when it could be shown that they had done so, they would be required to desegregate those institutions as a first step in remedial action. It was not clear what the next step would be, or even if there would be one. The focus was on the offense against the principle of equal protection of the laws. The facts gained relevance in relation to that principle. It was the first seriously formulated position whose implication was that racial equality required authoritative institutional desegregation. The dilemma emerged as it became increasingly clear that the effort to remedy discriminations based on race might require affirmative duties also based on racial considerations. As a result, the more efforts to remedy race discriminations were pursued, the more they gave rise to charges of "reverse discrimination." That is the democratic dilemma of constitutional duties.

These three dilemma views shared a perception of the American creed as a source of moral criticism when set against the prevailing race relations. There was, however, another view, the civic credo, which articulated a much more conservative understanding of the American creed. This civic credo, which was the established perspective among the civic elite in Chicago by midcentury, recognized that race relations were a problem, but because the American creed was already embodied in existing institutions, time and the normal functioning of those institutions would fulfill the promise of equality in the long run. Blacks were simply one more ethnic group, and democracy would work to bring them into the system just as it had brought opportunity to others. The advice stemming from this orientation was explicit: leave the basic institutions alone and let them do their work in an atmosphere of civic calm. The focus was on the dangers to progress posed by both black and white "irrational attitudes," which caused civic crises; but these were viewed as temporary aberrations to be dealt with by persuasion if possible, by the police if necessary. Because in principle the system was already open to all, the competition of individuals and interest groups would take care of the rest.

In actual practice this civic credo gave rise less to a dilemma than to a contradiction. Because it sought to protect the future by defending existing institutions, it ended up sacrificing future progress—which was its basic promise—to a defense of the structural status quo—which was its basic premise. Because it sought to secure progress in the future by denying the seriousness of conflict in the present, it guaranteed that the seriousness of the conflict would be carried into the future. In believing that the conflict was temporary, this civic credo traded off future progress toward civic peace and racial justice for a superficial and manipulated civic calm in the present.

9

In each case—Tocqueville's racist realism, DuBois's democratic dilemma of black dignity, Myrdal's democratic dilemma of white culture, the Supreme Court's democratic dilemma of constitutional duties, and Chicago's civic credo—we are interested not just in the abstract configuration of facts and values which each one presents but in the actions and interpretations to which each one tends to lead. That is, we are interested in them as moral ideas, as basic indications of what is and what is not at issue along the color line.

Moral ideas are not necessarily "good" ideas. How good they are requires rigorous moral analysis; but it is the function of moral ideas to establish and justify some "facts" as given and possibly even intractable, while exposing other "facts" as unjustifiable and requiring change. This relationship between facts and justifications in moral ideas serves to determine what actions are possible, rational, or requisite and what actions are impossible, irrational, or irrelevant. Morally speaking, therefore, justifications as much as facts are at the heart of the matter. Nowhere is this more clear than in the moral ideas about race in America, where the line between racism and realism has always been difficult to locate and to defend.

There have been only two times when even the wise dared to hope that Americans could summon their resources to expunge race as an issue from their common life. The first was during the Reconstruction period, 1865 to 1877. The second was during that moment known as the civil rights movement, 1954 to 1966. Both were marked by abolitionist success and marred by reconstructive failure. Reconstruction succeeded in abolishing slavery but failed to empower the freedmen with the full range of institutional capacities necessary for democratic citizenship. The civil rights movement succeeded in abolishing the Jim Crow system of legislated inequality but failed to achieve a desegregated society. In each case, an initial success in eliminating a major source of institutional inequality was undercut by an inability to carry the moral commitment to democratic equality constructively into the complexities of social, political, and economic policy. In each case, the reconstructive failure was an occasion for the resurgence of racist realism.

The Chicago civil rights movement was united in its opposition to racist realism and to discriminatory institutional practices. It was a coalition of individuals and groups who represented a coalescence of the three orientations we have called the democratic dilemma of black dignity, the democratic dilemma of white culture, and the democratic dilemma of constitutional duties. In this story, one would be hard-pressed to find a "pure type" of any of these persuasions. The civil rights movement was an emotionally charged experiment in the practical implications and creative extensions of these moral ideas, and, for most of the civil rights period, these ideas were understood to be differences in emphasis rather than in principle. An understanding of their diverse origins will shed some light on their divergent destinies when, after

1966, the coalition that had held them together under the discipline of common action began to come apart under the impact of a resurgent racist realism.

We shall tell this story from the perspective of yet another orientation, one that was formed in the midst of and as a result of the civil rights movement. Whereas the other perspectives are all addressed to the "Negro problem" and what is today called the "black problem," we identify the problem as the color line itself. We believe that the color line is the institution in American life which is at issue. Like the slavery from which it is descended by all the contingencies of institutional procreation, the metropolitan color line stands in complete moral opposition to liberal democracy, despite continued efforts to deny or smooth over that moral opposition.

The civil rights movement was driven by a heightened awareness of that moral opposition and a determination to press the confrontation between the forces of discrimination and segregation, on the one hand, and the potential of liberal democracy to mobilize and focus force for social change, on the other hand. United by a sense of moral opposition, the civil rights leaders developed and thereby transformed the dilemmas of democratic social change in relationship to the events and issues of their time. Here we can state these dilemmas in only a general way. In later chapters, we shall explore the specific forms they took, their interaction with one another, and their consequences, both for the movement and for the society at large.

Perhaps the democratic dilemma of black dignity became the most obvious of the three. The basic strategy of the civil rights movement was to mobilize a minority of the community to press for change, but to succeed required broad majority support or at least consent. As long as the regional issue of Jim Crow was the focus of concern, this was not a debilitating dilemma. When a national majority developed in opposition to the flagrant but regional practices of Jim Crow, and focus shifted, as it did in Chicago, to specifically metropolitan problems, this dilemma became much more politically debilitating and, perhaps, politically decisive.

During the civil rights movement, the democratic dilemma of white culture arose because, although groups and individuals might be unified in their moral opposition to imposed segregation and discrimination, that did not guarantee agreement about how best to secure equality—whether it should be pursued through an institutional integration that stressed the unifying themes of the national culture or through an institutional mobilization of black power that stressed the dignity and distinctive culture of blacks. It was on the horns of this dilemma that the civil rights movement finally lost its inner coherence.

The final dilemma of democratic social change—the dilemma of constitutional duties—arose because, although liberals were committed to individual persuasion, positive incentives, and nonviolence as the best means for achieving democratic social change, the color line is inherently coercive, collec-

11

tively harmful, and perpetually seething with violence. Thus there arose the dilemma of adapting individualistic sensibilities to institutional realities in the quest for effectiveness. Was the issue basically a police problem or a policy problem? Should the emphasis be on stopping harmful behaviors, on rectifying the damage they had already done, or on developing new redistributive initiatives? Were negative duties or affirmative actions the priority? These remained unresolved questions to the very end, and they were sources of considerable misunderstanding, both in the dialogue internal to the civil rights movement and in its communications with institutional actors beyond the movement.

The chapters in Part I of this book provide the historical, institutional, and intellectual background out of which the dilemmas of democratic social change emerged and against which they were defined. Part II is a narrative account of the making and the consequences of these dilemmas of democratic social change. Part III is an assessment of the weaknesses and a critical appraisal of the constructive possibilities of democratic social change in light of these dilemmas.

The story of the civil rights movement in Chicago could, of course, be told from other perspectives—for example, as an illustration of the problems institutions encounter in their efforts to accommodate group protest, as evidence of strains within the American societal community, or as a demonstration of the irrelevance of reform to the structural problems of late industrial capitalism.[9] Our focus on the dilemmas of democracy that arose in the course of opposition to the color line makes moral ideas, issues, and principles central. From our perspective, it was and remains a moral issue.

A PRAGMATIC THEORY OF MORAL ISSUES

In this study, the interaction of moral ideas, public events, and institutional structures is taken with utter seriousness. This study crosses the boundaries that are usually observed between the disciplines of ethics, history, and the behavioral sciences. "Ethics" usually is limited to the rational criticism of moral ideas abstracted from whatever roles they may play in actual events. "History" is usually limited to an account of events in which the substance of the ideas at stake in them is neglected in favor of an examination of the genealogy and function of the ideas involved in them. The behavioral sciences are usually limited to treating ideas as, at best, dependent variables in a matrix of structural "causes." Although we do not hold that ideas cause everything (obviously a bad idea), we do intend to carry the substantive analysis of ideas into the analysis of the events and structures in which they are implicated. That is one way to find out what ideas "mean." This is what is meant by the "pragmatic theory of meaning."[10]

Ideas become enmeshed in history and politics quite as much as anything else human. It is difficult, maybe impossible, to say how, in the main, the history and politics of ideas intersect with general history, but it is possible to catch moments of intersection and interaction. That is what we have tried to do in this study of the civil rights movement in Chicago. That movement was nothing without ideas. It was driven by ideas of racial justice; it was opposed by ideas of racial harmony; and it was defeated by encounters with issues that exceeded the reach of its ideas. If we do not take seriously the moral ideas of the civil rights movement, we cannot take that movement seriously except possibly as a case study in emotional excess and irrational behavior in which perhaps prestige was at stake for the actors but not much for the rest of the society, except their disturbed tranquillity.

It is the clash of ideas which provides the drama of this life. William James wrote, "Polarizing and magnetizing us as they do, we turn towards them and from them just as if they were so many concrete beings. And beings they are, beings as real in the realm which they inhabit as the changing things of sense are in the realm of space."[11] In this study we have tried to provide a narrative of ideas, to explain how ideas came together and were put forth, what roles they played in the ensuing events, what changes they underwent in the process, and what they served to show after all was said and done. This is intellectual history in a new key. It is "history" only in the loose sense that it deals with events now past. It is "intellectual" in the sense that it takes seriously the moral ideas put forth by the actors in those events. We treat those events as passages in a dramatic dialogue partly because that is what they were and partly because that is the most revealing perspective on what was at stake in those events.

Long ago Socrates taught that dialogue was a productive form for examining the meaning and adequacy of ideas, and he tried to show that this dialogue could be carried on almost anywhere—in everyday encounters, in all-night parties, in the midst of life, and in the face of death. Fortunately, Plato was often there to record some of those dialogues. Others he heard at second hand. Unfortunately, in writing them, Plato had to abstract those dialogues from "life" and put them in "books." There was no way around that if Socrates was to be remembered. Socrates was not forgotten, but in some ways his point was: dialogue about the meaning and adequacy of ideas can break out anywhere, and something important is at stake whenever it does.

The notion of dialogue, however, is as intimately linked to the presentation of dramas as it is to the examination of ideas. A play is nothing apart from its dialogue. And yet in plays the speech and the action are, for the most part, protagonists. In the end, the dialogue has to yield in some way to the sovereignty of the action—felicitously in the case of comedies, sorrowfully in the case of tragedies, impotently in the case of absurdist theater.

The civil rights movement was a dialogue in both the intellectual and the

13

dramatic senses. It was a movement of ideas, of actions, and of men and women who discussed their ideas and deliberated about their actions both in prospect and in retrospect. It was a movement that, by virtue of the problems it addressed and the actions it undertook, was under constant pressure to state its ideas clearly.

Clarity of ideas and intensity of action are not usually found in the same events. It is easy to lose track of ideas as they get absorbed in the passion and the web of interactions; and it is tempting to discount them altogether, especially in those events where they are decisively subjected to the sovereignty of action. For these reasons, it is sometimes said that the true meaning of ideas can be preserved only by protecting them from the impurities and ambiguities and compromises of action.

But action is the human *metier;* and if the meaning of ideas has anything to do with their humanity, then their possible and actual roles in events, in actions, in the fabric of interactions, in social institutions, and in personal habits are crucial to their meaning. Ideas may finally be subjected to the sovereignty of action in the course of actual events; but they give those events their qualitative character, their specifically human character. They cry out from the confusion of happenings: someone was here; this was a human event, not a falling rock or an explosion of gas.

It is a further peculiarity of ideas that neither victory nor defeat in the course of action is the final word on their value. Sometimes even in victory, ideas are found wanting in their adequacy and humanity; and sometimes even in defeat their transcendent value shines forth as a judgment on the events in which they were lost, and they retain their possibilities for another day. Ideas have to "work"; but that is not all they have to do.

This is especially the case with moral ideas, that is, ideas having to do with our well-being as individuals and as communities, ideas evaluative of how we treat ourselves and each other. These are ideas whose only purpose is to guide and evaluate action. Moral ideas are expressions of what is at stake for our humanity in the actions we undertake and in the situation in which we undertake them. Because of this character, moral ideas always involve two parts: a perception of what is at issue in some situation and the projection of a principle that would resolve the issue—that is, moral ideas are complex propositions in which both descriptive and normative elements are seeking the unity of action.

It is this peculiar, unavoidable, and potentially deliberate mixture of descriptive and normative elements which makes moral ideas both the most abstract and finally the most concrete of the constituents of action. For better or worse, it is this mixture of elements which stamps action as irreducibly and definitively human. Fragile, vulnerable, and incomplete as they may be, moral ideas assert themselves as claims to importance, as vehicles to a better life, indeed as instruments of life itself, as reasons for living.

In this last respect at least, moral ideas have an affinity and sometimes an antagonism with religious ideas. Whereas moral ideas look to some goodness that depends on human effort for its reality, religious ideas look to some wider goodness on which human effort depends for its reality and relative importance. The chasm between the two is utterly deep, but its width can vary enormously. They are "worlds" apart. The one is centered on matters that are thought to lie within our power, the other on matters that lie beyond our powers even though they may involve our ultimate well-being. But each of these worlds has its reality in the world of experience; and they have a way of melting around the edges and spilling over into each other, as it were, in the heat of action—where it is always a question how far our creativity might responsibly be extended and at what point we must yield to our constitutional limits and say, beyond this is beyond us, so help us God.

Ideas of justice fall clearly within the realm of moral ideas. They look to a goodness in the very structure of society, which depends on coordinated human effort for its reality. Retributive justice is concerned with the rectification of violations of established goods. Redistributive justice, for the most part, is concerned with controverted claims about goods that should be but are not established. Claims to redistributive justice, therefore, necessarily involve claims of historic or structural injustice as well as proposed principles of rectification. That is perhaps the most characteristic mixture of descriptive and normative elements in moral ideas: descriptive readings of what is wrong combined with prescriptive readings of what it would take to set things right.

It is this combined sense of what is the matter in some particular situation and what it would take to set it right that we call an "issue." Issues are moral ideas framed with reference to their relevance to particular problems. An issue is a proposal of both descriptive and normative reasons for acting in some particular way.

Race has always been an issue in American life; but it has not always been the same issue because widely varying descriptive and normative reasons have been proposed for action in relation to it. It is our intention to present the civil rights movement in Chicago as a narrative dialogue—in both the intellectual and dramatic senses—about the issue of race.[12]

HOW THIS BOOK IS ORGANIZED AND WHY

Part I, "The Making of an Issue," is an attempt to sketch a historical map of the major moral meanings that had been assigned to the issue of race in American life by midcentury. We have limited ourselves to describing the major configurations that in their coalescence and conflict were vital to the rise, development, and defeat of the civil rights movement in Chicago.

In Chapter 1 we describe the racial dilemmas of liberal democracy. We begin with Alexis de Tocqueville, who claimed that liberal democratic equality in America was for whites only because the prejudice and animosity of whites toward blacks was an insurmountable and unchangeable fact—the basic claim of racist realism. In opposition to both the ideas and practices of racist realism, two views were articulated which placed the issue of racial equality in the order of justice rather than of fate. The first was W. E. B. DuBois's democratic dilemma of black dignity, which held that blacks were morally obligated to assert their equality with whites regardless of whether those claims were honored. The second was Gunnar Myrdal's democratic dilemma of white culture, which held that whites would be obligated to yield equality to blacks because their liberal democratic values were too deeply ingrained and too pervasively embodied to be denied. These three orientations defined the national spectrum of ideas by midcentury.

In Chapter 2 we show how the national spectrum of ideas was filtered through local events and adapted to local institutions in Chicago. We do this by tracing the development of the multidimensional color line in Chicago, with special emphasis on the emergence and formulation of the civic credo, the articles of which intoned the high values of democracy to defend existing institutions and deny the moral and institutional seriousness of the color line.

Finally, in Chapter 3 we present the Supreme Court's introduction of the democratic dilemma of constitutional duties and trace its adaptation to local circumstances through the formation of a coalition of community groups focused on the issue of de facto segregation in schools and elsewhere in the city. We show how, by the end of 1962, that issue had fused proponents of the democratic dilemma of black dignity, the democratic dilemma of white culture, and the democratic dilemma of constitutional duties into a united front and had drawn the proponents of the civic credo into a conflict in which neither side could ultimately compromise without becoming morally compromised.

Part II, "The Pursuit of the Issue," is a narrative account of the conflicts that arose between the proponents of the de facto segregation reading of the issue and the defenders of the civic credo. It shows how the dilemmas of democratic social change emerged in those conflicts. The narrative is rooted in the de facto segregation perspective both because of the primary materials on which it is based and the sympathies of the authors. It describes the developments internal to this perspective—the formation of a coalition, the conflicts within that coalition, the ensuing arguments about principle and strategy, the responses of the general public as well as the civic and political elite, and the ways in which these responses provided occasions for reconsideration. Ultimately, it is a story of defeat for this perspective, of triumph for the civic credo, and of the implications of the dilemmas of democratic social change. In these chapters we have tried to preserve and convey the sense of what it was like to pursue this issue from the de facto segregation perspective.

At the same time, we have wanted to provide an analytical framework for assessing the narrative developments. Accordingly, each of the nine chapters in Part II concludes with a brief summary recapitulating the central events in the narrative based on seven questions: (1) How was the issue of the color line understood by the actors during this period? (2) What principles or grounds did the actors appeal to for addressing the issue as they understood it? (3) What strategies were undertaken to oppose, define, clarify, obscure, or defend the color line during this period? (4) What publics, both elite and citizen, were reached by these efforts? (5) What responses were elicited by these efforts? (6) As a result of the events described in this chapter, what were the consequences for the civil rights movement and for the definition of the issue? (7) Finally, what dilemmas of democratic social change emerged or developed in the course of these efforts to pursue the issue of the color line?

Part II concludes with the defeat of the de facto segregation reading of the issue, the political victory of the civic credo, and the full emergence of the dilemmas of democratic social change. In Part III we evaluate these events and their outcomes in terms of the moral ideas that were explicitly at stake in them. Because race was still an issue which liberal democracy had not expunged from the body politic, we call Part III "The Deepening of the Issue." In these chapters we recapitulate the narrative from the perspective of its outcome; we propose a reconstruction of the de facto segregation reading of the issue; we identify some of the normative resources and problems for the further pursuit of the issue of the color line; and, finally, we take our stand on a socially reconstructed version of the democratic faith.

This book is a study in the power of ideas, but it is not an argument for ideological determinism. Groups and individuals act according to their best lights. Sometimes base motives dim those lights; sometimes they are extinguished altogether by the winds of circumstance, by strong drafts from the unconscious, by gale-force fears, or by the vacuum that trails along behind sheer exhaustion. When this happens, the ideas have to bide their time until they make sense again. Many factors are involved in human events besides ideas; but apart from some ideas, bright or dim, examined or implicit, human actions are not undertaken and the urges toward justice make no sense.

This study was begun at a time when, because of the largely democratic and liberal ideas examined here, the drive for racial justice in America made sense to most Americans. Because of the events examined here, however, the drive for racial justice lost its "sensible" status. In view of the problems that remain in our common life, it is important that we find new ideas that not only make sense but also promise democratic social change and go beyond its dilemmas.

PART ONE

The Making of an Issue

CHAPTER ONE

The Racial Dilemmas of
Liberal Democracy

Ever since the first Africans were brought involuntarily to Virginia in 1619 on the ship *Jesus,* race has been a social, political, and economic issue but one that has never been susceptible simply to social, political, or economic resolutions. Pervading the sociology, the politics, the economics, even the psychology of race has been the persistent moral violation of black people as individuals and as a group. That is as much a fact as any statement about the human condition can be; and it is the fact that colors all the other facts about the color line.

The history of attempts to resolve this issue is not one of the glories of American culture. Rather, it is one of repeated moral failures. There is great potential for continuing and increased harm, both to blacks as a group and to the body politic generally, in trying to evade the full dimensions of the moral failures that are entailed in the continuing and adaptive power of the color line as a distributive rule in American life. For long periods of time both our culture and our politics have strained to avoid the morally problematic aspects of this issue, and the present time seems to be one of such avoidance. These periods reveal a chilling deficiency in the heart and mind of the culture.

Coming to terms with the moral claims, aspects, and dimensions of this continuing color line is not a simple matter because the interplay of fact and justification makes them not always what they appear to be. Understanding this interplay is the key to understanding the harmful resilience of the color line because the justifications have always worked to make the facts appear stubborn, and the facts have lent an air of realism and common sense to the justifications.

In this chapter, we shall examine three such configurations of fact and justification: Tocqueville's racist realism, DuBois's democratic dilemma of black dignity, and Myrdal's democratic dilemma of white culture. Although these themes were selected because of the role they played in the Chicago civil rights movement, they also provide exemplary case studies of the role of ideas in the making, bending, and breaking of the color line. In each case, we shall

21

see how the moral ideas involved served to justify or otherwise interpret and valorize the "facts" of the color line.

In important respects, Tocqueville, DuBois, and Myrdal were radically different. Tocqueville's ideas had the effect of justifying racial antagonism, or worse, and therefore served to perpetuate the denial of equality to blacks in America. DuBois found the indignities of the color line morally unacceptable, and therefore his ideas promoted increasing black protest of racial inequalities but without assuming that any immediate changes in the direction of racial equality would be forthcoming. By further contrast, Myrdal thought that basic changes in race relations were not only necessary but possible—and probably inevitable as well.

These three men stood generations if not centuries apart and therefore could be understood merely to have faithfully mirrored their times in their interpretations of the potential for change in the so-called facts of race in America. Indeed, it would be foolish for any analysis of these interpretations to argue entirely otherwise. Of course, facts change; indeed, this book is about the ways they do or do not change. Moral ideas about race, the way they justify or valorize the facts of the color line, is a crucial dimension in just how and why these facts change across generations and centuries. Yet, as we shall see, the patterns of justification tend to be much more durable than the patterns of fact on which they were ostensibly based.

As John Dewey pointed out, "No one is ever forced by just the collection of facts to accept a particular theory of their meaning, so long as one retains intact some other doctrine by which he can marshal them."[1] Thus Tocqueville's racist realism was not forced from the public arena by such fundamental changes in the facts of the color line as either the Civil War and the abolition of slavery or the civil rights movement and the elimination of the Jim Crow system. Indeed, each such abolitionist success quickly led to a resurgence of racist realism, which, even allowing for all the differences in time and circumstances that the generations and centuries required, was more like that of Tocqueville than different from it. DuBois's and Myrdal's dilemmas, too, were not only real in their own time but constitute continuing possibilities for interpreting the facts of the color line. And until the promise of liberal democracy is fulfilled, moral ideas and implications for action like those of Tocqueville, DuBois, and Myrdal will continue to serve as doctrines for marshaling the facts of the color line.

RACIST REALISM: ITS IDEAS
AND IMPLICATIONS FOR ACTION

Alexis de Tocqueville began *Democracy in America* in 1831, the same year William Lloyd Garrison began publishing the *Liberator,* dedicated to the cause of abolishing slavery. Garrison believed that abolition was the path to wider justice and equality in the American community. Tocqueville agreed that slavery was a great moral wrong— "God forbid that I should seek to justify the principle of negro slavery, as has been done by some American writers"—but he was not optimistic that its abolition would lead to any greater justice and equality between the races. Tocqueville invoked what he took to be the facts to justify his view. "Those who hope that the Europeans will ever mix with the negroes," he asserted, "appear to me to delude themselves; and I am not led to any such conclusion by my own reason, or by the evidence of the facts."[2]

Tocqueville's views are interesting if only because they are a clear and archetypal example of racist realism. Unable to justify the existing state of affairs, he also was unable to conceive of an acceptable alternative. "As soon as it is admitted," he wrote, that whites and emancipated blacks occupying the same territory "are placed in the situation of two alien communities," there were only two alternatives: "The negroes and the whites must either wholly part or wholly mingle." Although Tocqueville could not imagine the races "ever liv[ing] in any country upon an equal footing," he thought that racial equality was especially unlikely to develop in the United States because of the large number of blacks involved. "An isolated individual," he said, "may surmount the prejudices of religion, of his country, or of his race . . . but a whole people cannot rise, as it were, above itself." The abolition of slavery, he believed, would "increase the repugnance of the white population for men of color. . . . You may set the negro free, but you cannot make him otherwise than alien to the European." As Tocqueville explained, "We scarcely acknowledge the common features of mankind in this child of debasement whom slavery has brought among us. His physiognomy is to our eyes hideous, his understanding weak, his tastes low, and we are almost inclined to look upon him as being intermediate between man and the brutes."[3]

These "facts," Tocqueville asserted, created a racial impasse: "To induce the whites to abandon the opinion they have conceived of the moral and intellectual inferiority of their former slaves, the negroes must change; but as long as this opinion subsists, to change is impossible." He concluded, "The moderns, then, after they have abolished slavery, have three more prejudices to contend against, which are less easy to attack, and far less easy to conquer, than the mere fact of servitude: the prejudice of the master, the prejudice of the race, and the prejudice of color."[4]

Tocqueville may not have justified slavery, as some American writers had done, but by the time he got through, he had reduced it to the "mere fact of servitude," and he had gone far in justifying deep antagonisms and pervasive inequalities on a continuing basis. Tocqueville's view is a case study in the thin line between realism in matters of race in American life and the rationalization of injustice, the apparent justification of moral failure. Tocqueville was neither the first nor the last to blur that line. The facts of antagonism and inequality have always seemed so massive, the justifications apparently so thin, that the reasonable prospects for change have always been largely a matter of faith.

Tocqueville was basically interested in observing and reporting the many consequences of the pursuit and diffusion of democratic equality as a central dynamic in American life. He found its effects in every branch of human endeavor. Race was the exception that proved the rule. Equality was for the whites, and Tocqueville saw no way that it could be extended to native Americans or to blacks, both of which he treated in a single chapter.

Tocqueville's views were borne out by the events that led from emancipation through Reconstruction into the Jim Crow system of legislated inequality. The Civil War was an abolitionist success. The North, which began the war to preserve the Union, was, "as the hostilities dragged on . . . ineluctably driven toward incorporating emancipation and recognition of the black man as a man and citizen into the goals of the war and the postwar settlement."[5] Thus the Thirteenth, Fourteenth, and Fifteenth amendments (1865, 1868, and 1870) sought to extend the promise of liberal democracy to blacks by abolishing slavery, by bringing blacks under the protection of the Constitution, and by guaranteeing their right to vote. These civil and political rights were specified and enforced by a series of congressional enactments—civil rights bills, Reconstruction acts, and enforcement acts.

In addition, the Freedmen's Bureau, which had begun as a war measure, was continued after the war to provide former slaves with the material relief and economic capacities they required to actualize the promise of equality. Opposition by President Andrew Johnson, however, rendered the bureau unable to fulfill its commitment to forty acres of land for each male freedman—a prerequisite for some measure of economic independence—and the bureau was discontinued in 1868.[6]

These efforts to reconstruct the nation were remarkable in proposing to "raise over four million people just released from a legal servitude of special rigidity to a legal status of equality" and to do so "with the approval of an electorate who believed, except for an articulate dissenting minority, in the racial superiority of whites and the racial inferiority of blacks. . . . By legislative enactment and constitutional amendment, men who yesterday were property, subject to whatever discipline their owners might impose, were made the equal of their old masters in the right to due process of law, to contract freely, to hold property, to bear arms, to testify from the witness stand, to sit on juries, to enjoy public transportation, inns, and theaters, to vote both for local and national officials, and to themselves hold office." But Reconstruction did not constitute a pledge by the nation to complete racial equality. It was a Republican commitment in the face of opposition by northern Democrats and southern whites, and it was a commitment only to equality "in matters of public, as distinct from private, authority."[7]

Even these limited purposes could not be sustained, and Reconstruction was ended by the Compromise of 1877, a morally flawed but historically consequential arrangement that put Rutherford B. Hayes in the White House and removed federal troops from the South. This compromise consisted of an agreement to drop the Negro problem from the agenda of national policy questions. Hayes called it the "let alone" policy. It was similar to what others before him had called "popular sovereignty" and to what others after him have called "benign neglect." In each case it meant the same thing: no issue of justice was at stake and, therefore, national policy was not required to address the issue. Whatever the Negro problem was, it was not a public problem.

The Compromise of 1877 denied that the republic was in need of reconstruction. The burden of change was shifted, as Tocqueville had done, to the Negroes. The justification was that they were the ones in need of reconstruction, which, if it was possible at all—even the "best men" had doubts[8]— would have to be gradual. The problem was cast largely as an issue of self-help and separate racial development, encouraged and augmented, as circumstances and noblesse allowed, by private philanthropy, apart from any national commitment to social justice or structural change.

Rutherford B. Hayes acted out the symbolism of this morally flawed transformation in his own career. From the presidency of the United States, he went on to the presidency of the Slater Fund, one of the country's earliest large foundations, dedicated, among other things, to the betterment of the blacks' lot.[9] Likewise, the benign rationalization of the Compromise of 1877 was to move the Negro problem from national policy to private philanthropy.

After 1877, race relations developed within the framework of this destructive and profoundly deceptive euphemism. The federal government withdrew its protection, but the several states where blacks mostly lived were in no mood to "let alone." In the years that followed, they legislated what Rayford Logan called the "nadir" of the black experience in America.[10] "The strange career of Jim Crow" emerged to fill the void left by the abolition of slavery and the failure of Reconstruction.[11] Notions of "separate but equal," laced with "laws of natural selection," provided intellectual justification and, tragically, constitutional authority after *Plessy* v. *Ferguson* (1896)[12] for this new "peculiar institution," Jim Crow, with its many publicly enforced rituals of degradation.

Within the black community, Booker T. Washington was the outstanding leader who found creative ways of accommodating to this situation by pursuing strategies of black self-development with the aid of private philanthropists. In 1881, exactly fifty years after Tocqueville had foreseen that emancipation would place the burden of change upon blacks, Washington established Tuskegee Institute. Its purpose was to change blacks by providing them with agricultural and industrial education, beginning with growing their

25

own food and constructing their own dormitory and classroom buildings. Washington called this "taking advantage of the disadvantages."[13]

Washington's renowned address at the Atlanta Exposition in 1895 articulated two themes. The first, "cast down your bucket where you are," meant that blacks' efforts to change themselves should begin where they were, at the bottom of the occupational ladder, and that they should develop the agricultural and mechanical skills Tuskegee was founded to promote. For southern whites, "casting down their bucket where they were" meant helping and encouraging blacks to pursue these endeavors. They could do so in confidence that such black self-development enhanced rather than threatened the southern way of life. As Washington's famous second statement put it, "In all things that are purely social we can be as separate as the fingers, yet one as the hand in all things essential to mutual progress."[14]

Washington's speech, popularly known as the Atlanta Compromise, brought him rapid recognition as the black spokesman of the times. On this platform, he consolidated support for himself and his position among blacks and whites alike. For the next twenty years, until his death in 1915, Washington's leadership in race relations among supporters on both sides of the color line was unchallenged.

Although privately Washington financed legal challenges to the emerging Jim Crow system, his public acceptance of racial separation, his advocacy of black economic self-help, his flattery of whites, and his emphasis on the gradual achievement of equality, if and when blacks deserved it, meant that, like Hayes, he played out the role he was assigned by post-Reconstruction racist realism. As Tocqueville had anticipated, the abolition of the "mere fact of servitude" did not lead whites to abandon their opinion of the "moral and intellectual inferiority" of this "alien" and "debased" people. Blacks tried to change themselves and become worthy of white respect; some paternalistically inclined whites aided their endeavors. In both cases, however, the promise of democratic equality was stopped at the color line by deep-seated racial antipathies: "the prejudice of the master, the prejudice of the race, and the prejudice of color."

THE DEMOCRATIC DILEMMA OF BLACK DIGNITY:
ITS IDEAS AND IMPLICATIONS FOR ACTION

In 1903, when he published *The Souls of Black Folk*, W. E. B. DuBois was a lonely voice in his insistence that "the problem of the twentieth century is the problem of the color line." How, DuBois asked, "is it possible, and probable, that nine millions of men can make effective progress in economic lines if they are deprived of political rights, made a servile caste, and allowed only the most meager chance for developing their exceptional men?"[15] For him, civil rights was both a moral and a political problem that would not be solved by any amount of either charity or self-help.

DuBois challenged both the leadership and the philosophy of Booker T. Washington and, by 1905, found himself at the head of an important but short-lived organization, the Niagara Movement. His criticism of Washington was direct and pointed. "Mr. Washington's programme practically accepts the alleged inferiority of the Negro races," he said, because "Mr. Washington withdraws many of the high demands of Negroes as men and as American citizens."[16]

This theme was carried forward in the resolutions of the first meeting of the Niagara Movement, which took place on the Canadian side of the falls: "We want to *pull down* nothing but we don't propose to be pulled down. . . . We believe in *taking what we can get* but we don't believe in being satisfied with it and in permitting anybody for a moment to imagine we're satisfied."[17] So much for the philanthropic nonpolitical version of the Negro problem. This was a different tone from Washington's rhetoric of flattery, gratitude, and race debasement.

The Niagara Movement, with DuBois in the forefront, continued in existence from 1905 to 1909 or 1910. In the context of the time, the voice of the movement was unreasonably shrill in its determination to address the deficiencies of the political community.[18] Almost everything its members said was considered criticism of Washington, justifiably, for they saw Washington as standing between them and everything they thought should be said and done. Yet they were not specifically anti-Washingtonian. Deep personal feelings unquestionably animated both the Niagara Movement and the Washingtonians; but the former's political and moral interpretation of the problem set it apart not only from Washington but from the national consensus. Its members insisted on confronting the radical nature of the problem Washington seemed at pains to deny. They were willing to speak candidly about the deteriorating position of blacks at the hands of their "neighbors" and "political protectors." They were committed to protesting the disfranchisement, the lynching, the race hatred, and the political deals the major parties had made at the expense of blacks' rights. In short, they insisted on seeing the problem in the political environment and not simply in black people.[19]

Never more than four hundred in number, the members of the Niagara Movement searched for some rhetoric that would pierce the veil of degrading euphemism that obscured the politically and personally radical character of the Negro problem. In the heat of the moment, they called the Republican party of 1907 "the present dictatorship"; yet muckrakers and populists had called it worse. In 1908, their "fourth annual 'Address to the Country' blasted 'the Negro haters of America,' who had succeeded in excluding qualified men

27

from all areas of American life. Negroes were advised to get guns and prepare themselves for defensive action against white mobs." From cattle ranchers discussing the expansion of railroads across the plains, such a sentiment might have been understandable. From mill owners discussing labor organizers, it might have been even more permissible. But from blacks, it was too much—even though it had in common with these others its significance as a gesture of futility. When the Niagarans started talking that way, their movement was breaking up—not, however, before opening new moral grounds on which to oppose the Hayes-Washington rhetoric. Self-respect or "the determination to be men at any cost," as the fifth annual statement of the Niagara Movement put it, had come to seem intrinsically related to the open pursuit of civil rights for blacks in American public life. The moral question, the "determination to be men at any cost," was the propelling force of the Niagara Movement's political vision.[20]

The Niagara Movement perceived in the denial of political rights not a temporary setback to be accepted for purposes of expedience but an ultimate denial of common humanity and an affront to self-respect. The tension was unremitting, and it was not simply a tension between blacks and the society that treated them with disrespect. It was a tension within the black conscience itself. In *The Souls of Black Folk*, DuBois had expressed it as "a peculiar sensation, this double-consciousness, this sense of always looking at one's self through the eyes of others, of measuring one's soul by the tape of a world that looks on in amused contempt and pity. One ever feels his twoness,—an American, a Negro; two souls, two thoughts, two unreconciled strivings; two warring ideals in one dark body, whose dogged strength alone keeps it from being torn asunder."[21]

DuBois opened a perspective on both the color line and the American political community vastly at odds with the Hayes-Washington rules of the game/laws of nature/ethnic uplift approach. From the Niagara point of view, common humanity or brotherhood, as they called it, was not something to be earned by blacks and conferred by white people. They accused Washington of accepting the practical inferiority of blacks and believed the relations between blacks and whites could never be straightened out on that basis because it placed the burden for the existence of the color line on the blacks. Changing that relationship and that definition of the "Negro's place" required unremitting protest—the only incontrovertible proof that the blacks at least did not acquiesce in this assault on their humanity.

The Niagara Movement may have made an important contribution to the future, but it destroyed itself in the effort. The perspective was still too abstract and out of touch with the prevailing emotions in 1905–10. In calling for guns and the like the Niagarans misplaced the potential concreteness of their discovery. They may also have been incapable of growing into the fullness and richness of their own insight; but the beginning they made was destined to take root and grow during the first half of the century.[22]

Protest organizations following DuBois's Niagara Movement continued to assert this new standard of moral urgency. Interracial organizations, outcasts when the NAACP was founded with DuBois's support in 1909, managed to attract constituencies of a moderate to liberal complexion behind strategies of social change through litigation, political influence, persuasion, and economic development. The organization in the 1930s of racially inclusive unions, as well as all-black ones, made a point about equality and power. Social service organizations such as the Urban League, founded in 1911, were a constant source of information about living conditions, both social and political. The emergence and consolidation of black churches, fraternal organizations, businesses, and professional groups, which began in Reconstruction and continued under Jim Crow, expanded with the "great migration" of blacks from rural areas to urban centers beginning around the time of World War I.[23] The decisive shift of black voters into the columns of the Democratic party beginning in the mid-1930s gave their concerns a new political visibility. The federal government began moving into position for change. In 1939 President Franklin D. Roosevelt established the Civil Rights Section in the Justice Department.[24]

In 1941 A. Philip Randolph dramatized both of these developments—and added a new dimension with his March on Washington Movement. Randolph was president of the International Brotherhood of Sleeping Car Porters and a Roosevelt supporter. Like DuBois, he refused to be taken for granted. Early in 1941, he threatened a mass march on Washington unless Roosevelt would guarantee a fair employment practices policy. To back his demand, he organized local chapters of his March on Washington Movement and held large rallies in major American cities. He raised the specter of mass black activism aimed at immediate change in national policy—an entirely new possibility. And he seemed to have the means to make good on this threat. He set 1 July 1941 as the date for the march. To Roosevelt this seemed like a drastic move, and he tried to dissuade Randolph, who held firm. On 25 June 1941, Roosevelt issued Executive Order 8802 establishing the President's Committee on Fair Employment Practices.[25]

Then, in 1942, a group with a different orientation made its appearance— the Congress of Racial Equality (CORE), a nonviolent, racially integrated, direct-action, protest organization dedicated to opposing segregation and to exposing its existence and consequences in public life.[26]

Thus by the early 1940s, DuBois's lonely voice of 1903 had become a chorus united in the notion that whatever the facts of the color line might be, they were morally unacceptable. Black self-respect required protest. Thurgood Marshall, then director of the NAACP Legal Defense Fund, followed

29

the perspective on facts and justifications set forth by DuBois forty years before when he said, in 1944, "We must not be delayed by people who say 'the time is not ripe,' nor should we proceed with caution for fear of destroying the 'status quo.' Persons who deny us our civil rights should be brought to justice now. Many believe that the time is always 'ripe' to discriminate against Negroes. All right then—the time is always 'ripe' to bring them to justice."[27] But by 1944 such protests were neither lonely nor entirely ineffective. Indeed, in that year, the NAACP won a signal victory when the Supreme Court outlawed white primary elections, a common device for excluding black voters in the South from meaningful political participation.[28]

THE DEMOCRATIC DILEMMA OF WHITE CULTURE: ITS IDEAS AND IMPLICATIONS FOR ACTION

Gunnar Myrdal's *An American Dilemma* also appeared in 1944. The book opened yet a third perspective on the facts and justifications that surrounded the color line. Tocqueville had foreseen, and Washington had accepted, the notion that even in the absence of slavery racial equality was not possible because racial antipathies were too great. By contrast, DuBois had asserted, and Randolph and Marshall had creatively developed, the notion that black self-respect required the assertion of black equality because otherwise the racial indignities were too great. Now Myrdal argued that racial equality was possible because the internal dilemma of whites between their higher values and lower impulses was too great. Thus, where Tocqueville and Washington had seen a black problem, Myrdal saw a white one; where DuBois advocated a principled minority protest, Myrdal laid the grounds for a principled majoritarian strategy, which he expected to bear fruit in the immediate future. From Tocqueville morally justifying and expecting racial antipathy and thereby legitimizing the racial status quo, to Myrdal morally justifying and expecting racial harmony and thereby legitimizing racial social change, is surely an enormous reversal in just over a century—one that involved fundamental reinterpretations of both the facts and the justifications of the American color line.

Surprisingly enough, Myrdal's position was not based upon the developing militancy of black organizations. Much of the democratic dilemma of black dignity, from DuBois to Marshall, had become organizationally located in the NAACP and its efforts to enforce the Fourteenth and Fifteenth amendments through the courts. During the 1930s, however, under the impact of the Depression, a new group of black militants arose who emphasized a variety of economic approaches to the problem of black inequality and who were critical of all or part of the NAACP's legal strategy. Besides Randolph, who had always focused on this dimension of the issue, these economic militants included Ralph J. Bunche, who advocated coalitions of blacks and whites based on class, and DuBois, who by then sought economic relief through the creation of black cooperatives.[29]

Bunche's views had some influence on Myrdal's evaluations of black leadership and protest organizations. As part of the Myrdal study, Bunche produced a survey titled "The Programs, Ideologies, Tactics, and Achievements of Negro Betterment and Interracial Organizations," and he published an article, "The Programs of Organizations Devoted to the Improvement of the Status of the American Negro."[30] Bunche's analysis was devastating. "Minority groups, such as the American Negro," he wrote, "inevitably tend to become introverted in their social thinking . . . [and their] social perspective becomes warped."[31]

As a result, "Organizations devoted to the salvation of the Negro," Bunche continued, "have the following fundamental characteristics":

1. adherence to policies of escape, based upon racialism and nationalism;
2. lack of mass support among Negroes, and mass appeal;
3. dependence upon white benefactors for finance;
4. reluctance to encourage the development of working-class psychology among Negroes and avoidance of class interpretations;
5. tendency, directly or indirectly, to take their main ideological cues from white sympathizers;
6. lack of a coherent, constructive program;
7. lack of broad social perspective and the ability to relate the problems of the Negro to the main social currents and forces of the American society; and
8. pursuit of policies of immediate relief and petty opportunism.[32]

Bunche concluded that blacks needed associations and leadership that would organize them in large numbers around economic issues and make common cause across racial lines with all who were prepared to pursue those issues. "Under oppressive conditions," such leadership "would recognize that . . . identity of economic interests can overcome racial prejudices, and that black and white unity is possible."[33] His work constituted a second version of the democratic dilemma of black dignity. Like DuBois, Bunche was urging blacks to assert their rights and affirm their equality but, unlike DuBois, he felt they should do so on the basis of class rather than race.

Myrdal accepted important aspects of Bunche's analysis. An economist who devoted more than two hundred pages of *An American Dilemma* to economic issues, Myrdal felt the force of Bunche's critique of existing black protest organizations and of his call for more attention to the economic dimensions of the color line. But because Myrdal's focus was on the democratic dilemma of white culture, he emphasized "an obvious Negro interest and, consequently, a general American interest to engage as many white groups as

31

possible as allies in the struggle against caste." To this end of maximizing white allies, Myrdal affirmed "a whole set of [black] organizations specializing on different tasks and applying a different degree of opportunism or radicalism." As a result, Myrdal was able, as Bunche had not been, to endorse the programs of the NAACP and the Urban League. Still, Myrdal ended his discussion of black protest organizations on a note struck by DuBois and echoed by Bunche: "To the Negro people dishonest leadership is a most important cause of weakness in concerted action."[34]

If these emerging black protest organizations did not provide the facts that justified Myrdal's optimism, what did? This is an unusually pertinent question for Myrdal because his optimism about the prospects for change in American race relations set him apart from most other scholars of the subject. Since his expectations turned out to be surprisingly timely, the grounds for his optimism deserve careful attention.

Like Max Weber, Myrdal was well aware of the interaction between facts and values in social science research, and perhaps no social scientist since Weber had been more articulate on this question. More than Weber, however, Myrdal emphasized the way value premises determined the facts, and therefore he thought a value-free social science was impossible. Myrdal took this position because, unlike Weber, he did not believe that values were finally either subjective and personal or arbitrary. Because in this case, Myrdal's subject was the Negro problem and modern democracy, he adopted as the value premises of his study what he took to be the widely shared values that underlay American democracy. This choice was of great strategic import. He hoped that because all Americans shared his value premises, all might accept his conclusions. He called these American value premises the American creed.[35]

By the American creed, Myrdal meant the "ideals of the essential dignity of the individual human being, of the fundamental equality of all men, and of certain inalienable rights to freedom, justice, and a fair opportunity." Myrdal stressed that these were not abstract ideals that were merely given lip service, but that they were a living presence in American life—established in the founding documents of the nation, a part of the highest law of the land, regularly elaborated upon by national leaders, the subject of popular tracts, and the "foundation of national morale" in every war, including World War II, which was being waged as he wrote.[36]

His definition of the American creed, then, was the first basis of Myrdal's optimism concerning the Negro problem. This American creed was a fact in American life, embodied in institutions and appealed to by national leaders. It was a social force at work in our midst, "one of the dominant 'social trends,'" bringing all behavioral deviances from it increasingly under its sway. Of course, Myrdal knew that this American creed had yet to be applied in all areas of American life. Otherwise there would be no Negro problem. But he believed that "the Creed is expressive and definite in practically all respects of importance for the Negro problem. . . . In principle the Negro problem was settled long ago. . . . It represents nothing more and nothing less than a century-long lag in public morals."[37]

In this respect, at least, Myrdal agreed with the emerging black protest groups. From the perspective of the American creed, the Negro problem was a moral problem—and one that belonged to whites, not blacks. This moral problem constituted the American dilemma which Myrdal took as the title of his study.

> The American Negro problem is a problem in the heart of the American. It is there that the interracial tension has its focus. It is there that the decisive struggle goes on. This is the central viewpoint of this treatise. Though our study includes economic, social, and political race relations, at bottom our problem is the moral dilemma of the American—the conflict between his moral valuations on various levels of consciousness and generality. The "American Dilemma," referred to in the title of this book, is the ever-raging conflict between, on the one hand, the valuations preserved on the general plane which we shall call the "American Creed," where the American thinks, talks, and acts under the influence of high national and Christian precepts, and, on the other hand, the valuations on specific planes of individual and group living, where personal and local interests; economic, social, and sexual jealousies; considerations of community prestige and conformity; group prejudice against particular persons or types of people; and all sorts of miscellaneous wants, impulses, and habits dominate his outlook.[38]

Clearly, then, for Myrdal, the American dilemma was between two levels of valuation, which, though they were in conflict, were both internal to the American—"in the heart." This concept, too, was strategically important. Hearts, after all, might be more easily transformed than social, economic, and political institutions, especially in a culture whose primary religious processes focus on the importance of individual character.

Thus, for Myrdal, it was clear that the remedy for the American dilemma was an educational process through which "the illogicalities involving valuations become exposed to the people who hold them. They are then pressed to change their valuations to some degree or other." Myrdal concluded that "as the more general norms in our culture are given supreme moral sanction, this means . . . that the valuations on a more specific level (often called 'prejudices') will yield to them."[39]

By this process, through which "the need for logical consistency" among valuations is regularly (and increasingly rapidly) resolved in the direction of "the more general and timeless valuations [which] are morally higher" in Western culture, Myrdal had confidence that the triumph of the American creed would result in the timely resolution of the American dilemma.[40] This

33

was the second basis for Myrdal's optimism that democratic equality in American life would not be stopped by the color line. The American creed was not only a social force within American culture; it was a personal force within the individual citizen as well.

In important respects, this was his most important basis for optimism, for it explicitly broke with the reigning sociological interpretation of the Negro problem. Ever since William Graham Sumner's *Folkways* had appeared in 1906, Sumner's concepts of folkways and mores had been regularly invoked by social scientists to express their attitudes "that changes will be slow, or, more particularly, that nothing practical can be done about a matter"—in this case, the Negro problem. This was because folkways and mores presupposed, according to Myrdal, "a whole social theory and an entire laissez-faire ('do-nothing') metaphysics," which viewed society as "a homogeneous, unproblematic, fairly static, social entity."[41] For Sumner, like Tocqueville before him (and the civic credo after him), social values were immanent in society and served to promote and defend cultural continuity.

However useful this approach may have been in studying "primitive" or traditional societies, Myrdal found it entirely inadequate "when applied to a modern Western society in the process of rapid industrialization" and the rapid attitudinal changes accompanying that process. More particularly, Sumner's approach concealed from the social scientist the notion "that even within a single individual valuations are operative on different planes of generality, that they are typically conflicting, and that behavior is regularly the outcome of a moral compromise"—especially in periods of rapid social change.[42]

For Myrdal, social and personal values were diverse rather than homogeneous, and these values transcended some levels of social and personal life while, at the same time, they were embodied on other levels. Whereas Sumner saw values as the source of homeostatic equilibrium, Myrdal recognized their role as a source of tension—a tension he specified for race as the American dilemma. In seeking resolution, this tension became an engine of attitudinal and behavioral change in both the individual and the society. Thus Myrdal, in emphasizing those pluralistic, problematic, and transcendent dimensions of social and personal experience which Sumner had ignored, cast the weight of interpretation on social change and intrapersonal dynamics rather than on Sumner's social stasis and status quo. In both cases, we see how crucial the interplay of fact and justification is for the interpretation of social possibility. And, as we shall see, a similar conflict of interpretation was close to the heart of the struggle between the civil rights movement and the civic credo in Chicago.

Myrdal had a third reason for his optimism besides the social force of the American creed and the psychological dilemma it generated. He called it

34

the "Rank Order of Discriminations," and it embodied his assessment of the racial interactions whites and blacks disliked the most. For whites the rank order was as follows:

Rank 1. Highest in this order stands the bar against intermarriage and sexual intercourse involving white women.

Rank 2. Next come the several etiquettes and discriminations, which specifically concern behavior in personal relations. (These are the barriers against dancing, bathing, eating, drinking together, and social intercourse generally; peculiar rules as to handshaking, hat lifting, use of titles, house entrance to be used, social forms when meeting on streets and in work, and so forth. These patterns are sometimes referred to as the denial of "social equality" in the narrow meaning of the term.)

Rank 3. Thereafter follow the segregations and discriminations in use of public facilities such as schools, churches and means of conveyance.

Rank 4. Next comes political disfranchisement.

Rank 5. Thereafter come discriminations in law courts, by the police, and by other public servants.

Rank 6. Finally come the discriminations in securing land, credit, jobs, or other means of earning a living, and discriminations in public relief and other social welfare activities.[43]

Myrdal then noted an ironic situation: "Next in importance to the fact of the white man's rank order of discriminations is the fact that the Negro's own rank order is just about parallel, but inverse, to that of the white man." The question, in Myrdal's mind, was whether the whites would stick to their rank order when put to the test. "Upon the assumption that this question is given an affirmative answer, that the white man is actually prepared to carry out in practice the implications of his theories, this inverse relationship between the Negro's and the white man's rank orders becomes of strategical importance in the practical and political sphere of the Negro problem."[44] This was because those areas in which blacks were most needy and about which they were most eager to make progress, Rank 6, were the very areas that whites cared least about defending.

This is not to say, however, that Myrdal was proposing some sort of strategic lockstep on black protest organizations so that they all worked their way up his rank order of discrimination together. Myrdal also laid a fourth ground of hope for racial progress by what he called the "Principle of Cumulation." Myrdal pointed out that this principle, popularly known as the theory of the "vicious circle," whereby the insecure person eats and drinks more and more to cope with the increased insecurity of becoming overweight or alcoholic, worked in a reverse, positive direction as well. As it applied to race relations, he suggested that "a rise in Negro employment, for instance, will raise family incomes, standards of nutrition, housing, and health, the possibilities of giving the Negro youth more education, and so forth, and all these effects of the initial change, will, in their turn, improve the Negroes' possibilities of getting employment and earning a living." In other words, despite the massive racial discrimination and segregation in the American social order, progress on any aspect of the racial problem would, by the principle of cumulation, have positive effects on other aspects as well.[45]

This principle is particularly important for our study of Chicago because it provided a theoretical basis for the practice of coalition—the ability of organizations with disparate purposes, strategies, and resources to work together— that characterized the civil rights movement. As long as they believed in it, this principle of cumulation formed an important countervailing force to the sectarian tendencies that often characterize the politics of radical protest.

The fifth reason for Myrdal's optimism concerning the future of race relations in America was the new situation created by World War II, the beginning of which interrupted his study and which was still in progress when he wrote his concluding chapter. As he considered the shifts in social trends brought about by the war as well as those previously under way, Myrdal was convinced that a war fought for liberty and equality, and against racism in the form of fascism and Nazism, could only bring about a positive "redefinition of the Negro's status in America." Moreover, he saw black protest rising, "spurred by the improvement in education," to the point that "America can never more regard its Negroes as a patient, submissive minority. . . . They will organize for defense and offense."[46]

He perceived the North already moving toward racial equality although racial tension was increasing in the South. The national compromise between North and South on race was breaking down. And since "the North cannot well afford any longer to let the white Southerners have their own way with the Negroes" and "the Negroes are awarded the law as a weapon in the caste struggle," Myrdal took recent Supreme Court decisions, the New Deal, and other federal activities favoring blacks in the South as portents for the future. Good race relations at home, he thought, were important for maintaining America's leadership in the postwar world and especially for making the peace.[47]

Myrdal also anticipated greater social planning and an increased public role for social science following the war. This, too, he thought would benefit blacks, and it constitutes the sixth and final reason for Myrdal's optimism— his boundless faith in social science:

> In this spirit, so intrinsically in harmony with the great tradition of the Enlightenment and the American Revolution, the author may be allowed to close with a personal note. Studying human beings and their behavior is not discouraging. When the author recalls the long gallery of persons whom, in the course of this inquiry, he has come to know with the impetuous but temporary intimacy of the stranger—

36

sharecroppers and plantation owners, workers and employers, merchants and bankers, intellectuals, preachers, organization leaders, political bosses, gangsters, black and white, men and women, young and old, Southerners and Northerners—the general observation retained is the following: Behind all outward dissimilarities, behind their contradictory valuations, rationalizations, vested interests, group allegiances and animosities, behind fears and defense constructions, behind the role they play in life and the mask they wear, people are all much alike on a fundamental level. And they are all good people. They want to be rational and just. They all plead to their conscience that they meant well even when things went wrong.

Social study is concerned with explaining why all these potentially and intentionally good people so often make life a hell for themselves and each other when they live together, whether in a family, a community, a nation or a world. The fault is certainly not with becoming organized per se. In their formal organizations, as we have seen, people invest their highest ideals. These institutions regularly direct the individual toward more cooperation and justice than he would be inclined to observe as an isolated private person. The fault is, rather, that our structures of organizations are too imperfect, each by itself, and badly integrated into a social whole.

The rationalism and moralism which is the driving force behind social study, whether we admit it or not, is the faith that institutions can be improved and strengthened and that people are good enough to live a happier life. With all we know today, there should be the possibility to build a nation and a world where people's great propensities for sympathy and cooperation would not be so thwarted.

To find the practical formulas for this never-ending reconstruction of society is the supreme task of social science. The world catastrophe places tremendous difficulties in our way and may shake our confidence to the depths. Yet we have today in social science a greater trust in the improvability of man and society than we have ever had since the Enlightenment.[48]

So it was as a social scientist, as a social ethicist, and perhaps even as a revivalist that Myrdal concluded,

What America is constantly reaching for is democracy at home and abroad. The main trend in its history is the gradual realization of the American Creed. . . . America can demonstrate that justice, equality and cooperation are possible between white and colored people. In the present phase of history this is what the world needs to believe. Mankind is sick of fear and disbelief, of pessimism and cynicism. It needs the youthful moralistic optimism of America. But empty declarations only deepen cynicism. Deeds are called for.[49]

In sum, where DuBois had seen a black dilemma, Myrdal saw a white one, and where Tocqueville had justified the racial status quo, Myrdal legitimized racial social change. The interplay of fact and justification led Myrdal to such opposite conclusions for six reasons: the social force of the American creed; the trust that the American dilemma would be resolved in the direction of its rationally and morally higher and more general valuations; the rank order of discriminations; the principle of cumulation; the effect of World War II on

37

various social trends in America; and contributions of social science to improving people and institutions.

This is not to say, however, that Myrdal's optimism was unmitigated, and it is important for understanding subsequent events to realize what his reservations were. This can be seen best if we recall Myrdal's statement that the American creed "is expressive and definite in practically all respects for the Negro problem."[50]

The methodological seriousness of this claim is sometimes overlooked by readers of Myrdal, but it is absolutely central to his analysis. In each of the eight central sections of his study—on population and migration, economics, politics, justice, social inequality, social stratification, leadership and concerted action, and the Negro community—Myrdal explored the conflicts of beliefs and valuations concerning each topic and then explicitly specified the implications of his value premises, the American creed, for the topic. On population, for example, Myrdal noted that whites and blacks were in conflict: the former desired as few blacks as possible in America (provided acceptable means were found for limiting black population), and the latter wanted to increase the black population as much as possible. "It is implicit in the American Creed," however, Myrdal wrote, that "both white and black Americans in principle find it desirable to raise the quality of the Negro people." Therefore, "we can proceed safely on the value premise that the medical and health facilities and, indeed, all public measures in the field of education, sanitation, housing, nutrition, hospitalization and so forth, to improve the quality of the population and to advance individuals and groups physically, mentally, or morally, should be made just as available for Negroes as for whites in similar circumstances and with similar needs. This value premise has, in fact, sanction in the Constitution of the United States." In other words, "all . . . theoretically possible policies to effectuate the white desire to decrease the Negro population are blocked by the American Creed . . . and a unity of purpose [between blacks and whites] becomes established on the basis of the American Creed."[51]

By contrast, Myrdal found the American creed less definite and decisive on two topics of particular relevance to the subsequent chapters of the present study. First, on economic issues, Myrdal found "considerable confusion and contradiction even *within* this higher plane of sanctified national ideals [the American Creed] and not only—as elsewhere—*between* those ideals and the more opportunistic valuations on lower planes." In the 1930s this conflict was between "equality of opportunity" and the "liberty to run one's business as one pleases." As American economic liberalism moved from "rugged individualism" toward "gradually assimilating ideals of a more social type" under Roosevelt, however, the conflict increasingly was resolved in the direction of equality of opportunity. Thus, "the American Creed is changing to include a decent living standard and a measure of economic security among the liberties and rights which are given this highest moral sanction."[52]

As a result, he concluded that the American creed implied the following: "1. There is nothing wrong with economic inequality by itself. . . . 2. Somewhat less precise is our second value premise: that no American population group shall be allowed to fall under a certain minimum of living." This principle was less precise because "it is still undecided how high or low this minimum level should be. . . . 3. Our third value premise is bound to be the most significant one for our inquiry as it brings out the principal chasm between American ideals and practices: that Negroes should be awarded equal opportunities." Myrdal found this aspect of the American creed violated much more widely in the South than in the North, but he was aware that there was "plenty of economic discrimination in the North," and his subsequent ten chapters on aspects of economic inequality offered no clear hope for the future.[53]

The second area in which Myrdal found conflict within the American creed was that of "social inequality," by which he meant not the full range of relations between individuals but personal relations, "particularly those of an intimate sort." On the one hand, the equality of opportunity in the American creed prohibited any arrangement "which restricts opportunities for some individuals more than for others." This principle had already "been given constitutional sanction as far as public service and state regulations are concerned." On the other hand, "when segregation and discrimination are the outcome of individual action, the second main norm of the American Creed, namely, liberty, can be invoked in their defense. . . . If upheld solely by individual choice, social segregation manifested by all white people in an American community can be—and is—defended by the norm of personal liberty."[54]

Thus Myrdal's analysis left unresolved the questions of school desegregation and open housing, which are central to the story that follows. When these issues were pursued by the civil rights movement, would they be seen as issues of equality of opportunity and thus supported by the American creed, or would they be understood as issues of personal liberty and thus negatively sanctioned by the American creed? The answers were more nearly at hand than Myrdal could imagine in 1944. Surprisingly, for all his prescience in most matters, Myrdal assumed the continued existence of segregated schools, at least in the South, and he devoted his chapter on this topic to how these separate schools for blacks could be improved and made more equal to those for whites.[55]

As we have seen, however, on the whole Myrdal's *An American Dilemma* was overwhelmingly optimistic about the future. Not all scholars shared Myrdal's optimism. St. Clair Drake and Horace Cayton participated in the Myrdal project, but they also prepared a study of their own detailing the social development of ghetto life in Chicago. This study, *Black Metropolis: A Study of*

Negro Life in a Northern City, appeared in 1945. The authors agreed with Myrdal that "the problem which faced America was essentially a moral problem," but they saw America as "unable to deal with or even face the moral issue involved . . . frozen and paralyzed before its Negro problem." In their view, the American creed seemed much less potent a social force than it did to Myrdal. "It is conceivable," they concluded,

> that the Negro question—given the moral flabbiness of America—is incapable of solution. Perhaps not all social problems are soluble. Indeed it is only in America that one finds the imperative to assume that all social problems can be solved without conflict. To feel that a social problem cannot be solved peacefully is considered almost immoral. Americans are required to appear cheerful and optimistic about a solution, regardless of evidence to the contrary. This is particularly difficult for Negroes, who at the same time must endure all the disadvantages of the Job Ceiling and the Black Ghetto, as well as other forms of subordination.[56]

In the years that have passed since both these views were first presented, each has proved to contain important elements of truth. Myrdal was right in thinking that the time was ripe for a successful assault on the Jim Crow system. Drake and Cayton were right in thinking the nation would stand frozen and paralyzed in the face of the massing ghettos that were consolidating in every northern city.

For the moment, however, Myrdal carried the day. In the course of his study, Myrdal recruited the aid of just about every race relations scholar in America, drew from their previous work, commissioned dozens of new studies, and consulted with the leaders of American social science, people from all walks of life North and South, representatives of race relations organizations, and national and local political leaders. The high prestige and visibility of the study generated a new level of serious interest, both scholarly and political, in the American problem with race. Myrdal's study lived up to its mandate to be comprehensive; but it did more than that—Myrdal and his associates were able to formulate, for the first time since Reconstruction, a persuasive interpretation of the Negro problem as a moral, political, and national issue.

It was Myrdal's contribution to present the Negro problem not as an instance of sociobiology, as a quasi-Darwinian example of the self-development of a backward people, or even as an understandable outcome of ordinary majority-minority relations, but as a political issue centered in the moral values of the wider American community. The issue, as posed by Myrdal, was not that the American ideals and values were faulty but that they were insufficiently applied in relation to the Negro problem.

Myrdal's study certainly did not cause the many changes in American race relations which alternately emerged and erupted in the years following its publication, but it did provide an interpretive framework and a moral as well as a political perspective that made those changes seem not only desirable but even rational and inevitable. Myrdal's perspective provided sociological support for a politics of democratic social change. Through his appeal to the American creed, the moral resolution of the American dilemma, the rank order of discriminations, the principle of cumulation, the effect of World War II on social trends, and the ongoing role of social science, Myrdal succeeded in fashioning a bridge between the radical consequences of the color line and the moderate politics of democracy.

Myrdal's study tipped the balance of cultural interpretation in favor of a sociological justification of change as a rational expectation and a moral purpose. Existing race relations lost their reasonableness when reflected directly in light of the American creed and the rank order of discriminations. In Myrdal's interpretation, the conflict lay not in the bare relations of two different groups, black and white, minority and majority. Rather, it lay within the moral order to which Americans subscribed. The morality and the politics of the Negro problem were inseparable from this point of view; and for the first time since Reconstruction, the target for change was shifted back from black people to the wider political community.

In the civil rights movement that followed, Myrdal's formulation of the issue played a central role. The study may have been part of that gathering even from its inception. Myrdal, after all, had been recruited by, and his study had been financed by, the Carnegie Corporation, one of America's largest and most influential philanthropic foundations. Under the terms of the Compromise of 1877, such institutions were supposed to promote whatever advancement was possible in race relations; but under the terms of Myrdal's analysis the issue of justice in the community at large took priority over private charity as the national route to further advancement. Myrdal had formulated a comprehensive moral and intellectual platform for change, and an emerging civil rights movement was readying itself to pursue that agenda. The force and focus of that change, however, were destined to be quite unlike the educational process Myrdal had in mind.

The fear of change and the hope for change always seem to compete for dominance in the analysis of American race relations. The grounds for change seem to come into focus in radically different ways, depending on whether the analyst is more impressed with the massiveness of the facts or with the thinness of their justification. Ideas of what can be done seem to vary according to whether they are polarized by the supposed facts or by the apparent justifications. As we have seen, Tocqueville and Myrdal come down on opposite ends of this polarization.

For all their differences about what was possible, Tocqueville and Myrdal

41

appeared to agree about what was at issue in American race relations. Both of them believed that white prejudice lay at the base of the trouble. Tocqueville was not able to foresee any solution. Myrdal, however, was optimistic that political and cultural resources existed that could create democratic social change. To Tocqueville it seemed that "a whole people cannot rise, as it were, above itself," whereas Myrdal thought it was a matter of the people rising, as it were, to their own true level. "Fundamental changes in American race relations," he believed, "will involve a development toward American ideals."[57]

American thinking about race has perennially vacillated between these two fundamentally different attitudes; and what tips the balance from the one to the other is not some difference of judgment about the massiveness of the facts. As we saw with W. E. B. DuBois in *The Souls of Black Folk* and the Niagara Movement, it is the perception and articulation of what is morally at stake in those facts. We can see how this is so if we compare the different perspectives of Tocqueville, DuBois, and Myrdal in terms of how they perceived and articulated what was morally at stake.[58]

For Tocqueville, equality was the dynamic theme of the American experience, but it was limited to whites (and, writing in the 1830s, he might have added "male" to whites). Consent to the pursuit of equality was racially limited. DuBois complained that Washington seemed to accept this limitation, that he did not press "many of the high demands of Negroes as men and as American citizens." For DuBois, the issue was self-respect to pursue political equality and to express "the determination to be men at any cost." DuBois's appeal was to the universality of democratic equality as an appropriate claim for all Americans. In this, Myrdal agreed with DuBois. Myrdal stressed the centrality, the depth, and the pervasiveness of the American creed as the basis both for consent and for vitality in the American community.

For Tocqueville, accordingly, the American conscience was limited to intraracial considerations, bound by doctrines of race integrity. DuBois, on the other hand, articulated the "twoness" of the black conscience, caught between the high demands of equality as American citizens and the low evaluation inflicted by white Americans on blacks. Myrdal carried this "twoness" into the white conscience as well. It became the basis for his concept of an American dilemma that whites, too, were subject to the tension between their high valuations (the American creed) and the low valuations they acted out against blacks. This was a critical turn away from Tocqueville's interpretation of what was morally at stake for whites and toward DuBois's interpretation of what was morally at stake for blacks.

Whereas Tocqueville could see only a continued politics of enforced inequality, DuBois called for a politics of protest, demanding equal rights as citizens, the abolition of caste, and the freedom to pursue human excellence.

Myrdal sided with DuBois in principle but moderated his position in the direction of strategic prudence. His rank order of discriminations seemed to him to open up the possibility of pursuing a successful politics of racial equality without provoking an all-out black-white confrontation.

For Tocqueville the only initiatives that might lead to changes were those blacks might undertake to change themselves, to raise themselves in the opinion of whites. Tocqueville, however, had no reason to be hopeful that such would occur. DuBois, too, was impressed with the vicious circle in which blacks were caught by white perceptions. It was his conviction, nonetheless, that the only hope for breaking the vicious circle lay not in a bootstrap philosophy alone but primarily in reasserting the political claims of blacks to their rights as Americans. Myrdal agreed, and he was more hopeful than DuBois because Myrdal believed that the vicious circle could be turned around by the principle of cumulation. By taking opportunities that were opened by the rank order of discriminations, blacks could gain a substantial footing in both the society and the body politic.

Thus, whereas Tocqueville could see only separation of the races as he looked into the future, DuBois looked to assertive, rights-oriented protest groups to pursue the legitimate demands of blacks for equality as humans and as citizens. DuBois was at the center of the Niagara Movement, and after 1910 he was a central figure in the establishment of the NAACP. Again, Myrdal's advice followed and, to some extent, generalized the path laid out initially by DuBois. Myrdal counted on black groups and their white allies to press the claims of the American creed on the body politic at large.

Finally, whereas Tocqueville saw white people as dominated by prejudice—"the prejudice of the master, the prejudice of the race, and the prejudice of color"—DuBois, at least in his early career, appears to have believed that exposure of the facts could help to free the mind of prejudice. In his mind, at least, the facts exposed the lies of prejudice. Myrdal, too, believed that reason could transcend prejudice. He expected the educational process and scientific planning to play the crucial roles in bringing about change in the direction of a wider equality. For Myrdal the American creed not only pointed to what was right, it also pointed the way to what was rational, the final reason for his optimism. Reason supported and legitimated the demand for equality; therefore, the hope for change seemed to Myrdal to outweigh the fear of change because the grounds for change seemed so deeply rooted in the American experience and in the human condition.

43

CHAPTER TWO

The Development of the Color Line

in Chicago and the Emergence

of the Civic Credo View

If Myrdal was optimistic about the prospects for change, so, too, by midcentury, was Chicago's civic leadership, albeit for somewhat different and inferior reasons. Whereas Myrdal looked to the critical transcendence of the American creed to help resolve the democratic dilemma of white culture and create wider equality, Chicago's civic elite appealed to the immanence of the American creed in the normal functioning of urban institutions to produce a resolution of racial conflict in an atmosphere of civic calm. How this elite came to believe that change could be produced by defending the status quo is the story of the making of the civic credo, a story that cannot be told without giving an account of the making of the color line in Chicago. It is a story of how elevated beliefs, optimistically asserted, obscured the perception of what was actually happening to the structure of the community.

By midcentury all the dimensions of the color line were operating with full force: block-by-block separation of the races resulting in a ghetto with a population of half a million; subordination of blacks in access to basic life needs, standard quality public institutions, and political power; denial of ordinary status to blacks; the dynamics of fear and abasement; recurrent violence whenever blacks and whites openly competed for resources; and the rationalization of these interlocking dimensions in a consolidated civic credo, which, in the name of better things to come, served to obscure the seriousness of the status quo and to deny the need for basic change in the structure of race relations.

We will trace the institutional origins and consolidation of the color line in housing, education, and politics from its beginning on the margins of civic life to its domination of the center stage in a consuming drama of civic disruption and denial.[1]

44

THE MAKING OF THE COLOR LINE IN
HOUSING, EDUCATION, AND POLITICS

Chicago has not always been ruled by this color line. The practice developed before the theory and the theory before the disguise. The city had committed its destiny to the color line before its seriousness became evident. By then, however, denying its seriousness had become part of the problem. How that came to pass is the subject of this chapter.

The Ordinance of 1787 had declared the Northwest Territory "forever free." Although slavery was allowed in Illinois, there is no record of it in Chicago. Chicago had only 350 inhabitants when it was incorporated in 1833. The first school law, enacted in 1835, provided only for "all white children"; but black children did attend the early schools "even though no state aid was received for them."[2]

By 1837 there were 4,000 inhabitants, and Chicago received a city charter. The completion in 1848 of a canal joining the Chicago and Illinois rivers helped to assure the city's future as a transportation and commercial center. By 1850, the population had grown to nearly 30,000, of whom more than half were foreign-born and only about 300 were black. By 1860, the city's population exceeded 100,000, of whom about 1,000 were black.

In 1863 the Chicago City Council passed the Black School Law requiring segregated facilities, but this law was repealed by 1865. By 1870, blacks could and did vote in the land of Lincoln. Blacks constituted a little more than 1 percent of the city's population of 300,000. In 1876 there was a black representative from Chicago in the Illinois legislature.[3] Chicago's population continued to expand rapidly, reaching 1.7 million by the turn of the century and including 30,000 blacks.

In 1903 the Equal Opportunity League, which later became the Illinois branch of the Niagara Movement led by W. E. B. DuBois, was organized to oppose a proposal for segregated schools that was being considered by the new Chicago Charter Commission. By 1906, under the leadership of Dr. Charles E. Bentley, this segregation proposal had been defeated in the Charter Commission. The idea did not go away, however. In 1909, the Hyde Park Improvement Club, a model of sorts for the racist neighborhood protective associations of the future, was campaigning for segregated recreational facilities in Washington Park and was confidently asserting that "it is only a question of time when there will be separate schools for Negroes throughout Illinois." That same year the NAACP was formed in response to the race riot in Springfield, Illinois. Its first Chicago chapter appeared in 1911.[4]

In 1910 there were 44,103 black residents of Chicago, 2 percent of the city's total population. They were an object of tension and contention, but they were not a highly concentrated population. Two-thirds lived in predominantly white census tracts. Only four tracts were more than 50 percent black, and none was more than 61 percent. Only about a dozen blocks on the South Side were entirely black.[5]

During the years 1910 to 1919, Chicago's black population expanded rapidly, reaching 109,458 by 1920, 4 percent of the city's population. It had become significant enough to attract the attention of professional realtors, who viewed blacks as an issue of policy. At a meeting of the Chicago Real Estate Board (CREB) in April 1917, two officials raised the question of the "invasion of white residence districts by the Negroes." The board responded by appointing a Special Committee on Negro Housing to make recommendations for meeting this "threat."[6]

The recommendations of this committee inaugurated a policy of neighborhood segregation. With respect to the "great migration of negroes," the committee stated, "some feasible, practical, and humane method must be devised to house and school them." It is significant that housing and schools were linked in the realtors' minds from the beginning. The committee alleged that unscrupulous tactics of deceit and misrepresentation were "used by some colored agents in soliciting property." Therefore, the committee urged "block organization of owners, without delay, as the situation is primarily in their hands, and under their control." The Chicago Real Estate Board adopted the following policy: "Inasmuch as more territory must be provided, it is desired in the interest of all, that each block shall be filled solidly and that further expansion shall be confined to contiguous blocks, and that the present method of obtaining a single building in scattered blocks, be discontinued." This resolution was fateful not only for Chicago, where the practice of block-by-block concentration and expansion of the black population became an absolute rule, but also for other American cities whose real estate boards looked to the Chicago board for leadership and advice.[7]

In defense of this policy, the board pleaded the irretrievable loss of property values, estimated at from 30 to 60 percent, "the moment the first colored family moves into a block." It claimed that "promiscuous sales and leases here and there mean an unwarranted and unjustifiable destruction of values and the loss in the majority of instances is borne by the small owner whose property represents his life savings; the loss is not only individual, but public, inasmuch as reduced values means reduced taxes." Claiming to speak "in an unprejudiced spirit," the board concluded that both individual interests and the public good would be served by the policy of block-by-block expansion.[8]

If the realtors sincerely believed these claims, as they probably did, it was a remarkable coincidence of moral conviction and material interest. Money was to be made on both ends of the block—higher prices for the blacks whose access to housing was restricted by this policy and lower prices for the fearful

46

whites who would try to sell their houses in panic, with the realtors, who were the middlemen, profiting from both transactions.

The Chicago Real Estate Board recommended that its policy of block-by-block segregation be adopted as a city ordinance, but in November 1917 the U.S. Supreme Court invalidated racial zoning ordinances.[9] Not to be deterred from its policy, the board was quick to devise another means to the same end: "Whereas, there still remains a lawful method of protecting society and property values by block organization of owners, Now, Therefore Be It Resolved, that this board start a propaganda through its individual members to recommend owners societies in every white block for the purpose of mutual defense."[10] The realtors thus guaranteed that the more successful was their policy of concentrating the black population, the more the inevitable expansion of that population would be met by mobilized white fears.

Just as the realtors determined to organize and trade in racial fears, William Hale ("Big Bill") Thompson decided to organize and trade in black votes. Thompson was a Republican mayor from 1915 to 1923 and again from 1927 to 1931. Under his rule both black patronage and black officeholding increased. In 1914 blacks got a second seat in the Illinois legislature, and in 1915 Oscar DePriest was elected to the City Council from the Second Ward.

In 1921, the city adopted a fifty-ward system. Previously there had been thirty-five wards, each of which elected two aldermen. After that each ward elected one alderman to the City Council. The city's ward system, under which ward committeemen were major brokers of both votes and patronage, placed a premium on concentrating "manageable" blocks of votes, insofar as possible, on a ward-by-ward basis. Chicago was an "ethnic" city, and, in the calculus of ward committeemen and precinct captains, blacks were one more ethnic group.[11]

A black Republican organization began to emerge, which by 1928 sent Oscar DePriest to Congress; he was the first black representative since Reconstruction. By 1928 there were five black aldermen. By 1930–32, 2,785 blacks had gained appointive, nominally civil service positions.[12] Thus, during the same period that the realtors were developing a policy of rigid racial segregation in the housing market, the politicians were developing an interest in racial concentration of votes.

In 1917, East St. Louis, Illinois, suffered one of the worst race riots of all time, a riot from which the city never recovered. Chicago's expanding black population met increasing violence, and the fear of a major riot was endemic. In 1919 those fears materialized when Eugene Williams chanced to swim across an invisible segment of the color line which was drawn through the waters of Lake Michigan at the Twenty-third Street Beach. He was stoned to death by angry whites. The police arrested the blacks who protested the killing. Chicago was devastated for more than a week by open racial warfare. The riot prompted open calls for segregation as a solution to the problem of violence. In an outburst of racist realism, the *Chicago Tribune* warned that "so long as this city is dominated by whites . . . there will be limitations placed on the black people."[13]

In the aftermath of the riot, the governor appointed the Chicago Commission on Race Relations to study the situation that had led to the violence. The commission found that by 1920 there was a "Black Belt" on the South Side (Twelfth to Thirty-ninth streets, Wentworth Avenue to Lake Michigan) and another on the West Side (Washington to Kinzie streets, Ashland to California avenues). Even so, on the South Side, there were 43,000 whites living side by side with 55,000 blacks, while on the West Side there were 9,000 whites and 6,500 blacks. The commission found that most of the violence did not take place in these interracial areas.[14] It occurred on the edges of the areas, where black people were moving for the first time. Indeed, it was found that "a kind of guerilla warfare" had accompanied the consolidating and moving color line for the past two years: "In the twenty-four months before July 1919, twenty-four bombings occurred directed at new Negro residents or at real estate agents who dealt in transitional property."[15]

By 1920, then, even though the color line was not the absolute rule it was to become, its contours were sufficiently evident to produce the block-by-block disruption that would dominate the housing market in Chicago for years to come. Nonetheless, in 1921 the realtors reaffirmed the wisdom of their policy and voted unanimously that "immediate expulsion from the Chicago Real Estate Board will be the penalty paid by any member who sells a Negro property in a block where there are only white owners."[16]

During the 1920s the dual policy of block-by-block expansion of the black population accompanied by the organization of militant white neighborhood protective associations was augmented by the invention and promulgation of "restrictive covenants." These were devices, appended to property titles, by which an individual buyer entered into a communitywide compact not to sell or lease his or her property to certain classes of persons—always blacks, sometimes others as well.[17] These covenants were thought to be legally binding until in 1948 they were declared to be constitutionally unenforceable in state courts.[18] Between 1927 and 1929 almost four and one-half square miles of South Side property were enlisted into restrictive covenants. By 1948 this area had expanded to more than eleven square miles.[19] Apparently the neighborhood protective associations were the vehicles for disseminating these covenants and mobilizing community pressure for their adoption.[20]

By 1930 the black population of Chicago had increased to 233,903, almost 7 percent of the city's population, and the policy of block-by-block segregation had proven effective. About two-thirds of Chicago's black population

48

lived in areas that were at least 90 percent black.[21] In the emerging housing market the color line was no mere figure of speech. It was an increasingly solid reality.

By restricting and overcrowding blacks into older and less desirable housing, the color line created a differential quality and quantity of life, a practical inferiority or subordination for blacks characterized by "high sickness and death rates, a heavy relief load during the Depression, inadequate recreation facilities, lack of building repairs, neglect of garbage disposal and street cleaning, overcrowded schools, high rates of crime and juvenile delinquency, and rough treatment by the police."[22] In the words of Thomas Hobbes, ghetto life was "poor, nasty, brutish, and short."

And as the color line moved, violence, of course, was endemic as angry, frightened, and organized whites, in one neighborhood after another, tried in vain to "hold the line" against a growing black population that was being consolidated as a matter of market policy. This pattern of block-by-block black expansion meeting organized, frantic, and ultimately futile white resistance was set in the 1920s, and it continued to repeat itself.[23] The edge of the ghetto had become a major social reality, which, far from bringing interracial peace "in the interest of all," was a constant source of civic disorder and private agony on a block-by-block basis.

In 1918, Max Loeb, a member of the Chicago Board of Education, had addressed an open letter to the expanding black population in the pages of the *Chicago Defender*. "The colored population has increased largely since the War. Colored attendance in public schools has grown accordingly. How best can the Race antagonisms be avoided which so often spring up when the two races are brought into juxtaposition? Do you think it wise," he asked, "when there is a large Colored population, to have separate schools for white and colored children?" He solicited suggestions for how such a policy might best be begun "if under any circumstances it is wise." The readers of the *Defender* did not think it wise in 1918.[24]

By 1922, however, the Board of Education adopted a strict policy of neighborhood schools.[25] When combined with the real estate board's policy of block-by-block expansion of the black population, the neighborhood school policy guaranteed separate schools for black and white children and placed the schools in the middle of the disruptive dynamics of racial change. The link between housing and schools, contemplated by the realtors' Special Committee on Negro Housing five years earlier, had been formalized. Henceforth the disruptive dynamics of racial change in housing and in the schools would reinforce each other and tend to produce even higher profits for the realtors as they brokered sales on both ends of the block.

Other disruptive dynamics were also affecting the schools. From 1915 to 1923, the schools were consumed with graft, corruption, and land grabs as

49

well as confusion over who was actually a member of the Board of Education. "Big Bill" Thompson was in his second term as mayor of Chicago. His "solid six" on the Board of Education were convicted of conspiracy to defraud an honest superintendent of schools of his position in order to substitute one of their own. This legal action did not deter "the Thompson Board in its wild career of looting the schools between 1918 and 1923." Although old allies turned on Thompson and twenty-three persons were indicted for graft in the schools, Thompson and a political confidant of his were quoted as telling school board members, "We're at the feed-box now—and we're going to feed." In 1923 Thompson did not seek reelection, but he was elected again in 1927.[26]

In his study of machine politics, Harold Gosnell characterized the Thompson era as follows:

> As mayor of the city from 1915 to 1923 and from 1927 to 1931, he was hailed as "Big Bill, the Builder," Chicago's greatest booster, the defender of the weak, the champion of the people, while at the same time in certain newspapers the word "Thompsonism" came to be a symbol for spoils politics, police scandals, school-board scandals, padded pay rolls, gangster alliances, betrayal of the public trust, grotesque campaign methods and buffoonery in public office. He was a clown who distracted the people's attention while his political associates ran the city's business. He was a good clown and a firm believer in the principle that bad publicity is better than none. . . . As far as can be ascertained, he personally derived no pecuniary benefit from his activities in politics. He liked the game and the crowds.[27]

The 1920s were prosperous times in Chicago. Through 1927 rising property values were the object of a bipartisan "tax racket"; for a price, assessments could be reduced. Gosnell commented that "conditions grew so bad that the State Tax Commission ordered a reassessment in 1928," and no taxes were collected for more than a year while the reassessment was accomplished. The city ran on loans against anticipated revenue. When the reassessment was undertaken, it was a promise of increased funding for the schools. By the time the reassessment was completed, however, it was the beginning of financial disaster for the schools.[28]

Unexpectedly, "the real estate market lost its buoyancy in 1927. The volume of transfers, new buildings, and lots subdivided declined, apartment rents levelled off, and demand for vacant lots abated." The Depression, therefore, was a double disaster for the schools, which relied on property taxes. With large loans already outstanding, more were needed when back taxes did not come in and current revenues declined. "By 1933," according to one study, "teachers' salaries were months in arrears." Furthermore, in 1932 a business and banking consortium constituted itself as the Committee on Public Expenditures, with "immediate retrenchment" as its goal and the schools as one of its "primary targets."[29]

50

In 1931 the business and banking interests found a man in whom they had more confidence than the discredited Thompson. He was Anton J. Cermak, and, even though he was a Democrat, he was willing to impose austerity on the city budget and reform the tax machinery. He was also a tough party disciplinarian, who knew the value of patronage in building a political organization. At various times, he had been a state representative, alderman, bailiff of the municipal court, and president of the Cook County Board of Commissioners. Although Thompson badgered him in the 1931 election about having "saved six million out of a $10,000 salary," and there were stories about his bootlegging, gambling, crime connections, and real estate manipulations, nothing was ever proved. He was a master "at the art of conciliating business, labor, reform, nationalistic, and neighborhood associations."[30]

Cermak's policy orientation was conservative. That was his appeal to businessmen, but it was also his undoing. In 1932, Cermak cast his lot with the attempt to renominate Al Smith at the Democratic National Convention to the displeasure of Franklin D. Roosevelt and his patronage chief, James A. Farley. Even after the election, they refused to communicate with Cermak. In an effort at reconciliation with Roosevelt, Cermak went to Miami, where Roosevelt and Farley were vacationing. Still they would not acknowledge him. In desperation, the mayor of Chicago approached an open car in which Roosevelt was riding—just in time to be killed by an assassin's bullet meant for the president.[31]

But the organization he was building in Chicago was far from dead. When Cermak had become mayor, his friend Patrick A. Nash had become chairman of the Cook County Regular Democratic party—the political machine in the making. Nash was a prosperous sewer contractor who had been active in party politics for years. In 1933 he was seventy years old. As an economy move, the Illinois legislature empowered the Chicago City Council to name a new mayor, and Nash chose Edward J. Kelly, who with him shared Cermak's conservative policy orientation. Both men were committed to saving money in politically expedient ways. Kelly had been president of the South Park Board and chief engineer of the sanitary district. While he was mayor, it was learned that his income in 1926, 1927, and 1928 had been around $450,000. He paid the back taxes. His opponents got nowhere when they raised questions about how a lifelong public servant could have had such a high income.[32]

When Edward J. Kelly became mayor in 1933, he appointed five new members to the Board of Education, including James B. McCahey, who became president of the board, took personal charge of the budget committee, and made clear his intentions to make radical cuts in expenditures. In response, the Citizens Save Our Schools Committee, heavily influenced by the teachers, was organized. It later became the Citizens Schools Committee. As the teachers achieved stronger union organization, the Citizens Schools Committee became a gathering point for people concerned about the quality of the schools, their political abuse, financial irregularities, and, to a lesser degree, racial discrimination. This committee "held the mayor morally and, in a sense, centrally responsible for the condition of the schools."[33]

In the course of the 1930s, the banks got their money and the teachers got theirs. It is safe to say that at least some of that money was saved at the expense of the black children and their schools. "Studies made at that time showed that double shifts were almost all in Negro areas," and there were organized community protests about this situation late in the decade. Citizen research also revealed that "76 percent of the Negro children spent less time in school than white children. Inexperienced teachers were concentrated in Negro schools. Expenditures per pupil showed a racial differentiation. A sample study reported that in 1937–38, the Board of Education spent $86.07 per pupil in white schools, $82.02 in integrated schools, and $74.02 in Negro schools."[34]

During the 1930s the migration of blacks into Chicago tapered off, with fewer than 50,000 new arrivals. By 1940 Chicago's black population was 282,244. Both the physical pressure for more black housing and the financial means with which to get it were greatly reduced during the Depression. The 1920s and 1930s were a time of institutional development and consolidation of a black ghetto behind the color line.[35] The signatories of restrictive covenants might have believed that it was their action that had stemmed the tide of "invasion"; but the renewal of the great migration in the 1940s, on an unprecedented scale, was more than enough to disabuse any such idea.

One of the critical institutional developments that took place in the 1930s was the establishment of a strong black political organization within the Cook County Regular Democratic party. Previously, black politics was mostly Republican. In 1932 Herbert Hoover had carried the Chicago black vote. But in a surprising development, the Democratic organization was able to elect a little-known lawyer, Arthur W. Mitchell, as congressman from the First Congressional District, defeating the powerful Oscar DePriest. Mitchell's election was more of a national event than a local one. He was the first black to enter the Congress as a Democrat; but locally his election was more an indication of the growing power of the Democratic party. He had no organization of his own, and even though he served in Congress from 1934 to 1942, he never developed one.[36]

It was William Dawson who ultimately developed a black political organization within the Democratic party. Dawson was elected to the City Council in 1933 as an independent Republican after falling out with the DePriest organization. After Roosevelt claimed half the black voters in Chicago in 1936, however, Dawson moved into the Democratic party and with Mayor Kelly's support became the committeeman of the Second Ward in 1939. His influence spread from there. In 1942 he was elected to Congress, where he served until his death in 1970 at the age of eighty-four. In 1943 he was able to bring the Third Ward, in 1951 the Twentieth Ward, in 1955 the Fourth Ward, and in 1956 the Sixth Ward under his control, making him by 1960 the second most powerful individual in the party, second only to the mayor. Indeed, in the 1955 election, Mayor Daley owed his majority of 125,000 to Dawson's organization.[37] Thus Dawson moved into the Democratic organization just as the black population of Chicago was about to begin a massive expansion, adding 225,000 in the 1940s and another 300,000 in the 1950s. The patterns had been set. The color line was operating full force in housing, schools, and politics.

In the years between World Wars I and II the modern color line was formed, major institutions accommodated to it, and a black ghetto was established. The concentration of the black population was as striking as its expansion between 1910 and 1930, from 44,000, two-thirds of whom lived in predominantly white census tracts, to 233,000, two-thirds of whom lived in census tracts that were at least 90 percent black. The decision of the Chicago Real Estate Board in 1917 to pursue a policy of block-by-block expansion of the black population certainly was not the only reason for this concentration, but it did prove to be effective. The further decision to organize fearful whites into "hold-the-line" neighborhood protective associations and to promulgate restrictive covenants guaranteed constant conflict and endemic violence at the edge of the ghetto. The adoption by the schools of a strict neighborhood policy placed them in the center of that conflict and violence. Further, the existence of white schools and black schools gave the opportunity for discriminatory allocation policies, which were already a matter of record by the 1930s. The political system accommodated and perhaps enhanced the concentration of the black political ward organizations, first in Thompson's Republican party, ultimately in Kelly's Democratic party.

Thus by the late 1930s the full dimensions of the color line were in operation. Housing was segregated on a block-by-block basis. Blacks held a subordinate position in access to basic life needs through the provision of less desirable housing and less of it and at higher costs than whites paid;[38] in access to high-quality public institutions through discriminatory allocations to black schools; and in access to political power, though here the record is perhaps ambiguous. Down through the 1950s, the allocation of wards and patronage more or less kept pace with the expansion of the black population, but this political power was purchased at the price of not being able to affect the basic processes by which the black population was being segregated from and subordinated in the society at large. The denial of ordinary status was a recurring theme in all institutions, and blacks had become the object of special policies. The dynamics of fear and abasement were actively organized by the neighborhood improvement associations, institutionalized in restrictive covenants, and continuously exacerbated by the block-by-block expansion of the ghetto. The violence was endemic at the edge of the ghetto. The rationalizations amounted to various versions of racist realism: appeals to "natural" antipathy of the races, presentations of segregation as a way to minimize conflict and violence, beliefs that property values fell when blacks moved in, which were reinforced by the visible deterioration of the overcrowded ghetto housing and schools, appeals to "white solidarity" to hold the line "in the interest of all," and, of course, claims that blacks themselves preferred to live "with their own kind."

FROM RACE RELATIONS TO HUMAN RELATIONS:
RACIST REALISM IN SEARCH OF A THEORY

Between 1940 and 1950 Chicago's black population increased from 282,244 to 509,512. The conflict that accompanied this massive influx and the extension of the color line that went with it were cause for civic alarm. In June 1943 a race riot broke out in Detroit. The fear was widespread that Chicago might be in for the same. In July 1943, Mayor Edward J. Kelly appointed a blue-ribbon Mayor's Committee on Race Relations.[39] It was the first sustained attempt in Chicago to take official cognizance of the color line as a civic problem. Whereas the Chicago Commission on Race Relations had been created to study the causes of the 1919 riot, had been privately funded, and was transformed into a department of the church federation with the issuing of its report, the mayor's committee of 1943 was to lead to a permanent, publicly funded agency within the city government. Chicago was the first to establish this kind of human relations commission, and it was to serve as a model widely copied by other cities. In Chicago, however, it was to become merely the first in a long series of attempts to manage crises in the Negro problem through blue-ribbon commissions. (The Mayor's Committee on Race Relations existed through 1944. Its successor, the Mayor's Commission on Human Relations, continued its work during 1945 and 1946. A permanent city commission, the Chicago Commission on Human Relations, came into existence in 1947.)

Nonetheless, a distinguished group initially came together as members of the mayor's committee. Its first chairman was Edwin R. Embree, president of the Julius Rosenwald Fund, a philanthropy dedicated to the improvement of conditions for black people and the betterment of race relations. (Rosenwald had himself served on the 1919 commission.) At the same time that he was involved in the establishment of the human relations commission in Chicago, Embree was also participating in the transformation of the Commission on Interracial Cooperation into the Southern Regional Council and the founding of the American Council on Race Relations, an educational and consultative body available to local communities desirous of making positive changes in difficult minority relations.[40]

Another member was Charles S. Johnson, coauthor of the 1919 commission's report, who had in the meantime distinguished himself as a creator of the field of sociology of Negro life. Horace R. Cayton, journalist, scholar, and director of the most ambitious study of Negro urban life to date, and Robert C. Weaver, already on his way to becoming one of the foremost authorities on housing, an administrator experienced in the politics of equal housing in the New Deal, also served. Willard S. Townsend, international president of the United Transport Service Employees, CIO (Red Caps); Louis Wirth, one of the nation's leading theoreticians of urban sociology; and Melville J. Herskovits, anthropologist, whose studies broke ground for the field that would later be called black studies, were also active participants. The mayor's committee was an amazing array of thoughtful and experienced talent, which gathered to assess Chicago's potential for racial equality in the mid-1940s.[41]

In the beginning the mayor's committee was a remarkable instrument of civic self-criticism. Within six months of its appointment, it had called a comprehensive conference on city planning in race relations, which provided an opportunity for those who were concerned with solving the problems of race relations through democratic social change to meet with public officials who were responsible for devising ways and means of coping with the tensions generated by the color line. Mayor Kelly assured the participants that they were "not a meeting of idealists and dreamers to sketch a panacea." On the contrary, he said, "It is a meeting of the officials of the various municipal departments and of leaders in every branch of civil life to plan together wise and feasible steps toward the goal of democracy." In addition to the focus on "wise and feasible steps," the formal addresses all spoke in praise of pluralism, in dismay of discrimination, and in favor of an immigrant interpretation of the Negro problem.[42] Of all the city's services, the schools came in for the most pointed and sustained criticism.

It did not help when James B. McCahey chose to defend the school's racial policies in terms which to his critics seemed like an admission of the worst charges. "When Mayor Kelly was elected Mayor of Chicago in 1933," said McCahey, "he asked me to become a member of the School Board, with two thoughts in mind. One was to straighten out the financial chaos of the school board; and the other, that he knew well my sympathies as to the Negro people in the districts on the South Side."[43] If true, that was certainly the most damaging statement made about the mayor during the proceedings. By the time McCahey had finished his defense, everyone present knew well his sympathies "as to the Negro people."

By the 1950s, school officials would develop a stance of principled igno-

55

rance about the color of their schools. McCahey, however, spoke with candor about the "Negro schools" and conceded that "at the present moment they are slightly over-crowded." That problem was not, as he saw it, the board's fault. "If it were not for the war," he said, "and the limitations placed on account of materials that we cannot get, and the housing trouble on the Near South Side, the schools would be in top shape." The solution lay in building more schools in black areas, where the school population had nearly doubled between 1929 and 1943, from 21,564 to 40,572. He stressed that this increase had taken place at a time when enrollments were decreasing in "other areas," but changing population patterns did not suggest to him any alternatives for relieving the overcrowding. The board had built thirteen new schools and was projecting ten more in 1944 for a total increase of 23,000 seats for black pupils. In the meantime, he thought the board deserved credit for its efforts in a difficult situation. The pupil-teacher ratio in black schools had been reduced through the use of double shifts, to be sure; but he assured his listeners that "there is just one drawback to a double session—it means a shorter day." He denied any gerrymandering of school boundaries and that any vacant facilities existed which could be used to alleviate the overcrowding. The dramatic high point of his address came when he said: "The contrast between the opportunities provided these children now and before they migrated to Chicago is astonishing. . . . Down South they spend $37 a year for school buildings; in Chicago, $600 per pupil. . . . Ordinarily, children from other states would be required to pay tuition. However, these children who migrate to the city of Chicago from the South not having such advantages are immediately enrolled in our Chicago schools without the payment of tuition."[44]

The other participants in the conference were not pleased with this presentation, and it was clear from the responses that the racial condition of the schools had been at issue for some time. Irene M. Gaines, in speaking for the Chicago Council of Negro Organizations, said that that group had been "charging for the past 8 or 9 years . . . that the President of the Board of Education and his Superintendent of Schools are directly responsible for many of the smoldering resentments and hatreds that have been built up in the Negro community because of the rigid and terrible school facilities accorded our children." She claimed to have proof of gerrymandering, and she proposed that overcrowding be considered a sufficient cause for transferring students out of a school. John A. Lapp, president of the Citizens Schools Committee, said, "I just want to call your attention to the fact that there are 16,000 children in the elementary schools on the double shift system in the South Side, with practically none anywhere else in the city." Earl B. Dickerson, president of the Chicago Urban League, considered the South Side situation an emergency, and he wanted not only action but information as well. "We ask the President of the Board," he said, "to put into the open the number of schools in the city; and the districts in which those schools lie; so that we of the South Side, simple people, may understand the truth of the statement that there are no vacant seats and would no longer charge that there is discrimination."[45]

Edwin Embree concluded the day's proceedings by saying that "the schools appeared in these conferences to be the least satisfactory of the basic city services." In direct response to McCahey, he said,

It is not a proper answer to point out that children receive a better education in Chicago than they do in rural Mississippi—any more than it would be to point out our advantages over County Cork or the more dilapidated sections of Poland. Education in Chicago must be judged by Chicago standards.

This Committee recognizes the gains made by the present school administration. But it solemnly warns that public education is a chief pillar of American democracy, and that at whatever trouble and inconvenience, facilities for education must be equalized for all the people of Chicago.[46]

Even so, the day ended on a hopeful note. "The most important thing in the meeting, I think," said Horace Cayton, "is this: It has been shown that the Negro problem is not unique, not different from other problems Chicago has faced in the past. It has some differences. . . . But they are differences of degree, and the difficulties are not so great that they are incapable of solution. The problems of the Poles, of the Irish, the Italians, and many other people have been solved. And this first meeting demonstrates that a solution is possible for the Negro problem as well."[47]

The conference adjourned, and the committee set out to arrange its priorities. In June 1944 it was resolved that "in view of the basic importance of the housing problem to every other issue at the present time, and because of the favorable progress in other fields of our activity, this committee feels that the staff, without neglecting the other phases of our program, should concentrate most of its time and energy on the housing problem."[48]

In response, the Chicago Real Estate Board pledged itself to an increased building program of five hundred new residential units "for Negro occupancy on the South Side."[49] In not challenging that response, which was simply a promise of more, albeit better, of the same policy that had prevailed for more than twenty-five years, the committee failed to challenge the salesmen of segregation.

At the 1945 Conference on Home Front Unity, Embree and others were more sensitive to the problems of segregation in the schools. In his opening remarks he said, "Schools, our record here is nearly perfect—perfect zero." The building program had proceeded, and Embree conceded that "the school board has curbed, but not completely eliminated, the transfer system which has tended to build up de facto segregation of white and colored pupils."[50]

Speaking for the Chicago branch of the NAACP, Oscar Brown accused the schools of attempting to foster "as much segregation as possible." In illustra-

57

tion of this claim he cited the case of Washburne Trade School, "the only trade school, the only one that trains plumbers and lathers and other building trade workers." He claimed that the school "has a scheme whereby a person who takes that training must be an apprentice. The union has to name the apprentice to take the training. A Negro boy is never selected as an apprentice; consequently the very highly productive building trades exclude the Negro in those high categories of employment." The chairman of the session asked him, "You mean, in Chicago, the city provides a trade school available only to white people?" "That's the result of it," he replied.[51]

Another participant suggested that the unions, not the schools, were responsible for the situation. Brown responded that "the union ought not be given the right to control the schools."[52] Most of the participants sided with Brown, voted that the board should "open up Washburne Trade School," and requested the mayor's committee to pursue the matter.[53] In 1946, the commission reported that additional state legislation would be required to open up Washburne.[54] The situation remained unchanged down through the 1960s.

The first session of the Chicago Conference on Home Front Unity met during May and June 1945. In October and November it reconvened for the purpose of adopting the Charter of Human Relations to guide policy and express a civic consensus about the race problem. In keeping with its new emphasis, the committee became the Mayor's Commission on Human Relations.[55] At these meetings again there were lengthy discussions about the schools. Between the first and second sessions of the conference, there was a dramatic upsurge in interracial violence. By September some of this violence was focused in Englewood and Calumet high schools, where black students were enrolled for the first time and white students were on strike demanding segregated schools. As time went by, such incidents commanded most of the committee's attention and energy, but in 1945 they appeared to be blatant, irrational episodes rather than a pattern of future events.

At the time, framing the Charter of Human Relations to provide a comprehensive basis for city planning in race relations was the focus of attention. Indeed, the eruption of violence made that project appear all the more important so that the city as well as private agencies could identify their common ground for withstanding the irrational neighborhood pressures generated by the violence. Ironically, it was the violence that provided the needed common ground, for isolating and dealing with it became a major focus of the commission's work.

The reports for 1945 and 1946 show the commission, driven by neighborhood events and by the conception that the problem was a neighborhood one, defined its function more and more as crisis management and less and less as generating critical thought about the adequacy of the city's institutions.

58

Indeed, these reports began to shift from probing civic self-criticism to a self-serving stance of civic self-defense. And in the absence of a comprehensive policy orientation to the color line, the commission was driven into increasing reliance upon the police. For instance, instead of looking into the broad pattern of events and relationships surrounding the high school violence of 1945, the commission adopted a "virus" theory of racial disturbance. The schools of Gary, Indiana, were undergoing similar travail. "The situation in the Gary Schools," read the 1945 report, "has been an unfortunate source of infection. The school children of Chicago have gone to school together for a long time. They will continue to do so. Chicago will stand squarely for democracy in its public schools."[56]

Of course, the testimony at the Conference on Home Front Unity had demonstrated that not one of those assertions was true. When considering the immediate situation, however, the commission took notice only of the students' behavior, which it called "completely reprehensible, and absolutely opposed to the democratic tradition of Chicago." The violence was a police matter and a public relations problem. In addition, the commission took heart that the Board of Education was resisting the students' demand for segregation. At the time, it seemed a victory. "The mayor's committee looks upon this as a great gain in the life of the city," according to the annual report.[57]

A pattern of action and interpretation had been set. In 1946, the commission reported that violence "increased sharply over 1945 and became more serious in nature." In addition to schools, the commission found itself involved in volatile and violent incidents all along the color line. Teenage gangs were fighting, roller skating rinks were battlefields, and emergency housing for veterans was under siege, as militant whites, in each case, resisted the appearance of blacks in new territory. The problem, as the commission saw it, was in the neighborhoods, in the irrational fears of whites, whose behavior was becoming a police problem on a block-by-block basis.[58]

In an attempt to deal constructively with the problem as perceived, the commission turned its attention to community organizing techniques in the affected neighborhoods. Its answer to interracial violence was to form interracial groups. These groups came into being, however, only after the deterioration of relations was already well under way, and, in any case, they were no competition for the neighborhood improvement associations, which the realtors had sponsored and which were committed to holding the line no matter what.

By year's end, the commission was not encouraged with the results of its strategy. "This activity appeared to be fruitful," wrote the executive director, "only insofar as it contributed to the commission's knowledge of the area and as it pointed the way to an endless chain of people who were interested in the problem but were so gloomy about the prospects of even a potential solution that they considered any efforts in that direction a waste of time."[59] Under that interpretation, only the police remained as an effective force.

Meanwhile, the clouds that had been gathering around the schools burst all over the Chicago political scene. In 1946, a National Education Association (NEA) committee investigated the regime of James B. McCahey and General Superintendent William Johnson. The committee found irregularities in every area: the use of promotions and demotions for political reasons; a spy system at work among the teachers, reporting "disloyalties" to the administration; no merit system; nepotism; a superintendent dominated by the board president, who was an operative of the political machine, controlling appointments and contracts; fraud in the principals' examinations; a superintendent requiring the use of his own textbooks; evidence of bribes; board members with financial interests in the contracts they were approving—not always to the lowest bidder; and so on. The NEA committee identified McCahey and Johnson as the culprits but placed the responsibility on the mayor: "All the board members are his appointees and are to a considerable extent responsive to his wishes and cooperative with the city hall organization."[60]

Superintendent Johnson was expelled from the NEA. The North Central Association of Colleges and Secondary Schools threatened to withdraw accreditation from the Chicago public schools. The superintendent and a majority of the board resigned. The mayor created a blue-ribbon Mayor's Advisory Commission on School Board Nominations. It was meant to symbolize the removal of education from Chicago-style politics, even as the Mayor's Committee on Race Relations had been meant to bring good government to bear on the Negro problem.[61] Mayor Kelly, however, did not seek reelection in 1947.

Reform was the keynote of the year 1947. The Cook County Regular Democratic party, the sometime "machine," was by now a complex instrument of community mobilization, bargaining, administration, and governance—always ready with a reform program of its own. When Mayor Kelly had to step aside because of the scandalous school crisis of 1946, the organization came forward with its own slate of reform candidates. In 1947 it elected Martin Kennelley as mayor, and in 1948 it elected Adlai Stevenson as governor and Paul Douglas as senator. Colonel Jacob Arvey, county chairman, was able to present the organization as a reform party, even though some of its most prominent leaders were accused of malfeasance. In the midst of a crisis that might have been thought to spell its doom as a credible instrument of governance, this organization was able to expand its support and consolidate its rule under the banner of good government.[62]

This transformation is especially significant as it related to the schools. Because they had been the focal point in the exposé of patronage politics and the withdrawal of Mayor Kelly from office, they became a showcase of civic virtue. That education was nonpolitical became part of the civic credo. The Mayor's Advisory Commission on School Board Nominations became the sign and seal of the promise of nonpolitical purity in the administration of the schools.

A national search was undertaken for a new superintendent. The Illinois code was amended to make it a strong office, uniting business and academic responsibilities in the same official. In 1947 Herold C. Hunt was appointed to this office, and there followed an era of good feeling about the schools. Hunt created the Technical Advisory Committee on Intergroup Relations, which worked with Louis Wirth and his colleagues of the University of Chicago Committee on Education, Training, and Research in Race Relations. This group studied school boundaries and proposed revisions for about 30 percent of the elementary schools. The changes affected relatively few children.[63] In explaining the revisions, Hunt said that "complete use of all buildings is the one principle I hope will govern all boundary decisions. We have over-crowded schools in Negro areas, and vacant rooms and floors in neighboring schools that are predominantly white. Mixed schools exist in our system and no under-used school should be reserved as a white school."[64]

This public policy of equalizing the use of facilities did have some desegre-gating effects. As one student of the issue later commented, "Disparities be-tween Negro and white schools in class size and the use of rooms for auxiliary purposes were lessened. The number of surplus classrooms was lowered in interracial schools but not in white schools." To cope with the conflict that accompanied this desegregation, the board created a Human Relations Com-mittee to survey the system. This committee set out to organize local human relations committees and "pilot centers" for areas that were actively "experi-encing some community unrest . . . due to a growing Negro population." Advisory councils for these pilot centers and training programs in intergroup relations for the teachers were created. The Human Relations Committee has been called the "most complicated piece of machinery attempted by the Hunt administration."[65] But like the community organizing attempts of the Mayor's Commission on Human Relations, these local human relations committees were not effective in stemming the tides of racial change.

By 1953 the technical committee had prepared a plan for equalizing enroll-ments in Chicago's high schools. Hunt left the school system, however, and was succeeded by Benjamin C. Willis. He received the report on high schools, but he did not act on its recommendations, and he never reactivated the committee.[66]

Twenty years later, Robert Havighurst, who had worked on the technical committee and the boundary revisions, had some second thoughts about the project: "I think we should admit that we gave Mr. Hunt some bad advice. In general, our policy was one of being 'color blind.' . . . . What we did was

61

recommend the establishment of a strict neighborhood school policy which had the ultimate effect of driving white families out of certain school districts at a rapid rate. . . . If we had known that the Negro immigration would increase and remain high for a decade, we would probably have made other kinds of recommendations, perhaps including an open attendance policy."[67]

In the early 1950s, however, it was commonly believed that the worst was over and the road ahead would be smoother, especially in the schools. Since 1946, the schools had been "professionalized," meaning that they were freed from patronage politics; and they were administered along universal, not discriminatory, concepts of organization. They were thus cast as a reform institution.

THE MAKING OF THE CIVIC CREDO:
PREMISES AND PROMISES IN CONFLICT

The formation of the civic credo and the role of the schools in it is a case study in moral failure of a high order, the story of how high ideals, originally espoused as creative instruments for civic self-criticism, came to be used as weapons of civic self-defense, obscuring the realities of injustice, community disruption, and human suffering.

The developments that began with the appointment of the Mayor's Committee on Race Relations in 1943 and led to the creation of the Chicago Commission on Human Relations in 1947 played a key role in the making of this civic credo. From its inception the very existence of the commission seemed to imply an official recognition of the gravity of the Negro problem. But what was the Negro problem? As initially enunciated in 1944–45, it was the conflict between the actual conditions under which Negroes were living and the democratic imperatives for equality. It was a partial version of Myrdal's white dilemma of democratic culture. The original committee understood that its task was fourfold: to assess the adequacy of the city government's response to this problem and to make recommendations for improvement; to enlist the support of increasing numbers of groups in the recognition of the seriousness of the problem and to provide channels for their concerns; to elicit the widest possible cooperation in planning for better race relations; and to create an air of understanding in volatile situations of conflict. It was an evolutionary concept of the commission's role; and the founders, at least, seemed to envision a progressive relation between recognition of the problem, understanding its complications, and cooperation in working toward its solution.

In its early days, promoting recognition and understanding involved criticism and candor, especially about the schools. The schools were excoriated for their blatant racism. Ten years before the *Brown* decision, Embree enunciated for Chicago the same principle the Supreme Court was to espouse: "that public education is a chief pillar of American democracy, and that at whatever trouble and inconvenience, facilities for education must be equalized for all the people of Chicago."[68]

The principle was sound, but the commission's understanding of the empirical problem in the face of which it would have to be applied was seriously flawed. And that caused the downfall of this attempt to mobilize civic resources to counter the virulent effects of the color line. Even in its early days this flaw was evident. When the commission attempted to focus its program on housing, it failed to deal with the underlying dynamics of block-by-block expansion of the ghetto. Consequently, as its 1945 and 1946 annual reports demonstrated, its program was increasingly driven by events to become one of attempts to manage the violence and community crises precipitated by that block-by-block expansion—a move from a policy orientation to a police function.

Fear of imminent violence had caused the mayor to convene the commission in the first place, but instead of paying attention to daily violence that was a regular feature of the moving color line, the commission focused on the "irrational fears of whites," which, at that time, were thought to be temporary. The commission made no "edge of the ghetto" analysis and seemed not to realize that it was dealing with a social and commercial process that had been not only continuous but triumphant in the housing market since before 1920. Because of its failure to analyze this phenomenon, the commission's activities were reduced to various ineffective strategies for managing and containing the routine crises of neighborhood violence which were effectively shaping the political geography and the civic climate of the city. Consequently, even from the very beginning, the commission was out of touch with the actual dynamics of the problem.

This failure was not perceived by the participants because they assumed that they knew what the problem was. The theme was stated by Edwin Embree in his first annual report. "Negroes are simply the latest of the immigrant streams that have built this city," he said. "The problem is to give Negroes, as for the most part we have given other immigrant groups, full rights and free opportunities."[69] Whereas Myrdal's optimism was rooted in his understanding of the critical transcendence of the American creed, the optimism of the founders of the human relations commission was rooted in an understanding of the American creed as immanent in existing institutions, in the mayor's determination to "do the right thing," and in a conviction that the immigrant analogy provided a basic model for the black experience.

Accordingly, the commission assumed that racial conflict was a temporary problem that would be healed by time and the normal functioning of institutions. It further assumed, along with the most prominent sociologists of the

63

time, that the war-induced influx of blacks from the South would taper off in the 1950s. Neither of these suppositions was borne out by actual events. Consequently, this attempt to alter the dynamics of the color line failed.

In keeping with its assumptions, the commission adopted a majoritarian stance. Since both the deepest democratic values in the culture and the full authority of the city seemed to be committed to the resolution of the Negro problem, the commission framed its program to mobilize key elements of the community behind a broadly conceived campaign for civic consensus and to identify key sources of conflict against which the civic consensus and the municipal authority could be brought to bear. If an atmosphere of calm could be maintained, assimilation was only a matter of time. Other immigrant groups had been down the same road. The Negro problem was neither unique nor radical in its dimensions.

By the time the Chicago Commission on Human Relations became a regular department of the city government in 1947, its critical function was spent. It had become an agency for the identification of emerging trouble spots and for managing those inevitable crises which could not be averted. It was fated to deal with these disruptions as they occurred, and the ability to do so was henceforth considered an impressive achievement. This agency's mission had been misconceived.

By the early 1950s, the agency's activities were equally misdirected. At the end of its first five years as a government agency, the commission issued a report that was exuberant in its claims. Chicago, the report maintained, was firmly set on the path of progress in dealing with the evils of the color line:

> The five years of this report—1947 through 1951—have marked a dramatic change in human relations in Chicago. Five years ago Chicago might easily have exploded into racial violence. Today, with a professionally trained police force alert to human relations problems, no one any longer fears a riot. Five years ago Chicago's schools were charged with gerrymandering to segregate colored children, and curriculum indifferent to human relations did little about children's attitudes. Today the schools are the most democratic institutions in the city. Five years ago only one or two Loop hotels could be counted upon to give equal service to all people. Today discrimination in a major Chicago Loop hotel is the rare exception to the rule. Therefore if this report sounds optimistic it is so with good reason. The Commission is painfully aware of the unfinished business of democracy in Chicago, but the road ahead is unquestionably smoother. [70]

The idea that the worst was over and the disaster had been averted was supported by the assumption among demographers that the war-induced migration of blacks into the North would surely taper off in the 1950s. In keeping with the immigrant analogy, it was thought that reduced population pressure would allow time and space for the normal processes of assimilation to take over without the constant atmosphere of crisis. Selected neighborhoods were still convulsed from racial change, but in the absence of any analysis of the structural problems, the commission was reduced to theorizing that irrational attitudes accounted for the continuing conflict. The commission, therefore, conceived of its task as dealing with those irrational attitudes and their social consequences—by persuasion if possible, by force if need be. In this respect, at least, it reflected Myrdal's understanding that the American dilemma was a matter of attitudes and that those attitudes that were in tension with the American creed were, if not irrational, at least at a lower level of rationality.

By 1951, however, the commission seemed to be much more impressed and saddened by the irrational attitudes of blacks than by those of whites. Firm in its conviction that the "problems arising in communities undergoing change must be met by people living on the blocks in these areas," the commission expressed concern that the blacks were yielding to "segregated-mindedness" and losing the opportunities for desegregation: "The new, mixed community is the battleground for the removal of this 'segregated-mindedness' of the Negro, which he has adopted in defense against 'white supremacy' and 'white superiority' notions. In our new, inter-racial communities we have the opportunity to eliminate ideas of caste and prove the fundamental premise of our democratic faith, the equality of all in rights and responsibilities."[71]

The problem, as envisaged by the commission, was to get the message across to blacks that this equality was theirs for the taking. Unfortunately, the report explained, "Elements of the Negro community and the institutions which have developed within it as a part of the segregated pattern have found that there is a certain power in segregation. For one thing, it eliminates competition and assures a market, even though limited. There is a vested interest on the part of some Negro institutions in segregation." The commission did not discuss any other "vested interests" that might have developed along the color line. Instead, it bore down on the segregated-mindedness of a hypothetical "Negro real estate man": "He belongs to a segregated Negro real estate board . . . and is still . . . interested only in the listing and sale of properties to prospective Negro purchasers. He carries with him the whole tradition of fear about listing and trying to sell properties too far away from the established Negro community. His intention, like that of most of his fellow Negro brokers, is to list and sell properties on this block, house by house. Then he will sell the houses on the next block. And the segregated pattern has won again." Nor was this Negro realtor alone in his segregated-mindedness. His behavior, the commission went on to say, "can be duplicated in the Negro doctor, newspaperman, social worker, professional man and woman, and the ordinary workingman who moves into the new community."[72] Here we can see how, by 1951, the commission defined the Negro problem. In this perverse portrayal, blacks themselves, with their segregated-mindedness, were their own worst problem.

65

The commission took no notice of the continuing activity of white neighborhood protective associations, dedicated to opposing any expansion of black people into their territory. In 1951, the same year as the commission's progress report, a study of these groups concluded that they were far from spontaneous expressions of the popular will. Realtors might justify their policies as merely an accommodation to popular passions, but the study concluded that this "policy which appears to have been made by the small homeowners . . . is actually originated by those who have a business interest in real estate." And it was not the commission's hypothetical Negro real estate man which this study identified as the problem: "Realtors, builders, and mortgage bankers hold a great deal of interest in and control over neighborhood improvement associations. Less active on the local level, they dominate all of the regional and federated clubs in the city and also the city-wide organizations, and this is where the pressure comes from."[73] Nonetheless, the commission did not question the idea that time and the normal functioning of institutions would operate to assimilate black people into the mainstream of democratic participation in the life of the city if the blacks could but overcome their segregated-mindedness.

The schools, especially, were expected to play a vital role in this development, and by the early 1950s the schools were a matter of considerable civic pride as well as an emblem of hope. By 1951 it was a matter of sheer credulity to believe such a claim. That it was widely shared by the civic and intellectual elite of the city is testimony to the power of the civic credo that had been fashioned since the war.

The disruptions arising from the expanding color line in Chicago had been subsumed under a civic credo that authoritatively asserted that the issue was best described as the Negro problem, with the emphasis on what was wrong with blacks; this problem was analogous to that previously faced by other ethnic, immigrant groups; democratic values and the normal functioning of institutions would, in due time, produce equality of treatment for blacks; the worst was over, and the road ahead was incomparably smoother; and, therefore, further progress depended on pursuing nonpartisan, majoritarian, consensual strategies in an atmosphere of civic calm. The schools were cited as a prime example of this civic credo. They had been laundered by separating them from politics without examining their implication in the dynamics of the color line, and anyone who might subsequently want to address that problem was going to face charges of reintroducing politics into the schools.

A great deal more than an agency's mission had been misconceived. The new principles of civic order had been misconceived at such a high moral level that the will to believe began to substitute for the evidence of the civic senses to such an extent that the facts of civic life became enemies of the civic credo. Every one of the doctrinal assertions of the civic credo was at moral variance with the facts.

In fact, by 1950, Chicago had a black ghetto of more than half a million. During the 1940s the city's black population nearly doubled, and it was more segregated and more massively segregated in 1950 than it had been in 1940. The block-by-block movement of the color line was increasing rather than diminishing day by day. It was disruptively segregating the neighborhood schools as much as any area of life.

Yet the problem in the schools, as perceived in the early 1950s, was to protect their professional autonomy. That was the platform on which Benjamin C. Willis became the general superintendent in 1953. Within months of arriving in Chicago, Willis wrote what could be called the professional tenet of the civic credo.[74] His article "The Need for Professionalism in Education Today" asked such questions as "Shall we be errand boys or leaders?" and "Are we only to respond to trends and pressures?" He left no doubt about his own stance. "Much of what is wrong with education today," he wrote, "can be attributed to the fact that educators . . . have abdicated from positions of educational leadership, and have permitted themselves and their schools to be swayed by the winds of uninformed public opinion."[75] The politicians were as supportive of this platform as were the school administrators.

This situation boded ill for anyone who might become a critic of the schools. Insofar as criticism could be labeled political, the city's liberals and establishment could be expected to draw together to resist any such intrusion. It had cost all parties a great deal to separate the schools from politics, and the mere specter of any breach in that high wall of separation became a breach of faith, of the civic credo. And since blacks were considered an ethnic group, any issues of race pursued outside the normal functioning of the institutions became politics. The schools were perceived as doing their best, within the limits of what was professionally wise; demands for alternatives would be treated as irrational, unprofessional, and worst of all, political. Race had been reduced to a problem of housing, and the underlying dynamics of neighborhood disruption were, by virtue of the civic credo, perceived as merely temporary eruptions of the irrational.

When in 1954 the U.S. Supreme Court enunciated its principle in the *Brown* case that "separate educational facilities are inherently unequal," there was, accordingly, little concern for what that decision might mean in Chicago. What Anthony Lewis and the *New York Times* said about the North generally was true emphatically of Chicago: "As the racial revolution developed in the South, there was a certain amount of sanctimoniousness in the North. That northerners should feel morally superior on the racial issue was understandable, for they did not live in a society which was officially, legally dedicated to treatment of the Negro as a separate and inferior being—a society like the old South. The legal premise in the North was the opposite: Government was pledged against racial discrimination."[76]

Yet when Morton Grodzins surveyed the figures from the 1950 census and projected their trends, he was moved to portray "the metropolitan area as a racial problem." He pointed out, "If segregation is defined not in legal terms but in the number of students who attend all Negro schools, then it is undoubtedly true that more Negro students are segregated in the schools of New York and Chicago than in any other cities or some states."[77]

The combination of block-by-block housing segregation and a strict policy of neighborhood schools combined to produce what was called de facto segregation. To be sure, the segregation in Chicago was not de jure in the Jim Crow sense; but as this chapter has shown and as attempts to deal with it would later show, it was something other than what is conveyed by the simple term "de facto segregation." Chicago had an active color line, and block-by-block expansion of the ghetto was the social mechanism by which it was extending its rule. And Chicago had a civic credo that drew a veil of institutional innocence across the disruptive dynamics of the expanding color line.

CHAPTER THREE

The Emergence of the

De Facto Segregation View

In the course of identifying the moral meanings of the color line which were to be significant for the civil rights movement in Chicago, Chapter 1 described three major configurations of the fact and justification that had come to interpret racial issues by midcentury: racist realism, the democratic dilemma of black dignity, and the democratic dilemma of white culture. Chapter 2 traced the making of the color line in Chicago and the emergence of a civic credo that served to obscure the interlocking dimensions of that color line in name of better things to come. A fifth major perspective on the issue was set forth by the U.S. Supreme Court in its 1954 *Brown* decision—what we shall call the democratic dilemma of constitutional duties. This chapter traces the development of this view in Chicago into the de facto segregation interpretation of the color line.

The question before the Supreme Court in *Brown* concerned the provision in the Fourteenth Amendment that no state shall "deny to any person within its jurisdiction the equal protection of the laws." Did this doctrine apply to the color line in its Jim Crow form? Seventeen southern and border states and the District of Columbia had passed laws requiring or permitting school segregation by race. Was this a violation of equal protection of the laws and, if so, what remedies were appropriate?

These issues were difficult for the Supreme Court in 1954, and they have been controversial for the nation ever since. Initially, under the impact of Reconstruction, the Court had interpreted the Fourteenth Amendment as proscribing all state-imposed discrimination based on race.[1] In 1896, however, in *Plessy* v. *Ferguson,* the Court had given constitutional sanction to the racist realism of the times. It found that "in the nature of things it [the Fourteenth Amendment] could not have been intended to abolish distinctions based on color, or enforce social, as distinguished from political, equality." "Separate but equal" became the law of the land.[2] Thus to grant relief to the plaintiffs in

Brown, all parents of schoolchildren forced to attend separate black schools, the Court would have to take the unusual and difficult step of reversing itself and overturning one of its own major decisions. And beyond this question of precedent lay the even more serious fact that an entire region of the country had based its social and political arrangements on the *Plessy* doctrine.

In the 1930s, however, the NAACP had made educational discrimination the center of its long-term strategy to pursue the democratic dilemma of black dignity through the courts, and it was as a result of these efforts that the *Brown* case was before the Supreme Court in 1954. At first, the NAACP had attacked the obvious inequities of Jim Crow schools—low salaries and the lack of access to state graduate and professional schools. The organization hoped that making black schools materially equal to white schools would become so expensive that the system of separate schools would fall of its own weight.[3]

In *Sweatt* v. *Painter* (1950) the issue took a new turn as the NAACP persuaded the Court to consider such intangible factors as reputation of faculty, community standing, and interaction with future colleagues in finding that a segregated, state-supported law school in Texas was unequal.[4] This decision constituted a direct repudiation of the separate but equal doctrine, at least for law schools, and it prepared the way for the *Brown* decision, in which the black schools involved were, or were in the process of becoming, "equal" to white schools in such tangible respects as buildings, curricula, and teachers' salaries.

By 1954 a bare majority of the Supreme Court was prepared to overturn school segregation. The newly confirmed chief justice, Earl Warren, was convinced that the separate but equal doctrine rested on the premise of the inferiority of the Negro race and that *Plessy* could be sustained only on that basis. This notion was morally unacceptable in a post-Myrdal America. But the repercussions of reversing *Plessy* would be enormous, and it took all Warren's superb political skills to obtain a unanimous decision from the Court.[5]

Warren delivered the opinion of the united Court on 17 May 1954. This opinion did not claim historical evidence for overturning *Plessy* nor did it charge the South with illegal or immoral actions in practicing segregation.[6] It did find the practice no longer justified. Public education was now "perhaps the most important function of state and local governments," and it "is a right which must be made available to all on equal terms." Citing *Sweatt* and *McLaurin,* the Court argued that intangible factors prevented separate education from being equal, especially for black school-age children among whom social psychologists influenced by Myrdal had found feelings of inferiority generated by racial segregation. Thus, it concluded, "in the field of public education the doctrine of 'separate but equal' has no place. Separate educational facilities are inherently unequal."[7]

Still, the Court recognized the complex problem posed by formulating and implementing appropriate relief. Giving the South some time to adjust to this decision, the Court called for further arguments on the question of relief. Instead of trying to supervise this complex task, in 1955 the Court returned the cases to the lower courts, which had originally heard them, to ensure flexibility and consideration of local circumstances. The Court called for a process of desegregation to take place "with all deliberate speed."[8]

For all its diplomacy and statescraft, the *Brown* decision released a flood of controversy in which the Supreme Court itself rather than Jim Crow at times appeared to be the issue. White citizens' councils formed all across the South, and southern governors spoke of nullification. State legislatures authorized school closings, suspended compulsory attendance laws, and diverted funds to private schools in efforts to avoid school desegregation.[9]

As a result, the "deliberate speed" the Court called for did not materialize. Ten years later only 10.8 percent of the black children in the seventeen states immediately affected by *Brown* were attending desegregated schools. This situation was even more serious if the six border states and the District of Columbia are distinguished from the eleven southern states. In the border states, with approximately 3.6 million children in the public schools, 59.3 percent of the blacks were enrolled in desegregated schools. In the southern states, with 11 million public school pupils, however, only 2.14 percent of the blacks were in desegregated schools.[10]

Despite the compromises required to obtain a unanimous decision and the delays that occurred in implementing *Brown*, however, the Supreme Court had enunciated a new interpretation of racial fact and justification in 1954. Separate schools were inherently unequal, and the doctrines of racist realism that had argued otherwise were no longer a constitutionally acceptable basis for public policy. The Court explicitly supported proponents of democratic dignity and their pursuit of political equality and, more implicitly, it accepted the moral claims of the American creed as enunciated by Myrdal. But it went beyond Myrdal in finding that racial equality required at least some authoritative institutional desegregation. It put the American creed not just on the moral agenda of American hearts but on the political agenda of the nation's laws and its public life as well. In finding Jim Crow schools constitutionally unacceptable, the Court opened a new dilemma in American race relations, the democratic dilemma of constitutional duties.

Of course, the full meaning of the Court's decision was not clear to anyone in 1954, and as the Court and the country have encountered the dilemmas of affirmative democratic duties, the implications of the *Brown* decision have continued to spawn controversy.[11] But because the decision implied more than it immediately resolved, the stage was set for organized groups all across the land to explore its meanings.

Brown was addressed to legally segregated schools in the South. But what about other forms of legally established segregation—public accommodations, for instance? Countless groups across the South, including the one led in a bus boycott by a young Baptist minister in Montgomery, would pursue that question in the years immediately to come. What about racial segregation in the North? Was racial separation any less unequal or the damage it caused any less severe when it occurred without legislative enactment? Countless groups across the North would explore that question too. In short, although many factors produced the civil rights movement, some of which we have already examined, the *Brown* decision stimulated, legitimized, and focused a new round of civil rights activity. Consequently, we take May 1954 in Washington, D.C., as the birth date and place of the civil rights movement in its modern form. Before it was over, this movement would make "which side are you on" the national question.

DE FACTO SEGREGATION: THE CASE
AGAINST THE SCHOOLS

In Chicago the mayor saw to it that there were always two sides to every question. In 1953, Richard Daley became the chairman of the Cook County Regular Democratic party, and in 1955 he was elected mayor of the city of Chicago. He held both of those posts continuously until his death in 1977. Daley inherited the precinct organization that had begun to coalesce under Mayors Cermak and Kelly but had grown impatient under the "reform" administration of Mayor Kennelly.

Part of Mayor Daley's power, which was considerable, was that, from the very beginning, it was legendary as well as real. He was a master of the complexity of Chicago's political organization, and part of that mastery was a virtuosity in the orchestration of public issues so as to take advantage of that complexity. If Daley designated an issue as "local," that meant he expected the ward committeemen and their precinct captains to handle it. If he designated an issue as "citywide," that meant the mayor and his city administration would handle it.

Some citywide issues were, in his lexicon, "administrative." That meant they were subject to interest-group bargaining, with the mayor himself frequently arbitrating the bargaining and enforcing a settlement. Other citywide issues, however, were "nonpartisan." That meant blue-ribbon committees would be needed to handle them. Since it was partly a matter of his discretion into which category an issue should fall, the mayor seemed always to stand ready with a response for any issue that arose.

For the most part, Mayor Daley defined the issues generated by the moving color line as "local." In 1955 and 1956, he yielded control of two more black

72

wards to Congressman William Dawson. When other wards objected to the building of public housing units within their boundaries because of the racial implications, Chicago, never a city to eschew federally financed contracts, built two miles of sixteen-story concrete towers in the heart of the South Side. These Robert Taylor Homes were totally lacking in the necessities for the development of vital community life, and they became a symbol of what everyone meant by "ghetto." This was one local solution that became a city-wide object of attention.[12]

In keeping with the civic credo, to which Mayor Daley wholly subscribed, the schools were nonpartisan. Even though the mayor appointed the members of the Board of Education and the City Council confirmed them, a blue-ribbon committee, the Mayor's Advisory Commission on School Board Nominations, screened the candidates and recommended the nominees. The schools were above politics. That was the official stance.

This arrangement of issues was stubbornly adhered to by the mayor, the Board of Education, and the press, but it shed little light on what was actually happening in the city and did even less to promote any sense of alternative. For the first time in its history, Chicago's population declined by 1.9 percent between 1950 and 1960. The number of black people, however, had increased by more than 300,000, rising to 812,637, almost a quarter of the city's 3.5 million inhabitants. All predictions that the second great migration would level off after World War II had proven wrong. So had the policies that had been predicted on that assumption, although the full impact of this was not altogether apparent at the time. The color line, which had taken shape when blacks were only 4 percent of the population, by 1960 cut across the city instead of defining small pockets within it (see Map 1). It was a citywide issue in every way, except in official recognition. In the schools, it was creating havoc, not everywhere at once but in a steady progression of one neighborhood school after another.

As the civil rights movement gained attention and momentum in the South, there were those who searched for some way to frame a civil rights issue out of the massive segregation taking place in the North. The campaign for fair employment practices legislation initiated as part of A. Philip Randolph's March on Washington Movement in the 1940s was finally successful in Illinois in 1961. By the mid-1960s, continuing pressure for open occupancy ordinances had succeeded in Chicago and some suburbs, but these did little to alter the pattern of racial concentration and exclusion. Even effective community organizations such as those created by Saul Alinsky could not stem the tide of racial change on a neighborhood basis although they may have lowered the level of hostility, disruption, and exploitation that usually went with it.[13]

Still, the question of the schools remained. As long as de facto segregation seemed to arise simply from irrational attitudes in the neighborhoods, it pre-

73

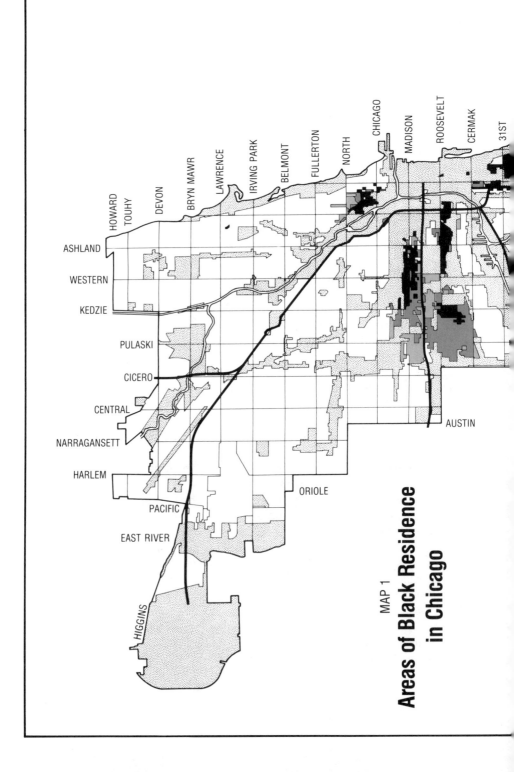

MAP 1
Areas of Black Residence in Chicago

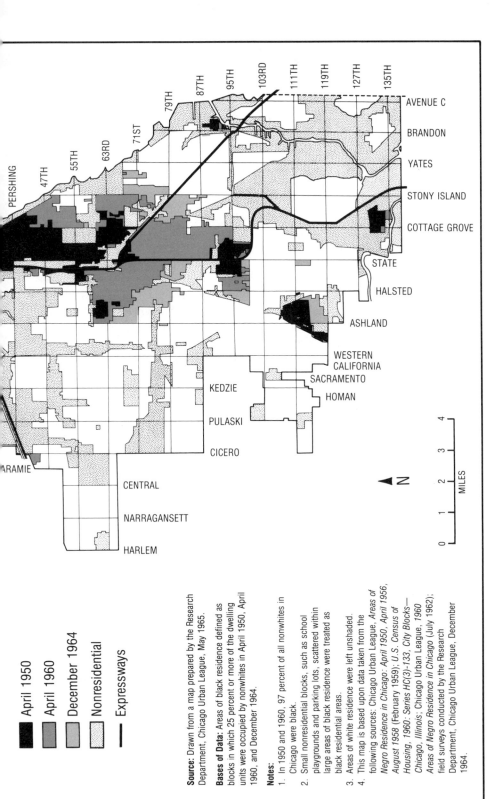

Source: Drawn from a map prepared by the Research Department, Chicago Urban League, May 1965.

Bases of Data: Areas of black residence defined as blocks in which 25 percent or more of the dwelling units were occupied by nonwhites in April 1950, April 1960, and December 1964.

Notes:

1. In 1950 and 1960, 97 percent of all nonwhites in Chicago were black.

2. Small nonresidential blocks, such as school playgrounds and parking lots, scattered within large areas of black residence were treated as black residential areas.

3. Areas of white residence were left unshaded.

4. This map is based upon data taken from the following sources: Chicago Urban League, *Areas of Negro Residence in Chicago: April 1950, April 1956, August 1958* (February 1959); *U.S. Census of Housing, 1960: Series HC(3)-133, City Blocks—Chicago, Illinois*; Chicago Urban League, *1960 Areas of Negro Residence in Chicago* (July 1962); field surveys conducted by the Research Department, Chicago Urban League, December 1964.

- ■ April 1950
- ▨ April 1960
- ▧ December 1964
- ░ Nonresidential
- — Expressways

MILES
0 1 2 3 4

N

PERSHING
47TH
55TH
63RD
71ST
79TH
87TH
95TH
103RD
111TH
119TH
127TH
135TH

AVENUE C
BRANDON
YATES
STONY ISLAND
COTTAGE GROVE
STATE
HALSTED
ASHLAND
WESTERN
CALIFORNIA
SACRAMENTO
HOMAN
KEDZIE
PULASKI
CICERO
CENTRAL
NARRAGANSETT
HARLEM
LARAMIE

sented different problems than did de jure segregation. In February 1958, however, an article appeared in *Crisis,* the journal of the National Association for the Advancement of Colored People, which tried to narrow this distinction considerably. Titled "De Facto Segregation in the Chicago Public Schools," it offered some disturbing data for those who thought the schools were innocently doing the best that could be expected from people of goodwill caught in a difficult situation.[14]

As we will see from this article, the thrust of this assault on de facto segregation stressed the segregation and questioned its de facto status. Writing in the same vein a few years later, Meyer Weinberg made clear the premise in his article "De Facto Segregation: Fact or Artifact?" There was no question in his mind that de facto segregation was an artifact of policy, not an accident of history: "So-called de jure segregation can be traced back to a statute or an ordinance. But every board of education is a by-law-acting and law-enacting body; it is an agent of the state and has taxing and other powers of a governing body. Its regulations have the force of law. A board of education decision to establish school boundary lines is de jure."[15]

In exploring the implications of the *Brown* decision along these lines, the 1958 *Crisis* article began to lay out what was to become a major alternative perspective to the civic credo interpretation of racial issues in Chicago. Like the Supreme Court in *Brown,* it emphasized institutional policies rather than individual attitudes; and unlike the civic credo, it focused on existing policies and practices of racial exclusion and discrimination, and it appealed to the values of the American creed to provide the grounds for democratic change.

This article resulted from the failure of the Chicago branch of the NAACP to secure any clear commitment from the Board of Education to integrated schools. The board stood firm on its commitment to the neighborhood school, which the NAACP was convinced was the source of increasing segregation. The NAACP, therefore, without the cooperation of the board, set out to estimate the extent of segregation in the Chicago public schools. It relied on the testimony of local groups and the observations of unofficial observers and reported its findings in the *Crisis* article.

"De facto segregation was considered to exist," said the report, "if ninety percent or more of a school's population consisted of Negroes and Puerto Ricans on the one hand, or of continental whites, on the other." On this basis it was estimated that "91 percent of the Chicago elementary schools were de facto segregated in the spring semester of 1957." Seventy percent (250 schools) were "predominantly white"; 21 percent (73 schools) were "predominantly Negro"; and 9 percent (32 schools) were mixed. These figures placed 87 percent of the black students in "Negro schools," 12 percent in "mixed schools," and 1 percent in "white schools."[16]

Correlative with this high level of segregation, the report found significant differences in enrollment depending on whether a school was "white," "mixed," or "Negro." "The average population of the predominantly white elementary schools is 669; of the mixed schools, 947; of the predominantly Negro schools, 1275." The black schools accounted for 81 percent of double-shift pupils and were assigned "a disproportionate number of inexperienced teachers," the report continued. "While some of the elementary schools are de facto Negro because of housing, none of the high schools is." Philips High School had been black since the 1920s; but DuSable High School "was built and districted to be Negro at a time when there were white schools east, west, and south of it"; Englewood, an all-black high school, "still has four white feeder elementary schools"; Carver, the smallest high school in Chicago and all black, "draws its students from a public housing project" exclusively. "In cost and quality of instruction, school time, districting, and choice of sites," the report concluded, "the Chicago Board of Education maintains in practice what amounts to a racially discriminatory policy." According to this study, the schools were more segregated than the city as a whole and the neighborhood schools were more segregated than their neighborhoods.[17]

These were serious charges, which the school administration never tried to refute in detail. Instead, General Superintendent Willis took the position that he was legally required not to know the racial composition of the schools and that, because he had no knowledge, he could not be held responsible. In 1958 the board reaffirmed its neighborhood school policy by tightening the requirements for transfers.

It was not only the board which drew back from the facts and the logic of "De Facto Segregation in the Chicago Public Schools." When this article was published in *Crisis,* the Chicago branch of the NAACP had an activist leader in the person of Willoughby Abner. The report was intended as an opening salvo in a campaign against de facto segregation in the North, but before any substantial support could be built for this argument against the schools, Abner was out of office. Congressman William Dawson's organization was instrumental in his defeat.[18] As a result, the local NAACP developed a reputation for being politically controlled and thereafter was suspect among civil rights activists for years to come.

Other groups used the data in the article in their testimony at school budget hearings and before state legislative committees, but concerted action was not forthcoming for several years. The pattern described in the study continued to prevail:

Such desegregation as occurs temporarily when Negroes move into new areas proceeds under the maximum disadvantages. No one who has watched the departure of the last white children in a matter of weeks from a transition school; who has witnessed the angry defiance of the Negro children declaring they are glad to see them leave; who has heard the sorrowful acknowledgment of the Negro parents who

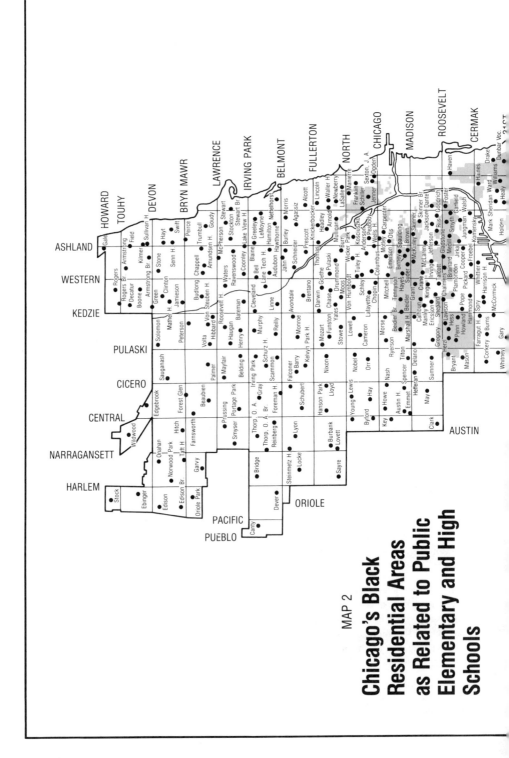

MAP 2

Chicago's Black Residential Areas as Related to Public Elementary and High Schools

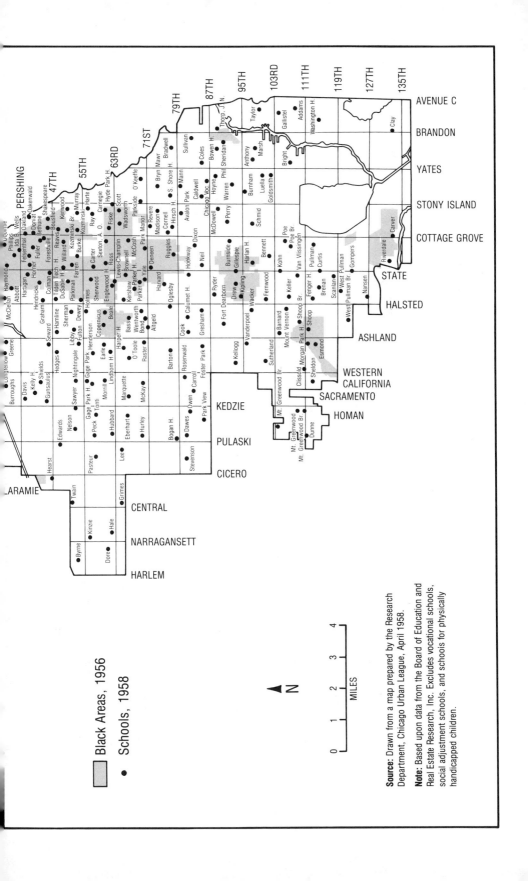

Black Areas, 1956

● **Schools, 1958**

Source: Drawn from a map prepared by the Research Department, Chicago Urban League, April 1958.

Note: Based upon data from the Board of Education and Real Estate Research, Inc. Excludes vocational schools, social adjustment schools, and schools for physically handicapped children.

understand what their leaving means, but who nevertheless want that extra seat for the crowded school; who has experienced the embarrassment of the white parents who declare that they are only moving because they cannot deprive their child of adequate schooling—no person who has been through all this will have any doubt that transition is the opposite rather than the equivalent of integration.[19]

In 1959 the U.S. Commission on Civil Rights labeled Chicago as the most residentially segregated large city in the nation. The color line was expanding disruptively across more and more neighborhoods at the same time, bringing havoc to the neighborhood schools (see Map 2). Between 1958 and 1960, enrollment at the Burnside School climbed from 1,138 to 1,773. According to Superintendent Willis, "Much of this recent increase was unanticipated because there had been but little new housing constructed in the area." At the Cornell School enrollment had climbed from 868 in 1959 to 1,212 in 1960. At the Dixon School, where enrollments had been declining during the mid-1950s, the numbers jumped from 1,338 in 1958 to 1,670 in 1960. At the Parker School, there were 1,397 pupils in 1955. By 1957 this figure had increased to 1,830; by 1960 to 2,791. These schools were situated in the path of the moving color line on the South Side.[20]

On the West Side, the Gregory School had 1,590 students in 1954. In 1956, this number had climbed to 1,864. By 1959, it was 2,115, and it ballooned to 3,862 by 1960. The Gregory School had only forty-six classrooms. By 1961, Gregory had 4,194 students, more than 3,000 of them on double shift. On the South Side, the Kipling School was built on Ninety-third Street at Lowe Avenue in 1961. It opened its doors with more than 35 children to a classroom because of what the general superintendent again called "an unexpected increase in population."[21]

The pattern was the same wherever the color line was moving—"recent, extensive, and unexpected" increases in enrollment. School officials maintained an official stance of "color blindness" and denied any knowledge of why these numerical disasters were befalling particular schools. The people in the affected neighborhoods knew perfectly well what was happening. The board claimed that the problem was unanticipated but temporary overcrowding. The people in the neighborhoods perceived a process of permanent racial change and all the consequences that historically went with it.

In January 1961 Federal Judge Irving R. Kaufman handed down a broadly conceived opinion ordering the schools of New Rochelle, New York, to desegregate. "It is of no moment," he said, "whether the segregation is labeled . . . de jure (according to law) or de facto, as long as the board, by its conduct, is responsible for its maintenance."[22] This decision was greeted by the formation of a group dedicated to the extension of that doctrine to the Chicago public schools. Attorney Herbert Fisher of the Chatham–Avalon Park Community Council understood *Taylor* as holding that "the school board

80

must act affirmatively to ensure integration regardless of the composition of neighborhood school districts."[23]

By then, the Chicago branch of the NAACP had a new executive director, the Reverend Carl A. Fuqua, who was supported both nationally and locally in his determination to take a strong civil rights stand on local issues. The NAACP Committee on Legal Redress accordingly associated itself with the drive to create litigation like that for New Rochelle in Chicago. In February 1961 the branch adopted a policy statement on education which recited the evidence of segregation and inequality and concluded with the resolve "to seek legal action" whenever "the Board of Education refuses or is reluctant to change its existing practices which, whether stated or not, result in a 'separate but unequal' school system in Chicago."[24]

The NAACP set out to coordinate the neighborhood dissatisfactions with the citywide drive for a federal case. In March the principal of a South Side school, Oglesby, called an assembly of only the black children and lectured them on their behavior. Some of them, she felt, were damaging the reputation of the school. The parents were incensed and held a conference to let the principal know it. In a letter to the Board of Education, Fuqua urged an investigation of all such incidents and offered "aid in uncovering" them. He urged the board "to take another look at its position on human relations . . . and to come up with some effective programs supported by a firm and factual statement of policy not cloaked in cliches."[25]

The *Defender* saw no hope for self-reform within the board: "The Superintendent and the Board demonstrate such abominable human relations themselves that it is no small wonder that no better techniques are used throughout." In a move that took a swipe at both the board and the NAACP, the *Defender* continued: "We commend the NAACP's alertness but would advise that sterling organization that the best way to insure democracy in the city's schools is in federal court. We've all talked enough and the words vanish on the wind. The powers that be in this city will react only to political pressure and court orders. We could have the one if we woke up to our strength, and could get the other if the NAACP lawyers get cracking."[26]

The NAACP was still suspect, but it continued to build toward a school suit. In April the NAACP asked the mayor to require from his school board nominees a statement of their positions on desegregation, especially on applying the *Brown* and *Taylor* decisions to Chicago. The mayor did not require such a statement. The NAACP then turned to the neighborhoods and began to organize task forces "to acquaint parents of local school problems and show how their children are being short-changed by the Board of Education." Speaking to parents in Chatham, West Avalon, and Park Manor, the southern boundaries of the South Side color line, Fuqua found audiences well acquainted with the turmoil of recent racial change (see Map 3). By mid-April,

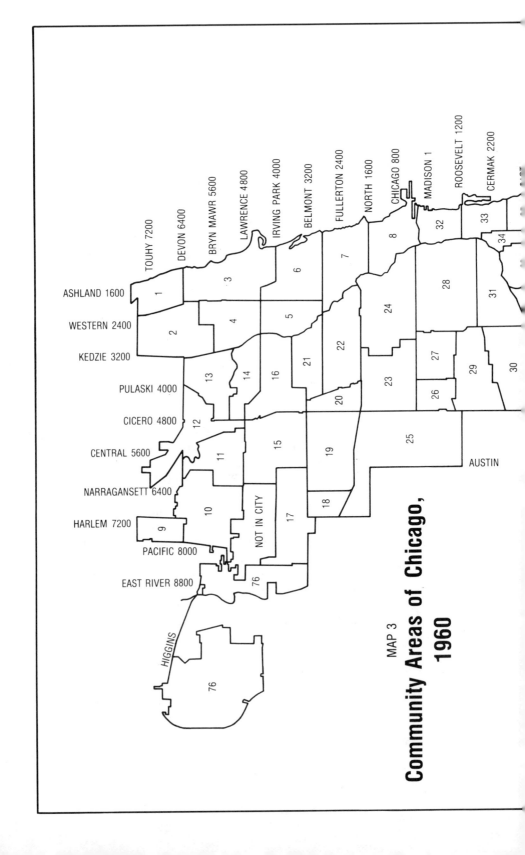

MAP 3
Community Areas of Chicago, 1960

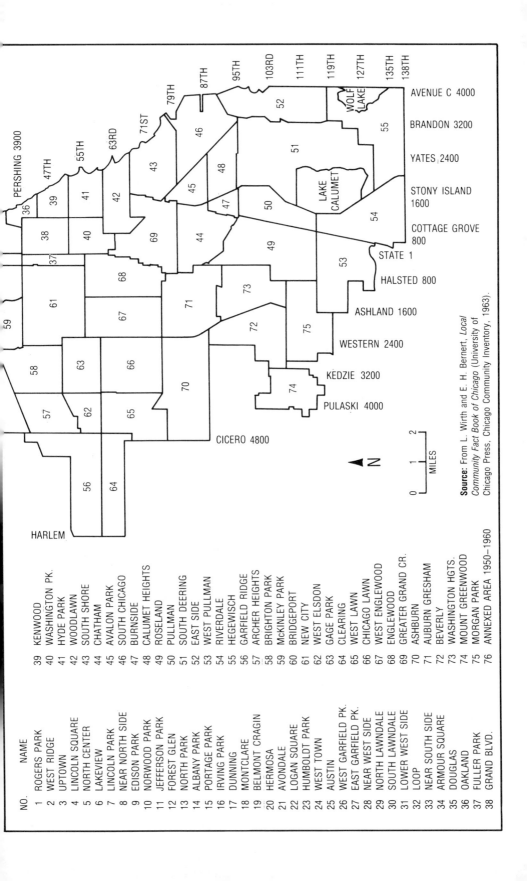

PERSHING 3900

47TH
55TH
63RD
71ST
79TH
87TH
95TH
103RD
111TH
119TH
127TH
135TH
138TH

AVENUE C 4000
BRANDON 3200
YATES 2400
STONY ISLAND 1600
COTTAGE GROVE 800
STATE 1
HALSTED 800
ASHLAND 1600
WESTERN 2400
KEDZIE 3200
PULASKI 4000
CICERO 4800
HARLEM

WOLF LAKE
LAKE CALUMET

N
0   1   2
MILES

Source: From L. Wirth and E. H. Bernert, *Local Community Fact Book of Chicago* (University of Chicago Press, Chicago Community Inventory, 1963).

NO.	NAME		
1	ROGERS PARK	39	KENWOOD
2	WEST RIDGE	40	WASHINGTON PK.
3	UPTOWN	41	HYDE PARK
4	LINCOLN SQUARE	42	WOODLAWN
5	NORTH CENTER	43	SOUTH SHORE
6	LAKEVIEW	44	CHATHAM
7	LINCOLN PARK	45	AVALON PARK
8	NEAR NORTH SIDE	46	SOUTH CHICAGO
9	EDISON PARK	47	BURNSIDE
10	NORWOOD PARK	48	CALUMET HEIGHTS
11	JEFFERSON PARK	49	ROSELAND
12	FOREST GLEN	50	PULLMAN
13	NORTH PARK	51	SOUTH DEERING
14	ALBANY PARK	52	EAST SIDE
15	PORTAGE PARK	53	WEST PULLMAN
16	IRVING PARK	54	RIVERDALE
17	DUNNING	55	HEGEWISCH
18	MONTCLARE	56	GARFIELD RIDGE
19	BELMONT CRAGIN	57	ARCHER HEIGHTS
20	HERMOSA	58	BRIGHTON PARK
21	AVONDALE	59	McKINLEY PARK
22	LOGAN SQUARE	60	BRIDGEPORT
23	HUMBOLDT PARK	61	NEW CITY
24	WEST TOWN	62	WEST ELSDON
25	AUSTIN	63	GAGE PARK
26	WEST GARFIELD PK.	64	CLEARING
27	EAST GARFIELD PK.	65	WEST LAWN
28	NEAR WEST SIDE	66	CHICAGO LAWN
29	NORTH LAWNDALE	67	WEST ENGLEWOOD
30	SOUTH LAWNDALE	68	ENGLEWOOD
31	LOWER WEST SIDE	69	GREATER GRAND CR.
32	LOOP	70	ASHBURN
33	NEAR SOUTH SIDE	71	AUBURN GRESHAM
34	ARMOUR SQUARE	72	BEVERLY
35	DOUGLAS	73	WASHINGTON HGTS.
36	OAKLAND	74	MOUNT GREENWOOD
37	FULLER PARK	75	MORGAN PARK
38	GRAND BLVD.	76	ANNEXED AREA 1950–1960

the *Defender* was calling the NAACP activities "a war against the Board of Education." In June the NAACP called on the board not to renew Superintendent Willis's $42,500 a year contract. Instead, the board did renew his contract and raised his salary to $48,500 a year.[27]

Over the summer, momentum continued to build toward a courtroom confrontation between the board and its critics. On 2 August 1961 the U.S. Court of Appeals upheld the New Rochelle decision, and on 29 August 1961 the U.S. Supreme Court refused to stay the court order. On 30 August 1961 Paul Zuber, attorney for the plaintiffs in New Rochelle, arrived in Chicago, invited by the NAACP and the Chatham–Avalon Park Community Council. His visit coincided with the announcement of Operation Transfer, a plan designed to demonstrate that segregation, not overcrowding, was the problem in the schools. Black parents had been organized to attempt to take their children out of overcrowded schools by registering them in nearby white schools that were not overcrowded. Knowing they would be refused, these parents planned to become the plaintiffs in a civil rights suit. A wide coalition of civil rights groups, community organizations, and church groups joined in sponsoring Operation Transfer.[28]

On 6 September 1961, 160 parents were denied their requested transfers. Although the operation had been widely publicized, the names of the target schools had not. The object was to avoid disruptive confrontation between parents that would take the focus off school policy. The operation went smoothly without any complicating incidents. On the same day, CORE sent the Board of Education a seven-page listing of schools alleged to have unoccupied classrooms. CORE advised the board to forget its neighborhood school policy and to promote instead a "fuller use of the school plant, racial integration, and equal opportunity."[29]

Raymond Pasnick, a member of the board, said that he had requested the information contained in the CORE communication from the school board staff and had been waiting eighteen months for an answer. "If the allegations are true," he said, "the board should be concerned about depriving children needlessly of a full day's education and about the tremendous waste of existing facilities. . . . These are facts that could easily be checked; not something that should be shrouded in mystery."[30] The same sentiments had been expressed in 1945 by Earl B. Dickerson at the Conference on Home Front Unity. It was to lift this cloud of mystery and to break the dialectic of unanswered allegations that the NAACP was building support for litigation.

The NAACP, however, was itself still under a cloud. Its credentials as the coordinator of the school issue were suspect. It did not have the confidence of all the participants in the coalition that was forming, some of whom wondered if it really meant to follow through or if it was being used by the political organization to siphon off discontent. These suspicions became decisive shortly after Operation Transfer. The legal redress committee of the NAACP favored a cautious approach to litigation—a broadening of legal resources and financial backing and more visible and organized community support for what was bound to be a lengthy process. Others, however, especially representatives of The Woodlawn Organization (TWO), favored immediate action. TWO was an Alinsky community organization, less than two years old at the time, and represented the new style of grass-roots militancy that was to become a major factor in the urban issues of the 1960s. Paul Zuber agreed with the TWO representatives. There were charges to be made, there were plaintiffs to make them, and the legal ground had already been opened up in New Rochelle. What more was needed to make a case?[31]

Zuber prevailed in a polarized atmosphere of mutual and debilitating suspicion. The *Webb* case was filed on 18 September 1961, but it failed to become the center of a coordinated strategy. According to Herbert Fisher, "Within a month, it was just one more poorly supported and competitive form of ineffectual protest. It failed to bring the schools under sustained public scrutiny."[32] After an exchange of pretrial motions and affidavits, the *Webb* case was dismissed 31 July 1962 on the grounds that the plaintiffs had not exhausted the administrative procedures provided by the state of Illinois. On 28 June 1963 the case was reopened as a result of a U.S. Supreme Court ruling which found that plaintiffs did not have to exhaust Illinois' elaborate administrative procedures to gain access to the federal courts.[33] On 29 August 1963 both the defendants and the plaintiffs stipulated that they had reached an out-of-court settlement of the complaint.[34] No law was made in this case, and the board's policies or intentions were not clarified.

DE FACTO SEGREGATION VS. UNEXPECTED OVERCROWDING: INTRANSIGENT INNOCENCE AT THE BOARD OF EDUCATION

The exchange of affidavits in the *Webb* case shed some light on what was happening in the schools, but the board took refuge in sophistry. It interpreted the charge of "racial segregation" in "scientific" terms and demanded to know what anthropological or biological system of classification it was being accused of using: E. P. Stibbe, W. C. Boyd, S. M. Garn and C. S. Coon, E. A. Hooten, or what? Each of them was the author of a scientific theory of racial classification. Obviously, the board engaged in no such ritual of scientific classification as would be required by adherence to any of these elaborate and comprehensive theories of race. With such distinctions in mind, Superintendent Willis claimed categorically: "I know of no attendance area that has been gerrymandered, no construction site that has been selected, no double or overlapping shift program that has been instituted, no classrooms that have been allowed to remain vacant, no upper grade center, elementary, or high school branch that has been established for the purpose of creating and maintaining 'Negro elementary schools' or 'white elementary schools' in Chicago, as charged by the plaintiffs' affidavit."[35]

The problem was not segregation, according to the superintendent. It was merciless and unanticipated overcrowding at selected schools. "The facts," he said,

> may be drawn into perspective by citing again the magnitude of the problems with which the defendants are faced. The Burnside, Cornell, Dixon, and Kipling Schools are located in District 16. Gregory is located in District 8. Parker and Bond are located in District 20. On 21 November 1961, 15,232 of the 22,374 pupils on double shift in Chicago . . . were located in these districts. . . . Over half of the 1951–1961 enrollment increase in these three districts occurred in the 24-month period between September 1959 and September 1961. The gain in this two-year period was 20,292 pupils; the total gain in the ten-year period was 35, 322.

As with the board of 1945, the board of 1961 was certain that relief for these overcrowded schools was only a few buildings away. Current construction plans, the superintendent promised, would "remove all of the 15,232 students in these three districts from double shift by February 1963."[36] Apparently neither the increases nor the points of their occurrence were entirely unanticipated.

The key difference between the board and the plaintiffs lay in questions of affirmative action. The board denied that it had any "affirmative duty" to provide either the city or its pupils with a "school system which is racially integrated."[37] The board never budged on that position, and its critics never ceased seeing its posture as a sham. Even supposing the best of motives on both sides, there was an inevitable and disruptive clash of perceptions between those concerned with de facto segregation and the proponents of the civic credo. At its best, the Board of Education moved in a world defined by individual schools and their problems. The board perceived no problems in the system as such; schools were being built as quickly as possible to relieve what the board claimed were temporary problems of overcrowding. In the meantime, the board relied on short-term measures such as double shifts to relieve the pressure.

The people in the neighborhoods, however, perceived these developments as ultimate, not in any way temporary. Most of these schools were in districts to which black people were moving in an effort to gain access to better housing and schools than they had found in the established ghetto. They did not see the deterioration of the schools as temporary but as a repeat of what they were moving away from. Neither did the whites see it as temporary. They saw it as the fulfillment of their worst fears of what happens when blacks move in. Black and white together found themselves caught up in the destructive dynamics of the color line in which the overcrowding in the schools epitomized what was happening to their neighborhoods. Two years might be a short time for the planners at the Board of Education, but it was more than enough time to settle the permanent location of a neighborhood on one side or the other of the color line. The people in the neighborhoods knew that even if the Board of Education would not acknowledge it.

On 16 October 1961 the Board of Education held a public hearing in an effort to quell the rising stridency of its critics. The session lasted eight hours. Only twenty-nine of the sixty-five petitioners were heard. After the first two presentations had consumed an hour each, the Reverend Arthur Brazier and his supporters from The Woodlawn Organization walked out in protest and began to picket outside the hearing. Inside, members of the board argued with the NAACP's charge of deliberate segregation and the Urban League's claim that there were systematic inequalities between black and white schools. By day's end, there was no sign that the board saw any need for alternatives. The charges that were being made constituted a fundamental challenge to the civic credo and its tenet of racial progress through the normal functioning of democratic institutions. Thus these charges were much too serious for the board, itself the premier example of the civic credo, to become a fair forum for their airing.[38]

Parents at the Cornell School, which by the fall of 1961 had more than thirteen hundred pupils, decided to boycott the school instead of protesting the overcrowding at the board's hearing. Mrs. Ernest Baker was an officer of the parents' group, a plaintiff in the *Webb* case, and a full-time teacher without tenure in the public schools. Before reporting to her assignment at another South Side school, she walked the picket line at Cornell. The next day she was called downtown, asked to explain her activities, and told that Willis would recommend that she be fired "for conduct unbecoming a teacher." Because she lacked tenure, this could be done without a formal hearing. And it was. Her firing was the occasion for the formation of Teachers for Integrated Schools, a group that would leave its mark on the developing school issue. Among the charter members was Albert A. Raby, a teacher at the Hess Upper Grade Center on the West Side.[39]

In November 1961 Willis gave his long-awaited inventory of classrooms. There were, he reported, 222 rooms not currently in use; but he recommended that 143 of these be used to reduce class size in neighborhood schools. Another 65 would soon be taken up by anticipated increases. Only 14 rooms could be considered truly vacant. Board members Mrs. Wendell Green and Raymond Pasnick expressed disappointment that the superintendent made no recommendation to reduce double shifts.[40]

Within a month, however, the Chicago Urban League released a report claiming that at least another 382 classrooms were vacant and that the board was guilty of segregation in its assignment of facilities. With this report, the Urban League, which previously had worked behind the scenes and in a conciliatory manner, moved to center stage of the community conflict over the schools. Public controversy was a new context for the league, and the transition was not made easily. *Chicago's American* editorially accused the league of creating "emotional confusion":

> If it is true, as Willis has declared in a press conference, that 84 of these rooms do not exist because they were in buildings that have been torn down, he is justified in denouncing the Urban League report as "invalid and misleading." But if the estimate were accurate, it would not show, as the Urban League says it does, that there is segregation. Segregation is always institutional. In places where it exists it is based on state or local law. There is no such law here: white and Negro children have always attended the same schools. The problem to be solved is not segregation, since there isn't any; the problem is overcrowding. Calling it segregation only adds emotional confusion to the difficulties of solving it.[41]

With these words, the editors of the *American* publicly recommitted themselves to the civic credo interpretation of the schools issue—even in the face of *Brown, Taylor,* and the mounting evidence compiled by proponents of the de facto segregation view. They were soon to be joined in this stance by the other three white dailies.

In late December 1961 the board appeared to be trying to improve the emotional atmosphere that had gathered around its practices. For several years the Citizens Schools Committee had been calling for an independent survey of the educational and administrative policies of the board. In October it had been joined by the regional Parent Teacher Association. At that time, Willis had flatly stated that "we do not need a survey to tell us that we could use more teachers." In December, however, the board authorized $100,000 for an independent survey of the schools, to be conducted by a panel of three experts. In another conciliatory move toward its critics, the board authorized a limited transfer plan under which pupils in schools with classes averaging more than forty could transfer to schools averaging fewer than thirty. Students were to provide their own transportation. Finally, in an effort to reduce double shifts, the board voted to buy mobile classrooms and install them around seriously overcrowded schools. By the end of 1962, 150 such facilities were in service.[42]

Each of these moves led to more controversy. It took eighteen months to get the survey under way, and by then it had ceased to be independent. Willis had insisted on being one of the three panel members. The others were Robert J. Havighurst of the University of Chicago and Alonzo Grace of the University of Illinois. The transfer plan proved ineffective in redistributing students. The mobile classrooms became known as "Willis Wagons," and controversy raged over whether they were being deployed to relieve overcrowding or to maintain segregation.

The year 1962 opened with the first sitin of the school controversy. Under dispute was a plan to transfer about thirty students from Burnside School, which everyone agreed was overcrowded. The board wanted to send the students to the Gillespie School, which was already black. The parents demanded that they be sent to the nearby Perry School, which was still white. Beginning on 2 January 1962 and continuing for more than two weeks, the protest encompassed teachins at Burnside School, arrests of parents, ministers joining the ranks of the protesters, dismissal of charges by a judge who openly sided with the parents, picketing of the Board of Education, conferences with Superintendent Willis, and, finally, another suit involving the racial practices of the schools. *Burroughs* v. *Board of Education* sought damages for the plaintiffs and an injunction against the maintenance of schools reserved for whites, such as Perry. As with the *Webb* case, this, too, was dismissed on 2 November 1962 on grounds that state administrative remedies had not been exhausted.[43]

Protests continued throughout February. Four mothers entered a branch of the Kellogg School to check on how much space was available. Theirs was one of a series of visitations that day. They were arrested on complaint of the principal, found guilty of criminal trespass on 15 May, and given suspended sentences on 5 June 1962.[44] Kellogg, Burnside, Gillespie, and Perry schools were all in what the board called District 16. Almost everyone else called Woodlawn. It was a lower- and working-class neighborhood almost completely traversed by the color line, but which, by virtue of The Woodlawn Organization, was known as a militant black community. TWO specialized in aggressive, direct action techniques that brought conflict into the open.

Also in February 1962 the Chatham–Avalon Park Community Council, a white-collar black community organization, held a public conference titled "Segregation in the Chicago Public Schools" to express the conviction that segregation was indeed the problem in the public schools and to begin to gather a coalition of like-minded groups. The invited speakers were Leon Despres, the alderman from the ward around the University of Chicago and a critic of the Daley administration; Raymond W. Mack, chairman of Northwestern University's Department of Sociology; Raymond Harth, an attorney for the plaintiffs in the *Webb* case; and Edwin C. Berry, executive director of the Chicago Urban League. They concluded that there was a need, in Mack's words, "to educate the people to the magnitude of the problem."[45]

A city-wide seminar was held on 24 March 1962, sponsored by the Chicago Urban League and a "committee of PTA leaders," and called "How to

Achieve Quality and Equality of Education in Chicago Public Schools." Representatives from community organizations, race relations agencies, organized labor, the Catholic Interracial Council, American Jewish Congress, Citizens Schools Committee, PTAs, public and private welfare agencies, Protestant ministers, City Council members, other political figures, attorneys, and even the Chicago Commission on Human Relations were involved in leading workshops.[46]

The participants heard Dan W. Dodson of New York University attack the concept of the neighborhood school. The president of the Cleveland Board of Education, an executive of the schools in Washington, D.C., and an attorney from Detroit all told of experiments in their cities which, by comparison, made Chicago sound retrograde. The Urban League presented the findings of its research on the history and current status of segregation in the Chicago schools. The focus was on the "northern problem." In the end, the conference resolved that "racially separate schools, no matter what the cause, have a harmful effect on the developing personality of all children and impede the ability of minority group children to learn." The resolution also called upon the mayor to appoint school board members "who are committed to providing a policy of integration of the schools."[47]

NEIGHBORHOOD SCHOOLS WITHOUT NEIGHBORHOOD SUPPORT: THE CIVIC CREDO IN CONFLICT WITH COMMUNITY ORGANIZATIONS

By April 1962 a coalition to pursue these resolutions was beginning to take shape. It included the NAACP, the Urban League, The Woodlawn Organization, Chatham–Avalon Park Community Council, and Englewood Council for Community Action. It was called the Coordinating Council of Community Organizations (CCCO), and it was to serve as a clearinghouse for exchanging information and coordinating individual strategies. For the most part, it was a behind-the-scenes organization, but even in the beginning it provided a common front for dealing with the mayor.[48]

Late in April the school board nominating commission nominated five men and a woman from whom the mayor was to select two members of the Board of Education. All were white and all had records of silence on the issue of segregation. The *Defender* fulminated in a front-page editorial that it was unbelievable that either chance or merit had produced such a slate after all the public clamor over the schools: "A bedtime story of this magnitude would lack credibility even to a feeble-minded child." Even Alderman Kenneth E. Campbell, a loyal supporter of the mayor, said, "By and large, the Negro community resents it."[49]

90

The schools were in trouble with the community. The voters had rejected a proposed bond issue. The *Defender* had called for Superintendent Willis's resignation on 18 March 1962. Even the blue-ribbon nominating committee was under fire. The CCCO organized a delegation to meet with the mayor on 25 April 1962, which the *Sun-Times* called "a protesting group of Negroes."[50] In fact, the delegation was integrated and included Chicago's six black aldermen (all Daley loyalists), Edward Marciniak of the Chicago Commission on Human Relations, members of the Committee for Equality in Education, and CCCO representatives. Mayor Daley agreed to try to reconvene the nominating commission and to review the composition of the commission itself.

Because he usually adhered to the civic credo, it was unusual for the mayor to admit any appearance of political influence on the commission or the Board of Education, and the *Sun-Times* was immediate with its editorial objection. "The protesting Negro groups," said the newspaper, "now want active partisans of their point of view, representatives of a block rather than proponents of an unprejudiced, over-all approach to school problems." The newspaper interpreted the situation as a group grab for power and called it a danger to "our ideas of good citizenship."[51]

In reply, H. B. Law, president of the Chicago Urban League, challenged this "ethnic politics," civic credo interpretation of what was at issue in the schools. "The necessary starting point, here," he asserted, "is frank realization that a very large segment of the city (and not just the Negro segment, by any means) finds disastrous inequities in the present conduct of our public schools and believes that these inequities pose an extremely serious threat to the welfare of the entire community." It was not that the nominees for the school board were white, as was Law, but that they "seemed to offer only uncertain representation for those who seek greater progress toward equality of opportunity."[52]

On the issue at hand, the mayor split the difference between these two conflicting concepts of good citizenship. The nominating commission did not reconvene. The mayor chose Bernard Friedman and Raymond Spaeth from the existing list of candidates. In September, however, the mayor did appoint the first black group to those represented on the nominating commission, the Cook County Physicians Association.[53] After all, the civic credo did not exclude all ethnic considerations; indeed, it insisted on seeing blacks as an ethnic group.

Thus by the spring of 1962, it was clear that the Board of Education was in trouble with sizable segments of the public. In response, in May the board elected the well-connected and diplomatic Clair M. Roddewig as its president. Over the course of his tenure in this role, he was to prove a conscientious and skillful advocate of the civic credo perspective. On assuming office he said, "One of the first problems that confronts every member is restoring the confidence of critical groups in the board. If we don't solve problems with people and their communities with mutual respect, we can have the finest courses in the world in our schools and it won't mean a thing." He conceded that an accurate inventory of school facilities was still "one of the things we have to get at," and he spoke hopefully of achieving "better understanding" with the NAACP, the Urban League, and TWO.[54] Throughout the spring and summer he led a major diplomatic effort to restore harmony between the schools and their communities.

In May and June 1962, however, TWO made an issue of the mobile classrooms by organizing a boycott of the Carnegie School. About 90 percent of the eleven hundred pupils stayed away from classes on 18 May 1962. Referring to the mobile classrooms as "Willis Wagons," Rev. Arthur Brazier asserted that "the whole Negro community is positively opposed to mobile classrooms because we believe this is a means of maintaining segregation." The district superintendent, Curtis Melnick, countered by deploring "the fact that TWO chooses to show its power by interfering with the education of youngsters and depriving them of opportunities which they badly need."[55] In the absence of relevant data on facilities, the situation descended immediately into an accusatory impasse.

Roddewig tried a more conciliatory approach on the West Side, when parents began a sitin at the Herzl School. Even though he was not prepared to reverse the order installing the mobile classrooms, he did meet with the parents. He pleaded for their patience, assured them that the mobiles were temporary, and promised them that the building program was being pushed as fast as possible. The protests continued.

In July, Federal District Judge Julius J. Hoffman dismissed the *Webb* case, but not without expressing himself on the substance of the issue. "Chicago cannot deny the existence of *de facto* segregation," he said,

> or excuse it on the pretext of a benign indifference. We can't say piously, as there was once a tendency to do, that we don't know what is the percentage of Negro pupils to a given school because we do not ask a child his race or make it a part of the school record. There is nothing pious about refusing to face a fact that has an important bearing on the training of a child and his relationship to the community. . . . I am certain that Superintendent Willis, whom I know to be a great man and a great educator, and a wise and courageous minister, will see to it that the Chicago schools will be fully integrated and equal.[56]

Roddewig promptly assured the press and the public that "we are going to do the right thing."[57] The *Chicago Daily News* interpreted this to mean that the board would undertake a serious study of the problems raised in the *Webb* case. In fact, there was no immediate prospect of any such review. Over the summer the board did adopt a new approach to its critics, but it did not alter its stance on their criticisms. At its 8 August 1962 meeting, when groups arrived with placards expressing their concerns, Roddewig took time to recognize their presence. "Will you all hold your signs up at one time so the members may read them?" he asked. "Thank you," he said after a pause, "and now put them down." Then, on a motion by Bernard Friedman, the board voted to set up mechanisms "for preventing publicly-announced good intentions from fizzling out and requests for action from the school administration from being forgotten before they are carried out."[58]

Affirming that he was still looking forward to an independent survey of the schools, Friedman explained his motion by saying that he also thought "we might better spot our own deficiencies now and try to correct them." At this same meeting, however, the board voted to create branches of the white Dawes and Hubbard high schools to prevent "overcrowding" at these schools. The branches were to be in black elementary schools. Aware that this action did nothing to relieve the existing overcrowding that was causing so much community conflict in already black schools, the board promised to have a transfer program ready to present at its next meeting.[59]

The transfer plan that emerged was similar to the one that had been announced in December 1961. The plan was "permissive," allowing any pupil who was in a school with classes averaging more than forty students to transfer to a school in which the classes averaged less than thirty. The transferring pupils were to provide their own transportation. The NAACP, the Urban League, CORE, TWO, and others pointed out that under this plan the board was guaranteeing some students that their class size would not be allowed to exceed thirty while guaranteeing other students that theirs could not fall below forty. Therefore, instead of calming the critics of the schools, the transfer plan became yet another example of apparent discrimination.[60]

The board's budget hearings in the fall of 1962 provided a public forum for groups to reiterate their criticism of the schools. At these hearings both the chapters of CORE and the Englewood Committee for Community Action became more vocal and visible; and in relation to these two groups especially, Roddewig seemed unable to secure the cooperation of the general superintendent in his diplomatic and conciliatory approach toward community critics of board policies and practices.

When the Reverend Philip Dripps read a statement for the Englewood group critical of the transfer plan, the general superintendent chose to belittle the speaker rather than respond to the complaint. Observing that the speaker "hasn't been out of college very long," Willis said, "it's too bad he doesn't visit some of the new schools in the area and see what's going on." Willis chided the audience for overlooking the assets the board was providing for the community, especially the junior college and the teachers' college. "It's high time," he continued, "the people in the community begin to say 'this is an opportunity for us.' As far as college education goes you won't find a more fortunate group of people anywhere than in this community. These are some of the things you should be talking about."[61]

Rev. Dripps's testimony in 1962 was but one in a series of finally futile efforts to demand good-quality institutions in a disintegrating neighborhood where the population was declining and the schools were increasingly overcrowded. Between 1950 and 1966 the white population of Englewood declined from 124,809 to 24,289, and the black population increased from 14,006 to 107,771. The change, in other words, was not only rapid but nearly total.[62] During this socially destructive process, the neighborhood was little more than a concept, and the neighborhood schools were much less than adequate institutions.

Meanwhile, in the fall of 1962, the school bureaucracy, following Willis's lead, stiffened its resistance to voices of community complaint. According to the *Sun-Times,* "there were growing complaints from P.T.A. leaders that principals and district superintendents were bringing undue pressure on them in an effort to control what they said at the budget hearings."[63] One district superintendent tried to prevent a representative from the local CORE chapter from speaking. The result was a tumultuous meeting with people chanting "let CORE speak" and demonstrators waving placards hailing "General Willis" and proclaiming "The Superintendent Belongs in Mississippi." Those who did gain the floor called for Willis's resignation, and the NAACP branded the hearings as "useless."[64]

The NAACP commented that "the practice of suggesting to speakers that they include complimentary remarks about the schools . . . [was] significantly revealing" and that "the conduct of the general superintendent of schools in these hearings has been disgusting, though not surprising."[65] Undaunted, Superintendent Willis threatened to walk out on one spirited hearing unless the audience calmed down. "If you want to know what I'm thinking about," he told the assembly, "get a copy of Kipling's 'If.' " ("If you can keep your head when all about you / Are losing theirs and blaming it on you; / If you can trust yourself when all men doubt you / And make allowance for their doubting too. . . .")[66]

Late in October 1962 the state superintendent of public instruction opened hearings into the charges of segregation which had been formally lodged by TWO. Since the *Webb* case had been dismissed from federal court on the grounds that the plaintiffs had not exhausted the administrative remedies available from state agencies, TWO determined to exhaust them. This hearing opened on 30 October 1962 and was continued 3–5 December 1962. The hearing was yet another replay of the controversy over whether segregation or overcrowding was at the root of the disruption in black schools. It did become clear in the course of the testimony that the Board of Education considered only neighborhood space as available space, hence its total reliance on mobile classrooms and an aggressive building program.[67]

In December Roddewig finally put the issue squarely as the board saw it: "If the courts would say that the neighborhood school policy violates the Constitution of the United States, we would change; but the courts have not said that." That was the most direct answer the critics of board policy had received. He was saying that it would take a federal court order to produce a reconsideration of the neighborhood school policy by the board. Incomprehensibly, the *Chicago Sun-Times* reported these remarks under the headline "Roddewig Promises Review of Neighborhood School Policy."[68]

The criticisms of the Board of Education achieved some official recognition and validation with the issuance of an investigative report by the U.S. Commission on Civil Rights. Authored by John E. Coons of Northwestern University, the report vindicated the principal criticisms that had been raised by advocates of the de facto segregation view since 1957, beginning with the NAACP report. Coons agreed with the 1957 NAACP's estimates of the scope of segregation within the system; and even though yielding that housing patterns were the underlying cause for racial concentrations in the schools, Coons still felt constrained to say, "On selected premises a case could be made against the school administration. Timely measures might have desegregated substantial numbers of classrooms, if that were the primary object. The administration has made no effort to aid in integration; indeed to the extent that it has recognized the existence of the problem, its policies probably have impeded rather than promoted integration." He conceded that "it is legitimate to inquire what solution within practical reach would have improved the situation in any substantial way."[69]

The concept of the neighborhood school had ceased to be either functional or descriptive in many areas of the city. "Practically speaking," Coons observed, "neighborhood schools do not exist in many of the crowded areas of Chicago, unless the requirements of that concept are satisfied by the mere existence of a building called a 'school' which is physically located in something called a 'neighborhood.' . . . The most serious charge against the administration seems to be that in many areas it has not been operating a neighborhood school system, but has acted as if it were."[70]

Coons devoted an entire section of his report to the "empty desk imbroglio"—the issue of how many vacant chairs and underused classrooms there were. The board's local critics learned that they were not alone in their inability to obtain a factual accounting of school resources. "At no point in this report or later," Coons reported, "was a complete inventory of all Chicago schools presented." Nonetheless, Coons concluded: "It is reasonably

95

clear from this mass of indirect evidence that substantial space existed in a number of areas of the city in 1961–62. The new president of the board readily conceded this in an interview."[71]

This policy of secrecy about available facilities had originated with the Willis administration. The *Chicago Daily News* pointed out that annual classroom inventories were routinely reported during the Hunt administration.[72] The lack of such data merely served to cast the general superintendent's motives under a cloud.

"During 1961–62," according to Coons,

> the administration, consciously or not, was faced with a choice. It was clear that the overcrowded schools had to be relieved. The issue was whether this should be accomplished by transfers to uncrowded schools or by the purchase of mobile units. When the superintendent took the position that there was no room in other schools for this purpose and the board did not dissent from this conclusion, the issue was foreclosed. Why the superintendent so concluded and why the board accepted his conclusion without inquiry in the face of the evidence is difficult to understand.[73]

Whatever the reasons, the results were far-reaching, and Coons's report did not draw back from the obvious conclusion: "From the point of view of racial discrimination or merely that of nonracial equal protection, the confinement of pupils in crowded classes when other facilities were underutilized cannot be justified. The effect of this action was not merely injuring to the children retained in crowded schools. Perhaps the most serious injury was suffered by the school administration itself through the loss of public confidence in its impartiality."[74]

Edwin C. Berry, executive director of the Chicago Urban League, hailed it as "a great report which substantiates the charges that have been made all along." Rev. Arthur Brazier of TWO called it a "vindication"of the efforts to fight segregation. "The Chicago Board of Education," he predicted, "can never more afford to sit on its hands and allow the evil practice of segregation to exist."[75]

Superintendent Willis, on the other hand, responded by putting the question of the neighborhood school before the board for a policy decision. While making it clear that he still preferred the neighborhood concept, he told the board he would prepare a transfer plan to use all the space available by 29 January 1963 if the board so wished. The board did not so wish, though it took several weeks to reach that conclusion.[76]

It was unlikely, in any event, that the board would have opposed its general superintendent on such a fundamental policy. Joseph Pois, who was a member of the Chicago board from 1956 to 1961 and who later taught public administration at the University of Pittsburgh, stressed the structural dependence of the board members on the general superintendent in his case study of Chicago's "school board crisis." He pointed out that the statutory structure of the board almost inevitably pulled it into the details of the day-to-day operations without affording any opportunity for general review and investigation. The board was responsible for the "general supervision and management" of the school system, but the statutes also vested in the board such specific and detailed responsibilities as "prescribing the course and methods of study, the employment of personnel, the appointment of the general superintendent and attorney, fixing of employee compensation, dividing the city into subdistricts for the purpose of apportioning pupils to the several schools, removal of educational and civil service employees, preparation and adoption of budget, acquisition of real estate, the disciplining of pupils, investment of school funds, and the sale of tax anticipation warrants and bonds." Furthermore, "statutory references to purchases and the expenditures of funds have been interpreted as making these functions direct responsibilities of the board."[77]

All this was expected of a board of eleven members who served without pay. Even though the statutes mandated that all the powers of the general superintendent should be exercised "subject to the approval of the board," in fact the board members found themselves almost completely dependent on the general superintendent and his staff to fulfill their functions. The distinction, therefore, between "policy" and "administration" was merely analytic. In operation, this distinction was rhetorical, perhaps mainly involving public relations, for it defined which party—the board or the general superintendent—had to face the public and be held accountable for policies. In offering to abandon the neighborhood school concept, Willis was shifting the responsibility for that policy from himself to the board.

In an atmosphere of conflict with the community, the Board of Education was placed at a distinct disadvantage. Although the board was the legal source of authority for the administration of the schools, its own authority with the public was almost entirely dependent on the behavior and performance of the administration. What was more, Willis held to a very high doctrine of "professionalism" and to a very low doctrine of lay participation in the formation of educational policy. "Much of what is wrong with education today," Willis wrote early in his Chicago career, "can be attributed to the fact that educators . . . have abdicated from positions of educational leadership, and have permitted themselves and their schools to be swayed by the winds of uninformed public opinion."[78]

Willis may have justified his arrogance toward protesters by his high principle of "professionalism"; but the fact is that his critics did not represent "the winds of uninformed public opinion." As it turned out, the complaining community rather than the positive-thinking superintendent was in better touch with the truth. While the general superintendent was berating Rev. Dripps for not knowing "what's going on" in the Englewood schools, a new class of children

97

was entering the first grade there. Of those children, only about one-fifth would be reading at their normal grade level by grade six. Of course, no one could prove that in the fall of 1962. Yet by 1967, it was a grim, statistically certified fact that 80 percent of these children had failed to achieve sixth-grade competence.[79] By then, Willis was gone, and the winds of public opinion had reached gale force. But the "temporary" problems in the Englewood schools had permanently affected the life chances of those children. And no one had any plan for reversing those results.

By 1962, there were organizations in increasing numbers of neighborhoods that could see "what's going on" and knew what it meant for their children. That was what the rising tide of protest was about, and it was not uninformed. When the Board of Education finally did cooperate in a racial inventory and analysis of its schools, as part of the out-of-court settlement in the *Webb* case in 1963, the findings were just as the NAACP had claimed in 1958.

In 1962, the Board of Education was in the center of a gathering storm of protest, and it was also in need of more money. Meeting the 1963 budget required an increase in the school tax. Further, the board needed additional bond money to continue its building program. The revenues from bond issues in 1951, 1955, 1957, and 1959 were running out. Almost $290 million had been spent on new and renovated facilities, but the public had been unable to secure an accurate inventory of these facilities or their availability to relieve the chronic overcrowding which the general superintendent claimed was the paramount problem in the schools.

In December 1962, the board decided to delay asking the public for another $50 million in bonds.[80] A similar proposal had been defeated in April, and in the meantime, Roddewig's diplomacy had failed to make peace between the board and its critics.

"It must be remembered," said Pois, "that the Board functions in an environment fraught with tensions, conflicting pressures, and insatiable demands. . . . It may be felt that procrastination and playing down issues will at least temper feelings of indignation and criticism. . . . The atmosphere apparently is more conducive to seeking emollients that, at least momentarily, ward off crises, tone down strident criticisms, and afford a veneer of harmony and smoothness."[81]

Harmony and smoothness may have been the goal during 1962, but they had not been achieved. Nor did they seem within reach for 1963 without a change in the board's policy.

The Supreme Court's decision in the *Brown* case put the American creed on the political agenda. Although that decision specifically applied to de jure school segregation in the South, its principles could be thought applicable to either de jure or de facto school segregation, North or South. Under the impact of the *Brown* decision, groups began forming in towns and cities across the nation to pursue the implications of the "equal protection of the laws" for their schools.

By the end of 1962, the issue of segregation in the Chicago schools had emerged into full view. It had been documented by the NAACP in its 1958 report "De Facto Segregation in the Chicago Public Schools," which claimed that "the Chicago Board of Education maintains in practice what amounts to a racially discriminatory policy." That report had analyzed the dynamics of racial change in the schools, including overcrowding, which increased the incentive for whites to leave as soon as they could. In affidavits filed in the *Webb* case, the general superintendent had confirmed this analysis by documenting the rapid increases in school enrollments in racially changing neighborhoods even though he claimed to be unable to explain these demographic catastrophes.

The *Taylor* decision involving New Rochelle schools gave legal standing to the grounds that had been implicit in the NAACP report, namely, "it is of no moment whether segregation is labeled de jure (according to law) or de facto, as long as the board, by its conduct, is responsible for its maintenance." The board's critics believed that *Taylor* imposed an affirmative duty on the board to pursue a goal of integrated education. The general superintendent, and ultimately the entire board, however, were firmly committed to the neighborhood school policy. Not only did they deny any affirmative duty to pursue racial integration, they even denied official knowledge of the racial conditions of any school.

The NAACP report of 1958 had been intended as part of a strategy to extend the logic of *Brown* to the schools in Chicago, that is, that in the matter of schools, separate is inherently unequal and affirmative rectification is, therefore, constitutionally required. That strategy was set back by the change in local NAACP leadership and was not revived until the 1961 *Taylor* decision. A renewed drive in Chicago for federal litigation against the schools was once again coordinated by the local NAACP Legal Redress Committee; but once again organizational problems resulted in failure to develop a coordinated and comprehensive legal strategy with community support. The *Webb* case was filed, only to be dismissed in 1962, reinstituted in 1963, and settled out of court shortly thereafter. No overall legal strategy for challenging school segregation in Chicago ever became an important part of civil rights activities or the school protests that were to follow.

Instead, strategic focus turned to coalition building among the various community organizations that were concerned about the color line and the schools. By early 1962, the nucleus of a coalition had begun to emerge. Called the Coordinating Council of Community Organizations, it included the NAACP, the Chicago Urban League, The Woodlawn Organization, the Chatham–Avalon Park Community Council, and the Englewood Council for Community Action.

99

At the time it was more a clearinghouse for information than a direct action group, although it did send a delegation to the mayor to challenge his school board nominees and the process by which they had been chosen in April 1962. For the most part, however, it functioned to provide research, publicity, and support for community groups, especially those that shared its interpretation that the school issue was one of de facto segregation.

The activities by which these concerns were expressed varied considerably: CORE, which had taken up the research capability on which the NAACP had relied in 1957, sent the Board of Education a seven-page letter telling the board where it had unused space (in white schools) to relieve the severe overcrowding (in black schools). In December 1961, the Chicago Urban League issued a study of available classroom space which corroborated the CORE claims. TWO began a strategy of sitins at disputed schools. Chatham–Avalon Park Community Council held a community education conference on segregation in the Chicago public schools. The Urban League sponsored a citywide seminar titled "How to Achieve Quality and Equality of Education in the Chicago Public Schools." These groups also testified at every public hearing held by the Board of Education. When the *Webb* case was dismissed from federal court on the grounds that the plaintiffs had not exhausted administrative remedies, TWO lodged charges of segregation against the Chicago schools with the state superintendent of instruction. Those hearings became yet another arena of confrontation between the board and its critics.

The responses to all these activities were complex. The mayor added a black group to his Advisory Commission on School Board Nominations. The Board of Education claimed to be an innocent victim of inexplicable overcrowding at selected schools. Both in 1958 and again in 1962, however, the board reaffirmed its commitment to a neighborhood school policy. In support of this policy, the board began to order mobile classrooms and place them at seriously overcrowded schools. With the question of available space still unresolved, this move became one more piece of evidence that the board was determined to solve its problem only within the bounds of a segregated system rationalized by the civic credo.

In May 1962, Clair M. Roddewig became the president of the board and pledged himself to "restoring the confidence of critical groups in the board." He attended community meetings and pleaded for understanding and patience. He was civil and diplomatic, but he was unyielding in his commitment to the neighborhood school policy. His position was that only a federal court order could change that policy.

The general superintendent was more confrontational. For Willis, the nonpartisan plank of the civic credo meant professionalism, elitism, and, frequently, autocratic behavior. Even board members were disturbed that he was not forthcoming with accurate data on available space. In community meetings he was insulting to speakers and groups. Through district superintendents he tried to rig public meetings to avoid or at least mute the criticism of the schools. Even the U.S. Civil Rights Commission was unable to secure his cooperation in gaining access to data.

By late 1962, the U.S. Civil Rights Commission had issued a report that agreed substantially with the de facto segregation critics of the schools. According to that report, even the president of the board had conceded that substantial space existed within the system to relieve the overcrowding in the black schools. The report also observed that the Willis administration "had made no effort to aid in integration" and had probably "impeded rather than promoted integration." The report concluded that the concept of a neighborhood school had broken down and was no longer a functional premise for policy. The board responded by reaffirming its commitment to the neighborhood school policy.

A year of controversy had not moved the board from the position articulated the year before by *Chicago's American,* the civic credo: "The problem to be solved is not segregation, since there isn't any; the problem is overcrowding. Calling it segregation only adds emotional confusion to the difficulties of solving it." Segregation or not, the board denied that it had any "affirmative duty" to provide a "school system which is racially integrated." The board did vote in December 1961 and again in August 1962 to allow voluntary transfers out of schools in which class sizes averaged above forty into schools in which they averaged below thirty. Neither of these plans provided much relief to many students, and they became controversial in themselves because of the double standard.

By December of 1962, therefore, the lines of conflict between the schools and the civic credo, on the one hand, and the advocates of the de facto segregation view, on the other, were drawing tight. The board had taken its stand for the neighborhood school and in support of the general superintendent. The advocates of civil rights had begun a coalition around the CCCO, had initiated local school protests, and had spoken at every available forum, but they had failed to sustain litigation that would bring *Brown* to bear upon Chicago. As a result, although they were certain that the discontent with the schools was widespread, they were uncertain as to the effective focus of that discontent. The report to the U.S. Civil Rights Commission had confirmed that more than overcrowding was at issue in the neighborhood schools that were being ravaged by the relentless, block-by-block expansion of the color line in Chicago.

In sum, as the de facto segregation view of the schools issue emerged, it held that the Chicago public schools were segregated; this segregation made black schools tangibly unequal; since the schools were more segregated than their neighborhoods, housing patterns did not entirely explain this segregation in the schools; school board policies were in large part responsible for these patterns

101

of segregation and subordination in the schools; and the school board had an affirmative duty to integrate and equalize the schools.

Like the *Brown* decision from which it arose, this de facto segregation view incorporated major elements of the perspectives that had developed from Du-Bois and Myrdal—clearly legitimizing the protests of black parents, for example, and regularly appealing to the highest values of the culture. In this appeal to the American creed, the de facto segregation view resembled the civic credo, but whereas the civic credo counseled acceptance of existing arrangements and institutions, those who saw the issue as de facto segregation demanded institutional change in the name of the American creed. Thus, even in its emergence, the de facto segregation view was in radical and inevitable conflict with the civic credo over the question of democratic duties in the face of a color line that cut across the entire system.

PART TWO

The Pursuit of the Issue

CHAPTER FOUR

The Issue Is Joined: 1963

Ihe annual report of the general superintendent of the Chicago schools claimed that "by January 1963 for the first time in Chicago public school history there was a seat for every child in the city's elementary schools."[1] The building program had finally caught up with the school population, but this achievement did not produce the satisfaction that had for so long been promised. It went largely unnoticed at the time, and had it not been included in the annual report, it might never have been known at all. Indeed, in January the budget still included outlays for new buildings, necessitating an increase in property taxes. In a letter to the board, CORE urged that these expenditures be dropped "until it is learned what the money is for." CORE contended that "we have been building segregated school buildings instead of educating children democratically in the buildings we already have."[2]

A contrasting position was taken by E. T. McSwain, the dean of Northwestern University's School of Education, who declined the honor of heading the long-delayed independent survey of the Chicago public schools. "You can always find weak spots in anything," he said, "but Chicago has a very fine system. Too much emphasis on what's wrong can lead to unrest and lack of confidence."[3] Undaunted, the board reportedly approached several other "leading U.S. educators," but they, too, declined the responsibility after discussing its prospects with Willis.[4] For the moment, the question of the survey could not be resolved, and the "success" of the building program remained unheralded, even by its proponents.

AN EXPANDED CIVIL RIGHTS COALITION: NATIONAL LEGITIMACY FOR DIRECT ACTION

Meanwhile, the National Conference on Religion and Race convened in Chicago with 657 delegates from across the country and sponsored by the National Council of Churches of Christ in America, the Synagogue Council of America, and the National Catholic Welfare Conference.

The meeting had the dual purpose of commemorating the centennial of the Emancipation Proclamation and of calling for "leadership of religion in ending racial discrimination in the United States." The participants met in workshops to plan programs to increase the commitment of their communions to the struggle for racial justice. The purpose of the meeting was to express a commitment to the gathering momentum of the civil rights movement, not to debate that commitment, and to issue an "Appeal to the Conscience of the American People." Warning that "racism is our most serious domestic evil," it took as its theme "action now" to eliminate racism. "We must eradicate it with all diligence and speed," the church leaders warned. "For this purpose we appeal to the consciences of the American people."[5] The meeting was notable not only for its unanimity on an issue that was as deeply divisive of local churches as it was of local school districts,[6] but also because it was the first time in American history that the official bodies of Judaism, Roman Catholicism, and Protestantism had jointly and publicly conferred to express their agreement on anything. It was a surprising event in which previously minority voices within the American religious communities emerged in an official capacity, complete with the mantle of ecumenicity—a symbol of the highest ecclesiastical status in 1963.

No doubt the participants in the National Conference on Religion and Race were a select group of those who were already prepared to commit the ideas and sentiments of their religious traditions to the goals and tactics of the civil rights movement. Following this conference, however, there was a dramatic increase in the public visibility as well as the inner vitality of religious groups committed to racial justice. The Presbyterian Interracial Council, the Interracial Council of Methodists, and the Fellowship for Racial Justice Now within the United Churches of Christ were established. The Chicago chapters of all these joined the CCCO before the summer was out, as did the Catholic Interracial Council (CIC) and the Episcopal Society for Cultural and Racial Unity (ESCRU). The CIC, founded in 1937, had concentrated its efforts principally within the Roman Catholic community before 1963. ESCRU, founded in 1959, was already controversial for its support of "freedom riders" in 1961.

The Ecumenical Institute, a combination "disciplined community" and lay training center operating from Chicago's West Side, was at the time a gathering point for socially concerned clergy of many persuasions, and it, too, joined the CCCO following the Conference on Religion and Race. In addition to legitimizing and stimulating these denominational caucuses, the national conference resulted in the Chicago Conference on Religion and Race becoming an ongoing organization dedicated to coordinating denominational responses to the issues of the civil rights movement and to creating a trifaith ecumenical presence in the city. In Chicago, at least, the national conference found a responsive ecclesiastical setting, and the immediate results were impressive whether they were representative or not.

The CCCO, which had met with the mayor in the spring of 1962 to protest the nominees for the school board, had, in September 1962, been rewarded for its efforts with the appointment of the Cook County Physicians Association to the roster of groups entitled to send a representative to the Mayor's Advisory Commission on School Board Nominations. In April 1962 the CCCO had been little more than a joint delegation of five groups, the Urban League, the NAACP, TWO, Chatham–Avalon Community Council, and the Committee for Equality in Education. These groups consulted together periodically with a view to developing a joint strategy on the schools. By October 1962 the groups were meeting more regularly and had formalized their relations with a simple one-page "Rules of Procedure."

In February 1963 the CCCO met once again with the mayor to discuss school board appointments. By then the Cook County Physicians Association, Cook County Bar Association, and Dearborn Real Estate Board, all black organizations, as well as CORE and the Englewood Committee for Community Action, had joined the council. Speaking for the group, H. B. Law was unwilling to discuss the content of the discussion, but he did say, "The mayor appeared sympathetic to our problems."[7]

During the same week, yet another neighborhood rose in protest against its schools. The board proposed to transfer children into an old warehouse that was not yet completely renovated. The parents established the 71st and Stewart Committee, boycotted the school, and prevented the board's action. The NAACP was instrumental in arranging meetings between Roddewig and the parents. For a time the situation was tense, and Roddewig seemed to be having trouble with his communications downtown. Reportedly, he hung up on Willis rather than continue their disagreement over the phone.[8]

Late in February the Illinois House of Representatives passed an amendment to the School Code of Illinois, which became known as the Armstrong Act, requiring affirmative action from school boards to prevent segregation in the planning of new schools and to rectify de facto segregation in creation and revision of attendance zones.[9] After this law went into effect in June 1963, the board found itself in the position of having to produce and publish "racial head counts" for schools and districts. It was the end of the board's "know-nothing" stance on the racial composition and distribution of the city's schoolchildren. According to the U. S. Commission on Civil Rights, this legislation was "the first of its kind" by a state legislature.[10]

"Then came Birmingham which changed all space and time." That was how one participant expressed what everyone active in the movement for civil rights experienced in April 1963.[11] Birmingham reshaped the national perception of what was at stake in the civil rights movement. Its effects were felt at

107

the highest levels of government and at the grass-roots levels of community action in hundreds of cities across the nation.

The crisis in Birmingham began on 3 April 1963 with modest demands for desegregated downtown public facilities, the breaking of the color bar in hiring clerks and secretaries, and the formation of a biracial committee to work out further details for the desegration of Birmingham. The movement was led by the Reverend Fred Lee Shuttlesworth, an associate of Martin Luther King, Jr., and Ralph D. Abernathy in the Southern Christian Leadership Conference. Shuttlesworth lived in Birmingham. King and Abernathy did not.[12] When the demonstrations began, they were widely interpreted, even by some factions of the Birmingham black community, as the work of outside, radical agitators. By the time the crisis had run its course—increasingly large mass arrests, the use of dogs and fire hoses against men, women, and children, the burning and bombing of black homes and property, the president's threat to use federal troops, the shrill defiance of Governor George C. Wallace even though a settlement had been worked out, the issuance of King's "Letter from the Birmingham Jail," and the mocking of nonviolence by Malcolm X— King, Abernathy, and Shuttlesworth emerged as rational moderates who had truly grasped the radical passions that had to be tamed with racial justice. And for a season, racial injustice became a dominating national concern. It was no longer *a* national problem. It was *the* domestic issue. Birmingham became the code word for all that racial injustice implied. Birmingham also became the model for persistent mass action among the opponents of the color line. Under the mood generated by Birmingham, if it was not massive, it was nothing.

Bayard Rustin was quick to catch the significance of this transformation. While the events in Birmingham were still working themselves out, he wrote that one could see a "new phase of the civil rights movement" emerging. It was, he said, "the phase of mass action—non-violent disobedience and non-violent non-cooperation." It confronted the South with a choice between integration or chaos. "This struggle," he concluded, was reaching decisive proportions in the South and was "only beginning in the North, but it will be a bitter struggle."[13]

In Chicago, however, the developments in April and May continued to be ambiguous and indecisive. On the one hand, the mayor appointed to the Board of Education Warren Bacon, who was black, integrationist, outspoken, and the vice-president of a steel company. He replaced one of the longtime conservatives on the board. On the other hand, Willis was still telling the press of his objections to an independent survey of the schools even though the board had selected Robert J. Havighurst of the University of Chicago to head the survey. Both the John Birch Society and the American Legion opposed Havighurst's appointment because of his long record of liberal and civil libertarian commitments. Board member Spaeth attacked the idea of a survey

108

because he thought it was being handled in a way unfriendly to the general superintendent. Although Willis did not name Havighurst, he was reported by the *Sun-Times* to have said that the board's "choice of director indicates a decision to reverse the policy of neighborhood schools."[14]

Somewhere between the majority of the board and the general superintendent there were lines of conflict. Some members reported that Willis threatened to resign over the choice of Havighurst. Others denied it. Finally a compromise was worked out. Havighurst was to be joined by Willis himself and a third party of their choosing in designing, supervising, and finally reporting the results of the survey. For the moment all parties were pleased. Willis had forestalled a survey of his work over which he had no control. Havighurst had a reputation for scholarship and integrity which inspired trust from even the most severe critics of the schools. Together they picked Alonzo Grace, dean of the School of Education at the University of Illinois, as the third party. He raised no controversy whatever.

The real meaning of this compromise, like the other developments of early 1963, lay in the future. For the present, they were ambiguous. For instance, did Roddewig's responsiveness to the 71st and Stewart Committee signify a new stance of openness to community discontent with the schools, or was it a tactical retreat from an obviously bad situation? Did Warren Bacon's appointment signify the mayor's intention to reconstitute the board into one that would deal candidly with its problems, or was it an attempt to pair Bacon with Mrs. Wendell Green, the other black member, who was avowedly pro-Willis, thus creating a stalemate over what the "real demands" of black people were? Should the overall meaning of the survey be read from the fact that Havighurst would direct it, or that Willis had secured a place for himself on the team? And was it more important that the Armstrong Act created an affirmative duty for school boards or that it was written in language that still presupposed a system of neighborhood schools? The answers to all these questions remained to be seen, but a wait and see attitude was not the order of the day in the summer of 1963.

In the South, Governor Wallace had raised himself to the stature of a symbol by fulfilling his pledge to "stand in the schoolhouse door" at the University of Alabama rather than acquiesce in federally ordered integration. President John F. Kennedy federalized the Alabama National Guard and forced the issue to a conclusion. On 11 June 1963 the president addressed the nation to explain his actions and to implore the country to do more. "We face," he said,

a moral crisis as a country and a people. It cannot be met by repressive police action. It cannot be left to increased demonstrations in the streets. It cannot be quieted by token moves or talk. It is a time to act in the Congress, in your state and local legislative body, and, above all, in our daily lives. . . . A great change is at hand, and our task, our obligation, is to make that revolution, that change peaceful and constructive for all. Those who do nothing are inviting shame as well as violence. Those who act boldly are recognizing right as well as reality.[15]

As if to seal the president's tone of urgency with senseless tragedy, the very next day Medgar Evers, Mississippi field secretary for the NAACP, was ambushed outside his home and shot in the back—dead at the age of thirty-seven. Symbolic of unyielding resistance, the police in Jackson, Mississippi, two days later arrested 160 mourners who were marching silently in memory of Medgar Evers.

In Chicago, Clair Roddewig was reelected president of the Board of Education on 12 June 1963. He took the occasion to express the new mood of urgency and solemnity as well as his own personal commitment to improve race relations. He acknowledged that "the schools have become involved," and he urged board members to ask, "Have we done the job we have to do?—thinking not necessarily about buildings or courses of study, but in terms of the school as a part of the community?" Ironically, as he spoke there were pickets outside the board building still protesting the exclusion of blacks from Washburne Trade School, a situation that had provoked protest for twenty or more years. He set the end of the year as a target for measuring progress "in creating better relations between these groups and the school board." It was not a question, he continued, of "whether they do or don't express the views of the Negro community." The point was that "the groups that express this dissatisfaction are the only groups asserting leadership among Negroes in this area. You are not going to wake up some morning," he admonished his fellow board members, "to find them gone and say to yourself, 'It was a bad dream!' "[16]

Nonetheless, after Roddewig had finished his remarks, Warren Bacon, the new member, and Superintendent Willis found themselves in conflict over how to respond to a new community conflict. The Englewood Committee for Community Action was demanding the ouster of a principal. Bacon wanted the parents to be heard. Willis claimed that was not necessary because he already had a "complete" report from the district superintendent. Bacon contested the completeness of the report, saying, "You have just one side. Both should be heard." He insisted that there was a breakdown of rapport between the school and the community, and "regardless of who is at fault" the board should hear both sides.[17] Willis did not consider his view of the schools "just one side." As we have seen, in his judgment, the "professional" view was the complete view. In the conflict with "uninformed public opinion," Willis was not prepared to have his judgment considered "just one side."

In mid-June, the weekend *Defender* published a feature article on Mrs. Wendell Green, for many years the lone black member of the Board of Education and a loyal and longtime supporter of Willis. The banner for the article

110

announced, "Talkative Mrs. Green Derides School Integration Issue, Sneers at Marches by Dixie Youngsters."[18] The lead paragraph quoted her as saying: "The biggest problem in Chicago's schools is not whether they are integrated, or not integrated, but motivating the individual child to study and to accept knowledge." Certainly that was not the prevailing articulation of what was at issue in the schools. Consequently, individuals from the Negro American Labor Council, Teachers for Integrated Schools, SNCC, CORE, and the NAACP youth council joined together to picket Green when she spoke at the graduation ceremonies at Dunbar Vocational High School. She was greeted with placards saying, "Willis and Green must leave the scene."[19] The demonstrators were not simply protesting Green. Dunbar Vocational itself was also an object of their concern. Dunbar was open to black students; in fact, it was mostly black; but graduation from it did not lead to union membership, as graduation from Washburne Trade School did. To the protesters, that seemed to be more of a structural than a motivational issue, and they were angry at Green for confusing the two.

At the school board meeting of 26 June 1963, Faith Rich, one of the authors of the NAACP's "De Facto Segregation in the Chicago Public Schools" but now representing CORE, appeared in the company of aggrieved parents. "We are protesting," she said, "the transfer of students from Farragut High School to Hirsch and the use of mobile classrooms because both moves are subtle plans to perpetuate segregation." To show that this case was not isolated, she cited the board's creation of a new high school at Orr on the West Side, thus removing the white students from Marshall High School. "This vicious circle would keep Marshall predominantly Negro," she charged. "It's the same pattern all over again—segregation."[20] Six years after the publication of "De Facto Segregation in the Chicago Public Schools," the data still fit the familiar pattern. It was significant, however, that by 1963 the data were accompanied by protesting parents from the affected communities.

Over the Fourth of July weekend, the NAACP held its Free by Sixty-Three national conference in Chicago. The slogan had been announced ten years before. Long considered the conservative among civil rights groups, the NAACP took a decisive turn toward direct action at this meeting.[21] Even though President Kennedy favored a moratorium on demonstrations while his civil rights package was before the Congress, leaders of the major national civil rights groups—including the NAACP—were going ahead with plans for a massive March on Washington for Jobs and Freedom Now. At its convention, the NAACP formally rejected the idea of a moratorium, and more than four hundred of the delegates joined a demonstration at the Chicago Board of Education to protest "the most segregated school system in the North."[22]

The idea of a moratorium in the summer of 1963 completely misconceived the passions and the momentum behind the often amorphous civil rights movement. Neither the old-line nor the newer race relations organizations were in control of the situation. Perhaps it was, to some degree, of their own making, but in the summer of 1963 the civil rights organizations were as much the objects as the subjects of the actions and passions of the movement.

The NAACP was caught up in these tensions. As part of its national convention, it called for a march through Chicago's Loop, ending in a rally at Grant Park to symbolize its new activism. Yet by inviting Mayor Daley to participate in the march and speak at the rally, the leadership opened itself to criticism from all sides. A caucus of about one hundred persons, organized by none of the established civil rights groups but drawn from several of them, including the ranks of the NAACP, prevented the mayor from speaking at the rally, much to the embarrassment of the NAACP leadership. Speaking from the convention's podium later in the week, James Meredith, hero of the struggle to integrate the University of Mississippi, chastised the new assertiveness in civil rights. "If we take on the same characteristics of our oppressors and enemies," he said, "intolerance, bigotry, and allowing no voice to speak out but those that say what we want to hear—I feel that certainly our course may well be doomed."[23] Once again, the NAACP leadership was embarrassed.

Nevertheless, the *Chicago Sun-Times* lauded the NAACP march and rally, viewing it as largely ceremonial, "a demonstration that a community has recognized a problem and is trying to solve that problem." The newspaper even contrasted the march in Chicago with the proposed March on Washington, which it saw as a "threat," a "demand," and an "exhibition of force to intimidate," carrying within itself "the seeds of violence." In Chicago, by contrast, "the presence of the elected head of government in the vanguard of the march is evidence that the whole community is part of the problem and the solution." The *Sun-Times* and the *Chicago Daily News,* which were considered to be Chicago's liberal newspapers, thus continued to editorialize in the spirit of the 1951 human relations commission report, reaffirming the civic credo that the worst was over, that the city was already committed to the purposes of the civil rights movement, and that, therefore, demands, demonstrations, and nonviolent direct action were unreasonable and out of place. Though granting that the city "still has a long way to go before it can say without fear of contradiction, that this is a city where all men enjoy equal rights," the *Sun-Times* took its stand on the affirmation that "Chicago has made great strides in race relations in the past 20 years."[24] In adopting this stance, the newspapers became active participants and partisans in the unfolding events.

On 10 July 1963 CORE began a sitin at the Board of Education building. The demonstrators remained in the board president's conference room continuously from 10 July to 18 July, when they were removed by the police. Throughout this time increasingly large groups of supporters and antagonists

112

gathered in and around the building until by 18 July the situation had become unruly. CORE had undertaken this dramatic tactic out of frustration with its inability to get any satisfaction through letters to the board, testimony at public meetings, or private conversations with school officials. The board was trying to have it both ways: there was a seat for every child in the schools, but it was overcrowding and not segregation that was disrupting the neighborhood schools.

The people in CORE were frustrated with the board, but CORE was also an organization in the throes of change. Like the NAACP, CORE was as much the object as the subject of the new activism. After years of existing with loosely coordinated small fellowship chapters, pacifist-oriented CORE was attracting large numbers to its meetings. It remained committed to nonviolence and integration in the summer of 1963, but many of its followers were increasingly angry with the established institutions, in search of a grassroots mass base, and inclined to emphasize the desire for various forms of black power. Its leadership was in flux. When Roddewig complained, "I don't know who is running CORE," it was not because he had failed to make the effort to find out.[25] Several persons publicly represented CORE during the sitin, and they did not all speak in the same voice. Before the summer was out, Samuel Riley, longtime chairman of Chicago CORE, resigned "for personal reasons." Although committed to aggressive direct action, Riley was also a skilled negotiator with a complex vision of the skills required for the politics of confrontation. By midsummer, however, it seemed that only the commitment to direct action was holding the factions in CORE together.

The newspapers fulminated against this new direction. The *Sun-Times* chided CORE for not understanding the inverse relationship between "rights and roughnecks," and the *Daily News* preached that "coercion isn't persuasion." The *Daily News* granted that CORE's charge of segregation was "important" but insisted that "it is also beside the point." The very use of direct action techniques raised the question "whether the real motives of CORE leaders are what they say they are."[26]

This confrontation actually produced several meaningful concessions from Roddewig. Even though there had been no editorial comment on the substance of CORE's concerns, Roddewig knew well what they were. On the same day that he called the police, therefore, he agreed to secure a racial head count of the schoolchildren by fall, to produce supporting data for proposed boundary changes, to recommend a transfer plan, and to provide a meaningful inventory of classrooms.[27] It was a better response than CORE had been able to evoke by less confrontational means.

In this atmosphere of increasing responsiveness to nonviolent direct action, more than eight hundred persons assembled at the Methodist Church in Woodlawn, under the auspices of the CCCO, on 20 July 1963 "to map a broad strategy for change in the field of human rights in our community."[28] By this time, the CCCO was a rapidly expanding coalition of civil rights groups: NAACP, Urban League, Cook County Physicians Association, Cook County Bar Association, Dearborn Real Estate Board, Teachers for Integrated Schools, Committee to End Discrimination in Chicago Medical Institutions, CORE, TWO, Chatham–Avalon Park Community Council, Englewood Committee for Community Action, Chicago Area Friends of SNCC, Negro American Labor Council, Catholic Interracial Council, Presbyterian Interracial Council, Episcopal Society for Cultural and Racial Unity, and Ecumenical Institute.

Speakers for the day were James Forman, national executive of the Student Nonviolent Coordinating Committe; Edwin C. Berry, executive of the Chicago Urban League; Rev. Arthur Brazier of TWO; and Dick Gregory. It was a balanced ticket of militant and moderate spokesmen. If any had expected a split along those lines, Berry, a moderate, set them straight. "Chicagoans should not be disconcerted by the presence of pickets and sit-ins," he said. "It is a healthy sign." Brazier interpreted the meeting as a demonstration that the black man "would no longer rely solely upon the white liberal to articulate his interests." James Forman bore down on the centrality of Mayor Daley if there were to be any changes in Chicago.[29]

The participants took part in workshops on welfare, housing, schools, employment, legislation, health, and leadership. The workshops produced resolutions supporting CORE's direct action and identified new targets: hospitals that refused to serve blacks or did so on a segregated basis, Motorola's employment policy, and a shopping center in the heart of Englewood in which blacks held only 53 of the 496 jobs. In addition, there were proposals to picket the homes of Chicago's black aldermen, who, because of their close relations with the mayor, had not been invited to the meeting. Several of these men had announced that they were setting up a civil rights office of their own to deal with education, hospitals, employment, and urban renewal.[30] This announcement was greeted with cautious skepticism, and nothing more was heard of it in the days to come. The CCCO groups were attempting to develop and coordinate their own agendas, and bickering with the aldermen was not high among their priorities.

At this meeting, the many voices of the civil rights movement in Chicago were trying to establish a common vision and vehicle that could enhance the pluralism of interests and approaches and minimize their conflicts with each other. When CORE returned to its discussions with the Board of Education on 25 July 1963, its position was bolstered, for the moment, by the wide support that had been expressed at the CCCO meeting. After a month of raucous tactical wrangling, it appeared that CORE and the Board of Education were ready to discuss the substance of the issues.

114

CORE submitted a twelve-point agenda covering atendance areas, maps and data on the schools, options in redistricting, Willis's philosophy of integration, problems in the integration of faculty and staff, the trade schools, and teaching materials.[31] On 30 July 1963 Roddewig, three board members, Willis, and representatives from CORE met to discuss these matters. During the entire meeting Willis said only that he and his staff would "review all matters." There was no discussion. While the meeting took place downtown, contractors were already clearing the ground to place mobile classrooms at Seventy-third and Lowe, one of the sites that was supposed to be under discussion. These negotiations between CORE and the schools, therefore, ended with yet another round of angry demonstrations in which more than one hundred persons, including Dick Gregory, were arrested. As with the earlier demonstration downtown, CORE was not able to maintain a nonviolent discipline among its followers. In the escalation of tactics from picketing, to blocking trucks from entering the scene, to chaining themselves to earth-moving equipment, the passions of the demonstrators got out of hand, and the police on the scene were cursed, kicked, and stoned.[32]

Once again attention to the substance of the issue—whether the board was engaged in segregationist practices, reserving some schools for whites in spite of unused space and overcrowding the black and racially changing schools— was overshadowed by a blurred vision of racial unrest. According to a Gallup poll, the polarization of the community was advanced, with 70 percent of the whites believing that demonstrations hurt the drive toward racial equality and 70 percent of the blacks believing the opposite.[33] It did not help the popular perception of the civil rights demonstrations that the ordinary violence accompanying the moving color line continued unabated during the summer. At the same time that CORE was demonstrating at Seventy-third and Lowe, whites were attacking blacks as they tried to move into housing in the previously all-white neighborhood around Fifty-seventh Street and Morgan Avenue. In the press as well as the public perception, these two stories remained vaguely identified as examples of a common theme: racial unrest. The specter of violence hung over it all.[34]

This specter loomed all the larger as the March on Washington drew near. The march had been proposed earlier in the winter by A. Philip Randolph, at seventy-three a veteran of the century's various struggles for civil rights. He wanted the March on Washington for Jobs to give a tangible focus to the nation's unrest. After Birmingham, King had taken up the idea and expanded it to "jobs and freedom" to underline the civil rights thrust of the movement. By midsummer, the NAACP, CORE, SNCC, and Urban League had joined in sponsorship. Throughout the summer, the march had remained low on the list of local priorities among Chicago civil rights groups. It was not even on the agenda of the CCCO's strategy meeting in July. Local responsibility for or-

115

ganizing a contingent of the march had fallen to Timuel Black and the Negro American Labor Council by virtue of their association with A. Philip Randolph.

As the event drew near, however, it became a symbolic test of loyalty to the civil rights movement. Predictions of violence abounded, from Malcolm X to the editorial writers at the *Chicago Sun-Times;* but the determination among civil rights groups to make the march a massive display of support for civil rights and a national example of the power of nonviolence was increasing daily. More than twenty-five hundred participants boarded trains in Chicago for the March on Washington. This foundling of the movement had been transformed into the most dramatic, massive, and affirmative test of nonviolence to date. By the time the march took place, religious and union leaders had joined civil rights organizations, Bayard Rustin had managed the details, both political and logistical, and President Kennedy had given his blessing and cooperation for the staging of the day.

On Wednesday, 28 August 1963, more than two hundred thousand persons joined hands, sang songs, heard speeches, and by their presence and behavior testified that nonviolence was still the better path to civil rights. King intoned his dream of an integrated America where all could live in equality and harmony. The *Chicago Sun-Times* reported on its front page that the march had been "a profoundly moving demonstration—so big, so orderly, so sweet-singing and good-natured, so boldly confident and at the same time relaxed—and completely right from start to finish." On its editorial pages, however, the newspaper continued to discredit the organizers and to reassert that "the time had come for the demands of Negroes to be taken out of the streets and into the conference rooms, as is happening in Chicago on school board complaints and job placements." The *Sun-Times* worried that the world would get the wrong impression from signs reading "Before We'll Be A Slave, We'll Be Buried In Our Grave." Bayard Rustin saw the march as the beginning of a period of "intensified non-violence." The *Sun-Times* hoped that after the march demonstrations would "taper off."[35]

THE CCCO AND THE SCHOOL BOYCOTT:
LOCAL LEGITIMACY FOR DIRECT ACTION

Indeed, it appeared that the conference room might very well be the scene of progress in Chicago. On 29 August 1963 it was announced that the plaintiffs in the *Webb* case had reached an out-of-court settlement with the Board of Education. The board agreed to adopt a resolution of commitment to eliminating inequities in the system, to appoint a study panel to recommend a plan for achieving this goal, and to produce a racial head count of

116

its pupils. At the same time, the board passed another limited transfer plan allowing the top 5 percent of students in high schools without honors courses to transfer to high schools with such programs.[36]

This transfer plan became the center of massive conflict. As many as seven hundred white parents at Bogan High School on the Southwest Side began to picket in protest on 9 September 1963. Twenty-five hundred met the next night at the high school with their alderman, James Murray (son of Thomas Murray, vice-president of the Board of Education). The parents claimed the school was already overcrowded. Alderman Murray made clear that the school was not the only issue. Although he was a sponsor of the city's real estate ordinance forbidding discrimination, he told them he was "against open occupancy . . . an encroachment on your property rights." The following day some two hundred of these parents carried their protest to City Hall and the Board of Education building.[37]

This time Willis proved responsive to community pressure. He removed fifteen schools, including Bogan, from the list that could receive transfer students, leaving only nine. The board ordered him to reinstate some of the schools. He refused, explaining that the decision must wait at least until 9 October 1963. At this point, parents from Hirsch High School on the Southeast Side secured a court order compelling Willis to carry out the board's voted policy. On 3 October 1963 Willis evaded service of the court order, slipping out the back door of his office and disappearing while the board attorney unsuccessfully appealed the order.[38] Rather than obey the court order, Willis offered his resignation on 4 October 1963. The board, he claimed, had infringed upon his administrative prerogatives.

Willis had become the issue of the moment. The *Chicago Defender* had devoted its front page on 15 August 1963 to an editorial headlined: "We Accuse." It was a bill of particulars against Benjamin C. Willis. A week later the black aldermen had informed Roddewig that "they were dissatisfied with their relationship" with Willis. But the civil rights groups had remained reluctant to define Willis as the issue. They wanted to focus attention on conditions in the schools and policies of the board—an increasingly difficult task. The *Sun-Times* greeted Willis's resignation as having been "inevitable for some months." He had "lost contact both with his board and with his public . . . had risked his prestige as an educator—risked it to impose his will on the board and the community—once too often."[39]

On 7 October 1963, however, the board voted not to accept his resignation and formed a committee, headed by Thomas J. Murray, to work out a reconciliation. Only two board members opposed Willis in public, and one of them announced his resignation. The North Central Association of Colleges and Secondary Schools came to Willis's defense. Twenty-three of Chicago's biggest businessmen wired the board supporting Willis.[40] Organized white

117

neighborhood groups, such as the Bogan parents, became outspoken in his behalf.[41]

On 9 October 1963, Lawrence Landry, speaking for the CCCO, announced plans for a boycott of the schools "in protest of the board's refusal of Willis's resignation." This announcement came in advance of the plan's formal adoption by the CCCO, but apparently that caused no serious dispute. Informally most of the groups had discussed the idea favorably. The date was set for 22 October 1963.[42]

For the first time in its history, the Board of Education formally adopted a policy of racial integration on 13 October 1963 and pledged "to effect the development of a continuous program to achieve this goal."[43] Although this resolution was in keeping with the board's agreement in the *Webb* case, no changes in the racial patterning of the school system or the deployment of resources emerged.

By 16 October 1963 the reconciliation had been worked out with Willis. The board agreed to develop a new set of ground rules for distinguishing between policy and administration. Plans for the boycott accelerated. Landry headed a Freedom Day Committee. The NAACP and other groups had held back on making a commitment until it was clear that the mayor would not intervene with the board. Willis's return closed that avenue, and the recruitment of churches to serve as "freedom schools" went ahead. As the day approached, the mayor expressed his opposition to the boycott, but the black aldermen came out in favor of it. A last-minute delegation to the mayor found him unyielding in his position that the schools were nonpolitical. Ever since the support for Willis had started building, the mayor had kept his distance from the dispute—at least in public.[44]

Landry and others were privately expecting a boycott by seventy-five thousand students. Publicly they were talking about possibly thirty thousand. "This will hurt the children and the school system and will hardly influence policy at the level where it is made," intoned the *Sun-Times* in anticipation of the boycott. "The time for serious conferences is overdue," the editors added, but it was not clear to whom they were speaking.[45] The CCCO published a list of thirteen demands, any one of which might have served to get "serious conferences" under way:[46]

1. Removal of Willis and an immediate nationwide search for a new superintendent of schools.
2. Immediate publication of a total inventory of school population, number of classrooms, classroom usage, including a racial count of students, teachers and principals, conducted school by school.
3. Have the Board of Education institute a basic policy of integration of staff and students.
4. Removal of Sterling McMurrin and Lester Nelson from the Committee to Study

118

Racial Composition of Chicago schools. (They are disqualified to serve, having declared themselves to be partisan to Dr. Willis and therefore cannot serve objectively.)

5. Addition to the Racial Study Committee of such persons as Dr. Kenneth Clark and Dr. Dan Dodson, two of the nation's foremost authorities on problems of school desegregation.

6. Immediate publication of pupil achievement levels on standardized achievement tests, grade by grade and school by school.

7. Dr. Havighurst to assume immediate and sole charge of the school survey.

8. Ask Mayor Daley to request federal funds on an emergency basis for a crash remedial program in all schools where achievement records show help is needed.

9. Immediate change in Board's hiring practices to permit hiring of social workers, counselors, and nurses without the present requirement for teaching certificates.

10. Abolition of all high school branches in elementary schools.

11. Board of Education to make trade and vocational education available to all students under instructors who are qualified in the trade or vocation areas they are to teach.

12. All available space in permanent facilities to be utilized fully; then, and only then, should mobile units be used, but *never to be used to perpetuate segregation.*

13. Finally, reconstitution of the Board of Education by the appointment of new members to the board who are publicly on record in favor of overcoming de facto segregation in the Chicago schools.[47]

When the day came, 224,770 pupils boycotted the Chicago public schools. Late in the afternoon between eight and ten thousand people gathered in the Loop to march from City Hall to the Board of Education and to hear the stunning news of their success. Signs reading "Willis-Wallace: What's the Difference" expressed the emotional focus of the day: Benjamin C. Willis had become an urban version of the man standing in the schoolhouse door.[48] Just as the Board of Education had become unified and solidified in its support of Willis, the CCCO had emerged as a unified and publicly visible coalition of civil rights groups opposed to Willis, his administration, and his policies. In October 1963 a conflict drawn along those lines was not likely to lead to serious conferences. The time for them may have been overdue, as the *Sun-Times* concluded, but the situation had been reduced to a series of power plays that made the rational discussion and resolution of issues altogether unlikely.

The *Chicago Tribune* issued a "friendly warning" to what it called "the reckless men at the head of the civil rights movement": "Do not mock the rule of law by using lawless tactics. . . . Do not destroy the good will of fellow citizens." The size of the boycott was unimpressive to the *Tribune* because "Negroes are still a minority in Chicago—only about one-fifth of the population." The CCCO "demands," therefore, meant nothing. "The mayor and the school board must refuse to knuckle under to such ultimatums from troublemakers." The boycott had been just so much "civil commotion."[49]

As the excitement of the moment faded back into business as usual, the *Tribune*'s analysis came to prevail, even though at the time it hardly seemed a serious response. Within the CCCO, the boycott seemed a sure sign of grassroots support and a mandate for the CCCO to pursue change aggressively. The leaders of the boycott began to plan for formal negotiations with the school board and for further demonstrations to continue the pressure.

The CCCO leaders were looking at a different set of figures from those that impressed the *Tribune*. On the same day as the boycott, the school system released the results of its first racial head count. It showed a total enrollment of 536,163, of which 50.9 percent were white, 46.5 percent were black, and 2.6 percent were "other." It further showed that 50.9 percent of the elementary pupils and 33.8 percent of the high school students were black and that 88 percent of the black elementary and 64 percent of the black high school students attended schools that were segregated (at least 90 percent black). When compared with the reported absences because of the boycott, these figures showed that the black schools had supported the protest overwhelmingly. From the CCCO point of view it was a victory, not only in showing support but equally in proving the case. The facts were no longer subject to dispute.[50]

THE CCCO AND THE BOARD OF EDUCATION: MEETINGS WITHOUT NEGOTIATIONS

Lawrence Landry became the chairman of the CCCO's negotiating committee. The CCCO found itself in a quandary as to which of its demands were negotiable. It assumed that it would enter into lengthy and complex formal negotiations with the Board of Education. The mood within the CCCO was that finally civil rights concerns would be taken seriously by the board and that the CCCO was the vehicle for pursuing those goals. The delegates voted to resume direct action if the negotiations proved ineffective.[51] It was not appreciated at the time that the same events that had propelled the CCCO to the center of the civil rights stage had also pushed Roddewig to the side at the Board of Education. In reconciling themselves to Willis, the majority of the board—Warren Bacon was the only holdout—had effectively agreed to side with the superintendent in any further disputes with the community at large. This spelled the end of the board's president, Roddewig, as an effective public person. His attempts to find room for diplomacy and conciliation between the board and its critics were henceforth openly at

120

odds with the majority of the board and with Willis, behind whom that majority was explicitly unified.

For the moment, events proceeded as if this were not the case—inexorably into confusion. The first informal breakfast meeting between Roddewig and the CCCO team resulted in a change of CCCO leadership. Charles Davis, convenor of the CCCO and an NAACP delegate, characterized the meeting as "useful." Roddewig had no public comment. In CCCO circles, Davis was accused of a "sell-out." His connections with the NAACP and the business community, his mild-mannered style and "behind-the-scenes" orientation were all at odds with the more militant mood of the moment. He was replaced as convenor by Rev. Arthur Brazier of TWO, who said that "all meetings with the board should have the full focus of public attention on them." Landry adopted a tough posture. "We shall not compromise any of our thirteen demands on the board," he said, "including the removal of Benjamin C. Willis as school superintendent."[52]

A second, formal meeting took place between Roddewig, two of his board members, and the twenty-member CCCO negotiating team on 9 November 1963. Roddewig characterized the session as "cordial," but Landry said, "We left on a note of protest."[53] Both sides felt the need to meet, it seems, but neither side had clear expectations about what the meetings could or should accomplish.

The CCCO was meeting every Saturday for extended deliberations aimed at solidifying its position and extending what the delegates considered their favorable position.[54] At its meeting of 11 November 1963, James Forman of SNCC assured the delegates that national attention was focused on their struggle, urged them to undertake further demonstrations, and promised them that he, as well as James Farmer of CORE and Whitney Young of the national Urban League, would be in Chicago on 24–25 November to help publicize their continuing actions. He suggested further school boycotts, a boycott of State Street stores, and other activities timed around the monthly anniversary of Freedom Day. He did not expect the negotiations to be quickly productive. Neither did Lawrence Landry, who wanted the strategy committee for the negotiations empowered to recommend further demonstrations if the next meeting with board members was not fruitful. This suggestion was approved unanimously. In response, the State Street Council invited Rev. Brazier to a meeting, but he refused. Roddewig, however, finally made clear that the board was offering the CCCO a "hearing" to air its concerns, not "negotiations" of its demands.

At its 16 November 1963 meeting, the CCCO rejected the idea of another "hearing," notified the press that "negotiation had failed," and called for further direct action against the school board. Landry issued a vituperative invective characterizing Roddewig as "unfit . . . either to preside over the Chicago public school system or to deal with us." He rejected yet another transfer plan, which the board had passed, as likely to "increase the amount of segregation in our schools." He told the board members, "Your greatest service to the American dream of equality can be only your immediate resignation." He held the mayor responsible for the board's intransigence and announced a public hearing on the schools, to which the Board of Education was invited, on 25 November 1963. He called for a boycott of State Street stores beginning 29 November 1963, telling the businessmen, "Maybe your ears will open better when your cash boxes are less active." As one of Landry's supporters said in disappointment: "When you needed to come up with a victory, he came up with a theory."

On 22 November 1963 President John F. Kennedy was assassinated in Dallas, Texas. The momentum of events in Chicago was suspended as the nation was engulfed in grief and mourning. "In this time of local tension and national tragedy," the CCCO urged the mayor to add civil rights organizations to his Advisory Commission on School Board Nominations. It had been a month since the great school boycott, and the CCCO still had no gains to show for its efforts.

By 30 November 1963, the CCCO was beginning to restrain Lawrence Landry. The zenith of his prestige as the originator and organizer of the boycott had passed. The CCCO refused to join in sponsoring SNCC's boycott of Loop stores, and it passed a resolution limiting Landry's role as its spokesman. CCCO delegates feared that the group was being committed to policies and programs by Landry's press releases. They amended their constitution to require a quorum of two-thirds and a vote of two-thirds of those present to authorize any action program in the name of the CCCO.

On 4 December 1963 the idea of negotiations between the CCCO and the school board passed into oblivion. A school board meeting on that day opened with Thomas Murray accusing SNCC of trying to kill him. Tempers flared as accusations were exchanged. When that quieted down, Roddewig acknowledged a communication from the Chicago Conference on Religion and Race urging the board to take the CCCO seriously and to commit itself to a policy of integrated education. Board members Bacon, Pasnick, and Friedman thought the request was reasonable. Roddewig, however, pointed out that the religious bodies were not in a morally advantageous position to be demanding integration from the Board of Education when they did not exemplify it in their own households of faith. On that note, the last in this round of meetings ended.

It was not until their meeting of 21 December 1963 that the CCCO delegates were finally confronted with how little the school boycott had affected either their position or the salience of their concerns among those with established positions. The physician who had gained a seat on the Advisory Commission on School Board Nominations through CCCO pressure forced recognition of this fact. When he told the delegates who the probable nominees for the school board would be, it was clear that the nominating commission was not responsive to the CCCO. He had to tell them the unwelcome news that "the Southwest Side is more active and influential than we are." In an attempt to cheer the shaken delegates, he proposed that the CCCO "should be ready to do something in April." For the moment, the issue was not being settled in its favor.

It was an inauspicious moment for the delegates to be confronted with their powerlessness. Militant anger contended with disappointed caution, and the delegates found it impossible to frame an acceptable response to the reported state of affairs. Expressing the sentiment "we must retaliate," Landry persuaded a bare majority to support the downtown boycott—not enough to make it official. Meanwhile, never expecting this turn of events, the CCCO had scheduled a meeting with the black aldermen for that afternoon to pressure for their support in the struggle with the mayor and the Board of Education. The delegates turned to a long and involved discussion of what they wanted from the aldermen. Ralph Metcalf was the only alderman to appear, and he advised them to "look for one decent egg" among the school board nominees. It was rather like the physician's advice, which had angered some of the delegates, to "take the least possible progress when it comes up." By the end of the afternoon, this meeting, which had begun with the assumption that the aldermen would attend, ended with the realization that it would be necessary to communicate with them by mail.

The mayor nominated Mrs. Lydon Wild, a South Shore socialite, and Cyrus Hall Adams, a State Street merchant, to the Board of Education. Neither of them had any conspicuous commitment to the concerns of the civil rights movement. The boycott of the schools had bonded the CCCO together as the civil rights coalition in Chicago, and it had convinced the members that they had grass-roots support in the ghetto, but it had failed to convince the Board of Education, the mayor, or his advisory commission.

The power that had been demonstrated in the boycott turned out to be useless and ineffective in forcing change. It had decisively shifted the year-long agitation about schools from the neighborhoods to downtown, but it had not produced even the prospect of change in either place. The U.S. Commission on Civil Rights asserted in its year-end report that "the tenacity with which Chicago has confined its Negro pupils to neighborhood schools, and refused to rezone attendance areas or to relax its no-transfer-from-zone-of-residence rules, is well-known."[55] By the end of 1963, it was so well known that, unlike the commission's report of the year before, this assertion failed to elicit comment. But at least the issue had been joined. In a school system that

123

claimed to have a seat for every child, the issue was not innocent overcrowding. It was segregation in some form, and the administration's own figures showed that it was at least de facto on a grand scale.

By the end of 1963, the issue was not only segregation in schools; it was also the Board of Education's manifest refusal to do anything to remedy that situation in spite of a massive public demonstration of discontent in the black community. General Superintendent Willis had become the symbol of what was at issue as much for militant whites as for civil rights advocates. He resigned his job rather than offend the whites, and he got it back when the board yielded to his distinction between policy and administration. In either case, the result was the same: not offending angry whites and not appeasing angry blacks. The first was policy, the second was administration.

Thanks to the Armstrong Act, the factual grounds of the civil rights protests at least were no longer in dispute. The board's own figures showed that 88 percent of the black elementary and 64 percent of the black high school students were in segregated schools, that is, schools at least 90 percent black. Almost 250,000 black children were enrolled in the Chicago public schools that year. The inequalities between black and white schools were undeniable, even though the CCCO was still demanding additional documentation. Civil rights groups appealed to the Armstrong Act as imposing an affirmative duty on the board to prevent segregation in the planning of new schools and to rectify de facto segregation in its revision of attendance areas.

Increasingly throughout the year, groups reached for strategies of direct, nonviolent confrontation with the Board of Education in an effort to negotiate or force those changes which the Armstrong Act seemed to require. The events in Birmingham and President Kennedy's response galvanized a sense of urgency and shifted the spectrum of moderates and militants decisively toward activism. The picketing of Mrs. Wendell Green raised the issue of Washburne Trade School's special relationship to the unions and lack of relationship to the black community. Four hundred delegates to the national convention of the NAACP joined a demonstration at the Board of Education building to protest "the most segregated school system in the North." The CORE sitin at the board, which lasted from 10 to 18 July, became unruly, but it produced the first concessions from the board president in the form of data relating to CORE's continuing charge of "segregation." By the midsummer CCCO conference, demonstrations were the norm by which commitment was measured. The March on Washington in late August expanded and dramatized the acceptance of that norm even though a Gallup poll showed a serious black-white polarization in attitudes toward civil rights demonstrations. This polarization was a major factor in the successful school boycott, which blacks supported overwhelmingly, but it was also a factor in the boycott's limited usefulness. Blacks still controlled only six wards.

In the events of the fall, General Superintendent Willis explicitly courted militant white support. The *Chicago Tribune* delivered a "friendly warning" that "Negroes are still a minority in Chicago—only about one-fifth of the population," and the *Sun-Times* continued to deplore direct-action techniques as inappropriate to the situation because "Chicago has made great strides in race relations in the past twenty years." Indeed, during the first half of that year alone, the mayor had supported the Armstrong Act in the Illinois legislature and had appointed Warren Bacon, an outspoken black civil rights advocate, to the Board of Education. Roddewig had continued his campaign of conciliation in agreeing to make data available to CORE and in reaching an out-of-court settlement in the *Webb* case. But that was the end of his effectiveness. The transfer plan, which was part of the *Webb* settlement, stirred a militant white response in the service of which General Superintendent Willis was willing to stake his job. Some of Chicago's most influential businessmen rose to the defense of what they considered a beleaguered professional. That the general superintendent was already back in his office by the time of the great school boycott meant that the board would not respond to any of the demands its organizers put forth. Policy and administration prevailed.

The events of 1963 had expanded Chicago's civil rights coalition, the CCCO, and had established nonviolent direct action as the norm of the movement and the standard of commitment. Church groups, labor groups, business and professional groups, new-style and old-line civil rights groups had all made the transition. By year's end, however, the success of the school boycott was more of a problem for the CCCO than it was for the Board of Education. The CCCO was unable to get the board to negotiate on the boycott demands or to make a mark on the Advisory Commission on School Board Nominations. "The Southwest Side is more active and influential than we are," the delegates were told by their representative on the commission. The CCCO had taken the center stage of civil rights activities in Chicago by virtue of the boycott; but in spite of this massive show of support, it was still a peripheral factor in the rooms where decisions were made, rooms to which the delegates had believed the boycott would give them access.

Early in 1963 the CCCO as an organized body was still pursuing the traditional strategies of nonviolent democratic persuasion—writing letters, testifying before the school board, and meeting with the mayor—although some community groups were adopting more aggressive tactics. Birmingham and the March on Washington made a turn to massive direct action possible in Chicago, just as the retention of Willis made it necessary.

With the school boycott, however, the paths of the national and local movements took different courses. Like Birmingham and the March on Washington, the school boycott demonstrated the CCCO's ability to mobilize a minority around civil rights aims, but, unlike the movement elsewhere, Chicago civil rights leaders were unable to translate this apparent mandate into majority support for, or even consent to, civil rights goals. As the year ended, therefore, changes in CCCO leadership (from Davis to Landry to Brazier) reflected the delegates' uncertainty about the path through and beyond the democratic dilemma of black dignity—whether to increase attempts to gain white majority support or to intensify efforts to mobilize the black minority.

At the same time, the CCCO also encountered related problems around the democratic dilemma of constitutional duties—the tension between persuasion and coercion as means for democratic social change. The white Chicago dailies had regularly called for the resolution of racial issues "at the conference table" and just as regularly condemned the more coercive forms of nonviolence (the March on Washington, the CORE sitins, and the school boycott) as "civil commotion," "lawless," and "violent." This reaffirmation of the majoritarian, consensual, and civic calm planks of the civic credo placed the CCCO in an impossible position. Civil rights leaders also had called for serious negotiations on the schools issue, but in the fall of 1963, it seemed clear that only these more coercive forms of nonviolence stood much chance of getting them to the conference table. The CCCO's position was complicated because some CORE demonstrators had crossed the emotionally thin but practically crucial line between coercive nonviolence and physical violence. With the failure of the school boycott to force the school board to the bargaining table, the CCCO found itself even more deeply entangled in the dilemma. Did the path ahead lie in ever more coercive forms of nonviolence in support of their full demands, as Landry argued, or should they return to means which were more dependent on persuasion and, as the physician suggested, "take the least possible progress when it comes up"?

Thus, by the end of the year, both the CCCO's strategy on the schools issue and its means for pursuing social change were in doubt.

CHAPTER FIVE

The Action Is Stalled: 1964

During 1963 the civil rights movement in Chicago had become progressively unified and aggressive in response to events in the community at large, events of national significance such as Birmingham and the March on Washington, and events of local importance such as Willis's successful defiance of and ultimate triumph over the Board of Education and the courts.

The CCCO had sponsored the massive school boycott, but it was more like an event that happened to the civil rights groups than one they could trace directly to their own doing. The boycott catapulted the CCCO into the center of prominence among local civil rights groups, and by early 1964 more than twenty groups were a part of the coalition.[1] It was a broad-based but not a mass-based organization. Its fame rested on a display of grass-roots grievance, but its mass support was neither organized nor represented in its membership. This deficiency increasingly resulted in contention within the CCCO as the delegates found themselves torn between conflicting strategies to reach and represent their grass-roots support and to deal with public agencies, which continued to treat the CCCO and civil rights demands as negligible political factors. During 1964 both inner coherence and public effectiveness seemed to elude the CCCO at every turn. By year's end and by an agonizingly centrifugal process, the CCCO was reduced from a partially successful coalition, determined to prove its mass support, to a small clique, uncertain that its own survival was worth the trouble.

FROM THE FIRST SCHOOL BOYCOTT TO THE SECOND: "WHAT DID THEY PROVE?"

In the flush of fame and feeling following the first boycott, none of the tensions inherent in the CCCO's position had been faced, nor had it seemed important that they should be. By January 1964, however, it was clear that the CCCO's demands of October 1963 had not made their way onto

127

the civic agenda. Consequently, the sense of achievement and momentum within the CCCO began to dissipate while the tensions began to surface and to focus around proposals for what action the group should take next. Four different strategies were presented over the course of the year: to display mass support once again, as in the boycott, and thereby develop the mass base of civil rights concerns; to present a low public profile while pursuing behind-the-scenes diplomacy and carefully coordinating the targets of demands; to engage in activities designed to gather the support of local communities on an organized basis and to increase public understanding of the schools issue; and to carry the civil rights strategy directly into the arena of electoral politics. Concerned with the dilemmas of black dignity and constitutional duties, the first strategy sought to mobilize the black masses to force change. The second focused on securing white majority support through persuasion. The third and fourth strategies were aimed at increasing both black mobilization and white support—the former through direct action, the latter through the political process. These strategies were frequently presented as mutually exclusive; but over the course of the year, all of them were tried and each in turn revealed some new weakness, not only in the CCCO but in the possibility of institutional desegregation in Chicago, especially in the schools.

At the first meeting of 1964, on 4 January, the tensions within the CCCO began to surface as Edwin C. Berry proposed a strategy of diplomacy and low-profile lobbying aimed at influencing the mayor. City Hall was the problem, as he saw it. The Board of Education was "Daley's board," but the CCCO had to deal with the existing board, even while working to change it. Therefore, Berry proposed meeting with the mayor to continue pressure for change in the composition and procedures of the nominating commission.

He also proposed lobbying with selected and presumably friendly members of the nominating commission to support integrationist candidates for the school board. Those he thought most likely to be persuaded were the university and labor representatives. He also thought that CCCO representatives should try to get other civic groups to support the civil rights demands and give them public visibility.

Landry, on the other hand, proposed to reactivate the Freedom Day Committee to consider another boycott of the schools. That proposal released many of the pent-up feelings about the first boycott as the delegates launched immediately into the question of a second boycott—which had not yet even been proposed. The delegate from the Cook County Physicians Association, also a member of the school board nominating commission, complained: "We hurt the kids. We hurt the school system. Don't go down the failure road again. Don't beat our brains out on the impossible." The delegate from CORE took a different view: "From ocean to ocean people are talking about the

128

school boycott. We are faced with a defeatist attitude . . . but our boycott had a great effect."

Although the motion to reactivate the Freedom Day Committee was passed, the discussion of its possible meaning and importance continued unabated, for Landry was not proposing just another boycott in Chicago. He wanted the committee to contact civil rights groups in other cities to explore the possibility of a coordinated, multicity boycott. Berry's proposal implied that because the first boycott had failed, the CCCO should draw back into the low-profile territory its leaders understood and work from there to increase white support through pressure and persuasion. Landry's proposal had a different premise: because a massive Chicago boycott had failed to gain recognition for the CCCO's demands, the next move should yield nothing in its militance but should repeat it on a grander scale and a wider stage. Such a strategy might or might not force white support; the emphasis was on mobilizing an even larger militant black minority. These proposals brought the tensions within the CCCO to the surface in a raging internal controversy about which course to follow. The question was no longer what to do about the mayor and the school board but what direction the CCCO itself should take.

At the CCCO meeting of 11 January 1964, it was announced that Rev. Arthur Brazier had resigned as the convenor and had been replaced, according to the rules of procedure, by Albert Raby, who had been the recorder. In fact, Raby had been in the chair since 21 December 1963, the same meeting at which the CCCO had been confronted with its failure to convert the boycott into tangible gains in the schools. Raby was a delegate from Teachers for Integrated Schools, a group that cast its lot on the side of militancy in the controversies surrounding a second boycott.

At this meeting, Landry, reporting for the Freedom Day Committee,[2] moved "that CCCO sponsor a one-day boycott 11 February 1964." He also announced that the Reverend Milton Galamison was convoking a multicity meeting in New York on 12 January 1964 "to explore the issues of various cities." A double-layered discussion ensued over whether to have another boycott in Chicago and whether to get involved in the national maneuvering among established and emerging civil rights groups. Some delegates were worried that the CCCO would be committed to a boycott by press releases from the New York meeting, thus embarrassing the group at home. Concern was also expressed that the CCCO might seem to be part of a move to undercut or bypass the established national civil rights leadership, thus embarrassing it in national circles. For the most part, however, the debate revolved around local considerations.

The first question was money. The treasurer, H. B. Law, reported a deficit of $833.73 still owing from the first boycott. The committee was unclear

129

about how to handle finances although it did suggest various fund-raising activities, including assessing its member organizations. The NAACP opposed the boycott because the financing and the national overtones were unclear. TWO supported the boycott if the financing could be cleared up. It was voted to establish a committee to raise a fund for the CCCO. The Urban League opposed the idea of a second boycott. This in itself was financially significant. Although the Urban League had not officially been a sponsor of the first boycott and had technically abstained so as not to jeopardize its tax-exempt status, unofficially the league had contributed informal access to funding sources, had allowed the use of its staff and facilities to provide less controversial services, and had encouraged the personal participation of its talented staff. Indeed, the decision to hold the first boycott had been made in Berry's apartment on the night that the Board of Education voted not to accept Willis's resignation. This time, however, Berry preferred his own strategy of diplomacy with City Hall and civic groups, whereas the NAACP wanted a push for voter registration.

The meeting was stalled by a long debate over the presence of a *Defender* reporter in the room. She was allowed to stay because she was there as a delegate from Chatham, but the decision was not easily made. The Freedom Day Committee continued its campaign for a second boycott. The issues, the materials supporting them, and the organizational structure were all laid out. The CCCO's moderation since the first boycott had not produced results. Failure to stage a second one would be an "abdication." But the NAACP and the Urban League were not the only groups holding back. "People say we haven't tried other things," complained the delegate from Roseland Heights. The time was too short, and "we don't know where we are going," demurred the delegate from the Presbyterian Interracial Council. The objection was raised that boycott materials were already circulating in the community with the warning that "you can't cram something down another's throat." At issue was the "grass roots," whether another boycott would be a display of support or an exposé of the CCCO's weakness. In the end, ten organizations favored the boycott, five were opposed, and two abstained. Because of the lack of the necessary two-thirds, the issue was scheduled for reconsideration the next week.

On 18 January 1964 Landry and others returned to debate the boycott, buoyed by their meeting in New York with Galamison and others. It was time to get to the "hard core ghetto issues," Landry asserted. Slum housing and rent strikes needed to be added to the agenda. For the moment, however, he proposed a school boycott for 25 February 1964. He felt opposed on two fronts, said one of Landry's supporters: "the white power structure" and "the more reactionary liberal groups." Landry was presenting the militant perception of the situation. The Freedom Day Committee agreed to incorporate Berry's proposal into its own and to send a delegation to the mayor. The financing remained unresolved, but there were suggestions for a "black feather fund," for "freedom rallies" with national figures participating, and for fund-raising activities by individual organizations. Everyone agreed that more than a boycott would be needed to change the Board of Education. Mobilizing support for the CCCO's demands was the primary goal. On that basis, the CCCO voted eleven in favor, three opposed, two abstaining, to call a boycott of the schools for 25 February 1964.

Instead of discussing extending the boycott to two days, as Landry had proposed, the meeting of 2 February 1964 was plunged into a lengthy debate over holding the boycott "in abeyance." As proffered by the Reverend James McDaniels of the Presbyterian Interracial Council, the purpose of this motion was to facilitate negotiations with the Board of Education. If the first boycott had not achieved that purpose, possibly the threat of another one might.

The Freedom Day Committee wanted to keep the original date, arguing that it was supported by local parents' councils and Baptist ministers. A thousand dollars was already in hand, and a fund-raising luncheon was planned with school board member Warren Bacon as a speaker. Plans for freedom schools were well advanced, and promotional materials had already been produced. The seriousness of the CCCO as a civil rights organization was at stake.

The majority of the delegates, however, were not persuaded. Most of them agreed with John McDermott (Catholic Interracial Council), who said: "Another boycott with no results would discredit our leadership. . . . We need success more than emotional exercises." Too many reservations, it seemed, had arisen about the boycott—reservations about the organizations' abilities to carry it off, about Landry's leadership, about the multicity alliance which Landry seemed to be forming, and about whether, even if the boycott worked, it would result in real changes. Eleven organizations favored holding the boycott in abeyance, seven were opposed, and two abstained. The motion carried, but it left a bitter division. On one side there was the feeling that "today Mayor Daley has divided us." On the other side it was said, "Many people think that form of action [the school boycott] is sacrosanct," and that the delegates were being boxed in by press releases, a reference to Landry's statements after each of the two multicity meetings. Yet another delegate said, "I have heard the word today. CCCO will fail for lack of concern."

The idea that the mayor was manipulating the situation arose because the judge in the *Webb* case (reinstated late in 1963 with Willis's return to office) had offered the plaintiffs more time, which they desperately needed to prepare their case—if the boycott were called off. A second vote to hold the boycott in abeyance was eleven for, ten against, splitting the coalition down the middle. In frustration, one delegate asserted that the one-third of the delegates who had not supported the boycott at the previous meeting "shouldn't come back and divide us." A feeling that everything was falling apart pervaded the meeting.

The CCCO did arrange a meeting with Roddewig for the morning of 9 February 1964. It was congenial but not productive. The CCCO met on that afternoon, heard the report of the meeting, and voted to hold the boycott on 25 February 1964. Seventeen organizations supported the motion, three were opposed, and one abstained. Planning for the boycott had never stopped. Landry was counting on a series of "parents councils," which had grown up around local school protests in the summer of 1963 and were loosely associated with SNCC. It was voted to meet with the mayor although not much was expected. In an attempt to secure more harmony within the CCCO, ESCRU pointed out that the Urban League was under attack by the press and needed the respect and support of the organizations within the CCCO. The *Tribune* was complaining that the Urban League was too political for a Community Fund agency, and the *Defender* was raking the league as too conservative for a civil rights agency.

By the meeting of 15 February 1964, the Board of Education had pledged to continue to pursue an integrated school system. CCCO delegates were not impressed with such a pledge. A delegation had met with the mayor, who made it clear that he wanted the boycott called off. He agreed only to "consider" the coalition's demands, although he took a hands-off attitude toward Willis. Any progress, he seemed to say, would come "after the Hauser Report." The delegation told the press that the mayor had given them nothing and chastised the Board of Education for its policy of continuity.

By 22 February 1964 a CCCO delegation had met with Judge A. L. Marovitz, who was by then hearing the *Webb* case. Roddewig had also been present in the judge's chambers. Marovitz wanted the boycott called off, but it was not clear how far, if at all, he was willing or able to mediate between the board and the CCCO. Raby had offered to call a special CCCO meeting to help establish the grounds for further discussion. Roddewig refused to do the same with the Board of Education. The CCCO, therefore, canceled further discussions—a decision for which it was chastised in the press.[3]

Meanwhile, work had proceeded on the boycott. Briefings had been held with non-CCCO organizations to present the rationale for the boycott. Money was coming in, though it was still unclear that income would match expenses. Leaflets were being distributed to the schools. Freedom schools were set. Speakers in local areas were active. Dick Gregory was helping with rallies. A downtown demonstration was in preparation. Support was building even in reluctant communities such as Chatham–Avalon. Still, two of the black aldermen, in cooperation with Congressman Dawson, had started an anti-boycott organization called the Assembly to End Poverty, Injustice, and Prejudice, and there was no telling how effective their organization might be.

The boycott itself was something of an anticlimax. It was credited with causing 175,000 absences. In October that number would have been considered massive, but in February it was a 22 percent decline in participation, and the CCCO had exhausted itself in the doing. Board of Education member Pasnick proposed that it was finally time for the board and the CCCO to meet and discuss the demands. Led by the objections of Mrs. Green, the majority of the board opposed such a meeting. The mayor expressed the official attitude toward the boycott when he asked, "What did they prove?" The same question bothered the CCCO delegates. Neither militancy nor diplomacy seemed to have advanced their standing with either the elusive "grass roots" or the equally elusive Board of Education. Shortly after the boycott, Roddewig announced his intention to retire from the board on 1 April 1964. A political commentator said at the time: "If this able and tireless public servant had any fault, it was that he suffered courteously the unsufferable too long."[4] Possibly so, but the CCCO, in quest of negotiations, was not apparently the major obstacle to the full service of Roddewig's considerable diplomatic skills.

Willis's only public response to the boycott was telling a news conference that "attacks on teachers and other major disciplinary problems occur in areas where the October 1963 and 25 February 1964 school boycotts were most effective." He also claimed that such problems had increased 50 percent since September. Speaking at a CCCO-sponsored "inter-group dialogue," Raby responded by observing that "a responsible administrator, sensitive to the public tendency to panic over alarms, would, if his basic thesis had any validity, address himself quietly and resolutely to setting his own schoolhouse in order without the fanfare of publicity." Raby contended that Willis "chose to inspire hysterical front-page stories even *before* he ordered principals and teachers to make systematic reports of incidents of violence." Raby's reply, however, was not front-page news. In the competition for public interpretation, Willis had won the round.[5] In the superintendent's view, it was the protesters rather than their grievances, the pupils rather than the schools, that were the problem.

AFTER THE SECOND BOYCOTT:
AN UNSUCCESSFUL SEARCH FOR NEW INITIATIVES

By the time the CCCO met again on 21 March 1964, it had been a month since the second boycott, time enough to recover a sense of strategic possibility. In an attempt to focus attention on the condition of the schools rather than on the protesters and on the vague but provocative prospect of racial unrest, the CCCO decided to highlight grievances at specific schools, one at a time, across the city. The plan was called the Spotlight

Campaign. It was intended to convey the actual situation to the public and to help mend the tattered fabric of local communities whose grievances could be remedied only by citywide actions; but the program never worked. Twenty-seven pickets showed up for what had been announced as a "massive march" on the mayor's office to spotlight his responsibility for the composition of the school board. The neighborhood activities suffered a similar fate.

On 31 March 1964, the panel headed by Philip M. Hauser of the University of Chicago issued its report on the racial condition of the schools and made thirteen recommendations for change. This report was done in accordance with the out-of-court settlement of the *Webb* case in August 1963. It found that 84 percent of the black pupils were in black schools (schools with at least 90 percent black enrollment) and that 86 percent of the white pupils were in white schools. It documented the comparative inferiority of the black schools in overcrowding, physical facilities, and the experience and education of the faculty.[6]

The report was equivocal, however, in accounting for these differences and in recommending remedies. It cited housing patterns as the basic problem and expected some improvement from ethnic mobility. Some of the findings appeared to document "lower mental ability" among blacks, but the panel took a generous view of their educability, their ability to profit from instruction as much as other groups. The panel was especially concerned that integration be achieved without increasing "white flight" from the city and its schools. Consequently, though recognizing that the neighborhood school system was a major source of segregation in the schools, the panel was willing only to recommend what it called a "Modified Open Enrollment" policy. Actually this was an expanded neighborhood school policy, pairing existing districts and allowing voluntary transfer within these expanded districts, with heavy emphasis on freedom of choice. The panel also proposed free transportation to convey students from overcrowded to underused facilities. Finally, the admission was made that such facilities existed. Special attention was urged to redraw boundaries and select sites for new schools to foster integration. Four recommendations concerned teacher training and the integration of facilities. Four more dealt with improved quality and effectiveness in educational procedures. There was a call for efforts to obtain additional funds and for the creation of a biracial group to be called Friends of the Chicago Schools to oversee implementation and to garner public support for it.[7]

Superintendent Willis prepared a "study guide" as an aid to "thoughtful reading" of the report. It consisted entirely of argumentative questions designed to justify the administration and to undercut the panel's recommendations. For instance:

> What do you think might be the advantages and the disadvantages of a program which required teachers to teach in certain schools not of their choice?

134

What can parents or the community do to make teaching in their schools desirable? . . .

What are the financial implications for taxpayers of free transportation?

How can school boundaries be drawn to maintain an integrated school as neighborhoods change?[8]

The Board of Education, nonetheless, unanimously approved all thirteen of the panel's recommendations "in general principle" and referred the ones on pupil integration to a new committee headed by Frank M. Whiston, board member and prominent Chicago realtor. Staff and committees were to prepare implementation plans "for prompt submission to the board for approval."[9]

Initially civil rights leaders hailed the report as confirming their complaints, but as its ambiguities translated themselves into no clear policy direction, CCCO delegates became disenchanted with its content and possibilities. In the CCCO discussion of the report, Raby, who had initially been impressed with the recommendations, decided, on reflection, that "we shouldn't be pleased until the child in the classroom is affected."[10]

In mid-April Raby had a public exchange with Hauser, which provoked him to draw the bottom line for him and for increasing numbers of civil rights activists. Hauser argued that "integration can not be brought about by force—it has to be lubricated with persuasion. The donkey and the carrot approach rather than the use of the whip will achieve more. . . . If steps taken next," Hauser maintained, "accelerate the white exodus to the parochial school system, or out of the city, you may be pursuing excellent principles—but there will be nothing to integrate."[11]

"If the white folks want to run from us," Raby retorted, "we will chase them wherever they go and integrate with them. We will transmit to our children—maybe—segregation. But also self-respect."[12] If there was a conflict between civil rights and self-respect, between gaining majority support and asserting black dignity whether effective or not, Raby like DuBois would take his stand with self-respect. For the moment, however, Hauser to the contrary notwithstanding, these two did not seem to be in conflict.

After all, the CCCO was still in quest of white support, planning a conference of civic groups for 2 May 1964 with the theme "Finding Common Paths." The CCCO was also involved, somewhat reluctantly, in planning a massive rally for civil rights, scheduled for 21 June 1964 at Soldier Field. Martin Luther King, Jr., Mahalia Jackson, and others were to lead this rally in support of the 1964 civil rights bill, which was pending in the U.S. Senate. The goal for that rally had been set at one hundred thousand by its cochairmen, Edwin C. Berry of the Urban League and Edgar H. S. Chandler, executive director of the Church Federation of Greater Chicago. Once again some delegates felt that press releases had committed them to a major test of their resources. At the same time, the CCCO was unable to agree on the membership application of the Muslim Brotherhood, a splinter group from the Nation of Islam. The issue of black nationalism was stirring among these civil rights groups in Chicago, but in the spring of 1964 it had not yet come into focus.

The mayor had appointed another black group, the Cook County Bar Association, to his school board nominating commission. There were three positions to be filled on the Board of Education, and Dr. Jasper Williams (the CCCO delegate who was also a member of the nominating commission) reported that the publicity and pressure from the CCCO were having an effect on the commission. "I don't think we can lose this time" he concluded.[13] This optimism was transmuted into frustrated anger, however, when the CCCO was called into a special meeting on 6 May 1964. The mayor had renominated Mrs. Wendell Green, the seventy-four-year-old anti-civil rights black. James Clement and Louise Malis were also nominated, and, though both were white and many delegates had doubts about each of them, Green was the center of attention. With much ambivalence it was agreed that the coalition should at least testify against her at the City Council hearings, but could something more effective be done as well? The delegates could not agree. Attorney William Cousins testified for the CCCO on 8 May 1964 against Green because of her demonstrated record of opposing integration in the schools and against Malis because of her lack of a record on integration in spite of years of citywide PTA activity.[14] Clement, it turned out, had been one of ESCRU's preferred candidates.

Testifying against Green at the City Council hearing was a gesture of futility, compounded by the countertestimony of a former Chicago branch NAACP president, who, two months later, was slated on the Democratic ticket as a candidate for circuit judge.[15] Further, the conference Finding Common Paths was poorly attended and poorly covered by the press. So far, nothing was working for the CCCO.

In response, the CCCO created a new program committee. At the meeting of 16 May 1964, this committee recommended that "CCCO has tried direct action and sitting around the table. We must now add action in the political arena." To do so, the CCCO should establish a separate political arm, like the unions, to protect the tax-exempt status of its affiliates. The committee was to consider alternative courses of action in relation to the November election. Landry, however, wanted another boycott, to last three days this time, 16–18 June, to organize support for the 21 June rally and to prepare for a "permanent boycott in the fall." Since he believed that there was "not going to be any real election in the fall," he proposed that civil rights groups "should simply boycott the election." The majority of the delegates, however, were ready to try the political arena. They were not willing to support another boycott, but they agreed that symbolic action was needed. For this, they turned to the idea

136

of a "month of mourning and mobilizing," to run from 27 May, when it was supposed Green would be confirmed, to 21 June, the date of the Illinois Rally for Civil Rights.

Two representatives from the CCCO tried to present the mayor with a black mourning wreath as he left his home early on 27 May 1964. They had to settle for a conference in his office, later in the day, at which the mayor defended Green as an able "senior citizen" and, his face reddening with anger, became incensed that anyone would mourn the absence of racial justice in Chicago. He thought his administration had a long list of accomplishments on that score. While four hundred "month of mourning" pickets circled city hall, the mayor went off to preside over the City Council.[16]

It turned into a confusing day. The council did not confirm the mayor's school board nominees but deferred the issue for a month on a motion by one of the administration aldermen. Later, the Board of Education met to elect a new president. With three seats vacant, one member absent, and three others wanting to defer the election of a president until the full board was present, it seemed that the board would have to wait to select its new leadership. But with Roddewig and Green present and voting even though their terms had expired, Frank M. Whiston, a prominent realtor and longtime friend as well as supporter of Willis's, was elected president of the Board of Education.

He immediately unveiled the "Willis-Whiston" plan, a thirty-page report, which rejected Hauser's expanded neighborhood concept and substituted another permissive transfer plan under which pupils could transfer from any overcrowded school to any underused one. The schools in each category were listed. Even the *Chicago Defender* reported, "Willis Throws in Towel, Okays City-Wide Integration of Schools."[17] Civil rights groups were more perceptive. Albert Raby and Rosie Simpson, chair of the Chicago Area Parents Council for Integrated Schools, branded the plan "a sham and a fraud," aimed at defeating the Hauser recommendations. "It is the duty of the board and superintendent to plan and administer a sound, city-wide program," they said. "The Willis proposal would relieve them of that responsibility, and place the burden for school administration on the parents instead."[18] They were mindful that similar transfer plans in November 1962 and December 1963 combined had affected a grand total of sixty-three children. When the Friends of the Chicago Schools Committee was called into its first session, ostensibly to oversee the implementation of the Hauser recommendations, it was presented with copies of the Willis-Whiston plan but not of the Hauser report.

Superintendent Willis granted a television interview and claimed the high ground for this new strategy. He maintained that black schools were not inferior; that even where there was no "mingling of the races" a student could still get a good education; that, in any case, Chicago schools were not segregated; that the neighborhood school was as old as Chicago; that it was the

137

board's policy, not his, that integration should apply universally and not just to selected schools as in the Hauser report; and that the question of the schools' legal and moral responsibility "is now before the courts." This statement caused even the *Chicago Daily News* to editorialize that Willis and Whiston "are building up a strong presumption that they do not intend to deal forthrightly with the problem of de facto racial segregation in Chicago's public schools."[19]

On 19 June 1964 the Civil Rights Act of 1964 passed the U.S. Senate, exactly one year after President Kennedy had first proposed it. It was with mixed feelings, therefore, that its sponsors approached the Illinois Rally for Civil Rights two days later. Successful nationally, they were still stalemated locally in their search for a strategy that would bring the issue to the surface in some publicly salient way. They were stymied too, in their attempt to make specific local grievances part of the Illinois rally.

Seventy-five thousand people turned out for the rally, which was a festive celebration of the passage of the civil rights bill. The program included Edwin C. Berry, James Farmer, James Forman, Father Theodore Hesburgh (president of Notre Dame and a member of the U.S. Commission on Civil Rights), Senator Paul Douglas, and Mahalia Jackson. Martin Luther King, Jr., exhorted that "after this rally . . . everyone in Chicago will realize the Negro in this community is determined to be free." It was the largest rally for civil rights the city had seen. (The mayor was invited, but he explained that he had to be with his family on Father's Day.) The rally concluded with the reading of "A Pledge of Action for Civil Rights," a statement of general support for nonviolent demonstrations, the Mississippi Summer Project, strong civil rights planks from the Republicans and Democrats, and "full civil rights and equality of opportunity" in Chicago and Illinois. It also called for a "timetable of action beginning in September 1964" and for integrated schools in Chicago, but it did not call for support for the CCCO, nor did it mention Willis.[20]

The *Chicago Sun-Times* interpreted the rally as symbolic of the need for no further civil rights demonstrations in Chicago. The rally proved to the *Sun-Times* that black and white could come together and work together cooperatively. Furthermore, "in areas where local laws already meet or surpass the objectives of the new civil rights legislation, and Illinois is one such, there is no moral reason for making this summer one of discontent and unrest." The rally, instead, "should stand as the first event in a summer of progress in Chicago." Chuck Stone, columnist for the *Defender*, took a different view, claiming that the rally was "a cruel hoax on the Negroes of this city and a futile gesture by a small band of white do-gooders with enormous guilt syndromes about the race problem." Stone claimed that the civil rights bill contained "nothing" for the North.[21] On that score, he was agreeing with the

Sun-Times while drawing an opposing conclusion about the local situation. It was common currency that the 1964 civil rights bill pertained to the South. Neither the *Sun-Times* nor the *Defender,* it appeared, had grasped either the significance or the pathos of the Illinois Rally for Civil Rights, a celebration of national victories set in the midst of local stalemate.

As the participants were going back to their homes in metropolitan Chicago, down in Mississippi James Chaney, Andrew Goodman, and Michael Schwerner were being kidnapped and murdered. The limits to festivity, celebration, and congratulations always hung low over the civil rights movement, North or South.

The Board of Education spent the rest of the summer amending the Willis-Whiston plan, substituting it for the Hauser recommendations, and deciding that it could not legally pay for the transportation of transferring students. Finally, in August, Murray, the vice-president of the board, could say: "I am going to vote for this because it doesn't commit us to anything."[22]

On the question of how to respond to Willis's well-orchestrated evisceration of the Hauser report at the 11 July CCCO meeting, Meyer Weinberg observed: "The civil rights movement always loses because we let Willis define the problem and make the proposals—to which we only react." The Willis-Whiston plan was a case in point. Similar plans in other cities had not worked; therefore, "we need to develop our own positive program for the public schools." There might be ways, he suggested, to invoke the Civil Rights Act against the school board's use of federal funds, to involve the human relations commission in the schools, or to urge the allocation of special funds for remedial desegregation. The CCCO appointed a committee to develop these ideas.

Nonetheless, the Urban League continued throughout the summer to make an issue of the Board of Education's failure to implement the Hauser report. Late in July the league sponsored a conference of civic groups and presented "An Analysis of the Stalemate in the Implementation of the Hauser Report." Berry exhorted representatives from 130 civic organizations on the need for community action.[23] Urban League board member Earl Dickerson, president of Superior Life Insurance Company, and state representative William H. Robinson unsuccessfully sought the group's support for a resolution demanding Willis's resignation. Instead, the groups formed an Ad Hoc Committee of Organizations, which bought space in all five of the Chicago daily newspapers and the two black weeklies. The committee's ad, which appeared 11 August, was a weak statement urging the Board of Education "to get on with the job" of implementing the Hauser report. "I can't understand what happened," Robinson told the *Defender.* "The ad, as I understood its initial conception, included all of the factors responsible for racial unrest, but somewhere along the line somebody watered it down."[24]

139

AN EXPANDING AGENDA FOR A DWINDLING GROUP:
A COALITION OVERWHELMED

Meanwhile, the committee on the politics of civil rights had constituted itself as the Coordinating Council Political Action Committee. This committee reported that it "was united on the conviction that we should enter politics, but was still thinking through strategy." That was an understatement in the summer of 1964. To be sure, representatives from more than fifty organizations had been present at the organizing meeting on 8 July 1964. One of their number, state representative Robinson (Freedom of Residence, FOR) had just returned from the Republican platform hearings in San Francisco. Those assembled were disturbed by his report of what could be expected from a Republican convention determined to nominate Barry Goldwater for president. Some of them had still not decided on a political route, and this report did nothing to persuade them otherwise. Some still wanted to work toward another school boycott in the fall; some wanted a strategy to "hurt Daley"; others wanted a push for additional civil rights legislation. The discussion ranged all over the political map, from a boycott of the polls through voter registration to an all-out endorsement of the Democratic ticket. By midsummer neither consensus nor priorities had begun to emerge in the political action committee.

The CCCO was losing its inner coherence and its external focus. The Committee to End Discrimination in Chicago Medical Institutions and SNCC had committed their energies to the Mississippi Summer Project. In the process SNCC had found other leaders to replace Landry. CORE was picketing Republican headquarters. The Citizens Housing Committee was fighting an urban renewal project. The Negro American Labor Council (NALC) was urging employment as top priority. The CCCO as such had no program for the summer of 1964.

Indeed, apart from the Mississippi Summer Project, and amid rising fears of a "white backlash," national civil rights groups had no highly visible program for the summer of 1964 either. The Republicans' nomination of Goldwater, signaling a victory for the right wing of that party, cast the national political issue in a new light: the *Defender* reported his nomination under the banner "GOP Convention, 1964, Recalls Germany, 1933."[25] The explosion of violence in Harlem on 18 July, followed over the summer by ghetto riots in seven other cities, did nothing to ease the self-perception of tenuousness among civil rights groups. On 29 July 1964, accordingly, the leaders of the major national civil rights groups met and issued a call for "a broad curtailment, if not total moratorium," on all forms of direct action until after the presidential election, 3 November 1964. Roy Wilkins (NAACP), Whitney Young (Urban League), Martin Luther King, Jr. (SCLC), James Farmer

(CORE), A. Philip Randolph (NALC), and John Lewis (SNCC) all joined in this unusual appeal.[26] The *Chicago Sun-Times* called it the "civilized approach" the paper had preferred all along and added: "We welcome Dr. King and his colleagues to that point of view." The *Chicago Tribune* was less impressed and branded the moratorium "a sudden, cynical respect for law."[27]

These events helped shape the direction of the Coordinating Council Political Action Committee, which by the CCCO meeting of 1 August 1964 had decided to form Freedom Democratic Clubs to parallel the Mississippi Freedom Democratic party. Albert Raby had been elected chairman of the Freedom Democratic Clubs, and an office was established in the Loop. A convention of the clubs was planned for early in the fall, and their initial project was to be voter registration to develop the protest vote against Goldwater. Officially the CCCO had recessed to discuss this report. The delegates expressed concern that the clubs be coordinated with such other independent political groups as Protest at the Polls, Independent Voters of Illinois, and Voters for Peace. There was also concern that voter registration be tied in with voter education, lest civil rights energies end up recruiting more votes for the Daley organization. The original impetus to take civil rights concerns into the electoral arena had been, after all, to show strength in the one area the mayor respected, not to get out more votes he could call his own. For civil rights advocates in Chicago, the Goldwater nomination had made electoral politics even more ambiguous than usual.

The formation of the Freedom Democratic Clubs was announced by a full-page ad in the *Defender,* 17 August 1964. The first order of business was a campaign to support the seating of the Mississippi Freedom Democratic party delegation at the National Democratic Convention. In the summer of 1964, Mississippi had become a symbol for both politically ensconced racial oppression and a determined, militant, and unflinching opposition to that oppression. In the Mississippi Summer Project, a clustering of SNCC, CORE, New Left activists, church groups, and some labor organizations seemed to be forming as the new vanguard of the civil rights struggle. In Chicago, the Freedom Democratic Clubs became the gathering place for a similar clustering of groups. For some of these, Mississippi was the symbol for what America really was. For others, it was the symbol for what America really rejected. In either case, there was an ambiguous relationship to the Democratic party: to use it as a vehicle to reach the grass roots and the public; and to confront it with the need for internal change and radicalize the liberals by forcing attention to "such needs as jobs—without discrimination; quality schools and decent housing—without segregation; adequate health and welfare legislation, not 'economy' squeezes to sub-human standards."[28] In this context it was neither a victory nor a defeat when the National Democratic Committee decided to allow the Mississippi Freedom Democratic party two at-large seats and the offer was refused. It was but another highly visible step in a militant majoritarian strategy for reaching the grass roots and the public, on the one hand, and confronting the Democratic party, on the other. The political aim of the Freedom Democratic Clubs was to register voters in ghetto precincts; but "when the regular organization fails to speak out on issues that concern the people—in Chicago, or Springfield, Illinois, or Washington, D.C.—we shall speak out."[29]

The CCCO continued to meet on a minimal basis. Most of its creative energies went into the Freedom Democratic Clubs. By mid-August, Superintendent Willis had decisively seized the initiative in the battle for the implementation of the Hauser report. By incorporating a proviso that the board could consider paid transportation for transfer students under special conditions and by agreeing to study a limited plan for clustering schools, he had succeeded in promoting the Willis-Whiston permissive transfer plan as the maximum implementation of the Hauser report that could be accomplished without additional funds. The theme, as stated by a black district superintendent of the schools, was that "we cannot do things overnight" because the students involved were difficult. "If they can't get to a school across the street on time," she said, "they can't get to one five blocks away." She was joined in this exoneration of the schools by the Reverend Joseph H. Jackson, president of the National Baptist Convention, USA, Inc., who reminded the public that "the Hauser report does not lay blame on any organization for the existence of segregation in fact in this city." Cyrus Adams, who was chairman of the board's Committee on Integrated Pupil Placement, said he was "inspired" by such voices from the black community. Even the mayor joined in, saying, "The board is approaching the Hauser Report in a satisfactory manner." When the Friends of the Chicago Schools Committee requested the board to reconsider its pupil transportation policy, Whiston ordered the group to support the decisions of the superintendent and the board "or be dissolved." Increased enrollment alone would cost $9 million more in the fall.[30]

When the CCCO met on 12 September 1964, Warren Bacon was present to share his perception of the situation. The board, he said, "lacks the will to pursue a policy of integration." He did not foresee "any significant change" because "there is a hardening of the lines now in the board." A "permanent minority" of five had developed, including Clement and Malis. Malis, he added, "has been a surprise, and I hope she is reappointed." Looking to the future, he reminded the delegates that "Willis's contract expires in August 1965." He warned them that "as presently constituted, the board will renew Willis's contract." He looked to the Havighurst report, due on 11 November, and the *Webb* case hearings, rescheduled to January 1965, to bring the basis for black and white complaints about the schools into the open.

On these latter, however, the delegates were less hopeful than Bacon. The

142

public was not aware of the conflict within the Havighurst panel and Willis's refusal to cooperate with such surveys or to provide data to the school board, but the attack on Berry by Paul Zuber, the attorney in the *Webb* case, was detailed in the *Defender*. A committee was appointed to try to iron out this latter conflict, even though it was believed that the *Webb* attorney's purpose was to create a way to get himself out of a poorly financed case that was going to face an unsympathetic judge.

Raby focused on the Freedom Democratic Clubs. Money was coming in, and he had taken a leave from the public schools to give full time to the clubs. He was speaking for many of the delegates when he said: "We need to reexamine the civil rights movement in this city. We have assumed that masses of people together with evidence of segregation would awaken the moral conscience of the people. But no appreciable change resulted from the boycotts. . . . There is no inherent power in demonstrations. We need to prepare to support the Mississippi Freedom Democratic Party in 1968 and enter the mayoralty campaign in 1967."

On 19 September, however, the CCCO delegates received telegrams saying: "Massive voter registration campaign has not gotten off the ground. Imperative that CCCO do its share. Must meet to coordinate and maximize everyone's efforts to register 100M." The delegates turned out in response and heard that the Urban League would provide staff for this "non-partisan" activity. "This voter registration drive lends itself to precise evaluation," Berry reminded the delegates. "Thus it cannot be allowed to fail." In turning to voter registration, the civil rights groups had put themselves on a new line.

By 17 October 1964, the results were in and the Urban League had prepared a precise evaluation. In the twenty priority wards (chosen for their high percentages of black voters) there was a total of 133,000 new registrations. An estimated 80 percent of Chicago's eligible black vote had been registered, compared with 68 percent in 1960. The black potential had been increased from 46 percent (1960) to 58 percent total of the registered voters in Chicago. A second phase in the campaign was planned for the weekend before the election. Martin Luther King, Jr., and other national civil rights leaders would arrive for a round of voter education rallies.

This success, partial as it was, stood in marked contrast to the fate of integration in the schools. Superintendent Willis had announced that out of 1,653 pupils eligible for transfer under the much-amended Willis-Whiston plan, only 28 children had chosen to apply. According to the *Sun-Times*, "He attributed the low application figures to a conviction by parents that crowding problems in school are not as great as before."[31] This development was not mentioned at the CCCO meeting following its announcement. For the moment, the CCCO's attention had decisively shifted from the schools. Its next meeting was consumed by internal dissension over whether to express a posi-

143

tion on the firing of Chuck Stone by the *Defender*. Some delegates valued his militant voice; others had felt the sting of his invective, not the least of whom were the Urban League and Berry. In the end, a moderate and inconsequential resolution was passed saying that the *Defender* "is not now an adequate voice" of the black community. It took so long to come to that statement that the rest of the agenda, which included "the future of CCCO," had to be postponed to another day.

The CCCO's public face, however, still appeared effective in spite of the disarray of its inner relations. It sponsored King's highly visible "non-partisan, voter education" campaign. Sixteen rallies were held on Saturday, 29 October 1964, at street corners across the black community. These rallies were joined by a large motorcade, and the atmosphere was festive and even triumphant as King kept saying it was "no secret" that he was not voting for Barry Goldwater. Later in the evening, at a suburban picnic dinner at which King was honored by the Catholic Interracial Council, he interpreted the election as a choice of "non-violence or non-existence; we will use negotiations, or we will walk through the future with chip-on-the-shoulder diplomacy."[32]

The continued failure of King's idea that nonviolence could lead to negotiations in Chicago, however, was not only driving the CCCO into "chip-on-the-shoulder diplomacy" but was also creating a sense of futility among the delegates. At its meeting of 31 October 1964 the CCCO was confronted with three situations over which it had little control. First, attorney Cousins had confirmed the report, first made on 17 October 1964, that a black family had been forcibly removed from an apartment at 3309 South Lowe, two blocks from the mayor's home. The building was owned by John Walsh, former president of Teachers for Integrated Schools (TFIS), but his real estate agent had removed the blacks' belongings and installed a white family on his own initiative. There appeared to be collusion with the local precinct captains and police. The CCCO voted to send a delegation to the mayor. Second, the delegates discovered that their committee could not get an appointment with the publisher of the *Defender*. They voted to threaten the *Defender*'s circulation if he continued his refusal. Third, Lawrence Landry returned to the CCCO, after an absence of five and a half months, to ask support for a boycott, which was already under way, of schools located in public housing apartments at the Robert Taylor and Washington Park Homes. The CCCO voted to endorse the boycott and to send a representative to meet with Charles Swibel, the chairman of the Chicago Housing Authority. The CCCO, however, was not able to respond fully to the appeal. The boycotters also wanted curricular materials so that the children could continue their education during the boycott, teachers, a school bus, canvassers to work in the projects, and money. A committee was appointed to look into these needs, but it was clear that neither Landry nor the CCCO, which had organized citywide boycotts in days not too far past, had

144

the resources to sustain even this limited local response to clearly shameful conditions.

These children were virtually imprisoned in public housing, without adequate protection (one child had been paralyzed after being hit during recess by an object falling from the upper gallery of the high-rise building), without proper toilet facilities (public housing apartments have only one bathroom), without proper ventilation, sometimes without heat, always without standard schoolroom facilities or educational materials, constantly subject to the distractions of a busy building, isolated from any contact with the outside world, deluged with substitute teachers whose attitudes were transient, without even milk in the classrooms. These were Landry's "hard core ghetto issues"; but it was not clear to him or to the rest of the CCCO how they could be addressed.

Raby testified at a Board of Education policy hearing on 5 November that "our overriding concern is that this concentration-camp existence is evolving into a policy of super-segregation for which these converted apartments now threaten to set a pattern."[33] By 7 November the CCCO committee had learned more about the situation. Eighty-six apartments were being used as schoolrooms, but support for the boycott was dwindling. The rooms violated the fire regulations and, because of their proximity to liquor stores, the zoning code. The teachers' union claimed ignorance of the situation. There was talk of bringing the problem to the attention of officials in Washington. But the CCCO was not in any position to take over the boycott, and Landry and the parents were in no position to sustain it.

On 12 November Robert Havighurst presented his report to the Board of Education. Philosophically it stood in stark contrast to the practices discussed above. "It is the proposition of this report," Havighurst told the board, "that the Board of Education and all who are concerned with the schools should accept the fact that actions taken with reference to the schools need to be considered in the light of how they affect the city as a desirable place for all kinds of people to live, as well as how they serve the educational needs of particular individuals. It is my conviction that the two interests, rightly considered, will not conflict."[34]

His report called for, and to some extent documented the need for, a socially responsible school system, but it also emphasized the difficulties of achieving that goal. The report avoided any direct confrontation with the issue of segregation, focusing instead on socioeconomic status as a factor in educational achievement. It recommended a vast expansion of compensatory education, the establishment of three large areas in which the schools and communities could work together to stabilize existing integration, the administrative grouping of schools according to their students' achievement levels, and a continuing program of research and development aimed at the interrelation of social and educational factors in the administration of the schools. Havighurst

145

estimated the cost of his recommendations at $50 million but said he saw no alternative if the schools were to deal with educationally disadvantaged and still serve and attract middle-class families.[35]

The CCCO spent more time discussing the Havighurst report than the Board of Education did. In fact, after its initial presentation, the $185,000 Havighurst report never again appeared on the Board of Education's agenda. Both Meyer Weinberg, editor of *Integrated Education,* and June Cooke, researcher for the Urban League, prepared extensive analyses of the Havighurst report. Both were critical of the emphasis on compensatory education because of its implied paternalism toward the poor and also because it was not accompanied by proposals for serious institutional change. Although finding strengths in the report's basic analysis of the schools' shortcomings, Weinberg thought it was "factually evasive." "It tries to avoid shocking the board," he said, "and tries to give the board what is realistic on the assumption they will accept it." But he concluded, "This won't work with the board." By year's end, even the newspapers agreed with him. Willis's budget for 1965 projected vast plans for a billion-dollar program sometime in the future but cut the existing appropriations for compensatory education and ordered more mobile classrooms. So much for Hauser and Havighurst. "It appears," said *Chicago's American,* "that Willis doesn't want to do anything about the Havighurst Report. We can't claim great surprise."[36]

During the year momentum on the issue of segregation in the schools had been lost. By December, the CCCO could not even find a sponsor for a conference on the crisis in Chicago education it hoped to use to begin a campaign opposing the renewal of Willis's contract. With the election over, money for the Freedom Democratic Clubs was drying up. The CCCO voted to endorse the challenge the Mississippi Freedom Democratic party was preparing for the Mississippi congressional delegation, but neither the CCCO nor the Freedom Democratic Clubs had enough money to send Raby to a strategy session in Washington. Some organizations were still coming to CCCO meetings to secure endorsement for their strategies. The United Citizens Committee for Freedom of Residence in Illinois, for example, wanted to hold an Illinois rally for freedom of residence law. The CCCO was still expressing its support for such action, but as Raby said, "We were only a small clique trying to get something going."[37] Neither the display of mass support, the pursuit of behind-the-scenes diplomacy, the organization of local grievances, nor the entry into electoral politics had proven effective as means of advancing the civil rights agenda in Chicago.

The year 1964 saw a national mandate and a local stalemate on the issue of segregation. In June the Congress passed the Civil Rights Act of 1964, a broadly conceived attack on Jim Crow practices in public accommodations. The event was celebrated in Chicago with a rally attended by seventy-five thousand people and addressed by luminaries of the national civil rights movement. It was a festive but ineffective event. Its call for a "time-table of action beginning in September 1964" for the integration of the Chicago public schools was destined for the dustbin of deliberate delay. Even though two prestigious panels of the board's own devising reported that the school segregation was massive and the resulting inequalities were monumental, by year's end the issue of segregation was not even on the board's agenda.

The events of 1963 had been predicated, both nationally and in Chicago, on the conviction that the time had come for decisive encounters with the shame of segregationist practices and institutions: the time had come for change, for desegregation, for integration, for equality. As it became apparent that change did not seem near in Chicago, a chasm of uncertainty opened as to the inner principle and ultimate grounds for further action.

In arguing for a second school boycott and associating himself with a movement for a national school boycott, Landry appealed to "ghetto mobilization" and "hard core ghetto issues" as the first principle of effective future action. He held to the same principle when he espoused the cause of children trapped in public housing schools. He was on the path that would later become a full-fledged black power movement, but in 1964 these concerns served only to confirm the lack of ghetto support for the local civil rights movement and the general weakness of the CCCO's resource base.

Berry and others realized the need for expanded white support. Therefore, he proposed that the CCCO present a lower profile, not stressing demonstrations but seeking more behind-the-scenes contact with the mayor and cultivating a broader spectrum of support for civil rights goals from civic groups.

The poorly supported conference Finding Common Themes, the massive Soldier Field Rally for Civil Rights, and the midsummer conference of civic groups, gathered to analyze the stalemate in the implementation of the Hauser report, represented attempts to expand white support. The two conferences were ineffective, and the rally highlighted the difficulty of converting general support for civil rights into local support for specific changes.

Raby remained open to building both black and white support. He had said, "We will transmit to our children—maybe—segregation. But also self-respect." He felt it was crucial not to remain silent or to allow inaction but to hold the coalition together as much as possible. For Raby and a few others, minding and mending the coalition became a principle of action—not an easy task when the tension between black power and integration, the democratic dilemma of white culture, was emerging but had not yet crystallized.

For each of these emerging differences of principle, there was a corresponding difference in what should count as effective action. The result was a strate-

147

gically incoherent year for the CCCO, which gained few results and even less support. The second school boycott brought out the emerging tensions within the CCCO, cost Landry any future role in the coalition, achieved no response from the Board of Education, and soured most of the delegates on any further citywide demonstrations for the rest of the year. The attempt to mobilize concern around local schools fared no better. The mayor was more responsive in his school board appointments than the CCCO delegates realized at the time because they were so offended by the reappointment of Green. The first day of the Month of Mourning and Mobilization was, for all practical purposes, its last day. The Illinois Rally for Civil Rights contributed little to the local movement. The CCCO Political Action Committee and its offspring, the Freedom Democratic Clubs, failed to become lasting organizations, although, spurred by the Goldwater presidential campaign, they did increase black voter registration. By the 1964 election an estimated 80 percent of the black voters in Chicago were registered, as compared with 68 percent in 1960. At 58 percent, blacks had become the majority of registered voters in the city. On the weekend before the election, the CCCO sponsored a series of voter education rallies, featuring Martin Luther King, Jr. It was a highly visible, numerically successful campaign, but the CCCO as a coalition was, by then, an empty shell with no strategy for the continued pursuit of the local issues it had done so much to dramatize. The strategic incoherence of the year had been accompanied by a dwindling of support even from the CCCO's constituent organizations.

None of their moves had provoked anything like the desired response. After the second school boycott, the mayor asked, "What did they prove?" Willis tried to link the boycotts to violence and disciplinary problems in the schools. The Hauser report gave the Board of Education an opportunity to pursue a cautious program of limited desegregation without the stigma of having been forced to do so by agitation in the streets. Instead, the board adopted the Willis-Whiston plan, another permissive transfer plan, a means of desegregation that had proved ineffective. When board member Murray said, "I am going to vote for this because it doesn't commit us to anything," he was right. The general superintendent's own report admitted that only twenty-eight children applied for transfers under the Willis-Whiston plan, the only plan put forth that year for the schools which achieved its purpose. Willis cited the low participation in the transfer plan as evidence that parents were not dissatisfied and that overcrowding was not really an issue. Meanwhile, eighty-six apartments in public housing projects were being used as makeshift classrooms. If the Hauser report was watered down, the Havighurst report, with its emphasis on the interaction of social and educational factors, was simply ignored. The board never discussed the inequalities of performance by the schools which the Havighurst report documented. A discussion of the need for the compensatory programs recommended by Havighurst would have implied a recognition of the inequalities they were designed to rectify.

By the end of the year, the CCCO had lost both the capacity and any strategy for pursuing the manifest segregation and inequality in the schools which, only a year before, it had wanted to address in direct negotiations with the Board of Education. The academic experts, Hauser and Havighurst, had fared no better through the use of moderate means. The issues were real and urgent, but there seemed to be no means at hand to pursue them.

In the absence of effective strategies directed toward increasing either minority mobilization or majority support, whether by coercion or persuasion, the dilemmas of black dignity and constitutional duties were being reduced to matters of self-respect and conscience. It remained to be seen what action was possible on those grounds.

CHAPTER SIX

The Defeat Is Disguised: 1965

In January 1965, A. Philip Randolph suggested that "the civil rights revolution has been caught up in a crisis of victory; a crisis which may insure great opportunity or great danger to its fulfillment." In the same vein, James Bevel of the SCLC proposed in August: "There is no more civil rights movement. President Johnson signed it out of existence when he signed the voting-rights bill."[1] Both of these statements were rationalizations for why the civil rights movement had been stalled in public and stalemated in its inner strategy councils for months, but neither begins to account for the disarray in Chicago, where there had been no victory to create a crisis and the voting rights act augered no significant political change. Perhaps these interpretations had some validity in the national and the southern arenas, but in Chicago a crisis of futility was paralyzing not only effective action but even concerted strategizing.

In an attempt to recreate the possibility of concerted action, the Chicago Urban League engineered a Leadership Conference on the School Superintendency on 6 February, at which six hundred community leaders heard Philip Hauser say: "If retained, Willis will undoubtedly continue to regard the Chicago school system as his own feudal principality."[2] In response, the conferees adopted a call for a new superintendent and then joined in workshops to discuss how to accomplish that goal. Before adjourning, the participants voted to continue the conference as an organization to coordinate the opposition to Willis. The effort quickly became no more than a letterhead with a mailing address and telephone number even though the question of renewing Willis's contract was a matter of intense and continuing public attention throughout the winter and spring, and even though within a week of the conference, Robert Havighurst added his voice to those opposed to Willis's retention.[3]

Still, Willis had defenders on the Northwest and Southwest Sides as well as the Reverend J. H. Jackson, a power among the ministers of the National Baptist Convention, USA, Inc., of which he was the president and for which he was taken to be the spokesman. He called the anti-Willis moves "mass hysteria" and told a group of conservative students it would be a "tragedy" if such emotions were to destroy a man of Willis's "professional calibre."[4]

There was a third group in the public lineup on the Willis contract. C. Virgil Martin, president of a State Street department store and frequently the spokesman for the State Street Council, chose not to criticize Willis but to focus on his age; he was sixty-four. Though careful to say that retirement was not mandatory, Martin pointed out that "business and industry usually change senior officers at sixty-five."[5]

While the public was thus divided on the substance of the question, the Board of Education was concerned with procedural questions. In October 1964 Whiston said the board should do nothing until it had learned whether Willis was interested in another contract, and Willis was in no hurry to express his wishes in this regard. In February the board attorney ruled that since the terms of two members expired in April, the board could not legally act on a contract for Willis until after that. Willis's contract expired on 31 August 1965.

It appeared that the question of Willis's continuation would be resolved in an atmosphere of relative civic calm. Late in February, the *Chicago Daily News* published an obituary of the CCCO. Speaking in the past tense, the *News* recalled the summer of 1963, "when the tempestuous civil rights movement alternately frightened or bored much of Chicago." The death of the CCCO had apparently been by suicide or at least accidental self-destruction. "The school integration issue backfired on the civil rights groups," the *News* intoned. "All had insisted that Negro parents should have the right to send their children out of their neighborhoods to better white schools." But the permissive transfer plans had laid that idea to rest. Parents did not want it. "Civil rights leaders," the obituary continued, "were put in the embarrassing position of saying that Negro families had to be 'forced' to send their children to integrate other schools." The *News* seemed to be offering an unfriendly version of the "crisis of victory" theory, as if the CCCO had won its demands only to find that "the people" did not want the spoils. Indeed, the *News* inaccurately attributed this view to Lawrence Landry while stressing that he and other former militants "have started settlement houses—a civil rights version of the old neighborhood centers that helped the early immigrants." Calling the CCCO "the super-group that tried to coordinate the disparate groups," the *News* concluded that it "still meets occasionally, but for all effective purposes it has expired."[6] With the CCCO gone, apparently all was quiet where formerly racial unrest had prevailed.

THE ROAD TO A THIRD SCHOOL BOYCOTT: EXTERNAL PRESSURE AND UNCERTAIN COMMITMENTS

Beginning with their meeting of 27 February 1965, the delegates to the CCCO engaged in a concerted effort to restore and expand the group as a civil rights coalition. Not only were they unhappy with their position in Chicago, but Timuel Black reported that a good deal of anger and frustration had been expressed at a national civil rights leadership conference because Chicago had not provided enough support for groups on the line in the South. After a season of preoccupation with the programs of their separate organizations or looking for an alternative to the CCCO such as the Freedom Democratic Clubs, the delegates were ready to try to make the CCCO work. A new planning committee was appointed, only about half of whose members represented established CCCO groups. The rest were new recruits to the anti-Willis camp.

In contrast to the movement in the South, civil rights activities in Chicago had not had clerical leadership or a religious style. Even with significant participation from church groups, the CCCO had a distinctly secular appearance, and it had never attracted large support from the black church leadership. An effort was under way in early 1965, however, to commit the black clergy more visibly to the civil rights movement in Chicago. Staff of the Church Federation of Greater Chicago and the Urban League worked as intermediaries between the CCCO and a group of black clergy to plan a series of Lenten demonstrations focused on the "sin of segregation" in the schools.

It was an elusive alliance. The Reverend S. S. Morris, who had been active in civil rights groups for years, organized Clergy for Quality and Equality in Education. Forty ministers picketed City Hall on Ash Wednesday, 3 March 1965, saying that "the present superintendent either cannot or will not eradicate these evils" (segregation) and asking "forgiveness for those who have perpetuated racial segregation in the Chicago public schools."[7] These clergy decided to hold weekly demonstrations during Lent and to work with the CCCO toward a major demonstration during Holy Week. They were drawn mostly from the religious groups already affiliated with the CCCO.

On 7 March events in Selma, Alabama, took on national significance. The beating of civil rights marchers by state troopers shocked citizens across the country, and its meaning was underscored for those who first saw the report immediately following the television premiere of "Judgment at Nuremberg."[8] Finally, substantial numbers of local black Baptist clergy came for the first and the last time to a Lenten demonstration; but as they subsequently discussed what to do next, their distrust of the CCCO became clear. Some of them wanted to sponsor their own "economic boycott," but all they were able to produce was a weak demonstration, largely peopled by white students, at Carson, Pirie & Scott department store.

Attention turned to Good Friday, and hope was invested in a demonstration that was to involve at least thirty thousand participants. City Hall was to be the target of this Good Friday Witness against Willis. Willis, for his part, was on the move again. At the board meeting of 12 April he presented a plan that promised to stabilize integration in South Shore. Even the Urban League said:

"Willis now appears to be responding to civil rights pressure."[9] Nonetheless, the CCCO and the clergy turned out only twenty-five hundred demonstrators for a poorly organized event that more or less marched from Grant Park to City Hall during rush hour only to have technical difficulties with the public address system. Hosea Williams of the Southern Christian Leadership Conference implied in his speech that King and the SCLC might come to Chicago and produce a real movement "in the North." That statement was one sign of hope in an otherwise depressing day.[10]

The defeat dealt to the CCCO by the Good Friday demonstration left the groups in consternation over what they could do next. The event had been planned as an expression of support and the beginning of a series of actions around Willis, but the delegates learned at their meeting of 24 April that "we have an $800 deficit from 16 April and that counts $500 of unpaid pledges." Meanwhile, Willis was issuing a series of confusing plans for changes in the schools, their boundaries, clusters, and programs. Some, their patience gone, wanted immediate civil disobedience. Others counseled waiting until King came later in the summer before trying more demonstrations. No decisions could be reached, and the CCCO did not meet for more than a month.

On 28 April, 125 university professors from the Chicago area released an open letter urging that Willis be replaced. The Urban League published a report documenting the increase in segregation during his tenure. The Chicago City Missionary Society called for a new superintendent. The state senate, however, passed a resolution praising the bureaucratic Willis for his "charismatic personality." And on 22 May eleven hundred persons gathered at the Edgewater Beach Hotel for a testimonial to Willis at which Democratic Congressman Roman Pucinski said, "The children of this city have had a rare experience from his profound wisdom and experience."[11]

On 27 May, after months of behind-the-scenes wrangling, the board had worked out a compromise. Willis's contract was renewed for the full four-year term with the understanding that he would retire by December 1966. Willis worried board members because he was equivocal about his intentions to retire.[12] Civil rights groups were outraged by his retention.

The executive committee of the Chicago branch of the NAACP voted to sponsor a week of protest, beginning 6 June, to include another school boycott. This action uncorked the chaotic contention that had been building among civil rights groups all during the past year of frustrating futility. The press interpreted the NAACP as calling for a week-long boycott. When the CCCO convened on 29 May, the atmosphere was charged with emotion and tension. Was another boycott a good idea? Should it last five days? Was there enough time to get organized? Was there enough support for it to work? Why did the NAACP announce the action before consulting others? What were the achievable goals of a boycott? Who was the target, Willis, Daley, or the

153

school board? What was the long-term strategy? Was all this just a momentary emotional response, destined for yet another failure? Would there be national support for action in Chicago? What could be done beyond a boycott?

The CCCO threaded its way through these highly charged questions by agreeing to hold a boycott on 10–11 June with a "nationally led" march on 10 June, even though James Bevel of the SCLC had expressed the opinion that the coalition lacked both the resources and the resolve to follow through.

Raby and Sidney C. Finley of the NAACP were named cochairmen (Finley, the Illinois field representative of the NAACP's national office, was acting director of its Chicago branch), and it was unanimously decided that "the boycott and march be sponsored by NAACP with CCCO support." The NAACP, therefore, was responsible for the event and accountable to the CCCO. It was also agreed to contact Congressman Adam Clayton Powell to secure hearings on the Chicago schools and the Chicago poverty program before his House Education Committee and to seek an appointment with Francis Keppel, U.S. commissioner of education, to challenge Chicago's compliance with the 1964 Civil Rights Act. When the meeting adjourned, doubts still remained, and one delegate raised the concern of many when he said that all the talk and planning was not going to "fill the vacuum of mass support."

The CCCO reconvened two days later, 1 June, to plan strategy for the boycott and march. The meeting was marred by opposition to the boycott from those who thought it could not be organized in the time allowed and from those who thought that a boycott was an old and ineffective tactic. Planning went ahead nonetheless. A headquarters had been set up. Dick Gregory spoke up in favor of an extended boycott but only as the beginning of a summer of demonstrations in the Loop. Raby was receptive to that idea but not as a substitute for the two-day boycott that had already been announced. A committee was at work planning to extend the boycott to Carson's, the *Tribune*, and the Illinois Central Railroad because they had supported Willis. Gregory volunteered to set up a demonstration for President Lyndon Johnson when he arrived to address the Cook County Democrats. During the meeting, he drafted a telegram to the president. It was decided that the march should begin at Soldier Field and proceed to City Hall and the Board of Education building, a distance of two miles. Raby said it should be a "socially disruptive march," but that proposal was not discussed. The freedom schools were to focus on "political education." Amid plans for the Johnson demonstration and in spite of a continuing undercurrent of discontent, the meeting ended with a sense that the die was cast and events were in motion.

School Board President Whiston announced the appointment of a committee to search for a successor to Benjamin Willis, calling it "one of the best evidences in the world, to the people talking about a boycott, that they have

154

fair representation." The *Chicago Sun-Times* asked again, "Of What Avail a Boycott?" as it had on 23 October 1963, still firm in the conviction that the conference room could be substituted for the streets and "the sooner the better."[13] President Johnson avoided direct confrontation with Dick Gregory and the 250 demonstrators who were outside McCormick Place while he was inside.

By Saturday, 5 June, it was clear within the CCCO that the planning for the boycott had not gone well and that the event was being paralyzed by internal dissension and frustrating disorganization. At a meeting that evening, the floodgates of invective, distrust, jealousy, despair, confusion, and disagreement were let loose. There were two basic issues: the lack of community support for the boycott and the role of the NAACP as its sponsor. The meeting was called because there was strong sentiment within the CCCO to call off the boycott. Raby's overriding concern was "that we might have a united front."

Timuel Black led off, cataloging the lack of support for the boycott which he had encountered among previous supporters. Others cast doubt on the good faith of the NAACP, citing rumors that it was attempting to take over and discredit the movement in Chicago. Information about the boycott had been difficult to obtain, the boycott office was frequently unresponsive, the leaflets had been printed at the last minute and in insufficient quantity, and there had been emotional disagreements over what they should say.

Was the NAACP unwilling to attack Mayor Daley? That became a litmus question. Some felt that the CCCO was already so committed to the boycott that it could not reverse itself. Others felt that the CCCO was trying to "ride this horse to the finish line even though there is no prize." Many were focusing on Daley, considering Willis a waste of time. "Civil rights forces of Chicago are the laughingstock of America," said one delegate. Getting "the national spotlight on Chicago," not on themselves, was the concern of many. Somewhat ominously, a man seasoned in the southern civil rights experience suggested that "the people in this room must embrace other leaders." Finley spoke for the NAACP, but he did not help matters—he seemed to belittle the CCCO, claiming the NAACP could act alone and denying that the boycott had ever been a "fifty-fifty" proposition between the two organizations. He seemed equivocal about the mayor. The CCCO voted to take itself out of the boycott and to pursue a yet-to-be-determined program of its own.

Before this decision became public, the CCCO reconvened the following evening to reconsider its action. The NAACP wanted a chance to reach a compromise. So did Dick Gregory. Finley was not present, and Dr. Andrew Thomas spoke for the local NAACP. Thomas had to field all the years of suspicion surrounding the NAACP as well as the recent controversy. With the help of Raymond Harth, he managed to convey the good faith, if not the good

155

judgment, of the current local board of that organization. He was joined by Dick Gregory, who had decided that even "if this boycott is only one old cripple with a picket sign, I'm with him." The NAACP agreed to a ten-point CCCO platform for the boycott, and a slim majority voted to reaffirm its sponsorship.

The meeting did not end harmoniously. The opposition was still convinced that the boycott would not be supported in the communities, and Raby stressed that "individual organizations have the right to participate or not." The press never knew that the CCCO had withdrawn its support of the boycott, but by Monday and Tuesday, 7–8 June, the newspapers were full of stories about dissension in civil rights circles.[14]

On Tuesday afternoon, 8 June, the Board of Education obtained an injunction restraining the boycott leadership from further activity. The mayor pleaded with parents to send their children to school, saying, "It is only through education that we will have the type of society we want."[15]

It was the first injunction the CCCO had had to face. For Raby the issue was clear. The line between strategy and self-respect had been dissolved, and the injunction had to be confronted. He had been arrested on Monday night while conducting a "pray-in" at City Hall. Gregory was still in jail from the same action. When the injunction had first been issued, Raby had made a point of making statements to the press which he considered in violation of the order. He was angry that the self-styled militants in the CCCO had failed to do the same. By the time the CCCO met on 9 June, Raby was determined to carry the organization into violation of the injunction and called for a motion to that effect. A long discussion followed, but the delegates reached no conclusion. Raby said he would "rather leave than have a philosophical discussion of the injunction," and in the course of the dialogue he nearly did leave.[16] The self-styled militants were drawing back because they felt "boxed-in" by other peoples' moves. The moderates were looking for some way to keep the action going without technically violating the injunction. Raby kept pressing both sides for commitment. Word arrived by phone that the NAACP would not violate the injunction but would fight it in court and would participate in the march, if not the boycott, and defend those arrested. There were cries that the delegates were "victims . . . of a scheme" who had been "left at the last minute holding the bag," but the basic issue of what the CCCO would do about the injunction remained unresolved. In the end, it was decided to go ahead with the march, which had not been enjoined, on the supposition that signs supporting the boycott, which had been enjoined, would be carried by the marchers. Raby was sent to make a statement to the press: "Take the position," it was voted, "that while we respect the power of injunction, we hope for a reversal . . . and we call on the people not to be intimidated and invite them to protest with us tomorrow."

156

SOCIAL DISRUPTION: THE ROAD TO INTERNAL
RESOLVE AND EXTERNAL SUPPORT

When the march set out from Soldier Field on 10 June 1965, Raby decided to settle in the streets what the CCCO had not been able to decide in its deliberations. He led the marchers directly into the northbound lanes of Lake Shore Drive, gradually spreading them out until they occupied all the lanes. They continued in this fashion down the busy Loop streets. The ranks of the march were swelled by shoppers and workers who spontaneously joined the line while police rushed to reroute traffic around the demonstration. It took more than two hours to reach City Hall. "I still wasn't satisfied," Raby recalled, "so when we reached City Hall I asked the marchers to kneel and pray—as I had the night I was arrested. Then I got my catharsis; I was free."[17]

While Raby and others entered City Hall to confront the mayor, who was not there, the demonstrators sat in LaSalle Street. From City Hall, the demonstration moved up LaSalle Street to the Board of Education building. More than one hundred thousand students had participated in the enjoined boycott. With the demonstrators outside, the Board of Education met inside, approved Whiston's injunction, and heard Willis say that "the answer to overcrowding lies not in cluster plans but in concentrating on a building program." He also told the board that he was not planning to appoint an assistant superintendent for integration, thereby rejecting another of the Hauser report recommendations.[18]

Both sides, it seems, were committed to tactics of social disruption. Raby's promise to conduct daily marches until Willis was removed opened a new phase in the Chicago civil rights movement. Publicly, it was the beginning of socially disruptive demonstrations, including civil disobedience, aimed at forcing government officials to deal with civil rights issues after years of ignoring them. Privately, it was a moment of catharsis for long pent-up feelings of frustration and impotence. The much predicted "long hot summer" was upon the city.

There were no arrests that day, but the mayor said such a demonstration would never occur again. The following day, 11 June 1965, 252 people were arrested, charged with obstructing traffic and disorderly conduct. In addition, Dick Gregory was charged with resisting arrest and assault and battery, on complaint of two police officers. By then, events were in control of strategy. The CCCO was committed to daily marches, confrontation with the police, and a focus on the mayor, none of which had even been voted by the organization. Strategy was being made in the streets. When Raby refused to meet the mayor because marchers had been arrested, the mayor retorted: "Who is this man Raby? He doesn't represent the people of Chicago." In announcing that

157

the Chicago branch was withdrawing its support for the marches, Charles Davis said, in effect, that Raby did not represent the NAACP either. It turned out that Davis's statement was unauthorized and untrue, but it made news.[19]

Raby himself was plagued by the question of who he did represent throughout the summer. Although the CCCO constituent groups continued, for the most part, to participate and to support the evolving action, the CCCO ceased to function as a deliberative and decision-making body. Many new groups joined the action without joining the CCCO. Raby and others searched unsuccessfully for a new organizational vehicle that could, as he put it, "lock in everybody and lock out dangers." In the absence of such a structure, Raby's leadership substituted for an organization, and he felt the burden of the responsibility. "I have authority without instructions," he observed at the end of the first week of marches.[20]

It was to remain that way even though the movement was able to open an office and secure a staff of volunteers and others serving on "subsistence pay." Money was channeled through the CCCO. But the larger problems of organizational responsibility and decision making continued to be handled on an ad hoc basis, from action to action, meeting to meeting, with an informal executive committee growing up in the interstices. The problems, though serious, were finessed whenever they seemed to impede the momentum of events by appeals to the "credentials of participation" coupled with incessant behind-the-scenes diplomacy. Raby did not shrink from his new role, but neither did he relish it. He constantly tried to broaden the circle of leadership, which was easier to do on a day-to-day basis than on a symbolic level. Both within and beyond civil rights circles, all the problems were projected back on Raby.

Still the marches went on. In two days 448 persons were arrested. On Monday, 14 June, amid much civic speculation, the CCCO held a rally at Buckingham Fountain but did not disrupt the Mayor's State Street parade welcoming America's latest astronauts. Dick Gregory's full persuasive powers were required to make that decision palatable to the impatient demonstrators. The next day there were another 67 arrests when a leadership group of interfaith clergy met with the mayor. On the seventh day, 6 June 1965, there were no arrests, and a delegation presented the mayor with a copy of the Havighurst report. In an attempt to clarify the goals and to gain relief from the burden imposed by mass arrests, Raby announced that although the marches would continue, he did not expect any arrests in the immediate future.[21]

The participants had never thought through either the philosophy or the ramifications of civil disobedience. After a week's experience, they needed time to do so, but the lack of any organized structure for deliberation made it difficult. At the expanded meeting of 17 June this question of principle was raised, only to be buried under tactical considerations and postponed until the

CCCO could be reorganized to incorporate the new groups whose representatives were crowded around the room.

For once there was a widespread feeling of exhilaration that a real "movement" was under way in Chicago, and all efforts were expended toward keeping it going and developing "discipline and strategy."[22] That problem had no available solution except constant interpersonal diplomacy and reaching out beyond the marchers for support. The mayor, after all, was actively campaigning for public sympathy. With tears in his eyes, he had appealed to the South Shore Commission to cooperate with public officials and to help develop understanding between the Board of Education and the community.[23]

As events unfolded, the Friends of the Chicago Schools held a meeting with only six of the twenty members present, and four of them resigned because Willis had scuttled the Hauser report, whose implementation the Friends were supposed to oversee. The next day, 23 June, Willis promised to retire at sixty-five and to aid in the transition to new leadership. The school board, meanwhile, had met for four hours with a group of thirty-nine black leaders. Organized by Edwin Berry to support the marches, this group wanted Willis out by January 1966. The board claimed it lacked the legal authority to make such a demand. Following the meeting, Whiston told the press that the board would not withdraw its injunction against the boycott and that its members disagreed about both the Hauser and Havighurst reports. In Washington, Congressman Adam Clayton Powell announced that he would conduct hearings on charges of de facto school segregation in Chicago. And *Chicago's American* raised a "red scare" about the civil rights demonstrators, but no substantial information was forthcoming to link events in Chicago with nonindigenous sources. Raby responded that "there is no political test in the civil rights movement."[24]

On 28 June a large delegation met for two hours with Mayor Daley. Raby called the meeting "fruitless," but it did lead to a meeting the next day with Daley, Raby, and the school board. It was agreed to hold a special session of the board on 7 July 1965. The mayor asked for "cooperation." Berry said, "We stand ready to cooperate . . . if the board will give us anything to cooperate with." Raby held out, called for "an intensification of the direct action campaign," and later in the day led a march in which sixteen people were arrested. The next day, Daley joined in charging communist influence in the marches. Delegates from the United Church of Christ General Synod almost joined the march; eighty delegates set out from their meeting at the Palmer House but failed to connect with Raby, Gregory, and the march they were leading elsewhere in the Loop.[25]

The first of three major efforts to reach out beyond the marches surfaced on 4 July, when the CCCO filed a complaint with the U.S. Office of Education charging that the Chicago Board of Education was in violation of Title VI,

159

Section 601, of the Civil Rights Act of 1964 and "should, henceforth be deprived of any and all Federal assistance currently being received, and any currently under consideration." The complaint, prepared by Meyer Weinberg, editor of *Integrated Education,* reviewed the evidences of de facto segregation, drawing from the reports of the U.S. Commission on Civil Rights, the Hauser panel, the Havighurst survey, the Urban League, and the CCCO's experience with Washburne Trade School and the Chicago Housing Authority. It also cited the fate of the Hauser and Havighurst reports as evidence of the board's unwillingness to deal with de facto segregation. Finally, the complaint cast the Chicago situation in its national context: "We are further persuaded that the ways and means of creating and perpetuating segregation in Chicago may become the handbook for southern communities seeking to evade the 1954 Supreme Court ruling. We are confident that federal intervention in this matter, through the withholding of funds, will help underline the high fiscal cost, as well as the immeasurable social cost, of segregation to Chicago and to the rest of the nation."[26]

Within two days the Chicago Commission on Human Relations entered the school controversy for the first time, submitting a six-point suggestion to the Board of Education to make public its plans for securing a new superintendent, to appoint an assistant superintendent for integration, to bar discriminatory unions from Washburne Trade School, to redistrict high schools, to be open to "concrete" ideas for implementing the Hauser and Havighurst reports, and to seek additional compensatory education programs.[27]

In the second move to reach out beyond the marches, instead of meeting with the Board of Education on 7 July, Raby held a joint press conference with Martin Luther King, Jr. King announced that he would be in Chicago for demonstrations beginning 24 July for the purpose of attracting white support. "There are white persons of good will who just don't understand the movement," he stressed. "There is a great job of interpretation to be done." King made it clear that his trip would be supportive of local civil rights leaders and efforts.[28] Behind the scenes, this announcement was taken to mean that Chicago might be the target of a "northern campaign" by the SCLC. With the passage of the Voting Rights Act ensured, King was actively considering such a move. It would provide the "national spotlight" local civil rights leaders needed.

The daily marches went on, the mayor expressed a desire to meet with King, the Board of Education felt unable to appoint an assistant superintendent for integration against Willis's opposition, and the fifteen marchers arrested on 7 July brought the total for the first month to more than six hundred. By 11 July, the U.S. Office of Education had verified most of the CCCO's grievances even though the investigator, John E. Coons, reported that he was "severely handicapped by Schools Supt. Benjamin C. Willis' lack of co-operation and unwillingness to provide information," which often made it necessary "to rely on nonofficial reports." A group of forty-eight influential businessmen urged the board to speed up the search for a new superintendent, insisting that candidates for selection agree to "a positive policy and program to eliminate segregation as an educational goal."[29]

King arrived for four days of whirlwind activities on Friday, 23 July. His purpose, he said, was "to get to see the people and get to know the leadership of the Chicago civil rights movement." On Saturday he held a breakfast for clergy at El Bethel Baptist Church, where he told an audience of mostly white ministers, "If you want a movement to move, you've got to have the preachers behind you." Then he was off to eight neighborhood rallies in the North, South, and West Side black communities, where he urged participation in a mass march on Monday. On Sunday King and his staff preached in local churches in the morning, resumed the neighborhood rallies in the afternoon, and finished the day with a large gathering on the Village Green in Winnetka, a well-to-do northern suburb. On Monday, he had breakfast with the Catholic Interracial Council, lunch with professional and business people, attended a rally at Buckingham Fountain, and joined a march of more than ten thousand to City Hall, where he promised to return to Chicago if he was needed.[30]

In the third attempt to reach out beyond the marches, for the next two days, 27–28 July, the focus of civil rights activities turned to Washington, where Adam Clayton Powell was holding his hearings on de facto segregation in Chicago schools. No new evidence emerged from these hearings; they simply transferred the conflict from Chicago to Washington. The discussion revolved around Willis and his charts and graphs versus Hauser and his charts and graphs. According to Willis, the problem was that children who lack "those pre-school experiences which do so much to prepare a child for the tasks of the first grade" were unable to pass the readiness tests. The schools, he claimed, were doing the best they could to teach these unready children. Hauser, on the other hand, attacked the schools and their superintendent.[31]

By the end of July, the CCCO strategy projected at the meeting of 28 May—to gain national attention for the Chicago situation by approaching King, Keppel, and Powell—had largely succeeded but had made no real difference either in the impact or the inner momentum of the movement. Participation in the marches was dwindling into a band of faithful few under the leadership of Dick Gregory. The marchers began to feel neglected by the civil rights organizations, and, indeed, "the march" had begun to take on a life of its own. On 29 July the marchers entered Mayor Daley's neighborhood, Bridgeport, thus opening a new dimension in the concept of the "socially disruptive march" and in the problem of organizing a movement.

The marches to Daley's home took place at night. The one on 1 August lasted until 3:00 A.M. The following day, the mayor's angry neighbors seemed about to riot against the marchers, whom the mayor accused of "trying to create tensions." The police, accordingly, arrested sixty-five of them. Police Superintendent Orlando Wilson defended the action of his men. Raby wired the U.S. attorney general asking for federal marshals.[32]

Local columnist Irv Kupcinet reported a deep split in civil rights circles over Gregory's leadership, but no such split existed.[33] The CCCO meeting of 4 August was attended not only by delegates from the formally affiliated groups but also by representatives of groups that had joined the demonstrations without joining the organization. There was a long discussion about how the decision to march on Bridgeport had been made, but those assembled were willing to support that decision and Gregory's role. Once again, a decision made in the streets was ratified on consideration, and processes were set in motion to solve the problems raised by the new tactic. The man who raised the most questions about the new move made his position clear: "I think it was good to go against Daley's neighborhood, but the way the decision was made leaves too much to be desired. There is a limit to how many faits accomplis we can support." Raby admitted that he had been reluctant about the marches at first, but the experience had convinced him that "there was race relations education going on in that community." He continued, "The time may come when the mayor's people can't control the mob. If I can't control the line [of marchers], that's our problem. If the mayor can't control the mob, that's his problem. . . . Those of us who hope and pray for some reasonableness have to take a second look. It is not just the school issue, as I realized last night. I realized where the fight has to be carried on. . . . I support philosophically the concept of marching into communities. It is clearer where the problems are."

Raby also reported that serious discussions were under way to bring King back to Chicago. "He thought maybe they would come back and dig in, not just for three days," Raby said. A joint SCLC-CCCO venture was also under discussion. Everyone agreed that even with the CCCO in disarray organizationally, King's July visit had gone well. "We need a similar understanding next time," Raby continued; "no attempt should be made for him to come in and take over." Raby and the others saw King's presence as an opportunity to build a durable and well-supported drive for civil rights in Chicago. They feared that the city might be used as the site for a national victory after which King would leave the locals where they had been before he came, as had happened in the South. Even though the members of the expanded CCCO were eager to have King come to Chicago, they agreed that such a visit should be arranged by careful negotiation.

Again the problem arose of getting the CCCO's own house in order. "If we can't agree that there have to be lines of responsibility, nothing will be gained," Raby warned. "How flexible is the question. And it cannot be re-

162

solved tonight. . . . Now it is the crucial question. . . . We say we don't communicate with the power structure, but sometimes we don't communicate with ourselves." The meeting closed with the first singing of "We Shall Overcome" at a CCCO meeting and the announcement that free meals and haircuts were available for the marchers.

Police Superintendent Orlando Wilson asked a group of religious leaders to call for a halt to the marches. Instead, after conferring with Wilson, they called on the mayor and CCCO to meet "at the earliest possible moment." They regretted the "long history of prejudice, discrimination, and segregation," which had led both to the marches and the reaction to them. They concluded, however, that "persons who interfere with peaceful demonstrations must be admonished, restrained, and helped to understand their duty to preserve constitutional rights."[34]

Planning for the future was stalled while the negotiations with King continued. By 10 August the line of marchers had dwindled again, and they felt they had no support. In the face of declining action, the CCCO was still trying to work out an expanded format for membership and a flexible formula for decision making. The *Daily News* reproduced an Urban League map showing "where Negroes live." It graphed the block-by-block expansion of the color line from 1950 to 1964. "The Urban League's point," said the newspaper, "is to show that Negro ghettos continue to expand according to patterns of segregated housing, on a block-by-block basis." The league also called attention to the inevitability of segregated schools and their increase during the 1960s because of reliance on a neighborhood school system.[35]

Then, while Watts was in turmoil and the focus of national fear and attention, violence flared in Chicago's West Side ghetto. A woman was killed when a fire truck swerved into a stop sign, knocking it over and striking her. ACT, a group led by Lawrence Landry, had been protesting this all-white firehouse in a poor black neighborhood all summer. Nevertheless, ACT members aided police in dispersing a crowd right after the accident. On Friday, 13 August, however, ACT called a protest meeting on the site of the accident. A melée developed in which more than three hundred persons clashed with the police and twenty-four were injured. A white motorist was attacked as he drove by. Two members of ACT were arrested. Raby, called to the scene by police, tried unsuccessfully to calm the crowd. "Oh, I'm sorry to see this," he said as he left the area in a squad car to call off the demonstration at Mayor Daley's house. The violence on the West Side continued until nearly dawn. By then, 104 persons had been arrested. Two thousand National Guardsmen were brought into position around Chicago in case they were needed on 15 August. The Reverend Shelvin Hall, a West Side Baptist minister visibly identified with the civil rights actions of the summer, organized a volunteer group of clergy to patrol the streets and urge the residents to avoid further violence. Raby hailed the restoration of peace but

163

called attention to the underlying causes of the rioting. "We're not going to be involved in keeping peace at the price of injustice," he warned, and called for a meeting with the mayor. Such a meeting took place on 17 August 1965, but Raby emerged saying, "This was not the meeting I had requested." The meeting had consisted of a series of talks by city officials explaining how much they were doing "for Negroes." The *Chicago Sun-Times* excoriated Raby for his statement about "keeping peace at the price of injustice," apparently unaware of its context.[36]

As the summer ended, the Board of Education gave up the fiction of implementing the Hauser and Havighurst reports and disbanded the committee charged with that responsibility. At the same time, however, Andrew Young, executive director of the SCLC, announced a northern campaign in Chicago in cooperation with the CCCO. It would begin with the problems of de facto school segregation and the ouster of Willis, but that was "just the smallest beginning in solving Negro problems in the ghetto." So far, the CCCO had found that issue anything but the "smallest beginning"; but in both Atlanta and Chicago hopes were high for this new alliance.[37]

The strength of the national mandate to eliminate Jim Crow segregation from the structure of American life, expressed in the Civil Rights Act of 1964 and the Voting Rights Act of 1965, seemed to highlight the frustration and inability of civil rights groups in Chicago to pierce the veil of innocence that still hid massive segregation, block by block, neighborhood school by neighborhood school. In the course of 1965, Willis, an accomplished manipulator of its deceptive powers, became the symbol of that veil. Willis became the issue of the moment because he had set himself up for the role. His derisive attitude toward the Hauser report, his total neglect of the Havighurst report, and his manifest contempt for critics of his administration made him the symbol of resistance as well as a powerful impediment even to admitting that segregation was in any way a problem in the Chicago public schools. The expiration of his contract as general superintendent in August 1965 guaranteed a division of the civic leadership over the question of his tenure. As it turned out, the leadership was less deeply divided on that question than it was by his contention that segregation was not a problem in the schools. Thus Willis and the veil of innocence that seemed to exempt urban segregation from the national mandate to eliminate Jim Crow practices were the entwined issues of 1965.

In both cases, the grounds for action bordered on the ragged edge of pent-up emotion. Anger and frustration sought release in producing effective action. When such powerful emotion was released, events seemed to propel the course of action; and the discipline of principle became a recurring problem, which, given the aims and organizational circumstances, was consistently resolved in morally and strategically creative ways, albeit on a moment-to-moment basis. The underlying principle was to pierce the veil of urban innocence and to bring the national mandate against segregation to bear on Chicago.

In support of this principle, the CCCO pursued three somewhat loosely interrelated strategic goals: to get moving, to get rid of Willis, and to get national attention.

To get moving required breaking out of the shrinking base of support that had paralyzed the CCCO for most of the previous year. The Urban League's Leadership Conference on the School Superintendency reached out to six hundred civic leaders and provided Hauser with a public forum in which to express this opposition to Willis after a year and a half of trying in vain to work with him. Within a week, Havighurst added his voice to Hauser's, and even the State Street Council, though not criticizing Willis, seemed to want him eased out. None of this activity, however, achieved any organized focus.

Just as the *Chicago Daily News* was publishing an obituary for the CCCO, efforts were under way to restore its vitality. New members joined, and old ones came back. The coalition reached out to the black clergy. Eighty ministers picketed City Hall on Ash Wednesday and, in dwindling numbers, each Wednesday during Lent. The aim was to build toward a massive Good Friday witness against Willis, a march from Grant Park to a rally at City Hall. Except for the week after "Bloody Sunday" in Selma, however, black clergy were reluctant as a group to support CCCO activities. The mass march on Good Friday was poorly attended and poorly organized. The CCCO seemed still stymied in its efforts to get moving.

Ultimately, the Board of Education provided the needed stimulus for the CCCO by renewing Willis's contract. In an emotional reaction, the Chicago branch of the NAACP voted to sponsor a week of protest including another boycott of the schools. Once again the CCCO became the arena for debate and strategy. The Board of Education obtained an injunction against the boycott. Amid much controversy, both the NAACP and CCCO decided to honor the injunction, but Albert Raby, along with others, had decided that the situation called for socially disruptive tactics and civil disobedience. Thus began a summer of daily marches and demonstrations downtown and ultimately into the mayor's neighborhood. The march took on a life of its own. Much of the actual strategy for the marches was made in the streets and debated later in the CCCO meetings. The marching served to create the sense of a southern-style movement in Chicago, but it also created serious and recurring problems of discipline and strategy.

Thus by late June, two of the strategic goals had been achieved: first, the Board of Education had appointed a committee to search for a successor to Willis, and he had publicly agreed to step down within the year, at age sixty-five; and second, in pressing for this result, the CCCO had become the center of an expanded constituency for direct action. By decisions made in the streets, the CCCO was committed to tactics of civil disobedience and social disruption to pierce the veil of innocence that still seemed to exempt urban segregation from the national mandate for racial justice.

By the end of July, the CCCO had also achieved some progress on its third strategic goal—getting national attention. A complaint had been filed with the U.S. Office of Education claiming that the Chicago public schools were in violation of the 1964 Civil Rights Act and should therefore be deprived of federal funds. In addition, Martin Luther King, Jr., had held a series of community rallies, culminating with a march of ten thousand persons from Grant Park to City Hall, where King suggested the prospect of a Chicago campaign by his Southern Christian Leadership Conference. Finally, Congressman Adam Clayton Powell held hearings in Washington at which Hauser rehearsed the unwillingness of the schools to take any effective steps toward desegregation of the system and Willis pleaded that it was the children, not the schools, who lacked readiness for effective education.

During the first half of the year, representatives of the business and academic communities had been added to the moderate voices calling for a new general superintendent. Under the impetus of the NAACP's call for another boycott of the schools, new groups of activists were attracted to the CCCO. Dick Gregory became the symbol of the marches. Martin Luther King tried to expand support for the CCCO program in both the black and white communities. Even the Commission on Human Relations, in response to the federal complaint, added its heretofore silent voice to those urging change in personnel and policy at the Board of Education.

Willis remained an object of ceremonial celebration, but by late spring even his supporters were working on easing him out of office. As word of another boycott circulated, Whiston appointed a search committee for Willis's successor. He also got an injunction against the boycott. The mayor pleaded for understanding between the board and the community. Late in June the board met privately with thirty-nine black civic leaders. Members resigned from the Friends of the Chicago Schools, a blue-ribbon committee to provide public support for the schools' integration programs, because there were no programs to support. Within the week, the mayor met for two hours with a CCCO delegation. Neither of these meetings was able to produce peace on the school issue. One of Chicago's newspapers and later the mayor himself tried to raise a "red scare," suggesting communist influence in the civil rights movement, but that charge was so insubstantial that it got nowhere. The mayor was on better ground when he asked, "Who is this man Raby?" It was perhaps the most honest response to the surprising events of the summer of 1965.

By his own description, Raby had risen to "authority without instructions"

166

in the Chicago civil rights movement. The sudden infusion of new groups and people and the emergence of new tactics of civil disobedience and social disruption had left the CCCO organizationally inadequate for its new role. Events were happening to it and through it, but organizational responsibility and decison making had devolved to an ad hoc basis. Its forum for deliberate planning had virtually collapsed as it had gone from dormancy in February to strategy in the streets by June. For the moment, Raby's public leadership and the behind-the-scenes diplomacy had to substitute for organizational structure.

By the end of the summer, Willis was on his way out; but even though the Friends of the Chicago Schools was defunct and the U.S. Office of Education was taking the CCCO complaint seriously, the veil of innocence was still intact for all but civil rights activists. To pierce that veil, the CCCO was arranging for King and his SCLC to join the action in Chicago. Meanwhile, violence had broken out on Chicago's West Side. The National Guard had been mobilized. Both the police and the mayor had tied that violence to civil rights activities.

For a brief moment in 1965, the dilemmas of black dignity and constitutional duties had been dissolved. The tension between minority mobilization and majority support, and between persuasion and coercion, which the CCCO had encountered in the first school boycott and had been ineffective in addressing in 1964, were lost from view amid the angry emotions with which the news of Willis's reappointment was received. Self-respect, more than strategy, and conscience, more than politics, led Raby and the marchers into the streets. At last a principle of action, or at least initiation, had been found.

In the events that flowed from that new beginning, however, the democratic dilemmas of social change reemerged. What strategies were Raby and the marchers pursuing? What publics were they addressing? Was civil disobedience an appropriate means to their ends? Although the marches had a life of their own barely subject to such considerations, and the CCCO as such seldom formally addressed these questions, on the whole the answers were clear and creative. The marches became a demonstration of minority mobilization around civil rights aims and an occasion to increase minority support for both the movement and its goals. At the same time, the movement in Chicago was appealing for white majority support—not in Chicago, to be sure, where civil rights leaders had lost confidence in the capacity of the local majority or its officials to support their goals, but in Washington and across the nation, where support for civil rights goals in the South might be brought to bear upon Chicago through the Powell hearings, the Office of Education complaint, and King's presence. As a result, the CCCO once again had a strategy and, possibly, the means to pursue it.

167

CHAPTER SEVEN

The Search for a New Beginning:

August 1965–July 1966

At the 1963 Conference on Religion and Race, Msgr. John J. Egan had said to the assembled religious leaders: "We cannot expect to be taken seriously on the question of race relations if we do not insist on being taken seriously on the question of the poor." The issues of poverty and racism, he said, were too closely related, both in the popular mind and in the social order, to be considered separately: "Historically, American antipathies toward the poor have blended with American antipathies toward minorities, and the stereotype still prevails."[1] Msgr. Egan had stated the problem that by 1965 had brought the Johnson administration and the civil rights movement to loggerheads and by 1966 had shattered the coherence and cohesion of the civil rights movement.

Both the logic and the passion of the national mandate for civil rights seemed to require not only new policies to remedy structural injustices but new concepts of social rights.[2] In February 1965, Bayard Rustin observed: "The civil rights movement is evolving from a protest movement into a full-fledged *social movement*—an evolution calling its very name into question. It is now concerned not merely with removing the barriers to full *opportunity* but with achieving the fact of equality."[3] President Johnson had anticipated this shift from civil rights to social rights in his Great Society programs. In March 1964, he proposed what became the Economic Opportunity Act of 1964, which, he claimed, "does not merely expand old programs or improve what is already being done. It charts a new course. It strikes at the causes, not just the consequences of poverty."[4]

President Johnson conceived of the legislation as the beginning of a "national war on poverty," and he called for "total victory." The aim of the legislation was not to provide temporary relief for the poor but to reach out and include them in the productivity of the economy. "The United States can achieve its full economic and social potential as a nation," the bill declared,

168

"only if every individual has the opportunity to contribute to the full extent of his capabilities and to participate in the workings of our society. It is therefore the policy of the United States to eliminate the paradox of poverty in the midst of plenty in this Nation by opening to everyone the opportunity for education and training, the opportunity to work, the opportunity to live in decency and dignity."[5]

President Johnson also conceived of the Economic Opportunity Act of 1964 as providing the social support necessary to make good on the commitments to equality embodied in the Civil Rights Act of 1964. It was meant to provide financial incentive for alternatives to Jim Crow practices and financial help for the cities to deal with the accumulated problems of poverty and discrimination. Race and poverty had become interrelated policy issues.

In either case, race or poverty, education was a critical concern, and President Johnson's Great Society programs included an unprecedented federal commitment to education, especially in areas where poverty and/or discrimination could be addressed with compensatory and/or supplementary programs. Johnson's legislative program for education was truly monumental. Some of its key elements were as follows: Vocational Education Act (1963); National Defense Education Act Amendments (1964); Higher Education Act (1965); National Vocational Student Loan Insurance Act (1965); Elementary and Secondary Education Act (1966); International Education Act (1966); Model Secondary School for the Deaf (1966); Education Professions Development Act (1967); Education for the Handicapped Act (1968); Higher Education Amendments (1968); School Lunch Act Amendments (1962, 1968); and Vocational Education Amendments (1968). The Elementary and Secondary Education Act of 1966 alone added $1 billion a year to the federal commitment to education.

Thus the issues of race, poverty, and education were at the center of President Johnson's domestic policy, and his administration was committed to the idea that they were closely related. It was clear that the cities were the most visible and critical embodiment of these issues and would require not only additional resources to cope with them but also a coherent urban policy on the part of the federal government. Urban concerns and problems were, accordingly, elevated to cabinet status in 1965 with the creation of the Department of Housing and Urban Development (HUD). President Johnson appointed Robert Weaver as the first secretary of HUD. He was also the first black cabinet member. When the Fair Housing Act of 1968 was added, the circle of Great Society issues was completed: race, poverty, education, and urban development, each interrelated with the others.

This program met criticism from many directions from the very beginning, but before we proceed to some of the difficulties it raised in Chicago, it is only fair to point out that the combination of Johnson's economic policy and his

169

social programs did achieve some remarkable aggregate results. As Robert Lampmann has pointed out, "Disposable personal income (DPI)—income after payment of taxes and after receipt of cash transfers—was 44 percent higher on a per capita basis in 1974 than in 1960." During the same period "black family incomes rose from 52 to 62 percent of white family incomes" and "the median educational differences between whites and blacks narrowed from 2.7 to 2.0 years, and the narrowing was even more marked for younger adults."[6]

One of the most controversial aspects of the Economic Opportunity Act of 1964 was the concept of Community Action Programs, the designated vehicles for devising local projects and for channeling federal funds into local communities. The legislation defined a Community Action Program by four criteria. First, communitywide public and private resources would be mobilized in an attack on poverty. A "community" was defined as any area "including but not limited to a State, metropolitan area, county, city, town, multi-city unit, or multi-county unit." Second, a program would be established to provide services or assistance aimed at "bettering the conditions under which people live, learn and work." Third, "maximum feasible participation of members of the areas and members of the groups referred to in section 204a ("low income individuals and families") would be encouraged. Finally, the programs would be administered by some public or nonprofit private agency "which is broadly representative of the community."[7]

In Chicago, Mayor Daley organized a Community Action Program shortly after the legislation was introduced. It was called the Chicago Committee on Urban Opportunity, and Deton Brooks was named its executive director. Brooks understood the Community Action Program as an extension and intensification of existing welfare agencies and services. "The Chicago Concept," as he outlined it, was a mobilization of existing welfare agencies, public and private. Program planning relied exclusively on welfare and social service professionals. A series of urban progress centers was established to coordinate the delivery of services to target areas. Participation by the poor was limited to their role as recipients of services or as local indigenous staff at urban progress centers.[8] Thus at the neighborhood level, it appeared that the War on Poverty in Chicago, instead of providing new avenues to independent action for the poor to deal with their political as well as their economic powerlessness, was designed to capture social service delivery as a new source of patronage.

By April 1965, when full federal funding was beginning to flow into the Chicago Committee on Urban Opportunity, Adam Clayton Powell led an attack in Congress on the Chicago Concept for its failure to secure maximum feasible participation of the poor at the policy level. In response, the mayor expanded the committee to an unmanageable size while Brooks cut down the number of urban progress centers and tightened central administrative control by elaborating the bureaucratic distinctions between "service systems" and "program divisions."[9]

The Chicago Concept prevailed, and thereby President Johnson's search for a new beginning in the pursuit of "social rights" resulted in new money being channeled into politically and professionally dominated social services on the old model. His victory in legislation was turned to defeat in implementation.

In the flush of legislative victory, the president delivered a commencement address at Howard University in June 1965. That address, "To Fulfill These Rights," was intended to emphasize Johnson's commitment to pursue equality of results as well as equality of opportunity in the field of civil rights. Instead, it was the beginning of a serious breach between the president and the leaders of the civil rights movement. It was a speech in which the president was not well served by his staff, and the consequence was a serious disruption of his working relationship with the civil rights leadership.

In that address, President Johnson reviewed his own record on civil rights legislation and proclaimed it "not enough." In "the next and more profound stage of the battle for civil rights," he said, "we seek not just freedom but opportunity—not just legal equity but human ability—not just equality as a right and a theory but equality as a fact and as a result." The problem that needed attention, the president said, was the "widening gulf" in the life chances of blacks and whites. "The harsh fact of the matter is that in the battle for true equality too many are losing ground every day."[10]

President Johnson identified two principal causes for this widening gap: "First, Negroes are trapped—as many whites are trapped—in inherited gateless poverty." His Great Society programs were designed to release individuals from that poverty trap. "But there is a second cause," he claimed, "much more difficult to explain, more deeply grounded, more desperate in its force. It is the devastating heritage of long years of slavery, and a century of oppression, hatred, and injustice." [11]

It was wrong to identify the increasing inequality of blacks with causes in the past. That very week in Chicago the president had avoided demonstrators who wanted him to do something about the present causes of inequality in the Chicago schools. To those demonstrators, the president began to sound like Willis when he suggested that, of all the causes of increasing inequality, "perhaps most important—its influence radiating to every part of life—is the breakdown of the Negro family structure." It is true that he added: "For this, most of all, white America must accept responsibility," but those words rang so strongly of paternalism that, far from enunciating a doctrine of "social rights," they seemed to threaten an invasion of black privacy by battalions of Deton Brooks's "mobilized" social workers.[12]

The president proposed to pursue the policy implications of his address at a

171

White House conference on the theme "To Fulfill These Rights." It turned out that his Howard speech had been written on the basis of a report by Daniel P. Moynihan, an assistant secretary of labor. The concepts expressed in the president's address came from the Moynihan report ("The Negro Family: The Case for National Action"). When subjected to scrutiny, this report was shown to be verbally facile, intellectually vapid, and politically opportunistic (a combination of characteristics that subsequently served Moynihan well in advancing his own career but that, in its first field test, sundered President Johnson's domestic civil rights coalition). The critique was led by Benjamin F. Payton, director of the Commission on Religion and Race of the National Council of Churches, but he was not alone. The speech had struck a sensitive nerve and seemed to many civil rights leaders to augur a dangerous turn in policy. The White House conference, scheduled for November 1965, had to be postponed to June 1966. By then, the alleged deterioration and pathology of the black family was off the agenda. It was not acceptable as the centerpiece of further federal effort in the field of civil rights.[13]

In a speech in October 1965, Martin Luther King, Jr., expressed the prevailing view in civil rights circles. "The Negro family," he said, "lived in Africa in nature's jungle and subdued the hostile environment. In the United States, it has lived in a man-made social and psychological jungle which it could not subdue. Many have been destroyed by it. Yet, others have survived and developed an appalling capacity for hardships. It is on this strength that society can build. What is required is a recognition by society that it has been guilty of the crimes and that it is prepared to atone. With that beginning, there need be no doubt about the end."[14]

Thus by the summer of 1965, in spite of securing the passage of the historic Voting Rights Act, President Johnson was confronted with criticism of and opposition to major pieces of his Great Society programs from the very quarters they had been intended to serve. The transition from civil rights to social rights had not been well conceived, at least from the perspective of workable programs that could both gather support and achieve their purposes. To complicate matters still further, by the summer of 1965 a similar shift in principle and programmatic focus was under way in civil rights groups. This shift was no more successfully negotiated in the civil rights movement than it was in the Johnson administration.

SCLC AND CCCO: PHILOSOPHICAL DIFFERENCES
AND PROGRAMMATIC DELAYS

The decision by Martin Luther King, Jr., and the Southern Christian Leadership Conference to mount a campaign in Chicago in conjunction with the local coalition, the Coordinating Council of Community Organizations, was a first step in that transition. Even that first step was not easily accomplished, largely because there was so much at stake for all concerned. It was clear by then that urban segregation posed problems both of principle and policy which differed substantially from Jim Crow. Something new was required. By the same token, although the CCCO's ranks had expanded over the summer of 1965, it was nearly exhausted of vitality by its unsuccessful, repeated attempts to find some effective way to expose the color line in Chicago and mobilize support for change. Therefore, the SCLC and the CCCO, each with its own strengths and weaknesses, tried to work out a relationship for action in Chicago that could build on their respective strengths and overcome their respective weaknesses. There was more at stake in that attempt for the future of the civil rights agenda than anyone explicitly realized at the time. Even so, it was a nervous time for everyone involved.

It took from September 1965 to January 1966 to establish an organizational structure within which both the SCLC and the CCCO groups could work, the Chicago Freedom Movement. From January to June 1966, it was a process of building support for this Chicago Freedom Movement and for working out the programmatic focus of its demands and activities. In each of these phases, unresolved issues of principle exacerbated the discussions of strategy and tactics.

Over the summer of 1965 the focus of CCCO activities had been on the Chicago schools, and in the early discussions with the SCLC, no one assumed that it would be otherwise in the fall. Raby told the CCCO delegates at their meeting on 10 August that he was urging King to announce a Chicago campaign in time to help organize a massive boycott of the schools when they opened in September. A steering committee was appointed to represent the CCCO in its collaboration with the SCLC and to develop a Fall Freedom Program. The assumption clearly was that the flow of action from the summer to the fall would be continuous, albeit intensified by the SCLC's presence. That assumption was unrealistic.[15]

The CCCO had serious problems with its own internal organization as well as uncertainties about its relations with the SCLC. During the summer marches, several organizations joined in CCCO demonstrations without formally joining the coalition. No formal CCCO meetings were held for several months; most assemblies included CCCO delegates and representatives of "cooperating organizations." Proposals to regularize this situation were discussed throughout the summer, but the committee appointed to deal with the problem was divided between those who wanted to reform and expand the existing CCCO structure and those who wanted to make a fresh start with another organization, which resembled a "movement" rather than an "organization."[16]

Some of this tension was evident in a lengthy debate precipitated by the question of Dick Gregory's membership status. Gregory had been an active

173

figure in the summer's deliberations, and he had been critical in conducting and directing the summer marches. To the CCCO delegates, he represented the spirit of the movement, the very purpose they were trying to achieve in Chicago. Gregory's contributions over the summer were not an object of controversy within the CCCO. But the proposal to make him a delegate brought to the surface all the uncertainties about just what the CCCO was. Some argued that his "credentials of participation" were more than enough to gain membership in the CCCO, but others, worried about the emerging amorphousness in the lines of responsibility, wanted to maintain the constitutional requirement that only organizations could join and be represented in CCCO. The debate on this issue was spirited and indecisive, but a compromise was reached that was acceptable to all: Dick Gregory was made an honorary member.[17]

The matter was further resolved for the moment when an increasing number of cooperating organizations, lured by King's presence, chose to join the CCCO; those joining on 21 August 1965, for example, included United Packinghouse, Food, and Allied Workers (District 1); Chicago Baptist Association Human Relations Committee; Maple Park Homeowners Association; Mile Square Federation; and West Side Federation. Joining later in the fall were American Jewish Congress, Englewood Christian Leadership Conference, Friendship House, North Central College Campus Church, and Jewish Cultural Clubs.[18]

Similarly, the prospect of an alliance with the SCLC was beginning to attract previously scarce resources to the CCCO. Earl Dickerson, president of the Supreme Life Insurance Company and a prominent black civic leader, had secured a number of pledges of $50 per month to the CCCO from black businessmen. This source alone was producing $1,000 each month; the goal was $25,000 per year. Also, the Urban Training Center for Christian Mission, an ecumenical agency preparing clergy for inner-city ministries, was paying the salaries of several civil rights workers, including a young seminarian, Jesse Jackson. As a result of such contributions, the CCCO now had a full-time paid staff of seven.

Throughout August, planning continued on the assumption that an action program could be launched to coincide with the opening of school; but at each step in that planning, the focus of the program became more and more blurred, either because of practical difficulties involved in carrying out the ideas or because of conflicts in strategy. For instance, at the CCCO meeting on 21 August, the steering committee submitted a new plan for the delegates' approval, which had been devised by Raby, Alvin Pitcher of the CCCO staff,[19] and Walter Fauntroy of the SCLC. The idea of a massive boycott of the schools had been scrapped because it conflicted with the Urban League's "back to school campaign." Instead, the new plan recommended that a permanent boycott be organized in a single neighborhood. For other areas it was proposed that a series of one-week boycotts of individual schools be organized, leading finally to a coordinated boycott. This idea may have avoided conflict with the Urban League, but it ran into other difficulties.

Dorothy Gautreaux (Altgeld-Murray Parents Council, AMPC) objected that once again the CCCO was developing plans for neighborhood groups without consulting those groups. Other delegates joined in the complaint. The plan was not adopted.

On 31 August the CCCO sponsored a conference to strengthen its relations with organized labor and to fashion a broader consensus for the fall program. The 220 persons who attended were divided into working groups on education, housing, employment, and labor support for the civil rights movement. Reports from two of these groups came before the CCCO delegates on 2 September. The housing panel requested CCCO support for the suit being brought by Englewood residents to stop urban renewal in their neighborhood. Since most of the residences slated for demolition were sound and 80 percent of them were owned or occupied by blacks, the suit was being brought in federal court under Title VI of the 1964 Civil Rights Act, which prohibited discrimination in federally assisted programs. The delegates agreed to support the suit.

The second report from the 31 August conference was from the education panel concerning the Fall Freedom Program. The panel noted that the public schools regularly administered standardized tests to evaluate the quality of education they were providing, but, despite repeated requests of civil rights groups, the schools refused to make these scores available to the public. Therefore, the education committee proposed that the Fall Freedom Program administer such tests itself as a device to organize local communities around the schools issue. It was hoped that once a community group saw how the pupils in its neighborhood stood in relation to national averages, it might become more available for mobilization by CCCO.

Serious practical questions were raised about the capacity of the CCCO to undertake such a project. Hal Baron of the Urban League reminded the delegates of the failure of Operation Spotlight, a similar CCCO project he had headed eighteen months before, saying, "We've had greater success with citywide projects than local ones." Other delegates thought it would be much easier to achieve public visibility for such projects once King was in town; it was suggested that the SCLC staff assigned to Chicago might conduct the program. Still others doubted the efficiency of a project that was expected to require the efforts of five to ten staff members for three weeks to carry it out in a single neighborhood. This plan, too, required further work.

There were reports about efforts to have the federal courts take jurisdiction over the numerous cases resulting from the summer marches and discussion of

175

recent police brutality toward CCCO demonstrators. Then Raby reported on his meeting in Atlanta with King, Young, and Bevel to finalize arrangements for the SCLC's presence in Chicago.

The SCLC had agreed to stay for a period of two or three months, possibly as long as a year. King had promised a total commitment to Chicago: "The future of SCLC will depend on Chicago." Ten SCLC staff members would be assigned to work under James Bevel in his new position as parish program director of the West Side Christian Parish (WSCP). Bevel was a seasoned SCLC staff member who had come to Chicago fresh from the stunning events of Selma, which had propelled the Voting Rights Act into law. Raby committed the CCCO to work in other areas and to incorporate additional groups. King had approved the Fall Freedom Program, but the content of that program was still unclear. A joint SCLC-CCCO staff retreat was scheduled for 8–9 September to bring the program into focus and to work out a division of labor. Raby did not think a program would be ready before October, when it was planned to hold a joint retreat of 150 participants. The problems of working out the relationship, rather than the opening of school, were now dictating the timetable.

The many questions that arose about the arrangements revealed problems in the emerging relationship between the SCLC and CCCO. "What will be the official relationship between SCLC and CCCO?" Raby was asked. He answered: "Young's press release said 'work under and with' CCCO." The two groups "will not conflict on policy questions." He was asked: "Do we set policy or recommend to SCLC?" He offered reassurance: "This [CCCO] is still the seat of final decisions, but we will accommodate our program to their resources and experience." Concerns were expressed that the SCLC might "take over," but Raby noted that it had not done so in the past, though it had "been criticized for not building up local leadership before they left."

Nathaniel Willis of the NAACP raised a specific problem. "In a recent interview," he reported, Bevel had said, "Superintendent Willis is not responsible for poor education" and the CCCO's "marches were unwisely conducted." Raby responded that he had mentioned this issue to King in a telephone conversation earlier in the day, but he had also assured King that the interview was "no problem." We "now have Bevel working with us," Raby reminded the delegates, and would want to "take his advice into consideration."

Irene Turner (CED), a longtime delegate from one of the CCCO's most active affiliates, stated emphatically, "We must retain leadership. Bevel should work under discipline. No one should speak for CCCO without authorization." Raby responded, "We must be as clear about the relationships as last time. Bevel has apologized for the mistake, and we can't beat a dead horse."

176

The CCCO steering committee met 6 September to finalize plans for using the issue of student achievement test scores to organize parents and to coordinate these efforts with the SCLC. James Bevel and Bernard Lafayette of the Chicago American Friends Service Committee (AFSC) were also present.[20] Both were critical of the CCCO proposal.

Lafayette preferred a "reverse boycott" in which high school students would refuse to leave their classrooms for a few hours. Bevel spoke for presenting slide shows demonstrating that no jobs awaited the graduates of ghetto schools. Both emphasized the importance of organizing in the neighborhoods and conducting workshops for students and their parents. Both were vague when Raby pressed for details on what staff were required and what schools were being targeted, but in truth, the details were not the crux of the matter. Raby believed that action had to be organized around understandable programmatic goals. In large part, Bevel and Lafayette thought that grass-roots organizing preceded determination of goals and strategy. Bevel said, "In your training program, once people get information, they will develop strategy. In the process of developing people, a strategy will evolve and tell you what to do." Lafayette supported him: "You feel the spirit of what the people are willing to do. I don't think we can write a program. Strategy will develop along the way." Their immediate aim was not a fall program but reaching one million ghetto residents by spring.

Raby disagreed with this approach. "We want an effective program," Raby said. "We have heard a philosophical approach with appealing examples. Now we have an urgency of time. I must go back to CCCO with a concrete program and sell them on it. First, we considered a boycott when the schools opened; then we agreed to undertake something in October. Now we are talking about a spring program. I think we need a concrete program as soon as possible."

Bevel countered, "I want to raise alternatives. I would prefer to say we had a discussion. Then have another discussion. Others must feel what we feel. I would rather get there and talk to them." Raby still wanted details: "You have spoken for a program of mobilization. What is the minimum staff and support required?" Bevel stuck to his question: "You need a philosophical agreement with everyone involved first." Raby stuck to his: "I need a program to pull out to convince people." Lafayette persisted: "We must not sell program first, but get more minds involved. We must have open, free discussions." Raby responded, "I can't say I'm really for this."

Some CCCO delegates, however, were more impressed than Raby with Bevel's approach. "If we agree with Reverend Bevel's proposal," Herbert Fisher (Chatham–Avalon Park Community Council, CAPCC) said, "we cannot get the answer to what the program is going to be. It is to set off a ground swell. From it the ultimate program will grow." John McDermott (CIC) found

177

Bevel's approach "realistic and a basic change. This program is oriented first to the Negro community. He is talking about massive strength." Finally, even Raby conceded that "the concept of mobilization is very enticing," but he was still dubious: "I've got to see it. The Chairman must be convinced about what we are doing." With that, the meeting called to finalize plans for the fall ended seeking plans for the spring, and it was the CCCO's last discussion of a fall program. The fall had come. The program was not ready, either in Raby's sense or in Bevel's.[21]

THE OFFICE OF EDUCATION AND THE BOARD OF EDUCATION: A DECISIVE TEST OF STRENGTH

This collapse of any concerted fall program was followed closely by a set of events which was to prove as disappointing to some officials in Washington as to the CCCO. In filing a complaint with the Office of Education in July, the CCCO had hoped to bring federal pressure to bear on the Board of Education. Chicago was slated to receive $32 million under the newly passed Elementary and Secondary Education Act. A showpiece of the Johnson administration, this unprecedented billion-dollar program of federal aid to local schools had been designed partly to lure southern school districts into willing compliance with Title VI of the Civil Rights Act of 1964. When the CCCO complaint arrived at the Office of Education, there was already considerable confusion inside the Department of Health, Education and Welfare about the application of Title VI to de facto segregation in the North, and this complaint seemed to offer a well-argued test case for resolving that issue.[22] It did, but not as expected.

The U.S. commissioner of education, Francis Keppel, initiated an investigation of the Chicago schools because the CCCO "had unquestionably submitted the most detailed complaint" received by HEW. It was reported that "those who read the Chicago document were deeply impressed by the thoroughness of the documentation and the seriousness of the charges." Before funding a major new federal program, it seemed important to deal as quickly as possible with these charges and with the issues they raised.[23]

In September, moreover, Commissioner Keppel was irritated at the recalcitrance of General Superintendent Willis in providing the information pertinent to the CCCO complaint requested by an HEW investigating team. At a meeting on 23 September, Willis had said he would have to check with members of the Illinois congressional delegation before he could decide whether to answer the HEW requests for information, and he had indicated that even if he did respond, "the answer might well be two months in coming—if that soon."[24]

178

Commissioner Keppel was also concerned about Willis's reported plans for using the new federal money. The education act was designed both to foster integration in the South and to provide compensatory programs for children of poverty, defined as families with incomes of less than $2,000 a year; but Chicago informants, including the CCCO research committee, had told Washington that two of the three areas targeted by Willis were all white and included census tracts with a median income of $8,000. The *Chicago Tribune* reported on 28 September that the state superintendent of public instruction, Ray Page, had already approved this Willis plan. This *Tribune* story was inaccurate, but it had consequences.[25]

In Washington, it seemed that Superintendent Willis was trying to confront the Office of Education with a fait accompli. Accordingly, on 30 September, Commissioner Keppel wrote to inform Page that the Chicago school system was in "probable noncompliance" with Title VI of the 1964 Civil Rights Act. Keppel said the CCCO complaint "must be satisfactorily resolved before any new commitments are made of funds under federal assistance programs administered by the Office of Education, either directly or through your office." Keppel diplomatically suggested that the matter could be resolved "in a relatively short time . . . with the full cooperation of the Chicago school authorities." In the meantime, however, he proposed to defer any new commitments of federal funds to the Chicago schools.[26]

The reaction to Keppel's letter in Chicago was swift and predictable. Willis, "bristling with anger," fired a telegram to Keppel, asking "What is 'probable noncompliance'? . . . When will you let us know?" The superintendent then called a press conference and denounced the fund deferral as "illegal, despotic, alarming, and threatening." Mayor Daley said the "indiscreet" action of Keppel had "done irreparable damage to the whole concept of federal aid to education." The mayor then said he would fire Keppel if he worked for him. The school board was split on the issue. Conservative members immediately objected to the federal action; others were eager to learn more about the charges and any remedies HEW might propose. Congressman Roman Pucinski (D.-Ill.), a strong supporter of civil rights legislation in its southern application but also a strong supporter of Willis in Chicago, called for a General Accounting Office investigation of the deferral warning that "Congress won't appropriate another nickel for education programs" if federal officials continue such "arbitrary and dictatorial" acts.[27] That threat was serious because Congressman Pucinski was chair of the House subcommittee that controlled education legislation.

Press reaction varied. The *Tribune* denounced "the unspecified complaints [which] apparently consist of nothing more than various charges made by . . . a self-appointed civil rights group whose principal mission seems to be to conduct street demonstrations and otherwise harass Supt. Benjamin C.

179

Willis and the school board." The paper joined Willis and Daley (and thousands of southern school boards) in raising the issue of federal control of local schools. The *Daily News,* however, commented that "Chicago, through a stubborn and contrary school superintendent and a school board without the courage either to fire him or bring him into line, blundered into this mess on its own hook."[28]

Civil rights leaders applauded this federal vindication of their long-standing claims, but they were in no position to provide meaningful support for Keppel's move. John McDermott called the deferral "another demonstration that the civil rights movement in the city has been telling the truth" about the school situation. Raby said he "felt wonderful. I hope that this is the first step toward building a school system that will make every Chicagoan proud."[29]

At the CCCO meeting on 2 October, Meyer Weinberg noted that finally "HEW has started to accept some of our arguments." These were the same arguments that had been made since 1957; but with wisdom born of the intervening eight years, Weinberg went on to caution, "The only thing that will satisfy us will be a change in our school board policy." Other delegates reacted to Pucinski's stance by urging the CCCO to confront the congressman on this issue. Telegrams of support for Keppel's action were approved, and a press conference was planned to interpret the CCCO's complaint to HEW, but there was no fall program to provide tangible support for this critical federal move.

The opposition, however, was not lacking in tangible means to support its position. Senator Everett M. Dirksen (R.-Ill.), the Senate minority leader, and Representatives Daniel Rostenkowski (D.-Ill.), John C. Kluczynski (D.-Ill.), and Roman Pucinski (D.-Ill.) all publicly opposed the Office of Education. Pucinski made use of his committee position to arrange a meeting between Keppel and the Illinois congressional delegation. President Johnson, concerned about his hard-won education bill as well as his relations with the Daley machine, ordered his domestic adviser, Joseph Califano, Jr., to investigate Keppel's action. Both the Justice Department and the White House legal staff questioned the legality and the wisdom of the deferral.[30]

On 3 October, the president and Mayor Daley met in New York when Johnson signed a new immigration bill before the Statue of Liberty. Daley expressed his concern about the HEW action; Johnson said he should have called the White House immediately and assured Daley that he was looking into the matter. The president summoned HEW Secretary John W. Gardner and Commissioner Keppel. "He gave them unstinted hell," said one observer. Gardner reported, "At no time did the President suggest we reverse our position. The President did encourage us to settle the matter promptly." The next morning, HEW Undersecretary Wilbur Cohen, an experienced negotiator, flew secretly to Chicago with instructions to get what concessions he could from the school board.[31]

He got very little. Essentially, the responsibility for investigating the CCCO complaint was transferred from HEW to the Chicago school board, the putative defendant. The board was to report its findings in sixty days, and remedial action, "if any is called for," was to take place as "promptly as possible" thereafter.[32]

Informed of these "concessions" by the school board, Pucinski claimed victory: "They're just a face-saving device for Keppel. This is an abject surrender by Keppel—a great victory for local government, a great victory for Chicago. Mayor Daley has done the people of the nation a service by standing firm against this intolerable federal intervention."[33]

It had taken less than a week to cripple a major test of how the national civil rights mandate should be applied to a large urban school system. The speed of the reversal undercut support for Keppel that was just crystallizing in Chicago. Four members of the school board were in the process of drafting a telegram endorsing Keppel's action, and the CCCO was completing a detailed justification of the deferral. Now all that was left to Raby was to express his dismay: "We are shocked at this shameless display of naked political power exhibited by Mayor Daley in intervening at the highest level—not to bring Chicago into compliance with the Civil Rights Act, but to demand federal funds regardless of how they are used. Mayor Daley ostensibly supported the Civil Rights Act and all the Democratic congressmen from Illinois and Sen. Douglas voted for it. Yet they are the first to squeal like stuck pigs when the bill is enforced in the North, while they applaud enforcement in the South." Within the week, however, the school board intensified its efforts to find a successor to Willis.[34]

Although the matter dragged on for several years, the use of Title VI in northern school segregation cases was effectively settled for some time to come. The Office of Education eventually had to reassume responsibility for investigating the CCCO complaint, but its report was not issued until January 1967, nearly eighteen months after the inquiry had begun. By the fall of 1968, HEW was not even monitoring the Chicago schools' performance. In Congress, a wave of amendments were passed limiting the enforcement powers of the Office of Education, with Congressman Pucinski and other big city Democrats in the lead. Southerners, having learned from Chicago that civil rights enforcement could be opposed successfully through political means, lent their support to these efforts. It was two years after this Chicago episode before HEW undertook any further investigations of northern school segregation complaints, and enforcement proceedings, previously successful in the South, lay dormant for the same period.[35]

This episode underlined some of the essential weaknesses in the national mandate for civil rights. It exposed the gap that had opened between President Johnson and the civil rights leadership since the Howard University speech in June. Johnson's White House conference, "To Fulfill These Rights," had already had to be put off from November to June, and it seemed to pose more problems than could possibly be handled. President Johnson was justifiably proud of the newly enacted federal commitment to education, and he had intended it to serve his commitment to equality of opportunity and to social rights for blacks. The charges from civil rights groups such as the CCCO that his education act was being used to perpetuate segregation had caused "a horrible fear of embarassment" within the administration.[36] By the same token, however, the War on Poverty, the creation of the Department of Housing and Urban Development, and the Elementary and Secondary Education Act all had the effect of making Johnson more dependent on the big city mayors because only through them could those programs be made to work on their intended scale. And Richard J. Daley was preeminent among the big city mayors. When the SCLC came to Chicago, therefore, the Johnson administration was faced with a difficult test of its loyalties, a test the SCLC was not likely to pass if the situation developed into an either/or choice.

SCLC AND CCCO: FORGING A MOVEMENT

Within days of this decisive display of Mayor Daley's power the joint CCCO-SCLC retreat convened at Lake Geneva, Wisconsin, on 8–10 October. By the time of this conference neither the organization nor the program for joint action had been worked out. The two hundred participants included CCCO members, SCLC leaders and Chicago staff, and representatives of organizations that had worked with the CCCO in the past but not joined, as well as others that were attracted by the SCLC. Elements from organized labor and several prominent black clergy were present for the first time. The coalition was still gathering, and the retreat was a council of potential allies in search of a common theme to bind them together.

At the opening session, Raby stated the purpose of the meeting: "We will get to know one another." It was a far cry from the original idea of having the retreat be the opening move in an action program. For most of those present, however, it was their first direct contact with King and the SCLC staff. Raby was hopeful about the contribution of each party to the new alliance: "SCLC needs us to help set a pattern for the entire nation, and we need them for their experience and inspiration."[37]

Throughout the conference the SCLC led with its strength, the philosophy of nonviolence, and the CCCO led with its strength, detailed knowledge and experience of the programmatic issues in Chicago. A panel of CCCO delegates commented and suggested action on the issues of education, jobs, politics, housing, public welfare, and the War on Poverty—the same agenda the CCCO had articulated in 1963. Problems with the police and the courts and the potential contribution of the black churches had a new urgency on the CCCO agenda. Following the panel, the Reverend Shelvin Hall of the West Side Federation, a recent and influential addition to the CCCO, introduced King, most of whose remarks centered on the nature and history of the nonviolent movement and the importance of "Negro-white alliances." He assured the conference that the CCCO provided "a strong basis here for a powerful movement," but he stressed the magnitude of the task: "Chicago represents all the problems that you find in the major areas of the country. . . . If we can break the system in Chicago, it can be broken any place in the country."[38]

King, like President Johnson, was impressed with the link between poverty and racism: "Negroes are impoverished aliens in an affluent society. . . . [This] is a civil rights concern. The nonviolent movement must be as much directed against the violence of poverty, which destroys the souls of people, as against the violence of segregation." He called for intensifying the War on Poverty by establishing a two dollar per hour minimum wage, extending fair employment practices to all workers, and initiating a massive public works program, but it was unclear how these policy concerns could be linked to a movement in Chicago.[39]

He anticipated that "the movement in Chicago [would] be different from that in the South. There will be fewer overt acts to aid us here; naive targets such as the Jim Clarks and George Wallaces will be harder to find and use as symbols." King concluded on an evangelical note: "There are giants in the land, but we can possess the land of freedom. . . . Let us be dissatisfied with things as they are. Then, in some bright future, we will say with a cosmic past tense, 'Deep in my heart, I *did* believe, we *would* overcome.' "[40]

During the remaining day of the conference, as several of King's themes were elaborated and extended, it became apparent that Chicago posed problems of principle as well as of strategy for the SCLC. More than geography was involved in its move from Selma to Chicago, from South to North. Andrew Young articulated the new theme: "We are not seeking constitutional rights, but human rights." King agreed: "Constitutional rights was the subject of the fight in the South. In the North, human rights is more the question." James Bevel carried the idea forward: "There is not a civil rights movement. . . . The passage of the civil rights bill and the voting rights bill ended it. Now we are talking about a non-violent movement. The question is, 'How should men live in the city; what is man?' This transcends civil rights."[41]

Part of this transition involved questions of scale. Andrew Young estimated that "we need a thousand trained, informed organizers; a hundred thousand marchers." Bevel had made similar estimates. Bevel reiterated his perception

183

that the details of strategy and programmatic focus would emerge from the very process of organizing a nonviolent movement: "Ideas will come out of the massive disciplined organization that we need. The direction will come from the people, not just from directors. Directors should be sensitive to the flow of ideas from the people." Andrew Young's version of power to the people was more pragmatic: "Try some argument on one corner. If it doesn't work, try another argument on another corner. Keep this up until you get a yes, then build on that. There has to be something that genuinely comes out of you—your own. This is the way you communicate with people."[42]

Where Young was consistently irenic, however, Bevel was frequently acrimonious: "We ought to be realistic enough to say that if we do in the next two years what we have done in the last two, we won't be any further along than we are now. . . . If Negroes can't break up a ghetto in fifteen months, they will never get out. . . . SCLC has people who are working . . . not just sitting around looking important."[43]

When the question was raised as to just what the Chicago SCLC staff was actually doing under James Bevel's direction, Andrew Young explained: "At the present time the west side organizations meet together on the staff level and decide. Now they are experimenting with organizational methods which have worked in the South. Leadership participation in all this is anticipated." More generally, he went on to say, "SCLC will not have an official office. We will work through existing organizations. We are not going to sell memberships or try to take over anything. We will be here for the duration until problems are effectively confronted. This means that we expect to be here full-time for at least a year and then be on call indefinitely."[44] The SCLC was still casting about for an organizational approach to its vision of an urban movement; but the attraction of grass-roots organizing and issues was irresistible as this movement searched for a politically visible constituency for change.

King raised the question of how much "black nationalist" sentiment might be encountered in the North, as distinct from the South. Bevel said that this was not a problem, but he admitted that even he was "not very interested in integration of the schools per se." He added, "I'm interested in quality education in the ghetto." That was a new theme from SCLC staff, and it was taken up by several of the Chicago participants, who affirmed that the overriding issues were the "ghetto issues," "grass-roots organizing," and being close to "the people." One speaker questioned the role of whites and the black middle class in such a movement. That challenge was not pursued, but the black power issue, northern style, was emerging as a stance independent of old-line black nationalism as attention turned to ghetto issues.[45]

The SCLC was counting on the philosophy of nonviolence to bridge whatever gap there might be between the issues of poverty and racism. Accordingly, the final evening of the joint conference was devoted to an address by C. T. Vivian of the SCLC on nonviolence. "Nonviolence," Vivian said, "is after a community of love, of brothers: a community wherein men move and have relationships with one another on the basis of mutual dignity . . . as a child of God." He spoke of the implications of this philosophy for a nonviolent movement's treatment of its enemies, not as evil persons but as products of an evil system. It was important to speak the truth, "the truth [of] what the system does to man." The power of this system could be confronted only with power, and "our power is people." After discussing the fears that might undercut such a movement and emphasizing the need for discipline, self-purification, suffering, and action, Vivian concluded: "Nonviolence is the only honorable way of dealing with social change because if we are wrong, nobody gets hurt but us, and if we are right, more people will participate in determining their own destinies than ever before. A new man is the end product; a new society will be in orbit. . . . We are seeking the kingdom of God in twentieth century terms. We want a society in which man can fulfill his potentialities. It does not yet appear what we shall be but one day we shall be like Him. We shall know the truth in the real thrust of the human spirit."[46]

Several long-term CCCO delegates were caught up by Vivian's eloquence. Herbert Fisher (CAPCC) responded, "I cannot see the relation between what most speakers have said and our past experience. What has been said seems to transcend anything that we have conceived of in terms of organizations and attitudes. . . . We must rely on SCLC to give us a new understanding for organization to create a new society." John McDermott (CIC) agreed: "Vivian has proposed a new thing, a theology and philosophy which is new to us. This will require a great deal of training on our part."[47]

Throughout its history, the CCCO had experienced tension among its delegates, the organizations they represented, and broad-based community support. At least since Bevel's arrival some months before, the issue had become organizations versus the movement, or even goals, issues, and strategies versus organizing the movement. Now a conference that began with the CCCO discussing the issues ended with it affirming the movement. It still remained to be seen how the movement would get back to the issues and, indeed, which issues it would get back to; but a unifying theme had been struck, and an elevating vision had been articulated.

Some time would pass before this unifying vision would be translated into a unified organization and strategy for action. When Bevel reported on his organizing efforts to a delegates' meeting on 2 November, one stated the sense of many that these efforts "seem to bypass CCCO and make unilateral decisions which could lead to dissension." Andrew Young, in his usual conciliatory manner, explained: "We can't contribute at your [CCCO's] level, but we can organize in the streets. We naturally tend to go where CCCO is the weakest. Bevel knew some people on the West Side and found it easier to organize there. . . . He does pretty well with the creative freedom we give him."

By the CCCO delegates' meeting of 11 December, relations between the CCCO and the SCLC had reached a crisis. Young was present to "reestablish contact." "Since the joint retreat at Lake Geneva," he said, "SCLC staff have been used to learn the community, strengthen existing community organizations, and mobilize troops for the movement. . . . But now," he continued, "we are about ready for another phase—a series of planning and strategy meetings in January, and a city-wide fund-raising event in February. . . . We [SCLC] have been bogged down in administrative concerns, reorganizing our southern staff after our southern programs. Now, however, Dr. King is beginning to spend two or three days in Chicago each week, and I plan to be here at least as much." John McDermott was concerned that there still was no "action program to unite SCLC and CCCO." He appreciated the SCLC leaders giving more time to Chicago, but "around what [issues] are we going to do things?"

William Robinson (FOR), a staff member of the Chicago Church Federation and newly elected treasurer of the CCCO, raised the question of directing the movement staff. "We need," he said, "lines of administration and authority." For example, Robinson concluded, "I'm in a workshop on the West Side but I don't know under whose auspices it is being conducted."

Young assured the delegates that he expected to work closely with Raby on such matters, but the SCLC did not have anyone else to send to Chicago, and he had "hoped we could hold on until I could get [here]."

Robinson underscored Young's potential role. "We need you here because we have been drifting. We need someone who speaks for SCLC." Young affirmed that every CCCO organization would have its "specific function" in the movement, "but we can't decide this for them." It is "the nature of a movement to drift," he said.

Father Thomas Milleau (West Side Federation, WSF), who had reported a decline in attendance at Bevel's workshops the previous month, said a plan of action was urgently required because "the West Side needs tightening fast." He cited plans by the American Friends Service Committee and SCLC staff to pull students out of Marshall High School the following Monday, which "could be dangerous" unless the students were informed and well trained. Young replied that he had instructed the staff to conduct "no further demonstrations without clearance" but said he would "check on the situation."

Raby was concerned about the lack of communication: "I was told that the Jenner School boycott was being promoted by SCLC. Now I hear that the north side staff is being reassigned to the West Side." Young considered such rumors "the most serious problem in the movement, a major source of disruption." "Some," he said, "are planted, some arise from our own insecurities. We should be aware of this, track them down, and go to the source."

186

Don Rose, a delegate from NALC and a long-term volunteer publicist for the CCCO and other civil rights groups, countered that the best way to "fight rumors was by early dissemination of concrete facts—which *we* don't even have."

Raby summarized his concerns: "I don't know if we can solve the problem of goals while we are continually worrying about these problems of staff direction. I do know that every organization needs some meaningful activity around which to mobilize. Otherwise, people may start things and can't switch [when a meaningful program is developed]." Young disagreed. He wanted to "let everything go on": "In Birmingham, lots of things went wrong, but in the course of various demonstrations, we dramatized ten aspects of the problem, and now there are ten titles in the civil rights bill. . . . Thus, in Chicago, we need different demonstrations to dramatize different aspects of the northern problem. The problem is systematic exploitation, not just schools or housing. Our job is to pull together—Dr. King and CCCO. When the grass turns green, we've gotta have something in the streets."

Bevel arrived as the meeting was concluding and seconded Young's remarks, but in a manner that provoked rather than placated: "Negroes can't speak because they have no platform. My job is to build such a platform; then Negroes can speak on many issues. It takes time to think this out. What is a 'slum'? How is it created? Most people in CCCO don't know and thus can't deal with it. What do you move in Chicago and get Negroes in Harlem to move? We need a national movement—$120 billion to eliminate slums."

Faith Rich (CORE) asked if Bevel felt ready to act in relation to events such as the school board budget hearing the following Monday.

"No," Bevel replied, "We don't go to meetings until we can create change. Spend your time developing your army. Then, instead of reacting to Jenner School, you can react to the whole system."

Actually, James Bevel was in no position to make such a statement in December 1965. At that time, he was in the process of retrenching his grassroots aspirations. A firsthand account of the West Side Christian Parish project, which Bevel headed, reported:

> The early activity of the fall, intended to begin that "movement" which would "remake the face of the city," was enthused by the victory spirit of Selma and consequently massive in design. The combined WSCP-SCLC staff was assigned to tasks that virtually covered the metropolis—from working with ghetto youth gangs and community organizations to mobilizing Chicago-area college students and suburbia. . . .
>
> By the end of 1965, the combined SCLC-WSCP staff found the initial design indeed massive. The victory spirit of Selma proved not durable enough to support the frustrations of trying to cover a multitude of fronts in Chicago's complex metropolis. After a series of prolonged staff meetings, Bevel then retrenched the staff

into one area of the West Side—that of Warren Avenue Church—in an attempt to develop there during the first half of 1966 a sizable community organization.[48]

The "system" may have been the object of change, but by December 1965 James Bevel, like so many before him in Chicago, found the lure of neighborhood-based organizations irresistible. At this CCCO meeting of 11 December, Bevel announced his strategy of "digging in" to four Chicago neighborhoods, Kenwood and Englewood on the South Side, and Lawndale and East Garfield Park, where he was working, on the West Side. These were to form the foundation of a "Union to End Slums."[49]

Englewood was a long-standing member of the CCCO, and Kenwood-Oakland had just begun organizing in the fall of 1965 under the direction of Jesse Jackson, acting as a CCCO staff member. Kenwood was a South Side slum on which the CCCO had decided to concentrate partly to compete with Bevel's projects on the West and North sides. The focus in Kenwood was on such ghetto issues as welfare, quality of education, and urban renewal. Some in the CCCO had felt that their credibility and influence in the alliance with the SCLC required such a commitment. In this case the competition between the CCCO and the SCLC for standing turned out to be creative for their alliance. Bevel had added a much stronger West Side wing to the movement's potential than the CCCO had ever achieved on its own, and the CCCO was driven to grapple with the complexities of organizing the unorganized. In the past, the CCCO had been a gathering point exclusively for the already organized.

It was not until January 1966 that King was able to present a plan for the SCLC-CCCO alliance. The SCLC and CCCO leaders met for two days early in January. The outcomes of that meeting were presented to the CCCO delegates on 6 January 1966. The search for a working relationship between the CCCO, SCLC, and other cooperating groups had eventuated in a new organizational structure, the Chicago Freedom Movement; King and Raby were named cochairmen. The search for a common program had resulted in a joint CCCO-SCLC Chicago Plan, which was overwhemlingly approved by the delegates present. By then, both developments seemed obvious.[50]

THE CHICAGO FREEDOM MOVEMENT:
FOCUS IN SEARCH OF STRATEGY

In presenting the Chicago Plan, King acknowledged the CCCO's past efforts to "get rid of Willis" but, in light of the "limited impact" of those efforts, called for "something new." This fresh initiative was conceived by analogy with the SCLC's work in the South, from which "two principles have emerged. One, the crystallization of issues, and two, the concentration of action." In Birmingham, "the issue was simplified deliberately to: Segregation," and action was concentrated on lunch counters. In both cases, the aim was to enable citizens of goodwill to respond to and identify with the movement's grievances.[51]

The SCLC staff, King said, had "given a great deal of thought to the crystallization and definition of the problem in Chicago in terms which can be communicated to the man on the street." "The Chicago problem is simply a matter of economic exploitation. Every condition exists simply because someone profits by its existence. This economic exploitation is crystallized in the SLUM— . . . the total pattern of economic exploitation under which Negroes suffer in Chicago and other northern cities." King identified twelve dimensions of this slum pattern: education, building trade unions, real estate, banks and mortgage companies, slum landlords, the welfare system, federal housing agencies, the courts, the police, the political system, the city administration, and the federal government.[52]

The parallel with the South broke down, however, as King discussed ways of concentrating action in Chicago:

> There are two possible ways to concentrate on the problems of the slum: one would be to focus on a single issue, but another is to concentrate all of our forces and move in concert with a nonviolent army on each and every issue.
>
> In the South concentration on one issue proved feasible because of a general pattern of state and local resistance. However, in Chicago we are faced with the probability of a ready accommodation to many of the issues in some token manner, merely to curtail the massing of forces and public opinion around those issues. Therefore, we must be prepared to concentrate all of our forces around any and all issues.[53]

It was clear to King that the movement's present forces, the member organizations of the CCCO and the staff resources of the SCLC, "must be supplemented immediately by additional power factors"—the church, college students, black high school students, and unemployed blacks. In selected neighborhoods, King said, "some type of union to end slums" was contemplated "to bargain collectively with landlords and the city in an effort to change the conditions which create slums."[54]

An educational and organizational phase of the campaign was planned for February. By March, "demonstrations should be scheduled at points which should reveal the agents of exploitation and paint a portrait of the evils which beset us in such a manner that it is clear the world over what makes up a slum and what it is that destroys the people who are forced to live in a slum." By 1 May the "massive action" phase would begin. Once again, King found the southern paradigm instructive: "Just as no one knew on January 2, 1965, that there would be a march from Selma to Montgomery by March of that year, so now we are in no position to know what form massive action [will] take in Chicago. However, as we begin to dramatize the situation, we will be led into forms of demonstration which will create the kind of coalition of conscience which is necessary to produce change in this country."[55]

King concluded by suggesting the objectives of the proposed campaign: comprehensive federal legislation addressing "the problems of slum life across this nation," state legislative reforms, and, on the local level, citizens and organizations "continually dealing with the problems of slum life." The programmatic focus was still unclear. (The most specific outcome envisaged was a cultural center and sports pavilion for underprivileged youth.)[56] As had James Bevel, King and the Chicago Freedom Movement had opted for a concerted focus on a strategy of nonviolent direct action protesting slum conditions.

During the next months, civil rights activities in Chicago gained visibility as King moved into a slum apartment in North Lawndale and regularly spent two or three days in the city each week. Most of his visits were organized around a public appearance, usually sponsored by a community organization and designed to highlight slum conditions in a particular neighborhood. Late in January, King heard testimony from residents of East Garfield Park on housing, school overcrowding, lead poisoning, and abandoned buildings. On 2 February, he participated in a mass rally that formally launched the Kenwood-Oakland Community Organization (KOCO); the issue there was the school board's decision to build a new high school near the University of Chicago, thus resegregating the all-black lower-class neighborhoods to the north and south. On 17 February, King urged neighborhood people gathered in a pool hall to join "the union to end slums." On 23 February, he addressed a rally of concerned parents and teachers at Jenner School and met privately with Black Muslim leader Elijah Muhammad to explain the goals of the nonviolent movement in Chicago.[57]

Meanwhile, SCLC staff continued their work with West Side community organizations and started a series of weekend workshops with college and high school students and teenage gang leaders. In February, Operation Breadbasket was begun, using the threat of product boycotts to force grocery chains and producers to hire more blacks. By March, the first Union to End Slums was under way in East Garfield Park. KOCO's welfare committee was working with the West Side Organization's Welfare Union, and a revitalized CCCO education committee was meeting to address a variety of school issues.[58]

A Chicago Freedom Festival was held on 12 March to raise funds for the SCLC and CCCO. Harry Belafonte, Dick Gregory, Mahalia Jackson, and Sidney Poitier entertained a capacity crowd of thirteen thousand at the International Amphitheater; King addressed the audience on ending slums. The cosponsors split $80,000 in net proceeds.[59]

190

Another front in the war against slums was opened on 23 February, when the SCLC and the West Side Federation "assumed trusteeship" of a rundown apartment building at 1321 South Homan. Terming the move "supralegal— one dealing with moral matters," King announced plans to withhold rents from the landlord to cover the costs of repairs and rehabilitation.[60]

Response by the Daley machine was swift. One county public aid official called the takeover "anarchy." "If every individual could say, 'I'm not going to pay any rent and fix up my building myself,' think what would happen in a city like Chicago." Mayor Daley also publicly disapproved of King's action. He said everyone recognized the need to clean up slums, but, he added, "We also recognize that there are legal ways and illegal ways of achieving our objective. None of us would say we should use illegal ways. We have our courts and our legislature—this is the place to proceed." The day after the building was taken over, the city filed suit against the landlord seeking $200 a day for each of twenty-three building code violations.[61]

The symbolism of this takeover was embarrassingly shattered when it was discovered that the building was the only source of income for an eighty-one-year-old childless invalid, who did not appear to understand what was going on. John B. Bender, the building's owner, wished King well: "All I want . . . is maybe a thousand dollars more than the mortgage."[62] He was hardly the symbol of an exploitive slum landlord.

Mayor Daley's response to the takeover was typical of the counterattack he had been waging since King's arrival. He promised to end slums himself by 1968 and invited King to join with him in this effort. Daley turned every wheel of his machine to neutralize the issue and its constituency. A hundred building inspectors were dispatched to the West Side. The Welfare Department suspended rent payments to forty owners of slum buildings. A rat control program was introduced. Garbage collections were doubled. War on Poverty programs were established in direct competition with civil rights organizing efforts. Parole officers warned their clients not to join in any civil rights activity or they "might get into trouble."[63]

In late March, Mayor Daley held a series of meetings with Chicago religious, business, and labor leaders to report on the city's progress against slums and to solicit their support in these efforts. "All of us," Daley said, "try to achieve the same objectives. That is ridding the cities of America, including his [King's] own, of slums and blight." The problem of poverty, he said, was not created in Chicago. "It was created a thousand miles away in Mississippi, Georgia, and Alabama." The mayor requested the clergymen to "deliver sermons on the moral responsibilities of landlords and tenants and how members of their congregations could get job training and improve themselves." Later Daley continued his offensive before the Cook County Democratic Central Committee. "We have no apology to any civil rights leaders

191

who come into our city to tell us what to do," the mayor proclaimed to the assembled committeemen. "The record of the Democratic Party on civil rights is clear."[64]

Daily News columnist Mike Royko summarized the progress of King's Chicago campaign:

> The issues aren't as simple to dramatize as they were in the South. . . .
>
> The tactics he used down South aren't effective here. . . .
>
> They might have had impact if King had a fresh issue, but he hasn't found one. He has, in fact, gone after an old standard—slums.
>
> For years, newspapers have been running regular anti-slum campaigns. One of Mayor Daley's favorite activities is tearing down slums as well as anything else that strikes his fancy. In Chicago, most people agree slums are terrible. Some of them even understand what causes them. Then they yawn. . . .
>
> Mayor Daley hasn't had him over to the house for corned beef and cabbage, but he has not been unfriendly. He simply says he can do what King can do—faster and better.[65]

Meanwhile, the CCCO was experiencing new difficulties. The delegates met on 2 April for the first time since January. The purpose of the meeting was to allocate funds from the Freedom Festival to projects proposed by the coalition's member organizations, but discussion kept shifting back and forth from particular projects to the funding criteria proposed by the steering committee. In the end, the delegates adopted guidelines for the use of this money, partially funded a single project (the federal suit brought by the Citizens Housing Committee against the Englewood urban renewal project), and called for a "congress" on 7 May to outline their program and demands to the general public.

At the 9 April meeting, an innocent motion to print and distribute the treasurer's report, which showed receipt of $40,000 from the Freedom Festival, led to a lengthy and acrimonious debate. Some delegates were concerned about their responsibility to donors, others wished to guard their proceedings from the press and opposition, and still others expressed anxiety about the integrity of the CCCO's accounting and disbursement procedures. It took three roll call votes, including an unusual motion to overrule Raby, to resolve the issue and decide to print the treasurer's report. This organization was not accustomed to having money in the treasury.

The delegates also expressed frustration and disappointment over their lack of a closer relationship with the SCLC. Raby admitted that there was some "ambiguity" in the situation and hoped that the proposed congress would improve the situation. One delegate cited the 6 January "plan to merge" the SCLC and CCCO in the Chicago Freedom Movement, saying, "We should hold SCLC to it." Another commented that "we invited those people here and they are beginning to treat us like kids."

By the meeting of 23 April, the delegates' relationship with their own steering committee was under attack. Having adopted guidelines that contemplated the use of Freedom Festival funds for projects of CCCO affiliates, the delegates were faced with proposals from member organizations which would immediately exhaust those funds. The steering committee recommended as an alternative that the festival money be used to expand CCCO staff operations by hiring a coordinator of community organization, a research coordinator, and two organizers in public housing projects. This proposal was bitterly opposed by delegates from CORE and the West Chatham Community Improvement Association (WCCIA), both of which had requested funds for projects, and the steering committee recommendation was approved by only a thirteen to ten margin. Once again, the relationship with the SCLC was discussed and a retreat was approved to deal with both problems—SCLC and the steering committee.[66]

In May, the delegates committed their efforts to two major projects. Mayor Daley had placed a $195 million bond issue on the 14 June ballot. The funds were designated for street lights, sewers, urban renewal, mass transit, fire and police stations, neighborhood health centers, and garbage disposal. The CCCO had already publicly opposed a school bond referendum scheduled for the November elections unless the "school board adopt [ed] a clear-cut citywide plan for desegregating the school system." Delegates from the Citizens Housing Committee argued that the same standard should be applied to the city improvement bonds: they should be opposed "until and unless the city administration acts to end housing segregation." At the meeting of 7 May, the delegates decided unanimously to oppose this bond issue also.[67]

At the 24 May meeting, the SCLC proposed a citywide rally and march in June. The CCCO and the West Side organizations with which the SCLC was working had not met together since January, and Andrew Young had considerable progress to report: "Eleven locals of the East Garfield Park Union to End Slums have some form of organization"; "efforts have been made to organize Lawndale on a block-by-block basis"; and "the movement has been working with churches, high school students, college students, labor, gangs, etc." Young concluded, "Now is the time to coordinate these activities, bring them together in order to evaluate our strength, present specific demands, and provide an opportunity for an orientation to the movement." Young suggested that a rally for all these purposes be held either 12 or 26 June.

The debate that followed turned not upon whether the rally should be held but upon the choice of date and its relationship to the 14 June bond referendum. Some delegates argued that the rally would stimulate opposition to the bond issue if it were held on 12 June; others thought that date would divert energy away from their efforts against the bonds. Still others supported the later date so as not to make the success of the rally depend on success in opposing the bond issue. In the end, 26 June was chosen.

The day before this meeting Benjamin C. Willis had announced his resignation as general superintendent of the Chicago public schools, four months earlier than expected. This move would have been greeted as a great victory only a year before, but it was only a minor incident when it actually happened. Meyer Weinberg marked the occasion by saying: "A man is going, but the system remains. A man is going, but the damage remains. A man is going, but the sponsors remain. Willis will be gone, but that does not change the system any. We must start working on a platform on how we want the schools run. The demands are: first, repair the damage already done, and, second, no more damage through the school system."

King closed the meeting by urging unity through the CCCO, and he asked nonaffiliated groups to join the coalition so "we can all be on the same path." He emphasized the importance of the 26 June rally: "We must find ourselves committed to social change, but realize there is another force committed to no change. Out of these two forces must come a confrontation. This is the essence of a nonviolent movement. If we are strongly enough committed, we can turn the entire city out for this rally and march. . . . This will begin the summer action program, and this action will continue until our demands are met."

If the bond issue was any test of strength, the Chicago Freedom Movement had a long way to go before its demands would be met. Daley struck deals with the business community to secure its support, bank depositors found pro-bond flyers among their canceled checks, police and firemen donned pro-bond buttons and distributed leaflets door to door, and Roman Catholic Archbishop John Cody plugged the measure from the pulpit. Even major CCCO affiliates, NAACP, TWO, Chicago Urban League, and Catholic Interracial Council, endorsed the bonds. The referendum was passed by a two-to-one margin.[68]

Nonetheless, the die was cast for confrontation beginning with the 26 June rally at Soldier Field. At a press conference on 27 May, King announced a "new phase in Chicago civil rights activity." The organizing work of the SCLC and CCCO "must come to an end," he said, "and we must get about the nonviolent action which we hope will dramatize the problems and call forth a solution."[69] But it was still unclear, even within the councils of the SCLC and CCCO, which problems would be dramatized or what solutions would be sought. The programmatic goals, so elusive and divisive from the beginning of this alliance, remained problematic down to the last moment.

A WHITE HOUSE CONFERENCE, A MARCH IN MISSISSIPPI, AND A CHICAGO RALLY: THE QUESTION OF GOALS

President Johnson's White House conference "To Fulfill These Rights," which was finally held on 1–2 June, showed that this programmatic blur was much more than a local problem in Chicago. The president's agenda, focusing on the black family, had been rejected by civil rights leaders. His hope of charting a new course of social rights to support the national mandate for civil rights had, by the time of the White House conference, been reduced to a strategy of avoiding criticism from civil rights groups and containing the damage the war in Vietnam posed for the president's domestic coalition and program.[70]

In light of the pending Civil Rights Act of 1966, whose major provisions would have extended federal protection to civil rights workers in the South, prohibited the exclusion of blacks from juries, and banned religious and racial discrimination in the rental, sale, and financing of housing, and of the impending SCLC-CCCO campaign in Chicago, one might have expected the White House conference to provide an occasion for coordinating support for both of these; but it was nothing of the sort. King and the Johnson administration were both going their separate ways to defeat in 1966.

Only a year before, the president had checked his Howard University speech with King before its delivery, but in the meantime King had repudiated the speech and attacked Johnson's war policies. At the White House conference, therefore, King was persona non grata. The president who had done the most to promote the civil rights and equality of blacks did not invite the most eloquent spokesman and effective organizer of civil rights claims to speak at his conference. On the eve of the conference, King said he expected it would deal with his civil rights concerns in Chicago, but "only on paper." Constant nonviolent pressure would be required "to make the power structure react to the needs of the people."[71] By September, the Civil Rights Act of 1966 had been abandoned in the Senate, and the nonviolent movement in Chicago had collapsed at the summit.

At the time of the conference, both the administration and the civil rights leaders saw a need to move beyond traditional civil rights concerns. The president's attempt to open new social rights grounds for further national action had misfired. The attempt within the civil rights movement to find some strategic way to expose and break the link between poverty and racism had not yet issued in any clear focus or policy thrust. This was the problem that the SCLC and CCCO faced in Chicago; and in the month preceding the summer campaign it was a very pressing problem indeed.

Relationships were strained all around. In Chicago, the 4 June meeting of the CCCO opened with a procedural controversy over the renomination of Albert Raby as convenor. He was ultimately reelected to his fifth six-month term; but as the CCCO stood on the threshold of its most ambitious action program ever, there were dissenting votes for the first time. As the summer approached there was dissatisfaction with the leadership and the direction of the civil rights movement, local as well as national.

Raby expressed his disappointment with the White House conference,

195

which he had attended; but he noted that the criticism was well taken that the civil rights movement had not been prepared with an alternative to the administration's proposals and "programmed consensus," as another observer had called it. Several of the CCCO delegates responded by stressing the importance of developing their own goals and demands for the 26 June rally; but with three weeks to go, those programmatic demands were still not ready for discussion.

That rally was about to be postponed to 10 July, but not because of events in Chicago. On 6 June, James Meredith was shot in Mississippi. Meredith had just begun a march from the Tennessee state line to Jackson, Mississippi, to encourage black voter registration. King, Floyd McKissick (recently elected national director of CORE), and Stokely Carmichael (newly elected chairman of SNCC) rushed to Memphis and, at Meredith's bedside, agreed to continue the march. The march, which lasted three weeks, was frequently attacked by whites and quickly became an ongoing debate ostensibly over nonviolence versus self-defense, the participation of whites in the civil rights movement, and support for Johnson's civil rights program. In Greenwood, Mississippi, Carmichael electrified a sympathetic crowd with chants of "black power." A slogan was coined, national civil rights leaders were openly split, and the media made both a cause célèbre across the country. King vainly sought to mediate the dispute between McKissick and Carmichael, the advocates of black power, and Roy Wilkins and Whitney Young, the advocates of integration.[72]

If the White House conference had shown the disorientation in the civil rights movement over its programmatic goals, the Meredith march showed it to be in a process of incipient disarray on its moral grounds. The perennial differences in emphasis between advocates of desegregation, integration, and black solidarity were threatening to become differences of principle. Persons and perspectives that had been united in their opposition to the color line were now, under the press of events, beginning to emphasize their distinctiveness rather then their commonality.

It was in this context of declining civil rights prospects nationally, the emergence of black power as a concept and a public issue, rifts among civil rights leaders both nationally and locally, and the specter of ghetto violence that the CCCO and SCLC sought to formulate the demands and strategy to be announced at the 10 July rally. The incipient disarray over the moral grounds of civil rights demands was amply illustrated in the alternative proposals for the summer program in Chicago.

Ever since the establishment of the Chicago Freedom Movement and the adoption of the Chicago Plan in January, the focus had been on the slum as the concrete crystallization of racism and poverty. The sheer scale of this focus made it difficult to imagine how the slum could successfully be dramatized through the use of the SCLC's well-developed technique of nonviolent confrontation. This technique involved the creation of a civic crisis by the mobilization of highly dramatic demonstrations designed to force a corresponding mobilization of civic resources to resolve the crisis. It was critical, in the use of this technique, to have a set of specific goals or demands ready for the time when resolution appeared possible.

The massive scale of the slum, however, was not the only problem this focus posed for the use of nonviolent techniques. Genuine differences of principle were also involved in the choice of targets to be dramatized and resolutions to be demanded. Throughout the winter and into the spring these differences of principle eventuated in three significantly different proposals both for the targets of action and for the demands of the movement. The process of clarifying and harmonizing those differences was an important source of delay in the projection of the programmatic goals of the Chicago Freedom Movement. That more effort was spent harmonizing than clarifying these differences, given all the uncertainties and tensions involved in preparing a Chicago campaign, was probably inevitable, but it was to leave the movement in a weakened position when the time for resolution appeared.

These differences in principle were exemplified in the development of three program directions, each aimed at identifying the strategic point of entry for producing change in the existing dynamics of the color line in the creation and perpetuation of the slum. The first program was James Bevel's Union to End Slums. This strategy commanded most attention within the Chicago Freedom Movement during the winter and spring. It was essentially a black power strategy even though it was not called that. It was a strategy of organizing power for the powerless in black communities, mobilizing the ghetto by organizing tenant unions to negotiate with slum landlords, and forcing local and national policy attention on the immediate condition and the underlying power relations that produced those conditions. King helped to dramatize this thrust by moving into a slum apartment on the West Side and identifying his presence in Chicago with grass-roots and ghetto issues. The CCCO's efforts at organizing in the Kenwood-Oakland area, the West Side Organization's move into "welfare unions," and the North Side's focus on the Jenner School were all efforts to join the strategy of nonviolence to the everyday issues of poverty and powerlessness in the ghetto.

At the same time, William H. Moyer was continuing the American Friends Service Committee's program of research into discrimination by real estate agents in Chicago. This research was part of a fair housing program which the AFSC had sustained since the race riots in Cicero in 1951. In January, this was only one of numerous issues and targets then on the movement's agenda, and it was by no means a high priority. In a report distributed by the AFSC in February, Moyer advanced three propositions: that the black ghetto was cre-

197

ated and maintained by the policies and practices of real estate agents; that such confinement of blacks to the ghetto, at a time when the black population was increasing, artificially created a low supply and a high demand for black housing; and that, as a result, blacks got less housing for their dollar than did whites. Moyer called this phenomenon the "color tax."[73]

Using figures from the 1960 census, Moyer found that both white and non-white families paid the same median monthly rent of $78, although the median income of white families was 50 percent greater than that of nonwhites. The median-sized housing unit occupied by whites was 3.95 rooms and that of nonwhites was 3.35, although the median white household had fewer members than the nonwhite household. The nonwhite housing was more likely to be dilapidated or deteriorated. In other words, Moyer said, "Negroes pay the same for slums that whites pay for good conditions." Moyer concluded, "The role of supply and demand will always hold true and Negroes will continue to pay a color tax for housing until the entire housing market is open."[74]

During the spring of 1966, the AFSC initiated a project along the lines suggested by Moyer's analysis. On 12 February, members of eleven black families went separately to eleven different real estate offices in Oak Park, a predominantly white Chicago suburb. The committee found that "all were refused service offered to white home seekers. Only one family was shown a house by a realtor—the house was located next door to one of the few Negro families now living in Oak Park." The AFSC conducted a series of such demonstrations "to reduce [this] social problem to its basic truth so that the public can understand it and respond to correct the evil." By May, some thirty black families had been refused service by Baird and Warner, the real estate agency that became the focus of demonstrations held outside its office every weekend.[75] The implication for policy and the inner principle of this strategy was a demand for the desegregation of the housing market, that is, to end the slums through desegregating access to housing, thus eliminating the built-in exploitation of blacks that was inevitable in a two-market housing system.

A third proposal toward ending slums was advocated by the Citizens Housing Committee, a longtime CCCO member. Although it, too, deplored the color tax in housing, this report focused on the housing needs of the entire society and the failure of government housing programs to achieve their objectives: "Despite seventeen years of government clearance, the actual number of poor housing units has increased. . . . After twenty-seven years of public aids to provide low-rent housing, less than 800,000 units have been built—and thirty-six million Americans, mainly of low-incomes, still live in inferior shelter. Though government has given financial assistance to the private housing industry for thirty-two years, it is more profitable to own and operate slums than to build new housing for America's moderate income majority." Therefore, because "better homes, improved communities, and a free

198

and open market cannot be achieved in a housing economy based on short supply and racial discrimination . . . the Freedom Movement must call for a complete redirection of government housing and planning programs at all levels. To meet our mounting needs we must, first of all, *build housing*—with a public priority on a dramatic increase in low- and middle-income units, and a postponement of clearance for all but the most hazardous buildings." This proposal represented an integrationist approach to ending slums. The implications of this priority were detailed in concluding sections of the report on federally aided clearance, low-rent housing, middle-income housing, urban renewal, slum profits, federal housing code standards, and "democracy in housing and planning," and the implication was that both the supply and the distribution of housing had to be altered if slum ghettos were to be ended.[76]

Whereas Moyer's research had focused on the role of real estate agents in the color tax, the Citizens Housing Committee's report emphasized the failure of government programs to expand the housing supply. Each document suggested demands and strategies different from Bevel's goal of organizing tenant unions to negotiate with slum landlords. Moyer's proposal to seek equal access to an existing social good, in this case housing, was a desegregationist goal. The Citizens Housing Committee's proposal to create an open housing market by providing more and better housing for the entire society was an integrationist goal. Bevel's proposal to improve slum housing by increasing the power of the indigenous community was a black power goal. Each of these positions differed in emphasis and possibly in principle, and each potentially led to a substantially different strategy for action and a different set of demands.

In contrast to these clear alternatives that emerged in relation to housing, the proposals developed by the CCCO's education committee included all three emphases in a single document. The major focus was on school desegregation, and the committee draft advocated improved enforcement of existing desegregation laws, federal and state funds for overcoming racial imbalance, additional litigation based on the Fourteenth Amendment, and similar proposals. The draft also had an integrationist thrust in its call for a "national budget for quality integrated education," emphasizing the need to increase the resources available as well as the distribution of existing ones. The demand that the school board nominating commission "represent, primarily, people with children in the public schools" and the threat that "if the 'authorities' fail to educate children, the parents must do so" correlated with black power aims, even though they did not go all the way to demand "community control."[77]

This same tension of alternative principles was evident in the first overall draft of the movement program in early June. It listed a total of fifty-three demands in the areas of employment-income-finance, housing, education,

199

public welfare, and health. Many called for lifting the barriers of discrimination from existing social goods, a demand for desegregation. Others, such as the demand for a guaranteed annual wage, advocated integrationist redistributive policies. The demand for an economic development program for inner cities could be understood in either an integrationist or a black power context, although the tilt was toward black power. The ambivalent ordering of these principles is reflected in alternative titles for this draft: one version was called "One Chicago and One America for All!"; another, "Demands for Creating an Open City."[78]

A second draft ten days later clearly articulated all three aims. It began:

The goals of the Chicago Freedom Movement are:
1. To provide power for the powerless.
2. To equalize opportunity and results.
3. To establish an open metropolis.

The first was a black power emphasis; the second, integrationist; the third, desegregationist.[79]

The first section of this draft described the "primary function" of the freedom movement as "a means of providing power to the powerless and freedom from intimidation for the subjugated." The examples given made clear the black power emphasis: strengthening black economic institutions; organizing welfare recipients, public housing tenants, and public school students and parents; and increasing black leadership roles in ghetto institutions and policy-making bodies. A second section focused on the slum as an underdeveloped region, a "reservation . . . isolated from the body politic" resulting from "neocolonial" exploitation. A massive social and economic program similar to the Marshall Plan was called for; Congress was asked to appropriate $250 million to $500 million for each of three redevelopment authorities in Chicago. Again, this demand could be read in both black power and integrationist contexts. A final section expanded the list of specific demands to seventy-five. Many, but not all, called for desegregationist policies.[80]

The committee planning the rally met on 29 June to complete its work on the program aware that no clear strategy had yet been developed for pursuing the demands. Bevel began the discussion by urging that housing be given priority. At present, he said, "Negroes are restricted to reservations. [But] he is a man and must have a house. [We] need to go for broke on this issue. This will give a logical action program . . . and helps us deal with the ghetto people."[81] McDermott agreed with the housing emphasis but on desegregationist grounds: "We should call for a program [by the real estate board] to discipline members or throw them out, and call upon [the] state to license realtors who pledge this." Raby was concerned to get "some things on this paper we can mobilize around," to get into position where "we can give 15 July as the day we send one thousand people to do this thing or that thing." Bevel then linked his black power aims to a desegregationist strategy: "Go to Cicero and demonstrate day and night on the realtor companies. Go into all white neighborhoods [and] demonstrate until [the] housing is open. Leaflet churches every Sunday. Start demonstrations in slums against paying rent. . . . [We need a] simple real action program so the whole world knows about Chicago. Otherwise we dissipate our energy."

With the rally less than two weeks away, neither the programmatic goals nor the strategic focus of the action were yet settled. King expressed concern at the state of the planning, but he was assured that the complete list of demands would be ready for the rally and that the committee was discussing "an immediate action program." King then expressed his preference for the "whole idea of an Open City": "Congress is debating this issue of open housing this session. You can present bodies or bring about creative tension to expose the problem most creatively. Also economic and school problems are bound to this open city idea." Andrew Young agreed: "We want one target that will make several other targets tumble. Whenever the negotiations start, you need to talk about the many other things that you want. 'Open City' is a good battle cry. . . . You got to stick with gut issues. Open City is better than housing. There are so many things you can mobilize around." In the end, the committee approved defining the issue as "open city" and made "open housing" the first target.

The final version of the Chicago Freedom Movement program, published in July, restated all three goals:

1. To bring about equality of opportunity and results.
2. To open up the major areas of metropolitan life of housing, employment, and education.
3. To provide power for the powerless.

The earlier drafts were summarized, and the long list of demands was included. But, the final section, "Selected Immediate Action Demands—Summer 1966," began: "For our primary target we have chosen housing. As of July 10 we shall cease to be accomplices to a housing system of discrimination, segregation, and degradation. We shall begin to act as if Chicago were an open city. We shall act on the basis that every man is entitled to full access of buying or renting housing that is sound, attractive, and reasonably priced." Fourteen specific open housing demands were listed. The first two were addressed to real estate boards and brokers: "all listings immediately available on a nondiscriminatory basis" and "endorsement of and support for open occupancy."[82]

For the sake of strategy, the die had been cast for desegregation as the thrust of the campaign.

Black power could not be ignored, however, and final preparations for the 10 July rally took place amid continuing controversy over it. It was announced that Floyd McKissick of CORE would address the Chicago rally, but King canceled his speaking engagement at CORE's national convention in Baltimore, which, as expected, repudiated nonviolence and affirmed black power. A television interview by King promoting the rally turned into a discussion of black power. "It is absolutely necessary for Negroes to have power," King said, but "it is absurd and impractical to think Negroes can make it alone." He did not foresee "any real future" for violent tactics because they do not "appeal to the majority of the black people."[83] Throughout that summer, King was much more concerned to defend nonviolence than he was to attack black power. The reason is understandable: black power was one of the major threads of his Chicago campaign. That is why King tried to mediate the dispute between black power and integration when it broke out on the Meredith march; and that is why he remained irenic toward black power advocates, even when they were attacking him, throughout the summer.

When Roy Wilkins of the NAACP also criticized black power, Illinois Democratic Governor Otto Kerner phoned to arrange a meeting with Wilkins to discuss "civil rights problems in Chicago." Kerner suggested that King "had not attracted the public support he expected in Chicago because of the inability of Negro organizations to consolidate their forces behind one man." Wilkins was not willing to be used that way.[84]

At the rally, King was introduced to the forty thousand people gathered by a statement from Chicago's Archbishop Cody in which the prelate identified himself with the struggle against "discrimination and injustice . . . here in Chicago" and made special pleas to the trade unions to open their membership to the business community to increase merit employment and job training for minorities, and to real estate boards to support open occupancy laws. His support was important for desegregationist goals.[85]

King's own address was a defense of nonviolence. His rejection of violence was cast in pragmatic terms: "The ultimate weakness of a riot is that it can be halted by superior force. We have neither the techniques, the numbers, nor the weapons to win a violent campaign." Instead, he called upon blacks to declare their "own emancipation proclamation and make any sacrifices necessary to change Chicago": to "decide to fill up the jails of Chicago, if necessary, in order to end slums" and to "decide that our votes will determine who will be the next mayor of Chicago."[86]

McKissick's speech defended the use of the term "black power." It "has no connotations of violence," he said. "It means economic and social programs through Negro unity," the very doctrine King had been preaching since he came to Chicago. In response, however, one hundred members of a Chicago street gang waved placards that combined the legends "We Shall Overcome" and "Freedom Now" with drawings of a submachine gun.[87] Such were the ambiguities of the black power slogan.

After the rally, many of those present joined King and Raby in a march into the Loop, where they posted the movement's demands on the door of City Hall. The action phase had begun in Chicago.

It took almost a year for the SCLC to make the transition to Chicago, to find a focus for its nonviolent campaign, to explore the alternative grounds for urban action, to fashion a strategy, to gain public attention, and to establish a workable alliance with the CCCO and other organizations; and each of these was still uncertain of accomplishment by the Soldier Field Rally of 10 July, the time set for a new beginning in Chicago. The transition had proved more complex than anyone had imagined. In early August 1965, the plan was that the SCLC would be in Chicago to intensify a Fall Freedom Program focused on the schools. By September, SCLC staff were anticipating an action program in the spring at the earliest. By July 1966, the pieces were barely in place for an open city campaign. A review of the general situation shows why this transition took longer than expected and was only imperfectly accomplished.

The issue of civil rights was in transition that year. The national focus was turning toward the many issues which the CCCO had found so elusive of resolution in Chicago—the institutionalized links between poverty and racism. President Johnson's domestic policy had linked poverty, racism, education, and urban policy, and the president tried to articulate a doctrine of social rights to support the gains that had been made in civil rights. On the link between poverty and racism, however, the president had taken a wrong conceptual turn in explaining the contemporary widening gulf between black and white as attributable to causes in the past, the heritage of slavery, and in identifying the Negro family as the source of present problems. As a result, he found himself increasingly at odds with the civil rights leadership. His attempt to make a new beginning in breaking the link between poverty and racism had misfired.

King's move to Chicago was a significant step in the civil rights movement's search for a new beginning in articulating and breaking the institutional link between poverty and racism. It was clear from the start to King and his associates that urban segregation posed problems both of principle and of policy which differed substantially from Jim Crow. In early January King decided to focus the issue on the slum as the most concrete consequence of poverty and racism. The problem then became twofold: to develop his techniques of nonviolent confrontation to dramatize the injustice of the slum, and

203

to develop a coherent set of demands so that, when nonviolent confrontation had created a civic crisis, ideas for its resolution would be at hand. Discussion of these two problems consumed the first half of the year 1966.

Developing a coherent set of demands gave rise to alternative grounds or principles for civil rights activities in Chicago. When Jim Crow had been the problem, ending legal segregation was the obvious moral imperative. Urban segregation presented an empirically and normatively more complex problem. In Chicago, with a ghetto of a million residents in 1966, some principle of black power obviously made moral sense. Before the Meredith march, this principle went under a variety of names: "grass roots," "ghetto issues," "power for the powerless," "participation in policy making," and the like. Yet in a society with racial discrimination the rule in schools, housing, jobs, and public services, some appeal to the principle of desegregation to eliminate arbitrarily imposed inequalities also made obvious moral sense. Finally, in a society with one political system and one economic system, both functionally coordinated, some principle of redistributive integration was morally requisite for breaking the institutional link between poverty and racism.

These three morally obvious principles, however, created serious problems for developing a coherent strategy because the advocates of each tended to discount or belittle the proposals of the others. Early on, James Bevel perceived the importance of the black power principle in Chicago, and he tended to discount any moves that were not grounded in it. He did not perceive, however, that the black power appeal was also Mayor Daley's strongest point. The mayor was an expert at distributing jobs, programs, and offices on an ethnic basis. To be sure, Bevel had a very different sort of "empowering the powerless" program in mind than the mayor did, but the two were directly competitive in an area in which the mayor had a considerable material advantage by virtue of his political organization and Lyndon Johnson's domestic program. This is one of the major reasons why, when it came to making strategic decisions for the action program, Bevel yielded his black power sentiments in favor of a desegregation strategy. But until the very last moment, he held out for an alternative, even if vaguely articulated, vision.

The integrationists, who had basically set the tone in the CCCO over the years, were faced with a similar collapse of strategy based on their principle. If black power ran into the realities of local politics in the summer of 1966, integration ran into the realities of national politics. Integrationist policies required large new federal commitments of resources to domestic problems and a corresponding commitment to deploy them in deliberately counterracist ways. Integrationists generally had supported President Johnson's Great Society programs because they represented such federal commitments; but by 1966, civil rights leaders were at odds with the administration because this money seemed to be paying for further segregation. The administration was at odds with the civil rights leaders, especially King, because their protests about the distribution of resources seemed to threaten the federal commitment per se. The CCCO complaint to the Office of Education, charging that the new federal commitment to education was being used in Chicago to extend a segregated system, and the administration's rapid retreat even from investigating the complaint, were especially dramatic examples of the weakness of integrationist policies, which had come to be perceived in Washington as directly competitive with and threatening to the president's Great Society programs. Integrationists were placed in a politically untenable position. Their vision required an effective national commitment, but the administration had come to view them as a threat to its program. With no place to go nationally, integrationists found themselves in an increasingly weak position locally.

Thus the desegregationist principle was left as the only politically viable and morally legitimate gathering point for a local coalition in Chicago and elsewhere. Even though desegregation had its problems, too, at least it provided common ground which both advocates of black power and integration could affirm, and it provided a strategic focus for action: policies and practices of racial discrimination and exclusion embodied in identifiable institutions such as the real estate profession. Thus, after nearly a year of tensions generated by the rising popularity of black power sentiments and declining prospects for integrationist policies, the Chicago Freedom Movement resolved the tension at the last moment by espousing the desegregationist principle and strategy under the slogan of an "open city" with "open housing" as the first target. The movement, as if by a process of elimination, was finally committed to an encounter with the problems of action based on the principles of desegregation.

That commitment had been arrived at by a difficult process of trial and error, made highly visible by the presence of Martin Luther King, Jr., and the SCLC. It attracted many new groups into the CCCO, especially prestigious black clergy and selected labor representatives. The mayor was careful to maintain a public attitude of civic welcome for King and to stress his own commitment to civil rights and, as the issue evolved, to ending slums. The mayor was not about to antagonize King or become the symbol of recalcitrant racism. King's move to Chicago, however, coincided with his loss of favor at the White House, as both he and the mayor knew. Thus when the Office of Education threatened to withhold federal funds from Chicago, the mayor was able to move quickly to counter it, knowing that there was little that King could actually do. The congressional repercussions of that episode, moreover, were severe for the prospects of further civil rights legislation because an occasion had been created for mobilizing big city white Democrats who had supported anti–Jim Crow legislation to propose serious limitations on the application of that legislation to the problems of urban segregation.

Thus, throughout the year, King had to cope with significant losses in his previous base of national support while trying to establish a significant base of local and politically visible support for a program whose focus remained as unclear to its supporters as it did to the public at large. The takeover of a slum building on the West Side backfired symbolically. It was owned by an old man who was himself impoverished, and it became an occasion for the mayor to show that he could do more about slums than King could. But King was still a popular and charismatic figure. His appearances at local neighborhood events and his fund-raising for the Chicago campaign attracted attention and created an expectation that something big was going to happen on the civil rights front in Chicago.

The mayor did not want to be on the losing side, and so he maintained the position that "we have no apology to any civil rights leaders who come into our city to tell us what to do." That was as abrasive as he got. For the most part, he tried to outpromise and outperform King, especially on the issue of slums. He even got a new bond issue, which was targeted on slum problems. The Board of Education, for so long the object of civil rights protests, did not want to be a victim either, so it got Willis out of office before the summer. The board did not care to become the symbol of recalcitrant racism. The Chicago Real Estate Board, however, failed to foresee the impact of King's movement. When the demonstrations began in Oak Park, neither the realtors involved nor the real estate board saw any need for accommodation. Their lack of perception would have consequences.

Throughout the year, however, the major developments were internal to the movement. The problem was to uncover sufficiently rich and agreeable grounds to allow the SCLC and the CCCO jointly to make a new beginning in the assault on urban segregation. Both relationships and principles were severely tested in the process. Though both the SCLC and the CCCO leaders were sincere in their desire to join together and make a new beginning, neither could afford—morally—to abandon its past. The CCCO admitted the failure of its previous efforts, but its leaders, especially Raby, were convinced that clear programmatic goals were necessary both to hold a coalition together and to avoid public embarrassment. The SCLC, on the other hand, was committed to the philosophy and tactics of nonviolent confrontation. The task of coordinating these with detailed and researched programmatic goals was complicated by the emergence of controversy over the ultimate principle of the action program—black power, integration, and desegregation, either singly or in some combination. Sorting through these conflicts was a difficult enterprise. There were those who believed that the failures of the past were traceable to any or all of the following: wrong leadership, wrong issue, wrong principle, wrong tactics. The addition of the SCLC was an attempt to upgrade the leadership. The switch to emphasis on the slum was an attempt to sharpen

206

the strategic issue. The alternative proposals for action embodied attempts to clarify the principle and promote the choice of one or another. Only on tactics was there broad agreement—the aim was massive nonviolent confrontation carried to a point of civic crisis.

Thus the projected purposes of the civil rights movement addressed the dilemma of constitutional duties by seeking to crystallize the issues in publicly persuasive ways and to concentrate the action so forcefully that public officials would be compelled to resolve the ensuing civic crisis, perhaps through civic coercion.

The course of the Chicago Freedom Movement had been less certain in relation to the dilemmas of black dignity and white culture. Whereas Bevel had regularly called for mobilization of the ghetto around distinctive issues of black manhood, King had repeatedly insisted on the role of the white majority and had proposed a human rights interpretation of issues, which appealed to common cultural values.

Here, too, the desegregationist principle provided a middle way. The black minority was to be mobilized, to be sure, but around the general theme of an open city, beginning with desegregating the real estate market—both goals more in line with the common culture and potentially more capable of attracting white consent and support than ending the slums.

These were the purposes that animated the rally of 10 July 1966, the beginning of the much desired new beginning in Chicago.

207

CHAPTER EIGHT

Confrontations with Violence:

July–August 1966

The day following the rally at Soldier Field, Monday, 11 July 1966, King and Raby met with Mayor Daley to present the movement's demands. Daley listened "sympathetically" but repeatedly cited the "massive programs" the city had already undertaken— "housing inspection, eliminating slums and blight, rodent and insect control, and merit employment." "What would you do that we haven't done?" he asked. According to Daley, King and Raby "had no answers." According to King and Raby, Daley had made "only surface changes, and the Negro community can no longer live with token changes."[1]

King emerged from the three-hour meeting to tell waiting reporters that the mayor had made no commitments and therefore "many more marches" would be held that summer. King said he did not think Daley understood "the depth and dimensions of the problem we are dealing with," but that did not mean the mayor was a "bigot": "The current programs are in good faith; they are just not broad enough to be effective."[2]

For his part, Daley recommitted himself to progress on the issues he had discussed with King: "These problems can't be solved overnight and no reasonable person believes they can. We have need for massive action. We will continue it. I am not proud of the slums. No one is. We will expand our programs." Daley thought he and King were in agreement on overall objectives: "Dr. King is very sincere in what he is trying to do. Maybe, at times, he doesn't have all the facts on the local situation. After all, he is a resident of another city. He admitted himself they have the same problems in Atlanta." Asked about King's statement that civil rights groups were prepared to fill Chicago's jails if necessary, Daley responded there was "no reason" for that, and, in any case, it would "not be tolerated in Chicago as long as I am mayor." Besides, the mayor concluded, "I don't think Dr. King would violate any law. He said he was not for violence."[3]

The positions of the spring had been reiterated; the lines for the summer had been drawn.

The Tuesday *Sun-Times* editorially applauded King's list of demands because they "reflect in general the sentiments of conscientious citizens" and "parallel proposals made by responsible persons in private enterprise and public life who believe that racial inequity and discrimination are not only morally wrong but economically unwise." This view, however, was not universally shared. The Chicago Real Estate Board, the Chicago Housing Authority, and the State Street Council all issued statements through their officers rejecting the demands that applied to them. Jack Kleeman, executive vice-president of the Chicago Real Estate Board, responded to the demand for open occupancy legislation by saying, "We're opposed to the use of the force of law in this area." Charles R. Swibel, chairman of the Chicago Housing Authority, responded to the demand that public housing be developed outside the ghetto by citing limitations in the availability and cost of land. Samuel J. Fosdick, managing director of the State Street Council, said he did not think a racial head count of employees would be helpful, adding, "The very idea of a head count is discriminatory."[4]

Indeed, the only enthusiasm for King's proposals came from Charles H. Percy, Republican candidate for the U.S. Senate; he found the demand for the replacement of absentee precinct captains "entirely justified." "There are a great number of absentee Democratic precinct captains in the city. Citizens cannot be served effectively when their captains live elsewhere." Third Ward Democratic Alderman Ralph H. Metcalf, however, thought it "not within the purview of outsiders to tell a political party how it shall conduct its affairs."[5]

As all these reactions came in, the Chicago Freedom Movement was still trying to determine its final plan of action. It had been announced at the rally that the campaign of nonviolent demonstrations would begin on the next weekend, 16–17 July; but in the wiser councils of the movement the strategic focus had not yet crystallized, and the leaders were still wondering what to do when the demonstrators who had been recruited at the rally reported for their instructions.

It was only during the rally weekend that it was discovered, through an analysis of census data, how low the housing costs were in white ethnic neighborhoods. During the week following the rally, a plan was developed to visit real estate offices in some of those neighborhoods. The right to be served equally and fairly by real estate agents seemed a simple demand around which to organize, analogous to the demand in the South for fair and equal treatment at lunch counters. Apparently there was some thought that these white ethnic neighborhoods might provide Chicago's equivalent to Birmingham's Bull Connor, but that was not the overriding concern in the choice of an action strategy. The determining factor was the apparent simplicity of the demand: equal treatment.[6]

Events, however, were about to force an unplanned but not wholly unanticipated test of the power and persuasiveness of nonviolence in the turbulent context of the West Side ghetto. Indeed, as King had expected, nonviolence was on trial in Chicago in 1966, but not perhaps in quite the way he had expected. The nonviolent campaign had to make its way, first in the context of black violence and open anger about the abrasions of ghetto life; then, as the demonstrations began, in the context of white violence and open anger about any breach in the color line. In the end, this release of anger created the civic crisis that had to be resolved by summer's end.

BLACK VIOLENCE: A CHALLENGE
TO KING'S PRINCIPLES

On the Tuesday after the Soldier Field Rally, 12 July, the fear of a ghetto riot—shared by movement leaders and city officials alike—began to materialize out of a minor incident.

Chicago was in the grip of a week-long heat wave, and children sought relief in the spray of open fire hydrants. Although a city ordinance prohibited turning on hydrants except in emergencies, generations of Chicago children have played in their waters, usually under the indulgent eyes of the police. Because the heat wave threatened to lower water pressure, Fire Commissioner Robert Quinn ordered the hydrants sealed. At the corner of Roosevelt Road and Throop Street on the near West Side, an altercation arose when two patrolmen repeatedly turned off a hydrant only to have it reopened. At one point, the gathering crowd of observers protested the arrest of someone turning on the hydrant. Rocks and bottles were thrown at the police car; the patrolmen radioed for help. The thirty squads that responded were confronted by a crowd growing larger and angrier by the minute. Five or six teenagers were bloodied when the police used their clubs; bystanders were shoved and beaten by the police in their efforts to clear the street corner.[7]

As the tension mounted, Chester Robinson and other staff members of the West Side Organization (WSO) tried to intervene—initially by urging that the fire hydrant be left open, then by moving the crowd to WSO headquarters two blocks away. Police refused when requested to release those arrested and to withdraw their forces while WSO workers attempted to calm the unruly crowd. King was scheduled to hold a meeting at 10:00 P.M. in nearby Shiloh Baptist Church. The crowds that gathered there were restless. As one observer reported, "Many on the outside refused to hear King, declaring they did not want to be talked to about nonviolence in the face of what they were convinced was police brutality." Inside, King told the hundreds assembled that they were there "because we are all concerned about conditions we face in the City of Chicago, and we are determined to do something about it." He charged that "some of our brothers in Chicago tonight faced serious police brutality. They were arrested unnecessarily and they were victims of the system that exists in this city." But King's call for nonviolence was ineffectual. Some listeners walked out. Others shouted, "End police brutality." In an effort to hold the audience, Robinson suggested a march to the police station, where he believed scores of arrested teenagers were being held. This idea was rejected by other civil rights leaders. The meeting deteriorated in confusion.[8]

Outside the church, the crowd had grown to more than a thousand. When three Puerto Ricans in an automobile blundered into the crowd, only the physical intervention of WSO workers saved their lives. The rioting on the West Side began in earnest. King and other civil rights workers made the WSO their headquarters as they tried to accomplish in the streets what they had failed to accomplish in the meeting: to stem the violence. These efforts were not successful. Ten persons were injured and twenty-four arrested that night as blocks of store windows were smashed and nine stores were looted.[9]

Wednesday morning, Mayor Daley refused to characterize these events as a "riot"—he used the words "juvenile incident." King, however, had no such reservations. He called it a riot and blamed it on the police and city administration. He and his staff spent the morning working with the WSO to organize a noon-hour community meeting of businessmen, ministers, gang leaders, and others from the disturbed area. There, teenage grievances against the police and local businesses were aired at length.[10]

The neighborhood remained on edge throughout the day, and passing police cars were the object of whistles and jeers. No attempt was made to stop water play in the hydrants, an activity which by then had definite connotations of defiance. In the evening, however, the hydrants were repeatedly and forcefully turned off. Once again, the bricks began to fly. Even the arrival of a long-awaited cool front did not dampen the mounting tension.[11]

That evening was the regular Wednesday meeting time for the WSO, and its storefront headquarters was packed. Teen leaders presented their complaints in the presence of Police Task Force Commander James Hackett. "Speaker after speaker made allegations of police brutality and insensitivity" relating both to Tuesday night and to countless previous incidents. The prevailing attitude was that the police had provoked the violence by their handling of a minor juvenile incident. The police, however, defended their actions and lectured the audience on morality, law, and order. Most of the gang leaders stalked out of the meeting. Andrew Young's call for nonviolence was interrupted by a teenager who shouted his impatience with so much "talk" and invited his "black brothers . . . out on the street." Several more left to cries of "black power." In

211

contrast, John Crawford, the WSO worker instrumental in saving the Puerto Ricans the night before, castigated the "cowardly," "irrational," and "purposeless" behavior of the gangs. In his eyes, both nonviolence and black power were irrelevant to ending the violence and police brutality. Eventually, white clergy and reporters were asked to leave so that the neighborhood people could "get themselves together." As they walked into the street, molotov cocktails and firearms were beginning to go off. In time, they all left the area shaken but unharmed. [12]

That night the violence spread a mile north to West Madison Avenue, the scene of rioting the previous year. Several stores there and near the WSO were fire-bombed. Firemen were stoned when they attempted to extinguish the blazes. Some sniper shots were fired from a public housing project. Dozens of stores were vandalized and looted. It was after midnight before the hundreds of police had restored order. Eleven persons, including six police, were wounded and thirty-five were arrested. [13]

On Thursday, Mayor Daley met with key members of his administration, among them, Police Superintendent O. W. Wilson, Fire Commissioner Robert J. Quinn, Edward Marciniak of the Chicago Commission on Human Relations, and Charles Swibel of the Chicago Housing Authority. The mayor presented no surprises following the meeting; he had decided to stand pat. Daley said that although he would not hesitate to call in the National Guard, Superintendent Wilson had assured him that "the police had the matter under control." Wilson charged that there were "elements in the community which seem to be intent on destroying the effectiveness of police by charging police brutality." Marciniak requested that community leaders not call any meetings for Thursday night. "The West Side Organization has been holding nightly meetings out there and in my opinion it has not helped," he said. [14]

Chester Robinson, however, continued his efforts. He held a meeting Thursday afternoon with local parents to "find out how we can keep people off the street" and organized two hundred teenagers to canvass housing projects that evening in a call for a rent strike against the city. "We are trying to channel their energies into constructive nonviolent programs," he said. "We don't have any good ball parks or swimming pools, so we are going to demand that we get facilities to keep the kids off the corners." He could have added that because of the impenetrable color line, blacks had access to only one of the four park district swimming pools located within walking distance of the incident Tuesday night. [15]

At a meeting late Thursday afternoon at Shiloh Baptist Church, 150 clergy from across the city heard King respond to O. W. Wilson's allegations.

> King's anger was controlled, but very intense, as he talked of his encounter with the mayor on Monday of that week, of the insensitivity of Daley's response to his pleas for correction of the police abuse and for provision of adequate recreation facilities

in the ghetto. . . . King gave credit [to] . . .the WSO staff for their leadership in helping to avert a situation far worse than had actually occurred. He acknowledged his fear of losing his own leadership among the people, because he hadn't been able to produce a victory for them through nonviolent means. President Kennedy's dictum was quoted: "Those who would make a peaceful revolution impossible make a violent revolution inevitable." Dr. King then said emotionally, "I'm trying desperately to lead a nonviolent movement. I must say I need some help in getting this faith across. . . . So many people have lost faith in a democratic society and in nonviolence." At this point the audience responded with a long and emotional expression of support. King repeated Robinson's request that if the ministers and nuns agreed to go into the streets that night, they should look for specific instances of police insensitivity and brutality, recalling that almost every recent major urban disturbance stemmed from an alleged misuse of police power. "On the streets one learns that there is bitterness and hatred of police. These feelings just didn't come from nowhere," he said.

After the meeting, some fifty clergy patrolled the neighborhood urging the restoration of peace. The WSO area was quiet that night.[16]

Two and three miles to the west, however, Lawndale and Garfield Park exploded. Stores were looted and fire-bombed. Shots were exchanged between police and snipers at a dozen locations. Two persons were shot to death. One was a fourteen-year-old pregnant girl innocently standing on her own front porch. In all, more than thirty persons were wounded and two hundred were arrested. Police morale plummeted as a thousand officers were unable to restore order. With cries of police brutality in the air, some of the police countered by blaming the situation on the restraints that had been imposed on them. As one officer said: "We could have stopped this rioting the first day by laying out one or two of those guys with guns. You wouldn't shoot at a kid ten or twelve, but if you laid out a couple of older ones, their friends would go home and stay there." At police area headquarters on West Maxwell, a hand-lettered sign was taped to the waste basket: "Drop badges here," it said. In a futile attempt to "do something," police arrested twenty-one members of ACT in a raid on a West Side apartment, charging them with conspiracy to commit treason and disorderly conduct. The charges were groundless, motivated by settling old scores left over from the riot of the year before.[17]

The looting continued past dawn Friday morning. Superintendent Wilson acknowledged that "the situation has grown beyond the capacity of the police to deal with it." The affected area was sealed off by police. Fire stations inside the cordon were evacuated. Mayor Daley requested mobilization of the National Guard. In his televised press conference announcing this action, the mayor blamed the riots on the SCLC: "I think you cannot charge it directly to Martin Luther King, but surely some of the people came in here and have been talking for the last year in violence and showing pictures and instructing people in how to conduct violence. They are on his staff. They are responsible in

213

a great measure for the instruction that has been given for the training of youngsters." Rev. J. H. Jackson agreed. "I believe our young people are not vicious enough to attack a whole city," he told a press conference. "Some other forces are using these young people."[18]

At the time King and Raby were at the Palmer House with a hundred business, labor, religious, and social agency leaders in a meeting called by the CCCO and SCLC to press Mayor Daley for a creative response to the violence. Raymond Simon of the mayor's office was present as an observer, but he was unable or unwilling to arrange for a delegation to see the mayor. King and Raby led a group to City Hall anyway. In an immediate response to the mayor's press conference, Archbishop Cody, Rabbi Robert J. Marx of the Chicago area Union of American Hebrew Congregations, and Donald Zimmerman and Edgar Chandler of the Church Federation went to the West Side to release a statement criticizing those "who have connected these disturbances with legitimate efforts by men of good will to correct the injustices which some members of minority groups are still forced to endure in our society."[19]

When King's delegation was admitted to the mayor's office, Daley was ready to oil the waters he had disturbed only hours before. "Dr. King," he began, "I want to make one thing clear. We know you did nothing to cause the disorders and that you are a man of peace and love." The mayor then asked what the group "thought could be done." According to Berry, "We were worried about now, right now, and so we didn't go back to the big problems." A five-point agreement was worked out and announced to the press. It called for installation of sprayer attachments on fire hydrants; equal access to parks and swimming pools, enforced by the park district and police; precinct captains to urge residents to stay off the streets in the riot area; construction of more swimming pools and playgrounds in the area; and appointment of a citizens' advisory committee on police-community relations. "We think this is a good step," King told reporters. He said the appointment of the advisory committee was "the most important concession," but it "falls short of the police civilian review board we requested."[20]

At 6:00 P.M., 1,500 National Guard troops moved into the West Side. Another 2,400 were mobilized in reserve. Except for a few isolated incidents that night, the riot was over. In all, 61 police had been injured and 533 citizens had been arrested.[21]

The next day's *Tribune* carried the stories of the Daley-King agreement and the end of the violence, but it subordinated both reports to Daley's allegations of SCLC responsibility for the riot. The headline was "Links Riots and King Aids." Editorially, the *Tribune* rejected all charges of police brutality and reasserted its own "white man's" version of law and order. The rioters should be sentenced "to get out of the city within thirty days and never to come

214

back," the *Tribune* intoned. "If a judge regards this as too tough a penalty, he doesn't deserve to be on the bench." If that was not possible because of "legal objections," the *Tribune* urged that police take matters into their own hands and "pick up known rioters whenever and wherever they are seen, making life so unpleasant for them that they will be forced to leave town of their own volition." Calling for "railroading" and harassment, the *Tribune* editorial page was as inflammatory as anything that had been said on the streets of the West Side.[22]

The mayor's enthusiasm for King's proposals knew no bounds. Columnist Mike Royko summarized the events of the next days:

Now there was a program, and Daley liked it. Give them water. He had a whole lake right outside the door. . . . City Hall embarked on a crusade to make Chicago's blacks the wettest in the country. Portable swimming pools were being trucked in. Sprinklers were attached to hundreds of hydrants, and water was gushing everywhere. The city's department of planning mobilized to launch a long-range program of black wetness. The Chicago Park District joined in. So did the Fire Department. Suddenly the entire city administration was thinking wet. One cynical civil rights worker said, "I think they're hoping we'll all grow gills and swim away."[23]

When the Chicago Freedom Movement Agenda Committee met on Saturday, 16 July, its primary concerns were how to respond to charges that civil rights activities and staff were responsible for the riot, how to pursue the issue of police brutality, and how to reinstate the issues and demands that had been put before the city at the rally only one week before. They had been swamped in the sea of violence during the intervening days.[24]

Indeed, the entire thrust of the movement had been placed on the defensive by this eruption of violence. One member commented that there was "no way to mobilize the masses without making statements which appear to the public as irresponsible." The riots threatened to undercut the support of "moderates" for civil rights goals. In the hope of recovering the initiative and positive public support, the committee decided to emphasize that the "machine" was the enemy and to be "gentle with moderates."

The violence, however, had raised the question of the role of whites in the movement. It was not an ideological question dictated by black power slogans but an urgent practical question dictated by events. Under conditions of violence, the visible presence of whites was probably not effective in calming the populace, although it may have exerted a moderating influence on the behavior of the police. John McDermott of the Catholic Interracial Council urged a tactical retreat for whites in leadership roles, suggesting that they take a "supportive role" with input "at the level of policy and consensus making."

King conceded that the riot had been a "set-back" for their efforts, but he urged his colleagues, "Do not say we have failed." Instead, he proposed concentrating the campaign to bring positive developments out of the violence. The West Side had become the "Watts of Chicago," King said. Perhaps, therefore, Watts-like efforts could be attracted to rehabilitate the West Side.

Raby disagreed with that approach, saying it would feed resources to "the machine." He felt that a less concentrated approach to demonstrations "gives the machine a problem" by keeping its response off balance. He proposed "organizing for action" as recently planned and moving ahead. That meant demonstrations in all-white neighborhoods, organized around segregationist realtors and racially exclusive recreational facilities. In the light of the controversies generated by the riot, it also meant sending a delegation to confront Police Superintendent Wilson with the charges of police brutality. The decision was made to go ahead as planned.

THE OPEN CITY CAMPAIGN: AN UNCERTAIN BEGINNING

Thus with the National Guard still patrolling the West Side, the demonstrations that were announced at the 10 July rally began on schedule. From an "action center" in all-black Englewood, an integrated group of 120 persons proceeded west to Marquette Park in the adjoining all-white neighborhood of Chicago Lawn for a Saturday afternoon picnic. On Sunday, 200 demonstrators were taunted by teenagers as they conducted a prayer vigil near St. Gall Catholic Church in all-white Gage Park, directly north of Chicago Lawn. The white youths greeted the demonstrators with shouts of "go talk to the police captain who got shot in the back" and "why don't you go down to 12th Street where you can do some good"—both references to the recent riot. Troy Freeman, pastor of New Friendship Baptist Church, said the marchers "had come to take a look at the community because this is where they plan to send their children to school and to live."[25]

Such plans as any blacks may have had to live in these neighborhoods were challenged the following day, 18 July, when two real estate brokers obtained an injunction to stop Governor Otto Kerner's executive order banning discrimination in selling or renting housing. This order, scheduled to go into effect 23 July, had been occasioned by the Atomic Energy Commission's search for a location for a $375 million atomic accelerator, a project sought by five states. Weston, just west of Chicago, was in the running, but the NAACP had objected to that site because of housing bias. At nearby Argonne National Laboratories, for example, only 2 percent of the black employees had found housing in the area. In that context, Kerner did what was necessary to keep Weston under consideration by extending his 1963 "code of fair practices" to include

216

the real estate industry. The realtors objected to the governor's order in openly racist terms: "All we are asking," said Robert E. Cook, executive vice-president of the Illinois Association of Real Estate Boards, "is that the brokers and salesmen have the same right to discriminate as the owners, who engage their services."[26]

With the action program already under way, the agenda committee met Friday morning, 22 July. Its first item of business was organizing the movement's structure. The agenda committee had been functioning on an ad hoc basis as the continuation of a group appointed in connection with the 10 July rally. A more permanent arrangement was needed to submit to the larger body of delegates the next day.

The committee decided to propose a four-part structure. First, a Chicago Freedom Movement Assembly was to be responsible for general policy. The only requirement for membership in the assembly was "a genuine concern for civil rights." King and Raby were to recommend membership, and the agenda committee would review their recommendation only if "an issue is raised." Second, an agenda committee was to be responsible for carrying out policies adopted by the assembly, but it also had the authority to innovate policy, if need be, between assembly meetings. Third, an action committee was to be responsible for the day-to-day logistics of the demonstrations. It reported to the agenda committee. Fourth, King and Raby were to be cochairs of the Chicago Freedom Movement, responsible for the public interpretation of the movement and empowered to make "on the spot" decisions when time did not permit a full discussion by the agenda committee.

The committee then considered several questions about the open housing demonstrations. Should they be continued in any particular community, such as Gage Park, until a victory had been won there, or should they move on, if necessary, without such results? Would they move people into these areas if the demonstrations were successful in opening them up for black residence? And should welfare recipients be proposed as new occupants, or should the committee "avoid obstacles" by feeding in people of the same educational and economic level as the existing white community? Raby and Bevel were emphatic on this last point. As Raby put it, with families in the slums living in four rooms when they needed seven, "the person on relief needs an open city more than anyone." The decision was made to press for results in Gage Park.

Jesse Jackson reported that Operation Breadbasket had completed its fifth successful negotiation, this time with Bowman Dairy for 45 jobs for blacks with an annual payroll of $350,000. This brought Operation Breadbasket's total to 224 jobs with an annual payroll of $1,800,000. King commented that this was the movement's "most concrete program," one with "tangible results," and the "public needs to know about it." "Why is the white press

217

holding back?" he asked. The ensuing discussion focused on the inadequacies of the *Tribune*'s civil rights coverage, with Jackson suggesting a boycott of that paper.

Raby reported on the organizers loaned to the Chicago Freedom Movement by the Industrial Union Department of the American Federation of Labor (AFL) for work with tenant unions on the West Side. "The two forces with the most potential," he reflected, "are the civil rights movement and labor. We must continue these efforts to organize the unorganized and underpaid, on the job and in their communities." Charles Hayes of the United Packinghouse Workers, however, warned the committee not to "swell the numbers of [some] union that does not support the freedom movement." On the other hand, Hayes continued, "we should be willing to work with any union that works with us."

A final report concerned the contract signed the previous week between the East Garfield Park Union to End Slums and the Condor & Costalis real estate management firm. The contract, which covered fifteen hundred tenants, was the first such collective bargaining agreement between landlords and tenants. Plans were already under way to withhold August rents in buildings managed by another rental agent.[27]

The committee then discussed the meeting set for the following week with leading Chicago banks. At issue were building loans to black churches: "Those beholden to the power structure can get loans," it was said, but "Mayor Daley can block any loan in the city."

The summer program was in motion on several fronts, but the meeting concluded on a somber financial note. Outstanding bills for the rally were $18,000 against a $10,000 balance in the treasury. Less than 1 percent of the pledges from the rally had been collected.[28]

The Chicago Freedom Movement Assembly opened on Saturday, 23 July, with a report on the open housing demonstrations. "Real estate agencies are operating illegally," said University of Chicago ethics professor Alvin Pitcher. "It has been illegal for two years not to show property [to blacks]— yet none has been shown. [Thus] the first phase of [our] action is to make clear the closed nature of the city." In Gage Park, 121 cases of housing discrimination had been documented, he continued, and the movement was about to test housing discrimination in the Belmont-Cragin area on the Northwest Side, the second of ten areas chosen for direct action. Pressure in Gage Park would not slacken. A major demonstration was planned there for Friday, 29 July. The purpose was to "stay there until we are shown some houses." In the meantime, picnics and church visits would continue in Gage Park.

Jesse Jackson underlined one dimension of the issue. "There are 150 rental units [available] now in Gage Park, and yet they are building a 150 apartment high rise" for public housing in Kenwood. Baron (Chicago Urban League,

218

CUL) reported that eleven new public housing sites in the ghetto had been approved by the Chicago Housing Authority and the City Council and that this action was being challenged in court by the American Civil Liberties Union.[29]

Andrew Ransom, chairman of the Tenants Action Council (TAC) in Old Town Gardens on the near North Side, reported on two and one-half months of demonstrations there. TAC represented two hundred of six hundred tenants and hoped to have four hundred when a rent strike began 1 August.

King addressed the meeting with his assessment of the current situation. He thanked the delegates for the success of the rally and reported that they "didn't get a cold reception" when they met with the mayor the next day. But they did not receive any commitments either, he said, and therefore, they had proceeded to announce the summer action project. With reference to the violence on the West Side, King said, "I am absolutely convinced the riots cause more problems than they solve. They intensify white fears and relieve their guilt." Although there were "precipitating factors"—the police and a fire hydrant in Chicago—"the causes are deep: housing, education, discrimination. I think we are in for some difficult days. No massive program of any mayor is yet grappling imaginatively and boldly on the scale needed."

"We must move on with our positive program to make Chicago an open city," King continued. "We have dual housing, a dual school system, dual everything. Our big job is to move outsiders into the mainstream. It isn't legal that people are kept out; a statute here makes open housing a reality, [yet] realtors are breaking the law every day. Therefore, I hope you will support the efforts now under way. We must build a record of proof that Negroes are rejected. We will escalate with an all-night vigil next week."

"We must not despair," King said. "We are getting undramatic victories." He cited Operation Breadbasket from which "the Negro has just enough power to make the difference between profit and loss," the Condor-Costalis contract, which "legitimizes rent strikes," and Kerner's executive order on housing discrimination—though King thought that "may be the right thing for the wrong reason." On the other hand, there were the *Tribune* and the schools. "I have seen nothing worse in southern areas than the *Chicago Tribune* editorials," King said. "Their implications [are] for the white community to rise up in violence." He also said that the new school superintendent "couldn't be worse."[30]

King concluded by defending his work with street gangs, one of the grounds on which he had been held responsible for the riot. "I do not feel apologetic about working with gangs. My mission is not on the boulevard nor in the heights of bourgeoisieness, but in the valleys and alleys of deprivation. Four thousand Negroes out of 900,000 were rioting. We can't ignore [them]. A destructive minority can destroy the well-springs of the majority. [We must demonstrate] the tactical value and efficiency of nonviolence as a strategy. We must get concessions and victories massive enough to show the despairing that changes can come."

Raby then announced the membership of the agenda committee and the formation of an action committee. Members of the agenda committee were King, Raby, Arthur Brazier (TWO), John McDermott (CIC), Edwin C. Berry (CUL), Kale Williams (AFSC), William Robinson (Church Federation), Charles Hayes (Packinghouse Workers), Archie Hargraves (Urban Training Center), Arthur Griffin (West Side Federation), James Wright (United Auto Workers), Clay Evans (the most prominent black Baptist minister to support King's campaign), and Chester Robinson (WSO). Staff appointed to meet with the committee were Andrew Young (SCLC), James Bevel (SCLC), Alvin Pitcher (CCCO), and Jesse Jackson (CCCO).

There ensued efforts to expand the agenda committee. The NALC wanted representation, but Raby overruled a motion to provide it because "membership is by appointment." A delegate from the Citizens Housing Committee challenged the basis of the appointments, and Cousins (CAPCC) protested the absence of women. Raby replied that he and King "received authority to make the appointments [and] we will consider your recommendations." Jean Williams (ESCRU) said her organization was very active and would like to be represented. With reference to the authority of King and Raby to make appointments, she asked: "Do we have the authority to take it away?" In the end, the appointments stood, and the nominating committee's slate of CCCO officers for the second six months of 1966 (Raby, Hogan, and Robinson) was reelected without comment.

With the direct action campaign entering its second week, a pattern was emerging in these activities designed "to expose and to dramatize the fact that this city has two separate housing markets": "testing" of realtors by individual white and black families to determine the availability of housing units for rent or sale; mass visits by groups of fifty to two hundred persons to selected realtors who had refused listings to blacks while making them available to whites; picnics in "white" parks by large integrated groups making full use of the public accommodations there; Sunday morning worship in churches by blacks; mass outdoor prayer vigils on Sunday afternoons; and efforts to gain support for open housing from indigenous whites by work with local churches and community groups.[31]

During the weekend of 23–24 July, the picnic in Gage Park was marred by minor damage to the automobiles of some of the two hundred picnickers. Also, one person was struck by a stone as he was leaving the picnic. In Belmont-Cragin, sixty-one blacks and forty-seven whites tested thirteen realtors and found a pattern there similar to that in Gage Park; if blacks were offered housing at all, the listings were back in the ghetto. One lone realtor was found

220

to have a policy of offering his regular listings to blacks—"the only positive experience" in either of the two communities.[32]

The mass test in Belmont-Cragin was followed by a picnic at Riis Park in the area; the swimming pool there was closed when the demonstrators arrived. Don Rose, the movement's press officer, described the situation with restraint: "Park officials said that there was glass at the bottom of the pool, but rights aids believed it strange that the pool was not simply cleaned in that case, rather than being closed on a hot Saturday afternoon."[33]

On Monday, 25 July, Mayor Daley appointed twenty-three prominent Chicagoans to the police-community relations committee he had agreed to create during the riot. The agenda committee, meeting the following Thursday, 28 July, opened in dismay over *Sun-Times* reports that morning that most members of the new committee did not consider police brutality to be within their purview. Jesse Jackson wanted to know what the committee could actively be expected to do as a whole or through "our friends" on it. If that was the question, McDermott was sure of the answer: "recommend a civilian police review board." Others joined in discussing ways to influence the committee. Bevel did not think a civilian review board was worth fighting for. Noting that many of those who had been "brutalized" had police records and thus would be unimpressive witnesses before any review board, he argued that the issue was political, not administrative. "Teach [the people] to use the political apparatus," Bevel said. "Unless the voting people control the [ward] committeeman, we cannot control" the police. In part, Raby agreed. "There is no question," he said, whether or not "the board will be their own men. They will report what he [Daley] wants." But Raby wanted to use the review board as one more mobilizing issue "to effectuate political change."

When the discussion turned to the open housing campaign, McDermott reported on his conversation with Father Edward Egan, a moderate priest prominent in archdiocesan affairs and frequent representative for the archbishop. Egan had criticized the movement's activities in Gage Park on several grounds. He objected to making St. Gall Catholic Church, where the prayer vigil had been held, the focus of demonstrations. Monsignor James Hischen, St. Gall's pastor, was, of all Gage Park clergy, the "friendliest" to civil rights aims. Not only had his church been a focal point for demonstrations, it had been done, McDermott reported, "without the courtesy of saying we were coming." Father Egan also was said to believe that the demonstrations were having "no significant effect [with] friendly forces" in the area and were leading to a "polarization of Negro community versus Gage Park." Egan was especially concerned about the "temper of the community"; he felt there was "danger of violent response to the demonstrations." In short, he was "afraid of a riot," and he was "not satisfied" that the demonstrations were either

221

"desirable or necessary." Should violence occur, Egan thought Archbishop Cody's support might be lost. The criticisms offered by Egan were taken to be an expression of Archbishop Cody's position.

Kale Williams responded that there was "a good bit of merit in these concerns. For two and one-half weeks now," Williams said, "we have not got in the press anything about what we are doing." In addition, he pointed out that no leaflets had been distributed in the streets interpreting the demonstrations and that the movement had contacted only two clergy in the area—William Cox (a Presbyterian minister) and Msgr. Hischen, albeit post facto.

Jesse Jackson responded that it was "accidental" that the demonstrations had taken place at St. Gall's; the "busiest corner" in the neighborhood had been chosen. He was critical of the staff who had been responsible for working with people in Gage Park, but he hoped they could "reestablish lost communication." Jackson felt that "imminent violence" was probably "unavoidable—unless people stop it."

McDermott, too, found "merit in Father Egan's criticism." He drew back, however, from Egan's conclusion that the demonstrations were neither desirable nor necessary. He thought the movement had been "fuzzy about what they were trying to get and in dramatizing injustice," but it was not wise to "go away without concrete results." He urged that "Hischen should be used to call together leaders, [while we] use demonstrations to strengthen his position." He cited Hischen's "interracial experience" as head of the Catholic Bishops' Committee on Migrant Workers as evidence that the monsignor was no stranger to the issues of justice. But now "he [Hischen] feels hurt." McDermott suggested that his Catholic Interracial Council had a "special role to play" in this situation, and he offered to assign his assistant to work with the action committee.

Jesse Jackson, impatient with this prolonged criticism of the demonstrations he had helped lead, said, "John, fellows like you have got to spend time with us [in Gage Park] instead of sitting here and discussing what we do."

King pressed McDermott to say whether he was suggesting "cessation of action." "No," he replied, he wanted "better research on who is who—don't lump [our] friends and enemies together."

King expressed hope that it would be "possible to pull forces of good will together tomorrow." He was "not optimistic about Cody going all the way down the line. Once [there is] confrontation, [we] may lose him. He has taken a lot of heat for his Soldier Field statement and for endorsing [our work]." King interpreted the report from Father Egan as a message from Archbishop Cody, saying, "You have not taken me into [your] confidence. He thinks St. Gall was selected by design."

The committee decided to accept the archbishop's request for a conference with King and Raby and to meet the next day with Msgr. Hischen. It was less clear about how to arrange a meeting with the two candidates for the U.S. Senate, incumbent Paul H. Douglas and Republican Charles Percy. After some discussion, it was decided to ask John Sengstacke, publisher of the *Chicago Defender,* if he would organize such a meeting.

The newspapers that week were filled with civil rights stories. President Johnson condemned the riots and defended his Vietnam policies. Roy Wilkins and A. Philip Randolph denounced action by the House to exclude owner-occupied home and apartment houses with up to four units from the civil rights bill then before Congress. Barry Goldwater blamed King and the president for the riots in Chicago and other cities. Forty-eight black clergymen published an extended statement on black power in the Sunday *New York Times.* "The fundamental distortion facing us in the controversy about 'black power,'" they said, "is rooted in a gross imbalance of power and conscience between Negroes and white Americans. It is this distortion, mainly, which is responsible for the widespread, though often inarticulate, assumption that white people are justified in getting what they want through the use of power, but that Negro Americans must, either by nature or by circumstance, make their appeal only through conscience." Locally, KOCO protested a Chicago Housing Authority proposal to build even more public housing in Kenwood. Five SCLC-CCCO–sponsored neighborhood tenant unions came together to form the citywide Chicago Tenants Union. A judge in Springfield issued an injunction exempting 154 real estate brokers, including 22 from the Chicago area, from the governor's open housing order on the grounds that the governor's order usurped legislative functions and violated the right of contract.[34]

The all-night vigil Friday at F. H. Halvorsen Realtors was called off after six hours because of fear of violence from a crowd of five hundred hurling verbal abuse at the fifty demonstrators. "We don't want violence," Jesse Jackson said, "so we are leaving." The press reported this episode but ignored the ten documented cases of discrimination by Halvorsen Realtors, which made the company typical of the twenty-three tested in that neighborhood.[35]

WHITE VIOLENCE: A CHALLENGE
TO MAYOR DALEY'S SUPPORT

The action returned to Gage Park on Saturday, 30 July. An integrated group of 450 marched from the action center in Englewood to Halvorsen Realtors. The marchers, carrying signs reading "end slums," "freedom 100 years overdue," and "a prejudiced child is a crippled child," were met by signs proclaiming "white power" and "nigger go home." Some in the crowd sang: "I'd love to be an Alabama trooper, and that is what I'd truly like to be, because if I were an Alabama trooper, I could shoot niggers,

223

one, two, three." Police used their nightsticks to restrain groups of whites from interfering with the demonstration. Bricks, rocks, and bottles were thrown at the marchers. Six persons were injured; seven whites were arrested.[36]

On Sunday, 350 marchers in Gage Park shoved their way through groups of white teenagers blocking their path. As the crowds grew and the marchers turned north on Kedzie Avenue toward Halvorsen Realtors, they were again bombarded with bricks and bottles, and an automobile was pushed into their line of march. One of the marchers described what happened next:

> The scheduled hour-and-a-half march turned into a four-hour nightmare as we wandered haphazardly through the neighborhood, unable to get through the mob and back to our autos. . . . A girl about ten years old and wearing shorts got me with a rock during the frenzied attack. When Sister Mary Angelica, a first grade teacher at Sacred Heart School in suburban Melrose Park, was struck in the head and fell dazed to the ground, a roaring cheer went up from the rabid hecklers on the opposite sidewalk. The cheering continued as other marchers scooped up her limp and unconscious form and shouldered their way to a police car. "We've got another one!" the hecklers screamed. . . . White persons in the line of march were targets of special abuse as the residents—especially older women—spat at us and called us "traitors, communists, white-niggers" and ranged a long list of sexual perversion charges against us. One man, apparently not yet master of the English language, shouted in fierce German which one marcher translated for me as: "I am an American; you are communists." Many youths cried, "Burn them like Jews," and "white power." Others yelled, "Polish power." Gallantly, a young man handed a stone to his girlfriend. She threw it at the marchers and then smiled up at her date, who kissed her. Priests and ministers who were moving among the hecklers hoping to be able to restore order, were met either by resentful silence or by taunts: "Are you one of those nigger lovers too?"

The police captain ordered his men to use their sticks, but the attackers followed the demonstrators yelling threats and crying "white power." One carried a noose and repeatedly screamed, "K.K.K."; others burned a cross in the street.[37]

By dusk, the mob had grown to four thousand, and the marchers' automobiles, ostensibly left under police protection, were attacked. Twelve cars were burned, two were pushed into a lagoon, and a dozen more were overturned. Among the thirty-one persons injured was a Catholic priest, one of nineteen Gage Park clergy who had gone into the streets to try to deter what the *Sun-Times* termed "counter-demonstrators."[38]

Another local Catholic pastor, a former vice-chancellor of the archdiocese, commented, "I can honestly say I wouldn't go near the mob again unless I was armed. You just can't realize the hatred manifested. We were there at the request of the police department . . . [but] we learned the sight of a Roman collar incited them to greater violence and nastier epithets."[39]

The *Chicago Tribune* was quick to link this new outburst of violence with the recent riots. "We don't condone this kind of violence, whether its authors are white, Negro, or Puerto Rican," the editors said. But it was clear where their sympathies lay. "It [the violence] will happen as long as there is incitation from one side or the other, and the demonstrators knew they were asking for trouble when they invaded the Gage Park community." The *Sun-Times* also condemned the violence editorially, hoping that "those who cry 'police brutality' whenever police have occasion to arrest Negro offenders will note that the police had to use the same kind of force against whites." Unlike the *Tribune*, the *Sun-Times* acknowledged that the marchers' "right to protest is constitutional" and, therefore, the paper called upon the people of the area "to live up to their reputation for being law-abiding, self-respecting persons." Still, the *Sun-Times* editors joined their colleagues at the *Tribune* in expressing sympathy for the attitudes of Gage Park residents, who were "understandably concerned when their area is made the target of demonstrations," who were "apprehensive about the outrageous statements being made by some of the extremists in the 'Black Power' group," and who "sincerely believe that demonstrators for open housing are being deliberately provocative."[40]

In its condemnation of the violence, the *Daily News* also affirmed that the marchers were entitled to legal protection. The paper criticized the equally "mistaken" notions which it understood to animate each side in Gage Park: on the one side, the ideas that blacks "lack initiative" and that "their homes . . . would be in jeopardy if their community were 'invaded' by Negroes"; on the other, the idea "that brute force, alone, can wrest the Negro's birthright from the whites." It was unfortunate, the *Daily News* said, that "people, no matter what their color, tend to 'think' with their viscera, not with their heads." The paper favored "creat[ing] an atmosphere where the races can come together in confidence rather than fear." It did not apply this insight to the current situation, however.[41]

In contrast to all three of these white dailies, which linked the Gage Park violence to the West Side riots, the *Chicago Daily Defender* put the matter in the context of open occupancy, the governor's open housing order, and the civil rights bill then before Congress: "Illinois as well as the rest of the nation must soon or late come to the grim realization that residential segregation is a root cause of racial unrest." And if an analogue for the violence was to be sought, it was not to the West Side that the *Defender* looked: "Here is a situation reminiscent of Mississippi or Alabama, and which could well develop into full scale race rioting. What is the white leadership doing about it?" the *Defender* asked.[42]

Whereas the white editorial pages blamed the people involved in these events, residents of Gage Park blamed the "racial unrest" on Mayor Daley, Archbishop Cody, the newspapers, and, most of all, "It's them—especially Dr. Martin Luther King, Jr." As one woman said, "They deliberately come in here. They knew they were going to have violence. I wouldn't go and live somewhere I wasn't wanted. Why do they? Why don't they clean up the slums if they want nice places?" Another resident, reflecting upon previous moves by Gage Park residents in the face of the advancing color line, said, "Now they want to come in and drive us out again. Well, we have to protect our neighborhood. This is a matter of self-preservation."[43]

Raby professed no surprise at these events and attitudes: "What happened demonstrated the latent hostility that exists and that most Negroes are aware of. We know that housing patterns are not accidental and that a racist psychology exists in communities such as Gage Park." He and King issued a statement accusing the police of being "either unwilling or unable to disperse the riotous mob that so brutally attacked Negroes and whites who had come to the community to seek open housing in compliance with the law. . . . We shall continue to demonstrate in every all-white community in Chicago in our nonviolent effort to open housing for all men," they said. Plans were announced to step up the demonstrations in Belmont-Cragin.[44]

Tuesday, 2 August, Superintendent Wilson countered charges that his men had failed to protect the marchers by asserting that civil rights leaders had not given the Police Department adequate advance notice of their plans. He said police learned of Sunday's demonstration only one hour before it began. He requested at least twenty-four hours' notice.[45]

Twenty-five clergy from Gage Park also commented on the situation there. After expressing concern for "the safety and stability of our neighborhood as well as the value of our homes," they condemned the violence, affirmed the constitutionality of the demonstrations, and declared their "stand for a just and open society where every man can live wherever he is able without respect to race or religion."[46]

Later that day, 500 demonstrators marched to Parker & Finney Realtors in Belmont-Cragin under the watchful eye of 180 police. Minor scuffles took place between police and white youths clutching bricks and bottles. Bevel and Jackson praised the improved police protection. The scuffling continued on Wednesday as police cleared the way for 250 demonstrators in Belmont-Cragin. Twenty-one whites from the crowd of a thousand were arrested; one demonstrator was injured in the eye when his windshield was smashed. In a new escalation of direct action, Jackson announced that King would lead the march to Gage Park that weekend.[47]

On Thursday, King and Raby met for three hours with leading black members of the Democratic organization to discuss the civil rights demands. Although the dozen aldermen and state representatives repeatedly claimed that Mayor Daley was already moving to resolve many of the problems with which King was concerned, they agreed on the need for open housing legislation, increasing bank loans to blacks, greater controls on building standards, and racial head counts of employees. The demand that absentee precinct captains be replaced was the only one flatly rejected by the group. Such demands as the recognition of welfare unions, school desegregation, and a civilian police review board were not discussed.[48]

This meeting with black leaders of the Daley machine was the first public indication that the mayor was seeking some accommodation with the demonstrators, at least to the point of exploring possible terms for a settlement. Privately, such feelers had been proceeding for some time. Weeks earlier, for example, Charles Swibel, chairman of the Chicago Housing Authority, had suggested that King "had gotten in over his head and needed a 'victory.'" Swibel proposed that King and the city could reach an agreement without confrontation in the streets. He promised reforms in the public housing he administered: elevator guards, one-year leases, door bells, an interracial committee to work on integrating public housing, and the construction or rehabilitation of 408 units. In return, King was asked to issue a statement praising the mayor's "wise administration" and "leadership," and "pledg[ing] his cooperation to Mayor Daley in implementing the positive programs the city has underway." King had considered this proposal but in consultation with Raby had turned it down. On 3 August, Daley and Swibel announced the reforms anyway.[49]

That they did so was a sign that the bargaining positions had so changed in the past week that the token concessions Swibel proposed were no longer significant. On the one hand, the civil rights movement had demonstrated its ability to dramatize an issue, albeit white hatred and violence rather than housing discrimination, and it appeared able to continue to do so almost at will. On the other hand, Daley might have waited out the demonstrations, if necessary, had the residents of Gage Park and Belmont-Cragin focused their anger on the marchers, or even on Archbishop Cody, but it was increasingly clear that the people in the neighborhoods were holding the police, Superintendent Wilson, and the mayor himself responsible. It was not the shouts of "nigger" and "white power" that bothered the mayor but those of "Wallace for president"—which suggested a breach in the ranks of Daley's precinct organization. The fall elections were only three months away, and Daley needed the votes of the ethnic neighborhoods such as Gage Park and Belmont-Cragin.

On 4 August, the Chicago Conference on Religion and Race issued a statement signed by twenty-one denominational leaders, including Archbishop Cody, which supported the marches and called upon "our fellow citizens of all convictions to respect those who seek to obtain their rights in a responsible way."[50] That statement might well have been addressed to the editors of the *Tribune,* who, with the march to Gage Park headed by King imminent, found their "patience at an end." Under the general rubric of "tumult and violence on the streets," the paper linked the civil rights demonstrations with an incident in which black teenagers had attacked two white firemen. The *Tribune* called for "the stiffest penalty that the law allows" for the teenagers and continued: "The same treatment should be accorded the imported prophets of 'nonviolence' who are seeking to incite trouble with marches into white neighborhoods. The Rev. Martin Luther King of Atlanta is expected to lead another of these forays into the Gage Park area, where whites were baited into a near-riot last weekend. . . . It would be well to advise King in advance that if he manages to produce a similar result he and his lieutenants can expect to find themselves in the lockup."[51]

The more moderate *Sun-Times* simply adopted recent criticism of the demonstrations as its own. "If the civil rights groups continue to stage marches without due notice," the editors said, reflecting Wilson's comments, "we can only conclude that their purpose is not to 'educate' white persons, as they say, but deliberately to stir up trouble." Similarly, the *Sun-Times* cited the statement by Edward Marciniak of the Chicago Commission on Human Relations that his agency, which was responsible for enforcing the city's fair housing ordinance, had not received any complaints concerning real estate agents in the Gage Park and Belmont-Cragin areas. The editors urged the "civil rights protesters [to] use legal machinery available to them to protest alleged discrimination." Until they did so, "it seems fair to conclude they are more interested in demonstrating for the sake of demonstrating than in opening up neighborhoods to qualified home buyers or apartment renters."[52]

Friday afternoon, 5 August, Raby and Mahalia Jackson led six hundred demonstrators in Gage Park. Twelve hundred police tried to protect them from a mob variously estimated at four to eight thousand. When King arrived and alighted from his car, he was struck on the head by a rock the size of a fist. Missiles—bricks, bottles, firecrackers, a knife—continued to fly as the march made its way to Halvorsen Realtors amid shouts of "Get the witch doctor," "We want King," and "Kill him, kill him." King said, "I have never seen such hostility and hatred anywhere in my life, even in Selma." Nor was the hostility and hatred all aimed at demonstrators. A police officer gave a similar assessment: "This night has to rate as one of the worst in our history. The outrageous cop-fighting we experienced here was about the most vicious I've ever seen in nearly thirty years of service." In all, thirty persons were injured and forty-three arrested.[53]

On Sunday, 7 August, the marchers returned to Belmont-Cragin. In the largest demonstration thus far, eleven hundred demonstrators were escorted by five hundred police. A crowd of five thousand whites harassed the marchers, throwing rocks and cherry bombs, as the marchers visited three churches on their way to the Parker & Finney real estate office. Three persons were injured, twenty-one arrested. Only a thunderstorm averted more serious violence.[54]

By then, the mayor wanted an end to the marches. At first he considered using the courts to stop them, but precedent was on the side of the marchers. The Supreme Court decision that had enjoined Governor Wallace from banning the march from Selma to Montgomery the previous year applied to Chicago as well, and the city's own ordinance requiring parade permits had not previously been used to stop sidewalk demonstrations. In any case, arresting demonstrators was likely to swell their numbers in subsequent marches and to alienate the black voters whom Daley also needed. Daley made his position official on Monday, 8 August, when he told Republican Alderman John J. Hoellen, who wanted to make the marches a partisan issue, that the city would not ban them. The Chicago Commission on Human Relations began trying to persuade realtors to open their listings to blacks in the hope that civil rights leaders might voluntarily halt the marches. Ironically, one of the commission's arguments was that blacks probably could not afford houses in the affected areas anyway.[55]

Then came a chorus of "End the Marches" editorials. "Why not," the *Tribune* asked, "a great petition, or a huge rally, to signify to King and his imported troublemakers that Chicago Negroes want an end to this campaign to stir up the antipathy of white people and want to give the races a chance to live in harmony?" The *Sun-Times* called for "a peaceful meeting" of "responsible citizens, the ministry, the elected city officials, the target real estate agencies, and others" with King and his followers "to talk out grievances." The *Daily News,* claiming the point had been sufficiently made that Chicago was "not an open society," proposed that King should himself end the marches—"stop asking for violence and start asking for manifests of responsibility and a willingness to cooperate in quiet, productive ways."[56]

These proposals were far from the mood of civil rights leaders, however, who announced plans for a further escalation of direct action—a march Wednesday into the Bogan area of the Southwest Side, long a hotbed of anti-black sentiment, where racially motivated protests over a school transfer program had set off the chain of events leading to Willis's resignation in 1963. With King out of town for the annual SCLC convention, Jesse Jackson speculated publicly about a march into suburban Cicero though there were no actual plans for such a move. Cicero had been the scene of rioting in 1951, when a single black family had moved in. More recently, in May 1966, a black youth had been murdered there while he looked for a job.[57]

The public response to these announcements was immediate and alarmed.

229

Police Superintendent Wilson warned of a race riot and attributed a 25 percent increase in the crime rate during the past two weeks to the diversion of police to protect demonstrators. Cicero officials requested a mobilization of the National Guard. The chief of the Illinois state police canceled vacations for his officers. Cook County Sheriff Richard B. Ogilvie revealed that he had "information that there would be violence in Cicero that would make Gage Park look like a tea party." Jesse Jackson affirmed that "we plan to go to Cicero before the week is over. It will be rough, but I'm going to Cicero."[58]

Meeting on Tuesday, 9 August, the Chicago Commission on Human Relations "agreed that some effort should be made" to convene a meeting of the mayor, civil rights leaders, the Chicago Real Estate Board, and other interested parties "to discuss the problems and to try to make some recommendations for solutions." Meanwhile, at his first press conference in a week, Daley said he would like to see the question of "whether certain real estate people have been violating the city ordinance on freedom of residence" resolved at the conference table. When the mayor met with the commission later in the day, it was agreed to convene the city's top leadership, but under other auspices than the mayor's. Daley called Ross Beatty, chairman of the Chicago Real Estate Board, who agreed to convene such a meeting.[59]

At the same time, top officials of the United Auto Workers (UAW) were engaged in efforts to arrange a meeting between labor leaders and the mayor to discuss a conference on open housing. With Daley's commitment to the meeting in hand, Robert W. Johnson, Midwest director of the UAW, called Raby on Tuesday to suggest suspending the demonstrations while the possibilities of negotiation were explored. UAW President Walter P. Reuther phoned the proposal to King at the SCLC convention in Jackson, Mississippi.[60]

When the action committee, which was responsible for the demonstrations on a day-to-day basis, convened late Tuesday night to consider the UAW request, members of the agenda committee were also present because of the importance of this decision. Raby left the four-hour meeting thinking the committee had accepted the proposal and would divert Wednesday's demonstration from Bogan to the offices of the Chicago Real Estate Board in the Loop. The next day, Bevel, Jackson, and Bernard Lafayette of the action committee were angered by press reports, attributed to Raby, that the march to Bogan had been postponed. They were under the impression that the final decision had been left to them and that, in any case, they were to announce the plans at the Action Center on Wednesday afternoon. Bevel wanted to go to Bogan anyway because they "could not tolerate such leakage" and because the press was interpreting postponement of the march "as a concession to those more conservative forces." As hundreds of demonstrators waited for march directions in the Action Center at Warren Avenue Congregational Church, upstairs Raby confronted the action committee to insist on the decision to march in the Loop. At one point, he "threatened a public and official break with the Action Committee if they decided to march in Bogan." Eventually the committee capitulated, but Raby's assertion of authority left scars. One member of the committee said, "Many of us saw this as a foreshadowing of the end of the movement and that the Agenda Committee had the capacity and control to stop demonstrations . . . under their conditions."[61]

At the office of the Chicago Real Estate Board later that day, Raby read a prepared statement to two hundred demonstrators. "We have decided to appear before the Real Estate Board office rather than march in Bogan today in order to make clear that the issue facing this city is whether or not the illegal and immoral practices of real estate agencies will continue," Raby said. "People of influence in business, government, and the press have a choice. Either they can move immediately to bring a cessation to illegal and immoral real estate practices or they can continue to cloud the issue by focusing on secondary concerns."[62]

Ross Beatty responded that the board would call a conference soon to resolve the dispute. Although agreeing that "people have a right to live in a decent neighborhood," Beatty denied that it was the real estate broker "who is at fault." "These demonstrations have made clear that . . . the problem is in the hearts and souls of the property owners."[63]

As Beatty's comment suggests, the Chicago Real Estate Board considered itself a third party to a conflict between the civil rights movement and small property owners, whom the realtors merely represented. This stance led two members of the human relations commission, William Caples and Hale Nelson, and a business associate, Paul Lund, to reconsider the board's sponsorship of the leadership conference. As a result, Lund and Caples undertook to persuade the Chicago Conference on Religion and Race (CCRR) to convene the meeting. This, however, created a new problem—convincing the board to participate as a protagonist rather than as the sponsor of the conference. When Beatty resisted appearing in that role, Lund finally told him, "Look, if you don't show up at that meeting, you're not going to have a city left to build in!" After four hours of debate, the board agreed, with the stipulation that other private and government agencies also be present to respond to the movement's demands.[64]

As the Conference on Religion and Race set about the arrangements for a metropolitan leadership conference, new pressure to suspend the marches came from Archbishop Cody, who asked movement leaders to reconsider continuing the demonstrations because of the likelihood of violence. The archbishop also called upon "civil authorities" to "convene immediately meetings between realtors and civil rights advocates in order to achieve a just and lasting resolution of the present crisis." Rabbi Marx and W. Alfred Diman, exec-

231

utive secretary of the Chicago Baptist Association, expressed support for the archbishop's statement.[65]

Raby responded, "In the absence of any effective program by public and private leaders against segregation, to ask us to stop marching is to ask that we surrender and acquiesce in this form of human degradation." In its first public break with the archbishop, the Catholic Interracial Council called Cody's request "unfair and unrealistic." It was like "asking a labor union to call off a just strike before a single grievance has been righted," the council said. Meanwhile, a downstate judge issued a temporary injunction banning the enforcement of Governor Kerner's open housing order.[66]

On Thursday, Daley met with seventeen Chicago labor leaders who had been brought together by the UAW. The mayor announced their support for ending the marches and convening a conference to discuss civil rights issues. "To take the demonstrations off the streets—this is our number one problem," Daley said. Civil rights leaders rescheduled the march to Bogan for Friday afternoon, and Raby and Berry flew to Jackson to confer with King about the emerging prospects for negotiations.[67]

Friday, 12 August, the Chicago Conference on Religion and Race issued invitations to a conference on civil rights problems to be held the following Wednesday. James W. Montgomery, bishop coadjutor of the Episcopal diocese and chairman of the CCRR, said the date had been set so King could attend. Later that afternoon, 725 civil rights demonstrators, guarded by 1,000 police, marched in Bogan without major incident. Raby credited a door-to-door canvass by community leaders with producing the relative calm. "Now what that same leadership has to do is convince people to accept the Negro into the community," he said.[68]

In the days immediately preceding the conference, civil rights leaders undertook two more rounds of demonstrations to show their power, focus the issue, and strengthen their bargaining position. On Sunday, 14 August, simultaneous marches were conducted in three Chicago neighborhoods. Gage Park and Bogan had been the scenes of previous demonstrations; Jefferson Park, on the far Northwest Side, was new. These actions were necessary, a spokesman said, to show that "this is a city with a pattern of discrimination on the part of realty brokers, and not simply something that occurs in an isolated community." A total of twelve hundred demonstrators, guarded by a like number of police, participated in these marches. The most serious incidents were in Gage Park, where, as men in business suits and women in their Sunday dresses held aloft swastikas, two of the marchers' autos were damaged and one marcher was stunned by a brick. Later, following an American Nazi rally, police were attacked by a white mob.[69]

On Tuesday, a series of small demonstrations took place at locations chosen to illustrate the specific demands civil rights leaders would carry to the conference table the next day: City Hall, where leaflets told passers-by, "The mayor must enforce the Chicago fair housing ordinance and the City Council must end segregation in its choice of public housing sites"; First Federal Savings & Loan Association, where picket signs read, "Loan to Negroes for housing outside ghettos"; the Chicago Real Estate Board, where leaflets said, "Real estate boards and brokers bear the primary responsibility for the closed city"; the Cook County Department of Public Aid, which Bevel said "does not try to find housing for Negroes outside the ghetto"; and the Chicago Housing Authority, which had failed to end "high-rise, high-density concentration camps" in the ghetto.[70]

The Chicago Freedom Movement's concentrated campaign of nonviolent demonstrations for an open city lasted from 10 July to 16 August 1966. By the latter date, this campaign had created a civic crisis, and the immediate issue for everyone was stopping the marches and relieving the threat of violence. Indeed, throughout the summer, this campaign, designed to raise the issue of racial discrimination and to force the adoption of desegregationist policies and practices, had been dominated by the confrontation of its nonviolent commitment with eruptions of anger, hatred, and vicious violence, first in the context of a West Side ghetto riot, 12–15 July, and then in the context of its own marches into militantly white neighborhoods, 16 July to 16 August.

The West Side riot, following so closely on the Soldier Field Rally intended to initiate the summer action program, threatened the grounds of the campaign in two ways: for whites, it reinforced the racist connotations of violence associated with blacks generally and the ghetto in particular, thus heightening the dynamics of fear, aversion, and abasement; for King and his movement, it presented a challenge to the power of nonviolence. King felt compelled to argue his case for nonviolence in the midst of the riot, despite the risk of associating his movement with the riot. After a season of arguing the importance of ghetto issues and ghetto mobilization, King was confronted with ghetto violence and the problems of ghetto-bred anger and hatred. In that context, King defended nonviolence as an effective and constructive approach to dealing with ghetto conditions. He was only partially successful.

On the issue of demonstrations, King had to defend nonviolence in the context of white violence. The demonstrators remained remarkably disciplined in spite of monumental provocation, and nonviolence remained the secure and, in the event, radical ground of the action. In this campaign for an open city, nonviolence proved to be an effective way to dramatize the exclusion of blacks and the depth of anger and racial hatred in militant white communities. Those demonstrations, however, were also intended to expose the "illegal and immoral" policies and practices of realtors and to build a case for

233

desegregationist remedies. Another aim was "getting the machine," disrupting Mayor Daley's secure precincts to force him into negotiating with the movement.

The strategies adopted during the summer proceeded directly from these grounds even though the flow of the action and the results achieved seem to have been dominated more by the course of events than by strategy. No one planned a riot on the West Side, but it served to challenge the movement's commitments to end slums, to an open city, and to nonviolence and to underline their urgency. It was essential that King carry his case for nonviolence even to those who were moved to violence by the ghetto issues and that he not only argue but show that nonviolence was the more effective way to attain change. Thus the movement associated itself with community groups such as the West Side Organization and the West Side Federation that were trying to end the violence and promote change. To do this required taking up the immediate ghetto issues of police brutality and recreational deprivation and confronting the mayor with the need for change as well as peace. Thus King both argued nonviolence with street gang members and mobilized business, labor, religious, and social agency leaders to support his platform of peace with change. Ultimately, the mayor agreed to this platform. For that moment, the changes demanded were minimal and immediate: recreational facilities and a citizen advisory committee on police-community relations.

The strategy of the marches was to dramatize the dual housing market, expose segregationist realtors, and force the mayor into negotiations of the movement's demands for open housing. It involved testing realtors by sending both black and white customers to request their services, demonstrating outside the offices of racially exclusive realtors, holding integrated picnics in "white" parks, conducting church visitations at Sunday morning services by blacks and prayer vigils outside churches, and attempting to find friends of the movement in these militantly white neighborhoods. The demonstrations were held in areas selected partly for their potential to disrupt the mayor's political base in these white, ethnic neighborhoods and thus to force him to negotiate much more serious commitments both to desegregation and to ending slums.

These demonstrations turned national attention to Chicago and tore the veil of innocence away from urban segregation—if only for a moment. For the first time in Chicago, the movement had reached into white, working-class, ethnic neighborhoods on a grand scale and had either provoked or exposed a truly shocking depth of anger, hatred, and potential for violence. By mid-August, the civic elite of the metropolitan area, heretofore safely ensconced behind the scenes of civil rights activities, were forced to surface and take responsibility for resolving a civic crisis of unprecedented proportions.

Throughout the summer the responses to the unfolding events were so much a part of the developing crisis that they gave very little indication of how it

234

was to be resolved. During the West Side riot, the mayor flirted for less than a day with the idea of blaming King for the violence and pursuing a stonewall strategy with the movement; on that same day, he and King worked out a package of promises. Simultaneously, the National Guard arrived and the violence virtually ended. No one knew which, if any, of these events had proven effective. For the next month, the mayor maintained his stance as the custodian of the civic peace and the protector of the demonstrators. By early August, he was moving behind the scenes to arrange negotiations to end the marches, if not the slums, but it was clear that he did not wish to be responsible for managing the negotiations. First, he asked the Chicago Real Estate Board to convene a meeting with the movement's leaders, himself, and other interested parties. When it became clear that the board was more interested in arguing its innocence than in negotiating a settlement, the mayor backed a suggestion to have the meeting convened by the Chicago Conference on Religion and Race. Although that organization and the principal representatives of religious bodies had been publicly supportive of King's campaign from the beginning, they were willing to call for an end to the marches in exchange for the prospect of serious negotiations in which the civic elite of the metropolitan area would agree to take responsibility for resolving the issues raised by the marches.

The major metropolitan dailies were largely outrageous both in their coverage and their editorial comment on the summer's events. The *Tribune* adopted a somewhat polished downtown version of militant white anger, first in relation to the West Side riot and then to the open city marches, expressing anger at the black ghetto violence and calling for a rough-and-ready frontier justice, while justifying the white violence on the theory that the demonstrators were "asking for trouble." The *Chicago Sun-Times*, firmly wedded to the civic credo of 1951, took a consistently "know nothing" attitude toward what the fuss was all about. The paper insisted that "responsible" leaders in Chicago were already committed to the movement's goals, thereby implying that the demonstrations were unnecessary and that the failure to achieve negotiations was to be laid at the movement's door. The *Sun-Times*, like the *Daily News*, did defend the demonstrators' constitutional right to protest; but, like the *Tribune*, the *Sun-Times* expressed editorial sympathy for the Gage Park residents, who "sincerely believe that demonstrators for open housing are being deliberately provocative." After all, that belief was shared at the editorial offices of the *Sun-Times*, which covered the demonstrations but did not report the cases against the realtors. The *Daily News* took a "pox on both your houses" stance, condemning the racism of the militant whites while characterizing the movement as committed to "brute force."

Only the *Defender* maintained the position that "residential segregation is a root cause of racial unrest" and that the burden of finding a solution was on

235

the white leadership. By mid-August, this leadership was aware of its responsibility even if the white press continued to focus on the marches. But it was unclear, on the eve of a precedent-setting conference of the metropolitan leaders, what could or should be done, first to resolve the immediate civic crisis and then to work on some of the underlying issues. The confrontation with urban violence had brought an urgency to civil rights issues in the North which they had never had before, but it was not a foregone conclusion that this new-found urgency would lead in progressive directions. In terms of the dilemma of constitutional duties, the summer's events had forced the civic elite to recognize that the violence posed a police problem, but it remained to be seen how concerned they were about the policy problem of an open city.

CHAPTER NINE

The Search for an Agreement:

August 1966

On Wednesday morning, 17 August 1966, in the Episcopal Cathedral of St. James, the civil rights leaders finally arrived at the long-desired conference table to negotiate with the civic leaders the issues and demands that had been dramatized in the streets of Chicago with increasing intensity for the past four years. Around the U-shaped table were gathered Mayor Daley, representatives from the Chicago Commission on Human Relations, various other city agencies, the business community, organized labor, the Chicago Real Estate Board, King and Raby, and the members of the agenda committee. At the head of the U were Episcopal Bishop James A. Montgomery, chairman of the Chicago Commission on Religion and Race and host of the conference, other religious leaders, and Ben W. Heineman, president of the Chicago and Northwestern Railroad. Heineman had chaired President Johnson's White House conference in June and had agreed to chair this meeting as well. Members of the press were excluded from this summit meeting of some sixty civic leaders. In the heat of the moment, representatives of the schools, for so long the object of civil rights concerns, were forgotten.[1]

Bishop Montgomery opened by affirming that the church needed to be relevant to the concerns of the time and that it should provide a meeting place for all people. He then introduced Heineman, who, he explained, had been chosen to chair the conference so that CCRR members would be free to speak in support of the movement. Heineman began by calling on Mayor Daley, inadvertently violating an agreement reached the previous night that King would open the meeting, Mayor Daley would speak next, and then King would present the movement's demands. The tension was such that the conference might have foundered at that point except that the mayor kept his remarks brief and formal. King said Chicago had "a dual school system, a dual economy, a dual housing market," and he appealed for "the help of the people with the real power . . . [in] transforming this duality into a oneness."

King turned to Raby, who said he was pessimistic about the negotiations because of previous experience with such efforts. He spoke of Cicero as symbolic of the difficulty to be faced:

> Fifteen years ago in Cicero a Negro family moved in; there was a riot, and they burned their house down. Fifteen years later when Negroes again say they may go into Cicero everyone is agreed that it will take the National Guard to protect any Negroes who go into that city. So there has not been any significant change through the natural process. The movement has exposed by its marches how we all have failed. We must admit that this dialogue that's beginning today would not have occurred without the marches. But there will be no resolution of this situation until we have a factual change in the circumstances of Negroes. We will not end our marches with a verbal commitment.

Ely M. Aaron, CCHR chairman, then introduced the city's eleven-point proposal supporting open occupancy, thus putting the real estate board on the spot, and called for ending the demonstrations, thus putting the movement on the spot and the mayor in a mediating position.[2]

A. L. Foster of the black Cosmopolitan Chamber of Commerce put in historical perspective the CCHR proposal that realtors support open occupancy. "You may not remember," Foster said, "that the Chicago Real Estate Board brought its proposals for establishing a network of restrictive covenants to the National Real Estate Board in Atlantic City and sold restrictive covenants, a device for racial exclusion, to the nation. So it is particularly appropriate that we demand of them that they now completely change their position and sell the national real estate industry on the proposition that it has got to support open housing rather than closed housing."

Ross Beatty, president of the real estate board, responded:

> This meeting is a good thing. The most important thing for us to understand is what the situation really is as it exists—not what we like it to be or want it to be, but what it really is. Also we must approach things of the past as past.
>
> My associates are decent honest gentlemen. They are leaders in their community. And now I want to tell you how they feel. This is our statement. We are not here to negotiate because the problem can't be solved between us and the civil rights people. You must understand that realtors accept property as an agent. The realtor doesn't own or control the property. It is this agency relationship—we are the agents—that binds the realtor under the law to the person for whom he is an agent.
>
> Now we have concluded after considerable experience that we cannot persuade property owners to change their attitudes about whom they want to sell their property to. And therefore we will reflect their attitude change. Now we know that there are problems and we are the ones who are easy to blame since someone is needed to blame. But the problem is not ours. The realtor is an agent; we must represent our clients. And therefore, because our clients are opposed to the open occupancy law, we must oppose the law if we are to honestly represent our clients.

238

We would propose that a market research corporation be hired to assess community attitudes to see whether or not the community is properly reflected by our position. We are asking also that there be conferences with community leaders to see if they will take the leadership in changing attitudes. The realtors cannot take the lead in this for various reasons. We would also like a clearer definition of the Chicago open occupancy ordinance. We will urge our people to obey the law, and we will ask our board to restate their position.

At that point Raby introduced the nine movement demands:

1. The Mayor should immediately launch a new program to enforce the Chicago Fair Housing Ordinance effectively and vigorously everywhere in the city. Specifically, we ask as 1st steps of such a good faith program:
   a) That the City policy of equal housing opportunity and a digest of the ordinance be required to be posted on the windows of all real estate offices in the city.
   b) That the City of Chicago test real estate offices for compliance with the law all over the city and on a year-round basis.
   c) That the City of Chicago launch a program of initiating complaints against violators of the ordinance all over the city and on a year-round basis.
   d) That the city hire additional people to enforce the law and act on complaints within 48 hours as is done by other city agencies where inspection reveals violations of liquor and food laws.
   e) That the licenses of real estate brokers found in clear violation of the law be immediately suspended.
   f) That the city seek the authority for a more powerful fair housing ordinance, one which would apply to property owners as well as to real estate brokers.
2. The Chicago Real Estate Board should:
   a) Immediately withdraw its support of the suit contesting the legality of the Chicago Fair Housing Ordinance.
   b) Withdraw its opposition to the Governor's fair housing executive order and to the fair housing provision of the 1966 federal civil rights bill and persuade other realtor groups to cease their warfare against the order and the proposed federal legislation.
   c) Pledge to support an effective state fair housing law, one which applies to property owners as well as brokers, in the coming session of the state legislature.
3. The Chicago Housing Authority should adopt a policy of no more high rise public housing projects in the Negro ghetto and in high density areas. All groups present should support the CHA in such a policy.
4. The Cook County Department of Public Aid should end the containment policy of seeking housing for and placing Negro families solely in ghetto communities.
5. The Urban Renewal program should adopt a policy of using its relocation services to break down segregation barriers and to promote an open city.
6. Savings and Loan Associations and other financial institutions should adopt an

239

effective policy of equal service and lend mortgage money to qualified Negro families for purchase of housing anywhere in the metropolitan area.

7. The Federal Deposit Insurance Corporation should suspend from membership any bank or savings and loan association which is found guilty of practicing racial discrimination in the provision of financial services to the public.

8. The Association of Commerce and Industry and the Chicago Federation of La-bor–Industrial Union Council should pledge support of these reforms, and initi-ate vigorous education programs among their members on the morality of an open city. Business and labor leaders should also use their financial resources to build integrated low and middle income housing in areas outside the ghetto.

9. Religion leaders should pledge support of these reforms and initiate vigorous programs in closed communities on the morality of an open city. Religious in-stitutions should also pledge financial support for the construction of integrated low and middle income housing in areas outside the ghetto.[3]

There was no immediate response to these demands. Instead, Leonard Foster of the Garfield Park Chamber of Commerce picked up where his father had left off. "I've heard Beatty's position," the younger Foster said, "and he says, 'we are not responsible,' yet he has in the real estate board the key people for setting trends. He says the board people are only agents, but . . . the agent-client capacity is not one in which the agent must do and does do anything the client wants. There are many directions that realtors take, or that clients take from their agents. Basically, they now assume that the client is discriminatory, and they take his listing as discriminatory unless the client indicates to the reverse."

Clark Stayman of the Chicago Mortgage Bankers Association then made the first concrete response to the nine proposals, saying that the demand that mortgages be made available "in all neighborhoods without regard to race or religion" could be "absolutely accepted" by the association.

Daley asked if the demonstrations would stop if the demands were met. King answered, "Yes, the demonstrations in the neighborhoods might stop, but we also have demands in the areas of education and employment. You are hearing here only our demands in the area of housing." Daley replied, "If we do all we can as a city, then why can't the marches stop? I thought this was supposed to be a kickoff for a conference table." King countered by asking the mayor if he agreed to the demands specifically addressed to him. Daley read each of the six items and agreed to them.

John Baird, of Baird and Warner Realty and president of the Metropolitan Housing and Planning Council, then suggested, "With all due respect, the mayor can't really do all the things he has said here immediately. Will the marches stop before the mayor has been able to accomplish the specifics?"

Rather than answering, Raby pointed out that only the mayor had said what he was willing to do: "We must hear from everyone."

Charles Swibel, to whom the third demand was addressed, responded: "I can't say that we will cease building high-rises in ghetto neighborhoods immediately, because I think the elderly should have high-rises. Also, we should ask the county and the suburbs if they would provide us land to build low-rises on. But we will agree that we will build non-ghetto low-rise as much as is feasible." Edwin Berry of the Chicago Urban League explained that the demand concerned high-rise apartments for families, not elderly, and raised the question of twelve sites then on the drawing board—all in the ghetto and most of them high-rise.

The mayor intervened to explain that federal regulations created the high-rises by limiting the cost per apartment. "Once you pay for land costs in the city, you have to build high-rise." Berry, however, was not satisfied. "The CHA always blames City Council" for ghetto sites, he said. "Can *you* get sites out of the ghetto?" he asked the mayor. Daley did not respond directly. "Well, let's get the slums out of our cities and replace them. I know about public housing," he said.

> We've got Negro neighborhoods where they don't want public housing, just like white neighborhoods. Now I don't want to concentrate all the poor people in one place, but we've got to put public housing some place in some neighborhoods.
>
> I can't see how we can keep lecturing to children that they live in ghettos because it gives them a ghetto mentality. We should say to them what we can do to make public housing a good place to live in even if it has been a mistake in the past. We're building up great frustrations in our public housing projects.

Edward Marciniak joined the discussion to point out that the problems of the housing authority were metropolitan problems. "Have you asked the Cook County Public Housing Authority," he queried the movement leaders, "about whether or not they will help give us vacant land sites? What is their response?"

At this point, Arthur Mohl, past president of the real estate board, wanted to speak for that group. "Let me make it clear," Mohl said,

> the Chicago Real Estate Board will obey the Chicago city open occupancy ordinance. In our view each member can interpret his action with his lawyer because we are a trade association, and what his legal position is will be defined between himself and his lawyer.
>
> Most of what we are doing here is nit-picking. Twenty-five percent of the rental housing in this city is actually controlled by realtors, and the rest is controlled by individuals who are not realtors who own buildings. Now, if we are going to be realistic, we must ask how can we deal with the bigoted attitudes in the neighborhoods. You can accuse us as though we created that bigotry until the end of the world, but we are not the creators, we are the mirror. We need a cooperative venture here, not bullying, but a program to sell people in the neighborhoods on the idea that the world won't end if a Negro moves in.

241

Mohl closed by saying that the Chicago Real Estate Board was not in the business of resolving social problems.

King replied: "I disagree. . . . All over the South I heard the same thing we've just heard from Mr. Mohl from restaurant owners and hotel owners. They said that they were just the agents, that they were just responding to the people's unwillingness to eat with Negroes in the same restaurant or stay with Negroes in the same hotel. But we got a comprehensive civil rights bill and the so-called agents then provided service to everybody and nothing happened and the same thing can happen here."

As several people addressed the chair, each wanting to make sure that a particular point would be discussed, Heineman announced, "I want to make it clear that I don't intend to recess this day until we have resolved these issues; I have no plans to recess except for lunch." That was a surprise because the meeting had been scheduled for two hours, but Heineman was following a mandate from the mayor that he should "get this issue settled today."

Thomas G. Ayers, president of Commonwealth Edison and of the Chicago Association of Commerce and Industry, agreed with King on the importance of law in changing behavior, citing the example of fair employment practices legislation, which the association had supported. He concluded by saying that the association backed "all the points in the proposals of the Chicago Freedom Movement." A spokesman for the Chicago Federation of Labor then also endorsed the proposals.

With the mayor, the business leadership, and organized labor now in agreement, Bevel turned the discussion back to the realtors. "The key problem," he said,

> is that realtors refuse to serve Negroes in their offices. And that must change. That is insulting and it is humiliating. And the burden is to change service to Negroes. If the city were opened then everyone would stop discriminating against Negroes.
>
> We have a big problem in Chicago; it's safer now in Birmingham than it is here in Chicago. Rockwell [head of the American Nazi Party] is leading this city, and the Chicago Real Estate Board should begin to lead it.

Beatty responded by saying there were only three real estate board members present; the full board would be meeting that afternoon. "All of the real estate industry must get together, not just ourselves. We're only a portion of it. . . . We can't sit across the table and bargain with the civil righters for something we don't have the power to give."

Another real estate board representative drew an analogy: "If King would come out against the fair housing ordinance, he would lose his supporters. He would lose his position and he would not be a leader. You've got to realize that you're asking us to do the same thing. When we ask our realtors to abrogate their position as agents, then you're asking us to do what you'd be

242

asking Dr. King to do if you told him he had to come out against the fair housing ordinance."

King tried to put the issue in the context of principle. "I must appeal to the decency of the people on the Chicago Real Estate Board," he said.

You're not negotiating this question with us. You are men confronted with a moral issue.

I decide on the basis of conscience. A genuine leader doesn't reflect consensus, he molds consensus. Look at myself—there are lots of Negroes these days who are for violence, but I know that I am dealing with a moral issue, and I am going to oppose violence if I am the last Negro in this country speaking for non-violence.

Now the real estate people must act on principle in that same manner, or they're not leaders. The real estate industry has not only reflected discriminatory attitudes, it has played a significant part in creating them. In fact, in California, the real estate people spent five million dollars to kill the open occupancy law there. Now don't tell me that you're neutral.

Yesterday, I spoke with Attorney General Katzenbach about another problem. He told me that, if the money that the real estate industry was using to fight the federal open occupancy law were available to the government, they could eliminate all the slums in one major city. I appeal to the rightness of our position and to your decency. I see nothing in this world more dangerous than Negro cities ringed with white suburbs. Look at it in terms of grappling with righteousness. People will adjust to changes, but the leadership has got to say that the time for change has come. The problem is not the people in Gage Park; the problem is that their leaders and institutions have taught them to be what they are.

Beatty was not moved: "Well, we will recommend to our board that we sit down with you and discuss this further. But we have got to be clear on what the Chicago open occupancy ordinance really requires." Persisting in his notion of just who was responsible for open occupancy, he concluded with a plea: "We must find a way of reaching the people."

Donald Zimmerman, moderator of the Chicago Presbytery and president of the Church Federation of greater Chicago, brought the discussion back to the actual demands: "I want to call us back to the three points [dealing with realtors] in the freedom movement demands. These demands are basically for the real estate board to change its present actions in regard to legislation and laws," he observed. "I think the Chicago Real Estate Board can act on these"—without waiting for a change of attitude in the neighborhoods.

Rabbi Robert Marx, of the Union of American Hebrew Congregations, argued that "we have heard this same thing from the real estate board over and over. They must understand that we must have a change now." Robert Johnson, UAW regional director, agreed. "This is an urgent situation. The real estate board must realize there must be a change now. . . . No one can stand in the road of progress. You can't go back now and do your business as usual."

243

Thinking that the meeting had proceeded as far as it could, Raby suggested that it adjourn. Daley, however, pressed for a resolution. "No, let's not adjourn the meeting. The Chicago Real Estate Board should get on the phone to their members and do something about these demands now."

Heineman summarized the proceedings: "Gentlemen, the big stumbling block here is the Chicago Real Estate Board and what it's going to do about the demands on it. And the representatives of the real estate board must realize that they are the key to this thing. The monkey, gentlemen, is right on your back, and whether you deem it as fair or not, everyone sees that the monkey is there. And the question is how are you going to deal with the demands placed on you."

With that, the meeting was adjourned until four o'clock, when the realtors were to report what they had been able to accomplish at the meeting of their board that afternoon.

The civil rights leaders met over lunch to discuss whether, and under what conditions, they were prepared to call a moratorium on the marches. They determined to focus on the reality of an open city rather than law enforcement and to insist on concrete results before halting the marches.

Meanwhile, Mayor Daley placed a call to Beatty at the real estate board office. "In the interest of the City of Chicago, you cannot come back here this afternoon with a negative answer," the mayor insisted.[4]

CHICAGO REAL ESTATE BOARD: A PHILOSOPHICAL CONCESSION

Beatty began the four o'clock session by restating the position of the Chicago Real Estate Board:

1. As a leadership organization in Chicago, we state the fundamental principle that freedom of choice in housing is the right of every citizen. We believe that all citizens should accept and honor that principle.
2. We reiterate our belief that progress in race relations can be produced only under a favorable climate and that the technique of street demonstrations will harden the bigotry and slow down the progress.

   If demonstrations don't terminate promptly, we may lose control of our members and be unable to fulfill the commitments we have undertaken.
3. We have decided we will—as a Chicago organization—withdraw all opposition to the philosophy of open occupancy at the state level—provided it is applicable to owners as well as brokers—and we reserve the right to criticize details as distinguished from philosophy—and we will request the state association of real estate boards to do likewise, but we cannot dictate to them.
4. We respond to the [Chicago] Human Relations Commission by stating we will effectively remind our members it is their duty to obey the Chicago Fair Housing Ordinance as their lawyers interpret its meaning. We do not accept the gover-

During 1961 and 1962, school protests frequently began in black neighborhoods where school board policies created racial segregation and overcrowding. Seventh-graders and their parents conducted the first sitin of the Chicago school controversy at Burnside School in January 1962. Enrollment there was more than forty-three pupils per classroom. (*Chicago Daily News,* 5 January 1962.)

By April 1962 a coalition of civil rights and community organizations called the Coordinating Council of Community Organizations (CCCO) had emerged, in part to organize school protests. Initially a low-profile organization, its first public meeting packed Woodlawn Methodist Church in July 1963. (Photograph by Jack Lenahan, *Chicago Sun-Times,* 21 July 1963.)

In August 1963, members of the Congress on Racial Equality (CORE) joined with local parents and children to block installation of mobile classrooms known as Willis wagons at Seventy-third and Lowe because there was already adequate classroom space in four predominantly white schools nearby. (*Chicago Daily News*, 2 August 1963.)

Left: In the face of growing protests, School Superintendent Benjamin C. Willis refused to change his policies and thus became the focus of criticism. On 15 August 1963, a front-page editorial in the *Chicago Daily Defender* called Willis "an emblem of racial segregation." Two years later, he was still defending the same policies. (*Chicago Daily Defender,* 4 August 1965.)

Below: Following the arrest of thirty-six members of CORE conducting a sitin at the Board of Education offices on 11 October, a wall was erected to prevent any further demonstrations there. This wall became a symbol of Willis's insulation from the public. (Photograph by Morgan Photo Service, *Chicago Daily Defender,* 21 October 1963.)

Willis resigned in October 1963 rather than implement a school board plan that might have brought a handful of black honor students to all-white Bogan High School—over the vehement objections of Bogan parents. When the school board backed down and persuaded Willis to stay, Warren Bacon was the lone "no" vote. (*Chicago Sun-Times,* 17 October 1963.)

The school board's refusal to accept Willis's resignation led CCCO to call for a boycott of the schools on 22 October. In all, 225,000 students participated. (*Chicago Daily Defender,* 17 October 1963.)

The school boycott brought public recognition to both CCCO and Lawrence Landry, the leader of that protest (center). Bayard Rustin (right) was the organizer of the march on Washington on 28 August 1963. (*Chicago Daily Defender,* 12 December 1963.)

When the CCCO was unable to translate its public support into any change in school board policies, it called a second school boycott for 25 February 1964. The Democratic machine actively opposed the boycott, including Alderman Claude W. B. Holman (bottom left foreground). One hundred and seventy-five thousand students joined in the boycott, but that was less than had participated in October. (*Chicago Daily Defender*, 25 February 1964.)

The seventy-five thousand participants in the Illinois Rally for Civil Rights at Soldier Field on 21 June 1964 made it the largest such demonstration Chicago had seen. Originally planned to push for passage of the 1964 Civil Rights Act, it met to celebrate the passage of that legislation two days earlier. This national mandate for civil rights stood in contrast with the civil rights stalemate in Chicago. (*Chicago Sun-Times*, 22 June 1964.)

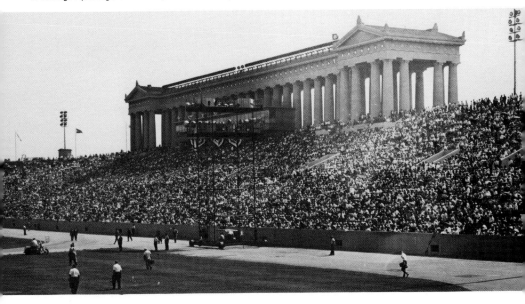

Above: The Reverend Samuel S. Morris, Jr., and Alan B. Anderson of the CCCO led forty clergymen, one for each day of Lent, as they circled City Hall on Ash Wednesday to dramatize their opposition to School Superintendent Willis. (*Chicago Daily News,* 3 March 1965.)

Left: The renewal of Willis's contract in May 1965 led to a third school boycott in June, daily marches in the Loop throughout the summer, and the arrest of hundreds of demonstrators for blocking traffic. Mayor Richard J. Daley refused to meet with leaders of the first march on 10 June: Dick Gregory (center), Father William Hogan, CCCO recorder (far left), Albert Raby, CCCO convenor (center rear), and Robert Lucas of CORE (right). (*Chicago Sun-Times,* 11 June 1965.)

For two days, King addressed a series of community rallies, mainly in black neighborhoods like this one at Orleans and Oak on the Near North Side. He asked the crowds to join him for a rally and march downtown the following Monday. (*Chicago Sun-Times*, 25 July 1965.)

Opposite: In July 1965, Martin Luther King, Jr., and members of his staff toured cities in the North exploring possible locations for a campaign on "northern issues." His three-day visit to Chicago was sponsored by the CCCO under the leadership of Albert Raby (left) and began with a meeting with two hundred Chicago clergy at El Bethel Baptist Church, 5657 South Lafayette. (*Chicago Sun-Times*, 25 July 1965.)

Opposite: More than ten thousand Chicagoans responded to King's call and marched with him down State Street to City Hall. The success of King's visit in July 1965 convinced him to make Chicago the base of his northern campaign the following year. (*Chicago Sun-Times*, 27 July 1965.)

Throughout the fall, Raby and the CCCO continued to build the case against Chicago's schools, charging an unresponsive school board with segregation, gerrymandering, and poor quality education at this hearing held by the West Side Federation. From left: the Reverend James Mack, Edgar H. S. Chandler of the Church Federation, author Lerone Bennett, Professor W. Alvin Pitcher of the University of Chicago, and Albert Raby. (*Chicago Sun-Times*, 1 August 1965.)

The Reverend James Bevel moved to Chicago in 1965, the first of King's Southern Christian Leadership Conference (SCLC) staff to do so. The Union to End Slums that he organized kept black power issues on the agenda as the CCCO and SCLC joined to form the Chicago Freedom Movement. (*Chicago Sun-Times.*)

Six months after he addressed this rally in Lawndale in July 1965, King moved into a nearby apartment on South Hamlin Avenue to dramatize the need to end slums. (Photograph by John Tweedle.)

Just as the Chicago Freedom Movement was entering its direct action phase, the West Side riot of 1966 began with youngsters seeking relief from the heat by opening fire hydrants only to have police turn them off. (*Chicago Sun-Times*, July 1966.)

The open city campaign began with demonstrators kneeling on the sidewalk in front of real estate offices in segregated, all-white areas—here, on West Sixty-third Street in Chicago Lawn. (Photograph by Jack Lenahan, *Chicago Sun-Times*, 30 July 1966.)

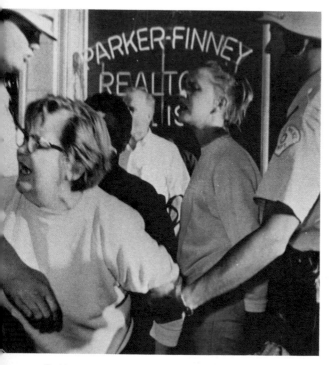

Twenty-one persons were arrested on 3 August in the all-white Belmont-Cragin area as police sought to protect 250 open city marchers from a white mob of 1,000 carrying rocks and bottles. Demonstrations there centered on the Parker and Finney, Inc., real estate agency at 5043 West Fullerton. (*Chicago Daily Defender,* 4 August 1966.)

Opposite, top: Swastikas, "white power" placards, and increasing violence greeted open city demonstrators in Chicago Lawn, Marquette Park, Belmont-Cragin, and here in Gage Park. (*Chicago Sun-Times,* 15 August 1966.)

Opposite, bottom: Behind the "white power lines," Raby addressed demonstrators outside a real estate office at 5434 South Kedzie in one of three marches that day as the Chicago Freedom Movement escalated its direct action tactics. (*Chicago Sun-Times,* 15 August 1966.)

Edwin C. "Bill" Berry, executive director of the Chicago Urban League, and Kale Williams of the American Friends Service Committee were among the Chicago Freedom Movement participants in the summit meetings of August 1966. (*Chicago Sun-Times*, 23 August 1966.)

Alderman Thomas Keane (31st), Alderman Ralph Metcalf (3d), and Mayor Richard J. Daley led the city's representatives at the summit meetings. (*Chicago Daily News*, 26 August 1966.)

King marched into Chicago's segregated East Side community while the summit agreement on open housing was being worked out. (*Chicago Sun-Times*, 22 August 1966.)

Below: Albert Raby and Martin Luther King, Jr., co-chairs of the Chicago Freedom Movement, announced that the open housing marches would be called off as a result of the summit agreement they had just reached with city leaders. (*Chicago Daily News*, 26 August 1966.)

Chester Robinson, leader of the West Side Organization, accused King and Raby of "selling out Negro interests" for "empty promises" and proceeded with a march into all-white Cicero on 4 September 1966. (*Chicago Sun-Times*, 28 August 1966.)

The tent-in at Weston, Illinois, on 22 June 1967 protested the decision to locate a large atomic energy research facility in an area not open to black residents. (*Chicago Sun-Times*, June 1967.)

nor's order as proper and will not ask compliance so long as it is under injunction.

We accept the commission's invitation to appoint a committee to help clarify the detailed application and meaning of the ordinance.

We object to the proposal by the Freedom Movement that the city or citizens engage in testing real estate offices. This is unwarranted harassment.

5. We cannot sacrifice principles we have espoused in our objection to the constitutionality of the Chicago ordinance—as requested by the Chicago Freedom Movement.[5]

Raby was not sure how to interpret this response. "We've heard your statement; we're not sure what you're saying," he said. "What is your position on our demands A, B, and C?"

"On your demand A," Beatty replied, "which is to withdraw our support from the suit testing the legality of the Chicago Fair Housing ordinance, No. B, to withdraw our opposition to the governor's fair housing executive order, No. C, to support an effective state fair housing law, No, but we will agree to withdraw our opposition to a law."

Bevel wanted concrete results. "Gentlemen, I don't think the important thing is what your position is about A, B, and C," he said. "The question is whether Negroes are going to be served at your office tomorrow morning."

William R. Ming, a member of the NAACP Legal Defense Committee present as a CCHR member, said that the city ordinance already required what Bevel was demanding. "The ordinance is clear," he argued. "Ever since September, 1963 every broker has been obliged to abide by practices which are in compliance with what it is that Mr. Bevel wants. The Negro is protected by this ordinance. He must be served under this ordinance by realtors."

Bevel, however, expressed his desire for something more than the law and its slow process of enforcement. He cited his experience in Memphis in 1960:

We had a series of marches to try to open up the restaurants and, finally, we had a meeting like this. What was agreed was not that they were going to pass a law or anything like that. The power structure said that they were going to see to it that we could eat in Memphis. One week later we went out and we ate and we have been eating in Memphis ever since. Now that's what we want here today.

I want to re-emphasize that we need Negroes to be served in real estate offices. And you people here can see that will happen. That's a conservative, simple, humane request, and let's not confuse the issue with all these A's, B's and C's.

Andrew Young agreed, giving a similar example from the Savannah civil rights movement, which had addressed school issues. "Legislation and a court decision affecting the schools followed," he said, "but we got the change before the legislation and the court decision. Now, we need leadership to bring a result. Where they have had ordinances and laws, they don't work

245

to produce the result we want. We need a plan to do right and not a law to stop wrong."

Beatty seized upon these statements about the insufficiencies of the law to claim support for his own position. "I couldn't agree with you more," the realtor said. "We should take the monkey off our back and put it on the back of all the people." That was hardly the point James Bevel and Andrew Young had been making.

Zimmerman of the Chicago Presbytery brought the discussion back to the realtors and the law. He asked Ming, "Does the ordinance provide that realtors should do what Mr. Bevel says, that is, serve Negroes?" Assured by Ming that the ordinance did so provide, Zimmerman turned to Beatty: "When you tell your people to obey the ordinance, will you tell them that they should serve Negroes?" Beatty hedged: "We're still not clear on some points of the ordinance. We can ask them to obey the law."

In the face of this continuing recalcitrance from the realtors, Raby turned to Daley. "Now I want to know," Raby asked, "when the mayor will see that an ordinance is enacted to require that all real estate dealers post in their windows the open occupancy law and a statement of policy on nondiscrimination." The mayor was flustered for he was not usually questioned so pointedly. "I said already this morning that I would do that. I keep my word and that will be done. Actually I've got my corporation counsel checking on it right now to see whether we can do it without an ordinance—whether we can just require it under existing law."

William Robinson, a former Republican state legislator and a member of the agenda committee, asked Daley about the state law. Daley replied, "The Democrats have always supported a state open occupancy law and the Republicans have fought it. We need a state law that covers the metropolitan area."

Rabbi Marx turned attention back to the realtors, citing the portion of their statement that said, "If demonstrations don't terminate promptly, we may lose control of our members." "You have been here all morning saying to us," Marx noted, "that you don't have control over your people and that, therefore, we are asking the wrong people to change. Now do you have control or don't you have control?"

At that point, Jesse Jackson tried to "go back to the basic issue," which, in his view, was religious. He talked of the theological dimensions of the matters before the group and concluded, "I'm not concerned about your law. Dr. King has told you what the needs are, and your law must come to a higher level than it has come. It must come to the theological level."

Raby put the basic issue more pragmatically: "I think we must ask, can a Negro walk into a real estate office and be served? If we find that in fact is true, then whatever it is that the real estate board is trying to say in its statement will not be of any concern to us because that's what we want. And if we find that's true in fact, then your statement is all right. If not, it is not."

Berry, however, found the real estate board statement "totally unacceptable" and asked the mayor, "If the Chicago Real Estate Board can't do something about our demands, can you?"

The mayor, however, was not about to become the focus or the issue in this discussion. He replied to Berry by coming to the defense of the real estate board—the first person to have done so all afternoon.

> I think they've done a lot. It shows a real change that they've come in here indicating that they will no longer oppose open occupancy. We will act as an agency through the human relations commission. We shouldn't ask the real estate board to withdraw its suit.
>
> We have agreed to virtually all the points here and everyone says that they are going to move ahead. Now let's not quibble over words: the intent is the important thing. We're here in good faith and the city is asking for your help.

Heineman also challenged Berry: "Bill, you said the statement is worthless, but isn't point three, the willingness of the board to stop opposing the state open occupancy law, a significant change?" Berry did not think so. "I've had a long experience with them. They will say that they will withdraw it, but they are still fighting the principle in court."

Heineman persisted in finding merit in the statement, however, and finally Berry conceded, "Well, on fourth reading . . . the third statement is something." Heineman said, "It is a concession."

King then expressed his own concerns about the limitation of law to achieve the movement's goals:

> I hope that people here don't feel that we are just being recalcitrant, but we do have a little history of disappointment and broken promises. I certainly wouldn't want to argue with Mr. Ming. Mr. Ming was my lawyer who saved me in court in Alabama from ten years in prison and he's my great counselor. But I would remind him that ten years ago we got a court decision and a law three years ago now that says that segregation is illegal, and we now have 5.3% of the children integrated in the South. And Bob Ming is telling me now that the ordinance will do the job! We see a gulf between the promise and the fulfillment.
>
> We don't want to fool people any longer; they feel they have been fooled. So we are asking today that Negroes can buy anywhere. When will that be? Tell us, so that we won't fool the people. We need a timetable, something very concrete. We want to know what your implementation is.

Heineman then summarized the negotiations to that point:

> The mayor has accepted your demands on him.
> The real estate board has stated that it will withdraw its opposition to a state open

occupancy law. This is a great victory, a major victory, and probably insures passage of that legislation.

The other demands have been mainly accepted. The only one that hasn't been involves the Federal Deposit Insurance Corporation and they aren't here. I can pass your claim along to them.

The chair feels that we are well on our way to realization and that the demonstrations could now cease until we see if these agreements are working out.

Bevel, however, returned to the difficulty of realizing the movement's aims through law:

Most all the laws have not been effective in providing men housing. We're asking the board of the realtors and the city of Chicago to go beyond that law. We don't want a commission investigation. . . . I can't suggest anything to the Negro people of this town until I can say to them, to a man, to a Negro man, "You can buy land from the people who sell land." Nothing less. Now white men don't go to commissions to get a house, and I'm a man like white men, and I go to a real estate office. Anything that you come up with, any scheme or game, that's short of that is inadequate.

Robert Spike (CCRR) then added his voice to Heineman's.[6] "I consider the change by the Chicago Real Estate Board profound. I don't think, on the other hand, that we should take Bevel's frustration lightly. But we've got to make clear here that the Chicago Freedom Movement didn't say, in its three demands to the real estate board, what Bevel is saying, and that is that Negroes would be served in all the offices. I think we need some terms here for a moratorium." As one observer noted, Spike was "the first person outside the establishment" who called for halting the marches. Spike seems not to have understood that in calling for the enforcement of Chicago's 1963 fair housing ordinance, the movement was demanding what Bevel was saying.[7]

Raby, however, did not think the group was "nearly so clear on all these things as Mr. Heineman says . . .—points three, four, and five, for instance." The discussion turned to these items, which concerned the Chicago Housing Authority, the Cook County Department of Public Aid, and the Chicago Department of Urban Renewal.

The public aid representative denied the movement's charge that his agency had a "containment policy" and placed "Negro families solely in ghetto communities." "We let people pick their own housing," he said. William Robinson, a former social worker, disagreed: "Negro families are encouraged by your people to find housing inside the ghetto."

Kale Williams, of the American Friends Service Committee and a member of the agenda committee, put the issue in the context of affirmative action by noting that all three points concerned public policies that had not heretofore had any effect on opening the city to black residents. The agencies involved

248

could open the city, Williams argued, if their tenant placement and site selection policies were affirmatively administered.

Young continued this theme. "The question is," he said, "Who is going to bear responsibility for desegregating the city? The society must change the patterns so that the individual can and will be moved out, rather than producing laws that put the individual in the position of having to move himself. We need a plan to aggressively desegregate this city, and we must take the responsibility here for implementing it."

Young underlined the urgency of his appeal by reference to the pathology of the ghetto:

As to your fears of violence, let me say that it is more dangerous in Lawndale with those jammed-up, neurotic, psychotic Negroes than it is in Gage Park. To white people who don't face the violence which is created by the degradation of the ghetto, this violence that you see in Gage Park may seem like a terrible thing, but I live in Lawndale and it is safer for me in Gage Park than it is in Lawndale. For the Negro in the ghetto, violence is the rule. So, when you say, cease these demonstrations, you're saying to us, go back to a place where there is more violence than where you see violence taking place outside the ghetto.

Daley reacted: "Did I hear you say that we are going to have more violence in this city?"

Young responded: "No, I'm saying that Negroes who are jammed into ghettos are people who are forced into violent ways of life. I'm saying the Blackstone Rangers are the product of what happens to people when you live in a ghetto. I'm saying that the ghetto has to be dispersed, that this city must be opened up, and this high concentration ended, or we will have violence whether there is a movement or not."

Daley rejoined: "The city didn't create this frustration or this situation. We want to try to do what you say."

Young answered: "Well, we need a program. We need to know how much is going to be accomplished in thirty days, and how much in sixty days. We will find families to move into twenty communities in the next thirty days. The United Auto Workers could find twenty or twenty-five families to move near their plants rather than being so far away. We've got to have a plan for an open city to take to the people."

Heineman was concerned at this apparent escalation of the movement's demands. "Now I think we've got to understand what we are talking about here," the chairman said. "We understood that your proposals were on these two pages, and it sounds now like you're changing things."

"No," Young answered.

What I'm talking about is a plan to implement what is on those two pages. For instance, we say that the Public Aid Commission will end its enforced ghettoization

249

of Negro recipients. So for the woman who lives in the apartment below our apartment, an aid recipient who works in a hospital on the North Side, the public aid commission would go out and look for a house on the North Side, near the hospital where she is working so she wouldn't be spending an hour and a half every day getting to work and an hour and a half going back. And the public housing authority would go out and find a site in Jefferson Park where we could build the next low-rise public housing units.

Swibel responded: "I will pledge to you that we will move people out," he said. "Take our word. I want to see these marches ended today. If we are dealing on top of the table, then call off the marches for twelve months. [At this, there was a groan from the movement side of the table.] We can't get an okay on Jefferson Park public housing sites in less time than that because the federal government will require so much red tape."

Charles Hayes, of the Packinghouse Workers and a member of the agenda committee, made a final appeal:

> I think that you need to be a Negro to really understand what the situation is here. I represent Negro people, laboring people. I am a Negro first: I was born that way; I'll die that way. I am a trade unionist since I was nineteen. I want you to know that there are a whole lot of people in this town who believe in Jim Bevel. No one here is holding anyone responsible, but what we're asking, what I'm saying here, is, we've got to see that we're in changing times and we can't go out after these negotiations and tell the guy on the street that what we got was an agreement from the Chicago Real Estate Board that they philosophically agree with open occupancy. The people want to hear what we're going to do for them now. If I as a union negotiator ever came back to my men and said to them, "I got the company to agree that philosophically they were in support of seniority," I'd be laughed out of court.

A fifteen-minute recess was then declared at Raby's request so the movement representatives could consult among themselves. At this caucus no one felt that the proposed agreements were sufficient grounds for calling off the marches.

CHICAGO FREEDOM MOVEMENT: NO MORATORIUM YET

When the conference reconvened, all eyes were on Raby, who stood to announce the results of the caucus. "We view this meeting as very important and significant," he began.

> For the first time there are verbalizations, at least, that show that we have some opportunities for change.
> But I would remind you that the important thing we stressed at the beginning of the meeting was the actuality, the implementation; that's the key. We can see the need for further discussions. In your mind the question may be a moratorium, but

we would have to say that we would have a moratorium on demonstrations if we had a moratorium on housing segregation. We would like to see a meeting one week from now to see what you're doing in terms of implementation. In the meantime we would meet in a sub-committee on specifics. I can remember everything this city did to see that a bond issue was passed, and we need that same kind of campaign on open housing. During this week we will have to continue our present plans.

Heineman asked if this meant there would be demonstrations during the next week, and Raby answered, "Yes. Demonstrations will continue for the next week."

Abruptly, Daley stood. "I thought we were meeting to see if there couldn't be a halt to what is happening in our neighborhoods because of the use of all the police and the crime rate rising throughout our city," he said.

I repeat, as far as the city is concerned, we are prepared to do what is asked for. I appeal to you as citizens to try to understand that we are trying.

I ask why you picked Chicago? I make no apologies for our city. In the name of all our citizens I ask for a moratorium and that we set up a committee. We're men of good faith and we can work out an agreement. The police can't give our people adequate protection now.

What's the difference between today and [a] week from today with men of good faith? We're defending your rights, and also there's no question about the law. Can't you do today what you would do in a week?

Ayers called attention back to the movement's demands: "We started on this document, and I don't think we should leave it now. We've gotten substantial agreement; we ought to make sure at least that we know what the outstanding areas are."

Raby responded: "Well, let me give you an example. Is the mayor going to ask for the legislation to require brokers to post the ordinance in their windows? Will he ask for that legislation next Tuesday and will he get it? Will that actually be implemented?"

The mayor, however, made his action contingent on the moratorium. "We've got to show the city council that you'll do something," he argued. "We'll pass what we said we'd pass if we get a moratorium."

Daley's statement angered Raby. "Some day I hope I can come before the mayor of Chicago with what is just, and he will implement it because it is right—rather than trading it politically for a moratorium!"

Heineman, trying to moderate the tone of the discussion, censured Raby: "In a cooler moment, I think you'll realize that the mayor cannot help but want fewer demonstrations; he's concerned about the safety of the people. And the mayor is accustomed to having his word taken."

But Raby angrily continued, spelling out just how unsatisfactory the agreements made so far were from the movement's perspective:

251

The real estate board hasn't done anything meaningful here.

I'm not clear on what the Chicago Housing Authority is really going to do about high-rises.

The Cook County Department of Public Aid has got to change. It can't tell us that it has all Negro recipients in one area and all white recipients in another area and that's an accident. That's an insult to our intelligence.

The urban renewal program is going to have to do something about its relocation policies.

I want to hear the details about what the savings and loan people are going to do.

I want to see companies and unions who have been asked to do something here kick out their members, kick out their employees who are acting like Fascists in the neighborhoods. If an employee stole something and was arrested, they would be fired immediately, but when they're stoning Negro cars and innocent Negro people nothing happens at all.

I am not going to go back to our people with a philosophic program. We want a real program; a moratorium on discrimination will bring a moratorium on marches.

Just as Raby had found James Bevel's substitution of a "philosophical agreement" for programmatic goals frustrating in the fall, so now in the summer, he found the real estate board's attempt to substitute a "philosophical" concession for behavioral change infuriating.

It was King who calmed this heated discussion with an eloquent and conciliatory statement. He began positively:

This has been a constructive and a creative beginning. This represents progress and a sign of change.

I've gone through this whole problem in my mind about demonstrations a thousand times, and let me say that if you are tired of demonstrations, I am tired of demonstrating. I am tired of the threat of death. I want to live. I don't want to be a martyr. And there are moments when I doubt if I am going to make it through. I am tired of getting hit, tired of being beaten, tired of going to jail.

But the important thing is not how tired I am; the important thing is to get rid of the conditions that lead us to march. I hope we are here to discuss how to make Chicago a great open city and not how to end marches. We've got to have massive changes.

Now, gentlemen, you know we in the movement don't have much. We don't have much money. We don't really have much education, and we don't have political power. We have only our bodies, and you are asking us to give up the one thing that we have when you say, "Don't march!" We want to be visible. We are not trying to overthrow you, we're trying to get in. We're trying to make justice a reality. Now the basic thing is justice. We want peace, but peace is the presence of justice. We haven't seen enough for the massive changes that are going to be needed.

To the Chicago Real Estate Board, I want to say particularly that your second point about the demonstrations being the wrong approach bothers me. Because the problem is not created by the marches. A doctor doesn't cause cancer when he finds it; in fact, we thank him for finding it. We are doing the same thing. Our humble marches have revealed a cancer.

We have not used rocks. We have not used bottles. And no one today, no one who has spoken, has condemned those that have used violence. Maybe there should be a moratorium in Gage Park. Maybe we should begin condemning the robber and not the robbed. We haven't even practiced civil disobedience as a movement. But we are being asked to stop one of our most precious rights, the right to assemble, the right to petition.

We asked Chicago to bring justice in housing, and we are starting on that road today. We are trying to keep the issue so alive that it will be acted on. Our marching feet have brought us a long way, and if we hadn't marched I don't think we'd be here today. No one here has talked about the beauty of our marches, the love of our marches, the hatred we're absorbing. Let's hear more about the people who perpetuate the violence.

We appreciate the meeting. We don't want to end the dialog. We don't see enough to stop the marches, but we are going with love and non-violence. This is a great city and it can be a greater city.

Young pointed out that the group could begin work on a more concrete program immediately and come back together in the near future. Johnson urged that the present negotiations continue: "We're talking about the future of America, and we can't work it out in one day. We should meet tomorrow. Let's find out by tomorrow night how much further we can get than where we are today."

In a surprising reversal of his resolve to meet until the issues were settled, Heineman appointed a committee, chaired by Bishop Montgomery, to "come back with proposals designed to provide an open city." He gave the committee ten days to accomplish its task.

A lengthy discussion then ensued about what, if anything, they had agreed to. Heineman suggested that he, in company with Bishop Montgomery, tell the press that they had "a full discussion, profitable but not conclusive," that a subcommittee had been appointed "to work out details, if possible," and that they would meet again the following week. About the demonstrations, Heineman proposed to say: "There was no commitment to terminate them in the interim, but the chairman hoped that whatever was done would be done with the view to the overall interests of the city, and that the movement would proceed with great restraint."

The civil rights representatives were concerned that nothing be said to imply any change in the marches. "Can't you just say," King suggested, "if there are demonstrations, you want to call on the violent people to be restrained?" Daley, however, wanted it made clear that no agreement had been reached at the meeting. Swibel made a final plea that the marches be called off, but Raby replied, "That question has already been answered."

253

The discussion returned to whether Heineman should say the movement would proceed with restraint. King said, "I think we've been restrained." Bevel suggested that Heineman not say he hoped the movement would be restrained but that Negroes would not be discriminated against. Ming wanted to include some demonstration of progress in the public report. He proposed saying that they all agreed that they could not solve the problems of the city while maintaining residential segregation and that the problems could not be solved by violence. As it became obvious they could not agree on a common statement, Daley stood up and said, "I think everybody should be allowed to say anything they want to, that it be made clear this is a continuing meeting, and that this has been a beginning." With that, the meeting dissolved in a babble; but a day that had begun with a clear focus on the recalcitrance of the Chicago Real Estate Board ended with a public focus on the refusal of the movement to suspend its marches.

The *Sun-Times, Daily News,* and *American* all editorially applauded the "summit meeting" as a "gain toward understanding" and looked forward to "further gains" from the work of the subcommittee. All three lauded the negotiating stance of the "power structure," but none of them discussed the movement's demands other than to suggest that "progress comes a step at a time" or that open housing "cannot be accomplished in one summer." As a result of this emphasis on the appearance of progress rather than its reality, all three papers made their major focus the refusal of the movement to halt the marches. Each counseled civil rights leaders to call a moratorium lest they hurt "their own cause," create "a reaction against their objectives," or "jeopardize the gains made thus far."[8]

Only outrage, however, came from the offices of the *Tribune,* which characterized the conference as "unproductive," distinguished only "by the effrontery of the 'rights' leaders in voicing their demands and stating their price for civic peace." The editors attacked King for requesting that the real estate board drop its legal challenge to the city's open occupancy ordinance and that it comply with the governor's executive order. It supported the claim of realtors that "decisions in disposing or renting property were up to the owners involved and that real estate men could not shove down their throats something which they regarded as distasteful. Rights in the city and country are not wholly one-sided," the *Tribune* said, "even though it may sometimes seem so. If King and his marchers have a right to take to the streets in provocative demonstrations, other citizens have the right to resort to the law and the courts, and they also have the power of decision over their own concerns."[9]

NEGOTIATING STRATEGIES AND PUBLIC POSTURES:
THE ROAD TO A SUMMIT AGREEMENT

The agenda committee met on 18 August to review the previous day's conference. Andrew Young had gained a new sense of the mayor and his relations with his inner circle of advisers. "People do not tell Daley the truth," Young said. "He is not a bad man."

Arthur Griffin (WSF) agreed. "I can't remember any meeting with as much potential," he said. "I have never known the mayor to agree to everything without quibbling or equivocation." But it was clear to Griffin that the mayor "could not understand Jim" Bevel. Daley was "befogged," for example, by Bevel's statement that he "would not recommend that a Negro go to the [human relations] commission."

King affirmed the "good climate" of the meeting, but he saw it as "basically concerned to get the demonstrations stopped." In King's view, this was because "the mayor feels [the demonstrations] are hurting him" in Paul Douglas's reelection campaign. Therefore, "if things are done [by the mayor], they are done to get the demonstrations stopped." Because he saw "no final good faith disposition to make Chicago an open city, [only] to do what was necessary in a token manner to end demonstrations," King emphasized the importance of "establishing the lines of communication [necessary] to get things on paper [and] implemented."

Arthur Brazier (TWO) challenged Griffin's reading of the mayor. "The mayor often agrees with everything" while one is in his office, Brazier said, but then "fails to follow through."

Griffin responded, "I know it sounds like I am running interference for Daley. . . . [There is] nothing in the book to say Daley will keep his word— unless it's power. I think that in all probability the course that has been taken is a good one. The meeting set the ground for negotiations."

Jesse Jackson also saw the civil rights leaders' need for power in the negotiations. The problem was that "the civil rights movement does not have sustaining power," he said. "We can't call the demonstrations off and on. We need to get a check and balance position vis-à-vis the mayor."

King agreed: "I never got the impression he meant to do the things he was promising." King then underscored his earlier analysis: "Katzenbach called me. Paul Douglas being hurt has created the crisis we have been talking about."

Bevel entered the discussion for the first time to repeat his attack on the human relations commission. "That commission," he said, "was set up to keep people from getting housing. It's a crying department for niggers."

King put Bevel's bitterness into a larger context. "They fail," he said, "to understand [the scope] of evil; they see it as a matter of individual intent rather

255

than societal sin." Although "in any movement," King continued, there are "symbols of antagonism . . . Daley is no bigot. Daley is about my son's age in understanding the race problem, [but] he is sincere." In this respect, King concluded, "the mayor and Archbishop Cody are alike. [But you] cannot say Cody does not believe Negroes are people."

After reflecting on Cody's experience in New Orleans, Young summarized: "Daley is in first grade; his excellency, in third." Young saw Cody as operating through "political relationships rather than theological." For that matter, he asked rhetorically, "What difference did the presence of clergy make" at the meeting? For Young, "the responsible leaders are being the mediators, not the religious leaders." Young concluded by suggesting a meeting between King and Cody and "asking the conference [on religion and race] to be with us." Bevel picked up the idea. He thought the conference could play two useful roles: "first, to educate Cody and Montgomery, and, second, to begin a propaganda campaign on the morality of open housing."

King then turned the discussion to the major task before them. "What," he asked, "do we plan to get out of the meeting next Friday?" He argued that it would "not be enough to make an agreement on paper. It must be a real plan [which] sees segregation as very real—sees that five Negro families move into Gage Park."

Bevel wanted to place the burden on the realtors. "We should ask," he suggested, "the board of realtors to have a delivery plan for opening up every community in Chicago." Brazier thought the problem was clear: "At our next meeting, draw up a plan to do what is necessary for open housing." Others were less certain, questioning the importance of numerical goals as part of the first steps or advocating being "flexible" and "leaving it to the [city] administration to implement." Brazier disagreed: "We must do it like we want it. We must give guidance; otherwise, they will provide roadblocks."

Kale Williams (AFSC) concluded the meeting on a surprising and potentially sobering note. "No one knows how to desegregate," he said. His own suggestion was to place emphasis on private agencies—the Conference on Religion and Race, American Friends Service Committee, and the like.

As this meeting ended, it was no clearer than it had been the day before under what conditions the movement would end the marches.

Reports were circulating that the mayor was considering legal moves to limit the demonstrations. "Daley, it was learned, considered Wednesday's high level civil rights conference a total disappointment since he failed to obtain agreement from leaders of the Chicago Freedom Movement on a moratorium on marches," said the *Sun-Times*. At the mass meeting Thursday night, Raby announced that fifty to one hundred real estate offices would be tested the next day. Bevel made clear that there would be no moratorium on marches: "We will demonstrate in the communities until every white person

256

out there joins the Republican Party." In fact, however, it was a deescalation in tactics to focus on testing real estate offices rather than marching in white communities.[10]

On Friday, 19 August, Daley obtained an injunction to restrain the marches. "If defendants are permitted to proceed with simultaneous marches," the city's petition in Circuit Court said, "it will be impossible for the Police Department . . . to protect . . . the life and property of the more than 3½ million citizens of the City of Chicago, who are not participating as marchers or as protesters to the marches, from the clear and present danger of riot, civil disturbance, and the deleterious effects of unreasonably overburdened police duties." The temporary order prohibited more than one demonstration each day and restricted that to a single area, limited the number of demonstrators to five hundred, banned marches at night or during rush hours, and required twenty-four hours advance notice to police.[11]

As Heineman had said at the first session of the summit meeting, "The mayor cannot help but want fewer demonstrations; he's concerned about the safety of the people." In an unprecedented live television address to defend his action, Daley reaffirmed his opposition to the use of injunctions and denied that the injunction sought "to prohibit or interfere with the constitutional rights of all citizens." But he had found himself "in a dilemma of balancing rights" to petition and to safety. This issue of conflicting rights, he said, "cannot be answered in the streets . . . but can only be answered around the conference table." King called the move "grossly unjust, illegal, and unconstitutional" and accused Daley of "bad faith" in asking for the injunction while negotiations were going on. "This is a time for statesmanship and I have not seen any of that." King said he would fight the injunction in the courts and hinted he might defy it: "I've been in dozens of jails all over the South and I'm not afraid to go to jail in Chicago."[12]

At St. James Cathedral, where the subcommittee was holding its first meeting, Robert Spike made a scathing speech questioning the "good faith" of the city's negotiators. Bevel, however, said he thought it was "rational logic" on the mayor's part to say, "If you will continue to demonstrate during the discussions, we have a right to seek an injunction during the discussion." Both Raby and Bevel said the negotiations would continue despite the court order. "The issue is still justice in housing," Raby said.[13]

By Saturday, the civil rights leaders had reshaped their strategy to meet the injunction. King announced that they would abide by the order pending the outcome of Friday's summit meeting, but if that meeting failed to produce an agreement "we will have no choice but to break" the injunction. In the meantime, a march would be held the next day, within the provisions of the injunction, into the South Deering section of Chicago. (South Deering had been the site of major race riots in 1953, when the first black family moved into a housing project there: for years afterward, the Chicago police maintained a special detail headquartered in one of the project's apartments to ensure the residents' safety.) At the same time, there would be additional marches into Chicago suburbs, which were not covered by the court order, to "satisfy persons who might want to join the protest in South Deering but were prevented from doing so" by the five-hundred-person limitation. In still another escalation, King announced that the freedom movement would conduct a march into Cicero the following Sunday, 28 August. Raby said "it is not a coincidence" that a final decision on the Cicero march would be made after Friday's summit meeting.[14]

With that, the stage was set for activity across the political spectrum. The marches on Sunday to South Deering, Chicago Heights, and Evergreen Park were peaceful because the hostile crowds were held down by heavy rains. In Marquette Park, however, where King had been stoned three weeks before, George Lincoln Rockwell, head of the American Nazi party, addressed a cheering crowd of fifteen hundred. Four robed Klansmen appeared at the Nazi rally, and when one was arrested, a mob of four hundred marched in protest to the police station where he was being held. Also arrested in the park was the Reverend Connie Lynch, a member of the National States Rights party. Meanwhile, at a Republican rally in a North Side amusement park, Charles H. Percy, Republican candidate for the U.S. Senate, said that black protests were directed "against the Democratic machines that have failed to back up their empty promises with performance." He predicted that blacks would "make their protest felt this November at the polls by switching to the Republican Party."[15]

Daley used the occasion to attack outside agitators and defend the citizens of Chicago. "The Commies are in there," he said. "You've got the Nazis. You've got everyone else. You've got the haters." Switching gears, he continued, "But these are not the people of Chicago. Anyone who says that does not know the people of Chicago. . . . We don't want any people who come into our city for the purpose of agitation regardless of who they are." Asked by a reporter if he was also referring to some civil rights leaders, Daley replied, "You can answer that." On the substance of the housing issue, Daley supported the right of any Chicagoan "to live any place he wants to." "But," he added, "let's not kid ourselves," and cited the existence of only seven integrated areas in the city. The problem, he said, was, "How do you integrate if other people move out?"[16]

The Chicago press, which had accused King of "playing to the galleries" and "demagoguery" when he hinted he might defy the injunction, was no more sympathetic now that he had decided to abide by it. The *Sun-Times* editorially reported that "the forces of good will in the community find it difficult to understand why Dr. King feels it necessary to continue making his point by staging simultaneous housing demonstrations" and recommended that he test his objections to the injunction in the courts. The *American,* acknowledging King's claim on "Meet the Press" that the demonstrations did not create hatred but "merely revealed it," warned, "Reverend King, that gun is loaded. If you go on pulling the trigger and it eventually goes off, it won't be the fault of the gun."[17]

The proposed march to Cicero became a cause célèbre in its own right. Cook County Sheriff Richard B. Ogilvie, two years later the successful Republican candidate for governor, responded so quickly that his call for dispatching the National Guard to Cicero was carried in the same editions as the march's announcement. By Tuesday he was requesting that the march be called off in the interest of public safety, warning that "marching in Cicero comes awfully close to a suicidal act." The *Daily News* joined in the call to cancel the march, which it termed "blackmail," a threat held over the coming session of the leadership conference. Failure to cancel the march, the paper said, "will be further evidence that the 'nonviolent' protest movement is seeking blood and martyrdom as a means of advancing its cause." And on Thursday, sharing headlines with Governor Kerner's decision to send the National Guard to Cicero, was Benjamin Willis's final meeting with the Board of Education. Prior to a standing ovation for Willis, the board approved the location for a new high school in Kenwood. Residents of the community were present to protest the site, which they said was occupied by "the only block of single-family Negro homes in the area." At the Board of Education, it was business as usual, undeterred by community protests, open housing marches, or summit meetings.[18]

In contrast to these local perspectives, some national observers thought the civil rights movement in Chicago was poised on the brink of success. Columnist Joseph Kraft said the open housing marches threatened Daley's political base among both the Eastern European immigrants who resided in the areas where the marches had taken place and blacks who had traditionally provided the Democratic machine with its biggest majorities. "Already," Kraft reported, "Charles Percy . . . has polls showing him with 20 percent of the Negro vote as against the 11 percent he took in 1964 as a candidate for governor." In this context, Kraft thought that the "true meaning of Dr. King's success in Chicago" was that "Negroes are not going to be satisfied only with improved housing, better education, and richer job opportunities. They are going to want, in Chicago and every other Northern city, a larger voice in the way the city is run."[19]

Peter Prugh of the *New York Times,* however, included the backlash factor in his analysis and found the outcome less certain. "Many Northerners," he said, "who trumpeted their support of civil rights drives in the South are, rightly or wrongly, now blaming Dr. King for the agitation in their own back-

yards." As a result, "it remains to be seen" whether King's Chicago campaign will "have the success or win the same wide support as the marches in
Selma. . . . Likewise, it's an open question whether the drive will strengthen
or weaken civil rights legislation in Congress this fall, or succeed in opening
many all-white areas to Negroes."[20]

Yet another perspective was brought by Bayard Rustin, in Chicago to address an American Federation of Teachers convention. Saying there was "no
civil rights way to get housing . . . education . . . [or] jobs," Rustin advocated a ten-year, $100 billion federal program to aid the poor being developed
by his A. Philip Randolph Institute. Publicly, he supported the Chicago housing marches as "an important element in building support for the forthcoming
proposal." Privately, he told King, "For God's sake, Martin, this [the
marches] is getting you nowhere! Settle for something."[21]

NEGOTIATIONS: IN THE STREET AND AT THE TABLE

The subcommittee that had been appointed to propose a settlement began its work Friday, 19 August, two days after the first summit conference. Its nineteen members included King, Raby, Bevel, Berry,
McDermott, and Williams representing the movement; Beatty and Mohl from
the real estate board; Montgomery, Spike, George Jones (president of Joe
Louis Milk Company), and the Reverend Robert Crist, all from the Chicago
Conference on Religion and Race; Thomas Ayers (president of both Commonwealth Edison and the Chicago Association of Commerce and Industry),
Leonard Spacek (Chicago Commercial Club), Thomas Faul (secretary-treasurer of the Chicago Federation of Labor); and Edward Marciniak representing the city.

The subcommittee took as its starting point the nine demands presented to
the summit conference by the freedom movement. Some members saw their
primary task as exploring and detailing the willingness of the various agencies
addressed by those demands to comply with them. Movement leaders, however, were aware of how limited their hastily prepared demands were in relationship to the goals of the movement, and they sought to press these larger
purposes on the subcommittee.

Accordingly, in addition to their previous demands, movement representatives submitted to the committee an additional proposal, Project Open City, to
create a continuing instrument responsible for implementing any agreement
that might be reached. In its initial form, this proposal called for the creation
of "a massive action program under the combined sponsorship of major public and private leadership forces of the community"—government, real estate, business, labor, religion, civil rights, finance, civic, mass media, and

education—"to achieve equal housing opportunity in the metropolitan area."[22]

Project Open City also sought to establish criteria to evaluate the success or failure of efforts to create an open city.

> The sponsoring groups accept the principle that the Project Open City must achieve measurable, visible change. It is accepted as a reasonable, specific goal that by June 1, 1967, the population of each closed community in the city and suburbs will change to become at least 1% Negro. Thereafter, as a result of the Project, the Negro population in these areas will increase at least 1% each year until by the end of five years, there will be no community whose population is not at least 5% Negro. Thereafter, it is assumed that an open housing market will have been achieved.[23]

In the subcommittee negotiations, the nine agencies addressed by the movement's demands were, for the most part, responsive to the civil rights requests. The first nine sections of the subcommittee's final report closely paralleled the movement's demands, differing primarily in two respects: the subcommittee's efforts to spell out these demands made its report much longer than the original demands; and demands the movement had addressed to the mayor were restated as commitments by the Chicago Commission on Human Relations.[24]

There was, however, one exception to this pattern. The Chicago Real Estate Board refused to make all real estate listings available to blacks on the grounds that it was still testing the validity of the city's fair housing ordinance in the courts. The real estate board agreed only "to remind its members of their duty to obey the ordinance and to circulate to them the interpretation of the ordinance to be supplied by the Chicago Commission on Human Relations." As a result, the subcommittee endeavored to strengthen enforcement of the city ordinance by the commission and looked to this, as well as the promise of the realtors to participate in the continuing body, to bring the realtors into line.[25]

The composition and role of this continuing body was itself an issue in the subcommittee negotiations. Originally envisaged by civil rights leaders as a massive action program involving city, state, and federal government agencies, it was transformed by subcommittee deliberations into a primarily educational effort conducted by private groups along the lines of the equal job opportunity committee already established by the Chicago Association of Commerce and Industry. And though early drafts proposed that the continuing body accept 1 percent housing integration within the year as a "reasonable, specific goal," the final report said only that "the group should in the immediate future set up specific goals for the achievement of fair housing."[26]

Here and throughout the subcommittee negotiations, the efforts by move-

261

ment representatives to expand their original nine demands were countered by accusations of "bad faith" from Ayers and Marciniak. Only gradually and reluctantly did the civil rights leaders realize that their initial demands had unalterably limited their bargaining position. As one member of the Chicago Freedom Movement negotiating team put it, "Our starting point became their ending point."[27]

The final issue faced by the subcommittee was the injunction limiting civil rights demonstrations. On Wednesday, 24 August, two days before the subcommittee report was due, movement representatives asked that the injunction be withdrawn in exchange for their promise to end the mass marches. Ayers, by now chair of the five-member group drafting the final report, considered this new demand another escalation. At the same time, he and most other subcommittee members continued to insist that any agreement had to include an end to the marches. At an impasse, with Ayers about to declare the negotiations a failure, the subcommittee settled for a report calling for "a cessation of neighborhood demonstrations on the issue of open housing so long as the program is being carried out" and was silent on the question of the injunction. In this as in other central issues, the subcommittee produced a report without at the same time producing the assurance of movement support for it.[28]

The full negotiating committee reconvened on Friday, 26 August, at the Palmer House. Ayers began the meeting by reading the report from his subcommittee, which he said had been unanimously accepted by the members, although movement representatives had indicated they would need to review it with other civil rights leaders.[29]

Heineman asked Daley for his comments. The mayor took the occasion to reaffirm his previous position:

> When men of good faith sit down and talk they can solve the problems. We said at the last meeting we would do everything possible as a city to meet the demands. I asked therefore for the assembling of a permanent organization to solve these problems at the negotiating table before there would be any further demonstrations. We want to recognize the right of people to demonstrate, but there isn't any reason why men of good faith can't bargain before there are any demonstrations.

Daley then moved a vote on the report. Raby, however, was not ready to end the discussion. "Just a minute here," he objected:

> We are all concerned in the freedom movement about the personal commitments of the individuals who are here. For instance, we want to know whether or not the churches will take responsibility for a specific number of Negro families in each all-white community. Will we be able to have one per cent Negro occupancy in every community in the city of Chicago by 1967? will there be a concrete date when the city and the Chicago Real Estate Board can guarantee us that the communities are

opened to all? And the ultimate question is still the question raised by Jim Bevel, "When do we foresee the time when a Negro can go into a real estate office in Chicago and be served?"

Silence greeted Raby's request for a timetable. Finally, Bishop Montgomery, Archbishop Cody, Rabbi Marx, and William Lee (president of the Chicago Federation of Labor) rose to reaffirm their goodwill and good faith—but no specific commitments were forthcoming.

Even Beatty of the real estate board tried to find something constructive to say. But when King questioned him about his public statement the previous day that realtors would go out of business if they were forced to sell and rent to Negroes, Beatty began to equivocate. "We'll do all we can," he said, "but I don't know how to do it. Frankly, I am confused. The last two weeks have been the most confusing of all my life. I think that there are a lot of specifics that we just aren't going to be able to work out here. But I hope that everyone will understand that we are all not bums. Real estate dealers are people and we need commitment from all people in this community, but on the other hand we are not hedging on anything."

With this, many around the room became apprehensive that the realtors were finally going to qualify their consent and undermine the agreement; Mayor Daley's distress was evident. Montgomery, however, committed the churches to support the realtors in their efforts, Johnson of the UAW promised labor support for the agreement, and the anxious moment passed.

Raby, however, introduced new uncertainties. "I think we should understand this vote is indicative of our intent to facilitate the agreement," he said. "We can't accept a vote that is binding. It should only be an indication of sentiment." Heineman pressed for a commitment. "I would think," he said, "the Chicago Freedom Movement would want a unanimous and a binding vote. On the other hand, I am sure that those who are committing themselves to the movement's demands want also to see a commitment."

As the discussion generated pressures for commitment, there was increasing uneasiness on the movement side of the table. Raby called for a fifteen-minute recess. In the movement caucus, those closest to the marches had doubts about either the desirability, the possibility, or both, of actually stopping the marches. But King and Raby prevailed. When the meeting reconvened, King spoke first:

We have decided that we are prepared to vote on the issue before us, and we want to agree that this is a most significant document. However, we have one or two questions that still remain.

First, while we recognize that this was not a matter involved in these negotiations, we are much concerned about the injunction we face. We feel that injunction is unjust and unconstitutional. Thousands of people were deeply hurt as a result of

263

that injunction. Now if we want to have a great meeting at Soldier Field and to march to City Hall with thousands of people as we did then, we can't do that. If we want to have a great march, only 500 people can march and thousands of people will be denied their freedom of assembly. We are acting in good faith and, since we are, we will agree to limit the demonstrations. And therefore, we want to know if the city will withdraw the injunction; we make the request of the city, "What will you do?"

Second, we are very concerned still about implementation. Maybe we are over-sensitive, but there have been so many promises that haven't been materialized that this is a great thing in our minds. We want to know if the continuing body that will be established to hammer out the specifics will be an action body or whether it will be just a forum. We want to know how soon it will be underway. Because ultimately we want to know how soon a Negro can go to a real estate office and feel reasonably sure that he will get fair treatment, that he will be served. And we also want to know how we can deal with the Negro that is not being served.

Montgomery responded to King's question about implementation. "On Monday," he affirmed, "we hope to have the organizing body set up as an action group and ready to roll."

Zimmerman addressed the question of the injunction:

This matter of an injunction has troubled me. I remember at our last meeting we heard one individual who said that he did not like the legal recourse as an approach to resolving these problems; he felt that he wanted to go to a real estate office and be served and not to a commission.

However, recourse to the courts is the basis of our society, and indeed it is a right and an obligation to use the courts. I would like to see this injunction tested in the Supreme Court of the United States, so that we can know, finally, what rights people have to assembly and petition.

King interrupted. "I'm sure you're aware," he said, "it will take at least three years and $200,000 of the movement's resources to get an answer."

Raby joined in the reply:

I am forced to respond here.

I don't see that the judicial process has really helped the Negro. I think it is very gratuitous of anyone to suggest that we suffer this injunction for three years just to get a legal opinion, because legal opinions haven't done us much good. The same process, the process of legal opinion, got us twelve years ago a decision of the United States Supreme Court that we would have integrated schools, that segregation would be done away with. And the result of that legal opinion twelve years later is largely insignificant.

We want from the city an answer and not a debate. I felt it was bad faith for the city on Wednesday to say that they would negotiate with us and then go out on Friday and seek an injunction against us.

264

Daley responded:

Last Friday I acted on the recommendation of the Superintendent of Police of Chicago.

I want you to know that I was raised in a workingman's community in a workingman's home. My father was a union organizer and we did not like injunctions. I know the injustice of injunctions.

But I also faced the decision of what to do with three and a half million people. The superintendent of police had said that the crime rate was soaring as his police resources, his crime-fighting resources, were being thrown into protecting the freedom movement. He also told me that the freedom movement wouldn't cooperate on giving him the routes or giving him advanced notice or in any way helping him in an effort to provide protection. So the decision had to be made.

There were many people who were demanding that we stop the marches entirely, but we said that they had a right to the marches. The course I took was the only one that I could take. I took an oath to preserve law and order and the Constitution.

Now as far as this agreement and injunctions are concerned, if this agreement is made and everybody keeps to it, you will have no worry about the injunction because you won't need to march. And if we agree to the document, then the injunction means nothing to you. We don't want long litigation and legal fees either; and I think this matter can be heard as an emergency matter before the continuing body. It was with heavy heart, yet firmness, that I sought that injunction. There was no other course for me.

King was conciliatory.

I appreciate what Mayor Daley has said, and I know he made the decision with heavy heart. I don't want to stress bad faith. I hope we are operating here by the law of life which is that reconciliation is always possible. But I think I've got to say, that if that injunction stands, somewhere along the way we are going to have to break it. We are going to have to break it tomorrow, or in a week, or in a month, or sometime as the movement proceeds.

Heineman did not think the injunction was a problem: "As I see it, this agreement has to do with the cessation of neighborhood demonstrations, and I think, Dr. King, that you are saying that this injunction isn't limited to enjoining neighborhood marches, but to assemblies as well. Now, Mr. Mayor, would you be willing to sit down with the legal representatives of the Chicago Freedom Movement to negotiate a modification that will allow them broader demonstration rights outside of neighborhood demonstrations?"

Mayor Daley responded: "The city will sit down and talk over anything with anybody. Speaking specifically, I know, as a lawyer, we can amend our injunction." The mayor again called for a vote. There was a hurried conference around King as the civil rights representatives considered their position.

265

Finally, King spoke: "I don't think that we can accept a conference to modify the injunction, because we are opposed to the injunction totally. However, we would accept a separate negotiation through the continuing body on this issue."

With that, the vote was taken. It was unanimous.

Heineman and Daley thanked the participants, but the final moment belonged to King:

> There comes a time when we move from protest to reconciliation. We have been misinterpreted by the press and by the political leaders of this town as to our motives and our goals, but let me say once again that it is our purpose, our single purpose, to create the beloved community. We seek only to make possible a city where men can live as brothers.
>
> I know this has been said many times today, but I want to reiterate again, that we must make this agreement work. Our people's hopes have been shattered too many times, and an additional disillusionment will only spell catastrophe. Our summers of riots have been caused by our winters of delay.
>
> I want to stress the need for implementation and I want to recognize that we have a big job. Because I marched through Gage Park, I saw hatred in the faces of so many, a hatred born of fear, and that fear came because people didn't know each other, and they don't know each other because they are separate from one another. So, we must attack that separation and those myths. There is a tremendous educational job ahead of us.
>
> Now, we don't want to threaten any additional marches, but if this agreement does not work, marches would be a reality. We must now measure our words by our deeds, and it will be hard.
>
> I speak to everyone on my side of the table now, and I say that this agreement must be interpreted as a victory for justice—and not as a victory over the Chicago Real Estate Board or the city of Chicago. I am as grateful to Mayor Daley as to anyone else here for his work. I think now we can go on to make Chicago a beautiful city, a city of brotherhood.

At that, applause, the only applause of either meeting, filled the room.

Heineman invited all the principals to join in a statement to the press. At the mayor's suggestion, however, Heineman spoke for them all. "This is a great day for Chicago," the chairman told waiting reporters. "We all gathered here and, through the great democratic process, we have worked out an agreement."

One civil rights worker turned and walked away. "Democratic process, shit," he said. "It was forced out of them."

As the metropolitan leadership conference, open housing conference, summit meeting—it was variously known—convened, Chairman Ben Heineman, following the mayor's lead, expressed hope that the assem-

266

bly would "get this issue resolved today," but as the day progressed, the perception of what constituted the issue was shifted significantly. At the end of the first session, the Chicago Freedom Movement had presented its demands and they had been accepted in principle by everyone to whom they were addressed except the Chicago Real Estate Board. The mayor requested the realtors to come to a second meeting with a positive response. At the same time, however, movement leaders were deciding to insist on agreements for implementation, not just agreements in principle, before stopping the marches. Although the realtors came to the second session still refusing any of the particular demands addressed to them by the movement, they had agreed to "withdraw all opposition to the philosophy of open occupancy at the state level"—a carefully limited statement if ever there was one; but the movement representatives had returned to press for the details of affirmative responsibilities entailed in the morning's agreements as the condition for ending the marches. At first, it seemed to the chair and others of the civic elite that the realtors had made an important concession but that the movement had escalated its demands. The burden of the meeting shifted to the movement's conditions for ending the marches. As the movement's representatives pressed for details to implement the agreements in principle, it became clear that it was vain to hope for a resolution of these issues in one day. The chair, therefore, appointed a committee to "come back with proposals designed to provide an open city." He gave them ten days. Thus a day that had begun with a clear focus on the recalcitrance of the Chicago Real Estate Board ended with public attention on the refusal of the movement to suspend its marches. The issues had been raised but not resolved.

Because the movement had taken its stand on the grounds of "peace with justice," everything depended on what affirmative changes would satisfy the principle of desegregation. King and his colleagues were convinced that the mayor and his colleagues were interested only in stopping the community demonstrations. In fact, however, as the issues moved into subcommittee negotiations, neither King and his colleagues nor Mayor Daley and his colleagues knew for sure what solution would stop the demonstrations. Even in the movement's agenda committee, it was said, "No one knows how to desegregate." In deciding to press for affirmative responsibilities, the movement had entered the maze that led from urban segregation to the metropolitan color line. It was an effective strategy for forcing negotiations, but there was no corresponding strategy for the negotiations themselves.

As the movement tried to get the focus of the demonstrations back on the realtors and their policies and practices, the mayor went into court to get an injunction limiting the size and number of the demonstrations. The movement decided to abide by the injunction but to plan additional demonstrations in suburban communities not covered by it, including the announcement of a march into the much-dreaded Cicero, which, by then, had become the symbol of white anger and potential violence. The strategy to force negotiation was in full effect.

As the subcommittee began its work, however, the movement's strategy for negotiations was still not fully formed. As long as there were no clear criteria for implementing any agreement that might be reached, there were no clear criteria for ending the marches. The movement initially presented a proposal that called for "measurable, visible change," aimed at a metropolitan area in which "by the end of five years, there will be no community whose population is not at least 5% Negro"; but the subcommittee was unable to specify the affirmative responsibilities by which that goal could be achieved. Discussion, therefore, turned to the creation of a continuing body that could mount and monitor programs aimed at metropolitan desegregation. Even the question of specific goals was deferred to that body, which, when it was finally conceived, was less an action body involving city, state, and federal agencies than it was a private agency committed to educational and diplomatic efforts to desegregate the metropolitan area. As this proposal took shape in the subcommittee, the movement's representatives were not sure they could support it, but they lacked any developed or practical alternative.

When the full meeting reconvened on Friday, 26 August 1966, it was still uncertain whether an agreement had been reached. Albert Raby wanted to get some specific goals on the record, and the subcommittee had not dealt with the disposition of the mayor's injunction. As it turned out, both of the issues were finessed in the final agreement, much as they had been in the subcommittee, with each side agreeing to work them out in the near future.

King called the final agreement "a victory for justice," but it was something less than that. The conference had not been able to move from agreement in principle that desegregation was desirable to the identification of affirmative responsibilities that would make desegregation a real possibility in the metropolitan area. The marches had gone as far as they could in dramatizing the reality of racial closure, but they had not created even the prospect of an "open city."

Faced with the Jim Crow color line in the South, the civil rights movement had regularly and appropriately focused on the behaviors that had to stop in public accommodations, the schools, and voting practices—that is, negative democratic duties. As it turned out, the summit conference had also focused on stopping specific behaviors—discrimination by the realtors and de facto acceptance of the color line in the policies of public and private agencies. Regarding the metropolitan color line, however, affirmative rather than negative democratic duties are the heart of the matter, as we shall argue in Part III.

The Search for an Agreement

Without a positive vision of democratic social change in the central political and economic structures of our society, attempts to rectify the behavior of specific actors and agencies fail by misconceiving the nature and the scale of the metropolitan color line. Marching into neighborhoods was the only behavior the summit agreement actually stopped.

269

CHAPTER TEN

Confrontations with Futility:

August–December 1966

When the summit meeting convened, both the mayor and the movement needed an agreement that would stop the marches. The demonstrations had succeeded in precipitating a civic crisis, but the movement was operating near the outer limits of its ability to sustain them.

From the mayor's point of view, the marches were inflicting a high political cost because he had to send the police to protect the marchers against the militant whites on the Northwest and Southwest sides. The social control role of his political organization was strained beyond its ability to perform. He believed that only the Republicans stood to gain from his dilemma, and by mid-September, public opinion polls showed just that. In the areas where the marches had taken place, normally Democratic voters were abandoning Senator Paul Douglas, lifelong liberal and champion of civil rights, for Republican Charles Percy, and they were swinging toward Republican Sheriff Richard Ogilvie in his candidacy for president of the Cook County Board of Commissioners.[1]

The effect of the marches on Senator Douglas was, of course, entirely unintended from the movement's point of view. In a year when he was up for reelection, however, a threat to Mayor Daley's political base was also a threat to Senator Douglas's chances. From within the movement, moreover, there were compelling strategic reasons for finding some way to end the marches. They had served their purpose of creating a civic crisis. It was late in the summer, and a significant source of energy for the movement came from students, who would be going back to school. Events had been at an emotional high pitch for weeks, and exhaustion was threatening both the leadership and the "troops." The churches and unions were moving away from support for continued action and beginning to favor negotiation. In short, the time was ripe for bargaining.

Negotiations with the responsible agencies in the city and in the metro-

270

politan area had, after all, been the strategic desire and the tactical problem that had brought a civil rights movement together in Chicago. Yet when the attempt to achieve those negotiations was finally forced by the SCLC's non-violent techniques for creating a civic crisis, the Chicago Freedom Movement had failed to put its full agenda on the table.

The nine open housing demands which Raby presented at the first session of the summit meeting had been formulated only the night before they were presented. The leadership did not think of them as the Chicago Freedom Movement's total position. They were drawn up because the agenda committee realized that something specific was needed. Nor were those demands approved or even discussed by any larger body. Had they been discussed by the CCCO or the Freedom Movement Assembly, there is no doubt that they would have been approved; but it is equally certain that the negotiators would have been instructed to present a wider platform, one that at a minimum would have included education and probably employment issues in addition to housing issues.

It is a basic principle of bargaining that one never gets more than one puts on the table; and it is considered bad faith in a bargaining situation to make demands and then not settle for a reasonable compromise. Only gradually, first in the main session of the summit and later in the subcommittee negotiations, did the representatives of the Chicago Freedom Movement come to realize that they were stuck with their initial demands and that they had cut themselves off from their larger agenda. It was a bargaining error, and the civic elite was more than ready to take advantage of the narrow focus it afforded.

This is not to say that the Chicago Freedom Movement might have won a victory but for this tactical error. It does, however, begin to account for the limited form the agreement finally took and for the subsequent problems of justifying it to the movement's adherents and, indeed, of finding any meaningful way of implementing it. The agreement was an achievement of the moment that extricated each of the parties from an otherwise impossible situation, but it was destined to generate recrimination from all sides.

The problems of justifying the agreement intensified the organizational disarray of the movement and gave rise to a sense of betrayal. The problems of implementation intensified the search for alternative future directions and gave rise to a sense of futility. By December, even the leadership was enunciating the theme "Nothing has changed."

271

THE AGREEMENT AND ITS IMMEDIATE AFTERMATH

The agreement consisted of ten points. The Chicago Commission on Human Relations was committed to enforcing the city's 1963 open housing ordinances, and the mayor agreed to work for the adoption of state open occupancy legislation in 1967. The Chicago Real Estate Board agreed to withdraw its opposition to the philosophy of open housing and to urge its members to obey the law. The Chicago Housing Authority pledged to seek "scattered sites" for public housing and to limit new buildings to eight stories. The Cook County Department of Public Aid promised to search out "the best housing available" within its cost ceilings for recipients "regardless of location" and to report any discrimination encountered in this effort. The Department of Urban Renewal made a similar pledge in the management of its relocation projects. The Cook County Council of Insured Savings Associations and the Chicago Mortgage Bankers Association affirmed their readiness to provide mortgage money on an equal opportunity basis. The U.S. Attorney General's Office promised to investigate the policies and practices of the Federal Deposit Insurance Corporation and the Federal Savings and Loan Insurance Corporation. The metropolitan religious leaders pledged to begin educational and support programs in the field of racial justice as well as to establish one or more "housing centers" to broker desegregated opportunities for minority families. The business and labor groups that were parties to the agreement pledged their support for the program and promised to educate their members as to its importance. Finally, the Chicago Conference on Religion and Race was charged with organizing a continuing council of metropolitan leaders to oversee the implementation and extension of the agreement.

King called it "the first step in a thousand-mile journey, but an important step." He said it was "one of the most significant programs ever conceived to make open housing a reality." For his part, Mayor Daley said: "I'm satisfied that the people of Chicago and the suburbs and the whole metropolitan area will accept this program in light of the people who endorsed it."[2]

On the day the agreement was reached, however, most eyes were focused not on its ten points but on its resulting in the Chicago Freedom Movement calling off its projected or threatened march into Cicero. Both the *Chicago Sun-Times* and the *Chicago Daily News* breathed editorial sighs of relief. "The end of housing marches in Chicago and the deferment of the Cicero march should mean a finale for civil rights demonstrations for a long, hot summer of 1966," said the *Sun-Times*. "A sensible compromise has finally been reached in the open housing battle that has threatened to tear Chicago apart," concluded the *Daily News*. "Strict adherence to the terms of the compromise is now essential to provide a respite from the tensions and turmoil of this hot summer of 1966."[3]

The *Chicago Defender,* however, was more inclined to justify the demonstrations than to celebrate the promise of civic calm: "The demonstrations, so loudly denounced by City Hall and most of the press, have proved their justification beyond the shadow of a doubt. . . . It was the demonstrations and the inflexible determination of Negro leadership as spearheaded by the Rev. Martin Luther King that caused the city of Chicago to acknowledge its mistakes and agree to rectify them."[4]

Archbishop John P. Cody celebrated the agreement: "I am delighted that our committee has been able to work out an agreement which will bring back peace and tranquility to our community and lead to the greater achievement of justice. . . . As the archbishop of Chicago I know that all our fellow Catholics are thankful to almighty God for this day. And we shall continue to pray and work for peace, justice and equality for all our citizens."[5]

Yet as King was reporting to a mass meeting on the West Side that the agreement was "a significant victory in justice, freedom and democracy," Chester Robinson, leader of the West Side Organization and an uneasy supporter of the summer campaign, was accusing King and Raby of "selling out Negro interests" for "empty promises." Robinson announced plans to go ahead with a march into Cicero, and he was supported by the Chicago chapter of CORE and the Student Nonviolent Coordinating Committee, both of which were, unlike WSO, members of the CCCO. The plan was to march to Cicero as originally scheduled, two days hence. Sheriff Ogilvie said that the march "would be a disaster for the civil rights movement" and warned that "if Dr. King is not able to control such groups as the WSO, then we have a chaotic situation."[6]

King, of course, was not the only party to the summit agreement for whom it caused trouble. The president of the South Suburban Real Estate Board claimed that the Chicago board had let it down but added, "I doubt we'll relent our opposition to open occupancy legislation." The president of the Evanston–North Shore board expressed similar sentiments. And by Monday morning the mayor was being picketed at City Hall by irate Southwest and Northwest siders claiming that "Daley Sold Out Chicago." These militant whites were demanding that "our Chicago aldermen must repeal the forced housing ordinance." They also wanted a grand jury probe into communist influence in the freedom movement.[7] Meanwhile, they called on politicians "not to surrender to mob violence and Communist agitation in the civil rights movement."[8]

It was King's dissidents, however, who made the most news. A march into Cicero had become an act of mythic proportions whose mere mention activated rituals of lamentation and apocalyptic expectations. The threat of such a march was the one issue that had been definitively settled at the summit meeting: King had called it off. When he learned of Chester Robinson's intention

273

to conduct the march anyway, King said: "I hope he reconsiders. I don't think it's necessary to march alone. Whenever it's necessary to go to Cicero, we should go together." He dispatched Andrew Young to talk the dissidents out of the march. Young achieved partial success. The march to Cicero was postponed one week to 4 September 1966, and Chester Robinson softened his criticism of King. In announcing the postponement, he said: "We respect Dr. King and leaders of the Chicago Freedom Movement, but, like the airline mechanics union, we must reject the first negotiation. Too little was secured to call off the Cicero march."[9]

This move, however, had as much to do with the alignment of groups within the Chicago Freedom Movement as it did with any disagreement about the negotiating goals. The march to Cicero became a symbolic gathering point of groups that were not included in the summit process and had not been consulted about the agreement. King and the leadership of the Chicago Freedom Movement had originally announced a march into Cicero as a part of their negotiating strategy with the metropolitan elite. It was an exercise in pure symbolism. Now Chester Robinson of WSO, Robert Lucas of CORE, and Monroe Sharp of SNCC were using it as an expression of their disaffection from the movement. It was still an exercise in pure symbolism, but the grievances expressed were real, as were the potential consequences of acting out the exercise.

That these public dissidents were not the only ones who felt shut out of the agreement process became clear at a meeting of the action committee on 30 August. The committee had planned and organized the logistics of the demonstrations over the summer, and it considered the agreement "very bad" and believed that the future task was "to show that the various agencies will not abide by the implications of the agreement."[10] This meeting was a sustained critique of the summit agreement and the process by which it had been framed.

The agenda committee was criticized for assuming the decision-making role and for not consulting with others. Like Chester Robinson, the committee members thought that the march on Cicero had been given up too easily and for too little. They found the agreement too vague. Their principle would have been "Do not accept proposals and items which do not relate to achieving goals (always ask 'if this recommendation is put into effect would that be necessary and meaningful to achieve good'). Do not propose items which do not meet that standard."

William Moyer, whose work had prepared the ground for the open housing campaign, was not pleased with the results. He had been consulted only once during the negotiating process, and his advice had not been taken. He had wanted the real estate board to agree to one sentence: "No realtor can carry a discriminatory listing." He was upset that the board had agreed only to drop its "philosophical" opposition to open occupancy. "Now two months can go by, some committees can be formed, and civil rights people can say there has been no progress while the power structure can claim one hundred percent progress because we have no guidelines."

The committee was guided in its deliberations by a written account of the dialogue and exchanges in framing the real estate language at the summit meeting. The action committee thought it was a "basic mistake" to have allowed a subcommittee to settle such an important matter and that, as a result, the movement had been trapped in the "false assumption" that the problem lay in the "philosophy" rather than in the "preachings and practices" of Chicago's ten thousand full-time realtors.

Nevertheless, the action committee was not prepared to join the dissidents' public revolt against the agreement. The committee resolved instead to "outline clear goals, benchmarks with time tables, which the Action Committee and the Agenda Committee can agree on."

The establishment of goals became the theme of the moment. Both King and Raby were sensitive to these criticisms from their most loyal workers. In an open letter "To All Marchers," they stressed that "the agreement contains specific commitments," and said further: "We must be vigilant now to see that these commitments are actually carried out. We must be prepared to resume our demonstrations if necessary, but we must also do everything we can to make the agreement work."[11]

Even as he was presenting the open housing agreement to a rally of his followers, however, King was already beginning to enunciate a shift in his own emphasis. Well aware of the limited impact of the summit agreement, King began to call attention to the "economic problem" as fundamental: "Where Negroes are confined to the lowest paying jobs, they must get together to organize a union in order to have the kind of power that could enter into collective bargaining."[12] As he spoke, there were cries of "black power" in the audience. Some members of the audience had come prepared to demonstrate against King, and they distributed the following broadside to persons as they entered the meeting:

WHO SPEAKS FOR THE BLACK MAN IN CHICAGO?
Our main problem in Chicago is that the Black man has no representation because the Democratic machine has a stranglehold on the ghetto. King says SCLC cannot participate in politics. The fact is SCLC always has and still is actively working for the election of Democratic candidates in the South. For example, this year SCLC backed a rabid racist, Wilson Baker, ex-chief of Police in Selma, for Sheriff in Dallas County, Alabama against Independent Black candidate Samson Crum. King didn't tell you that, did he? Isn't King actually helping Daley to exploit the Black man in Chicago by "refusing to get into politics"?

WAKE UP, BROTHER! DECIDE FOR YOURSELF—WHO SPEAKS FOR YOU?
King was marching in white neighborhoods for an "open city" to solve the problems of the ghetto. Even if we got an "open city" without money for Black people

275

to build and buy homes an "open city" is meaningless. The ghetto remains the same. Is token integration the solution to our problem? Would you move your family into Gage Park? Who is kidding who?

WAKE UP BROTHER! DECIDE FOR YOURSELF—WHO SPEAKS FOR YOU?
Daley blew the whistle and King stopped the marches just when Nazi Rockwell threatens a march through the ghetto. Cicero, Illinois was so afraid of nonviolent marchers they asked Governor Kerner to call out the National Guard! Why didn't King fight the injunction? Protest marches are guaranteed by the Constitution. Doesn't a "movement" fight unjust laws? Why did our "leadership" back down?

WAKE UP, BROTHER! DECIDE FOR YOURSELF—WHO SPEAKS FOR YOU?
King says we should celebrate a "significant victory" tonight because he got some concessions from the city. These concessions were just more empty promises from Daley, a man who has lied and lied to the Black man in this city for years. Many people are calling it a sellout. Did you read the so-called concessions? How are they supposed to help the man in the ghetto?

WAKE UP BROTHER! DECIDE FOR YOURSELF—WHO SPEAKS FOR YOU?
WAKE UP, BROTHER!
WE GOT TO GET US SOME BLACK POWER——
SO THE BLACK MAN CAN SPEAK FOR HIMSELF!

S.N.C.C.   4165 S. Ellis Avenue   924-6781

King responded by inviting Monroe Sharp of SNCC to take the microphone and make his point. Sharp said that black power meant "you don't have to deal with Mayor Daley and say you'll go into Gage Park. You make sure first that you can stand on your own corner, and that it belongs to you. Black power means that you tell the man to get out, not that he must hire some more Negroes or sell better merchandise."[13]

King replied, "The longer we wait to solve this problem, the more we're going to hear these misguided cries over and over again. I'm interested in human power, not black power or white power. When Pharoah wanted to keep the slaves in slavery he kept them fighting among themselves." Suddenly King launched into a sermon. At one point he even smiled and said, "I didn't mean to act like a Baptist preacher"; but that is what he was, and for the next few moments all the tensions of recent days found eloquent release in his rhythmic reflections on suffering and discouragement at the slow progress of civil rights. Finally, he was soaring: "I'm not worrying about Chicago. I'm not worrying about the freedom movement. Mine eyes have seen the glory of the coming of the Lord." King sat down, stunned by the release. The audience was moved to ecstasy. That was the King everyone loved. Tears of joy and frustration mingled with the strains of "We Shall Overcome." The summer of 1966 had been hard on everyone.[14]

Events had moved so fast in the previous week that the Chicago Freedom

Movement barely noticed the departure of Benjamin C. Willis from the Board of Education. Indeed, the events of the summer had taken on such a life of their own that the schools were not mentioned in the summit agreement, and no representative of the Board of Education had been invited to the meeting. Only a year before, Willis and the schools, not the real estate board and open housing, had been the object of the demonstrations. He received a standing ovation at his last board meeting. The *Sun-Times* commented that "Willis never seemed to understand that one order was passing and another taking its place. He became the idol of white supremacists and the villain of the civil rights advocates." The *Sun-Times* never seemed to understand that this polarization was the new order of the day. [15]

As the 1966 election season opened, the Gallup Poll reported that the Vietnam War, racial problems, and inflation were the top concerns of Americans and that confidence in the ability of the Democratic party to handle them had declined considerably since the presidential election of 1964. In 1964 49 percent of those polled preferred the Democrats, 22 percent the Republicans, 17 percent saw no difference, and 12 percent had no opinion. By the late summer of 1966 only 28 percent favored the Democrats, and 21 percent the Republicans, but 35 percent had come to see no difference and 16 percent had no opinion. [16] A big change had occurred in a short time. The season for political settlements was coming to an end. The Democratic party was about to become as uncertain of its constituency's support as the civil rights movement was of its own best direction.

The march into Cicero took place on 4 September 1966, the Labor Day weekend. Two thousand National Guardsmen, Cook County sheriff's patrols, and a contingent of Illinois State Police were deployed to keep order. Governor Kerner complained of the "inconsiderate decision of the march leadership" and expressed his "deep disappointment" that it had "ignored appeals to cancel or postpone this demonstration." [17]

Three thousand men protected 250 marchers from a furiously militant white mob estimated at 3,000. Rocks and bottles flew, but only one demonstrator appeared to be hit. National Guardsmen bayoneted six white youths. Another forty-two were arrested. Sheriff Ogilvie called the marchers unruly and reported that "they retaliated against onlookers with profanity and by throwing missiles back." The marchers chanted, "Black Power." The march stopped at the place where Jerome Huey had been beaten to death the previous May by four white youths who had nothing against him except that he was black. With his parents present, prayers were said in his memory despite the taunts of a crowd of seven hundred whites. This episode was a depressing display of the indecent emotions that were sweeping through white communities concealed under the label "backlash."

Backlash was the new order of the day. It was a frontier on which the

277

"fringes" seemed to set the tone. Within days of the Cicero march, George Lincoln Rockwell was in Chicago to hold "white power" rallies and marches into the ghetto. At the Chicago Coliseum, scene of the Democratic National Convention in 1968, Rockwell addressed an audience of sixty-five—his Nazi party was more visible than real.[18]

Nonetheless, the Chicago Freedom Movement found it difficult to structure a process either for justifying or for implementing the open housing agreement in such a hostile atmosphere. It was not until 16 September 1966 that the leaders held a meeting of the delegates in whose name they had entered into the agreement of 26 August 1966. The meeting was dominated by the tensions within the movement, which had been heightened by the agreement.

INNER TENSIONS OF THE MOVEMENT I:
POLITICAL DIRECTION AND ORGANIZATIONAL CONFUSION

The agenda committee met on 15 September to prepare for the next day. The question of the mayor's injunction limiting marches was still unresolved as was the problem of bail and defense for summer demonstrations. The SCLC was trying to raise money from national sources to cover these expenses. The committee discussed the Civil Rights Bill of 1966, under consideration in the U.S. Senate, where it appeared that a majority favored the bill but not the two-thirds required to break a filibuster. It was proposed to send a telegram to Charles Percy, Republican candidate for the Senate from Illinois, urging him to make a public statement for the bill and for cloture. No one knew whether he could influence Senator Everett M. Dirksen, Senate minority leader, to support cloture. The decision was left to King and Raby. Representatives of labor were reluctant to give Percy a chance to look good on civil rights because he was running against Paul Douglas, one of the oldest friends of civil rights in the Senate. King was concerned that the housing section of the bill had been so watered down in the House of Representatives "that you may institutionalize present housing patterns." He was willing to drop the housing section until another time, but the Leadership Conference on Civil Rights, a consortium of national groups that had maintained a more or less united front in Washington since 1949,[19] had taken an all-or-nothing stand on the bill, and the administration was worried about backlash. That King was willing to drop the housing section showed how serious the pitfalls were in the issue of open housing.

The discussion moved to the problems of enforcing the housing provisions of the summit agreement. William Moyer was spearheading a follow-up committee. He had drawn up a set of guidelines for the Chicago Commission on Human Relations to follow in meeting the obligations of the agreement by clarifying specific responsibilities and procedures. The key provision called for the commission to engage in "testing" two hundred realtors a week and to initiate complaints "when discrimination is suspected." The agenda committee approved Moyer's proposal.[20]

It was recommended that meetings of the Chicago Freedom Movement Assembly be held every two weeks, even though the assembly's role in implementing the agreement was unclear. The pressing issue seemed to be membership on the agenda committee because it had become the policy center of the movement. It was agreed that each organization in the assembly could send one person to the meetings of the agenda committee, provided notice was given. As the meeting ended, Raby proposed that dealing with "the life and organization of the CCCO" was at "the top of the agenda" for the next meeting.

When the delegates convened the next day, 16 September 1966, these organizational confusions dominated the agenda. King presented the summit agreement: "We have a tremendous job ahead of implementing the great demands of an Open City. It would have been better if we could have discussed all the points in the agreement with all of you delegates, but it was an error of the head, not of the heart. This was a 'first round' battle, but it was a victory. The power structure capitulated for the first time to the Movement. The power structure had to sit down and make some real concessions." He concluded, "We still have a long way to go and the Valley of Disunity is the greatest danger now." He was right about that. The meeting took an immediate, acrimonious turn. King was criticized for associating black power with violence. He had to make clear that he was not accusing Congressman Adam Clayton Powell and CORE Director Floyd McKissick of advocating violence, but he claimed that that was how the slogan was interpreted "in the streets."

The discussion turned to organizational discontent with the "undemocratic" role the agenda committee had assumed—and without authority, according to many delegates, not just black power advocates. A retreat to work out these organizational matters was suggested, but, as one delegate said, "More than a retreat is needed. Democracy is better. We have a right to give advice and counsel to the leadership. It must be built into this organization." In reference to the summit agreement, this delegate observed, "The Chicago Real Estate Board went back to its Steering Committee. We can agree to compromise, but we must have the right and understanding that this is a democratic organization."

King was concerned. "One thing we can do," he said, "is argue, flail, let everybody leave angry or we can constructively move on to rectify the errors of the past. . . . We should have done just what a labor union does. We should have gone back to the members and voted. . . . It never occurred to me until later that afternoon. I said to Andy Young that we had made a mistake."

279

The meeting proceeded to a review of the summit meeting and the plans for implementing the agreement, but that led back into an acrimonious discussion of authority and organization, centered on Moyer's proposed guidelines for the Commission on Human Relations. Some delegates believed that the commission, with its do-nothing history, was hopeless and should not be treated as even potentially responsible. Therefore, it was moved to reject the Moyer proposal. Raby ruled the motion out of order because the agenda committee had already authorized the report to go to the commission.

A discussion of the organizational confusion ensued. "Do we have three, two, or one organizations?" asked one delegate, and "What is the relation of the CCCO to the Chicago Freedom Movement?" It was a good question because the Freedom Movement Assembly seemed to have supplanted the CCCO as the delegate body, but it had been ineffective as a policy instrument and deliberative body. The assembly had been "the brainchild of the CCCO," but the CCCO seemed to have been left behind. Two distinct points of view were expressed, even among moderate and long-term CCCO supporters. William Robinson (FOR) said, "There would be no Chicago Freedom Movement without the worldwide power and charisma of Martin Luther King. You go to the conference table with Martin Luther King and he is worth ten CCCO's." William Cousins (CAPCC), however, said, "Let's look forward. We must carry on after SCLC leaves. We need clearly defined structures. We must call CCCO meetings as such. Then we will have a solid case."

The final question was "Is this a meeting of the Freedom Assembly or the CCCO?" Raby ruled that it was the Freedom Assembly. He conceded that "the CCCO needs to get together this week," but no arrangements to do so had been made. He proposed to take account of what had been said at this meeting and move ahead. Some wanted to suspend the continuing negotiations, consequent to the summit agreement, but in the absence of any formal charter for the Freedom Movement Assembly, the delegates seemed to lack the authority to issue such a mandate.

Discussion turned to providing bail money for Robert Lucas of CORE and Frank Ditto, two of the dissident Cicero marchers. There was a motion that it be "the declared policy that any member or members of civil rights organizations be rescued from any legal entanglements having to do with their civil rights activities if their activity is part of the Freedom Movement activity." Raby warned that "such a responsibility could break us, break the movement." It passed 25 to 17. It was agreed to raise money for Lucas. Ditto reportedly had already turned down an SCLC offer to bail him out.

The delegates agreed to hold a freedom movement retreat in late October "for the purposes of structural organization and policy formation."

It took two weeks to convene a meeting of the CCCO. The agenda committee met twice in that time to discuss fund raising, straightening out the lines of organizational responsibility, and implementing the summit agreement. The financial reports showed that the CCCO account had expended $7,400 in July, $2,200 in August, and $1,200 in September. Income for the period (including cash on hand as of 1 July 1966) had totaled $13,200. As of 1 October, there was a balance of $2,400. Still, the agenda committee wanted to raise $100,000 before Christmas to serve the overall movement with half the proceeds each for the CCCO and SCLC. The hope of raising so much money was unrealistic, but the agenda committee explored the problems that would be involved: being compromised by "the forces that control community money," the need to formulate a budget for its use, organizational competition if the funds were secured, the need for a committee to head the drive. Nothing came of this idea, and money continued to be tight for day-to-day operations.

On the organizational question, John McDermott of CIC, an active member of the agenda committee and a participant at the summit meeting, affirmed what the critics had said: "The movement has not operated in a truly democratic fashion." He saw the need for a clear proposal to coordinate both the Chicago Freedom Movement, SCLC, and CCCO and the staff functions that had evolved over the year. By 29 September the agenda committee had agreed that the issues were whether the agenda committee should be elected by the Chicago Freedom Movement Assembly or appointed by King and Raby and approved by the assembly, or whether its members should be partly elected, partly appointed; when the election of officers should take place; what should happen to the CCCO as a legal entity; and how the criteria of nonviolence and interracial cooperation should be maintained. A committee was appointed to work on these issues.

During this time, a civil rights bill died in the U.S. Senate for the first time since 1957. Majority Leader Mike Mansfield (D-Mont.) blamed the failure on the turmoil of "this simmering summer." Senator Dirksen called the "open housing" section of the bill "full of mischief." Senator Paul Douglas and the national Civil Rights Leadership Conference assailed the Senate's cloture rule.[21]

About one month after the summit meeting, the Leadership Council for Metropolitan Open Communities was beginning to organize with James W. (Joe) Cook, president of the Illinois Bell Telephone Company, as its chairman. He was new in town, having arrived from Connecticut in April. He had a reputation as a hard-driving "realist," and he did not have a long local history that could be held against him.[22]

The follow-up committee was not hopeful about the immediate prospects for this council. Conversation with representatives of the Chicago Commission on Human Relations had made clear that the commission did not accept the proposal that it should test realtors and initiate complaints against those that appeared to be discriminating. Conversations with representatives of the

Cook County Department of Public Aid had not produced much evidence of commitment to find nonsegregated housing for welfare recipients.[23]

INNER TENSIONS OF THE MOVEMENT II:
ORGANIZATIONAL DIRECTION
AND A SENSE OF BETRAYAL

On 1 October 1966 the CCCO, as distinct from the CFM Assembly, met for the first time since 23 July 1966. Thirty-three organizations were represented. It was voted to make it a "closed meeting." The proposal of six new groups for membership led to the appointment of a membership committee, but unanimous consent was needed to admit these groups to that day's meeting, and it was not forthcoming.

Only two substantive matters came before this meeting, which was abruptly adjourned just as it was about to reconsider the decision not to admit the new groups into the day's deliberation. This move cut out the "new business" section of the agenda, which included the proposal for a retreat to consider programs, the formation of a committee on structure, a proposal for voter education, the matter of bail bonds, and a report on labor and political issues from representatives of the Industrial Union Department (IUD) of the AFL-CIO and the NALC.

One substantive issue that was discussed was the report from the CCCO education committee. This group was preparing for a meeting with the new general superintendent of schools, James Redmond. The group was also recommending that the CCCO officially oppose the $25 million bond issue for the schools on the 8 November ballot. During September, the Chicago Urban League had released its report, "Racial Segregation in the Chicago Public Schools, 1965–1966." This report claimed and documented that "Chicago public schools continue to act as a highly efficient system of segregation. . . . A higher proportion of white schools now have 'their Negro.' . . . The racial barriers are no longer as absolute as they once were, but this change was accomplished in a way that did not diminish the racial isolation of the vast majority of Negro pupils."[24]

Although Berry of the Urban League had already publicly supported the bond issue for the schools, the CCCO education committee proposed a motion that read like an indictment and reflected a long history of frustration with the Board of Education:

WHEREAS the Chicago Board of Education is seeking the passage of a $25 million school building bond issue in the November 8, 1966 elections without specifying the uses of the money;

282

WHEREAS the Chicago Board of Education has failed to this date to implement requirements of the 1963 Armstrong Act both in redrawing school boundaries and in selecting new sites, and a change in the Superintendency does not in itself mean a change in current Board of Education practices of segregation;

WHEREAS schools built by the Board in the past and nearly all sites adopted in its 1966 budget and sites proposed since then will continue the pattern of segregated student bodies;

WHEREAS the newly released Chicago Urban League report on "Racial Segregation in Chicago Public Schools, 1965–1966" reveals that Negro students are more segregated in Chicago now than they were two years ago;

WHEREAS studies of Chicago's schools and the latest report of the U.S. Office of Education demonstrate that new buildings in themselves have not resulted in improved quality of education in Negro-segregated schools;

WHEREAS the National Convention of the NAACP in July, 1966, adopted a resolution declaring:

"We call upon our branches to oppose school construction plans, budgets and bond issues if the plans for new schools or additions to existing schools fail to correct segregation or will result in new segregated white or Negro schools whenever alternatives are administratively possible";

WHEREAS the civil rights movement of Chicago cannot endorse further financing for the Board of Education's building program without concrete evidence that this money will be spent for construction on sites located so as to maximize integration in conformity with the Armstrong Act,

BE IT RESOLVED: that in the absence of such evidence the Coordinating Council of Community Organizations calls for the defeat of the proposed school building bond issue on November 8th.

A condensed version of this motion passed 12 to 2 with 4 abstentions.

The committee also reported that it was preparing for a meeting with Redmond at which it intended to make "quality education" the central issue. The committee had prepared a thirteen-point program that could be adopted with existing resources and within existing statutory authority, a six-point program requiring additional administrative and legislative changes by the city, and a twelve-point program requiring changes at the state level of administration and legislation.

The other substantive matter to come before the meeting was the report from the Englewood Action Committee, which had gone to court to prevent the Green Street Urban Renewal Project. The city had asked for a continuance in the case, but it had also issued condemnation orders. The group was seeking support from local businessmen, but it was not clear which way they would go. Public protests of the city's action had been poorly supported. Andrew Young said: "The crucial point is urban renewal with no voice from the people . . . but there is an advantage here because it is a clear-cut issue of

283

homes being removed for private business parking lots. That business community is the second largest in the city and is entirely dependent on the Negro community. A boycott could be fifty percent effective." The committee, however, was not so sure, and the other delegates were hard-pressed to come up with any meaningful support.

The meeting eventually returned to the question of the new groups that wanted to join the CCCO but had not been allowed to stay in the meeting. There was considerable uneasiness about this issue, and just as the meeting was about to reverse itself and admit them, there was a motion to adjourn, which passed. It seemed like a move that had been prearranged by the leadership. Raby left, but some stayed and continued to discuss the new business that had been announced on the agenda.

More than irony was involved in the inability of the CCCO to get on with new business. The disgruntlement over the summit agreement, its content, its implementation, and the procedures surrounding it; the resentments about the authority of the agenda committee; and the general frustration about both the programmatic and ideological direction of the civil rights movement were beginning to crystallize into a revolt against the leadership—especially Berry and Raby.

In mid-September, Timuel Black (NALC), one of the most faithful and thoughtful of civil rights activists over the years, had written an open letter to Berry. It signaled a stinging break in the ranks. Black asked:

> What form should the movement take and what vehicles it should use, what tactics it should employ and in whose hands should be entrusted the responsibility for bringing the "Freedom Ship" in—safely and victoriously? . . . It is my opinion, shared by numbers of other people involved and interested in civil rights, that the above questions are basic, crucial and really need *immediate* attention—lest the movement be betrayed for a "mess of pottage." Bill, do you remember the story of how Jesus Christ was betrayed by one of his own for a few pieces of silver? Some of us believe that Dr. Martin Luther King is now historically related to this same problem. We believe that we have ample evidence, based upon past experience, to support our fears.[25]

A sense of heartbreaking betrayal pervades this ten-page open letter. "Because of this," said Black, "I am very frightened for the welfare of Dr. King, SCLC, CCCO and the whole civil rights movement in this city." He then reconstructed the events since 1963 and interpreted Berry's role in them as having been consistently devious and self-seeking. Nor was this sense of betrayal limited to Berry's actions. "The summer of 1963 saw the beginning of Rev. Brazier's observed frequent visits to Mayor Daley's office *ALONE. Your* single visits to his honor's were to be noted later—in early 1966—just before the Mayor's Bond Issue Drive and just before the Black-Newhouse state senatorial *SELL-OUT.*" This latter is a reference to Berry and Raby having supported another candidate than Black for endorsement by the Independent Voters of Illinois, but it would be wrong to think that Black was merely expressing "sour grapes." The letter was animated less by a sense of personal betrayal than by a sense that the entire movement had been politically betrayed—rather like, according to Black, the political takeover of the NAACP in 1957.

Black interpreted Berry's insistence that the CCCO remain nonpolitical as a political ploy. Independent Voters of Illinois, Protest at the Polls, and Voters for Peace had all been kept out of the CCCO on the grounds that their membership would endanger the tax-exempt status of organizations like the Urban League, Catholic Interracial Council, and NAACP. Yet all three of these "nonpartisan" groups had found some way to support the mayor's bond issue in spite of CCCO opposition. Black wanted the politics out in the open, not hidden behind a nonpartisan, tax-exempt status. "With all of the above—and more—as evidence of the past and with more evidence piling up in the present, it is my conclusion that you are neither Pro-Negro nor Pro-Civil Rights."

"Al Raby," on the other hand, "is, fundamentally, a fine 'guy' and has all the ingredients to become a great local leader. Quick fame and success have, temporarily, made him a bit power 'happy.' I think—and hope—he will recover. One thing may retard the recovery and progress. It may be that he has become influenced and enamoured with your *style of living* and your urbane sophistication. This trend has caused him to become sidetracked from real and dynamic grassroots leadership. I hope that he will come through without a severe hangover from the 'Bill' Berry Intoxication." Black concluded: "I shudder when I think how close you are, as an advisor and confidante, to Dr. King. . . . I hope that Dr. King, SCLC, Al Raby and CCCO will become wary of your motives and tactics and will remove themselves from the danger-zone. To fail to do so, just might prove to be disastrous and perhaps even *fatal.*"

In keeping with this attack on Berry, Black had proposed the admission of New Breed, a black political group, to the CCCO at the meeting of 1 October 1966. He was prepared to precipitate the political question as new business at that hastily adjourned meeting. By the time of the 14 October meeting, Raby, too, had fallen behind the veil of suspicion, and a caucus was organized to dump him as the leader of the CCCO.

A memo prepared by this caucus proposed the following scenario for the 14 October meeting:

> First, let all arguments grow out of the natural proceedings. Make every effort to appear natural and give an appearance of spontaneous response to issues. CAUCUS LITTLE OR NONE and, when necessary, give sign for the person to leave room or write note:

285

A. Innocent question raised by ——after the reading of minutes—that we take into consideration the actions of the Convenor at the last meeting.
DISCUSSION WILL ENSUE AND GENERAL FEELING OF ALL WILL BE VALU-ABLE. . . . DISCUSSION MUST ULTIMATELY LEAD TO:

B. *MALFEASANCE OF OFFICE CHARGES*.
Each person must speak to several charges—and if the person designated on this paper is NOT PRESENT, PLEASE ACCEPT THE RESPONSIBILITY to see that the items are all covered. Judge by discussion and watch for signals. PRESSURE MUST REMAIN SO THAT THE GOAL OF ASKING FOR A VOTE OF CONFIDENCE is attained. AFTER vote is attained, someone must MOVE that a temporary chairman be elected for the Retreat, where a permanent structure will be derived.

Eleven charges were listed; they focused the frustration of the moment on Raby:

1. Improper handling and lack of respect to delegates and their organizations on the part of the office staff—except when asked to support CERTAIN projects.
2. Cliques—in and outside the Agenda Committee. . . . Improper conduct in Agenda Committee. Too much consorting with one or two groups and the delegation of fundamental powers to these organizations. [read: Urban League] Cliques are detrimental to the democratic process.
3. Role of the Convenor to preside, not opinionate or emotionally attack any delegate.
4. Convenor assigns others to serve as spokesmen for CCCO. Also the fact that he enters into contractual agreements and reaches decisions of monumental importance—WITHOUT approval of delegates.
5. Summit.
6. Failure to call meetings according to Constitution—Setting up Chicago Freedom Movement Agenda Committee and giving delegates who dissented the answer that they could work all summer at Action Centers.
7. Convenor paid by forces outside CCCO—monies don't come through CCCO treasury. . . . Also hiring of Executive Director.
8. Unsavory practices where FINANCES ARE INVOLVED. No reports or audits.
9. Flagrant usurpation of role of Convenor—when delegates have specifically voted up or down an issue—especially criteria for funding organizations, Bond Issue (Urban League).
10. No attempts to organize Grassroots communities so they can relate.
11. Declaring meetings CLOSED—removal of people to hallways. Failure on part of Convenor to attend Ex Officio at ensuing Committee meetings.

The revolt against Raby, outlined in this caucus scenario, did not take place at the 14 October meeting even though the grievances and frustrations expressed in it did materially enter the delegates' deliberations. After the hasty adjournment on 1 October, a rump session had agreed to hold a CCCO retreat on 21–23 October at the Ecumenical Institute. Committees had been appointed to plan the retreat, and the agenda for 14 October called for the ratification of these plans and reports from the committees that had been working in the meantime. Raby came to the meeting prepared to support the decision to hold a retreat as agreed at the agenda committee meeting on 6 October. Black presented the report from the rump session and explained that "the reason for the retreat was a strong feeling that we have structural and functional difficulties, that we need to see what CCCO is and ought to be." John McDermott suggested that "the basic idea is to get away to heal the tensions and divisions." Therefore, he recommended that "an angel should supply us with beverages."

Even though this was basically a reconciliatory meeting, the tensions and divisions still surfaced as the group tried to agree on the arrangements for the retreat. Although it was agreed that the retreat was strictly a CCCO affair for the purpose of getting its own house in order, still there was the problem of what to do about the cooperating organizations such as SCLC, IUD, and WSO. In the end, they were invited to participate but not to vote on the structural or programmatic issues. But the delegates rejected a proposal to include "political" groups such as the Independent Voters of Illinois or New Breed. As originally proposed, the session on programmatic direction for the future was focused on the emerging black power or ghetto issues—welfare, gangs, tenant unions, urban renewal, organizing the unemployed, hospital organizing, and race and class conflict within the movement. The importance of these issues was affirmed, but schools and housing, the two main CCCO concerns at that moment, were brought back to the top of the agenda, though only after considerable discussion. Thus a meeting that had begun under the threat of an open break in the ranks of the Chicago Freedom Movement had turned to a search for ways to keep the undesirable disputes "within the family."

INNER TENSIONS OF THE MOVEMENT III: WHERE DO WE GO FROM HERE—SOME PROPOSALS

In its public activities, the CCCO was still able to maintain the appearance of assurance and a sense of purpose. On 18 October 1966 a large delegation met with the new general superintendent of schools, James F. Redmond. Their agenda was contained in a four-page presentation of "demands," grouped under seven general headings: implementation of the Armstrong Act (with special reference to the board's upcoming bond issue); establishment of uniform minimum achievement standards throughout the school system; citywide integration of students and faculties; a high-quality, integrated citywide

287

curriculum; improved working conditions and job security for teachers; procedures to acquaint and involve the public systematically with the needs, problems, and achievements of public education; and active support by the Board of Education and superintendent for local, state, and federal measures to strengthen and integrate Chicago's educational program.[26]

These demands were prefaced by a concise statement of the premises that had motivated concern with the schools for years:

> The laws of our state and nation entitle every child to the best possible education our society can provide. The Coordinating Council of Community Organizations accepts as law the Supreme Court's 1954 decision that "separate education is inherently unequal." Twelve years after that decision, segregated education is being illegally maintained for the 90% of Chicago's public school children who attend racially separate public schools.
>
> Segregated education harms all children in Chicago. It has resulted in inferior education for Negro children. It has damaged white children, as evidenced in the Swastika-waving youth that shamed Chicago's streets this past summer.
>
> Our goal and our demand is quality education for all of Chicago's children. We refuse, however, to consider this goal separate from the issue of integrated education. Those who plead for such separation are asking us to repudiate the lessons of history and the findings of unimpeachable research. To separate quality from the context of integration is to restore the discredited philosophy of "separate but equal," and to rob still another generation of Americans of their democratic rights.

After the meeting with Redmond, Raby said, "I am looking forward to a new era and an end of the crisis in Chicago schools." It was the first time any spokesperson for the CCCO had emerged optimistic from meeting with any official of the Chicago public schools. Superintendent Redmond had agreed to set up task forces consisting of his staff members, CCCO representatives, and, as needed, outside experts to produce concrete recommendations in each of the seven areas of CCCO concerns. It remained to be seen whether Redmond's response represented a substantial change in policy direction at the Board of Education and whether these demands by the CCCO education committee represented the directions and purposes the delegate body was prepared to sustain for the future.

At the CCCO retreat 21–23 October, both the directions and purposes to be pursued in the future were vigorously debated. Nothing was settled, but all the serious tensions of the fall were brought out and discussed. The recurring theme was, Are we going to be able to work together? The question had several sides, depending on the meaning of "we" and "together." There was some urgency to the question, Can black and white work together? And even supposing they could, at what level? As peers? The dissidents were concerned, as one of them put it, that "the purpose must be sharply defined— where whites and middle-class Negroes belong in the organization." For him, this meant dealing with the issue of "white supremacy" within the CCCO.

Black was more concerned about the stance than the future composition of the CCCO. "It cannot be a catch-all of organizations," he said. "If political activity is necessary, then organizations that cannot deal in politics should not be in." This was not, however, the prevailing view. There were too many cross-cutting choices to allow for simple resolutions—black or white, middle class or "grass roots," political or nonpartisan, umbrella organization or direct action coalition. And still the problems remained of relating the CCCO to other cooperating organizations, the SCLC, and IUD. Most of these issues were shunted off for consideration by the constitution committee.

When the steering committee met on 27 October, some dissatisfaction with the retreat was expressed. To the dissidents' question, "Can we work together?" some members of the steering committee were prepared to say "No." The dissidents were called "angry, frustrated . . . parasites on the movement," who would "continue to disrupt until we get rid of them." But the prevailing view was to "keep them in," to avoid a public "blow-up," on the theory that expelling them would only "help them build a counter-movement." By the steering committee meeting of 8 November, Raby reported that "the fight is going out of the dissidents," but he advised the committee to "proceed as if they were still strong" in preparing for the delegates' meeting on 12 November.

The one part of the retreat that made news was the report of the follow-up committee, which someone leaked to the press shortly after the retreat. The report was moderately composed, but a "spokesman" for the CCCO had charged that the implementation process for the summit agreement was a "slowdown," characterized by "administrative incompetence." The steering committee was upset both by the leaking of the report and by the unauthorized characterization of the process.[27]

The report had focused on the public agencies that were parties to the summit agreement. It noted that "as of today, the CCHR has not met any of these commitments," that "there has been no indication that the Department of Urban Renewal (DUR) has actively participated in an open city," that "it seems that the Chicago Housing Authority (CHA) policy is still to have different waiting lists," that investigation of the Cook County Department of Public Aid "has not found any change from the past practices," and that, in general, "there has not been much evidence that the agencies in the summit agreement have altered their program to foster or participate in open housing."[28] Raby and other members of both the steering and follow-up committees were annoyed about the leak because they had hoped to bring the report out jointly with the leadership council. As Raby said, "Now we have to repair our relations" with the council.

At least three different responses were given to Jesse Jackson's question

"What is so bad about getting the truth out?" John McDermott said it was the wrong question: "The movement needs collective discipline—democratic, collective decisions." He felt that as a matter of policy "no reports should be presented anywhere until they are presented here." King's concern was personal: "I agree this should get out, but it was embarrassing to me." He had not heard of the report, but "I can't admit to the press that I know nothing about it." He was also concerned because "we know we will not solve these issues in a year or two and this report gives the impression that there is no serious attempt to implement" the agreement. Raby, as we have seen, was concerned because the leak upset his strategy of broadening the base of pressure on the city agencies. "I am not always for the truth," he said. Rather, timing was the crucial point.

The members of the steering committee were sensitive to any appearance of disorder in their own house. The leadership council, which was to oversee the implementation of the summit agreement, was still in the process of formation, and any hopes for implementation rested on the stance that body finally adopted. It met over election day. In an "emergency" meeting with union leaders only a week before, the mayor had charged that King was deliberately stirring the backlash issue for the benefit of Republican candidates. "We know the forces that are on foot to divide people, but they never will divide our people because of the labor movement of the city of Chicago," the mayor had proclaimed. Berry had responded immediately by saying, "This business about Dr. King's coming here to stir up a racial backlash is silly."[29]

But it was not concocted out of whole cloth. During the summer, James Bevel had said, "We will demonstrate in the community until every white out there joins the Republican party." Both Bevel and Jesse Jackson had continued to make speeches in that vein. King had told the press that "this does not represent the thinking of all" in the movement, and King did his best to disassociate his own activities from Bevel's position. King denied the charge of stirring up the backlash on the grounds that "it is not backlash, but a surfacing of basic hostilities already present." He made this statement in the midst of a demonstration at a real estate office when rumors of a new round of marches into all-white areas were circulating. The rumors were untrue, but they had originated from movement sources.[30]

In October, Raby had written his interpretation of these events for the *Hyde Park–Kenwood Voices:*

> It is clear that a careful campaign is being waged to undermine the gains of this summer's rights activities. Two techniques are being used: wedges driven between the various facets of the movement, and legal harassment.
>
> Tales of dissension and splits in the movement are rampant. Often they are based on partial realities, such as simple disagreements that occur in any broad-based social movement. But these grains of truth are puffed up like breakfast cereal by the opposition.

Recently a nationally-syndicated column and a local newspaper were in the fore-front of the attack. Hatchetmen Rowland Evans and Robert Novak, who half destroyed SNCC through red-baiting and a stream of virulent attacks, let loose on Dr. King, Rev. Jim Bevel, and me. While never attacking Dr. King directly, the effort to get him was clear.

The burden of their assault was that this summer's open-housing drive was something dreamed up out of desperation to heal an alleged rift in the local movement. This is a clear slap at SCLC's president, implying that his major campaigns are top-of-the-head decisions aimed at internal problems rather than national issues.

Meanwhile, they totally ignored a year's building of tenant unions, the creation of more than $2 million worth of jobs for Negroes, the fusion of parts of the labor and civil rights movements, increased support of the churches, and most of all, a nation-wide focus on open housing through a debate on the ill-fated 1966 Civil Rights Bill. It is likely that columns such as theirs helped create a climate for the bill's defeat.

Another wedge was driven into the movement by Chicago's American in an article setting up the Urban League's Bill Berry as the "No. 1" man, manipulating everyone in the movement from behind the scenes. While sounding like a pat on the back for Berry, the effect was to isolate him. The League represents a more conservative portion of this movement; overplaying Bill's role in this manner clearly creates distrust and suspicion among the more militant organizations.

Those groups, such as CORE and the West Side Organization, were treated as wild-eyed outcasts in the article, lying in wait to do in Dr. King and seize the revolution.

It is not hard to play on the fears and suspicions of movement people who have endured difficult struggles and have known betrayal in the past. It is even easier to deceive the general public, which gains most of its information through the mass media.

There is little need for a lengthy defense of the movement's essential integrity and unity of purpose. Suffice it to say that virtually any individual in the movement may disagree on any given action, but when the time comes to stand up and be counted, we stand together.

Bob Lucas led a march into Cicero. Most of us disagreed with his action, but we believed in his right to go and in the justice of the march itself.

When he was arrested, our enemies hoped we would stand aloof. We did not.

Which leads to my next point, legal harassment. Isn't it strange that the city suddenly decided to jail Lucas right after the Cicero march—on charges that had been hanging for more than a year—then re-arrested him as soon as he was bailed out, for failing to appear in court while he was in jail?

Isn't it strange that I was recently convicted on State charges—added to a host of City charges—that emerged from a single, year-old demonstration?

Isn't it strange that Frank Ditto was jailed?

It's not strange if you consider that this is a new line of direct attack on movement leadership. It is more blatant than most, but only because the movement is growing in strength and represents more of a threat to the power structure. . . .

If you are concerned about this, your job is to stay close to the movement and get the facts. You can't rely on pundits, gossips, or rumors in this time of crisis.[31]

291

By November, therefore, in spite of pressure from the delegates for the CCCO to be more political, the steering committee was being driven by external events to take an increasingly strong nonpartisan position. Jackson explained that he and Bevel had been trying to explain that a one-party system leads to dictatorship, but as John McDermott pointed out, in Chicago "if we are talking about a two-party system, we are asking for a Republican vote." Those had not been Bevel's actual words. "Mayor Daley has got to realize," he had said, "that there are one million Negroes in this town, yet the Democratic Party has refused to recognize or adequately deal with the problems and indignities they are forced to live with."[32] Brazier said there was "no doubt the Chicago Freedom Movement is being manipulated by the Republican party," and he saw no solution. But King said the inescapable problem was the accusation "of getting money from the Republican party."[33] This was a problem in Chicago, but, as Andrew Young observed, it was also a problem for the SCLC in Georgia, where its tax-exempt status was in jeopardy.

It was a strange discussion. By then, neither political party wanted to be affiliated with the Chicago Freedom Movement, but each was determined to turn the discontent that had surfaced over the summer to its own electoral advantage. In the November election, the Republicans gained the advantage, electing Charles Percy to the Senate and Richard Ogilvie to the chairmanship of the Cook County Board of Commissioners, but the Chicago Freedom Movement gained no appreciable advantage from either of them.

The steering committee had to contend with other political problems in addition to the election. King had expressed a desire to organize hospital workers, and by early November found himself involved in a battle between two unions, neither one of which had been noticeably friendly to civil rights aims—the Building Service Union, whose president, William McFettrige, was close to the mayor, and the Teamsters. Norman Hill of IUD said that neither his people nor the American Federation of State, County and Municipal Employees (AFSCME) "would even sit down at a table" with either one of them.

King admitted he had a dilemma. He said that he "had not anticipated an inter-union conflict" even though he "should have." He said that he should have tried "to negotiate a compromise before engaging in an internal fight" between rival unions. He had "planned a meeting with Hoffa"; but at the urging of other steering committee members, he decided to call Jerry Wurf, president of the AFSCME, "to see what commitment he would make with the hospital workers before talking again to either the Teamsters or the Building Service Unions." He concluded by admitting, "It's a mess." In fact, it was similar to the dilemma with the Republican party. Neither of these unions, which stood to gain from King's support, had expressed support for the civil rights movement.

292

The clergy presented another problem. King said that "for the long haul, we need to draw more clergy into the movement." He especially meant the black clergy. "They want to be closer to the policy level," King said. Something should be done, he stressed, "especially in the light of J. H. Jackson's actions."

The Reverend J. H. Jackson, not to be confused with the movement's Jesse Jackson, was president of the National Baptist Convention of the USA, Inc., and the pastor of a socially prominent congregation on Chicago's South Side. Jackson had never agreed with King's confrontational activism. On 3 November, he had held a national convention of black religious leaders from his own and other denominations. It had clearly been an anti-King gathering. It issued a "manifesto of moderation," condemning confrontational tactics and stressing the need to begin by changing the attitudes of Negroes. "We must not allow the failure of others to embitter our spirit" was the double-edged thrust of this manifesto.[34]

At the same time, the Chicago Conference on Religion and Race was issuing its plans to aid in the implementation of the summit agreement. An educational Crusade for Justice was planned from 15 January to 28 February 1967 to build support for implementing the agreements reached in August 1966. The program was aimed at "the broad uncommitted middle."

The struggle for church support at the congregational level was on; and though the basically white denominations had been represented in the CCCO since 1963 by their interracial councils, support from the black churches had been much harder to acquire. King suggested that Operation Breadbasket might provide the necessary link. "Breadbasket is an affiliate of SCLC in Atlanta," he said, "and I have nothing from them to get the impression they would not want to be affiliated with CCCO." King wanted to pursue that route even though Jesse Jackson warned that the black clergy "wanted to make certain their actions would not be inhibited." Breadbasket was becoming Jackson's organization, much as the SCLC was King's.

At its meeting of 10 November the steering committee returned to the problem of partisan activity. The November elections were over, but the March primary for City Council and mayor was coming up, and pressure was mounting for a voter registration campaign. Raby acknowledged that some groups could not engage in partisan activities and that the CCCO itself could not be political in the electoral sense, but it could "initiate strategic positions." In addition, he thought that there should be a "political arm of the movement." Brazier agreed on the "need for political power." The CCCO, he said, "has a base of power other than marching, but the elected officials don't recognize us." "A positive base" was needed so "the political structure listens to what we are saying." McDermott thought the CCCO needed "to be in on selecting candidates for aldermanic races." Kale Williams cautioned that "if the free-

293

dom movement is going to get into politics, let's do it with a real appraisal of the possibilities." He would, he said, "rather elect two good people than run forty and lose." The resources for a voter registration campaign were not yet in hand. That would require major new initiatives.

Meanwhile, the process of implementing the summit agreement was proceeding very slowly. On 15 November the leadership council met to assess the progress to date. The Chicago Conference on Religion and Race reported on its efforts to distribute copies of the agreement to clergy and laity in the metropolitan area, to interpret the agreement to suburban leaders and communities, to form a Home Investment, Inc., to purchase homes in the metropolitan area and make them available for resale on a nondiscriminatory basis, to initiate an educational program for applicants for real estate licenses, to open a Housing Information Center to maintain listings already available on a nondiscriminatory basis, and to prepare a general public relations program to build support for the agreement.[35]

The Commission on Human Relations, in its report to the leadership council, stressed "the multiple problems present in the housing situations in the metropolitan area of Chicago." Recurring to its old civic credo refrain, the commission reported that "attempts have been made at educating the white community to the moral and economic bases for open occupancy, but the attitudes of the people of the community leave much to be desired." Nonetheless, the commission reported that it had processed seventy-four complaints against realtors since 1 August and that most of them had either been resolved or were in the process of "conciliation." Only six were still under investigation; it was "checking" firms to determine their compliance with the city ordinance; it was paying special attention to firms against which there had been multiple complaints; it had added two persons to its housing staff; it was looking into the legal problems involved in testing realtors; it had appointed five attorneys to preside over conciliation conferences; and it would urge the adoption of a state fair housing law in the 1967 session of the Illinois General Assembly.[36]

The Cook County Department of Public Aid had added three housing consultants to its staff, but neither that agency nor the Chicago Housing Authority could report any changes in either policy or practice.

At the steering committee meeting on 17 November, Berry gave his evaluation of these reports. Even though he was not optimistic, he thought the movement should "be prepared to devote considerable energy to make the agreement stand up." He counseled a "positive attitude," saying, "I do not think we should assume it will not work." He did not want the committee to adopt "a position of yacking and arguing." He did think it might be possible to get a committee member appointed as executive director of the leadership council.

John McDermott was concerned that the council adopt a citywide approach to the problem and not get bogged down in "individual cases." But Jesse Jackson wanted to discuss "the effect of our going back into the streets." McDermott cautioned, "If we go back without a sign of complete failure, I do not know what they will do." He was, he said, "disappointed at the slow pace." He acknowledged that the black family who had bought a house in Chicago Lawn, scene of the summer demonstrations, had been bombed and no official action had been taken, but he affirmed, "We have the ingredients for something good." Jackson countered by saying that "the system has not changed" and that people see "no special reason for accepting Negro people." He saw the profit motive as an impediment to open housing. "So for us," he concluded, "the problem is to remain sensitized to immoral behavior" and not be "lulled to sleep just because we have no weapon."

The next item on the agenda was a report from the SCLC's staff conference at Frogmore, South Carolina. King said that Hosea Williams was willing to come to Chicago for a "massive, crash, voter registration campaign." He recommended concentrating in one area, either Englewood or the Fourth Ward. The problem was money. The SCLC had been in touch with the Taconic Foundation, a sometime source of movement funds, but King reported that "Currier is not as responsive as his assistants were." That was bad news because it was Stephen Currier's money the foundation gave away. Berry agreed to call him. King also thought that Charles Percy might help the drive through his connections at Bell and Howell. King wondered about the procedures "from this point," that is, how to take this proposal to the delegate body. Raby assured him that "the response would be positive and unifying."

Berry reported that the White House Task Force on the Problem of the Cities was looking into the possibility of rehabilitating property in slum neighborhoods so that the tenants could own it. He reported "one hang up: if it is possible to do this." He also wanted to know, "What is our perspective?" since the program, if it could be done, would involve "tying people to segregated situations." King replied: "We have a two-fold job: to go all out for open cities or to make the ghettoes more livable." He reported that Secretary of Housing and Urban Development Robert Weaver had responded positively to the idea of building condominiums, but he was unclear whether HUD would be the best agency to institute such a program. Berry said that HUD "is problematic" and that "the regional HUD people should not participate." Archie Hargraves suggested that people at the Ford Foundation had indicated an interest in community corporations and that these might be instruments for implementing the program.

McDermott thought the entire process was lacking in a proper sense of urgency. In particular, he said, "Cook [chair of the leadership council] does not have the same sense of urgency as the people who conducted the negotiations." In his view, it was "either a blood bath or real open housing"—and

295

time was running out. Hargraves warned that even open housing "will not stop the riots." In his view, "riots are a generational phenomenon," and they would happen anyway.

The meeting ended with a discussion of fund-raising. Jesse Jackson was about to go on a national tour to raise money for the SCLC. The CCCO would have to raise funds in Chicago; it needed $2,000 each month for staff and operating expenses. The question was raised whether the supply of money would be threatened "if we have an action group endorsing candidates." It was a question to which there was no answer.

The meeting of CCCO delegates on 19 November 1966 consisted mostly of reports from constituent groups and standing committees. The Citizens Housing Committee and the Englewood Civic Organization reported once more on their continuing efforts to oppose the city-sponsored urban renewal program at Sixty-third and Halstead.[37]

Jesse Jackson reported a significant victory for Operation Breadbasket after a month of negotiating with the Hi-Lo grocery stores. Each of its fourteen ghetto stores (20 percent of Hi-Lo's business) agreed to open accounts at the black-owned Seaway National Bank. These stores also agreed to "display Negro products—e.g., Joe Louis Milk, Parker House Sausage, Stewart Bleach." The chain also pledged 183 new jobs for blacks. Jackson said that National Tea Company, another grocery chain, was the next target, but he claimed that there was a "blackout in the newspapers" on Operation Breadbasket. The committee on constitutional changes said it was planning a special session devoted exclusively to constitutional revision. Albert Raby reported on the session with school superintendent James Redmond. The education committee was empowered to participate in joint task forces with members of the superintendent's staff but was instructed "to make it clear that we ask for priority on issues as CCCO sees them." The delegates voted to "find the mechanism and vehicle to have expansive and effective voter registration campaigns, etc., on the political front" and instructed the convenor to "find a way to set such a program in motion." Raby reported on the position he would take at the Citizen's Committee to Study Police-Community Relations. He would advocate a civilian police review board, to be composed of fifteen to twenty members, with a staff of its own. Its meetings should be open to the public. The report on the follow-up to the summit agreement was brief, the main points being that the Conference on Religion and Race needed $25,000 to carry out its proposed programs and the leadership council was expected to name an executive director within two weeks. One delegate protested: "This committee should be exposed for being what it really is—a cover up."

On 25 November, with a tax-raising budget before the City Council, Alderman Thomas E. Keane, the mayor's City Council floor leader, denied that any agreement existed between the city and the civil rights movement on the question of open housing. The agreement, he claimed, consisted only of "certain suggestions put down and goals to be sought." King responded: "I hope this does not mean the administration now governing Chicago intends to break faith with all those who reached the agreement. Hundreds of thousands of Chicago citizens live in slums today awaiting the severities of winter. Last summer they were given the hope that their hardship would come to an end, that the slums could be eliminated, and that decent homes would be made available to all families in all neighborhoods. Any attempt to destroy that hope is an act of cruelty and a betrayal of trust. The people will not stand for it." Even Seymour Simon, the Democratic president of the Cook County Board, accused Keane of using "trickery of words to step away from" the commitments made at the summit meeting. Alderman Keane denied any such intention.[38]

By early December, it was clear that the leadership council was not coalescing into a powerful agency. At the steering committee meeting 1 December Raby said: "I have lost faith in the agreement. I have lost faith in those who are going to implement it. Nothing is being done. The chief problem is the Commission on Human Relations. We need a meeting to decide what we are going to do. Should we put Cook's committee on the spot? It is certain we could not start demonstrations in this weather." Bevel suggested that the organization plan to "do something by March, aimed at the mayoralty election in April." Jackson said it was necessary to "document the case in public." Hosea Williams offered his staff of fifteen, and he appealed for community organizations to cooperate and wondered how to enlist the people who had marched in the summer. He reported that the funding was still tenuous. The American Foundation on Nonviolence had put up $5,000. A conference with Stephen Currier at the Taconic Foundation was set for the following week, and "the Republican National Committee has some interest in putting money into the campaign." (The Republican money never materialized. Taconic gave a token grant.)

The discussion ranged broadly over the general problems of a voter registration campaign in Chicago. It began and ended with the unresolved question of the relation of a voter registration drive to the Daley political organization, the same ambivalence the CCCO had demonstrated in the short-lived Freedom Democratic Clubs two years before. It was clear to everyone that voter registration in Chicago was a partisan activity. It was decided to concentrate on wards where movement candidates were available and there were community organizations to support them. Bernard Lee (SCLC) proposed running movement candidates, fighting white candidates rather than getting involved in

297

"black on black" situations, and supporting candidates who were already in the field rather than trying to recruit new ones.

Kale Williams said that the movement staff in East Garfield Park came from AFSC and WSCP. AFSC staff, he said, "will not work on political campaigns" even though Lester Jackson, a candidate for City Council, "is a member of AFSC and a member of our Executive Committee." It was accepted that AFSC had to protect its tax-exempt status.

The committee agreed to set up a freedom voters league and to make an issue of voter registration procedures by demanding that the Board of Election Commissions provide neighborhood and night-time opportunities for registration instead of restricting registration to business hours downtown as announced. It was pointed out that in 1964 neighborhood registration had been conducted for a month. Charles Hayes (United Packinghouse Workers, UPHW) emphasized that a registration drive "has to spring from the broadest possible publicity to be effective." He thought the "political persecution of the movement" should be stressed as a "springboard to get people to have the desire to negotiate." Raby had been sentenced to three months in jail and a $500 fine whereas others convicted of the same offenses had been levied $25 fines. Hayes thought Raby's conviction should be publicized "to arouse the Negro community."

The discussion kept coming back to the partisan intention of a voter registration drive. Hosea Williams said he wanted "to motivate people in a nonpartisan drive," but the issues at hand were partisan: "the inadequacies of the machine" and "the inadequacies of life in the ghetto." Aware of black voting patterns in Chicago, he said, "a large, uninformed electorate is worse than none." The problem was how to control the voters the movement registered: "We can't get allied to the Republican Party without alienating our allies." It was a new problem for him: "In the South we have not lost the people we have registered." Again, the need for a freedom voters league, supporting movement candidates, was mentioned. James Bevel, however, was skeptical. It could be "poor and dangerous to run independent candidates," he said. "The movement has a political, social, and economic philosophy. Men run on issues, but the movement *preaches* issues."

Some of the issues were clear enough: night-time and neighborhood registration; the persecution of Albert Raby; the fate of the open housing agreement; the Green Street alternative to the Englewood Urban Renewal plan; and the creation of a new, segregated high school at Forrestville. But as the discussion ended, Hosea Williams was still uncertain, asking: "When we launch our drive, to what degree should it be an attack on the Daley machine?" As the meeting ended, King said that he was taking the month of December to write a book. When it finally appeared the next fall, it was subtitled *Where Do We Go from Here?*

298

THE MOVEMENT TAKES A STAND:
NOTHING HAS CHANGED

The organizing of the leadership council to implement the summer's agreements proceeded with less speed and more difficulty than anyone had imagined in August. It was 29 November before Edward L. Holmgren was named as executive director.[39] When his appointment was announced, the organizers still believed that he would have a budget of $500,000 for the first year of operation, but when the Leadership Council for Metropolitan Open Communities was officially launched only one week later, the first $100,000 was still not in hand, and only nine suburban village presidents had joined the council. Mayor Daley drew cheers when, in an attempt to reverse the sense of dwindling momentum, he discarded his prepared address to the council to make an emotional reaffirmation of his pledge: "I shall and will give every bit of my effort, dedication and devotion to carrying out the terms of the agreement put together by well-intentioned men in August 1966."[40] To underline his seriousness, the mayor brought Alderman Keane with him and named him as one of the charter members of the leadership council. It was clear at this founding session that the officials of the city and the leaders of the business community were more convinced than the suburban politicians that open housing was a metropolitan problem. In the suburbs, it was still an urban problem, if not *the* urban problem.

At this meeting, whereas the mayor chose to stress his commitment to the summit agreement, Raby chose to express his skepticism about its implementation. "I have waited three years," he said, "to see change in the social structure of Chicago. I was hit by rocks in Gage Park, and a man was bombed out of his home on the West Side recently, and I know that not one thing has changed in Chicago." Such a view, uttered at the founding of a new congregation organized to proclaim the civic credo, was heresy. *Chicago's American* rose at once to the defense of orthodoxy. Chicago had been making "progress in race relations" at least since 1951, as Raby should know, believe, and say. Discouraging words were out of place:

> It is his apparent belief that, because such things still happen in Chicago, nothing at all has changed; that race relations in the city are exactly where they were three years ago, and that talk of "progress" is meaningless as long as individual race haters continue to throw rocks or plant bombs.
>
> If that attitude were widely shared, it would effectively doom any progress at all. As Raby seems to define it, "progress" would mean remaking the city overnight into a paradise of racial justice where violence is never committed by white against Negro or Negro against white; and since that has not happened, no progress is being made. A more negative and discouraging viewpoint than that would be hard to imagine.

299

A great deal has changed in Chicago, and the rate of change is accelerating. The thing for Raby to do, it seems to us, is to encourage the changes—not to deny they're happening.[41]

But the silence had been broken, and Raby followed up his remarks with two lengthy public statements, one addressed to the *American,* the other to the Board of Education. In each case, the theme was the same: nothing had changed.

RABY TO *CHICAGO'S AMERICAN:*
NOTHING HAS CHANGED

Your editorial of December 8 challenging my remarks to a recent Leadership Council meeting concludes at the point at which it should have begun if your criticism is valid. You say: "A great deal has changed in Chicago." A list of examples was in order, but you offered none.

Let me dispel your editorial writer's doubts. I spoke as a Negro, and I did mean literally that "not one thing has changed in Chicago" to assure Negroes of their legal—let alone moral—rights to equality of treatment as Americans and as citizens of this city.

What I tried to tell the meeting was that the inequality becomes more pronounced, viewed against the pledges made at the summit meetings in August. Since then, the Holmes family was bombed out of the home on Oakley Street; another Negro family across the street was burned out Thanksgiving eve.

Assaults of a similar nature are occurring almost daily in our city. The Holmes family ordeal received publicity because their three sons are in or on their way to Viet Nam. The other cases are rarely mentioned.

There are no outraged headlines, no word of any apprehension of the arsonists and vandals and, to my latest knowledge, no public announcement of any intercession by Chicago's Commission on Human Relations. Has anything changed since the days of Trumbull Park?[42]

Has the quality of justice changed in Chicago? Compare the heavy fines and jail sentences meted out to nonviolent civil rights demonstrators (as late as November 28) and the token fines imposed on violent racists who burned cars and hurled rocks in Gage Park.

Has there been any change in our public school system? The bulk of our school building budget for 1967 is proposed for buildings and "Willis wagons" designed to keep Negro children out of "white" schools—in violation of state as well as federal law. The schools' superintendent is new—but the school board's policies are unchanged.

Since the summit meetings, the only officially reported change is that eight Negro families have been moved out of the ghetto. We are trying to verify this report. Even if true, it is more a reaffirmation of my position than it is evidence of change.

I opened my remarks to the Leadership Council with the comment that our only ultimate measurement of the success of the summit agreement can be tangible

300

change in our segregated housing pattern. Eight families moved out of the ghetto is no tangible change for a city of one million Negroes!

Where is the change of this city's three-year failure to enforce the fair housing ordinance of 1963? Realtors violate this ordinance every day in every white community in Chicago. To this date (December 16) the mayor has taken no action on the single complaint against a real estate company ever filed by his Commission on Human Relations. It is dated July 12, 1966, and calls for suspension of the license of Ryan & Co.

Your own editorial is further documentation of my charge that there has been no change. Once again you attack the complainant rather than the agencies and officials guilty of inaction. Once again you charge us with impatience, with defining "progress" as "remaking the city overnight."

Let me say first that instant protection of rights is the basic implication of a society that calls itself democratic and fortifies itself with a system of police and courts of justice for that end. In this context even "overnight" is too long for American Negroes, that "overnight" is three centuries too long.

The main point of my statement was that for the Negro in the Chicago ghetto—where the majority of Negroes live—there has been no change. I said that if there is any hope of change short of that wrought by nonviolent action in the streets, the hope rests with a determined and forceful implementation of the pledges made at the summit meetings.

Neither a chorus of civic leaders nor a fanfare of newspaper headlines can make enough magic with the words, "Summit Agreement," to clothe the still naked king.

The agreement remains a facade without substance. It looks good in front. Unless its sponsors—and the city's tax-supported agencies and political leaders—begin laying the bricks behind it quickly, it will have toppled by next summer.[43]

RABY TO THE BOARD OF EDUCATION: NOTHING HAS CHANGED

The proposed school budget for 1967 reflects no change in Board of Education practices which have provoked so much concern and protest from the civil rights community over the past years. Once again, we are being asked to approve more of the same status quo stew that has kept Chicago's school children educationally undernourished and anaemic.

When we met with Superintendent Redmond two months ago, he assured us he intended to "live up to the letter and the spirit of the Armstrong Law." But Section 320 of the proposed budget lists over $17 million for planning and construction, ignoring the requirements of that law that schools shall be districted to avoid racial segregation. Section 320 vindicates the reasons why CCCO opposed the recent school building bond issue. We opposed the bond issue because the Board had failed to inform the public where new schools and additions would be built with these funds, and failed to give any evidence that the money would be spent in conformity with the Armstrong Law. In the absence of such evidence, we could only assume

301

that the old pattern of building segregated schools would continue. The public still does not know where its $25 million will be spent—but Section 320 of this budget tells us the pattern of segregation has not changed. For example:

The largest single item in the building budget is $5,850,000 for a new school in District 14—the Kenwood High School. This will redistrict almost every white student out of Hyde Park High School, leaving Hyde Park High a 99% Negro-segregated school. If this Board is intended to observe the Armstrong Law, it would have recommended adding this amount to the $2 million assigned for the rehabilitation of Hyde Park High, to launch an educational park centered around that school which could serve an integrated student population drawn from Kenwood, Forrestville, Hyde Park, Woodlawn and parts of South Shore.

As the new Kenwood proposal now stands, the Board will spend almost $6 million to accommodate 2,000 students, including almost every white student who would otherwise have been enrolled at Hyde Park High! But less than a mile away from that Kenwood site is the Forrestville school compound, where, by Dr. Willis' own figures last year, high school space is needed for an expected high school population of 8,000, and a present high school population of almost 2,000. Right now over 1,600 children are attending the so-called "Forrestville High School"— an old upper grade center converted to high school use three years ago, but still lacking a gym, laboratories, or any of the other facilities that distinguish a high school. To meet this crisis situation, your budget offers only a planning item of $10,000—$50,000 less than it offered—but never spent—last year. Rumors in the community are that an unsatisfactory site in the heart of the segregated Forrestville district is being favored for a new segregated high school, some day.

Compare how this budget treats Kenwood and Forrestville, and you realize that nothing has really changed in this Board's segregationist practices! Most of the budget's line items of $10,000 remain cloaked in mystery, no locations are named, but the clues are there: like the item for a new school to serve three overwhelmingly segregated white high schools: Gage Park, Kelly and Kennedy. Or the items for schools to contain Negroes: one for Harland, Hirsch and Calumet; another for Farragut and Marshall. The list of examples is long—at the elementary as well as high school level. The old ways—the Willis ways—continue, even down to the $240,000 for more mobile units—Chicago's "Willis Wagons"—to keep schools mainly white or mainly Negro, rather than use empty classrooms. The budget continues to ignore the hundreds of unused classroom seats, and the possibility of bussing children from crowded schools to utilize this space.

Our gerrymandered school boundaries long ago discredited the myth of the "neighborhood school" as a fixed and unchangeable entity. Our practice of bussing handicapped children to special schools long ago destroyed the myth that transporting children to school is educationally undesirable. Yet both of these myths are invoked here to "protect" communities from integrated school populations!

C.C.C.O. asks the Board of Education to hold up action on this budget until it has heard the recommendations of the task forces on which we have agreed to cooperate with the Superintendent. When our delegates voted recently to accept Dr. Redmond's proposal, they did so with the clear stipulation that a test of the good faith of

302

this Board would be its attention to the task force proposals. We have informed Dr. Redmond we are ready to meet with his committee next week, to consider first ways to implement the Armstrong Act with funds provided in this budget and in the recent bond issue. We can tell you now—in advance of that meeting—that we are convinced only educational parks can effectively improve the quality and promote the integration of high school education in Chicago. We propose as a beginning an educational park for the Hyde Park, Kenwood, Woodlawn and nearby South Shore communities; an educational park for Forrestville and adjacent areas; and expansion of Waller High School immediately into an educational park, to help this highly diverse, integrated school maintain its stability. These are programs in the spirit and letter of the Armstrong Act.

For its failure to honor its obligations under the Armstrong Law, for its failure to provide for use of empty classroom seats, the C.C.C.O. repudiates the proposed budget as an unlawful use of public funds.

We condemn this budget equally for its failure to provide the tools to accomplish the goals it claims to be furthering. For example: Section 400 tells us a function of the Department of Integration and Human Relations is to work for "high quality integrated school programs" . . . including "increased integration of schools and faculties." The recent student and faculty head-counts disclosed that the overwhelmingly segregated pattern of students and faculties continues in Chicago. Yet the 1967 budget proposes a $50,000 cut in the department's appropriation. Nor does the budget reflect any program to strengthen the department's work with the kind of city-wide planning necessary to insure quality, integrated education for the whole city.

If the Board or its administrators plead they can provide quality education more quickly than integrated education, where is the evidence in this budget that they are moving in this direction? Where does the budget provide for additional psychologists, counsellors, remedial courses, special textbooks, better paid teachers, smaller classloads—all indispensable to raise the quality of education throughout Chicago, and particularly in the neglected ghetto schools?

Where is the Board's first attempt to enlarge educational horizons for our high school population with an educational park that can offer a richer variety of programs?

C.C.C.O. rejects the proposition that quality and integration can be separate goals. All history and all research demonstrate the imperative unity of these objectives.

By the same token, policy and budget are also inseparable. You cannot proclaim a policy of quality, integrated education, yet fail to provide the funds and programs to implement that policy. If you are worried over the lack of funds, we remind you that where policy reflects determination to fulfill legal and moral obligations, the public will demand funds for its implementation. Highways are rarely left in disrepair, regardless of a community's treasury, because lives are at stake.

Young lives have been at stake for too long in our city—in a hazardous educational program that produces illiterate graduates, dropouts who can find their identity only in gangs, and teenagers who chant racist epithets as they wave a Swastika.

303

It is to this disrepair that the Board must give top priority in its use of funds today. The cement for that repair lies in intensive programs to establish quality, integration and equality of opportunity throughout our public school system.[44]

NOTHING HAD CHANGED: GOING THROUGH THE MOTIONS

Nothing had changed; but the search for alternatives continued to preoccupy the freedom movement. In September, King, the CCCO, and a United Church of Christ–sponsored agency called the Community Renewal Foundation had submitted a proposal to HUD for $4 million to rehabilitate slum housing in two West Side neighborhoods (Lawndale and East Garfield Park) and one South Side neighborhood (North Kenwood–Oakland). The concept called for turning the rehabilitated buildings over to the tenants on a cooperative ownership basis. Some such idea had been in the air ever since King had taken control of 1321 South Homan in February. Then in July, King had cleared the general idea with HUD during the West Side riot. When this proposal was funded in December, it caused an organizational and strategic problem.

At the 8 December meeting of the steering committee, Raby raised "two basic questions: 1) should the civil rights movement be involved in rehabilitating housing?" 2) "what are the goals of the movement in rehabilitating housing as compared to other agencies?" He said that there had been "so much time spent, so much confusion" that "organization on the West Side ceased" to function. Kale Williams commented that Bernard Lafayette "is spending practically full time in these meetings." He was concerned about "how to relate this rehabilitation program to further tenant organizing, and to Negro businessmen and to continuing community organizations."

The Reverend Donald Benedict, executive director of the Community Renewal Society, parent organization for the Community Renewal Foundation, saw the problem differently: "Is the movement ready to move to an operational aspect of the problem rather than protest?" He thought it was time to "bring in skilled people," start training programs, and "face the complexity of the problem."

Raby commented wryly that this program "may make us look as bad as Swibel." Benedict thought that the difference lay in the goal, which was "to let tenants have more control of their living situation." Benedict proposed to see this program "as the movement getting the means of control." It would "take away from the ability to mount protest," but he thought the goal was worth the price. Both Raby and Kale Williams expressed reservations about "the decision-making process" at the local level. It required a lot of meetings, and Raby said it was "not such a way to operate a business," while Williams said it was "wasted energy with not much coming out of it." Raby was also concerned that "there was no programmatic description of the goals." He was not interested in actions for the mere sake of participation. "How do you get housing for the poor? How is that done?" He doubted that the answer lay in rehabilitating a few houses and turning them into tenant cooperatives.

Another question involved lines of responsibility. At the moment, there were three loci of accountability—the steering committee, the local communities, and the Community Renewal Foundation. "Who decides," Williams wanted to know, "about representatives from the local communities?" Raby said that "experts have to be responsible for realizations"; therefore, it was imperative that the goals be clear. He proposed that a meeting be held to deal with goals and to report back to the steering committee.

John McDermott reported that the constitution committee was prepared to recommend that the steering committee be partly elected by the CCCO and partly appointed and that the CCCO accept into membership all the groups that had been participating with the SCLC in the Chicago Freedom Movement.

Raby reported on the official launching of the Leadership Council for Metropolitan Open Communities, at which "Joe Cook made a good statement." At the end of his remarks Cook had quoted from a letter written by the son of a prominent steel executive. Writing from the battlefields of Vietnam, the young man had described the sentiments of Pfc. Milton Olive III, a black GI, "who, in a campfire colloquy with his fellow soldiers, concluded, 'You got to care. You just got to care!'" Several weeks later, he threw himself on a grenade to save his comrades. Posthumously, he was awarded the Congressional Medal of Honor. That was Cook's theme for the leadership council: "You got to care." Raby also assessed Edward L. Holmgren as "a good appointment" to the post of executive director. He said there were "not as many labor people" on the leadership council as he had hoped. In addition, he had a question about the "size of the civil rights representation." In summary, he said "Cook runs things" in a "high-handed" way.

William Robinson agreed with that characterization of Cook and added pointedly that he was "negative about criticism." The story was that, in recruiting the council, he had run into "overt resistance to open occupancy" and that the council would not endorse open occupancy legislation because "certain groups would not join if they did." Kale Williams suggested that "Cook is not high-handed, but inexperienced." Williams expected him to become more sensitive. He said there had been a series of reports at the previous Friday's meeting. Williams had done the report on the Chicago Housing Authority. "The follow-up committee," he said, "felt that it is at a point where it needs more liaison with the public agencies." To this end, the follow-up committee was proposing weekly meetings with the second- and

305

third-level leadership in these agencies. Raby agreed this should be done, but John McDermott said, "It depends on the type of relation." Unless that was clear and the "power of the Leadership Council" was brought to bear on these agencies, these meetings "might undercut the role of the freedom movement representatives." Williams said the follow-up committee wanted to meet once a month. That appeared to receive general consent.

The report on voter registration called for a budget of $45,000, which had not been raised. Hosea Williams would kick off a citywide drive with a "mass meeting" on 20 December. Williams's plan was to activate organizations in eighteen of the fifty wards, work relatively hard in eleven or twelve wards, and concentrate on six of these. The plan was to organize around issues, but Williams said it was up to the steering committee to develop the issues. Williams stressed his conviction that "people vote against before they vote for—urban renewal, welfare, education, economic exploitation." McDermott reminded him that they were "fighting aldermen" more than issues and asked, "Registration for what—to give Daley more votes?" Raby responded that there were "different issues in different communities." He thought citywide confrontation on neighborhood registration could be produced.

The steering committee meeting of 13 December began with a report from William Moyer on behalf of the follow-up committee. In essence, he said there had been "no change in participation in an open city by the major agencies which were party to the agreement." There was still "violence every day in racially changing blocks." He cited the Holmes family, whose windows had been broken on Thanksgiving Day at 105th and Green streets. Similarly, a family who had moved into Chicago Lawn was greeted by violence and property destruction.

What was needed, he said, was a "strategy in the movement with each of the agencies." The big question in his mind was to decide whether to "just wait" or "work along with Ed Holmgren" or "elicit information and say what we have found." Archie Hargraves wanted to know "what would constitute a giant step" and "how can we force a philosophy that builds pressure for that giant step?" Moyer, fresh from his encounters with the public agencies, suggested that his committee "could set up minimum standards for each agency" and "call them giant steps" if these agencies met them.

Jesse Jackson reported that agreements with National Tea and Del Farms had produced 383 new jobs. The supermarket chains also agreed to market the products of fifteen black-owned enterprises and to transfer the accounts of their ghetto stores to Seaway and Independence banks, both of which were black-owned. "One of the most significant projects we can do this winter," he said, "is a bank-in movement, asking concerned whites to put money in

Negro banks. The money could extend their lending power. The whole money market could change.''

The other problem on Jackson's mind was training programs. He wanted something independent of Operation Breadbasket. "The Urban League," he said, "needs a full department" to train people for Breadbasket-negotiated jobs. Breadbasket, he said, had "turned into an economic movement." It was "understaffed" and needed "help and suggestions." The Urban League representatives agreed to see about adding staff "to coordinate, recruit, place, and follow-up on Breadbasket jobs."

Another of Breadbasket's ventures was a project called Operation Love, an idea that was apparently as subject to misunderstanding as its name. It had been presented as a proposal to Coca-Cola. Rumors immediately spread that Breadbasket was demanding money, presumably under threat of demonstrations. Jackson said the proposal had been given to Coke for criticism and revision. The object was to raise some $5 million for new Negro businesses. About $260,000 was targeted for a media campaign to promote change in the presentation of blacks. Jackson tried to clarify the nature of Operation Love, but the relation of the steering committee to this project was not clear.

It was also announced at this 15 December meeting that the opening rally for the voter registration drive had been moved to 2 January 1967.

Meanwhile, on the Far West Side, yet another neighborhood, Austin, was beginning the painful process of block-by-block expansion of the ghetto. The Austin Community Organization was a group originally dedicated to creating an integrated neighborhood instead of one subject to rapid racial change. By December 1966, it had been in operation for more than two years, having launched highly visible attacks on slum landlords, real estate panic selling, block busting, and segregation in the neighborhood schools. Since October, the group, which now consisted of only forty dues-paying members, had attempted to make the open housing agreement mean something in Austin. In December it sent a report to Archbishop Cody of its unsuccessful attempts to find integrated housing for a black Catholic family in the Austin area. The group reported that it failed to get cooperation both from realtors and from local parishes. The report recalled Cody's "strong statement of support for open housing," but claimed that, "as far as local pastors are concerned, those are nothing more than statements and not matters of clear policy—that in fact, no directives or explanations of the housing agreement had been received at the parish level as late as 2 November 1966." When a *Chicago Daily News* reporter called a local pastor to check the report, he was told, "I've got all I can do now. Is it my particular job to find places for people to live? You have to balance rights against feelings."[45]

Just before Christmas Archbishop Cody announced a comprehensive six-month program of study and action for the 459 parishes in the Archdiocese of Chicago. It had been worked out as a response to the summit agreement by a thirty-five-member Commission on Human Relations and Ecumenism. Pastors and laymen were asked to spend the first four months of 1967 meeting and studying racial problems, especially in the areas of housing, education, and employment. This period of study was expected to eventuate in the formation of "committees on community life." During May and June 1967 these committees would begin a dialogue on open housing with local realtors and banking and savings and loan officials, a dialogue on high-quality integrated education with local school officials, and a dialogue on fair employment with businesses in their area.

At the same time, the Presbytery of Chicago announced a similar program for its 150 churches. Raby greeted these plans with enthusiasm. "We are overwhelmed by the comprehensive nature of the archbishop's program," he said. "If they are carried out to their logical conclusion, it will be a major stride toward achieving harmonious race relations in Chicago and could be another major victory against segregation. Had such a dialogue begun ten years ago we might easily have avoided many of the serious problems of the last few years."[46]

As the year ended, however, the Louis Harris poll showed that blacks and whites were at serious odds in their assessment of whether King had helped or hurt the cause of civil rights. Exactly half of the whites surveyed believed that King was hurting the cause, 36 percent thought he was helping. Among blacks, however, 64 percent said he was a help and 27 percent said he was hurting the cause. Even among blacks, the survey recorded more negative feelings about King than previously, especially among middle-income groups, who said he was "too militant" on the issue of open housing.[47]

After the massive school boycott of October 1963, the CCCO had been plunged into an enervating inner turmoil by its inability to convert that show of popular discontent with the schools into meaningful negotiations. After the high-level negotiations of August 1966, the CCCO *cum* CFM was once again plunged into an organizational crisis of conscience, which made it impossible to pursue its new negotiating position with organizational strength. At issue was the agreement itself, the process by which it had been arrived at, the process by which it was to be implemented, the adequacy of its provisions, and the people who had made it. The question whether that agreement would actually advance the goals of the civil rights movement was also raised. By December 1966, even its supporters in the movement had concluded that it would not. When Raby said, at the first formal meeting of the Leadership Council on Metropolitan Open Communities, "Not one thing has changed in Chicago," his words had a larger meaning. Not a week before, he had told the steering committee, "I have lost faith in the agreement. I have lost faith in those who are going to implement it. Nothing is being done."

Throughout the fall, the Chicago Freedom Movement had been embroiled in the question, Can we work together? One reason for raising that question was interpersonal animosities and long-suppressed grievances suddenly released by confrontation with futility overlaid with feelings of betrayal. The integrity of the movement was under attack from within and without. The black power wing was unhappy with a desegregationist agreement. The desegregationist wing was unhappy with its vagueness. The integrationist wing was unhappy with its divisiveness and the downgrading of the leadership council from an instrument of public policy to a vehicle for private projects. By December, principled unhappiness with the agreement was the prevailing mood within the movement, even among those who still wanted to try to make it have some meaning. In August, only the dissidents but by December all parties felt that the movement had been compromised by the summit agreement.

The possibilities for further action on any grounds seemed constricted. Attempts to reunite the coalition managed to quiet the rebellion but did not achieve reconciliation. Attempts to strengthen the emerging leadership council's mandate backfired when the movement's assessment of the city agencies surfaced in the press before they could be used in behind-the-scenes diplomacy. The SCLC's attempt to move into housing rehabilitation seemed unrelated to any larger strategy and promised little gain on the open housing agenda. Similarly, the SCLC's support for organizing hospital unions deadended in the rivalry and political connections of competitive unions. Although the discussions with General Superintendent Redmond about the schools opened hopefully in October, the budget he submitted in December promised no change. The SCLC was more enthusiastic about a voter registration project than were any of the local groups. The churches' promise of a Crusade for Justice to aid in the implementation of the summit agreement came just as faith was being lost in the agreement. Only Jesse Jackson's Operation Breadbasket seemed to have a clear agenda on which progress was being made, but he held his organization aloof from the Chicago Freedom Movement even though he sat on the steering committee.

In the midst of all this casting about, the U.S. Senate killed a civil rights bill because of its open housing section, and Senator Mansfield blamed King in all but name. In the November election, the Republicans reaped votes from the Southwest and Northwest sides, thus gaining a seat in the U.S. Senate and the presidency of the Cook County Board. By year's end, even middle-income blacks were beginning to voice the perception that King was too militant on open housing.

The Republicans were not eager to thank the movement for their electoral

309

success, but the Democrats were more than ready to blame. The movement was left in political isolation. Both Mayor Daley and the civic elite had a common interest in exploiting that isolation; and the Leadership Council on Metropolitan Open Communities was emerging as an effective instrument for that purpose. Thus the mayor was emphatic in his commitment to the council just as the movement was becoming critical of it.

As a result, the movement was strained internally and isolated politically. The leadership was uncertain of its mandate, its possibilities, and its support. All that was certain was that the summit agreement would not be an instrument of change. And if it was a question of balancing rights against feelings, the path was unclear in every direction.

Once again, in the open housing marches, the Chicago civil rights movement had mobilized a minority, but it had gained broader civic support more in name than in fact. None of the various combinations of persuasion and coercion it had attempted had proved effective. The movement had been unable to specify affirmative duties and unable to enact negative ones. The tensions among advocates of integration, desegregation, and black power had become open rifts. Thus, whether the terms were those of black dignity, constitutional duties, or white culture, the Chicago movement was encountering futility in relationship to every aspect of democratic social change.

310

CHAPTER ELEVEN

The Politics of Failure:
January–April 1967

The Chicago Freedom Movement was on a downward slope. Committed to a voter registration campaign, it had turned the local elections in February and April into a direct competition with the mayor in which it would be easy to measure victory for City Hall and impossible to calculate success for the movement.

The steering committee meeting on 3 January 1967 was concerned entirely with the voter registration campaign. On 9 December 1966 Hosea Williams had written to the Board of Election Commissioners requesting that six registrars be assigned to each ward for the entire month of January in anticipation of the 28 February primary for mayor and City Council and the 4 April election. On 29 December Commissioner Sidney T. Holzman had denied this request, claiming it would cost a million dollars. Hosea Williams believed that the commissioners had a statutory obligation to provide for neighborhood registration but said the movement was willing to settle for fifteen wards and he had offered to supply both offices and workers. The commissioners had said that they could not appoint "volunteer registrars"; anyone working on voter registration for the city had to be certified and sworn in. Williams had committed his group to finding certified registrars.

Meanwhile, 5 January 1967 was set as the date for the rally to initiate this voter registration drive. Congressman John Conyers from Detroit, Ralph Abernathy, Robert Henry (the mayor of Springfield), and Charles Evers of the Mississippi NAACP had all agreed to address the rally, which was to be followed by a meeting of the workers. The target for a massive turnout for registration at City Hall was 9 January. The staff reported that 129 telegrams had been sent to clergy, 2,000 letters had gone out to publicize the campaign, 55 special delivery letters had gone to community organizations, a phone campaign had been started, and the project was getting radio coverage. But only $18,169 had been raised for the project from a combination of the Tac-

311

onic, Stern, Field, and Ford foundations. The staff expected an equal amount in contributions of cash and services from local groups. It was not much money, considering that the SCLC had maintained a staff of eleven in Chicago for this project since 28 November 1966.

The basic strategy was to try "to show strength downtown." Arthur Brazier (TWO) thought sixty busloads of new registrants could be brought to City Hall. In 1961, TWO had sent fifty busloads of people to City Hall to register every week for four weeks. Berry suggested that the goal should be fifty thousand new registrations, but as William Robinson pointed out, "Registration alone is not enough." The problem was to tie the registration to the freedom movement's issues.

As the year of 1967 opened, it seemed that the pace of the action was about to pick up. As Raby said in announcing a 7 January CCCO delegates meeting, "The 'breather' is over . . . and the coming months pose a challenge to each of us who claims any right to be identified with Chicago's civil rights movement. The challenge—to your Convenor first of all—is to assess where we stand—five months after the Summit Agreement—four months after the departure of Ben Willis—two months before the aldermanic elections."

At that 7 January meeting of the CCCO, Raby was renominated as convenor, Father William Hogan was renominated as recorder, and Robinson was again nominated as treasurer. The absence of a quorum, however, prevented their election.

The report on the voter registration campaign reiterated the discussion in the steering committee, adding that Oscar Brown, Jr., had agreed to do a benefit concert at Orchestra Hall for youths, called "From Hoodlums to Heroes," on 13 January.

The report from the education committe recommended breaking off participation in the joint task forces with the Board of Education. They had met three times; had found that the board representatives always appealed to "real estate considerations" in the selection of school sites; had been unable to entertain, let alone articulate, any principle of integration for site selection; and had rejected all alternative sites proposed by CCCO representatives. Accordingly, a motion was passed that "the task forces schedule no further meetings" with the Board of Education representatives and that Superintendent Redmond be notified of this fact and the reasons for it.

The feeling was that litigation under the Armstrong Act was probably not advisable at that time because a similar case arising from Lake County was then under appeal. The approach chosen was to put pressure on Superintendent Redmond, to point out that he was still relying on the old staff gathered under Willis, and to compare his program unfavorably with the problems of the past five years.

Groups opposing the urban renewal project in Englewood were reported to

312

believe that their call for a boycott of stores during the Christmas season had had a negative effect on the volume of sales. Raby said that he would be ready with a policy statement on the open housing agreement at the next CCCO meeting. It would, he said, show that "nothing has changed in Chicago."

On 9 January the U.S. Office of Education issued a report on the Chicago public schools as part of its ongoing investigation resulting from the CCCO complaint of July 1965. This report did not threaten any cutoff of federal funds, but it did identify four problem areas and gave the Board of Education until 1 April to respond. The four problem areas were school boundaries, faculty assignment patterns, apprenticeship programs, and vocational trade schools. The report recommended that the board hire specialists to prepare a plan to eliminate the high degree of racial segregation that resulted from "residential segregation combined with the board's neighborhood school policy." It also recommended the integration of teacher assignments both by race and by years of experience. It said that "only a start" had been made in integrating the Washburne Trade School, and it called on the U.S. Department of Labor to review the apprenticeship programs there because of probable civil rights violations in the existing practices.[1]

Raby and Berry hailed the report as vindicating the CCCO's charges. At the Board of Education meeting on 10 January, Superintendent Redmond promised swift and comprehensive efforts to meet and "to go beyond federal regulations." "We shall be back," he told the board members, "with a blueprint of these aims for the consideration and approval of the board." At that same meeting the board approved applications for $3,179,341 in federal planning grants.[2]

Neither the CCCO nor the Chicago Freedom Movement of which it was a part was in a position to pursue this vindication of its complaint against the schools. With the Republicans in power at the County Board, William Robinson, the CCCO treasurer and a former state senator, was appointed director of the Cook County Department of Public Aid, but not much else was going their way. Robinson's last financial report to the CCCO showed an income of $4,840.20 for the month of January, payments of $4,739.04, and outstanding bills of $1,210.54. Ten of the constituent organizations had still not paid their dues for 1966. The voter registration drive was consuming time and effort for uncertain purposes. A crisis was brewing over the summit agreement. Energies once available for civil rights were beginning to gravitate toward the growing antiwar movement.

By the end of February it was clear that the voter registration campaign had not yielded any significant results. In the aldermanic elections on 28 February the most dramatic developments came in wards where the open housing marches had taken place. Thus, in those traditional Daley strongholds, the regular Democratic candidates were forced into runoffs with Republicans, who campaigned on the theme that the Daley organization was soft on open housing.

James Bevel, who by then was spending all his time on the Spring Mobilization Committee for Peace in Vietnam, told an audience at Northwestern University that the marches had ended too soon. "We should have continued the demonstrations until the city, county, state, and suburban governments passed an effective open housing law." Apparently forgetful of the strategic decisions to which he had been an influential even though reluctant party, Bevel implied that civil rights leaders had "succumbed to Daley's blandishments."[3]

The *Chicago Daily News* was editorially astounded at Bevel's ruminations and used them as an occasion to reassert the civil credo. Regarding the aldermanic election returns and the backlash sentiment they seemed to express, the *Daily News* granted:

> We agree with Bevel that the sentiment represented is mistaken and destructive of social progress.
>
> But the overriding question is: How can progress be made? The answer, if it is to mean anything, must deal with reality, rather than theory.
>
> One thing that strikes us as sure is that renewed demonstrations will have no other result than to widen still further the gulf between the races. Another is that whatever is to be achieved in improving housing, education and job opportunities for Negroes will come faster and more certainly in an atmosphere of calm.
>
> The results gained so far by the Chicago committee set up after last summer's "summit" meeting between Dr. Martin Luther King and Mayor Daley have been less than dramatic. But there has been progress, and the efforts continue day by day.
>
> In the Legislature a movement for a housing bill that will go at least part way in striking down discrimination is gathering support. If Bevel and his followers consider half a loaf worse than nothing they can doubtless create conditions in which all progress is stifled. We hope they will see that justice comes faster through cooperation than through confusion.[4]

Thus the media were committed to the idea that "there has been progress" and the movement was equally adamant that "nothing has changed." In mid-March, the follow-up committee charged that the city had "clearly and flagrantly" broken the summit agreement: the Chicago Commission on Human Relations "has met none of the four key commitments" made in August 1966. William Moyer and Elbert Ransom claimed to speak only as individuals, but in fact they were expressing the discontent of the movement's leaders. They accused the commission of defaulting on its commitments to obtain compliance with the city's open housing ordinance, to start a year-long program of testing realtors, to act promptly on all complaints, and to revoke licenses when cause was shown. Moyer called the commission's testing program "ridiculous." As for the brokers, Moyer said, "There has been absolutely no change in 1967 from real estate practices of 1963." The attack was full scale. "Neither the ordinance nor the summit have created any change." Not to avoid the point, Moyer added, "It's understandable. The city administration is not in open housing. It's not political to be so."[5]

Within a week, the leaders had expressed the same view publicly. Raby, Berry, McDermott, and Kale Williams joined the attack in a five-page report to the leadership council detailing charges against the Chicago Housing Authority, the Department of Urban Renewal, and the Commission on Human Relations. The housing authority was accused of continuing "existing patterns of segregation" and of creating two new segregated projects since the summit meeting. Charles Swibel, its chairman, claimed that segregation in the projects was the result of applicants' preferences. "It's not even racial," he said, "as much as geographic." The Department of Urban Renewal was criticized for continuing to push the Englewood project and for relying on segregationist brokers in its relocation programs. Lewis Hill, the commissioner of urban renewal, insisted that his staff "always sought out the best available housing in the city" and claimed that since the summer services had been expanded to include the suburbs. The Commission on Human Relations was found lax because "no offending brokers have had licenses suspended or revoked." Edward Marciniak, director of the commission, said his staff was enforcing the ordinance. James W. Cook, chairman of the leadership council, said that this freedom movement report was one among many his staff was studying.[6]

THE FREEDOM MOVEMENT AND THE
WAR IN VIETMAN: FUSION OR CONFUSION?

From Atlanta, King said, "Nothing much has changed. I'm afraid we're going to get a repetition of last summer." Although the summit, "was a marvelous agreement on paper . . . not much has been done." Inaction only intensified the discontent in the slums. The SCLC had decided to organize slum residents, and Chicago would be a prime target in King's quest for "a base of power in order to bring enough pressure to bear to bring about a guaranteed annual income." Within a day, in late March King was back in Chicago, calling for a new round of demonstrations. He said it was "absolutely necessary to march into Cicero this summer," for Cicero was "the symbol of resistance to housing integration. . . . Just as we confronted the colossus of Selma in the South, we are going to confront the colossus of Cicero in the North."[7]

King denied that his movement was "politically inspired," as Mayor Daley had charged in the heat of his drive for reelection. "Certainly my visit here has nothing to do with any political activities. The issue in Chicago is in-

315

justice. It was injustice before Daley was elected. If he is reelected, it will be injustice again." The mayor had called the movement's criticism of the city agencies "outlandish," but King repeated the criticisms: "I must express our growing disillusionment with the foot-dragging negative actions of agencies such as the Chicago Housing Authority, Department of Urban Renewal and Commission on Human Relations." Actually, it was in Daley's interest for the white voters on the Southwest and Northwest sides to hear this criticism.[8]

King's visit to Chicago was "politically inspired" in a different sense than Daley had in mind. King had come to Chicago that weekend to speak against the war in Vietnam at the peace parade and rally on 25 March. Only a month before, King had given his first speech devoted entirely to the war, and this appearance in Chicago was one of several that month focusing on this issue. King shared the platform with Benjamin Spock, Emil Mazey (international secretary-treasurer of the United Auto Workers), Michael James (a Students for a Democratic Society community organizer), and A. A. "Sammy" Raynor, Jr. (Chicago's newest black alderman). The rally platform called for an end of the bombing in North and South Vietnam, an immediate cease-fire, direct negotiations with all parties including the National Liberation Front, and a clear commitment to U.S. troop withdrawal. The sponsoring organizations were a curious mixture of Old Left, New Left, and pacifist groups.[9]

King's appearance at this rally gave rise to many questions about the connection between the movement for civil rights and the movement against the war. In his address, King drew a fairly direct connection. He did not believe it was possible to win the War on Poverty while prosecuting the war in Vietnam: to be "a hawk on Viet Nam means being a dove on the war on poverty."[10] In a letter to his supporters before the rally, King seemed to be urging them to take the civil rights movement into the antiwar movement. Addressed to "Dear Friend of Freedom," the letter, which later became controversial, read as follows:

> Your dedication to the cause of freedom has been evidenced by your continuing support of the Chicago Freedom Movement. I have been greatly heartened by your contributions.
>
> I am sure you realize that there is a growing threat to the achievements sought by the Movement. The escalation of the war in Vietnam is drawing concern, effort and funds away from our goals of justice and equality, and directing them toward destruction. More and more of our young people are taught that it is good to kill and destroy, and every day all of our citizens are shown the spectacle of this killing and destruction. The effects of this war can be seen in the growing acceptance of violence and the difficulty in obtaining funds for desperately needed housing, training and anti-poverty programs.
>
> Thus, a most important part of our work for Freedom is to do what we can to effect an end to the war. I urge you to take part in the Mass Rally being held in Chicago on March 25th, for which a leaflet and tickets are enclosed.

I further ask that you contact the members of your organization and urge them to participate in the March and Rally. The Rally, which is to be held at the Coliseum at 2:30 P.M. on March 25th, will be preceded by a march, starting at Wacker and State Streets, at 12:00 noon.

I feel that you share my concerns and will act to urge your members to participate in the Rally and March.[11]

A similar appeal from Albert Raby began: "I agree with Dr. Martin Luther King, Jr. that freedom and peace cannot be separated." It continued: "We who are part of the freedom movement have a special obligation to swell the ranks of the peace marchers. We know that the billions of U.S. Dollars being spent on destruction in Viet Nam are at the expense of all Americans, and particularly of Negro Americans who are still waiting for their long-denied rights to education, jobs, housing and health. We know the special price Negro youth is paying, fighting and dying in Viet Nam in far greater numbers than their proportion in the U.S. population."[12]

In the week that followed, local Chicago issues were still in the forefront. On Monday, 27 March, the leadership council received a staff report criticizing city agencies involved in the summit agreement; but the chairman of the council, James W. Cook, took the occasion to speak against King's talk of a new round of summer demonstrations. Raby, Berry, McDermott, and Kale Williams immediately issued a seven-page response to Cook and defense of King: "We must emphatically disagree with Mr. Cook's reported comments on Dr. King. Nothing can be achieved toward improving the climate of race relations in trying to separate Dr. King from Chicago's civil rights leadership, by criticizing him and praising us. We are firmly united. Dr. King was expressing the firm conviction of all associated with the Chicago Freedom Movement that progress has been inadequate. He has hopes of reforms and so do we. But we see no significant evidence yet of reform on the part of the three city agencies." Once again, they detailed their complaints about the practices of the three city agencies—Chicago Housing Authority, Department of Urban Renewal, and Commission on Human Relations. They spoke positively of the efforts of the leadership council and the churches but warned: "The three city agencies and the real estate brokers have the power in themselves to destroy the pattern of housing apartheid that is strangling this city to death. If they do not act now and act positively, the best supportive actions of business, labor, church, and civic organizations will have little effect for decades."[13]

During this time, the CCCO, as a constituent organization, was barely existent. In announcing a meeting for 1 April, Raby pleaded for a quorum to "take care of this year's unfinished business—election of officers and revision of the constitution." He assured the delegates that "Dr. King has announced he will be back with us soon, and asks CCCO—you and your organization—

to help determine the Freedom Movement's progress for the months ahead."[14]

At that meeting, Raby explained the decline in attendance as caused by the "problems, disillusionments, and concerns" of people with the CCCO. He asserted, however, that the "CCCO is a manifestation of the problems of all civil rights groups." It was subject to ups and downs. He reminded the delegates that "there was no activity in 1964" except the second school boycott and the ill-fated Freedom Democratic Clubs. It was "important not to be parochial about CCCO." The community organizations were still working. Operation Breadbasket was growing. Local school groups such as the parents' protest at the Crispus Attucks School were springing up. It was true that "voter registration failed in CCCO." Hosea Williams had been brought in to help the independent candidates, but he "took off on his own" and CCCO "had no developed alternative." Now, he reported, "we are trying to develop a program for Dr. King with regard to urban renewal." He estimated that it would take one or two months "to develop an urban renewal platform" around which to organize. It was a risk, he said, "because the new movement in community organization may destroy CCCO."[15]

The rest of the agenda, containing items titled "Urban Renewal Committee Principles" and "Proposed Curriculum for School of Community Organization," had a distinctly New Left thrust. Indeed, the curriculum proposal was presented by Rennie Davis, who, at the time, was closely identified with the New Left. The urban renewal principles were more in line with traditional civil rights programs, but the assumption was that they would be brought to bear through New Left organizing strategies.

By this 1 April meeting both the pull toward the antiwar movement and the push toward the themes and strategies of the New Left had crystallized as practical issues for the CCCO, and Raby was right to wonder whether the coalition could survive these strains in addition to the frustrations of its established agenda. The financial report for February and March showed an income of $5,953.70, expenses of $5,818.64, a balance of $135.06, and outstanding bills of $1,473.34. Ten organizations had still not paid their dues for 1966, and only three organizations had paid their dues for 1967.

A distinct shift was perceptible in the public atmosphere surrounding civil rights groups and purposes. The House Un-American Activities Committee was planning another investigation of the civil rights movement. In the past, these had consisted of exposing the communist associations of minor figures in civil rights groups. In addition, the Illinois General Assembly seemed much more ready to pass a "stop and frisk" law than an open occupancy bill. The American Friends Service Committee proposed holding a conference on the open city as a way of remobilizing the metropolitan elites to support the implementation of the summit agreement and of stressing the need for moderates to take responsibility in a deteriorating situation.

318

On 4 April, Martin Luther King, Jr., mounted the pulpit of Riverside Church in New York City to join his voice with that of Clergy and Laymen Concerned about Viet Nam.[16] It was a major statement of his position, and it is presented in detail here because its consequences for the Chicago Freedom Movement were both serious and immediate.

Affirming that "my conscience leaves me no other choice," King admitted that "we are always on the verge of being mesmerized by uncertainty." Opposing the war in Vietnam was "often a vocation of agony" because, he said, "we are deeply in need of a new way beyond the darkness that seems so close around us."

King said he had been asked: "Why are *you* speaking about the war, Dr. King? Why are *you* joining the voices of dissent? Peace and civil rights don't mix, they say. Aren't you hurting the cause of your people, they ask?" He offered seven answers to these questions. First, the War on Poverty was being sacrificed to the war in Vietnam. "I knew," he said, "that America would never invest the necessary funds or energies in rehabilitation of its poor so long as adventures like Vietnam continued to draw men and skills and money like some demonic destructive suction tube." His second reason for joining peace and civil rights was "the cruel irony of watching Negro and white boys on TV screens as they kill and die together for a nation that has been unable to seat them together in the same schools." This, he said, was "cruel manipulation of the poor." Third, the war was a challenge to the power of nonviolence: "I knew that I could never again raise my voice against the violence of the oppressed in the ghettos without first having spoken clearly to the greatest purveyor of violence in the world today—my own government." Fourth, he reminded his listeners that the SCLC motto since 1957 had been "to save the soul of America." Opposing the war was a way of "working for the health of our land." Protest and dissent were King's path to patriotism. Fifth, he said, "I cannot forget that the Nobel Prize for Peace was also a commission—a commission to work harder than I had ever worked before for the 'brotherhood of man.'" National allegiance was not one's highest duty. This was reinforced for King by "the meaning of my commitment to the ministry of Jesus Christ." Because of his ministry, King said, "I sometimes marvel at these who ask me why I am speaking against the war." Finally, King was motivated by his understanding of the Christian faith: "Beyond the calling of race or nation or creed is the vocation of sonship and brotherhood, and because I believe the Father is deeply concerned especially for his suffering and helpless and outcast children, I come tonight to speak for them."

He accused the United States of carrying on French colonialism "with our huge financial and military supplies to continue the war even after they had lost the will." He called the government in Saigon a "junta" and asked, "What do the peasants think as we ally ourselves with the landlords and as we

319

refuse to put any action into our many words concerning land reform? What do they think as we test our latest weapons on them, just as the Germans tested out new medicines and new tortures in the concentration camps of Europe?" The American presence was provocative and destructive of the family and village, "their most cherished institutions," of their land and their crops. "We have corrupted their women and children and killed their men. What liberators!"

The United States had initiated this violence. Even our own troops "must know after a short period there that none of the things we claim to be fighting for are really involved. . . . Somehow this madness must cease. We must stop now. . . . If we continue there will be no doubt in my mind and in the mind of the world that we have no honorable intention in Vietnam."

King then called on the U.S. government to end the bombing, declare a unilateral cease-fire, curtail the military buildup in Thailand and Laos, accept the National Liberation Front as a political fact in the future of Vietnam, set a date for the removal of all foreign troops, grant asylum in the United States to any Vietnamese who feared the new regime, and make reparations "for the damage we have done."

Even granting these concessions, King said, we would not be set right as a people because

> the war in Vietnam is but a symptom of a far deeper malady within the American spirit, and if we ignore this sobering reality we will find ourselves organizing clergy and laymen–concerned committees for the next generation. . . . I am convinced that if we are to get on the right side of the world revolution, we as a nation must undergo a radical revolution of values . . . the shift from a "thing-oriented" society to a "person-oriented" society. . . . There is nothing, except a tragic death wish, to prevent us from re-ordering our priorities, so that the pursuit of peace will take precedence over the pursuit of war. . . . This kind of positive revolution of values is our best defense against Communism.

King viewed communism as the Old Testament prophets had viewed Assyria—as a judgment against America's failure to keep the faith with the oppressed. "Communism is a judgment against our failure to make democracy real and follow through on the revolutions that we initiated. Our only hope today lies in our ability to recapture the revolutionary spirit and go into a sometimes hostile world declaring eternal hostility to poverty, racism, and militarism."

The time had come to choose: "Shall we say the odds are too great? Shall we tell them the struggle is too hard? Will our message be that the forces of American life militate against their arrival as full men, and we send our deepest regrets?" The war in Vietnam was forcing the choice: "The choice is ours, and though we might prefer it otherwise we *must* choose in this crucial moment of human history."

320

The *Chicago Daily News* concluded that "Dr. Martin Luther King has begun to sound like a demagog." Opposing the war in Vietnam while threatening to march on Cicero was more than the editors could accept. "His latest attack on the government's conduct of the Vietnam war—urging a 'boycott' and comparing American atrocities with those of the Nazis in World War II—displayed the same intemperance as his earlier call for marches into Cicero next summer. Civil disobedience won't cure either Vietnam or civil wrongs at home. And if King plans to continue his campaign against the Vietnam war he should get out of the civil rights controversy, because playing both games simply stirs fresh animosity and diminishes the prospect for understanding on either issue."[17]

The same advice came from Ralph J. Bunche, undersecretary for political affairs of the United Nations and America's other black Nobel Peace Prize winner, who said King should "positively and publicly give up one role or the other." King protested that he had been misunderstood. "A myth credits me," he said, "with advocating the fusion of the civil rights and peace movements. I hold no such view."[18]

A CONFLICT OF ROLES: KING WITHDRAWS FROM CHICAGO

In fact, however, King had the same doubts about the compatibility of his two roles as the *Daily News* and Ralph Bunche, and he voiced those doubts at a meeting of the Chicago Freedom Movement Steering Committee.[19] A director and a decision-making process for the summer program had to be determined, as well as King's role in it. He reminded the group that he had first opposed the war in 1965 even though his public position had only recently become controversial. Asking, "Is it wise to join the civil rights and peace movements?" he responded, "I work on both of them but separately." The war for him was "a matter of conscience." It was "impossible to merge the two organizationally but there can be a coalition without merger. From the perspective of content, they are *one*. There is no peace without justice and no justice without peace."

"We want to integrate schools and housing," he continued, "but we have to be concerned for the survival of those to be integrated. We cannot segregate moral concerns." He considered the Nobel Peace Prize a "commission to work for peace," which carried a moral obligation. But "when the guns of war are a national obsession, it is impossible to mount a social revolution." He asserted that "the war has hurt the civil rights movement more than my stand on the war has hurt it." Furthermore, "the SCLC board was unanimous in support" of his stand.

King was raising his pacifism for discussion. In reply, John McDermott

321

suggested that "force can be used in responsible ways." Speaking for the Catholic Interracial Council, he added that "the board and myself cannot take on any more enemies."[20] He wanted to keep the war and civil rights separate. The Catholic church had a long tradition of thought which held that war could be morally justified under limited conditions, and he did not believe he "would have been a pacifist in the face of Hitler." He acknowledged that the Gallup poll showed "twenty-two million explicitly opposed to the war in Viet Nam" and that "thousands of men are unwilling to serve." He predicted that "one year from now, one hundred thousand will be in jail."

At that point in the discussion, Raby suggested that the "CCCO ought not to take a peace position." King responded by asking, "Does my position on the war in Viet Nam create serious problems organizationally? Does this board feel that continuing relationships among civil rights groups in the city of Chicago would be jeopardized by my position on the Viet Nam war?" Edwin Berry replied that although "there are some people who feel the issues should not be joined," he did not think "any member would force the issue by asking for a severance of relations."

Archie Hargraves said that the small number of people he had spoken to felt that both civil rights and opposition to the war "challenge the 'white man's burden.'" King agreed: "It always brings ghetto audiences up by mentioning the war."

Kale Williams agreed, too. He said it was "important to keep the black, alienated, anti-American group a part of the nonviolent movement." It was an antidote, he said, to the "Carmichael—hate America" syndrome and gave an opportunity to demonstrate "the importance of nonviolence without hate." He thought it was essential to provide "an organization of anti-war feeling" on a constructive nonviolent basis: "King represents a revolution in values, a radical redistribution of economic and political power. The opposition to civil rights will not go with us anyway, and they will use peace as the excuse." But in addition, he warned that "many people who were with us in Selma and Birmingham will not be with us in the new phase." The country was "seriously compromised in Peace Corps countries because of the war in Viet Nam." The situation in those countries, he said, was already "almost hopeless."

Arthur Brazier said, "The ghetto is against the war, but we do not want a split in the civil rights movement. Dr. King must take a stand as a movement figure, that one day the United States must pull out." He was, he told King, "not going to criticize your stand." But he asked, "Would you want to persuade the freedom movement to join the peace movement?"

Raby intervened: "I hear that organizations are not prepared to take a position to support linking the issues" but that they would "not attack or criticize you." Brazier did "not see how Dr. King could have taken any other position." He added, "We may not be able to join the peace movement, but we should support Dr. King. We are for him one hundred percent. But it would be wrong if the price of admission into the civil rights movement is support of the peace movement." Kale Williams agreed: "We have no control over what is going to happen in the peace movement." Alvin Pitcher asked about the attitude toward James Bevel, Jesse Jackson, and others who were devoting major time to the peace movement. Archie Hargraves dismissed the issue as a "differentiation of roles."

Andrew Young pushed the discussion in the direction that King had been trying to take it all evening. "Peace is a problem," he said. "We do not have enough staff. Calls go unanswered. To maintain unity on civil rights issues requires Dr. King's time to offset the attacks on his war position." What was more, "the problems in the cities are so complicated, the evils so entrenched, that we cannot create a massive enough nonviolent movement in Chicago alone to bring a federal approach to bear on them. Perhaps we cannot go much further in Chicago until other cities get at least this far. How massive can a movement be in Chicago? In St. Louis, it might take six months to win a victory, in Houston maybe two or three days, but Chicago. . . ."

King assured the group, "We will continue to work in Chicago. We need a director and an administrator. But we need to get several cities moving." Without saying so, King was withdrawing from Chicago. He wanted to leave a staff behind and to keep the movement going, but he was withdrawing. His leaving was, perhaps, a strategic retreat as much as it was a new thrust. On 4 April 1967 Mayor Daley had been reelected for his fourth term by a landslide. He had campaigned against "outsiders," who were disturbing the civic peace. He never directly attacked King, but he left little doubt about his meaning. In analyzing the election results, a *Sun-Times* political writer concluded that "Dr. Martin Luther King, Jr.'s Chicago Freedom Movement has been pretty much of a political bust." He noted that the mayor had been reelected in 1963 by only 140,000 votes, a majority provided largely by his solid vote from the black wards. Yet his reelection in 1967 was by more than 500,000 votes, which showed that he had remained strong in the black wards and run wild in the white, ethnic ones that had been split only four years before. That Congressman Dawson's black Democratic organization had held its votes seemed to indicate "there is little reason to believe that the great majority of Chicago's Negroes are much more interested in integrating neighborhoods than their ethnic white fellow Chicagoans have been."[21]

This analysis presented the mayor as a civil rights statesman as well as a shrewd politician:

Last summer after the Negro riots and the civil rights marches led by the Chicago Freedom Movement, Daley attempted to come to terms with the Negro civil rights

323

leadership by offering them token integration in housing and massive aid in other areas of need. But he was unable to get the message to the ethnic whites in time to stave off defeat at the polls last November. It is of crucial importance of course, to move rapidly and effectively to give Chicago's Negroes, not tokenism, but genuine, full-blown equality of opportunity in education, employment, housing, recreational facilities and political participation. But it is not imperative to bring about integrated neighborhoods today or even tomorrow.

The mayor, it seemed, wisely understood the need for caution: "Daley is not only sensitive to, but reflective and representative of the predominant sentiments of the people of his city, both Negro and white."[22]

Colonel Jack Reilly, the mayor's press secretary, could not have said it better. The demonstrations had made a statesman of Mayor Daley, an honor he had previously found elusive. He had become the defender of the civic faith. It made no difference that there was not one shred of evidence that the mayor had offered to trade tokenism in housing integration for "massive aid in other areas of need," so great was the will to believe that "the road ahead is unquestionably smoother." Revisionism had already taken hold of the civic imagination; and in the new version, King and the Chicago Freedom Movement had become civic problems, disrupters of the atmosphere of calm so necessary to progress, and the mayor had handled them wisely. The disturbance of militant whites was "understandable," but the demands of the Chicago Freedom Movement were "irrational."

The civil rights movement in Chicago was essentially over. The issues it had raised remained unresolved, but the civic credo was there to promise their resolution in the future if citizens would look about the city with the "eyes of faith." The leadership of the civil rights movement was, by those civic standards, visually impaired.

By early April, Mayor Daley had been reelected by his largest majority ever. The voter registration campaign had clearly failed. King was withdrawing from Chicago, whether to pursue the peace movement or campaigns in other cities was unclear. The CCCO and the Chicago Freedom Movement consisted of little more than a group of leaders. The issue of racial justice in the metropolitan area had dropped from the civic agenda.

King had taken his stand on nonviolence, that principle he would not relinquish because his own integrity was at stake. The war in Vietnam posed a triple threat: to the principle of nonviolence, King's creative and long-standing resolution of the dilemma of constitutional duties; to the base of support of civil rights, as it had been developed as a result of DuBois's and subsequent efforts to address the dilemma of black dignity; and to the nation's priorities and their implications for the dilemma of white culture. King could not remain bogged down in the politics of failure in Chicago with so much at stake on the national scene; but neither did he want to abandon his relationships and commitments there. Therefore, he continued publicly to suggest the possibility of new demonstrations in the summer. Open housing having failed, a guaranteed annual income seemed to be emerging as his next domestic goal.

Albert Raby, on the other hand, was locked into the local situation. Although he joined King in opposing the war, he looked to new alliances on the community organizing front to rebuild an activist coalition around urban renewal issues. The logic seemed to be that if there was no possibility of opening the periphery of the ghetto, resources should be sought to renew and empower the neglected center. Raby had taken his stand on building a coalition for civil rights if possible, preserving self-respect in any event. With his loss of faith in the ability of the summit agreement to produce change in the conditions for blacks, he gravitated to issues and groups that at least affirmed self-respect.

It would be difficult to characterize either King's path or Raby's, at this time, as a strategy. Both were reacting to the shrinking prospects for their deepest aims and to the declining base of support for civil rights goals in Chicago and in the country at large. The dilemmas of democratic social change had been reduced to questions of political integrity and public survival.

It was the mayor and the civic elite who were riding high. Even when the federal government chastised the Board of Education on the very points raised by the CCCO, the general superintendent got the credit for promising action. Both the mayor and Superintendent Redmond were elevated to the status of civic statesmen as they increasingly adopted the script required by the civic credo—the worst is over, the road ahead will be incomparably smoother, time and the normal functioning of institutions will make all things right, those who obstruct progress are irrational, civic calm is the best guarantee of progress, and so on.

The civil rights movement was being shut out as black claims to rights were put down as irrational in the face of white expressions of feeling, which, though angry, were chalked up as understandable.

CHAPTER TWELVE

The Collapse of the Movement:
April–September 1967

When in April the Board of Education offered yet another "permissive transfer plan," the CCCO Education Committee complained that it benefited whites, did not equalize the use of facilities, and did not even protect what little integration existed in the system. When the parents at all-white Bogan High School protested its inclusion as a possible "receiving school," it was dropped from the list.[1]

The education committee said: "Last fall, the CCCO opposed passage of the $25 million building bond issue. We held that there were sufficient seats for all students, provided all branches and mobiles were used. The school administration then denied our claim. Now, by its own figures, the school administration shows that the existing school plant—*even without any branches or mobiles*—can accommodate all students on an extended day. This is illogical enough. But the administration further proposes to manipulate branches and mobiles so as to further fasten the system of segregation upon the schools."[2]

On 21 April, Mayor Daley was inaugurated for his fourth term. He said that "a relative handful" of civil rights groups had used "calculated appeals to hatred and emotion" to the detriment of "law and order." And he pledged that "as long as I am mayor, law and order will prevail." At the same time, he envisioned a program of capital expenditures for the city totalling $75 million. "The paramount objective of this administration is to eliminate slums and blight from every neighborhood." Open housing was not part of the mayor's blueprint for the future, but the election of two independent black aldermen from the South Side, William A. "Bill" Cousins, Jr., and A. A. "Sammy" Raynor, Jr., had more to do with the future of electoral politics in Chicago than the mayor's landslide did.[3]

On 24 April, James Cook, president of the Leadership Council for Metropolitan Open Communities, told the City Club that "Chicago is becoming a

Negro city at the rate of nearly five blocks a week, according to real estate experts." He warned, "It is not an either-or proposition. To cure the ills at the center of the infection of the ghetto while letting its periphery spread unchecked makes no sense." He appeared to differ with the mayor's sense of priority. In the same speech, he predicted that the Illinois General Assembly would "probably" pass an open housing law in its current session. The reason for this optimism was that the Atomic Energy Commission was proposing to build a large research facility in Weston, Illinois. Cook, along with many others, believed that the Congress would not authorize such a large federal facility without open housing legislation. In the question and answer period following his speech, he denied any disagreement with the mayor.[4]

In early May, Rennie Davis announced the creation of the Center for Radical Research, sponsored by a coalition of civil rights and New Left groups. The prospectus, prepared by Davis, Albert Raby, and Curtis Hayes said: "Demonstrations, while valuable in bringing ignored issues to public consciousness, do not, by themselves, provide the skills and experience necessary for disadvantaged urban residents to become controllers instead of pawns of their environment." The program proposed to train radical, indigenous community organizers to mobilize the urban disadvantaged classes. It was the logical extension of the drive toward grass-roots politics. The proposal would require about $7,000 to get started and $60,000 for the first year of operation. It was a case of the disenchanted reaching out to the disadvantaged on the assumption that they had a community of interest.[5]

STALEMATE ON ALL FRONTS:
THE FUTURE OF THE SCLC IN CHICAGO

In early May 1967, Pierre de Vise, a lecturer in urban affairs at DePaul University and the director of research for the Hospital Planning Council for Metropolitan Chicago, began to make public the results of his community studies, which he ultimately published as *Chicago's Widening Color Gap*. He ranked communities in the metropolitan area according to their economic status and social prestige, using median family income and median home values along with other variables. By these criteria the ten top communities in the metropolitan area were all-white suburbs: Kenilworth to the north, which de Vise characterized as "the most stratified community in the area, and the most segregated imaginable." Out of its population of about three thousand he estimated that it had one Negro, three Jewish, and five Catholic families. "This is Chicago's true WASP community." It also had a median income of $29,400. All the other top ten were similarly white.[6]

The ten most impoverished communities were, by the same criteria, black

327

and inner-city. The poorest community was the public housing reservation known as Altgeld-Murray Homes on the Far South Side. Dorothy Gautreaux had represented the citizens organization from Altgeld-Murray in the CCCO since the early days. The second poorest community was Oakland, which had been the object of the CCCO's first effort to sponsor a community organization. The third was an area called the Near South Side, and fourth was Douglas B, the area which included the Robert Taylor Homes, two miles of sixteen-story public housing units. Fifth was Grand Boulevard, the area west of Hyde Park and Kenwood, enclave of the University of Chicago. Sixth was the Near West Side, home of Chester Robinson's West Side Organization. Seventh was East Garfield Park, home of Bevel's tenant unions. Eighth was Fuller Park, west of Grand Boulevard. Ninth was Woodlawn, of which no more need be said in this story. Tenth was North Lawndale on the West Side. It had gone from 10 percent black in 1950 to 10 percent white in 1960.[7]

De Vise corroborated the claims of Moyer and the Chicago Freedom Movement of a year before: "Negro families are one-fifth larger than white families and have only two-thirds the income, but they occupy units one-fifth smaller, five times more dilapidated and three times more substandard than white housing units." He continued, "Here, however, the inequality ends. Negroes enjoy full equality with whites in respect to payment for these somewhat unequal packages of housing quantity and quality. Median rents are identical for white and non-white unites—$86."[8]

De Vise documented not only the contrasts between black and white communities but the near absolute separation of the two except in areas undergoing block-by-block racial change, five new ones each week. The pattern was intact in 1967. The civil rights movement had not altered it.

Still, in mid-May the Leadership Council on Metropolitan Open Communities announced Project: Good Neighbor. It would be, the council proclaimed, "a movement for equal housing opportunities throughout the entire Chicago area." Setting itself apart from the civil rights movement, "it calls for a totally different approach, for something other than laws and marches." It was to begin with a luncheon at the Conrad Hilton Hotel and proceed to discussions in local communities to "establish broad support for cooperative, constructive solutions to this very critical problem."[9] In Illinois, it was not a prudent time to suggest that there was "something other than laws" to deal better with the question of open housing, but there it was, sponsored by the Leadership Council on Metropolitan Open Housing just when the Illinois Senate's position on a pending open housing law was in doubt.

In a trial run of Project: Good Neighbor, Edward L. Holmgren, executive director of the leadership council, spoke to the members of the Gage Park Civic Association. This effort was a replay of those of the human relations commission in the late 1940s. Holmgren told them, "I want to explain to you

328

how open housing can be a boon to Gage Park." His "boon" was answered by cries of "boo." The meeting never got beyond that level. The leadership council was accused of being "outside agitators" from Kenilworth. Holmgren had to admit that the charge raised "an interesting question." It was no question as far as his audience was concerned.[10]

King praised the effort as a "serious attempt to make the housing agreement work" and he even called it "one of the most creative steps to make open housing a reality that is being taken anywhere in the country." James W. Cook described it as an effort "to help create the climate which will make it possible for every man to live where his heart and his purse will take him."[11] It was patterned after the programs previously announced by the religious bodies, absent the confrontational aspects. The project was carried out in the week following 4 June. It left no notable mark on the civic geography.

Indeed, as Project: Good Neighbor was taking place, the Louis Harris poll reported its latest findings. The movement in opinion had been retrograde. "White people split almost evenly in 1966 over the question of a federal open housing law," it reported. "Now whites are more than three to two in opposition to measures that would outlaw discrimination in housing. In addition, the number of white people critical of Negro demonstration tactics has risen sharply—from sixty-three to eighty-two percent." On the other hand, "On open housing, Negroes are seventy-eight percent in favor." Indeed, 85 percent of the Negroes wanted to "speed up civil rights progress."[12]

In a speech in Washington, King was not hopeful. "It's much more difficult now," he said. "Things are dark in the civil rights field. We are not going to have as many allies." On the president's proposed legislation for open housing, King said, "I've come to the conclusion it's going to be defeated this year as it was last year. This is very tragic—a social disaster." Still, he cited the program in Chicago as a reason for doubting the prospect of mass demonstrations there during the summer.[13]

On 10 June 1967 there was a meeting of CCCO delegates. William Robinson had still not been replaced as treasurer, but the financial report for April– May 1967 showed an income of $2,478.46, expenses of $2,211.19, and a deficit of $2,000 "from the summer of 1966." It also showed that nine organizations had not paid their dues for 1966 and only six had paid for 1967.

The two most significant items on the agenda concerned strategy proposals for open housing legislation and a report from King on the state of the movement. The "Action Proposal Re: Open Housing Legislation" said: "Despite unprecedented support for this year's campaign for a state open housing law from newspapers, religious leaders, businessmen and the Weston project, it appears probable that reactionary Senate Republicans are prepared to kill any meaningful bill. Clearly, some new, strong pressure is needed if open housing legislation is to be salvaged this session."

329

There were two proposals:

A) . . . that CCCO in cooperation with the NAACP and the Illinois Committee for
a Fair Housing Law sponsor a large and impressive mission to Washington to 1)
see Senator Pastore (chairman of the JCAE) and other friendly members of the
Joint Committee on Atomic Energy and 2) see Glenn Seaborg (chairman) of the
AEC to demand that the Weston project be dropped if Illinois refuses to pass a
fair housing law.

B) . . . that CCCO enlist a team of volunteers to set up tents either on the ground
designated for the Weston project or in the town of Weston itself, and attempt to
live there for a time to demonstrate dramatically that Du Page County's housing
is closed to Negro families and that the Movement is prepared to take extraordinary measures to attack housing segregation if the legislature refuses to take
ordinary measures. . . . Volunteers should be prepared to be arrested.

This proposal was adopted along with some criteria for acceptable legislation. The aim was a bill that would cover at least 50 percent of the housing in
the state and would provide enforcement by a statewide agency, either an
independent commission or the state attorney general, and sanctions against
violators, including authority for the courts to issue cease and desist orders
against violators.

When King rose to speak about "the future of SCLC in Chicago," it was
already known that he was planning a campaign in Cleveland for that summer.
Emphasizing what had been accomplished in the year and a half of SCLC-
CCCO collaboration, King highlighted Operation Breadbasket as a new, successful, and promising program, looked to the tenant unions as a new instrument of local control with a high potential, and foresaw a new focus on the
schools in the fall. The HUD housing rehabilitation program was a project to
be pursued, and political education was a long-range goal. He viewed the
open housing agreement as a positive step. Then King explained that he was
turning to Cleveland, where the SCLC would "make a different start than
Chicago." There, he planned to "organize the organizers" rather than become
engaged in a direct campaign of action.

Throughout the entire Chicago campaign, King had been sensitive to the
frequently leveled charge that the SCLC moved into local communities, used
them for its own national purposes, and then pulled out, leaving the locals in
vulnerable disarray. In fairness, it should be said that King made every effort
to avoid that outcome in Chicago; and his review of the accomplishments that
would remain in Chicago even though the SCLC turned its attention to
Cleveland was intended to underline the positive effects. Whatever else might
be said about the difficulties both the SCLC and the CCCO experienced in
fashioning a cooperative working relationship, it could not be said that the
SCLC exploited the Chicago situation merely to advance its national position.
In Chicago, the reputations of both groups had been at stake, and both came

330

away from the joint effort in considerable disarray and with increased vulnerability to those who opposed their purposes.

As if to symbolize this new state of affairs, on 14 June the Joint Committee on Atomic Energy voted to approve preliminary work on the nuclear accelerator at Weston. Senator John Pastore had asked the committee not to act until Illinois had passed a fair housing law, but in an unusual move the committee had overridden its chairman by a vote of eleven to three. Within a week, open housing legislation was dead in the Illinois General Assembly.[14]

The "tent-in" at Weston, which had been proposed at a CCCO meeting, began on 22 June 1967. As it opened, four Chicago religious leaders, Episcopal Bishop James Montgomery, Rabbi Robert Marx, executive director of the Union of American Hebrew Congregations, Msgr. John Egan, director of the Office of Urban Affairs, Catholic Archdiocese of Chicago, and Edgar H. S. Chandler, executive director of the Church Federation of Greater Chicago, asked Governor Kerner to call a special session of the Illinois General Assembly for the sole purpose of passing open housing legislation. The tenters pledged to stay in Weston until the Congress completed its work in the hope that the authorization for the Weston site could be blocked from the floor. The governor did not reconvene the legislature, and the Congress did not block the Weston appropriation.[15] At the same time, the Illinois Supreme Court dealt yet another blow to the civil rights movement by striking down the 1963 Armstrong Act. Raby called the decision "particularly cruel."[16] The legislative route to change seemed blocked at both the state and national levels.

Still, the *Chicago Daily News* editorialized that the "Tent-Ins Miss the Mark." In a ringing reaffirmation of the civic credo, the *Daily News* proclaimed:

Intelligent Negro leaders know as well as anybody that, leaving emotion completely aside, it is economics that will pull the Negro out of his abyss and give him the parity he seeks and deserves. The cure lies in jobs generating money creating the ability to reach out and get a better life. Education sparks the process. Much of the progress toward racial justice in the South has come, not because of laws or sweet feelings among the whites, but because as industrialization has advanced the Negro has become an increasingly important factor in the productive complex.

The struggle in the North has in some respects been more frustrating than that in the South. The Republican-dominated Illinois legislature might have been sitting in Montgomery, Alabama, for all the difference in point of racial bigotry.

But wrong-headed legislators are not going to be converted by tent-ins at Weston any more than by march-ins at the Board of Education or rocks through the windows of neighborhood shops. They simply have to be out-distanced as the progressive part of the community moves forward.[17]

It did not seem to blunt this peculiar statement of faith that the North had led the way in industrialization and Chicago had led the way in the Midwest,

331

and still both "intelligent Negroes" and "the progressive part of the community" were hard-pressed to identify any particular "moves forward" in the struggle against the racial bifurcation of the city and the metropolitan area.

In fact, it seemed that even the full resources of the city were unable to rehabilitate one slum building at 1321 South Homan Avenue. That was the building King had seized in February 1966 as a symbol of the slums. It turned out that it was a more fit symbol of the slum than had appeared in the first blush of irony, which had greeted the discovery that it was owned, not by a high-living slum landlord but by a poor old man who subsisted on its meager rentals. By July of 1967 that building was soon to fall to the wrecking ball. Initially the courts had assigned a receiver to refurbish the building. He was unable to accomplish the task economically. When the owner died in April 1966, the building went to a bank, which held an $8,500 mortgage on it. The fate of the building went in and out of court as each new plan for its rehabilitation collapsed at "the bottom line." The Chicago Dwellings Association, a municipal agency, intimated that the cost to rehabilitate this building would be $43,750, but the bank was willing to sell for $6,500. In August 1966, U.S. Gypsum Company offered to make the building a showcase of what it could do in rehabilitating urban apartments, but the company abandoned the project within months. The Chicago Housing Authority had spent over $4,000 on utilities, protective services, and relocation of the residents. By July 1967, the dwellings association was planning to knock it down and start over. The building had truly become a symbol of the slums.[18]

Unable to renew the core, unable to open the periphery, both the mayor's program and the civil rights movement were at an impasse. In a letter to the editor, John McDermott replied to the *Daily News* editorial and expressed the movement's understanding of what was at stake in the Weston tent-in. He wrote:

> The tent-in at Weston was not based on any "upside down notion" that what is good for whites is bad for Negroes. Rather, it was based on the sound notion that what is bad for Negroes is also really bad for whites, and that what is bad for America is also bad for Illinois.
>
> It will be bad for America if we allow the integrity of the law of the land to be ignored and eroded. This is precisely the issue at Weston. Thanks to the supreme irresponsibility of our Legislature on the issue of fair housing, there is now no honorable way for Illinois to lay claim to the Weston project. Title VI of the 1964 Civil Rights Act clearly requires that the benefits of a federal project like the proposed Weston nuclear accelerator must be equally available to black Americans as well as white Americans. In particular, it requires that there be equal job opportunity.
>
> But in an area like Du Page County where Negroes constitute only a tiny fraction of the population and where there is ample evidence of widespread housing discrimination, job opportunity is intrinsically related to housing opportunity. There cannot

be genuine equal job opportunity unless Negro scientists, technicians and other personnel are able to live within reasonable distance of their jobs.

The Chicago Freedom Movement is not anti-Illinois. We, too, want Illinois to prosper, but not at any price. Too many people seem to want the Weston project at all costs. But there are some costs too high for honorable men to pay. To make a mockery of the solemn commitments of our government is too high and too dangerous a price to pay for this project.[19]

But McDermott was defending a defeated position, true as his claims may have been. The next week, King was back in Chicago, not to push for open housing but to announce plans to turn Operation Breadbasket into a national program. Some two hundred ministers from forty-two cities attended a conference to launch Breadbasket into the national arena. It was said that in Chicago alone, Breadbasket had won 2,200 jobs worth more than $15 million in annual income for blacks. Breadbasket was the success story of the Chicago campaign. King drew headlines, however, for his kind statements about the progress in Chicago. "We have seen new developments, a new desire to implement the open housing agreement," he said. As evidence, he cited Project: Good Neighbor, "a most significant step forward." It was King's way of explaining why there were and would be no massive demonstrations that summer in Chicago. "Our weapon is noncooperation with economic injustice," he explained. That was the new thrust, and Operation Breadbasket was the vehicle.[20]

BURNING CITIES AND BURIED HOPES:
THE LOSS OF VISION

As the conferees went home from the national launching of Operation Breadbasket, the Newark riot was just breaking out. The pattern of ghetto violence that was destined to dominate the summer of 1967 had begun in mid-June. In Tampa, it had been set off when police shot and killed a black burglary suspect as he tried to escape custody. In Cincinnati, it was triggered by the conviction of a black man for the murder of a white woman.[21] The disturbances in Tampa and Cincinnati were followed by an outbreak in Atlanta. The Newark riot was destined to be followed by one in Detroit before the month was out, each apparently more destructive than the one before. The disorder in Newark "spread" to fourteen other New Jersey communities. The violence in Detroit was accompanied by disturbances in seven other Michigan communities and one in Ohio. Before it was over, there had been eight "major disorders," thirty "serious disorders," and ninety-eight "minor disorders" in June and July—all ghetto riots. The "minor disorders" continued into August and September. Only three "serious disorders" were recorded in August.

333

By the end of July, the nonviolent civil rights movement had been effectively displaced from the center of national attention.[22]

Late in July, President Johnson named Governor Otto Kerner of Illinois to head an eleven-member advisory commission to investigate the circumstances surrounding these disturbances. The president, at least, realized that "the looting, arson, plunder and pillage which have occurred are not part of a civil rights protest." He admonished a fearful and anxious public that "this is not a time for angry reaction. It is a time for action: starting with legislative action to improve the life of our cities. The strength and promise of the law are the surest remedies for tragedy in the streets. . . . There is a danger that the worst toll of this tragedy will be counted in the hearts of Americans; in hatred, in insecurity, in fear, in heated words which will not end the conflict, but prolong it. So let us acknowledge the tragedy, but let us not exaggerate it."[23]

Looking back, it is no exaggeration to say that the violence of 1967 altered the shape of political space and time along the color line. It altered and constricted the limits of possibility and legitimized the voices determined to make virtue out of those limits and vice out of every attempt to get beyond them. There was no riot in Chicago that year. The violence came to Chicago the following year on 4 April 1968, when news of King's assassination in Memphis spread throughout the tearful and angry South and West sides. During the summer of 1967, poll after poll discovered that whites and blacks were polarized in their views on every subject having to do with civil rights and the issues of black equality. The Gallup poll showed this division. The Lemberg Center for the Study of Violence at Brandeis University showed the same results in a six-city survey.[24] The Inter-University Social Research Committee–Chicago Metropolitan area documented it in its report, "Militancy for and against Civil Rights and Integration in Chicago: Summer 1967."[25] A CBS News poll a year later confirmed the depth and durability of these racially polarized perceptions of the social order.[26]

In this atmosphere, it was to be expected that the white press would praise as progress and the CCCO would reject as fraudulent the plan for school integration which Superintendent Redmond proposed in late August. The Redmond plan proposed to substitute racial quotas for racial change in schools along the moving color line in an attempt to assure whites that their schools would not go all black. He therefore also proposed to bus blacks to schools in outlying regions when a given school reached its quota. He would integrate the teaching staff both by race and teaching experience and provide additional training and aid for inner-city teachers. The plan also called for the building of five educational parks over the next eight to ten years and the creation of citywide magnet schools offering excellence and specialized programs. The plan promised increased integration at vocational schools, the development of vocational programs in neighborhood high schools, and the establishment, once again, of an advisory committee to look into the problems of the Washburne Trade School.[27]

The *Sun-Times* called the plan "courageous"; the *Daily News,* "bold, imaginative, even revolutionary." It was seen as something "the progressive part of the community" could support and believe in.[28]

The Redmond report was a response to the criticisms from the U.S. Office of Education of 6 January 1967, part of the continuing effort to adjudicate the CCCO complaint of 4 July 1965. The CCCO found the report unresponsive to its original complaint and to specific problems raised by the Office of Education. The following is only one example of the CCCO's response:

> The thrust of the Redmond-Board Report is racist. It implies that a black Chicago would be undesirable and that Negroes will always be underpaid. It is designed to keep the whites and limit the Negroes to a quota in newly integrated schools. What will be the effect on the non-white child when he realizes that a viable portion of him is say one-quarter?
>
> The quota for dealing with transition schools ignores the long miles of adjacent Negro and white schools or the triplicate series of Negro, mixed and white schools on the edges of the ghetto. It ignores the Chicago Housing Authority rooms misused for schools. It ignores the mobiles in the segregated Negro schools. It ignores the segregated upper grade centers, the white center Chopin in West Town, and the white center Cooper, both bordering Negro strips of the near West Side. The only integration of interest in the Redmond-Board Report is in the areas of active racial transition.[29]

The CCCO rejected both the good sense and the good faith of this report and concluded: "The federal government must, therefore, step in and enforce the Civil Rights Act and the U.S. Constitution. Never before have the facts been so clear. Never before have the government's ability and obligation to act been so evident."[30]

The *Sun-Times* labeled the CCCO response an "uncalled-for attack" and accused its authors, both of whom were white, of "racial touchiness." The *Daily News* called the CCCO's statement an "almost Pavlovian response in the negative to every plan the school board proposes." Both newspapers stressed the long-term impact the plan could be expected to achieve and faulted the CCCO for not appreciating its potential.[31] Still, eleven years later, in 1978, the NAACP was unable to detect the progress that had been promised in 1967, 1971, or 1976.[32] Segregation was still the rule; and the CCCO's critique had proved a more accurate indicator of what the Redmond plan actually portended than had the editorial enthusiasm of the civic credo.

On 19 September 1967 Albert A. Raby announced his intention to step down as the leader of the CCCO and return to school. He was thirty-three years old. For three years and nine months he had headed the movement for civil rights in Chicago. He was not quitting the movement, but he was suffer-

335

ing, he said, from "battle fatigue." He wanted time to rethink his position. Even in retiring, he was a leader, setting an example which many others found they had to follow. "It is tragic," he said, "that after so many young people have marched, and some have died, we find ourselves with the same kind of problems as when we started, and with little hope of change."[33] The always slender thread of hope for change had broken.

The *Chicago Daily News* saw no occasion for tears. In commenting on "the Raby resignation," the editors pontificated: "One trouble with Chicago's civil rights leadership—exemplified by Al Raby's attitude—is that its needle has got stuck; it has no other tactic but to damn, damn, damn. Thus, when an education integration plan with real promise was set forth, Raby's automatic response was to demand that all federal funds be cut off from the Chicago school system."[34]

If this study has shown anything, it is whose needle was stuck. Twenty years later, it seems obvious that the compulsive optimism of the civic credo is at least as debilitating as chronic depression. While consistently self-righteous and judgmental of others, editorially the white dailies were consistently and profoundly wrong.

By the fall of 1967, there was no place for the civil rights movement to go except "back to school." The civil rights movement had been defeated in Chicago and in the nation. It had lost the hope that it could create change. In place of hope, fear had moved to the fore. The stunning violence of the summer seemed to legitimize the fear and to rationalize the de facto situation: so what if it *was* segregation?

There were both radical and conservative versions of that question. The radical version asserted that white people were unreliable and that blacks did not need them, that self-respect lay in racial solidarity and pride. The conservative version asserted that ethnic cohesion had always been the American way, that people should not force themselves on each other, that pluralism was the bulwark of democracy, and that preferential treatment for one group only disturbed the natural order of ethnic diversity. In neither case did de facto segregation appear to be much of a problem. So much for the dilemma of white culture.

The framework for rationalizing the metropolitan color line had snapped into focus. The color line was still on the move, five blocks per week. The Redmond plan was a bureaucratic daydream, an attempt to assure whites that their schools could be spared the ravages of the color line. It was bold, especially in its disregard of the facts, relentlessly documented in *Chicago's Widening Color Gap* by Pierre de Vise. But that bureaucratic daydream of avoiding trouble had displaced King's communal dream of children walking

336

hand in hand as the guiding light in American race relations. So much for the dilemma of constitutional duties.

The CCCO's critique of the Redmond plan was the last exhausted gasp of a collapsing movement, cut off from any effective assertion of black dignity by the events of the past year. The battle had been lost at the polls in April, a landslide of ethnic politics. It had been lost at the leadership council in Project: Good Neighbor, an assertion of sentimental and mendacious euphemisms. It had been lost in the U.S. Congress in the refusal to link civil rights to the Atomic Energy Commission. It had been lost in the Illinois General Assembly, which could read the writing on the wall. It had been lost at the Illinois Supreme Court in an inversion of logic so embarrassing that even the justices could not live with it for long. It had been lost in the press, which persisted in seeing progress where only loss was evident and continued to attack the messengers who brought the news. It had been lost in the violence that frightened a nation. Consequently, it had been lost in the battle for public opinion. But underlying all of these, it had been lost in the continuing power of the color line to dominate the structure of community life in the metropolitan area.

Tragically, it was lost even in the CCCO's exhausted gasp. For the first time in its existence, the CCCO was flailing in public for its own grounds. On the one hand, it complained of Redmond's selective interest in integration; but on the other hand, it was willing to concede that a black Chicago might be desirable. Was segregation the issue or not? That was the final loss, the loss from which the civil rights movement in Chicago could not recover, the loss of its own principle. Raby was right. It was time to rethink the position. And it was not going to be easy.

337

PART THREE

The Deepening of the Issue

CHAPTER THIRTEEN

The Triumph of the Civic Credo

The 1960s are almost as controversial in retrospect as they were at the time. The decade in retrospect has taken on mythic proportions as the time when something important went wrong. For guilty and radicalized liberals it was when the hollowness of American culture was exposed. For self-righteous conservatives it was when the hollowness of American liberals was exposed. Liberals, conservatives, and radicals have competed as much for the interpretation of the 1960s as they did for influence at the time. As a result, the degree to which fantasies about that era have come to be the prevailing wisdom about what happened in that mythic moment is amazing.

The impression is irresistible that the conservative fantasies are the ones that have won the competition for interpretation. It is not uncommon to hear that the 1960s were a "liberal Camelot," a period of unrestrained social experimentation, that the country spent its way into unmanageable debt in the futile pursuit of social reform, that blacks were subjected to unrealistically high expectations and, at the same time, unjustifiable preferential treatment, that the youth of the country threatened our cultural foundations with personal and political anarchy while the liberals applauded—that it was, in short, a time when liberalism reigned supreme and rode roughshod over all counsels of prudence.

This is not the version of the 1960s that we have reported here; but there may be some explanation from this story as to why interpretation has drifted to the right. That decade was characterized by dramatic liberal initiatives, aborted purposes, unresolved issues, and the retreat to if not the triumph of conservative ideas. This mixture made the 1960s a time of unusually passionate events; but those events were neither so severed from what had gone before nor so alien to present difficulties as they seem in the light of current interpretation.

Issues were raised which exceeded the grasp of existing ideas. Disagreement and conflict erupted at several points on which a majoritarian consensus had been assumed. At least three of these conflicts have remained significantly

341

unresolved in the meantime, and attempts to resolve them simply by reasserting the existing stock of ideas have served only to deepen them.

Each of these conflicts crystallized in the events of the 1960s. The climax and collapse of the civil rights movement is one of those events, the one to which we have given extended attention here. The other two are complex events, which, though related, can only be mentioned. The rise of widespread opposition to the war in Vietnam signaled a breakdown in the national consensus about the proper role of the United States in the international arena, and we have continued to live with many deep antagonisms about what our role there should have been. In the midst of the collapsing civil rights movement and the rising antiwar movement, the Roosevelt coalition came apart as the southern vote and the blue-collar ethnic vote in metropolitan areas began to float, no longer securely anchored to the Democratic party as it had been since the 1930s. The search for a new majority coalition capable of governing had begun, and it has not yet come to a stable resolution.

The relationship between the collapse of the civil rights movement, the rise of the antiwar movement, and the disintegration of the Roosevelt coalition, both in the 1960s and since then, is, of course, a matter of controversy. We have seen how, at least in its collapse, the civil rights movement was affected by the other two. We have also seen how, in its origins, the civil rights movement was affected by the consensus about America's role in world affairs and by the place of blacks in the Roosevelt coalition.

In the mid-1940s, Gunnar Myrdal had appealed to America's role in the international arena as one of the reasons for his optimism. "America can demonstrate," he had said, "that justice, equality and cooperation are possible between white and colored people. In the present phase of history this is what the world needs to believe. Mankind is sick of fear and disbelief, of pessimism and cynicism. It needs the youthful moralistic optimism of America. But empty declarations only deepens cynicism. Deeds are called for."[1] He looked to the United States as a leader in extending the democratic ideals of the American creed both at home and abroad, and he was not alone in that perception.

By the same token, we have seen that the transition of black voters into the Democratic party was well under way in Chicago by 1940 and that they were a decisive factor in President Harry S. Truman's election in 1948 and Mayor Daley's rise to power in 1953. But we have also seen that ever since A. Philip Randolph's March on Washington Movement, significant black leaders had realized that it would take more than the normal functioning of the Roosevelt coalition to produce priority attention for civil rights concerns on the national agenda. For that, a civil rights movement was called for.

The civil rights movement was a complex series of events, only some of which come into view in the Chicago story; but it did, for a time, make those issues a priority on the national agenda. This movement was not only a struggle to influence national policy. It was also a battle of ideas. Indeed, without its ideas, the civil rights movement would never have taken place. What happened to those ideas in the course of the movement is an important and essential chapter in the story of what happened in and to the movement itself and in the assessment of what happened in the society as a consequence of those events.

And what were these ideas whose conflict and competition constituted the civil rights movement as we have described it? They were moral ideas in the sense that we described in the Introduction, that is, they provided a perception of what was at issue along the color line in Chicago and the projection of a principle that would resolve the issue. They were ideas of social justice in that they identified a potential goodness in the structure of society which depended on coordinated human effort for its reality. They consisted of descriptive readings of what was wrong combined with prescriptive readings of what was required to right those wrongs.

We have identified five such sets of ideas which came into dialogue, competition, and conflict in the events of the civil rights movement in Chicago: racist realism, the civic credo, the democratic dilemma of black dignity, the democratic dilemma of white culture, and the democratic dilemma of constitutional duties. Each was a complex set of ideas; and this dialogue and competition provides an occasion to review them comparatively and to give an account of how the civic credo triumphed over the others.

In Chapter 1 we showed how the racist realism of Alexis de Tocqueville set the official framework for inducing and interpreting events along the color line following the Compromise of 1877. Within this framework, inequalities along the color line were pervasive and progressively institutionalized, but they were not approached as problems of justice. Indeed, under the guise of the "separate but equal" doctrine, the color line was legislatively enforced on the theory that antipathy and inequality were the natural conditions for black-white relations. It was left to private philanthropy to do whatever it could to promote developments in the black community which might eventually raise these backward people up to the standards of the majority population. Within the framework of racist realism, these amelioratory efforts were strictly acts of charity. The chances of their actually accomplishing their purpose were not considered likely. It is not possible to describe racist realism without uncovering its inherent cynicism.

Both W. E. B. DuBois and Gunnar Myrdal defined their approaches to the color line against this framework of racist realism. Both agreed that philanthropy would not solve the problem because each saw the issue as one of justice in the community at large. Both called on the democratic values embedded in national institutions to challenge the treatment of blacks in Ameri-

343

can life. DuBois articulated the democratic dilemma of black dignity and called attention to the "twoness" experienced by blacks. Myrdal articulated the democratic dilemma of white culture and called attention to the conflict "in the heart of the American."

Each of these approaches was an attack on racist realism in the name of democratic justice. As citizens of a democracy, blacks had legitimate claims to equality of rights. Denial of these rights was an issue of justice. DuBois emphasized the dilemmas generated for blacks by the denial of these rights; Myrdal emphasized the dilemmas generated for whites. Although each of these perspectives gave rise to somewhat different strategic priorities, they were joined in their appeal to the transformative possibilities of the American creed.

Just as DuBois's *Souls of Black Folk* had been a major turning point in black thinking about the color line, so Myrdal's *An American Dilemma* was a major turning point in white thinking about race. Sponsored by the Carnegie Corporation, a major philanthropic foundation, the Myrdal study seemed to mark the end of intellectual respectability for the Compromise of 1877. Myrdal proclaimed that the Negro problem was an issue of justice. Charity was not going to solve the problem of the color line. It was the legitimate object for a politics of democratic social change in which the rational ideas of the culture, the American creed, were on the side of change.

Further, as we have seen, Myrdal was optimistic about the prospects for resolving the American dilemma. In the struggle between the inclusive values of individual dignity, fundamental equality, and inalienable rights to freedom, justice, and fair opportunity, on the one hand, and the personal and group prejudices that made blacks an exception to the implications of this American creed, on the other, Myrdal was confident that the former would prevail. Culturally, the American creed was not merely an abstract ideal but a social force by virtue of its embodiment in major American institutions. On the personal level, the press for logical consistency among an individual's values would lead to the triumph of the higher, more universal and rational values of the American creed over prejudices and local interests. Socially, Myrdal thought change was possible because of his theory of the rank order of discriminations, ranging from miscegenation to economic discrimination, which was identical but inverse for whites and blacks. Thus blacks could pursue what they most wanted to change, beginning with economic discrimination, without immediately threatening what whites most wanted to preserve, racial purity. Finally, Myrdal's theory of cumulation argued that because of the interdependence of all the factors in the black situation, progress in one area, such as employment, housing, or education, would produce progress in other areas as well.

344

In Chapter 2 we showed how the civic credo view of the issue was a rationalization of the color line in Chicago. It is true that the civic credo view assimilated Myrdal's emphasis on the conflict between rational ideals and irrational attitudes, but it failed to take the measure of the structural segregation that was relentlessly cutting its way across the city on a block-by-block basis. It posited the American creed as already adequately embodied in the normal functioning of institutions—and especially in the schools—but it failed to account for the increasing number of all-black schools or for their manifest inferiority. The immigrant analogy allowed it to vacillate between understanding the "irrational attitudes" as either a police problem or a natural but temporarily insurmountable problem that only time and the normal functioning of institutions could overcome. It tended to locate these irrational attitudes, along with all other aspects of the problem, in the black community (it was a Negro problem in that sense), and it looked to nonpartisan, majoritarian, consensual strategies pursued in an atmosphere of civic calm to produce racial progress in the long term. In other words, it was a whitewash of the issue.

In Chapter 3, however, we showed how Myrdal's emphasis on the American creed was both adopted and transmuted by the U.S. Supreme Court in the *Brown* decision of 1954. With *Brown,* the Court posed the democratic dilemma of constitutional duties. The doctrine that "separate educational facilities are inherently unequal" emphasized institutional rather than attitudinal dimensions in the descriptive definition of the issues. Although this doctrine was clearly aimed at de jure segregation, that is, the use of the law and the authority of the states to mandate racially separate and unequal schools, it was not clear whether this doctrine could be extended to include any and all racially separate and unequal schools, referred to as de facto segregation.

In Chicago a group formed explicitly for the purpose of developing and pursuing this issue of de facto segregation. It was related to the black and white dilemma views insofar as it continued to rely on the American creed as pointing the normative way to justice; but it substituted a much more focused descriptive reading of what was at issue: institutional policies and practices that produced, extended, and justified the continuing separation of the races and consigned the black students to inferior schools. From this perspective, the problem lay in making institutions, initially and especially the schools, more democratic, that is, more equal, more open, and more dedicated to developing the productive potential of each and every child. Like Myrdal, the proponents of de facto segregation also subscribed to a principle of cumulation, believing that gains in one area would support and encourage gains in others, but they applied a fairly strict institutional measure of what should count as gains. The problem from this perspective was to identify de facto

345

violations of democratic equality commensurate with the de jure violations addressed by *Brown* and to identify democratically defensible duties that would actually remedy the situation.

One of the most amazing aspects of the civil rights movement was the apparent absence of normative conflict among its constituents. The American creed seemed clear and decisive in the mid-1960s to all but Elijah Mohammad and Malcolm X, both of whom mocked the hopes of the civil rights movement. The strategy of the proponents of de facto segregation, however, was less clear. Were these moral ideas best advocated by the minority protest strategies of DuBois, by following Myrdal's attempts to develop and apply the higher values of a white majority, or by seeking an authoritative resolution in the courts? Since each of these strategies derived from and appealed to the American creed, however, they were not mutually exclusive, and thus the de facto segregation heirs of DuBois, Myrdal, and *Brown* made use of all these various means for advancing their principles. Each was to have its day in particular strategic situations.

DE FACTO SEGREGATION AND THE CIVIC CREDO: IDEAS IN COMPETITION

The civil rights movement in Chicago was basically a competition between de facto segregation and the civic credo and the various ways both of them drew on the American creed to interpret the city's problems. It is important to bear in mind that ideas do not always win because of their power as ideas. More often than not, they win because of the power of the persons who hold them. Yet they rarely win for that reason alone. They have to be seen as in some way plausible and persuasive interpretations of experience. There can be no doubt that in the competition between de facto segregation and the civic credo, it was the latter that had friends in high places; but the fact is that the civic credo won the competition for popularity as well as the competition for power. Some explanation is called for.

As the competition opened between these ideas of what was at stake in the issue of race, there were some important areas of agreement between them. Myrdal had subtitled his book *The Negro Problem and Modern Democracy,* and both the de facto reading and the civic credo reading agreed that it was the Negro problem for which a solution was required. They did not, however, have the same Negro problem in mind.

Myrdal, along with DuBois and the Supreme Court, was clear that the Negro problem was a white problem for two reasons. Morally, it was the white person who had the American dilemma between the general valuations

346

of the American creed and the specific valuations that made blacks an exception to the creed's provisions. Empirically, it was a white problem because "the white majority group . . . naturally determines the Negro's 'place.' " "All our attempts," Myrdal wrote, "to reach scientific explanation of why the Negroes are what they are and why they live as they do have regularly led to determinants on the white side of the race line."[2]

This was the line developed by the proponents of the de facto segregation reading of the issue. To them the Negro problem was segregation, pure and simple, and it was an institutional problem. The thematic focus of this perspective was laid out in the 1958 article which appeared in *Crisis*, "De Facto Segregation in the Chicago Public Schools." "In cost and quality of instruction, school time, districting and choice of sites," this article claimed, "the Chicago Board of Education maintains in practice what amounts to a racially discriminatory policy." The schools were more segregated than the city as a whole, and the neighborhood schools were more segregated than their neighborhoods. In the *Crisis* authors' understanding of the institutional dynamics, whites as well as blacks were hurt by this Negro problem. It was a situation of conflict in which everyone involved got cheated.[3]

The civic credo view, on the other hand, began with the doctrine that "Negroes are simply the latest of the immigrant streams that have built this city . . . and the problem is to give Negroes, as for the most part we have given other immigrant groups, full rights and free opportunities." By 1951, it was part of the civic credo that this goal had been accomplished (the schools were the prime example) and "the road ahead is unquestionably smoother." By then, according to the civic credo, the Negro was the Negro problem. Negroes had "found that there is a certain power in segregation." Negro realtors, doctors, newspapermen, social workers, professionals, and workers had to find some way to overcome their "segregated-mindedness." Further progress depended on pursuing nonpartisan, majoritarian, consensual strategies in an atmosphere of civic calm. From this perspective, those who raised racially motivated complaints about institutions were thought to be impeding progress because of their unregenerate segregated-mindedness.[4]

Another matter on which both proponents of de facto segregation and of the civic credo agreed was that the solution to the Negro problem lay in applying the American creed; but this agreement brought them into conflict in their understanding of contemporary institutions. For the proponents of de facto segregation, the American creed provided a normative critique of existing segregationist policies and practices. For the proponents of the civic credo, the American creed provided the substance of existing institutions. This meant that those who criticized existing institutions had, in some way and for some reason, forsaken the American creed and become the bearers of ulterior

347

motives. Formally, a similar case held for the proponents of de facto segregation: those who could not accept the critique of the American creed had something to hide. The importance of the American creed for both of these positions raised the question of bad faith to a position just beneath the surface of
all the conflicts that arose.

Since the civic credo was articulated first and had set the established ideas
for understanding the issue, the de facto segregation view came into the political arena in Chicago as a dissenting opinion. The substance of the de facto
segregation position was weighty. It claimed major institutional malfeasance,
but because it seemed to lack support as weighty as its claims, even its proponents were uncertain how to proceed initially. Just when their charges about
the schools first appeared in print, they lost the support of the local NAACP,
which was taken over by the Daley-Dawson machine because of its "militant"
criticism of Congressman Dawson. The perception of the political machine
was not wrong. The publication of "De Facto Segregation in the Chicago
Public Schools" did portend an outbreak of civic heresy.

It was not until a federal court began to approach the de facto segregation
reading of the issue, however, that real initiatives based on this civic heresy
were undertaken. In 1961, the *Taylor* decision in New Rochelle, New York,
held that "it is of no moment whether the segregation is labeled *de jure* (according to law) or *de facto* as long as the board, by its conduct, is responsible
for its maintenance." In response, a coalition coordinated by the local
NAACP formed to frame a case against the Chicago public schools. Although
a suit was filed, the *Webb* case, the strategy floundered on organizational
problems.[5]

The case never came to trial and never made any law. It did, however,
become a testing ground in the conflict between de facto segregation and the
civic credo. The plaintiffs charged "segregation." The schools pleaded "overcrowding." The pattern was clear. Schools in the path of the block-by-block
expansion of the color line underwent devastating increases in enrollment that
caused the color of their pupils to change 100 percent in a year or two. The
Board of Education pleaded ignorance, "color blindness," and claimed that
race had nothing to do with this pattern; it maintained a principled and official
ignorance of the race of its pupils. The board pleaded that it was dealing with
temporary, unexpected increases in enrollment in selected schools. The solution lay in building more schools. In short, the board claimed to be a victim of
unanticipated circumstances, and it denied that it had any "affirmative duty"
to provide "a school system which is racially integrated."[6]

Thus the lines of conflict between de facto segregation and the civic credo
in relation to the schools were drawn around the controversy generated by
claims of segregation, countered by pleas of overcrowding. The proponents of

de facto segregation were convinced that the facts were on their side. The U.S. Commission on Civil Rights confirmed their claims. But it was unclear how to press these claims. The courts were foreclosed until the protesters exhausted administrative procedures.

In this conflict, the Board of Education found protection in the doctrine of the civic credo, which allowed the charges of segregation to be cast as irrational. *Chicago's American,* 19 December 1961, stated the case succinctly: "Segregation is always institutional. In places where it exists it is based on state or local law. There is no such law here; white and Negro children have always attended the same schools. The problem to be solved is not segregation, since there isn't any; the problem is overcrowding. Calling it segregation only adds emotional confusion to the difficulties of solving it."

In the absence of both a legal strategy and an organizational vehicle to pursue it, the proponents of de facto segregation turned to coalition building among the various groups protesting the impact of the color line on their neighborhood schools. Despite the variety of strategies, tactics, and scale among civil rights organizations, they saw the cumulative possibilities in this diversity, and the CCCO coalition emerged, as an alternative to the NAACP, to coordinate these protests. Although they believed that both federal law and sound social science were on their side, they had to make their way in a civic atmosphere that cast them as, at best, a special interest group and, at worst, irrational troublemakers.

For their part, proponents of the civic credo placed their faith in the normal operations of the school system and claimed that the problem in the schools was overcrowding, not segregation—a problem which, as we saw in Chapter 2, had been thought to be inherent in schools at the edge of the color line since at least the 1930s. Mobile classrooms, soon to be called "Willis Wagons," were placed at those schools to relieve the problem that the civic credo called inexplicable overcrowding.

As it was in the beginning, however, here too the saints of the civic credo adopted both priestly and militant stances toward the unorthodox. School Board President Roddewig assumed a conciliatory approach and diplomatically sought to persuade dissident groups of the catholic substance of the civic faith, which required only their patience and understanding to reveal its truths. School Superintendent Willis adopted the opposite approach, and, however universal in principle his "professional" approach to school problems could have been, in practice he had neither time nor sympathy for his "uninformed" and unregenerate critics—be they local parents or federal agencies. Either way, school officials reaffirmed their commitment to neighborhood schools and their inexplicable overcrowding, and they suggested relief from this overcrowding only in the form of a permissive transfer plan that

349

was discriminatory on its face. Meanwhile, the mayor reaffirmed the ethnic, nonpartisan character of the issue by adding a black organization to his blue-ribbon School Board Nominating Commission.

During 1963 the civil rights movement continued to expand as new groups joined the coalition of de facto segregation proponents—many by CCCO's conference in July. At this same meeting, the CCCO sought to expand the range of issues in relation to which its interpretation of de facto segregation might be explored: employment, housing, welfare, politics—another expression of Myrdal's principle of cumulation. This potential expansion of concerns was not pursued that year, however, in part because of Willis's insistence on making the schools, and ultimately himself, the issue. Perhaps even more important in shaping events that year was the emergence of a particular strategic focus in the civil rights movement—first nationally, then in Chicago.

In 1963 nonviolent direct action and, increasingly, massive nonviolent direct action became the standard of effective efforts in the civil rights movement—the means by which it sought both to demonstrate widespread protests of discrepancies between the promises of the American creed and the actual conditions of blacks and to press for the actualization of the creed's promise. Fired by Birmingham and fueled by the March on Washington, massive direct action in Chicago took the form of the first school boycott, supported by 250,000 students, half the total school population. The school board's own figures, first released the day of the boycott to meet requirements of the newly enacted Armstrong Act, officially confirmed both massive racial segregation in the Chicago public schools and identified the civil rights movement's public base. The boycott was completely successful in black schools, partially successful in some transitional schools, and almost universally ignored in white ones.

Even before the racial head count was published, Willis had decided to take his stand as the hero of the militant whites. He rejected a limited transfer plan, which would have introduced a few black honor students from high schools that did not have an honors program into previously all-white schools that did. Rather than implement this plan, as both the school board and the courts had instructed him, he resigned, claiming the board had infringed on his nonpartisan administrative prerogatives.

For a brief moment, even such scribes of the civic credo as the editors at the *Sun-Times* thought Willis had "lost contact with both his board and with his public" and had "imposed his will on the board and the community—once too often."[7] Lay adherents of the civic credo, however, from the city's most prominent business leaders to white parents, had no such reservations about their newly martyred saint, and the board worked out a reconciliation with Willis, which effectively subordinated its role in policy to his responsibility for administration.

When the school boycott occurred a few days later, therefore, the civic priests were back to the orthodox line. The *Tribune* reaffirmed the ethnic nature of the problem with its "friendly warning" that "Negroes are still a minority in Chicago—only about one-fifth of the population," and the *Sun-Times* blamed boycott leaders for "keeping children out of school"—an action that could only hurt the children but could not "influence policy at the level where it is made."[8] The largest civil rights demonstration against school segregation in the nation's history thus had no effective results.

Even though the CCCO had demonstrated both separation and subordination in the schools and massive black dissatisfaction with this situation, the school board was in no position to respond to those institutional claims. Newly reelected School Board President Roddewig offered "hearings" rather than the negotiations the CCCO expected after the boycott, perhaps the best he could do with Willis clearly in charge of the schools. The CCCO responded by replacing the moderate style of Charles Davis with the militancy of Lawrence Landry. The sectarians were now in charge on both sides.

This was, for the moment, more a problem for the CCCO than for the school board. In 1964 a national mandate to abolish the color line in its Jim Crow form was concretely expressed in the Civil Rights Act, but in Chicago, 1964 was a year of stalemate for the CCCO on the issue of de facto segregation. The public success and practical failure of the school boycott had to be reckoned with. Some, like Landry, thought the path to progress lay in deepening the CCCO's base in the ghetto, and they undertook a second school boycott for that purpose in February. The mayor, increasingly aware of his role in articulating the civic credo, asked of the school boycotts, "What do they prove?" and underlined his ethnic understanding of the issue by appointing a second black to the school board. Meanwhile, Willis tried to link the boycotts to violence and disciplinary problems in black schools, as though protests against conditions there served only to intensify the Negro problem.

The mayor's question was a good one, however, especially for those in the CCCO who thought the path to progress lay in broadening their support in the white community. Indeed, it was a strategic question inherent in the de facto segregation reading of the issue—whether, at any given moment, increasing white consent to the American creed or encouraging black protest of conditions was the strategic priority.

Both the moderate proponents of de facto segregation and the proponents of the civic credo had long anticipated school board–sponsored studies of segregation and the quality of education in Chicago schools. The former hoped for definite confirmation of their claims of inferior segregated education; the latter editorialized in the midst of every protest, "Wait until the Hauser and/or Havighurst report." The Hauser report in April did indeed substantiate every civil rights claim, but it also provided the school board with the opportunity to

351

pursue modest proposals for desegregation at its own initiative in an atmosphere of civil calm. It was an attempt to reconcile the claims arising from de facto segregation with the doctrines of the civic credo. It did not work.

Under Willis's leadership, over a period of months the proposal was watered down into another ineffective transfer plan. When only twenty-eight children took advantage of it, Willis used that fact as evidence that black parents were satisfied with the education their children were receiving and that overcrowding was not a problem, that the normal operations of the schools were satisfactory to their immediate clientele.

The Havighurst report was also an attempt to reconcile the established facts of de facto segregation with the doctrines of the civic credo by offering the board an opportunity to expand both its revenues and its prestige through the adoption of compensatory programs. The Havighurst report died a merciful death in November because the school board, after investing $185,000 in its preparation, never discussed it. Apparently even discussing the compensatory programs it proposed would have implied a recognition of the inequalities they were designed to rectify. Outside the church of the civic credo there was no salvation, only chaos; and inside there was no room for compromising with the claims of de facto segregation.

The CCCO's only success for the year came from its move into the political arena, conducting voter registration and voter education campaigns, which helped reelect Lyndon Johnson. The CCCO-sponsored Freedom Democratic Clubs, which achieved this success, had been designed as long-term vehicles to develop an independent black vote, but they did not survive the election, and the CCCO itself barely survived the year. By the end of 1964, the national proponents of civil rights appeared poised for a victory over Jim Crow, but locally all they had to show for their efforts was an increase in the already overwhelming electoral margin of an incumbent president. In Chicago, Willis was more firmly entrenched than ever, dressed in the vestments of the civic credo.

In 1965, the national mandate for racial justice culminated in the voting rights bill. In Chicago, however, Willis was in control and continuing to use the civic credo to draw the veil of innocence over segregation in the schools. The CCCO, the coalition that came into being expressly to pursue that mandate and to pierce that veil, was only a shell of its former self. Through a variety of CCCO initiatives the previous coalition began to reassemble, but these programs, which now clearly had Willis as their target, were ineffectual. National progress in the struggle against de jure segregation seemed to undermine further the local plausibility of the de facto segregation claims.

It was the school board itself which, in the spring of 1965, galvanized the proponents of the de facto segregation issue to action as the board prepared to extend Willis's contract four more years. When the NAACP called for a week

352

of protest, the CCCO again became the center of debate and strategy concerning both the intentions of the still-suspect NAACP and the renewed search for effective forms of action. In this context "effective" took on new meanings in expressing the pent-up emotions of the previous years as well as in getting rid of Willis. The school board enjoined the boycott but not the associated marches, and those marches were effective on both counts. Raby led the march into the streets, tying up traffic for miles, and vowed to march daily as long as Willis remained. In the name of civic order the mayor ordered the arrest of civilly disobedient and socially disruptive demonstrators, and hundreds of demonstrators were indeed arrested. At the same time, however, the school board, with support from the Chicago business community, limited Willis's tenure to age sixty-five and began searching for someone to replace him the following year. These proponents of the civic credo had finally come to see Willis as contributing to civic unrest that made nonpartisan, majoritarian, consensual strategies difficult to pursue. His blue ribbon had faded, and the civic credo now required that he be replaced with another professional whose credentials were intact.

The daily marches were, of course, deplored by the other purveyors of the civic credo in addition to the mayor, and even some in the CCCO doubted their continued usefulness as questions of strategy were settled in the streets and questions of principle were left unresolved. Still, the marches provided an ongoing activity that attracted national attention and resources to the issues in Chicago, which seemed unresolvable until the national mandate was applied there.

A complaint was filed with the U.S. Office of Education, claiming that the Chicago schools were in violation of the 1964 Civil Rights Act and that, therefore, federal funds should be withheld from them. Martin Luther King, Jr., fresh from his victories in Birmingham and Selma and in search of a point of entry into northern problems, was impressed by the vitality of the Chicago movement. The CCCO used King as the centerpiece for successful community rallies and a downtown march during a weekend visit to Chicago, and he held out the prospect of a Chicago campaign by his Southern Christian Leadership Conference. Congressman Adam Clayton Powell held hearings in Washington at which the charges of de facto segregation and the civic credo's interpretations of the situation were directly debated. Willis used the occasion to suggest another version of the Negro problem—that black children were not ready for the schools rather than the other way around.

By the end of the summer, Willis was on his way out; the blue ribbon committee appointed to implement the Hauser report had resigned because there was nothing to implement; but the CCCO's complaint to the Office of Education was being well received there. The veil of innocence spread over the color line by the civic credo had not been pierced, but the plans of King

353

and the SCLC to join the CCCO held out the hope of a new beginning for the proponents of the de facto segregation issue in Chicago.

NATIONAL RESOURCES AND LOCAL RESISTANCE: MARCHING TO THE SUMMIT

At the beginning of King's Chicago campaign in the fall of 1965, the CCCO assumed that he would lend his experience, resources, and leadership to the school desegregation issue, which had dominated the coalition's agenda since its origins. That was not to be, however, in part because of difficulties in coordinating the energies of the CCCO and SCLC. There were differences of style to be worked out, but there were also differences in the intellectual landscape of the two organizations to be negotiated. Although the SCLC was familiar with and adept at pursuing the campaign against de jure segregation and the ugly emotions that underlay it, it was a good deal less at home in the world that came into view and had to be addressed if de facto segregation was the issue.

In addition, at the same time as serious tensions were emerging between King and President Johnson, the president was being drawn into ever closer alliance with the big city mayors. As a result, the president was obliged to minimize the importance of the CCCO complaint about the Chicago public schools. Therefore, just as the veil of innocence concerning the schools was about to be raised by the U.S. Office of Education, it was once again drawn across the schools by the unwillingness of northern big-city Democrats to accept the same desegregationist policies in their home districts which they had supported across the South. The mayor, the Illinois congressional delegation, and the Chicago white dailies defended the Chicago schools, which, they again insisted, were not segregated in any de jure sense, and attacked the CCCO and the Office of Education for even suggesting that much needed federal funds be withheld from the schools in Chicago. According to these civic leaders, if segregation existed, it lay below the Mason-Dixon line. In Chicago, the civic credo interpretation of the schools held firm, and, for all practical purposes, the rejection of the CCCO complaint settled the school issue in the North, not only in Chicago but across the country, for some years to come.

The reversal by the Office of Education was tied to the Johnson administration's strategy to specify affirmative duties by linking civil rights issues with poverty. This poverty was to be addressed by a new round of Great Society programs, which depended on northern liberal support for their enactment and the social work establishment for their implementation—even at the cost of

354

subordinating the concern for desegregation to poverty programs. The aim was to establish "social rights." It was the Johnson administration's attempt to provide material means and incentives for institutional changes at the local level. It was a major transition in the framework of national policy.

The civil rights movement was also in transition during this period. This transition was publicly marked by King's move from south to north and verbally noted in his shift in language from "civil rights" to "human rights." But what these human rights were and how they could be dramatized in Chicago to provoke the civic crisis required for negotiations posed major problems in setting the programmatic goals of such a campaign. Inside the movement, these questions led in a variety of directions—all of which can be understood as an attempt to reassert the normative supremacy of the American creed, which the CCCO and SCLC shared, and to explore the empirical and moral potential of that perspective for northern problems.

King moved north thinking that, in principle at least, his work in the South was completed. After all, his Birmingham campaign had produced the 1964 Civil Rights Act, which addressed public accommodations and schools, political disfranchisement, and discrimination in employment—items 3, 5, and 6, respectively, in Myrdal's rank order of discriminations. And when Title I of this act failed to increase black voter registration, King's Selma campaign led to the Voting Rights Act of 1965, which dramatically increased the black vote in the South. These were all de jure Jim Crow issues, however. In retrospect, therefore, both the president's ill-conceived poverty program and King's vaguely conceived approach to the link between poverty and racism in the North appear as efforts to lay a course of democratic duties which would remedy the damages of racism. Both President Johnson and King appeared to be returning to Myrdal's rank order of discriminations in relation to de facto issues—beginning with something like Rank 6, "Discrimination in securing land, credit, jobs, or other means of earning a living, and discrimination in public relief and other social welfare activities." But a variety of complex matters were included here, and, in any case, it remained to be seen just what might constitute the white rank order of discrimination regarding de facto issues in the North.

Where the issues had been de jure, as they were in the South, desegregation was the obvious import of the American creed. In Chicago, however, most CCCO members had long taken integration as their goal, but the black power strategies, first of Landry and then of Bevel, also made sense in a city with a ghetto of more than a million inhabitants. What did the American creed require: the creation of strong, self-respecting black communities able to negotiate their own interests; equal access to whatever goods the society offered; or affirmative duties to create equality of opportunity and, possibly, of outcomes

355

for all citizens? The question was a good one then, and it is still unresolved today. The American creed was less decisive normatively in the face of de facto segregation than DuBois, Myrdal, or many others had supposed.

In 1966, however, the question was settled in practice. The national resources needed for integrative redistributive policies were already committed to the Great Society, which meant in Chicago that those resources were coming to the aid of the civic credo. Bevel's version of black power was unable to compete with the Daley machine at its strongest point, the local black precinct. Thus desegregation, the only relevant principle in the South, became the middle and only viable principle in Chicago. The issues of the King campaign, which had begun to form around the slum, a black power and/or integrationist issue, finally took shape as the desegregationist demand for open housing—equal access to housing in opposition to the blatant and illegal discriminatory practices of realtors.

Despite the criticism this definition of the issue has received from revisionists, participants and historians alike, it was not an insignificant or irrelevant goal. The point of William Moyer's research had been to show that blacks paid about the same price for slum housing in Chicago as whites did for adequate housing. Indeed, as early as 1963, studies based on 1960 census data showed that income differential accounted for only 12 percent of the housing segregation in Chicago; this differential represented a decrease from 14 percent in 1950. In other words, purely racial, as distinct from economic, housing patterns were becoming worse.[9]

De facto segregation was the human rights issue in Chicago, and the Chicago Freedom Movement was constrained by the situation to adopt it. King became its prophet. Mayor Daley, on the other hand, became the high priest of the civic credo. Throughout the year, he welcomed King to his own ongoing war against slums (a considerable revision of his 1963 statement that Chicago had none),[10] and he backed his words with deeds—token actions, frequently enough, but always highly visible. His honor did occasionally wonder why King had chosen to assist in the struggle against slums in Chicago rather than in his own home town of Atlanta, but, on the whole, Daley's ability to maintain the cool, high road of the civic credo was remarkable in the midst of events that stirred heated passions on all sides. And it worked. Daley, the high priest, welcomed the concerns of King, the prophet; but as high priest, his honor asserted his responsibility for all the faithful. Even the ever-cynical *Daily News* columnist Mike Royko scored the opening rounds of the King-Daley bout solidly for the mayor. Thus when the summer action program was officially kicked off by King at Soldier Field on 10 July, the rally's slogan, "We're on the move," was more a hope than a reality among the proponents of de facto segregation.

The summer of 1966 was filled with unexpected developments that severely strained both the de facto segregation and the civic credo interpretations of the situation. When the West Side ghetto riot took place 12–15 July, just two days after the civil rights movement had begun the action phase of its nonviolent campaign, it was not easy for King and Raby to continue to advocate the effectiveness of their nonviolent approach to actualizing the American creed, but they did so, at considerable risk to both their persons and their program.

It was even more difficult for the mayor to maintain his claims of steady progress in ending slums in the face of widespread ghetto anger and violence, but he did so—initially minimizing the extent of the riot by calling it a juvenile disturbance. As the seriousness of the riot became undeniable, he considered blaming King for the outburst on the old southern theory that "our Negroes were happy until those outside agitators arrived." In the end, however, the simultaneous arrival of the National Guard and a modest promise by Daley to civil rights leaders to provide recreational facilities and to establish a citizens' police advisory committee restored peace to the West Side.

Likewise, no one expected nonviolent demonstrations designed to expose the discriminatory practices of realtors to initiate white riots in ethnic neighborhoods across the city. Apparently, maintaining all-white neighborhoods, like maintaining all-white schools, was high in the white rank order of de facto segregation.

These white riots were both a gain and a loss in the nonviolent pursuit of the American creed. On the one hand, King and Bevel had never counted on finding in Chicago the equivalent of Birmingham's "Bull" Connor or Selma's Sheriff Jim Clark, but Gage Park, Chicago Lawn, and Belmont-Cragin all demonstrated the same depth of anger and violence that had produced civic crises in the South. This very anger and violence, however, threatened to overwhelm the issues of housing segregation that the demonstrators were trying to raise.

This campaign showed that when the direct abuse of the law was not obviously involved (as it was in Jim Crow situations), the American creed lost its force and Myrdal's American dilemma was resolved in favor of the lower rather than the higher valuations. In the streets of Chicago and elsewhere (if the Congress and the Illinois General Assembly were at all representative), valuations were massively resolved in favor of the lower animosities and fears rather than the higher values—especially in matters that were considered private, like neighborhoods.

To some extent, this reaction was to be expected. Since Myrdal had written his study in the 1940s, many studies in social psychology had shown that, in the absence of structural change, persons and groups will tend to resolve their value conflicts in favor of their ordinary behavior rather than their higher values. In the jargon of psychologists, "cognitive dissonance" (the essence of Myrdal's formulation of the American dilemma) tends to be resolved, other

357

things being equal, through the justification rather than the alteration of behavior. In the summer of 1966, this behavioral tendency was dramatically acted out in the streets and rationalized in the newspapers and other pulpits of the civic credo.[11]

Certainly the Chicago white dailies followed this scenario. The *Tribune* defended police violence during the West Side riot, and then it justified white violence on the theory that the "demonstrators were asking for trouble," a clear statement of its version of the civic credo that whatever happened was always a Negro problem. The more moderate *Sun-Times* chose to emphasize the "civic progress in an atmosphere of civic calm" tenet of the civic faith and characterized these demonstrations as unnecessary (as all previous ones had been) because "responsible" leaders were always ready to discuss black grievances. Only the *Defender* supported the de facto segregation view that "residential segregation is the root cause of racial unrest" and that the burden was on "the white leadership" to do something about it.[12]

By mid-August, the white leadership recognized its position even if the white dailies did not. The mayor, after an increasingly uncomfortable month in his role as custodian of the civic peace and protector of the demonstrators, responded to the continuing white violence, a tangible symbol of his loss of control in the ethnic precincts he needed for the November election, and began moving toward negotiations. Likewise, Chicago's civic elite, usually hidden behind the "normal working of existing institutions" tenet of the civic credo, was forced to the surface by this civic crisis of unprecedented proportions and joined Daley in preparing for negotiations with civil rights leaders.

Thus urban violence had given the issues of de facto segregation an urgency in Chicago which they had never had before, but it was not clear to anyone whether this new-found urgency would focus on the immediate crisis or the underlying issues—whether, in other words, it would lead toward reaffirming the long-term optimism of the civic credo or resolving the structural issues of de facto segregation.

From early in the first session of the summit conference, it was clear that the priority of the mayor and other civic leaders was to restore civic calm by stopping the marches. For a short time pressure was placed on the recalcitrant realtors, who, for the day, were as much in violation of the civic credo as they had been, for years, in violation of the American creed. The realtors' verbal concession following the afternoon recess led to agreement "in principle" not to oppose desegregationist policies as required by both the civic credo and the claims of de facto segregation, but civil rights leaders were not interested in restoring civic calm until the affirmative responsibilities of implementing the American creed in housing were worked out.

As a result, the mayor acted unilaterally to enjoin the marches while these questions of implementation were referred to a subcommittee, which was to report to a second session of the summit conference ten days later. It was in the subcommittee that King and the CCCO representatives encountered the empirical and moral limitations of their interpretation when it came to specifying affirmative duties for de facto issues. The various public agencies involved did agree to change their policies and undertake new procedures, but movement proposals for "measurable visible change"—a metropolitan area in which, "by the end of five years, there would be no community whose population is not at least 5% Negro"[13]—were referred to a "continuing body" responsible for implementing the agreement. After all, insofar as desegregation was a matter of lifting barriers, who could promise how many might choose to cross them? And as the subcommittee changed this continuing body from the public action agency the movement had in mind to a private voluntary organization, it remained to be seen if the civil rights movement could accept proposals for which it did not have clear alternatives of its own.

In the end, it did, reluctantly, to be sure. The final agreement followed the subcommittee's lead in referring unresolved issues to a leadership council yet to be organized. The marchers had been successful in demonstrating the discrepancies between the American creed and the real situation in Chicago, but they produced little more than an agreement in principle to the desegregation they sought.

CIVIC CREDO:
POLITICAL VICTORY AND MORAL FAILURE

As it turned out, the summit agreement of August 1966 was a victory that spelled defeat for both the aims and the organization of the civil rights movement in Chicago. It took a little more than a year for the full dimensions of that defeat to emerge with the consequential finality of Albert Raby's resignation. As a result of the summit agreement and the implementation process it required, the movement became an overriding issue both for those who wanted to be in it and for those who viewed it as an external object. Dissension within and attacks from without became the order of the day. In addition and perhaps more important, there was genuine uncertainty within even the inner circle about both the grounds and the strategies for further action.

The summit agreement was a desegregationist document, yet the process of trying to implement it seemed to show that, as a practical matter and as a political option, the desegregationist position had lost as much of its ability to advance the civil rights agenda as the integrationist and black power positions. When the Congress refused to pass the Civil Rights Act of 1966 with its desegregationist thrust, it appeared that even this principle was being curtailed

359

in the national mandate for racial justice. The national policy was moving toward a new legitimacy for separation, justified by appeals to ethnic diversity, a policy in keeping with the civic credo, which had been operating in Chicago since the late 1940s. The dilemma of black dignity, the dilemma of white culture, and even the dilemma of constitutional duties were all being dissolved into a vision of virtuous ethnic diversity. There were both conservative and radical versions of this vision, but in either case, once this perception had been sealed with the fires of urban violence in the summer of 1967, it meant that a reconstructed principle of racist realism had become both the popular perception and the effective framework for national policy. This represented a defeat at the deepest level for the civil rights movement.

The cries of black power that came to the fore just as national policy and perception were reverting to a reconstructed racist realism gave rise to an agonizing ideological confusion. The civil rights movement had been a coalition of proponents of black power, desegregation, and integration from the beginning, but as the national framework snapped back into a resurgent racist realism, not only did the coalition come apart but its former members began to find fault with each other. Black power advocates berated "integration-mad" proponents as trying to break into a burning house. Desegregationists bewailed the surrender of black power advocates to the blandishments of racist realists. Integrationists could not see the difference between black power and racist realism. All that was certain was that the civil rights movement could not fit itself into a framework that amounted to the acceptance of separation in exchange for promises of equality and the assertion of pride.

King dealt with this problem by emphasizing his nonviolence rather than his race. He was accused of diverting the energies and attentions of the civil rights movement with his endorsement of the peace movement, but actually his antiwar activities were as much a response to a narrowing of the civil rights framework as they were an expansion of it. His activities might have been questionable on strategic grounds, but his moral grounds were both articulate and continuous with his previous commitments.

The CCCO was caught in this constriction of the civil rights framework. The summit agreement committed it to the implementation of desegregationist aims for which affirmative duties had not been specified. Agreements in principle without the specification of responsibilities that fulfill the principle are fertile grounds for revisionism, and that was the fate of the summit agreement. As the national mandate for racial justice drifted from desegregation to an ethnic diversity version of racist realism, so did the official interpretation of the summit agreement. The mayor was hailed as a statesman for carrying the agreement in that direction; the CCCO was left with nowhere to go and, as the *Daily News* appropriately noticed, not much to say but, "damn, damn, damn."[14] With the change in the framework for public policy and perception,

360

the withdrawal of King from Chicago, and the plaguing problems of implementing an agreement that had been revised beyond recognition, the CCCO as an organization, like its leader Albert Raby, suffered "battle fatigue" and a need to "rethink" its position. Individuals can, with good fortune, solve these problems, but coalitions generally cannot, and the CCCO did not. It ultimately died of them.

The year between the summit agreement and Raby's resignation was one of strategic trial and error for the Chicago Freedom Movement. Attempts to split the elites through a consensus-seeking implementation process did not work. Attempts to embarrass the elites through public complaints about foot-dragging, bad faith, and incompetence did not work. Attempts to make a visible dent in the mayor's electoral base worked accidentally to elect Republicans in November but had no impact when deliberately pursued in February and April, the local elections that really mattered to the mayor. Attempts to hold militant black power voices within the coalition failed early. Attempts to prevent conservative racist realists from capturing the civil rights agenda failed in the end. In Chicago, at least, attempts to broaden the civil rights coalition to include antiwar and social change groups did not work either. Overtures toward the New Left further narrowed the civil rights constituency. King put his confidence in Operation Breadbasket because that was the closest his principles would allow him to come to the new black power framework for civil rights—jobs for blacks, noncooperation with economic injustices, black pride that pays off; but Operation Breadbasket had held aloof from the CCCO and looked to a future of its own based in the black clergy.

In entering into the summit agreement in August 1966, the leaders of the Chicago Freedom Movement believed that, at the least, they had managed to recruit significant civic elites to the civil rights agenda for desegregating the metropolitan area. Granted, that agenda was not well developed, but it was plausible to believe that important segments of the power structure had become committed to its development. King found this a difficult idea to express to his established public in the movement; and as time went by, he found it an increasingly difficult idea to substantiate, although he continued to try, even at some expense to the truth.

As it turned out, the summit agreement and its implementation process were more like a play by Harold Pinter in which the movement's purposes were assimilated to the civic credo, which had always been the preserve of the civic elites, than a conversion of the elites to the perspectives and agenda of the movement. Even though both the movement's leadership and the civic elite had been equal parties to the making of the summit agreement, the elites captured the implementation process through the establishment of the Leadership Council on Metropolitan Open Communities. As a result, the mayor was able to emerge as a heroic and sensitive statesman carefully balancing

361

"interests," while the movement's leaders were cast once again as just one of those interests—irrational when they complained, always having to be balanced off against the understandable irritation of other ethnic representatives, specifically, angry whites.

Increasingly throughout the year political perceptions became racially polarized in the general public; and these perceptions were fixated, as it were, by the widespread ghetto violence of June and July 1967. This profound shift in the balance of political perception, attitude, and opinion portended doom for any further progress along the lines of the civil rights agenda. The Illinois General Assembly followed the Congress by nine months in refusing to legislate nondiscriminatory rules for the housing market. By then, only civil rights groups were upset by the refusal, and the Chicago Real Estate Board's view of the matter had become the prevailing political view: even if irrational attitudes could not be changed, at least they could be exploited. Project: Good Neighbor was strictly for downtown consumption. It did not work in the neighborhoods, as the leadership council learned.

The consequences of all this were the end of the civil rights movement in Chicago as an effective or even viable coalition, the triumph of the civic credo, and submission to the rule of the color line for years to come.[15]

In the year following the summit agreement, the CCCO was withered by its increasingly ineffectual role in the implementation process, the withdrawal of King from Chicago, and the loss of that slender thread of hope which had kept the movement going during other periods of low morale and apparent futility. That loss was dramatically symbolized by Albert Raby's resignation as the leader of the CCCO. The CCCO tried to function for yet another year or so, but it never had more than a semblance of its former vitality. Its hold on life was finally severed by the loss of its own motivating principle and perspective: that de facto segregation was the problem and that the American creed pointed the way normatively to its resolution. The American dilemma had suffered the fate of cognitive dissonance. De facto segregation was compromised by its inability to specify affirmative duties. The civic credo had triumphed politically. The collapse of the civil rights coalition was news, but the moral failure of the civic credo was not. Expectations had been lowered and so had civic standards.[16]

We have presented here a study in comparative and competitive moral ideas, colliding in that no-man's-land where moral ideas intersect with political rhetoric, on the one hand, and with religious appeals, on the other. Given the normative centrality of the American creed for both the civic credo and the de facto segregation reading of the issue of race, it was inevitable that the proponents of each would battle just as hard for justification as they did for power and that an important part of their conflict would become involved in

362

theological appeals to the "true" nature of the civil religion; that is, what did the American creed actually require by way of a body politic to represent it? At a high level of abstraction and emotional intensity, that was the issue.

Both sides had some difficulty bridging the gap between that high level of abstraction and the actual facts of the matter. The proponents of the issue of de facto segregation had a difficult time convincing the general public that the facts they cited had the general significance they claimed. The proponents of the civic credo, however, cast in the role of defenders of the faith, had a much easier time convincing the general public that the immediate facts did not matter because, given time, all would be well. Religiously, the civic credo had the upper hand in the competition for political rhetoric, for it had taken its stand on the appeal of the power of positive thinking, what William James called "the religion of healthy mindedness." Religiously, the proponents of the issue of de facto segregation had a more profound but more demanding position in the competition for political rhetoric, for they had taken their stand on the human capacity for critical transcendence, on the ability of people to stop wasting their substance in riotous living and to say, "We do not have to live like this. We are better than this." But this meant that they were cast as the critics while the proponents of the civic credo were cast as the defenders, not just of the status quo but of the nation's deepest values, the American creed.

In this conflict, therefore, even though the proponents of the issue of de facto segregation fully believed that they were defending the American creed, they were constrained to undertake strategies of protest, to raise up the ugly facts of life along and behind the color line, to question the good faith of the civic elite, and ultimately to disturb the civic peace in an effort to open the possibilities of critical transcendence. The proponents of the civic credo, occupying positions of authority, undertook strategies of denial in the face of protest, of reassurance that progress was coming in the face of ugly facts, of questioning the motives and good sense of the protesters, and of short-term efforts toward conciliation whenever the civic peace was disturbed and the police were not able to restore calm.

The general public was much disturbed by this conflict, and ultimately public opinion polarized along racial lines. As it turned out, the high degree of support for eliminating de jure segregation was not transferred to the issue of de facto segregation. The civic credo, which had been a preserve of the elites, became a popular interpretation of what was best. The claims arising from the de facto segregation reading of the issues had mobilized white liberal and black energies for a time, but after 1966 or 1967 they lost their power to polarize and magnetize. It was no longer clear what they demanded or where they led. The civic credo functioned to obscure the resurgence of racist realism, and the civic elite, whatever their response to black power rhetoric, had no problem accommodating to black power projects. Those demands could always be compromised by appeals to the ethnic calculus, and that was Chicago's home field.

With this shift in the framework of the issue, the civil rights movement disappeared as a factor in civic life. The civil religion adopted the theology of virtuous ethnic diversity. The power of positive thinking had swamped the capacity for critical transcendence, a slender reed at best. Some of the same church leaders who in 1963 had been certain that the prophetic will of God was "desegregation now" were proclaiming by 1966 the transcendent imperative for black power, but in the context of the resurgent racist realism that was an ambiguous imperative. What had been acted out religiously in the course of the civil rights movement was similar to the conflict that had been going on in the churches: critical transcendence versus the power of positive thinking. The outcome was similar in both places. Whatever its merits religiously or morally, positive thinking was the effective political rhetoric.

The consequence for the civil rights movement was its termination. The consequence for the issue of race we take up in the next chapter.

CHAPTER FOURTEEN

The Rule of the Color Line

The triumph of the civic credo sealed the fate of the civil rights movement in Chicago, but it left the relentless dynamics of the color line completely unaltered. It rationalized but did not resolve the issue of race. Rather, the civic credo obscured and mystified what was actually happening as the color line claimed five more blocks per week in its sweep across the metropolitan area. Under those conditions, the idea that time and the normal functioning of institutions would promote progress toward equality for all in an atmosphere of civic calm was actually an impediment to cogent thinking as well as to timely action.

The collapse of the civil rights movement in Chicago had a national significance which is difficult to state with precision. It was a defeat all around that was claimed as a victory by the leadership of both the civic elite and the Chicago Freedom Movement. The civil rights movement in Chicago ended at the same time the national movement did. The emotional and intellectual collapse, so strenuously denied in the summit agreement, was decisive for everything that was to follow in Chicago and across the country.

The civic credo functioned less as a body of ideas about what to do than as a platform for denying the seriousness of the situation—the same function it had always had. Segregation was still the rule, but the will to end it seemed to have been broken. Ideas ceased to function as means for channeling emotions into social purposes that could be deliberately pursued; instead, they began to function as mere statements of sensibility, expressions of feeling, identity badges signifying new cohesions formed in the vacuum left by the dissolution of New Deal liberalism. In the name of positive thinking, denial supplanted affirmation as the driving social force. If defeat could be victory, then events could mean anything. Patterns of words were substituted for configurations of facts as the sources of social orientation.

In this chapter, we shall discuss the consequences of this development for the social structure and for the accepted wisdom of what was at issue. In the next chapter we shall discuss the impact of this development on the national sense of normative direction. There we shall deal with the question of what

365

became of the American creed. In the final chapter we shall propose some directions for meaningful change, attempting to take seriously both the state of the social structure and the normative resources for the pursuit of democratic social change.

THE COLOR LINE AS AN INSTITUTION:
AN INTELLECTUAL PROBLEM

The long-term consequence of the collapse of the civil rights movement and the triumph of the civic credo for the social structure was the unchallenged rule of the color line. The long-term consequence for the accepted wisdom about what was at issue was the resurgence of racist realism, the rationalization of the undisputed rule of the color line.

This color line is no mere figure of speech. It is an institution that functions both as a distributive rule and as a symbolic universe. That is why time and the normal functioning of institutions will never lead to a future beyond the color line. Only social change deliberately pursued will do that. To understand why this is so, in this chapter, we will examine the color line as a distributive rule; in the following chapter, we will address it as a symbolic universe.

The failure to understand the color line as one of America's institutions was fatal to the civil rights movement in Chicago, but it was a failure of both the civic elite and the movement's leadership, and it was present in the scholarship as well as the leadership. It was a pervasive and consequential failure, a cultural flaw, and a religious problem. This is a large claim that cannot be proved in a few pages. We can, however, clarify the scope, the limits, and the basis of this claim by bringing the color line into focus as an institution that has identifiable characteristics and predictable consequences.

Probably the most peculiar fact about the issue of race in American life has been its persistence and resilience. There is no period of our history, from the earliest days to the most recent moments, when race has not been a source of social conflict or has not entered materially and consciously into the social, cultural, and institutional outcomes by which we periodize our history.

No other issue of social conflict has both required and eluded political resolution in every period of our national life. Slavery, Reconstruction, Jim Crow, urban ghettos, metropolitan color lines—we have lived with all of them, approaching each one first as a solution to the issue of race and then as the very embodiment of that issue. We have spent our history defending and then attacking these supposed solutions, but in the end we find ourselves as deeply in bondage to this issue as ever.

Although there are important differences between and among these faulty solutions to the issue of race, they have certain common and continuous dimensions, which are striking in their transcendence of time, place, circumstance, region, and prevailing economic structure, and in their adaptability to the shifting patterns of political power, community structure, cultural symbolism, and interpretation. In short, the issue of race appears to have had a life of its own in our culture, dominating finally even the efforts to resolve it. It appears to be one of the more continuous institutions with which we live and by which we shape our destiny.

The notion of institution can have either of two meanings. An institution may be a highly specific structure of enduring relationships, behaviors, and functions, such as slavery, Jim Crow, the urban ghetto, the nuclear family, or even the Department of State or the U.S. Supreme Court. An institution may also be a highly generalized structure of relationships, behaviors, and functions, such as the color line (which includes slavery, Jim Crow, and the urban ghetto), the family (which may be nuclear, extended, communal, or single-parent), the foreign policy community (which may include any number of actors and within which the Department of State may play a variable role), and the rule of constitutional law (of which the U.S. Supreme Court is, in some ways, but the tip of the interpretive iceberg). At this more generalized level, institutions are best described by the rules they embody and enact in their various particularizations. At this more generalized level, we can tell whether institutions are changing by observing whether the rules they impose are changing.

To understand institutions, therefore, it is important to grasp the rules they impose on those who come under their sway as well as the specific relationships, behaviors, and functions that embody them. The rules tend to be more durable than the specific relationships, behaviors, and functions. Institutional change can take place at either or both of these levels and, without an empirically adequate description of the general rules at the heart of an institution, it is extremely difficult to assess either stability or change in institutions. The issue of race provides a striking illustration of this problem and, as the civil rights movement collapsed, this distinction became an important consideration in understanding its demise.

If we take the three major specific institutionalizations of the issue of race in our history—slavery, Jim Crow, and the metropolitan areas—it is obvious that they differ enormously at the level of specific relationships between blacks and whites. Slavery was based on direct paternalistic oppression, Jim Crow on direct antagonistic oppression, and the metropolitan color line feeds on the indirect oppression that results from the combination of public civility, private discrimination, and ritual avoidance. They also differ enormously at the level of specific behaviors. From the perspective of what is required of blacks, slavery demands total submission in the presence of whites, Jim Crow demands consenting humiliation in the presence of whites, and the metro-

367

politan area structures a minimization of interaction between blacks and whites and some conflict of interest when these interactions cannot be avoided. At the level of functions, the differences become more difficult to describe because functions border on generalized rules. Still, there are particular differences. In slavery the function of blacks was to make money directly for whites. In Jim Crow at least part of the function was to certify status for poor whites. In the metropolitan areas, the function of blacks is much more ambiguous or polymorphous, for they provide both an underclass to absorb the inelasticities of the employment market and a vanguard middle class to symbolize the threats to white middle-class longing for economic security.

The differences between slavery, Jim Crow, and the metropolitan area as peculiar institutions could be elaborated forever. There are, nonetheless, some general rules that are common to all these differences. Arriving at an empirically adequate statement of these general rules has been one of the most vexing moral, intellectual, and political problems posed by the issue of race over the years. Lacking such a statement, we have more than once become disoriented both in our efforts to assess the relevant continuities and to project the relevant changes that would free us from bondage to this issue. It is, therefore, morally, intellectually, and politically crucial to derive an understanding of the issue of race which is at once both sufficiently general to cover the changing relationships, behaviors, and functions that have characterized this institution and yet sufficiently empirical to guide the contemporary search for relevant details and possible alternatives. This is what we have tried to do with our notion of the color line as a multidimensional institution.

Both now and in the past it appears that the institution of the color line has been both the cause and the outcome of the following set of dynamic dimensions:

1. continued or increasing separation of the races;
2. continued or increasing subordination of black people in their access to
   a. basic life needs,
   b. high-quality public institutions, and
   c. structures of political freedom and power;
3. continued or increasing denial of ordinary status to nonwhites within the social order and within the culture;
4. continued or increasing abasement and fear of nonwhite life by the dominant white society;
5. continued or increasing legitimacy for, expectation of, and recourse to violence in the making and keeping of the color line and as a consequence of it; and
6. continued or increasing rationalization of these dimensions, their consequences, and their claim to a future.

368

It is not possible to say in a few words exactly how we have derived this statement of the issue. The experience of the civil rights movement, narrated in Part II of this book, suggested each of the dimensions. Our examination of the development of the interracial structure in Chicago in Chapter 2 served to clarify and confirm the reality of these interacting dimensions. In this chapter our social analysis of how these dimensions actually function as a unified institution underlines their characteristics as a set of rules. Finally, as we shall show in the next chapter, anthropological considerations, both moral and religious, also enter into the structuring and specification of these dimensions and illuminate their cultural meaning and political functioning as a set of rules.

Some years ago, Dorothy Emmet pointed out that although the social and behavioral sciences are committed to the understanding of society as a "going concern," they are less than likely to realize that "to study human society . . . is to take account of conduct which is partly at least rule directed." It is not "just regularities, but regulated conduct" of which they give some account; and their functional and structural explanations, therefore, assume a proto- or quasi-moral status, at least to the extent that they render as reasonable any particular regulation that "is explicitly seen as a *moral* rule" by the population at large.[1]

It is interesting that the only entry on "rules" in the *International Encyclopedia of the Social Sciences* pertains to the notion "rules of the game" and discusses its doubtful applicability to the operations of democracy, except perhaps as a tool for understanding the behavior of legislative bodies.[2] Nor has the idea that social structures function as behavioral rules been much explored in the meantime; but social structures can "rule" events quite as much as and frequently much more than individuals, government agencies, or other purpose-pursuing agencies. (We know, for instance, that social class can function this way although we could certainly use much more empirical data and conceptual clarification on how that actually works.)

According to the *Oxford English Dictionary,* the verb "to rule" means "to control, guide, direct, exercise sway or influence over (a person, his actions, life, etc.)" and the noun is "a principle, regulation, or maxim governing individual conduct."[3]

To say, then, that the color line is a rule is to affirm that it is not just a description of regularities in human conduct, but that it is an institution which regulates such human conduct and behavior as comes under its sway. It is not just a generalization of regularities; it is itself a regulative reality, an active rule commanding the allegiance of "common sense," distributing "rewards" for obedience, and inflicting "costs" for noncompliance.

369

AN INSTITUTION UNOBSERVED: A POLITICAL PROBLEM

The collapse and the aftermath of the civil rights movement as an organized force for change in the structure of American race relations is a case study in the power of this color line to dominate events, to undermine any sense of alternative, and to paralyze the powers of empirical as well as moral analysis. This intellectual paralysis is, perhaps, the most surprising of the powers exerted by the color line, and as long as it persists the power of the color line to dominate events and undermine any sense of alternative remains unchallenged.

In the absence of a comprehensive concept of the interacting and mutually reinforcing dimensions of the color line, each of these dimensions—the separation, the subordination, the denial of ordinary status, the dynamics of fear and abasement, the violence, the endless rationalizations—presents itself in some shocking event as the key to the problem. Yet each of these dimensions, when attacked in abstraction from others, leads to an impasse, thus undermining the sense of alternative and promoting the idea, so central to racist realism, that nothing can be done to change this color line.

Intellectual bafflement was certainly not the only problem that developed in the mid-1960s, but it was a major problem and one that was completely unexpected. Until the Chicago campaign, it had seemed that new levels of commitment to well-established ideas, not new ideas, were needed to set the country on the path to racial justice. Over and over, Martin Luther King, Jr., and others had bemoaned the "paralysis of analysis," by which they meant that both the problem and its solutions were well known. Insofar as Jim Crow was the problem, they were right, but insofar as the problem was the color line drawn across the metropolitan areas of America, they—and the rest of the country with them—were not right.

New ideas were needed. They have not come easily, and what they should be is still debatable. We propose the concept of the color line as an institution that functions both as a distributive rule and as a symbolic universe. We will illustrate the comprehensiveness of this concept by recounting some of the problems and events that came to prominence in the aftermath of the civil rights movement. As we shall see, when liberals and the Supreme Court lost their way amid the uncharted dimensions of the post–Jim Crow color line, a resurgent racist realism arose to make peace with the color line in its metropolitan form.

In the first instance, the collapse of the civil rights movement was a problem for liberals of various sorts. There was enormous reluctance to accept the demise of the movement, especially by those liberals whose primary focus had been on the problems of Jim Crow. From their perspective, the civil rights movement came to a culmination, not a collapse, in the mid-1960s. The pas-

370

sage of the 1964 Civil Rights Act and the 1965 Voting Rights Act, along with President Johnson's Great Society programs, seemed to promise a better future for blacks and to prove that deep in the American character there were indeed wells of decency and democratic ideals that could be brought to the fore in shaping a better future for all. Much had been accomplished in a short period of time, and people of this persuasion saw the events in Chicago as a classic case of trying to go too far, too fast, with too little preparation. For them, it was a time to regroup forces for change at a new plateau of commitment. It was a time, not to push for new commitments, but to make good on the important ones that had been made, to follow through on the abolition of Jim Crow—a large agenda with much still to be accomplished. Had the Jim Crow system been the only form of the color line in America, this view would have been adequate.[4]

Unfortunately, those liberals whose primary focus was on the massive and growing urban ghettos saw little prospect for relevant change and saw the civil rights movement as falling into a state of collapse rather than enjoying a moment of culmination. From their perspective, the ugly emotions displayed in the streets of Chicago, the superficiality of the summit agreement, and the retreat even of the Johnson administration from the Civil Rights Act of 1966 seemed to guarantee a national retreat from the pursuit of racial equality and to prove that the American creed was more a ritual incantation said over sores it could not cure than a social force capable of shaping a future.[5]

Those who were impressed with the culmination of the civil rights movement had trouble seeing the collapse. To them it was a time for revising strategy and tactics and keeping the coalition together.[6] Those who saw the collapse of the civil rights movement as the key to the future had trouble even acknowledging that there had been a culmination in any important sense. To them it was imperative to shed the deceptive illusion of progress and face the fact, as Raby stated, that nothing had changed.

Thus both the culmination and the collapse of the civil rights movement posed a crisis for American liberalism. In either case the appeal to the American creed to provide legitimacy and direction for change was a fading prospect. One side said it was time to stop pushing for further change while the other said that no meaningful change had taken place. Where did that leave liberal egalitarianism, which had been the common ground between movement and mainstream politics?

Liberals had acted on the premise that equality before the law, equality in the marketplace of opportunity, and equality of human dignity were shared national values and that their pursuit would be adequate to produce interracial justice; but the weaknesses of this platform were everywhere apparent as this vision of liberty and justice for blacks in a progressively open society collided with the recalcitrance of the color line in the metropolitan areas. The norms of

371

this liberalism seemed at odds with social reality and the drift of political power.

The cities posed a new set of problems in which race was one of the most tangled issues, but neither the liberals nor anyone else had a developed agenda for these problems, as they had for the Jim Crow problems. Indeed, they did not even have a clear concept of what these new problems were. Many liberals had believed that urbanization itself would be a solution to the problems of racial discrimination and antagonism rather than the massively institutionalized racial problem that the metropolitan areas had become.

The shift in attention from the regional peculiarities of the Jim Crow system to the massive facts of the metropolitan areas involved a good deal more than an extension of the strategies developed to oppose de jure segregation.[7] De facto segregation did not, it turned out, begin to express the social and cultural seriousness of the situation.

The events in Chicago dramatically showed that even as the commitment to abolish Jim Crow took definite shape at the national level, this achievement, momentous as it was, did not promise the end of the color line. Instead of a moment of rejoicing and reunion, it became a moment of divisive shock.

When ghetto riots erupted in more than two dozen of America's major cities during 1967, President Johnson appointed the National Advisory Commission on Civil Disorders, headed by Governor Otto Kerner of Illinois, to investigate the causes of this shocking outbreak of violence. The expectation was widespread that its sources would be found in the pathologies of the black community. Liberals expected the commission to identify sociological pathologies; conservatives expected to find criminal ones. Instead, the Kerner commission, as it came to be called, identified white racism as the underlying cause of the trouble: "This is our basic conclusion: Our nation is moving toward two societies, one black, one white—separate and unequal. . . . What white Americans have never fully understood—but what the Negro can never forget—is that white society is deeply implicated in the ghetto. White institutions created it, white institutions maintain it, and white society condones it."[8]

This conclusion suggested that the disorder in the streets was principally symptomatic of the disorder in institutions. Sad to say, however, the report would have been quite different if this thesis had been the organizing principle of its work rather than an unsupported conclusion. Which institutions were implicated in the maintenance and extension of the ghetto? How did they function? How had the racist pathology of the social order come to share an identity with the destiny of our American cities? Because the report did nothing to advance answers to such questions, its discussion of white racism was doomed to a vagueness that continued to veil the realities of the color line to which the conclusion gave such dramatic testimony.

372

The report of the Kerner commission did not significantly affect national action on the issue of race, and no changes in the racial condition of the society can be traced to either the existence or the recommendations of that body. The language of "two societies" and "white racism" was emotionally highly charged, but it made no contribution to either urban or racial policy thinking. The report was principally an official recognition and certification of the unspecified depth and seriousness of the issue of race. Because this language of two societies and white racism was so lacking in its point of reference and explanatory power, it was also void of normative direction and guidance. In the end, the doctrine of two societies weighed in on the side of white racism as a fate beyond the power and wisdom of human effort to alter. At the very moment when the civil rights movement was being deflated by the experience of futility, failure, and collapse, a commission of the official society was locating the blame in the white community and calling it white racism but was utterly baffled about what could or should be done to change it.

The Kerner report might have achieved no standing at all had its publication not been followed so closely by the murder of Martin Luther King, Jr., on 4 April 1968. King's public career had represented the hopeful and determined pursuit of purpose in the midst of racial injustice; his death symbolized the loss of that purpose. Only the injustice remained. With the report of that bullet in Memphis, suddenly the gates were blown open on the gathering American racial chaos. And the Kerner report, with its unexpurgated (but also unexegeted) doctrine of white racism was within easy reaching distance for this desperate moment in search of a rhetoric to redeem itself from absurd meaninglessness.

Racism, white racism, institutionalized white racism, northern urban institutionalized white racism—it all came out in the rhetoric of accusation, as a eulogy to King and the movement he had once symbolized for so many. It was like a second Selma, except there was no Martin Luther King, Jr., and there was no movement and there was no clear idea of what to do next.

Only the Supreme Court seemed to be able to maintain a sense of the empirical relevance of segregation and of normative direction in the face of it, and this was because the Court was still addressing itself to situations of de jure segregation.

In 1954, the United States Supreme Court had taken its stand on the constitutional and empirical importance of desegregation. That "separate is inherently unequal" was a statement both of principle and of fact. The "separation" at issue in *Brown* was a legislatively mandated and publicly enforced inequality. In ordering the rectification of this inherently unequal separation in 1955, the Court left it to the discretion of local authorities to determine just what affirmative duties would be entailed.

For this stance, the Court was criticized from all sides. Herbert Wechsler

373

accused the Court of trying to enforce integration, which he favored, but he could think of no "neutral principles" to legitimize the Court's pursuit of it. Raoul Berger accused the Court of trying to force changes for which only the ballot box could provide legitimacy. Alexander Bickel accused the Court of importing a progressive egalitarian view into the Constitution and then subjecting the nation to a "continuous assault of moral imperatives."[9] Much more intemperate charges were made too.

It is true that in ordering desegregation without specifying affirmative duties to achieve it, the Court had not taken either a morally or a legally complete stand; but in denying legitimacy to Jim Crow arrangements, it seems that the Court had taken a constitutionally sound stand even if it did leave many questions unresolved. It should be remembered that there were and are empirical as well as constitutional questions involved in desegregation. It is well to recall also that distinguished voices were raised in defense of the Court's position. Archibald Cox and Ronald Dworkin both defended the Court's legal wisdom as well as its humanity in *Brown* and the subsequent school desegregation decisions.[10] In *Brown*, the Court placed the full weight of constitutional interpretation and its constitutional authority against the Jim Crow system of the color line. Another way to state the case could be that, in *Brown*, the Court withdrew the weight of constitutional interpretation and its constitutional authority from the separate but equal doctrine, as enunciated in *Plessy* v. *Ferguson* (1896).

In this endeavor, the Court was finally joined by both the federal executive and legislative branches in the civil rights legislation of the 1960s. By 1968, in *Green* v. *County School Board of New Kent County*, the Court was prepared to put aside its cautious invocation of "all deliberate speed" and to declare that school boards had "an affirmative duty to come forward with a plan that promises realistically to work *now*."[11]

By the mid-1970s, the Court, its constitutional interpretation, and its constitutional authority had prevailed over the Jim Crow system of legislatively mandated inequality, even in the face of a newly reluctant executive branch. The strength of the Supreme Court's course of action vis-à-vis Jim Crow was the strength of the desegregationist position: an unwavering focus on the behaviors that had to stop. That was enough, given a coalescence of political support for the Court's constitutional interpretation, to break the rule of Jim Crow. When in *Swann* (1971) the Court allowed busing as a remedy for dual school systems, it may have seemed to some as "the final step in the South's subjugation."[12] In fact, it was the final step in the subjugation of the Jim Crow system which the South had built under the shadows cast by *Plessy* v. *Ferguson*. The processes set in motion by *Brown* had a regional focus because the Jim Crow system of schools, which was the empirical point of reference from

374

Brown to *Swann,* was regionally embedded in seventeen southern states; and the Court's insistence on a constitutional mandate to desegregate those schools was adequate to effect the demise of that system. By 1972, the Supreme Court had substantially made good on its promise in *Brown* to eliminate Jim Crow school systems; and in 1979 the U.S. Commission on Civil Rights reported that it was in states north of the Mason-Dixon line that schools remained at a "high level" of segregation.[13]

Because of a case arising from the Detroit public schools, however, the Court found itself at the national impasse by 1974. In September 1971, the Detroit schools had been found guilty of de jure segregation. After extensive hearings, the federal judge had determined that no plan that was limited to the Detroit schools alone would remedy the situation. Accordingly, he had held additional hearings on proposed metropolitan solutions, thus mixing the issues of de jure and de facto segregation at the point of identifying a remedy. In June 1972, he ordered a plan that involved the Detroit schools and fifty-two suburban school districts—approximately 780,000 students. In December 1972, this ruling was upheld by a three-judge panel of the Sixth Circuit Court of Appeals. In June, it was upheld by the full Sixth Circuit Court, three members dissenting. In July 1974, the U.S. Supreme Court, by a vote of 5–4, reversed this order on the grounds that only the Detroit Board of Education had actually been found guilty of de jure segregation, and therefore the remedy must be confined to the city itself.[14] The Supreme Court could not find the grounds for a metropolitan remedy, and the local courts could not find the means for a municipal remedy. The courts said, in effect, that they were unable to produce an effective remedy for a proven injustice.[15]

By 1974, however, this impasse was much less shocking in fact than might be supposed in the abstract. By then the civil rights movement was long spent as a force in American life, and both popular perception and the effective framework for national policy had accepted racist realism as the premise of what was at issue and what should be done about it. How this had come about is a story of serious loss in the understanding of what was both descriptively and normatively at issue in the metropolitan areas and in the color line that cut across every one of them.

THE DECLINING SIGNIFICANCE OF LIBERAL IDEAS

Racial separation was an obvious fact of every metropolitan area. Neither time nor the normal functioning of institutions, however, held out any promise that this separation would diminish. Neither the de jure nor

375

the de facto notion of segregation provided a sufficiently empirical understanding of what was at issue in this racial separation. In the absence of an explanatory empirical focus, the normative question was unsettled at a very deep level.

The civil rights movement had been predicated on the sense that this racial separation was wrong, that it was at odds with democratic values; but more than that, the civil rights movement had been driven by a vision of life beyond the color line and a conviction that democratic egalitarian values would prove stronger than the antagonisms of the color line. When this liberal democratic faith was lost in the collapse of the civil rights movement, there opened a political, cultural, and ultimately religious vacuum into which a resurgent racist realism rushed to rationalize the rule of the color line.

Because the weaknesses of the liberal democratic faith were so apparent in the collapse of the civil rights movement, both conservatives and radicals could join in excoriating the liberal democratic faith. From the left, the ideas of the late Malcolm X, his attacks on the liberal faith in America, and his calls for deliberate separatism received new currency. From the right, the Nixon administration attacked the deliberate pursuit of social change and favored a racial policy of "benign neglect." For all their differences, both counseled an acceptance of racial separation.

From Malcolm's point of view, separation was a good idea for blacks. America was not a land of rational ideals at war with irrational attitudes toward blacks, he claimed, not a land that had "better angels" to which appeal could be made. He therefore castigated "integration-mad Negroes" because they did not understand American culture or their position in the world. "Since Western society is deteriorating," he said, "it has become overrun with immorality, and God is going to judge it, and destroy it. And the only way the black people caught up in this society can be saved is not to *integrate* into this corrupt society, but to *separate* from it, to a land of our *own,* where we can reform ourselves, lift up our moral standards, and try to be godly."[16] Race was not an American dilemma. It was the American indictment, the test that showed the American creed for what it really was, a cruel and corrupt white lie.

The Nixon administration led the attack from the right. Daniel P. Moynihan, sometime secretary of health, education and welfare in the Nixon administration, had managed to reverse himself completely since the days when he was an assistant secretary of labor in Lyndon Johnson's Great Society administration. In 1965 he had found "a case for national action," but by 1970 he counseled a stance (it can hardly be called a policy) of "benign neglect."[17] To the extent that there was any theory involved in this stance, it appears to have been that whatever the problem of blacks may be in this society, it is beyond the reach of policy. Time would take care of it. Deliberate change, purposefully pursued, does not seem to work. He counseled the Nixon administration to pursue a program of "lowering expectations," as if their elevation had been the major problem in prior years. Race had become a problem of too much too soon, not an American dilemma. America was great because it was good. The trouble was that blacks received too much attention. They should be thrown back into the ethnic swim.

In spite of their opposing premises about American values, the views of Moynihan and Malcolm X could and did find some common ground in their recourse to the "ethnic analogy." For Moynihan, it was a reason for the retreat from redistributive policies whereas for Malcolm X it provided a model of cohesion and a path to self-respect. "As other ethnic groups have done," he advised, "let the black people whenever possible, however possible, patronize their own kind, hire their own kind, and start in those ways to build up the black race's ability to do for itself. That's the only way the American black man is ever going to get respect. One thing the white man can never give the black man is self-respect! The black man never can be independent and recognized as a human being until he has what they have, and until he is doing for himself what others are doing for themselves."[18] Those words were music in the ears of the Nixon administration. Counsels of self-help had never created an American dilemma.

Malcolm X articulated popular strands of sentiment in the black community. Nixon-Moynihan provided a euphemistic articulation of the popular strains of white sentiments such as those that had been activated by the open housing marches in Chicago. They had in common their sense of the political importance of the racial factor, but both asserted that it was an ethnic factor. In this, they were both assimilable to the civic credo in Chicago.

Both of these positions, like the civic credo, took their stand on the ethnic analogy not only to explain but to justify racial concentration and separation. Malcolm X, the Nixon administration, and the civic credo were united in their claim that ethnic cohesion, far from being a problem, was the key to equality and social dignity. By the late 1960s that idea had been in circulation for a long time. It was popular with blacks as well as whites, but it did not fit the facts very well.

Gunnar Myrdal had discussed this "immigrant analogy" in *An American Dilemma*, but he had shown why it could neither explain nor justify racial separation.

> In trying to reconcile conflicting valuations [between the American creed and minority groups excepted from it] the ordinary American apparently is inclined to believe that, as generations pass on, the remaining minority groups—with certain distinct exceptions which will presently be discussed—will be assimilated into a homogeneous nation. . . . *The Negroes, on the other hand, are commonly assumed to be unassimilable and this is the reason why the characterization of the Negro problem as a minority problem does not exhaust its true import.* . . . Even by their

377

best friends in the dominant white group and by promoters of racial peace and good-will, they are usually advised to keep to themselves and develop a race pride of their own.[19]

Thus Myrdal's understanding of this "anti-amalgamation doctrine" (which we call the denial of ordinary status) explained why the immigrant analogy did not present a true picture of either the causes or the prospects for racial separation.

Subsequent research validated Myrdal's claims in this regard, while simultaneously demonstrating the empirical bankruptcy of the immigrant analogy. Limiting our discussion for the moment simply to the issue of housing, an analysis of census data for 1940–70 provided no evidence that Chicago experienced any significant housing desegregation during this period. In 1940 the index of racial segregation for Chicago was 95.0; in 1950, 92.1; in 1960, 92.6; and in 1970, 93.0—greater than that of any other large northern city. By 1980, this index still stood at 92.0.[20]

Nor can this phenomenon be explained by the fact that blacks were the last immigrant group to arrive in Chicago and that continuing immigration kept them at the bottom of the social ladder. Newer immigrants, for example Puerto Ricans, "were in 1950 of very low status compared to the other immigrant groups, and their residential segregation from native whites of native parentage was the highest of all the immigrant groups." Yet by 1960, "residential dispersion [had] already begun" for Puerto Ricans—and this was not because of social mobility in the usual sense. "On every socio-economic measure," in 1960, "the Puerto Rican population [was] less well off" than the "non-white populations of the city of Chicago"—"it is less educated, of lower income, more crowded, less likely to be homeowners, less well housed, and living in older buildings. Yet Puerto Ricans are significantly less segregated than Negroes." Thus the 1963 article that gave this information, "Is the Negro an Immigrant Group?" concluded with a resounding "No!"[21]

Neither the language of the two societies nor the immigrant analogy proved adequate to express what was happening or what was at stake in the metropolitan areas of America. Each pointed to a partial truth. The racial separation was severe enough to produce something like two societies, but they were both part of a common political and economic system. The problems lay in the relationships between these two societies. The color line joined them together while seeming to keep them apart.

The immigrant analogy, on the other hand, stressed the unifying aspirations in American society without accounting for the rejectionist dynamics of the color line. Each of these ideas, unable to account for the full sweep of the racial issue, became a justification for racial separation. Left and right seemed to coalesce around the idea that racial separation itself was not the problem

378

and perhaps there was some virtue in it after all—a clear case of empirical confusion generating normative confusion.

If the two societies were not the problem and if the immigrant analogy did not express the solution, then what was at issue in race? In a stunning coup de grace, which came after a decade of this impasse, William Julius Wilson offered an interpretation that attempted to discredit any lingering liberal impulses toward racial justice and to co-opt the sensibilities of the left into the concepts and programs of the neoconservative right by announcing "the declining significance of race."

According to Wilson's theory, shifts in the structure of the economy had largely transferred the problems that remained for blacks—and that were vitally important—from race to class. From this perspective, it was not racial injustice that needed national attention but the economic oppression of the late industrial underclass in which blacks, for historical reasons, were overrepresented. Although there is much that could be useful in the analysis which underlies this view, its major message appeared to be that race was not the issue because the direct oppression of blacks by whites was not the fundamental cause of current problems. It had the virtue of pointing out that most blacks were still, for whatever reason, on the wrong side of the "payoff" line. It transferred the policy focus from the problems generated by race to the conditions generated by class.[22] Or, to put the matter bluntly, the color line itself was no problem.

Wilson's criteria for arguing the declining significance of race are similar to Myrdal's rank order of discriminations, which everyone can agree are passé as the live issues between black and white. They were part and parcel of the Jim Crow code, and that code has been broken; but it boggles the mind how the continuing rule of the color line in the economy—which Wilson's argument amply showed—could be construed as a case for the declining significance of race.

THE COLOR LINE AS THE
STRUCTURAL BASIS FOR RACIST REALISM

Certainly the significance of race in the social order has shifted since the heyday of Jim Crow. Nonetheless, race is still very much a factor in American life, more institutional than attitudinal, more collective than interpersonal, more national than regional, and therefore more pervasive than ever. The color line is a definable social structure that functions as a rule and directly challenges the rule of democratic rights wherever it appears. This color line places at issue both the canons of fairness to individuals and the standards for responsible democratic control within the social order generally.

The first problem both for scholarship and for leadership has been to see this color line for what it is, a unified institution that functions as a distributive rule and as a symbolic universe. It is the structural basis for racist realism. When the several dimensions of the color line are not understood as the interacting elements in a unified institution, each of them appears to be a good reason for the continuing rule of the color line; but when the several dimensions are understood in their unified interaction, it is possible to see the color line as the social cause of the problems it is supposed to solve.

The color line is a problem for thought as well as for action as long as efforts to explain it continue to function as justifications for it. That is the essence of racist realism, the pervasive rationalization of the separation, the subordination, the denial of ordinary status, the dynamic of mutual fear and abasement, and the endemic violence of the color line.

It is essential to understand how this rationalization works in order to get a clear view of the unity of the color line, which is the source of its power to dominate events, to undermine any sense of alternative, and to paralyze empirical and ethical analysis. This rationalization works fairly simply even though its consequences are agonizingly complex.

We all know that massive racial separation is the general rule. No individual could possibly feel personally responsible for its existence. It is a structural feature of the world each of us enters. The separation appears to be nothing but a fact, but it is a fact with sweeping consequences for the personal destinies of individuals as well as for the social order generally. It sets the likely terms for personal identities and for interpersonal associations. This separation is so pervasive that, one way or another, it will function as a personal and social principle.

It may function as the simple and apparently innocent principle that people like to live with their own kind. As simple and innocent as that principle may seem, however, it is one of the most serious rationalizations of the color line. It explains the separation as a free act, completely overlooking the coercive and invidious factors that produce the separation. It begs the question of what is meant by "their own kind." This apparently simple and innocent explanation is actually a morally loaded and politically divisive justification for the color line, rooted as it is in the unspoken denial of ordinary status to nonwhites. In plain English "their own kind" means "they are different, they are not like us."

This separation and its implicit moral justifications set the terms for the dramas of interracial interaction. The underlying reality is that it is a derogatory principle, but the immediate reality is that it is a social fact with which black individuals and groups have to live and which they cannot help but turn into a principle of some sort.

380

The black community which is created by this separation has to find ways to counter and deny the morally derogatory principle that is implicit in the separation while still affirming vitality and self-respect in the midst of the immediate reality. Thus begins the search for some form of black power which can effectively challenge the moral insults as well as the material dangers that inhere in the color line. A dilemma arises from having to assert black dignity under the conditions imposed by the color line without thereby either implicitly or explicitly accepting the moral legitimacy of the color line itself.

The white community which is also created by this separation is much more diverse and has other principles than color available for its cohesions, even though the color line as a morally derogatory principle has always originated from the white side of the line. Whereas the black community has the need to assert its dignity without affirming the implicit derogatory principle, whites tend to affirm the separation as a fact while not wanting to take responsibility for its moral implications. It is the blacks, they wish to say, who are always raising the issue of color, thus in effect blaming the blacks for the separation. It is pure rationalization when white support for integration disintegrates in the face of demands for black power. Given the separation, it is inconceivable that any integration could possibly be accomplished without black empowerment.

The separation, however, does not exist in abstraction from the other dimensions of the color line. It sets the stage for "us" and "them" competitive relations in which subordination is the rule for nonwhites. This subordination extends to their access to basic life needs, to high-quality public institutions, and to structures of political freedom and power, thus converting both the destiny and everyday interactions of these groups with the larger society into peculiar policy problems for the public at large.

This subordination is not incidental to the separation. It is an inherent aspect of it. It is how the morally derogatory principle surfaces. It makes clear the discriminatory character of the separation. It is structural discrimination, but it has served as the basis for all sorts of claims of racial inferiority. This subordination, which is regularly documented by the Government Printing Office for all areas of life from infant mortality to longevity, from unemployment to types of employment, from value of housing to commercial ownership, has been just as regularly rationalized in so many ways that it is difficult to name them all. One theory after another claims to find the basis of this inferiority in heredity and intelligence while another claims to find it in character deficiencies of blacks such as poor work habits. Still others claim to find it in institutional deficiencies such as the alleged instability of the black family. These theories rationalize and justify the subordination by locating the problem in some putative defect of the blacks rather than looking at the dis-

381

criminations that impose these deficiencies. The subordination is real, and its consequences for black individuals and black communities are grave, but the causes can never be understood as long as discrimination is put aside in favor of "natural causes." The subordination may be a general rule, but it has moral and not natural causes.

Because it is a general rule, however, its operation has been converted into statistical generalizations. Banks, insurance companies, and realtors at all levels of the industry have converted these statistical generalizations into principles to guide and justify their own operations. To them it seems like realism to which they are only responding, and they are offended that there are people who call this behavior "red-lining" and see it as an active cause of neighborhood disruption.

Nor does the justification stop there. It extends to public institutions as well. The schools, crucial as they are to the children's future possibilities, are but a case in point. For more than thirty years now, plaintiffs have been proving in court that their children are caught in segregated and inferior schools. The conditions that affect these children are systemic to the metropolitan area as a set of interacting institutions, but attempts to remedy the situation on the scale that it exists appear to be forced and artificial resolutions. They will continue to be perceived that way as long as the color line, of which this subordination is such an important dimension, does not appear to be the problem. This subordination in access to high-quality institutions results both from and in subordination in access to political power as well. Within the world of the color line, all this seems natural, merely matter of fact. In the metropolitan areas, the Supreme Court has trouble finding discriminatory intentions at work. It is just the way things are.[23]

Of course, almost half of black teenagers cannot find work. It is just the way things are. When the subordination is considered in abstraction from the other dimensions of the color line, that is the final phrase—"It is just the way things are." Only people who do not want to understand can accept that explanation for anything. Yet because the subordination is so massive and regular, that is the most dangerous of its rationalizations. It cuts off the search for alternative explanations in the name of innocent simplicity. If it is just the way things are, then what could possibly be done about it? That is the perfect rationalization for discrimination. The evil can continue while innocence is maintained, as it always is, at considerable cost to the truth and in the name of being realistic.

The highly visible and massive separation and subordination, then, appear to provide a factual and reasonable basis for the denial of ordinary status. Experience seems to confirm that "those people are different." As a general rule, the status of the group as a policy problem results in the practical denial

382

of ordinary status to any individuals who are seen to fall within it, producing perceptions and interactions that accentuate the ways in which "they" are different.

Those who can take their ordinary status for granted are free to focus on the problems of individual achievement and personal mobility, while those who find ordinary status withheld can never be sure that even their positive achievements will count on their behalf. Enlightened self-interest seems to lie in making the most of this status, which is ascribed on the the basis of color.

This denial of ordinary status is the hidden premise of the separation, but the separation and the subordination are regularly cited as reasons for the denial of ordinary status. Thus it is that one dimension of the color line is rationalized by its association with the other dimensions. This gives the color line the character of a self-fulfilling prophecy of antagonism, inequality, and community-rending encounters. The cycle does not stop there, however. The differences of experience on either side of the color line are cited to justify the discontinuities of status; but these are not morally neutral differences. As a general rule, these accentuated differences are invidious. Each side, as a matter of common sense, defensively attends to what is most dangerous and destructive in the other, thus giving rise to a dynamic of fear and avoidance through which personal experience tends to confirm the mutually feared invidious differences.

Given the separation, the subordination, and the denial of ordinary status, we seem to have a situation in which it makes sense to ask questions of better and worse. Because of the subordination, there is a situation of practical superiority for whites, and this affects the social psychology of race relations and the perceptual structure of the interactions. Whites do get better jobs, housing, schools, public services, and the like, not apparently through any special treatment but (at least as they see it) through working hard as individuals within the system. Their inclination, therefore, is to look for (and to find) special deficiencies in those groups who do not better themselves through working hard as individuals within the system. They focus, not on their own good fortune but on the practical inferiority of others.

This practical inferiority—the statistically demonstrated higher frequency of poverty, family and community disorganization, lower scholastic achievement scores, higher crime rates, and the like—represents everything that Americans want to avoid. Whenever these symptoms appear, they spread an atmosphere of fear, a social psychology of avoidance and threat, and a social dynamic of mutual abasement in which each party, in peering across the color line, sees and provokes and responds to what is worst in the other. In an atmosphere of threat, avoidance becomes the most sensible policy.

But violence becomes the most likely outcome. As a general rule, the dy-

383

namic of mutual fear creates a "legitimate" expectation of violence, which can be turned in almost any direction depending on situational factors—that is, when mutual avoidance succeeds it may be turned inward, but when avoidance breaks down or subordination is challenged, the violence may erupt from either side.

Violence has been endemic to the color line in all its forms—slavery, Jim Crow, and now the metropolitan areas. Nobody wants to live under the daily threat of great bodily harm. Common sense, therefore, dictates that families and businesses have a propelling interest in putting as much distance as possible between themselves and the violence of the color line. Translated into practical alternatives, this means that blacks, for instance, will try to move, if they can, beyond the violence of the ghetto and that whites, if they can, will want to get away from nonwhite areas or, failing that option, will try to prevent the movement of blacks into their areas. Either way, the violence goes on; and the people caught up in it, far frbm having any interest in opposing the color line, seem to have an urgent interest in extending it.

As a general rule, these other rules are interpreted as a function of something else than each other; for example, as functions of natural inequalities, or of historical atavisms, or of capitalistic requirements, or of "neutral" economic developments, or of intergroup relations, ethnocentricity, minority relations, and the like—that is, as anything but an internally coherent, historically continuous, socially causal institutionalized rule in its own right. The attempt to understand the more proximate factors that go into the making and keeping of these socially effective subrules should not distract us from probing, with full rational seriousness, the internal linkages among them that add up to the rule of the color line.

This search for deeper reasons for the color line leads to its rationalization. It does not require bizarre claims on nature, history, or the divine to rationalize the color line, although these may be invoked and called upon to buttress its defense and provide yet another layer of justification for the color line's claim to a future. As we have seen, however, the simpler rationalizations are both more powerful and more common. In either event, the socially structured and produced facts become reasons for their own existence, values calling for their own continued existence, symbols interpretive of our common humanity, rituals of degradation and justification, and principles governing the forms of association that prevail—from the most intimate to the most corporate, from the utterly private to the most fully public. These all add up to an apparently rational, albeit racist, realism whose moral universe is disguised as nothing but matter-of-fact common sense. These rationalizations prevent us from taking the full measure of this color line because they sustain and support the basic structural and perceptual foundations of the color line itself.

384

THE COLOR LINE AS A DISTRIBUTIVE RULE: WHO BENEFITS?

It is clear from our description that the color line is a discriminatory rule, but is this color line a zero-sum rule, such that any attempt to alter it must deprive whites of their rewards and inflict additional costs on them? That is the common view, and in 1970 it was espoused by the U.S. Commission on Civil Rights in its publication *Racism in America and How to Combat It*. In that view,

> overt racism persists mainly because it still yields significant psychological, economic, and political advantages to millions of white Americans—and even to a few nonwhites. Successful efforts to combat racism will necessarily reduce or eliminate these benefits, thereby imposing a significant cost upon people who now enjoy them. That is why attempts to combat racism have been so strongly resisted. Moreover, such resistance is far more widespread than most people realize because so many whites receive significant but only dimly-realized benefits from the subordination of non-whites.[24]

From this perspective, it appeared that the only hope for change was that white people could be persuaded to forego their benefits for the sake of a wider justice. Although the commission did not say so, the only option to that unlikely prospect is to engage in direct reverse discrimination, which, as we all now sadly know, was the battle of the 1970s. Is the rule of the color line such that those are the options for combating it—either repentant whites or abused whites? If so, it is a rule that, however unjust, seems likely to prevail over either of the proposed remedies.

There can be no doubt that there are substantial zero-sum elements in the rule of the color line, but there is considerable question how these elements are distributed, and substantial matters of truth as well as strategy are involved in the specification of those distributions and the understanding of their operations. There can be no doubt that the rule distributes substantial disadvantages and direct costs to most blacks and to blacks as a group, but it is a real and somewhat empirical question: To which whites does the rule distribute advantage? And are there also identifiable groups of whites to whom the rule distributes disadvantage? The truth about this rule as well as strategic wisdom in the face of it depends on the answers to those two questions.

To take but one sphere in which the rule of the color line continues to distribute disadvantage to blacks as a group, the employment market, what do we find? "If you examine the employment position of blacks," according to Lester Thurow,

> there has been no improvement and perhaps a slight deterioration. Black unemployment has been exactly twice that of whites in each decade since World War II. And the 1970's are no exception to that rule. Whatever their successes and failures, equal

385

opportunity programs have not succeeded in opening the economy to greater employment for blacks. Given this thirty-year history, there is nothing that would lead anyone to predict improvements in the near future. To change the pattern, there would need to be a major restructuring of existing labor markets.[25]

But a restructuring of existing labor markets simply for the purpose of benefiting blacks, especially if it must be done to the disadvantage mostly of whites, is beyond the range of political wisdom as well as political possibility. If all whites are threatened by policies and programs aimed at improving the opportunities and the performance of blacks in the labor market or in the institutional arenas of education, politics, and the like, there will be no such policies and programs—even though there may be some annual ritual of swearing legislative and executive intent.

It may be, however, that this very view of the matter, that blacks can be advantaged only by threatening disadvantage of most whites, is a further extension of the rule of the color line rather than an opening of alternatives to it. It is not, after all, so easy to say exactly which whites benefit most and most directly from the rule of the color line. That some do is certain. And it does not help the empirical task of identifying them when the air is full of mass confessions of white guilt, antiphonated with hysterical protestations of white innocence. The fear of the color line is empirically much more solid and general among whites than are the benefits of it.

The disadvantages imposed on whites by the rule of the color line appear not to have been widely explored; and yet, in a curious way, these may be the key not only to the truth about the rule of the color line but also to the directions in which to look for strategic alternatives. In the rule of the color line, however, it is not an easy matter to identify, let alone to isolate, the disadvantages that flow to whites from its operations because of the dynamic of fear which is such an essential dimension of it.

When fear prevails, the rational calculation of advantage and disadvantage is radically distorted, the more so whenever we have a situation in which experience tends to confirm the legitimacy of the fear. In classic cases of paranoia, for instance, we know that the paranoid is rarely wrong; people do not like him/her. It is the paranoid's sense of causality that is distorted because he/she cannot see that it is his/her own behavior that provokes the feared and despised rejection of others. We also know from the study of social situations that it is much easier to create a dynamic of fear than it is to bring it to a successful halt.

We live in a culture that is institutionally committed to the calculation of costs and benefits as an essential part of rational problem-solving; but we find that this methodology tends to break down whenever substantial elements of fear enter the equation—as in the color line or nuclear power—because there arises substantial dispute, indeed genuine confusion, as to which are the costs

386

and which the benefits. This may be one of the reasons why so little attention has been paid to the disadvantages imposed on whites by the rule of the color line, and conversely, why so little hard evidence has been forthcoming on which whites actually benefit the most and the most directly from the rule of the color line. Only the disadvantages to blacks appear to have been clear and distinct, and even on that score, there have been recurrent arguments that perhaps blacks, if they were savvy, could turn the rule of the color line to their advantage.

Still, it seems possible to identify some serious disadvantages and heavy costs which are imposed on whites, sometimes selectively and sometimes as a whole, by the rule of the color line. For instance, whenever the rule of the color line is being extended—in the housing market, the schools, the economy—whites as well as blacks are caught up in the violence as its victims and not simply as its perpetrators. By then, of course, it is virtually too late to create alternatives. It is a moot question whether the dynamic of fear causes or is caused by the violence. Whenever the one appears in reality, the other becomes an immediate prospect. Although this dynamic of mutual fear permeates the rule of the color line, it hardly appears to be advantageous to anyone, except those who know (or think they know) some way to exploit it for financial or political gain; but again, this can be done only at the expense of some whites. Nonetheless, it seems clear that it is not whites generally but particular whites and some few blacks who benefit materially from this dynamic of fear.

We have turned entire cities over to this dynamic of fear and avoidance and constant threat. In restricting the movements of others, most whites have lost their own ability to come and go freely. They end up abandoning and buying property and paying and receiving prices based on the proximity of that property to the color line. So much for the rights of private property under the rule of the color line. There are streets on which most whites fear to drive. There are schools, restaurants, theaters, parks, and museums to which they stop going. Even the freedom of association is surrendered as churches and other centers of community activity break under the strain of strife and flight. None of these appear to be advantageous. To the people caught up in these dynamics, the consequences appear to be forced on them. Even libertarians know that fear and freedom cannot coexist. Where the one rules, the other must be put to flight. Everything about the color line is forced, and it does not start with busing—Nixon et al. to the contrary notwithstanding.

Nor does the denial of ordinary status to blacks appear to provide much benefit to most whites. In a competitive society such as ours, in which so much depends on achievement, luck, and the quest for stable private satisfactions, the systematic ascription of basic difference to others seems more like a guaranteed source of threat and resentment than a guarantee of belonging. In

387

creating an "us or them" atmosphere, the color line may obscure the more discriminate perception of actors, actions, and consequences that are unsettling in their effects on everyday life, rather like George Orwell's Snowball in *Animal Farm*.

It may be thought, though, that the disadvantages of the violence, the fear, and the denial of ordinary status are more than counterbalanced by the clear economic, social, and political advantages of the subordination of blacks; but even here the case is not as clear as the rule of the color line and its associated roving bands of racial realists would have it. It is simply not true that subordination of the access of some to basic life needs, high-quality public institutions, and structures of political freedom and power thereby assures to the many an increased access to these goods. The case can be made, on orthodox grounds, that the costs of maintaining subordinated populations inflict dramatically depressing opportunity costs on the nonsubordinated populations, too. This case was made in the 1960s in the A. Philip Randolph *Freedom Budget*, and it has been made more recently in Lester Thurow's *Zero-Sum Society*.[26]

By the same token, the alleged benefits of separation are necessarily purchased at considerable cost to those whites who are caught up in the dynamics of the ever-moving color line. They find their personal and communal lives disrupted yet decisively cut off from any sources of public support that could prevent their losses. They are truly harmed, often physically, always emotionally and economically.

In calling attention to these disadvantages which accrue to whites from the rule of the color line, it is not our intention to argue that "whites have it just as bad." The point is simply to establish the full sweep of this rule in its empirical consequences as a preparation for assessing the full sweep of its moral consequences.

What was lost in the collapse of the civil rights movement was any sustained pursuit of the full sweep of the empirical reality, the moral foundations, and the public consequences of the continued rule of the color line. If this color line is what the issue of race is about, then its significance as a force in American life is certainly not declining. What has declined since the mid-1960s is any comprehensive vision of what is at stake in submitting to the rule of this color line.

The normative problems posed by this color line are twofold: first, seeing through the justifications that inhere in the operation of the color line itself as we have done in this chapter, and second, establishing alternative moral claims that can justify remedial policies on a scale appropriate to what is at issue in the operation of this color line. Unless this color line is a problem of justice, it is not a problem but only a possibly peculiar arrangement by which Americans choose to order a part of their lives. But we can no longer posit, as the civil rights movement plausibly could and did, a unified American creed which is clear, unambiguous, and definite in its opposition to this color line. We turn to this problem in the next chapter.

388

CHAPTER FIFTEEN

American Creeds in Competition:

A Problem of Faith and Justice

The collapse of the civil rights movement was accompanied by a moment of acrimonious confusion as to what the deepest values and ideals of American life are and should be. It is easy in the heat of such moments to take values and ideals lightly, to focus on the confusion and its attendant ironies and absurdities, and to lose track of the profound truth that entire communities, like individuals, cannot help but embody some values and ideals even in the midst of confusion and disorientation—values and ideals by which they will be judged by others, whether they want to be so judged or not.

The pursuit of justice in the community is not, after all, a part-time occupation or sometime thing. It is the everyday reality of every human community, and it has everything to do with what life is like for the community as a whole as well as for the groups and individuals who live there.

From the beginning to the end, the civil rights movement was based on a perception and conviction that the deepest values and ideals of American life were a settled matter and were well expressed in the Declaration of Independence: "We hold these truths to be self-evident, that all men are created equal, that they are endowed by their Creator with certain unalienable rights, that among them are Life, Liberty, and the pursuit of Happiness." Myrdal had properly called these values and ideals the American creed. It did not assert, "We happen to be a people who believe these things." It asserted that these values and ideals were in the nature of things, were God-given, were unalienable. It was, in this sense, a serious religious affirmation.

This American creed, as it turned out, was not "expressive and definite in practically all respects for the Negro problem" in the way that Myrdal had supposed. It is true that he had reservations about just how expressive and definite this American creed was when applied to economic matters or to the issues of interpersonal intimacy. Maybe that left the outcome of claims for equal access to schools, housing, and jobs doubtful. If so, the American creed suffers from a debilitating permissiveness with regard to the actual dimensions and consequences of the color line.

There may be an indefiniteness in the values and ideals of the American creed, but there is nothing indefinite about the color line that is drawn across each and every one of our metropolitan areas in the continental United States. Nor does this color line seem to lack for justifications that range all the way from "It is just the way things are" to "It is just about the way things ought to be." There are, in post–civil rights movement America, very few voices saying that we ought to forge a future for ourselves free of the color line. Since there were so many voices saying that during the civil rights movement—it was the dream at the Washington Monument and at the Washington Park YMCA, where the CCCO met—its absence requires some explanation.

What became of the American creed in the midst of the civil rights movement and its aftermath? Did it simply fail to produce the justice that it promised? Did it turn out to be little more than a pious wish? Did it come up against a stronger social force than itself? Was there more confusion than was thought about just what it did promise?[1]

DuBois, Myrdal, the Warren Court, Martin Luther King, Jr., Lyndon Baines Johnson, Albert Raby, and most of the groups in the CCCO had seen the American creed as the expression of a liberal democratic faith, as a promise of equality for all Americans; but the more this promise was pursued, the less clear it was what form of equality this liberal democratic faith promised and what means were legitimate to achieve it. All the adherents of the liberal democratic faith were agreed that the Jim Crow system of using the law to enforce inequalities was wrong; but on the issue of the inequalities of de facto segregation deep differences developed both about what could and what should be done. Some continued to look to negative duties of nondiscrimination as sufficient to open the way to democratic equality. Others believed that black power was the indispensable condition for democratic equality. Still others affirmed that only the integration of blacks into the full range of institutional life could assure democratic equality on a regular basis. Each of these views expressed a different sense of priority about what could and should be done to make good on the promise of democratic equality.[2]

The first answer to the question about what happened to the American creed in the midst of the civil rights movement and its aftermath is that even for those who saw it as an expression of a liberal democratic faith, it was not expressive and definite in when it confronted the full dimensions of the color line. There was not only uncertainty but conflict about what the promise of democratic equality ought to mean in the face of the color line.[3]

This is not, however, the whole answer to the question. Not everyone understood the American creed as the expression of liberal democratic faith. The adherents of the civic credo were as fully convinced as the adherents of the liberal democratic faith that theirs was the true representation of the American creed, that the civic credo expressed the democratic promise of existing American institutions, the promise of peaceful and manageable progress. Whereas the adherents of the liberal democratic faith emphasized equality, the adherents of the civic credo staked everything on liberty. Their notion of progress was largely utilitarian, the promise that more and more people could achieve what they wanted without having to force too many people to put up with things that they did not want.

There is a second answer to the question about what became of the American creed: the adherents of the liberal democratic faith came into conflict with each other and with the adherents of the civic credo. And still that is not the whole answer to the question. The civic credo and the liberal democratic faith were not the only contenders for the meaning of the American creed. There was also what Thomas Luckmann called the "invisible religion," whose adherents were committed to the pursuit of happiness as the major article in the American creed.[4] From this perspective, the American creed promised to respect the transcendent dignity of each and every life and to protect individual autonomy and the circles in which it is fostered—families, friends, churches, neighborhoods, and social clubs. The adherents of the invisible religion may well have been the "swing vote" in the conflict between the adherents of the liberal democratic faith and the adherents of the civic credo.

Each of these, the liberal democratic faith, the civic credo, and the invisible religion, is a socially structured faith in the promise of American life, the American creed—equality of rights, liberty, or the pursuit of happiness—and each looks to aspects of the present as the key to the future.

The civil rights movement had represented a concerted and aggressive pursuit of the liberal democratic faith. When the civil rights movement collapsed, however, this liberal democratic faith lost its inner coherence. Its adherents found themselves in conflict with each other about what should be done, indeed about what could be done, in the face of the color line. Some said the promise for the future lay in black power, others wanted to hold out for integration, and still others wanted to stay the course with desegregation and see where it led. Each of these argued that the promise held out by the others was not only unwise but dangerous to pursue. There were some, of course, who simply walked away and adopted the civic credo or disappeared into the invisible religion. In any case, the collapse of the civil rights movement involved a loss of faith that has left the color line without any serious and comprehensive opposition.

The American creed, once believed to be a unifying force in American life and a source of national direction and inspiration, became the cause of sectarian conflict within the body politic and the occasion for disenchantment with the national direction. The themes of equality, liberty, and the pursuit of happiness were set against one another as partisan banners. The semblance of a common faith expressed by an American creed was lost.

391

A loss of faith may seem like a small thing in a secular age, especially if most people see it as the loss of someone else's faith; and since the loss of liberal faith was most immediately evident in the collapse of the civil rights movement, neither conservatives to the right nor radicals to the left were inclined to mourn it. For them it was a rhetorical opportunity and a political opening of pre-Rooseveltian proportions, and they did not stand paralyzed in the face of the prospect. From both perspectives, the strategy was the same: first get the liberals, then get power.[5]

Racist realism became one of the tools of the trade. The color line was effectively downgraded from an issue to a fact in American life. For the conservatives it was a fact that, if any change at all was required, time and the normal functioning of the market would set right. For radicals it was a fact that proved that the entire system required change. Only the liberals had believed that justice required the deliberate pursuit of democratic social change to break the rule of the color line—and that it could be broken.

The liberals, it turned out, were easy to get, and so was the power. The radical vision of changing the system was domesticated into books that were read by people who were forever "feeling good about themselves," disillusioned about their society, and politically immobilized by their own ideas.[6] Ultimately, in other words, they withdrew into some branch of the invisible religion.[7] Though the conservative vision of "virtuous ethnic diversity" succeeded in retiring the color line from the national agenda, it left the country as a whole more deeply in bondage to the color line than it had been before. King's question of the mid-1960s, "Where do we go from here?" was answered by a different "we" than he had in mind.

The cry of the civil rights movement had been "we shall overcome." It was not clear at the time who "we" was. On reflection it seems that it was those who had faith in the reconstructive powers of liberal democracy. As long as that faith was intact, the problem of justice was in focus. When the civil rights movement collapsed in the mid-1960s, however, it was an open question whether it was the color line or the liberal democratic faith that was on trial at the bar of justice. In effect, both were; and in fact, both still are.

The collapse of the civil rights movement in Chicago and the resurgence of racist realism nationally narrowed the normative vision to only those goals that could be accomplished within the basic terms dictated by the color line. Liberal strategies were debunked as either ineffective ways to move the majority or as denigrating ways to treat the minority.[8] Attempts to force change through nonviolent activities were said to be irrational and counterproductive provocations of white anger.[9] Attempts to force redistribution of educational and economic opportunities were said to pose problems of "reverse discrimination."[10] Attempts to press the rights claims of blacks on a statistically significant scale were said to be policies of "preferential treatment."[11]

Submitting to the rule of the color line, however, does not purchase the peace, the progress, or the personal happiness that it promises. It poses moral problems because the color line is a socially structured distributive rule that violates the well-being of individuals and of the community. It stands in direct opposition to the democratic order of community. It poses religious problems because it violates the transcendent dignity of individual human beings and the covenants of being human. It is a structure of faith that stands in opposition to any of the democratic faiths. The more the color line prevails, the more democracy seems like a pious wish or a cultural lie.

SOCIAL STRUCTURES OF FAITH:
A PROBLEM FOR EMPIRICAL ANALYSIS

We live in the midst of competitive structures of faith. It is essential to understand them as social structures if one is to assess their power potential.

Uncovering those socially embodied and culturally articulated structures of faith is a primary task for social ethics.[12] Raising them up to a level of awareness through disciplined discourse is an important prerequisite to the clarification of the moral problematic. Although it is true that the religious and the moral are not the same, it also seems to be true that each requires the other to be understood and enacted. These structures of faith elude perception not because they are so abstract but because they are so concrete. Their doctrinal assertions are not printed in books. They are imprinted in our institutions. They are embedded in apparent "facts."

It has gone largely unnoticed that the color line is itself a structure of faith, and that has been one of the principal reasons why there has been so much difficulty, both intellectual and political, in coming to terms with it as a factor in American life. This color line, in other words, the institutional basis for racist realism, is one of the American creeds in competition with the others. Like the others, it appeals to aspects of the present as the key to the future, and like the others, it claims to represent values that are in the nature of things and truly unchangeable.

To understand these American creeds and their competitive relations, we have first to understand that they are not simply individual and subjective stances distributed at random among the American people. They are socially structured, action-oriented response stimuli in which facts and meanings are interchangeable. Understanding these structures is as much a descriptive task as understanding the patterns of kinship, the distributions of political and social power, the status system, the class configurations, or the machinations of self-interest in the society.

393

Such structures can be found wherever there are social relations that embody, imply, or evoke principles, values, beliefs, symbols, rituals, and associations that represent claims as to what is the most important consideration in the life of the community. There is no need to assume that there is or can be only one such structure of faith in any given society, certainly not ours. It may be that in archaic communities a monolithic social structure also functioned as a structure of faith; but in modern, pluralistic societies, there is more than one such structure.

There are two ways to approach these structures. The first is to see how the world appears from within their terms. This is not easy to do for those who do not participate in these structures on a believing basis. The second is to see how one of these structures appears from the standpoint of another. Both ways are essential to understanding what these structures really mean.

The ultimate worldly meaning of social structures of faith lies not only in the activities and social relations they engender but also in the comparative standing one of them achieves in competition with others. The advocates of any given structure of faith have always understood this. That is why so much "theological" energy has so often gone into polemics about the opposition.

Whatever the standing of faith claims to the absolute and universal may be, in this world it is comparative advantage that counts; and in matters of faith, comparative advantage presupposes a pluralism of options and competitive relations among them. Comparative advantage goes to that structure of faith which is most persuasive in the competition to give meaning and priority to the unresolved issues of this life. It is through the competition of faiths that the question of what is really true is kept alive in modern societies as the advocates of each faith try to persuade others that their vision is indeed true, which is to say that it represents the best possibilities available.[13]

When we say that these social structures of faith represent claims as to what is the most important consideration in the life of the community, it does not mean that all the complexities of community life are reduced to one issue. Faiths are not necessarily simple-minded just because they are single-minded about what is the most important consideration in the life of the community. The most important consideration here is not necessarily that characteristic at the center of everyday attention. It is the one that tends to prevail whenever it comes into conflict with its competitors.

This is the key to understanding the color line as a social structure of faith. Whenever the color line comes into conflict with competitive structures of faith, it tends to prevail, reinforcing the comparative standing of racist realism as the American creed. In the rest of this chapter we will examine the competitive relations and comparative standings of these American creeds—racist realism, the liberal democratic faith, the civic credo, and the invisible re-

394

ligion—to ascertain a comprehensive answer to the question about what became of the American creed in the midst of the civil rights movement and its aftermath.

We have seen in Chapter 14 how the color line functions as a distributive rule, but it also functions as a symbolic universe or as a structure of faith. Each of these functions tends to reinforce the power and obscure the reality of the other. It is as a symbolic universe that the color line poses religious problems and as a distributive rule that it poses moral problems. As a distributive rule, it is a constant source of harm to individuals and to the structure of the community, inhibiting the free pursuit of legitimate public and private purpose, unfair in its distribution of goods and opportunities, disregarding of legitimate claims to rights and obligations, imposing structures of control that do not meet the canons of democratic responsibility. We will now show that, as a symbolic universe, this color line is a structure of bad faith.

We call the color line a symbolic universe because it is a set of mutually reinforcing and apparently self-explanatory facts. The subordination, denial of ordinary status, dynamics of fear and avoidance, and violence all appear to be reasons for the separation. The separation and subordination seem to justify the denial of ordinary status, and the denial of ordinary status, in turn, seems to justify the dynamics of fear and avoidance, and so on to the violence and its rationalization.

Faith and justice, like facts and values, may be logically distinct or at least distinguishable, but they are nonetheless everywhere found mixed in activities, events, and structured contexts. Indeed, they are found so mixed that it is always an open question which is which. And this is not an easy question to settle in particular cases. It is some advantage just to know that there is a question.

In the case of the color line, unless the question of faith is dealt with, the question of justice cannot even come up. Racist realism is a case in point. Racist realism asserts that however one may feel about the color line, in fact there is nothing to be done about it. It is beyond the power and wisdom of human effort to abolish it. Whatever else it may be, the color line cannot be a question of justice because justice is limited to what human effort can accomplish.

As John Dewey said so nicely, "No one is ever forced just by the collection of facts to accept a particular theory of their meaning, so long as one retains intact some other doctrine by which he can marshal them."[14] Thus we see that as long as the color line functions as its own reasons for being and continuing, there is not even any sense of a need for alternatives, let alone a real sense of alternatives. The color line is a socially structured doctrine of its own inevitability, a self-fulfilling prophecy of helplessness with regard to our common humanity. As long as that doctrine remains intact, the damage goes on.

This may seem an unusual use of the word "faith." In most minds the idea of faith is primarily identified with elevated beliefs about the meaning of the world beyond this life, and that may be true, depending on what is intended by the phrase "beyond this life." For many in the West it is the idea of immortality, of life after death, of the supreme destinies and transformations for which this life is a preparation of some kind. For others, it is an idea about the depth, the richness, and the ultimate meaning of this life, not in its egocentricity but in its wider reaches.

In either case, faith is a primitive and primordial orientation toward the nature and the significance of the human enterprise. And that is what the color line represents: a primitive and primordial orientation toward color as a legitimately determining factor in the nature and significance of the human enterprise. It is some measure of the hold this faith exerts to notice that, in America, it is easier to believe in life beyond the grave than it is to believe in life beyond the color line.

In sum, the color line creates a world that, on its own terms, makes sense. That is its most important characteristic and the source of its normative function. It will help to explain this otherwise elusive and seductive characteristic if we approach the color line not only as an institution and a distributive rule—which it clearly is—but also as a set of socially structured religious meanings, a structure of faith, a structured universe of principles, values, beliefs, symbols, rituals, and associations by which color is defined as a preferred and preeminent mode of being around which it makes sense to organize significant aspects of our common humanity. If, however, we approach the color line as a social structure of faith, it is not for the purpose of justifying it but for the purpose of showing that it is bad faith.

SOCIAL STRUCTURES OF FAITH:
A PROBLEM FOR NORMATIVE ANALYSIS

Ours is a religiously pluralistic society, which means that more than one social structure of faith is competing for attention and importance. And the major choices are not restricted to the usual rubrics of Protestant, Catholic, Jew, and other. Those have become more like emblems of personal identity than comprehensive faith orientations. Organized religion has been swept along by the "modern bargain," an arrangement by which public institutions agreed to be denominationally neutral while the traditional religions agreed to restrict their particular claims to the private sphere, in which they could ostensibly compete for the attention and loyalty of individuals without coming into direct conflict with one another and without disturbing the civic peace.

The result of this modern bargain has not been a religiously neutral culture of secular humanism as some may suppose. Instead, the result has been the development of a society in which religious attention has centered on concerns about the interior life of the individual as the only matter of ultimate importance, identifying that life as a private matter, indeed, as generating and occupying a private sphere. Under this bargain the churches have prospered, denominations have proliferated, and a rich array of ultimate meanings has increased the individual's apparent freedom to choose those symbols and beliefs that seem most deeply to express individual orientations toward what ultimately matters. This orientation represents a deep commitment to the pursuit of personal happiness, one of the three major articles in the American creed.

Thomas Luckmann has analyzed this development in his study *The Invisible Religion.* According to Luckmann, individuals stand as consumers before a vast array of historically developed ultimate meanings, filling their lives, like shoppers with market baskets, with prepackaged religious meanings selected from the transcendental shelves of our supermarket culture. In his view, this modern orientation has shifted the focus of sacred meanings from the world to the self. This sacralization of the individual is articulated as the autonomy of individual being, mysteriously atomized in a private sphere of family, friends, and such meanings as they can share and sustain as they construct their personal but private identities. The preferred and preeminent modes of being are the private ones. The nature, limit, importance, and content of common humanity are seen in terms of their availability for private uses, in this world and any others.

This preoccupation with the private as the preeminent may be somewhat descriptive of advanced modern cultures, but it is also problematic. The social world remains intrusive especially at the normative level as the bearer of competitive religious meanings. The anomaly of this orientation toward the autonomous individual is that the pursuit of an ultimate privacy has produced the most powerful and extensive collective structures ever erected by any culture. These collectivities make conflicting claims on the interior as much as the exterior life of the individual. Ironically, the focus on the private individual tends to obscure the social structure of the orientation and to mystify the consequences of this orientation for the shape and content of our common humanity. Neither in its focus of attention nor in its corresponding inattentiveness is this orientation well equipped either to grasp the significance of the color line or to envisage a world of meanings beyond this life, if by "this life" we mean a life ruled by the color line.

The world-creating and world-limiting powers of the color line assimilate somewhat unconsciously with the invisible religion of the private sphere. Even though much of this assimilation may be unconscious, we need not assume that the unconscious is always deeply buried in the psyche of the individual. It may just as well be pervasively enacted in the social structure. To be sure, the color line produces attitudes (the dynamic of fear and abasement is one of its dimensions), but attitudes are known to vary significantly with changes in the structure of situations. It is at least an open question where the unconscious is located. Some of it is deeply embedded in the psychic structures of individuals, but some of it is pervasively embodied in the social structures of cultures.

To see the color line as a socially structured faith is first and foremost to see it as what it is, to see it whole, and to take seriously the power it exerts. But it is also the first step in relativizing that power. Like other dismal forces in the human condition, the color line gains power and dominance the more it functions unconsciously as an unseen force, explained away by the racist realism that it generates.

One of the lessons of cultural relativity is that in every age and climate realism wins the day. It is the fantastic array of realisms that needs to be explained. There never was a realism that did not have a moral universe of some sort embedded in it and, consequently, enacted through it. That moral universe, however, is not easy to find because it is disguised as common sense, and it is protected by socially embodied and culturally articulated structures of faith. So it is with racist realism.

The color line is a set of facts, but it is also a socially structured doctrine about the meaning of those facts. As a doctrine, it is a socially structured assertion about the moral meaning of those facts, disguised as nothing but matter-of-fact common sense. As long as the social structure remains intact, sheer inertia remains on the side of the moral doctrine that it asserts. It has a credible claim to be the "real world."

If we think of the "faith factor" in a culture only in terms of the abstract ideas by which the various faiths may be expressed and overlook the concrete behaviors through which they are also expressed, and if we focus only on the subjective states they produce without inquiring into the anthropological structures to which they appeal for their veracity, we are left with a completely irrational factor into which it is not possible to inquire in any disciplined way; and this major aspect of any culture, this source of energy, this center of attention and sense of limits must remain beyond the reach of analysis. By reducing faiths to abstract ideas and subjective states without relating them to concrete behaviors and anthropological structures, we declare the very basis for relative importance to lie beyond the compass of reasonable discourse. In this way, the dynamics of persuasion expel any questions of truth as well as any reasonable grounds for relative justice. When patterns of words are abstracted from the events in which they function, both the words and the events lose their capacity to bear inherent meanings that can be understood.

In such a world, claims to rights, for instance, cease to be claims to human importance. Instead they become instruments or weapons for simply getting one's way. Any American creed is thereby unmasked as a rationalization for getting, for keeping, and for concealing power, and it is left as a body of variable values incapable of rational explication or defense.

We need not drink from this dry well if we will pay more serious and disciplined attention to the faith factors in our own culture and in the cultures of others. Faiths are, to be sure, various and variable, but their structures and consequences are not incalculable or unaccountable if we know where to look.

Whatever their ultimate objects may be in the nature of things or by way of gods, on their behavioral and anthropological sides faiths are reasons for exercising certain basic human capacities in certain ways; and the arguments that are proper between faiths are arguments about whether one way of exercising these capacities is better than another and also about whether some of these ways may be wrong, that is, bad faith.

As long as we attend only to the abstract ideas and subjective states of faith, it might appear that the notion of bad faith does not mean anything except that a given faith fails to persuade us, but we shall see, when we attend to the behavioral and anthropological structures of faith, that this notion is crucial to considerations of justice.

It is true that there is no neutral ground from which to engage in the analysis of structures of faith. Either one is explicating the world from the standpoint of a faith or one is explicating the structure of a faith itself, either from within or beyond its standpoint. This is a good deal less of a problem for objectivity than is commonly supposed. Apart from its objectification from an alternative standpoint, each faith is not subjected to the question of its veracity and of its effect on others.

This is both the power and the weakness of the color line. On its own terms it makes sense. Its absurdities, mendacity, and injustice appear only from the standpoint of an alternative faith. The less it is subjected to this objectification, the greater its claim to common sense and the more the questions of truth and justice are put aside. That is why the period of confusion about the American creed following the collapse of the civil rights movement has resulted in widespread acceptance of the color line as an arrangement that should not be fundamentally changed.

As long as the color line enjoys this status, it is effectively in the competition to be the American creed or, at least, to be one of its more secure and socially structured doctrines. Ever since the collapse of the civil rights movement and the elimination of the Jim Crow system, the question before the

399

house and dividing the house has been whether the inequalities entailed in this continuing color line are a legitimate result of the free pursuit of individual preferences in a democratic society or whether they result from a violation of the equal rights which are an essential element in the democratic promise. It is a question, in other words, whether the color line or the democratic promise is on trial at the bar of justice.

For several decades, the color line in the metropolitan areas has been operating not only on the power of its own rationalizations but also under the normative protection of putative democratic values as a legitimate outcome of the normal functioning of democratic institutions. This is what the civic credo claims and proclaims. We believe that this proposition is morally wrong because, as we showed in the last chapter, it is empirically wrong in its idea of what is going on, that is, because of the failure to understand the color line as itself an institution and the continued reliance on the misplaced immigrant analogy.

The civic credo does appeal to genuine democratic values, but it appeals to them in a morally as well as an empirically confused manner. The moral confusion in the civic credo seems to arise from an improper identification of the democratic principle of consent with the general notion of preference. This confusion has deep roots in the liberal tradition, but it has deleterious consequences for democratic aspirations. It goes to the heart of the democratic promise.

The genius of democratic theories of the state lies in their recognition that the persuasions of the mind are many and diverse. Consequently, the principle of consent occupies a central place in democratic theory as an essential component not only for political order but even for justice. The paradox of democracy may be that although any vision of justice requires coercion, democratic justice also requires consent. It may be a paradox, but it is also the strength of democracies to conceive of justice as a work of the state and of the citizens themselves, the highest form of self-government.

Because of the crucial importance of consent, a democratic society gives wide berth to the free pursuit of preferences, viewing them as basically benign and generally productive both of individual satisfactions and of social goods. John Locke argued that magistrates should not extend their coercive powers into the "inward persuasions of the mind." Adam Smith's *System of Natural Liberty* consisted almost entirely of the proposal that the state should stand back and provide only the minimal framework required to release and protect the free pursuit of individual preferences. Jeremy Bentham's utilitarianism argued that persons basically seek to maximize their own pleasure and to avoid pain, or in the modern idiom, to maximize benefit and minimize cost. John Stuart Mill adapted these ideas into arguments for representative democracy and universal education. The point in each case was that the people know best what they want in this life and that the state consists of the minimal arrangements necessary to allow the release of individual energy for the free pursuit of preferences.

Now the question is whether the color line is merely an outcome of the free pursuit of individual preferences. It does not appear to be. Insofar as the tendencies to violence, fear, and abasement are essential dimensions of it, the color line appears to be a coercive rule, no matter how slavishly it is either obeyed or internalized. Even if a plausible case could be made that the color line, especially in its contemporary form, is merely the outcome of the free pursuit of individual preferences, however, it would not necessarily follow that it meets the democratic standards for consent. Consent and preferences are not the same thing.

Both historically and ethically, Western democracies are rooted in the affirmation and protection of rights universally ascribed to each and every person. These rights form the basis for the claim of equal citizenship in a self-governing body politic. Both historically and institutionally as well as ethically, the color line is a denial and violation of rights on the basis of variously elaborated categories of color. We have already come to this judgment in the case of slavery and Jim Crow, even though each in its own heyday found defenders who tried to argue around the rights violations perpetrated in those forms of the color line. Now we have before us the case of the metropolitan color line; and once again, rationalization in the name of preference is the order of the day, obscuring the causes of disorder in the community.

DEMOCRACIES AND RIGHTS:
AGREEMENTS AND CONTROVERSIES

In its appeal to rights, democracy is as much an anthropology as it is a political theory or system. This is because rights identify certain basic human capacities as deserving political protection both for the sake of the individual and of the community at large. Thus in the encounter with the color line, we are driven to reexamine the anthropology as much as the institutions of democracy. Although democracies are committed to the free pursuit of individual and group preferences insofar as that proves to be possible and socially productive, this relatively free pursuit of preference is limited by the free exercise of these basic human capacities.

The democratic vision maintains that the individual has a right to the free exercise of these capacities and, as a result, the community incurs the social obligation to shape institutions and policies that do not violate and in fact facilitate the free exercise of these capacities. These human capacities translate into both individual rights and social obligations by virtue of the claim

401

each of us necessarily makes to their free exercise. At a minimum, the democratic vision includes the following capacities as providing a basis for rights:

1. The capacity for association is the ability we all have to join with others for mutually agreed-upon reasons. This is the right to pursue purposes of our own choosing in the company of persons of our own choosing. The freedoms of speech and assembly are crucial exercises of this capacity. We have the social obligation to provide an orderly (legal) framework within which associational life of great diversity can flourish and within which the conflicts arising from associational life can ultimately be adjudicated.

2. The capacity for initiation is simply the ability each of us has to be the cause of his or her own behavior, to be the source of our own choices and actions. This is our right to be self-determining, including—if you will—the right to make our own mistakes. There is no social obligation to see that each of us gets his or her own way, but by virtue of this right there is social obligation to see that individuals are not discriminated against in their access to goods, services, and opportunities that are basic to the pursuit of personal well-being, material and otherwise, and are generally available.

3. The capacity for consent is the ability to give and withhold assent to and participation in the structure and/or direction of one's actual or potential relationships, public as well as private. This right not to be forced into direct relationships translates into a social obligation to proceed in the pursuit of purposes and relationships only within the boundaries set by the other rights and on the basis of free and timely expressions of desire and approval and with proper safeguards for the protection of unconsenting parties.

4. The capacity for conscience and self-respect is simply the recognition that each of us carries on a subjective life of his/her own in the course of which one comes to one's own judgment about the merits of the self and others. The right of conscience asserts the unavoidability of this domain and underlies the stringent social obligation to institutionalize only socially inclusive and equitable criteria for social participation, while allowing self-exclusion for reasons of conscience.

5. The capacity for political interaction arises from our ability to respond to the effects and consequences of the actions and transactions of other persons and groups on ourselves. We have the right to organize institutions that transcend interpersonal interactions and to fashion common purposes to control the effects of those interactions and to provide means for the peaceful settlement of conflicts arising from those interactions. The right to participate in these matters imposes the social obligations to minimize violence, to exercise coercion only within the bounds set by the other rights, and to provide fair and due process for the pursuit of these matters.

6. The capacity for reason, the ability to think, to know, and to understand, requires great care of discipline and development. The right to think freely

and for oneself, therefore, imposes a social obligation to provide universally available institutions for the development and expression of thought and to provide an institutional order hospitable to deliberation both in its structures and in its policies.

The rational and political specification and defense of these rights and obligations is subject to continuing controversy and diverse theories about what these rights are and what they require in the body politic; but it is the existence of these "rights questions" which imposes the problem of equality on democratic politics. Because of the rights question, democratic societies place themselves under the obligation to justify inequalities by showing either that they arise from or that they do not violate or abridge the free exercise of rights. The democratic notion of equality is rooted, in the first instance, in the claim to equal rights. Therefore, the democratic notion of equality stands or falls on the rational explication of these rights and the specification of the institutional arrangements required to protect and advance such rights as may be rationally defensible and situationally specifiable.

Both the rational defensibility and the situational specifications of rights are debatable. On the rational side, theories of rights seem most notable for their differences from each other. They do not seem to agree on fundamental definitions and ground rules. Neither do they seem to coalesce around common conclusions as to why either general or particular courses of action should be endorsed, undertaken, eschewed, or forbidden. Libertarians may look upon inequalities of power and privilege and see only the natural and legitimate results of the free pursuit of individual preference whereas liberationists may look upon the same situation and see the injustice of rank oppression. Utilitarians might look upon the inequalities and ask if they serve to promote the greatest good for the greatest number before deciding whether they can be justified, whereas Rawlsian egalitarians will look upon the inequalities and ask whether each person, nonetheless, has an equal right to liberty and whether these inequalities can properly be understood to be to the advantage of all. Some rationalists would want to know if the inequalities were such as to deprive persons of those basic goods necessary to the exercise of their generic rights—voluntariness and purposiveness.[15]

How can rights occupy a central place in democratic politics and polities when there are such wide differences in their rational explication? There are at least three important responses to that question. The first is that these rational differences, far from canceling each other out, serve to underline the philosophic as well as the political importance of rights questions. Second, it is part of the democratic vision that justice in the community at large need not and will not be the work of one theory alone. Justice is as much a community effort in its conception as it is in its enactment. Third, when we apply any of these theories to the structure of the color line, whatever their differences of

403

theoretical orientation, none of them is able to justify the rule of the color line as we have described it. Each of these developed moral theories provides grounds for undertaking extensive redistributive policies in the face of the color line,[16] but no such redistributive policies will ever be undertaken or even seriously proposed as long as the color line is believed to result from the legitimate exercise of these capacities of association, initiative, consent, conscience, political interaction, and reason, which is to say, as long as it maintains its integrity as a social structure of faith. As matters stand, the color line passes as a brand of common sense that is not in profound and comprehensive conflict with the other competitive American creeds.

In fact and in principle, however, the conflict between the color line and the other major competitive American creeds is both profound and comprehensive. The separations of the color line violate and abridge the free exercise of the capacity for voluntary association. The subordinations of the color line violate and abridge the free exercise of the capacity for initiation, collective as well as individual. The denial of ordinary status on the basis of arbitrary color categories violates and abridges the free exercise of the capacity for consent. The dynamic of fear, abasement, and avoidance violates and abridges the capacity of individuals to be the morally responsible agents of their own lives. The legitimation and expectation of violence violate and abridge the free exercise of the capacity for political interaction. And the rationalizations of the color line violate and abridge the free exercise of the capacity for reason.

If the conflict between the color line and the democratic faiths is so direct, profound, and comprehensive, then why is the opposition to it not equally direct, profound, and comprehensive? To answer this question, we look at the social structures of the alternative creeds, their internal dilemmas, and their competitive relations.

COMPETITIVE FAITHS: DILEMMAS OF
DEMOCRATIC SOCIAL CHANGE

The invisible religion of the autonomous individual seems to assimilate rather unconsciously with the color line. With its focus on the private sphere, the tendency is to accept separation based on family, ethnicity, and any condition of likeness as desirable components of identity. With its focus on the self, the tendency is to discount social causes of inequality and look to pride and the marshaling of personal resources as the proper response to disadvantage. It leads with an interpersonal rather than a political notion of consent. Conscience appears as an instrument of self-development rather than as a source of transcendent judgment about the merits of the self in relation to others. The realm of political interaction, so disruptive to the private sphere, seems to require management rather than participation. The primary focus of reason in the invisible religion is to scout the world for resources that can be used in the construction and reconstruction of the self—and, therefore, in defense of the self. It is a structure whose underlying theme is the denial of vulnerability. It is an orientation of high expectation for the interpersonal world and aversion to the impersonal world.

The thematic unity of the invisible religion lies in its commitment to the transcendent dignity of each and every life, regardless of circumstance. Its great strength lies in its refusal to see differences of circumstance as humanly significant differences of kind. But that is also the source of its weakness vis-à-vis the color line. There is a built-in tendency to underestimate or entirely neglect socially structured moral meanings, to view them only as occasions for individual response and not as serious problems in and of themselves, requiring alterations in the public order.

This leads the invisible religion directly into the dilemma of democratic dignity in its competition with the color line. Insistent on the transcendent dignity of each and every human life, this faith yields conflicting imperatives about what to do when faced with social forces that would deny that dignity. First, forget it. Find your own strength. Get on with your life by making the most of your own resources. Second, fight it. Do not put up with these indignities. Challenge them wherever they raise their ugly heads.

In either case, the principle is personal and interpersonal. The focus of attention is on the existential rather than the structural aspects of the color line. The tendency is to look to personal change and group advancement as the answer to the problems posed by the color line but not to the color line itself as the source of difficulty. The assertion of black dignity takes priority, but the problem of what to do about the majority remains unresolved. Thus in the end, the invisible religion can be tragically assimilated, in the name of its own highest value, to the color line.

The civic credo, on the other hand, takes the majority problem as the key, liberty as the theme, and consensus as the principle. The tendency here is to rely on voluntary associations as expressions and organizations of private interests and to look to individualistic initiatives to advance those interests. This individualistic and interest-oriented understanding of associational activity generates a strong doctrine of patriotism as the bedrock of consent. Since material progress and a share of political power are the promise of democratic institutions, any fundamental criticism of existing institutions is suspect. The slogan "America: Love It or Leave It" is never far from the emotional center of the civic credo because the civic credo relies on the impersonal but emotionally charged notion of progress as the promise of patriotism. The intellectual content of this notion is largely utilitarian, that is, the greatest good for the greatest number at the least harm to the fewest—in the long run.

405

Conscience is largely a matter of ethnic and/or denominational preference, a very private matter from within the civic credo. Any level of deep personal feeling is taken to be a matter of conscience, and the civic credo is strict in forbidding political interference in matters of conscience. By the same token, however, political nonexpression is also the rule when conscience is at stake. Matters of conscience are left to the individual. As long as democratic institutions are operating, the individual should not intrude matters of conscience into the public business, and political institutions should not interfere with truly private matters.

Consequently, the principle for politics is consensus. The public agenda should be restricted to those matters on which agreement is possible and near at hand, and the political arena should remain officially neutral in the midst of the competition between and among interest groups. Indeed, politics is the balance wheel, ensuring only that one interest group does not gain any unfair advantage over the others, that is, impose its preferences on unwilling groups. The goal of politics is the accommodation of as many organized preferences as possible and the authorized use of police powers to enforce the accommodation. Private violence is anathema, but public force can be exerted very strongly whenever the consensual order is threatened. Police and other armed forces play a major role in the civic credo.

Given this dual orientation toward the unremitting competition of interest groups, on the one hand, and toward a politics of consensus, on the other, the civic credo gravitates toward a managerial notion of reason. Therefore, any conflict is perceived as an irrational threat to public order.

This leads the civic credo directly into the dilemma of white culture in its competition with the color line. Insistent on the liberty of each and every group to pursue its own preferences and interests as vigorously as possible within the framework of public order, this faith yields conflicting imperatives when faced with problems in the order itself. First, trust the order to make good in the long run. Do not make demands that are presently unmanageable. Second, question the motives of those who question the order. Distrust them.

The civic credo is thus left in a terminal dilemma when events along the color line force a choice between black power and integration. Because of its reliance on interest groups as the engines of social progress, it promotes black power as the way into the public order, but because of its reliance on managerial techniques and administrative resolutions, the demands for black power seem to undercut the long-run integration which the civic credo promises.

In either case, when the principle of motion is organized group preference and the principle of resolution is the amelioration of intergroup conflict in an atmosphere of civic calm, the tendency is to identify public order with consensus and to perceive disorder as willful and/or ulterior rather than structural and social. The inclination is to find ways to calm the offended parties, either through some new balance of interests or through the use of the police, rather than entertain strategies of deliberate institutional reconstruction. Thus the civic credo is unable to cope with the demands for black power it generates or to deliver the integration it promises. In the end, therefore, the civic credo, too, in the name of its own deepest principles, tends toward a tragic assimilation with the color line.

Finally, there is the case of the liberal democratic faith, which is clear in its opposition to the color line but unclear about the affirmative policies that would actually liberate the body politic from this structural defect. Secure in its emphasis on rights, it seems to lead directly into the dilemma of constitutional duties.

With its focus on equality of rights, the liberal democratic faith looks to the realm of voluntary associations as the fountainhead of alternative public policies and political creativity. It is true that through these associations Americans create various forums for exercising their freedoms of speech and assembly in relation to all manner of issues to persuade friends and enemies alike of the rightness of their concerns and to test as well as to display the strength of their purpose and resolve. Hardly an issue in American life has not gained access to public attention through the formation of associations determined to be the voice of the people. This is one of the most competitive aspects of American life. Even large corporations, in other ways so unquestioned in their exercise of power, find it necessary to defend and advance some of their most important interests in this arena.

For all the American individualism, real and alleged, there is a built-in behavioral connection between the perception of issues and the formation of associations. In the everyday world, this is what Americans mean by their natural rights. Freedom of speech, action, and even religion translate as a matter of common sense into the opportunity to pursue issues as one sees them in the company of others who more or less agree. The liberal democratic faith looks to this voluntary sector for the initiative in articulating, criticizing, and reforming public purpose.

It is taken for granted that all this should be within the law, in some sense, even when changing the law is part of the purpose. Since the laws are considered amenable to orderly, democratic change by means of pressures generated within this voluntary sector, it is also taken for granted that activities are to be limited by respect for the rule of law. This is the source of consent, not to the status quo but to the promise of the law to deliver an equality of rights through legislative, judicial, and executive institutions.

At the same time, both the law and the people in general relate to persons as individuals. At least for moral purposes, each person is considered—and on the whole, considers him/herself—as a morally responsible agent of his/her own life. This is taken for granted in everyday activities, and it has to be proved in

407

some way if there are circumstances that might mitigate this forcefully structured assumption. That each person is the bearer of his/her own conscience tends to be the center of explicit moral concern.

At the same time, the liberal democratic faith looks to the official organs of the society to function as a national conscience. The distinction between formal procedures and substantive purposes cannot finally be maintained in a rights-oriented society. To make good on legitimate rights claims, the body politic must pursue and ensure at least some substantive purposes and be judged by the purposes it does and does not pursue and ensure.

The liberal democratic faith is, consequently, committed to a politics of conscience. This is its great strength and its great weakness. Conscience is insistent, judgmental, and not necessarily right; and no one knows this better than the devotees of the liberal democratic faith. There is, therefore, in the liberal democratic faith a strong drive toward persuasion as the overriding political principle, although its emphasis on rights also gives it a deep legitimation for the use of coercion.

When the liberal democratic faith comes into conflict with the color line, the dilemma of constitutional duties arises. The negative duties seem clear and the use of coercion legitimate. That is, the deliberate discrimination and the political violence of the color line are proper objects of public power. By the same token, some reparation for the victims of those discriminations and that political violence is in order; but reparation requires affirmative duties. Insofar as such reparation requires imposing solutions on resistant and otherwise innocent parties, the liberal democratic faith is caught in the dilemma of constitutional duties. Like its other competitors, it yields conflicting imperatives in the face of the color line: because rights are at stake, use coercion to rectify the situation, but because conscience is at stake, use persuasion to rectify the situation. Thus paralyzed, the liberal democratic faith, like its competitors, can tragically be assimilated to the color line.

Each of these versions of the democratic faith—the invisible religion of dignity, the civic credo of liberty, and the liberal democratic faith in equal rights—represents values that are violated by the color line. Yet each of them also ends in apparently unresolvable dilemmas when confronted with the actual dimensions of the color line. We also see that each of them is rendered weak and defensive when they pit themselves against each other. They share the democratic aspiration to create a self-governing community of self-respecting individuals, but they inhibit each other when the drive for equal rights, for liberty, and for the pursuit of happiness are conceived in opposition to each other.

The conflict among these competitive religious meanings is the key to understanding both the scope and the context of our moral problems and the resources available for the constructive pursuit of alternatives. If we have

408

learned anything of general significance from the past century of studying the history of religions, it would seem to be that it is the humanistic import which shines through and is enacted through the diversity of socially structured faiths. The varieties of religious experience, encounter, and expression that prevail among a people are significantly what makes that people a people or, what is the same thing, faiths are best understood as providing structured and symbolic definitions of the nature, limits, importance, and content of a people's common humanity. It is by turning to the actual forms of common humanity that we gain access to the meaning of these diverse orientations and that we are in some position to judge the acceptable and legitimate range of religious pluralism, on the one hand, and to see bad faith for what it is, on the other.

The constitution of the everyday world in terms of its preferred and preeminent modes of being lies at the worldly outcome of faith orientations. It is, therefore, by their contribution to the constitution of the everyday world that faiths must ultimately be judged by others if not by their adherents. This is the only basis on which they can be judged by others. The transcendental mysteries and deliverances of various faiths are inaccessible to nonadherents, but the everyday consequences constitute a sphere of responsibility for adherents and nonadherents alike. It is thus not true to say that faith is an utterly private persuasion beyond the legitimate judgments of those who do not share the persuasion. Faiths are socially structured claims about what ultimately matters in this world or any other, and though there is room for incredible differences of persuasion on that count, still there is a limit to the toleration that can be or should be allowed—and that limit is the test of justice.

Bad faith is any faith that requires and thus justifies harm to others in its very expression, that promotes in its adherents and imposes on the wider community the sacrifice of others in the name of innocence, purity, and rectitude. It is one thing if we choose to sacrifice ourselves to some transcendent good. It is quite another matter if we choose to sacrifice others—and it makes no difference whether we do it for some transcendent good or for some selfish good. It is all the same—bad faith.

Justice, not faith, is the final appeal in the midst of the pluralism of persuasions to which we are subject. Appeals to faith are not the final appeal in matters that affect the community at large. In such matters the final appeal must be to considerations which are in principle accessible to all, a condition that appeals to faith alone cannot meet. To the degree that the everyday consequences of structures of faith constitute a sphere of responsibility for adherents and nonadherents alike, common rules are required for adjudicating what is to be allowed and what is to be done. To the extent that what is at stake is good faith, there is no problem in principle because the final appeal of faith is to its persuasiveness, and to the extent that bad faith is at stake, the only decisive way to demonstrate the claim would be to show that the harm it is said to impose constitutes injustice.

Ideas of justice may well be as controversial as affirmations of faith, but at least in principle they can be discussed by everybody. They call for evidence which is publicly available, and they eventuate in rules of public order. Ideas of justice are not basically ideals to be pursued. They are rules to be accepted or imposed. Problems of justice are, accordingly, problems in the rules by which communities order their collective lives and the lives of the individuals who participate in them. One of the defining characteristics of problems of justice is that they concern not only the unjustifiable harm done to individuals but the unjustifiable harm done to the order of the community.

Ideas of justice are propositions whose subject is first and foremost the state and whose predicates are intended to discriminate legitimate from illegitimate uses of coercion. Coercion is not a problematic notion. It means forcing someone to do something that he or she would prefer not to do or prohibiting someone from doing something that he or she would prefer to do. It means placing limits on the unrestrained pursuit of preference.

If the inequalities represented by the color line pose genuine rights problems, then the search for relevant equalities will require redistributive solutions. The question is whether the positive forces of the liberal democratic faith, the civic credo, and the invisible religion can be brought back into a reconstituted American creed that might yet prove expressive and definite in practically all respects in the conflict with the color line.[17] The problem is redistribution. Each of the democratic dilemmas arises from a reluctance not only to force redistribution but even to consider it as a possibility.

Justice may be the final appeal in the midst of the pluralism of persuasions to which we are subject, but it will not be pursued, as we have seen, if its dictates seem to run counter to the deeply structured faiths by which the life of the community is ordered and moved. It matters a great deal, therefore, whether the redistributive dilemmas of these democratic faiths are merely circumstantial or whether they reveal a tragic flaw in the heart of the democratic promise. That is why the competition for the American creed is a problem in faith and justice.

We believe that the normative resources exist for a meaningful pursuit of democratic social change through a serious encounter between the actual dimensions of the color line and the real possibilities of the democratic promise. In the next chapter we will try to indicate how this encounter might constructively be aimed.

410

CHAPTER SIXTEEN

Breaking the Rule of the Color Line: A Problem of Democratic Social Change

The color line imposes continued separation of the races, the subordination of blacks, the denial of ordinary status to nonwhites, the dynamics of fear and abasement between the races, an ever-present potential for violence, and mind-boggling rationalizations whose point is always the same whether the appeal is to science, religion, or common sense: there is nothing to be done about these injustices except to live with them. As a result, harm is done to individuals and to the structure of the community. The highest values of the democratic vision—equality, liberty, and the pursuit of happiness—are all violated by the operations of this color line, but attempts to convert these high values into positive directions that would oppose and overcome the persistence of this color line as an established American institution have revealed the dilemmas of democratic social change. Assertions of black dignity seem to undercut majority support for structural change and even to undermine any perceived need for it. Organized assertions of black interests seem to undercut any promise of institutional integration and even to undermine any perceived need for it. The search for persuasive affirmative duties seems to undercut the legitimacy of coercion in the pursuit of change and even to undermine any perceived need for it. In each case, these democratic values seem to lose their power as they approach the redistributive problems posed by the color line. There seems to be more reluctance to envision and pursue redistributive policies than there is to accommodate the color line. This is the problem of democratic social change.

Is this a strategic or a substantive problem? This chapter is an exploratory essay into the possibility that it is a strategic problem and that there are sufficient resources in the array of democratic values to pursue redistributive social

411

change and to open a future free of the color line. We do not claim that America will pursue such a future. The best anyone can do under existing circumstances is to explore the possibility.

THREE STRATEGIES FOR CHANGE: DESEGREGATION, INTEGRATION, AND BLACK POWER

There are only three basic strategic options for opposing the color line, and, as we shall see, none of them is likely to be effective at the structural level unless all of them are pursued. These options are desegregation, integration, and black power.

Desegregation is a strategy that would rectify the color line by prohibiting discriminatory behavior and undertaking compensatory efforts on behalf of those who have been harmed by it. Desegregation strategies are strong in the identification of behavior that should be stopped—dual school systems, white primaries, and racial exclusion from juries, jobs, and public accommodations. Desegregation is weak, however, in identifying affirmative duties and in defining adequate compensatory programs. The more desegregation is pursued, the more it forces the question of affirmative duties. The civil rights movement in Chicago was a case study in this very dynamic. The movement came apart when proponents of integrationist affirmative duties and of black power affirmative duties came into conflict with each other, each critical and skeptical about the efficacy of the others' proposals. As far as efficacy was concerned, both were right to be skeptical.

Integration is the strategy that hopes to fulfill desegregation through the institutionalization of broadly inclusive rules of participation in all areas of social life—in schools, housing, jobs, politics, commerce, culture, and interpersonal relations. The integrationist strategy is strong in its pressure for common rules and in its realistic emphasis on the unity of the social, economic, and political systems and, therefore, in its drive to secure equality of consideration and participation for blacks in all the institutions of national culture. But integration is weak in the apparent conflict between its search for common rules, on the one hand, and the empirical necessity for group-oriented compensatory programs if those common rules are to be fulfilled, on the other. Whereas desegregation requires the breaking of the racially discriminatory use of color categories, integration requires the use of color categories for measuring rectification. Therefore, the more integration is pursued as a strategy, the more it generates both the need and the imperative for black power.

Black power is the strategy that aims first to redistribute power and initiative to the black community as the reliable leader in breaking the rule of the color line and to the advancement of blacks as a group as the relevant measure

412

of rectification. The black power strategy is strong in its realistic focus on the actual position of blacks in the society and on both the hardships and the creative resources of black people. It is also strong in its morally imperative resistance to leaving the legitimate destiny and self-identity of blacks to the definitional powers of whites, but it is weak in the apparent conflict between its opposition to discrimination, on the one hand, and its emphasis on black cohesion, on the shared history and destiny of the black community, and on the claim to distinctive grounds for self-respect in the black community, on the other.

None of these strategies alone is sufficient to deal with the complexities of the color line and thus to point a way beyond it. If we absent the drive for desegregation and integration, black power can degenerate into another accommodation to the separations imposed by the rule of the color line, yet another version of separate but equal. Again, if we absent the drive for black power, the integration strategy can degenerate into another version of white assimilationist supremacy. Finally, if we absent a drive toward integration and black power, desegregation dead-ends in negative and abstract imperatives without affirmative duties. In the concluding events of the civil rights movement in Chicago, we saw all of these happen.

The civil rights movement had not been only a coalition of these three normative principles. In some ways it had been a consolidation of them. In the events and deliberations of the movement they seemed more like differences of emphasis than of principle, different but compatible ways to make democracy work for racial justice. That was the thread that held things together and kept them moving.

It came as a shock when that thread broke and these differences of emphasis reemerged as differences of principle, with the partisans of one taking aim at the partisans of the others, each camp at pains to show why the principles of the others had failed and would fail to make democracy work for racial justice. (And indeed each group did have telling evidence to support the perceptions of deficiency in the others.) In the South, desegregation, even with the backing of the federal courts, had not produced impressive results by the mid-1960s; in the North, with the triumph of the civic credo, it had been rejected as a relevant principle. Even its potential as a principle seemed limited to de jure segregation.

Integration, too, had been rejected by its inclusion in the millennial dream of the civic credo, that is, by the assertion that time and the normal functioning of democratic institutions would inevitably produce it. The facts were against that assertion. The schools were an obvious example. By 1966 it was clear that the U.S. Office of Education was no more inclined than the Chicago Board of Education to challenge those facts. Consequently, integration seemed to be a principle with no political potential. The principle of black

413

power seemed to be all that was left, but under the circumstances it was an ambiguous principle. Insofar as it was used to attack policies of desegregation and integration, it played into the hands of the resurgent racist realism. Insofar as it was used to defend and mobilize the dignity of black people in a hostile society and an alien culture, it emphasized the ways in which blacks, rather than the larger society, had to change. Its constructive potential as a principle was limited to the black community.

The retreat to black power was a sign of serious loss of faith. For those within the movement, it was as far as they could go without surrendering their rights claims altogether. For those in the larger society, it was as far as they could go without rejecting the rights claims altogether. But in both cases, it was a relinquishing of any drive toward structural change. The impasse was complete. The power to define the issue had shifted from the civil rights movement's framework of redistributive claims to the national framework of resurgent racist realism.

From within this framework, the problems of blacks and their relation to the larger society were conceived largely as involving ethnic interests, that is, as problems for which blacks themselves would have to take moral and tactical responsibility. They might have a dilemma about whether to conceive their well-being in terms of integration or black power; but henceforth, it was their problem, not the society's. Whatever the weaknesses of the civil rights movement may have been, at least it was clear that the position of blacks in American society posed an issue of justice that would require a marshaling of national resources to rectify and resolve. Under the framework that has been in place since the late 1960s, the position of blacks in American society has been conceived in terms of ethnic competition, such that efforts to rectify segregation must face charges of being either forced (as in busing) or preferential (as in employment) or reverse discrimination (as in any attempts to overcome past, imposed inequalities). To the extent that there is any question of national justice from within this framework, it is resolved by an appeal to balancing ethnic interests.[1]

The collapse of the civil rights movement resulted in the loss of any effectively articulated understanding of the full range of justice issues entailed in the position of blacks in American society. The justice issues had not been resolved, and the way to address them had become unclear.

The collapse of the civil rights movement ended what had been a concerted drive for democratic social change in the structure of American race relations. As it turned out, the system of Jim Crow race relations was decisively broken. The abolitionist phase of the movement was a partial success. The use of the law to create and enforce racial separation and discrimination was ended, but the civil rights movement, as much as the official organs of the society, was stymied by the constructive tasks that remained if we were to create a racially open society. The result was a massive display of the principle of cognitive dissonance: unable to see how behavior could be altered in the direction of a wider justice, American policy turned to the justification of the behavior in question, thus leaving the color line not only intact but actually buttressed by a new level of justification.

For the second time in American history a major institutionalization of the color line had been abolished, but the issue of race had not been resolved. As with slavery, the abolition of Jim Crow had come abruptly, even though both had been vigorously defended to the end. As late as 1863 it was not clear that the Union was prepared to abolish slavery. Nor was there any clear idea as to what form a future without slavery would or could take. Similarly, as late as 1963, southern resistance to the attack on Jim Crow still prevailed while scholars, newspapers, and politicians argued over whether segregation was a southern or a national problem. Then the Civil Rights Act of 1964 and subsequent legislation and court orders decisively abolished the Jim Crow system. The abolitionist impulse had won the day once more.

But once more, there was no clear idea as to what form a future without Jim Crow would or could or should take. The major form it has taken is the racially bifurcated metropolitan areas ruled by the color line and the attendant assignment of a disproportionate percentage of blacks to an economic underclass. Today we look out upon these metropolitan areas and their attendant job markets and take it for granted that the color line is an essential ingredient in their institutional arrangements. Indeed, serious scholars look upon this situation and find evidence for the "declining significance of race."[2]

We draw a different conclusion. Looking back on the successful abolition first of slavery and then of Jim Crow while also looking out over the metropolitan areas of the country, we conclude that abolition without redistribution has not worked to produce the hoped-for wider justice. Further, in the metropolitan areas, it will not be possible to abolish the rule of the color line in any sense without redistribution. It seems that as Americans we have consistently looked for a cheap way out from under the rule of the color line only to find that we have chosen the much more costly option.

It is too optimistic to say the translation of rights claims into redistributive economic policies is one of the great pieces of unfinished national business both at home and abroad. At the moment it is a rejected piece of national business. President Johnson's War on Poverty and his other Great Society programs were an attempt to make good economically on the civil rights commitments of the 1960s, just as Martin Luther King, Jr.'s Poor People's Campaign was intended to represent an alternative conception of the relationship between economics and rights.[3] Since both of these conceptions of redistributive policy have suffered political repudiation in the meantime, the question of redistribution has been under a cloud.

415

As it relates to the rule of the color line, however, redistribution is a very broad notion; for this color line distributes differential experiences of the social order, invidious statuses, fear, eruptive violence, political power, educational and economic opportunities, community disruption, and color-bound bondings. Therefore, although it is important to understand that redistribution is the requisite imperative to break the rule of the color line, it is equally important to distinguish one kind of redistribution from another and to distinguish the grounds for one kind of distribution from another.

We cannot expect to break the rule of the color line without facing the moral and practical complexities of redistribution. It was on the rock of those complexities that the gathering national commitment to break the rule of the color line in the 1960s crashed, splintered, and fell to the ground.

When pursued fully, all three strategies for breaking the rule of the color line generate affirmative duties and redistributive consequences. Desegregation generates affirmative duties on an institutional basis, duties to open access for all people to generally available goods, services, and opportunities that are basic to the pursuit of personal well-being, material and otherwise. It also generates affirmative duties to protect the fabric of consent in relationships. Even though the appeal is often made to prejudice, as if yielding to that were the equivalent to protecting consent, we all know that consent cannot be protected when ordinary status, that is, equal citizenship, is not granted to all. Equal citizenship and open access to the structure of opportunities require redistributive policies to be more than empty promises. That is the sharp edge of desegregation.

Black power, too, generates affirmative duties on an institutional basis to break the dynamic of fear, avoidance, antipathy, and abasement. To do this requires policies aimed at the reparation of damage done to blacks as individuals and as a group, that is, true empowerment. It also imposes affirmative duties to provide universally available institutions for the development and expression of the true pluralism of thought. Individuals and groups are entitled to appear as what they are, one among many. They should not be forced to appear only as what others say they are. To have the power of reason is to have the capacity to speak in one's own voice. Black empowerment requires redistributive policies of affirmative action, not empty phrases about blacks "doing their own thing" with "their own kind." That is the sharp edge of black power.

Finally, integration generates affirmative duties on an institutional basis to secure equal protection of the laws and equality of institutional treatment—whether it is in the schools, the job markets, the legal system, the housing market, the medical system, the political system, or whatever. It also generates affirmative duties to expand the possibilities of nonviolent coercion in the face of the violence that is endemic to the rule of the color line and to fashion

416

peaceful political alternatives for settling the conflicts that arise from inter-racial interactions. Integration requires redistributive policies that will actually bring the common institutions and the shared events of this society under common rules. That is the sharp edge of integration.

In the collapse of the civil rights movement, we lost the inner thread that leads from desegregation to affirmative duties.[4] As we face the future, our problem is to recover the comprehensiveness of the issue and the relevance of principle to fact. Until we learn to break the rule of the color line, we are condemned to live under its power at great harm to individuals and to the very structure of community life as well, which is to say, to our aspirations for a creative democratic community.

CIVIC AND ECONOMIC WELL-BEING: IS THERE A TRADE-OFF?

When Gunnar Myrdal surveyed the issue of race in America, the Jim Crow system prevailed in the South. Yet he discovered some reasonable grounds to expect change when he observed the rank order of discriminations and found that blacks and whites did not attribute the same importance to the discriminations in the Jim Crow code. Whites, for instance, worried most about interracial sexual relations while blacks desired that the least of all the prohibited activities. Blacks, on the other hand, were most concerned about securing their economic well-being—land, credit, jobs, income—while whites were least committed to denying them those things. This inversion in the rank order of discrimination seemed to Myrdal to open possibilities for change in the general level of well-being for blacks, provided they were pursued with some prudence.

There was some wisdom in that observation and in the strategies that flowed from it for cracking the Jim Crow system from within. In the metropolitan areas, however, the prospects for democratic social change will ultimately depend on identifying and developing concerns shared by blacks and whites.

Racist realism denies that there are any such shared concerns; but the only way to move beyond the color line is to demonstrate that as a practical matter this is not true. As long as "black interests" and "white interests" are arrayed against each other in a "winner-take-all" atmosphere, the only redistributions undertaken will be punitive in their effect if not in their intent. There is no getting around this redistributive dead end as long as the color line is the policy premise.

The color line does damage to individuals and to the community at large. The damage done to the community at large cannot be rectified unless common interests can be identified and pursued across the color line. The color line generates interracial disadvantage in at least three broad areas: the violence and the fear generate civil disorder on such a regular basis that they undermine institutional confidence and disrupt the civic peace; the subordination and denial of ordinary status generate a chronic disruption of full employment in the economy; and the result is retarded economic growth, purchased at the price of continued separation and its rationalization.

Redistributive policies will never be undertaken until we see with some clarity the costs that are currently being exacted from the community at large by this continuing submission to the rule of the color line. It is costing us our civic peace. It is frustrating full employment policies. It is retarding economic growth. Those are common concerns, and it is only our bondage to racist realism that prevents the perception of them.

It is curious but potentially tragic that a democratic society would attempt to manage its economy in abstraction from the social structure of opportunity, without regard to the inhibiting consequences for all constructive activity imposed by regularly structured political violence, and oblivious to the simple truth that maximum performance cannot be achieved on the basis of excluded participation. Interest rates, money supplies, tax programs, and budget deficits and surpluses all have a role to play in the production of economic well-being,[5] but so does the state of the social order, the level of education, the readiness and morale of the people to create and to seize opportunities and, indeed, the general horizon of possibility that serves as the lure to action. The interplay between civic and economic well-being is not a one-way street.

The color line presents a very strong case of this two-way interplay between civic and economic well-being. Probably the most telling criticism of President Johnson's Great Society programs is that they were premised on the idea that we could buy civic progress and peace with the dividends from economic growth. Even though that strategy achieved some partial successes in redistributing money, it quickly led to a backlash of resentment that ended in political disaster for the strategy because its proponents had no effective answer to the question, Why should my productivity support somebody else's advancement? The premise itself proved to be politically self-destructive.

The argument thereafter polarized around the concept of redistribution instead of focusing on reconceiving the problem of economic growth and its relation to civic well-being. The Johnson policies, along with the mainstream of welfare liberalism, were premised on the idea that economic well-being comes first and can pay for civic well-being. Those policies were rejected with only a minor change in the major premise. What triumphed politically was the idea that economic well-being does come first and that civic well-being will have to take care of itself with help from the police. Law and order replaced redistribution on the national agenda.

418

Since then the political and, to an alarming extent, the intellectual debate have been framed to assume and assert that, for policy purposes, civic and economic well-being stand in a trade-off relationship with each other. We can, we are told, pursue either equity or efficiency, but not both.[6]

As far as the color line is concerned, this choice is forced by considering the productive possibilities in abstraction from the constraints imposed by the political violence of the color line, the constricted structure of opportunity, and the excluded vitalities. In this situation the practical consequences of our conceptual apparatus do not work out in either direction. If we pursue efficiency or growth and try to use the dividends to increase equity, the strategy self-destructs politically. If we pursue efficiency or growth and disregard the equity problem, the strategy falls way short economically—the one place it was supposed to pay off.

What is an alternative? Is there some way to pursue civic well-being and economic well-being in an integrated manner without playing one off against the other?

In these final pages, we cannot hope to outline a complete strategy for democratic social change, but we do intend to explore a few of the considerations that make redistributional equity a more reasonable means to democratic goals than it has seemed in the recent past. Redistributional equity is not, after all, a goal in itself. It would not even come up as a problem if it were not for the existence of structural injustice. Yet as matters stand now, it is the promise of a democratic society which generates the redistributive imperatives and the realities of the color line which block the redistributive possibilities. Is there a way out of this impasse? There may be if we take the political violence of the color line seriously and if, at the same time, we explore the possibilities of nonviolence just as seriously.

NONVIOLENCE AND INTEGRATION: CONSTRUCTIVE POSSIBILITIES

It seems that even during the civil rights movement, and certainly since then, the importance of nonviolence as a strategy of combating the color line has consistently been underestimated. For King, of course, nonviolence was both a moral and a religious principle to which he was ultimately committed and from which he would not be moved. A study of his followers in Chicago showed, however, that for them nonviolence was more a strategic option than a moral commitment.[7] For the proponents of the civic credo (in Chicago and elsewhere), nonviolence was just another way to disturb the civic peace and provoke violence in others.

419

There are several reasons why nonviolence has not been taken as seriously as perhaps it should. We have not taken the measure of the intimate connection between violence and separation in the making and keeping of the color line. Violence is repugnant. Everyone in his/her right mind wants to avoid it. To the extent that violence is identified with whites, blacks want to avoid them. To the extent that violence is identified with blacks, whites want to avoid them. Hence racial separation is the goal, but it is always incomplete. There is always a region where the races meet. The greater the separation, the higher the self-fulfilling expectation of violence. The separation and the violence feed on each other in a cannibalism of the body politic.[8]

Neither have we taken the measure of deliberate strategies of nonviolence, designed not only to expose but to counter, to isolate, and to neutralize the effect of the structural violence which is so essential to the rule of the color line. Even after the experience of the civil rights movement, which used aggressive tactics of nonviolent direct action, too many people still think of nonviolence as merely passive nonresistance.

On the positive side, there has begun, largely thanks to the monumental work of Gene Sharp, an exploration of nonviolence as a strategy for wielding power, for building democratic support, and for forcing change. Although this work has only begun to explore the strategic possibilities of nonviolence, it is nonetheless an encouraging beginning.[9] Sharp documents the versatility of nonviolent strategies in the face of the full gamut of political regimes and problems. Here we are mainly interested in it as an important and needed supplement to the everyday politics of liberal democracies like ours.

The combination of underestimating the continuing importance of violence in the making and keeping of the color line and of underestimating the potential of nonviolent strategies for countering that violence and its dreadful political consequences has, time and again, brought defeat to hopes for change. The violence of the color line is more than a police problem, as our own history proves. The police have never been able to prevent it or its political consequences. This is not because the police are racist, though in many cases they have been. Rather, it is because there is only so much control that the police can be expected to achieve and maintain, and that control does not generally extend to the causes of political violence.

At some point, citizens have to take some responsibility for opposing political violence. By political violence we mean physical harm, threatened or executed, to persons and property, carried out in such a manner as to force the community to alter its life in ways that would not freely be chosen. At most, the police can deal only with the direct perpetrators of such acts; the police cannot be expected to deal with the alterations of community life that are thus forced. In the absence of politically structured alternatives, people try to move away from violence, they restrict their activities to avoid it, or they arm themselves for defense. Every one of these alternatives forces a way of living on the community which would not otherwise be chosen. It is a serious blow to democratic politics that aspires to be the politics of self-governing communities.

Political violence is the most serious challenge to democratic politics because it is an attack on the freedom of association and on the self-governing potential of the body politic. The question is how citizens can take responsibility for opposing political violence. Without an answer to that question, the democratic prospect is measurably and dramatically dimmed. If violence is allowed, legitimated, and accommodated, there is no way finally to break the rule of the color line. The hidden premise of racist realism is the affirmation of political impotence in the face of political violence.

It is, therefore, impossible to believe that we can break the rule of the color line unless we can develop effective ways of countering and neutralizing the violence that is an essential dimension of it. We cannot expect Americans of any color to give up their historic orientation that violence is the legitimate last resort in the face of threat unless it can be shown that there is a more effective last resort. It is not enough to point out that violence cannot effectively be countered by violence as long as people continue to believe it is the only real bottom line of commitment. Nor will we be able to counter violence as long as it is believed to be the legitimate result of frustration, anger, and rage.

Frustration, anger, and rage are some of the raw materials of the color line, and it is not to be expected that they will disappear under any circumstances. That they are perennially possible states of personal feeling, however, does not sanction any particular political expression of them. We do not sanction murder just because the agent was in the grip of frustration, anger, or rage. Nor should we sanction more collective actions that appeal to these motives and distort the very shape of the political order and social geography. These passions will not go away. The problem is to develop politically constructive channels for them. In the absence of socially structured alternatives for their expression, the frustration, anger, and rage only deepen the rule of the color line.

Building politically constructive and aggressive nonviolent channels for the expression of frustration, anger, and fear is the only alternative we have to being governed, indeed coerced by the political violence of the color line. What other means do we have to reassert the dignity of individuals and the decency of democratic political order, to reassert our right to organize institutions that transcend interpersonal relationships, to fashion common purposes to control the effects of those interactions, and to provide means for the peaceful settlement of conflicts arising from those interactions?

Of course, the counterquestion is whether we have any such means. Do we

421

even have such a possibility? Didn't the collapse of the civil rights movement prove that nonviolence does not work? That is probably the deepest challenge of the color line to any democratic hopes for a wider justice.

At this point, no one should venture too certain an answer to these questions. Those who say we do not have even the possibility of aggressive nonviolent alternatives to the present situation shut off the exploration of what may be our most important option. Those who say that we can develop effective nonviolent means of combating the political violence of the color line speak far beyond the presently structured possibilities. The question of developing our nonviolent capacities is the question on which the future of the color line hangs as well as the future prospects for democratic social change. It is at the moment the crucial missing piece.

We do have resources that could be developed, and fortunately we do not have to suppose that everyone or even a majority needs to be converted to nonviolence before anything will be possible. We do have a thriving sector of voluntary associations, and historically they are the birthplace of social and political novelty. And among those voluntary associations a variety of both national and local groups are concerned with the problems generated by the color line—race groups, civil rights groups, and social change groups. None of these is, at the moment, looking hopefully to the immediate future. The problems that concern these groups all seem much larger than the resources available to deal with them, but the groups all have in common (even when they are so ideologically divided that they will not even speak to each other) a desire to find some way to break the debilitating rule of the color line.

If nonviolence is ever going to make a comeback, it will have to be on a basis different from the moral and religious basis on which it was defended during the civil rights movement. The only basis on which nonviolence will get a new hearing, and, we believe, the only basis on which it deserves a new hearing will be on the practical belief and demonstration that it actually works as a method of gaining support, forcing change, and defeating the political violence of the color line. It will have to be developed as a way of meeting head-on those forces that frighten people and distort the community: drug pushers, youth gangs, pimps, bigots, house-burners, slumlords, corrupt officials, and the like. Nonviolence cannot be restricted as a strategy to forcing governments to "do something" as it largely was during the civil rights movement. That was an appropriate and successful strategy against de jure segregation, but it is not likely to be productive against the metropolitan color line. That is what the open housing marches in Chicago proved.

What is called for now is nonviolent vigilantes, organized groups of people determined to reclaim the freedom of the streets, the freedom of association, the freedom of citizens in their own country. Black and white alike, we are living like prisoners in our own country, afraid to walk our own streets and threatened by the structure of our own society. Some whites may believe that blacks are the threat, but blacks are the most threatened of all by this violence. They are already bearing the greatest burden, but they may have to provide the leadership for others to follow.

This does not mean, of course, that they will have to do it alone. There are whites in this society who will join the effort to counter the violence of the color line and who understand that, to some extent, there is a public need for integrated strategies to break its coercive rule. "Black and white together, we shall overcome" is the truth of the matter even when the possibilities of it seem remote.

Only by directly confronting the dimension of violence can we hope to break the rule of the color line. As long as that goes unchallenged, our fate is sealed. If, on the other hand, we can begin to isolate the violence and its perpetrators instead of being atomized and made impotent by it and by them, then we have a chance of achieving the levels of desegregation and black power necessary to break the rule of the color line.

By facing the simple fact that there are some kinds of protection that citizens cannot buy, the creative use of nonviolence can strengthen the rule of law without turning the society into a police state. There is no substitute for the organized vigilance of citizens. Civil rights groups, churches, community organizations, urban business groups, and even insurance companies and banks already have a community of interest, albeit a presently disorganized one, in developing the potential of effective nonviolent vigilance and intervention in the political violence of the color line. It would be foolish to suggest that isolating, countering, and neutralizing the violence of the color line is anything but a chancy enterprise, but there is so much at stake in it for everyone in the society that, sooner or later, it is a chance that some of us will have to risk.

Public institutions cannot serve public needs when the citizens themselves, through their own voluntary associations, do not give emotional force and political focus to what those needs are. It is hard to say which needs come first, but it seems unlikely that we will make much headway on either desegregated opportunities or black empowerment unless at the same time we are committed to creating integrated resolutions of the conflict which the vigorous pursuit of either desegregation or black empowerment will generate.

In addition, black and white alike suffer directly from the violence of the color line and from its effects on the political community, and efforts will be required from both sides of the line as well as integrated efforts to defeat the violence and rebuild the political community that has been fractured by it. Surely such initiatives will have to originate in the voluntary sector, but the resolutions will have to be institutional to be effective.

The violence of the color line is a concern that is truly shared on both sides of it. Time and the normal functioning of institutions will not cure this violence. Civic peace is not on the horizon as long as this violence is both rampant and accepted as the way things are. It will require extraordinary efforts, additional commitments, and great risk to those groups who set out to oppose it. It is not a realistic goal. Civic peace involves a redistribution of power from the color line to the democratic faiths.

DESEGREGATION AND FULL EMPLOYMENT: EQUITY AND GROWTH

Difficult as it will be to overcome the political violence of the color line, important as it may be to isolate this problem and deliberately try to break the cycle, the goal of redistributing power from the color line to the democratic faiths cannot be achieved by focusing efforts only on the violence. It is doubtful that groups would undertake the extraordinary efforts, make the additional commitments, or take the great risks that are involved in opposing violence unless they see it as part of a larger movement to restore the promise of democratic equality for everyone.

No sane person could possibly believe that substantial headway can be made in limiting violence while half of the black teenage population had neither employment nor the hope of it. Those energies need to be drawn into the productive economy for the sake of the youngsters and for the peace of the community. Unless we can open up substantially more employment possibilities and provide the educational support needed to take advantage of those opportunities, a black child born in the late twentieth century faces a much bleaker future than that child's grandparents did. We are in great danger of repeating the pattern that was set in the late nineteenth century—a generation of high hopes and some opportunity followed by a tightening of the color line and declining fortunes for those caught on the wrong side of it.

Unless there is deliberate intervention to alter the course, that is the path we are on. This observation is near the heart of Lester Thurow's analysis in *The Zero-Sum Society*. "If you examine the employment position of blacks," Thurow wrote, "there has been no improvement and perhaps a slight deterioration. Black unemployment has been exactly twice that of whites in each decade since World War II. And the 1970's are no exception to that rule. Whatever their successes and failures, equal opportunity programs have not succeeded in opening the economy to greater employment for blacks. Given this thirty-year history, there is nothing that would lead anyone to predict improvements in the near future. To change the pattern, there would need to be a major restructuring of existing labor markets."[10]

Indeed, as matters stand now, Thurow's analysis indicates that economic

424

performance is likely to decline generally and the position of blacks to deteriorate into a deeper inequality. He showed that between 1947 and 1977, although the distribution of family income, calculated for quintiles, remained somewhat constant, the distribution of wage and salary earnings showed a tendency to shift in favor of the top two quintiles. He accounted for this relative stability in the distributional profile of the country by the combination of transfer payments to the poor, tax loopholes for the rich, and government-sponsored jobs and amenities (roads, schools, parks, and the like) for the middle class. Political pressure to deal with inflation and the increasing demands for economic security, however, threaten that "troika of benefits" because of the counterdemands to cut back on government expenditures. "Any cutback," Thurow predicted, "will increase the economic pressures on the poor (fewer income transfer payments) and the middle class (fewer good jobs)."[11] The double result he foresaw was increasing inequity in the distribution of economic benefits and retarded economic performance for the economy as a whole.

To those who are committed to the idea that growth and equity have to be traded off against each other, the retarded economic performance will seem to argue for increasing inequity. Periods of low growth, they say, are a poor time to press for the desegregation of labor markets, and they seem to have common sense on their side. After all, desegregation of labor markets is a difficult problem at best, and it is at maximum disadvantage if it is pursued as a program of redistributing unemployment. That is guaranteed to bring out the worst in everyone, as we have seen wherever affirmative action programs have been followed by reductions in force.

The assumption in those circles is that social justice is a luxury that the country may buy with the dividends from prosperity. That assumption, however, may betray a profound misunderstanding of the macrorelationship between equity policies and economic growth policies. The A. Philip Randolph Institute's Freedom Budget of 1966 was based on the opposite theory, namely, that the serious inequities imposed by the color line (and other forms of discrimination) actually impede the performance of the economy as a whole, that they impose opportunity costs on the productive capacity of the economy, thus leaving everyone less well off.[12]

A variation on this perspective is developed in Lester Thurow's *Zero-Sum Society*. It is his thesis that "if we cannot learn to make, impose, and defend equity decisions, we are not going to solve any of our economic problems."[13] If this is true, then desegregation of the labor markets could generate benefits as advantageous for whites as for blacks.

The clear implication of this insight is that blacks and whites have a common concern for the desegregation of employment opportunities. Without it, we cannot achieve the full employment which is the engine of economic growth. The equation, in its simplest terms, is that discrimination in the labor markets prevents full employment and thereby retards economic growth. Thurow's is a utilitarian argument for desegregating the opportunity structure, that is, aggregate good is being sacrificed to unjust distribution and, therefore, the aggregate good—full employment leading to increased economic growth—requires redistribution of opportunities.

There is no law in nature or history that says protecting rights for groups and individuals must bring disadvantage to the community at large. And as we face the problems of the contemporary economy, it may well be that protecting rights of groups and individuals, especially by breaking the rule of the color line, may be the key to achieving advantages for the community at large.

We are a long way from protecting rights as a first priority in economic policy. Desegregating the opportunity structure, as complex as that would be, is but one step in breaking the rule of the color line, but it is the key to freeing the now suppressed capacities for initiative in the black communities and for releasing the now muted capacities for consent to the building of an equitably rewarding common life. The systematic and arbitrary subordination of blacks and the denial of their ordinary status as citizens, neighbors, workers, and human beings generally not only exact a price from its direct victims but also impose harm on the community at large. The affirmative duties therefore must meet two criteria: to provide a remedy for the direct victims and to rectify the harm to the community at large.

We all know that these affirmative duties will not be embraced simply as a result of an outbreak of goodwill in the white communities toward the black communities of America. These affirmative duties stand a better chance of being embraced if they do not require massive self-sacrifice of material interests and if they promise material benefits not just for blacks but for Americans generally. It appears that blacks and whites do have a common interest and stand to gain materially from a desegregation of the opportunity structure in the country. At the moment, however, this is an unorganized interest which runs contrary to common perception. That is a serious problem. The common perception is that gains for blacks can be achieved only at the expense of losses for whites through what is called reverse discrimination and preferential treatment.[14] This is emotionally loaded language, all the more so because it purports to be morally serious language.

The implication of charges of reverse discrimination is that we have two parties, one of whose rights have been violated, but there is no remedy short of violating the rights of the second party. If this is a true description of the situation, and if it is what commonly happens in finding remedies for discrimination, then rights may be a political problem but they will not serve as fundamental grounds for political life. Something else will have to be de-

426

cisive. Somebody's rights will have to be sacrificed. Rights may be self-evident, but they cannot be God-given or unalienable because both the neighbors and the government may legitimately override them. In short, if the concept of reverse discrimination is allowed to stand unqualified as a general description of what happens whenever a remedy is sought for a rights violation, then the idea of rights loses all force as a fundamental claim to human importance.

It is much the same with charges of preferential treatment. The language itself is a denial that there is any rights claim at stake. The implication is that power is being exerted without reason to bring advantage to someone at someone else's expense. If the concept of preferential treatment is accepted as descriptive of the situation whenever remedies for discrimination are sought and as a true equivalent for the concept of affirmative action, then any question of rights, their violation, and remediation is effectively excluded from consideration. Rights are reduced to one more weapon in the irrational but eternal battle for advantage—a truly Hobbesian view.

AFFIRMATIVE ACTION AND BLACK POWER: COMPETITIVE EQUALITY

Is there room for a rights-grounded concept of affirmative action? Both the aggregate of goods available in the community at large and the distribution of goods to individuals within the community seem to depend on an affirmative answer to that question. Blacks and whites may indeed have a common interest in the desegregation of employment opportunities, but that common interest is merely fanciful unless there is a course of affirmative actions by which that interest can be legitimately actualized. The lack of such a course of common action has kept this common interest unorganized. If there is to be a legitimate concept of affirmative action, it will have to arise from the conjunction of this common interest with genuine rights issues.

In a study of the federal court decisions on desegregation, Robin Lovin suggested that by 1978 the courts had evolved four "norms for the practice of desegregation." Lovin identified these four norms as follows: protection of rights is the first priority; affirmative rights entail affirmative action; systemic wrongs require systemic remedies; and public institutions must serve public needs. Lovin argued that these norms defined "a practice of desegregation with sufficient complexity and precision to assure a degree of uniformity in desegregation procedures across the country."[15]

It appears that this latter contention was true only in regard to de jure or Jim Crow desegregation. These norms may provide a starting point for the future, but they have led the pursuit of desegregation in the metropolitan areas into complexities of black power and integration, and these unresolved problems

427

seem to have stymied even the further pursuit of desegregation. The problem is to specify the kind of equality which is required to make good on a successful rights claim.

The pursuit of desegregation focuses on the problem of achieving equality of consideration, the pursuit of black power on achieving competitive equality, and the pursuit of integration on achieving equality of participation. In each case, it is problematic what is meant by "equality," especially as it bears on the consequences of moral principles for economic consideration, competition, and participation. It may be problematic, but the question should not be avoided because the color line is a problem of justice largely because of its political and economic consequences.

How often has it been said that morality cannot be legislated? And what could be further from the truth? What cannot be legislated is personal virtue. But morality extends to considerations of social, economic, and political justice, and they mean nothing if not enforced within the framework of law. The U.S. Supreme Court has been subjected to controversy and abuse for affirming that simple truth especially in its desegregation decisions. It is true that social, economic, and political justice require more than legal enforcement, but surely not less if one is serious.

The courts have a continuing role to play in the desegregation of this society because there are groups and individuals who can show by all the rules of evidence and procedure that they have been victimized by institutional policies that discriminate against them on arbitrary grounds of color and deny them the ordinary status to which they are entitled under the Constitution. Although that is a police problem, to fulfill these criteria means that the protection of rights is a policy problem as well. The courts cannot find constructive remedies to these problems unless their findings are supported by remedial policies aimed at desegregating the institutional structure of opportunities, which is a policy problem. These criteria cannot be met with one or two simple strokes or without considerable debate and conflict. It seems clear from our experience, however, that what is at stake in both the police and the policy problems is our ability to mount and sustain a full employment policy, on the one hand, and a rights-regarding policy, on the other.

At a minimum, then, if the norm of protecting rights is to be upheld, victims of discrimination are entitled to remedies at law. The remedy will surely take the form of at least a negative duty—stopping the discrimination—but it may require affirmative duties as well to make some restitution to the individual who has been discriminated against and to require some change in the policies of the institution in question, at least to the extent that the violation arose from defective policy and not simply from individual arbitrariness.

A commitment to desegregate opportunities, therefore, is but a first step, which poses further problems both of principle and of policy. The real test of

428

desegregation lies in the affirmative duties undertaken to achieve equitable results. Equality of consideration has to be measured by equality of results.

This brings us to Lovin's second and third norms, that affirmative rights entail affirmative actions and that systemic wrongs require systemic remedies. Merely opening up the future does not wipe the slate clean. In fact, unless the slate is cleaned in the direction of more equitable results, it is not possible to open the future. A full employment policy that still left blacks disproportionately massed at the bottom of the system would still reinforce the rule of the color line. Affirmative action programs, pursued on a hit-or-miss basis and not as an integral part of economic policy over the past decade, have led to cries of preferential treatment and complaints of unfairness. Such programs have not met the systemic test.[16]

There may be many reasons why absolute equity or strict statistical egalitarianism cannot be achieved overnight and is not even desirable or justifiable, but that does not alter the fact that systemic inequities based on color (or sex or any other arbitrary category that delivers privilege to some by denying opportunity and access to others) are both unjust and unjustifiable. Any pattern of social distribution that displays and enforces such categorical inequities—and the issue here is enforced, categorical inequities—is prima facie unjust and unjustifiable, however well entrenched it may be. The systemic wrongs are these enforced categorical inequities, and the affirmative duties can be fulfilled only as we move toward nondiscriminatory patterns of distribution.

If we are ever to accomplish this, we must be clear about the standard for measuring and judging equality of results. Surely Thurow is right when he says that the fully employed white male represents the standard of material advantage against which others measure their success and treatment in the economy. The question is whether the material advantages of the fully employed white male represent a privileged status that is necessarily purchased at a cost to all the others or whether this standard of achievement and reward represents a generalizable possibility. Thurow thinks that an economy which performs as well for everyone as it does for fully employed white males is an achievable goal.[17] It is not a radically egalitarian goal, with its five-to-one spread in earned income averages between the top and bottom quintiles, but it would be a considerable advance over the current twenty-seven-to-one spread.

This is an ideal standard for breaking the rule of the color line. In the first place, it recognizes that the discriminatory impact of the color line has been collective and will not be broken by merely individualistic resolutions. Discriminatory impact has to be measured by comparing groups, and progress in rectifying that impact has to be measured by group standards. In the second place, as long as the profile of the black community significantly departs from the profile of the fully employed white male, it puts to rest debilitating claims about preferential treatment, at least at the macro level of the argument. In the third place, it serves as a challenge and stimulus to the economic system to perform for everyone—a possibility its defenders claim is its virtue, but a test it has yet to meet.

The goal here is not preferential treatment but competitive equality, which will test whether the white community has vested its self-respect in occupying a privileged position. No doubt some whites have, but it is a dubious proposition that most whites have. It seems that relative equality of the sort proposed is the necessary condition for combating the dynamic of fear, avoidance, and antipathy. Whites, like blacks, fear poverty and its effects at least as much as they fear color, and the black community needs the resources of relative equality to be able to deal in its own way with the sources of fear, avoidance, and antipathy, to deal with the situation from a position of relative equality, and to speak with its own voices of reason. It takes relative equality to make the voices of conscience and reason effective in practical affairs and not simply the last refuges of the human spirit in the face of impotence and injustice. Competitive equality, in other words, is another name for black power, which, as a practical matter, cannot be achieved in the economy short of integration, that is, short of equality of participation in economic life, its opportunities, and its rewards.

It is true that competitive equality for blacks should not—and as far as we know, need not—be purchased by imposing inequalities of either competition or participation on whites, but this is an area in which great care will have to be exerted. As matters now stand, there are those whose expectations include the unconscious premise that discrimination will continue to work in their favor. That premise should be disappointed to the extent that they expect rewards to which they may not be entitled.

On the other hand, since group-oriented remedies are required, it is not only possible but likely that others who have perhaps innocently benefited from the color line may either feel or be treated unfairly by the proposed remedies. Until or unless there are effective and regular due processes for adjudicating such claims and for providing compensation to successful claimants (instead of retreating from group-oriented remedies), we will have no end of resentment, frustration, anger, and rage. We cannot break the rule of the color line if claims of reverse discrimination continue to be a political impediment to constructive efforts at eliminating root discrimination.

The emphasis has to be clearly on equality of competition and participation, following the same rules for everyone. If it is true, as we have every reason to believe it is, that desegregating the economy is a major step in the direction of effective full employment policies and sustained economic growth, we will have the resources to compensate individuals who may stand to be harmed by the pursuit of this important public purpose.

430

This brings us to the last of Lovin's norms, that "public institutions must serve public needs." "Public" is a loaded word in democratic theory and societies, just as the concrete meaning of the word "needs" is subject to the deepest possible conflict. Over and over, it has been said that the public needs racial separation as an inducement to civic peace, but constant violence as an essential dimension of the color line seems to create this need and to enforce the separation. What the public needs is an effective antidote to this violence, which deprives us of civic peace, and to this discrimination and exclusion, which deprive us of full employment and economic growth consonant with our capacity.

No policy of black empowerment either can or should succeed unless it includes provisions for generous compensation to individuals who stand to be demonstrably harmed by this pursuit of a broader equity. Such compensation would go a long way toward overcoming resentments which such a policy would otherwise provoke. There is no reason in principle why serving public needs should create further forced disabilities. Given sufficient institutional creativity, we should be able to work out integrated resolutions that deliver equality of competition and participation.

The provision of integrated and equitable resolutions is the third and final answer to the question of what kind of equality we are prepared to pursue and enforce. It is true that such resolutions may be expensive and may become most politically feasible when the economy is in a growth mode. But the case has been made that the ability of our economy to sustain a growth mode may well depend on the equity decisions needed to break the rule of the color line.[18] Growth depends on bringing groups into the productive economy, not on keeping them down and out. The harmony between individual and community well-being may not be preestablished, but it can be worked out if each citizen has an equal voice. That is the perennial work of justice, however partial and ambiguous the day-to-day achievements may be.

DEMOCRATIC SOCIAL CHANGE: FROM DILEMMAS TO DIRECTIONS

We will know that the protection of rights is the operative priority when the prevailing principle of private cohesion is friendship, that unique combination of chance, personal desire, and mutual consent, and when the prevailing principle of public cohesion is integrated participation in all phases of institutional life, that is, when no opportunities in the society at large are closed to anybody on account of race or any of its associated euphemisms. Only under these conditions will persons be truly free to choose their associations, to nurture and extend their cultural heritages, to shape their own

431

lives, and to contribute as they will and can to the richness and diversity of society as a common enterprise on a nonindividual basis.

In this chapter we have tried to show that these are not hopeless goals, that indeed they are reasonable purposes, and that, if they are properly pursued, blacks and whites have a common interest in them.

We began with the dilemmas of democratic social change: that assertions of minority dignity seemed to undercut majority support for structural change; that the drive for black power seemed to undercut any promise of institutional integration; and that the inability to specify persuasive affirmative duties seemed to undercut the legitimate uses of coercion in the pursuit of social justice. Each of these dilemmas arises from a reluctance to pursue redistributive policies which are essential to forging a community no longer in bondage to the color line. The problem, therefore, which we have explored in this chapter, is whether these dilemmas constitute a terminal impasse for democratic values in their confrontation with the color line or whether it is possible to envision a course of democratic social change to open the future for an American community free of the color line.[19]

The test was to see if there were rational and empirical grounds for turning these dilemmas into directions for democratic social change. It was an exercise in identifying new possibilities. No effort has been made in these pages to say what it would take to bring these possibilities to pass. That would require a great deal of strategic calculation, political skill, and organizational competence. But it seems that none of that important energy will ever be expended unless there is a convincing case that it could be expended effectively on behalf of real possibilities.

According to our analysis, there are such possibilities. We argued for them by showing that the color line inflicts costs on the community at large by seriously disrupting the civic peace, by frustrating the desire for full employment, and by retarding economic growth. We further argued that there are ways to turn these costs into concerns that can be shared by black and white alike and that there are reasons to believe that the community as a whole, not just one racial group, could benefit from pursuing these common concerns.

In relation to the political violence of the color line, it is possible that a renewed redevelopment of aggressive nonviolence could be used in conjunction with (and not as a substitute for) established agencies of the law to reclaim the freedom of the streets and the property rights that are now so regularly violated by the unchallenged rule of the color line. In that case, at least, it is possible to reestablish a progressive relation between coercion and persuasion that restores some promise to the notion of democratic social change.

In relation to the other dimensions of the color line, it is not so easy, and it may not be wise, to abstract them from each other for purposes of discussing their liability to change. The major point is to show how they function not

432

only to violate the rights of blacks but also to frustrate full employment goals and retard the level of economic growth. Viewed in this context, there is a possibility of majority enrichment and, therefore, majority support for demands for black recognition and competitive equality. Viewed in the light of economic performance, the imperatives for black power and for integration, far from being in real tension with each other, come to the same program as a practical matter.

It takes wise social policies as well as sound court decisions to maintain a rights-regarding and self-governing democratic community. From what we can see, this is not an unreasonable aspiration even for a community such as ours, which has lived so long in bondage to the issue of race. The actual pursuit of democratic social change for the purpose of moving ourselves beyond the color line is, however, as much a matter of faith as it is of justice. According to this analysis, the democratic faiths, whether they focus on equality, liberty, the pursuit of happiness, or all three, are seriously violated by the continuing rule of the color line. We should be able to count on them as reservoirs of emotional energy and support for well-framed courses of action aimed at breaking the rule of the color line. What is missing is a politics of democratic social change that conjoins the rational possibilities with the structured emotional forces of the democratic faiths.

CONCLUDING OBSERVATIONS

The color line is a problem of faith and justice. It is a socially structured rule. In this final chapter we have explored some of the grounds that may be available and some of the policies that will be required to break the rule of the color line. We have emphasized the redistributive imperatives that follow from any serious commitment to democratic equality: desegregated opportunities, black empowerment, integrated and equitable relations. We have given a hopeful reading of the prospects for democratic social change at least by discussing it as a real possibility. In Chapter 1, we said that "the facts of antagonism and inequality have always seemed so massive, the justifications apparently so thin, that the reasonable prospects for change have always been largely a matter of faith." At this point, perhaps, the best we can do is give a brief account of the faith that has informed and sustained this inquiry.

The collapse of the civil rights movement was a serious loss. It marked the loss of any vision of what might lie beyond this life dominated by the rule of the color line, the loss of that slender thread of hope for change in the structure of American race relations. It opened an abyss of doubt about both the power and the substance of democratic values in American life. By the late 1960s, Myrdal's optimism about the power and substance of the American creed had

433

come to seem hopelessly misplaced, and in typical American fashion we went from optimism to cynicism about our prospects for democratic social change. Amid the triumph of the civic credo and the counsels of benign neglect, racist realism reasserted itself as the national framework for disposing of issues of racial justice. Only occasional cries of black power remained as echoes of the moral urgency that had so recently been the driving force of the movement, but even those voices were swept along in the tide of civic cynicism.

It may be that the recovery of reasonable hope is our most difficult problem. At least that has been the underlying purpose in our exploration of the problems of faith and justice. We know that the optimism of a Myrdal cannot be recovered; but what is more, we do not believe it would be desirable even if it were possible. American life, it turns out, is much more religiously complex than Myrdal supposed in his reading of the American creed, and the color line is much more structurally pervasive and articulated than he supposed in his reading of the American dilemma.

Like Myrdal, we have tried to open a rational way to press moral claims against the structure of the color line, to provide a disciplined approach to the value conflicts that eventuate in and emanate from the color line, and to uncover a realistic moral basis for a politics of democratic social change. Myrdal solved these problems by attributing social force and centrality to the American creed and then placing the fact of the Negro problem in that context. He was thus able to avoid direct confrontation with the normative problems raised by the color line. Values remained facts for him. It was their power which allowed him to rely on them. But what if high values are out of power? Then what? That is our problem. But it is also a problem for the disciplines of social inquiry on which we rely for understanding ourselves as a society.

We cannot afford to purchase hope at the price of neglecting or suppressing the seriousness of our problem. False hopes can be as detrimental to the community as bad faith. Reasonable hope proceeds from unflinching recognition of the facts, whatever they may be, and a commitment to pursue the alternative possibilities, however slim they may seem. Perhaps we can make clearer our grounds for hope by contrasting them with Myrdal's grounds for optimism.

Normatively we have relied on what we called the democratic anthropology, the generic human capacities for consent, conscience, political interaction, initiation, association, and reason. At the end of Chapter 1 we compared and contrasted the ways Tocqueville, DuBois, and Myrdal read the potential of these capacities in relation to the color line. Here we shall compare and contrast our own reading of these capacities with Myrdal's; in this way perhaps we can explain why we are not optimistic about the prospect for democratic social change even though we do see some grounds for reasonable hope.

434

As Myrdal understood it, the American creed represented the deep value consensus that held America together in spite of all manner of contradictory impulses. He believed that the American creed, with its commitment to the dignity and equality of all persons before the law and under the Divine, would ultimately demarcate the level to which the American people were going to rise in their relations with each other. That was the promise of American life. It was the American faith. We see now, however, that it is but one of the American faiths and it is not as decisively contrary to the continued rule of the color line as Myrdal supposed. The democratic faith is more pluralistically articulated in American life than Myrdal's American creed, and it stands in a competitive relationship with the bad faith of the color line. We cannot say with Myrdal that "in principle the Negro problem was settled long ago." It is exactly at the point of principle that the matter remains unsettled in American life. As long as the color line rules, the denial of ordinary status to blacks seems to be a natural condition. Equal rights and equal citizenship may be recognized as the valid basis for claims; but we cannot say that the American public is on the verge of breaking the rule of the color line simply because the equal rights and equal citizenship of blacks are violated by it. Rights claims will continue to provide the transcendent basis for movements and policies aimed at democratic social change, but it is no longer possible to believe, if it ever was, that such claims will carry the day by virtue of their transcendent dominance in the culture. They may be worth fighting for, but their success is not assured.

By the same token, the issues of conscience seem much more complex than Myrdal's portrayal of them as an American dilemma. Because of the dynamics of fear and abasement, many Americans, far from experiencing any dilemma between their higher values and lower impulses, feel justified in behavior that not only reinforces but extends the color line. Although we propose group-oriented remedies of affirmative action as the antidote to this dynamic of fear and abasement, we have to realize that such proposals are far from self-evident as solutions to the problems of conscience generated on both sides of the color line. And we can be certain that, however beneficial such remedies might prove to be, they will never be adopted on a relevant, societal scale without the renewal of a comprehensive vision of a larger social good that lies beyond the color line.

Therefore, like Myrdal, we too have a rank order of discriminations; but whereas Myrdal geared his to the protocols of Jim Crow, ours is attuned to the realities of the metropolitan color line. It is our judgment that limiting, isolating, and countering the violence of the color line is the number one priority for blacks and whites alike. Because of his rank order of discriminations, Myrdal believed that the prospect for a politics of democratic social change depended on blacks and whites having an inverse order of priorities; in other

435

words, that blacks cared most about things that concerned whites the least. In our view, the prospects for change will ultimately depend on finding and developing concerns shared by blacks and whites, beginning with the issue of violence.

A second priority which blacks and whites potentially share is a concern for full employment. Affirmative action programs that raise the average of black participation in the economy up to the level of white participation do not stand a chance except in the context of resolutely pursued policies of full employment. Nor do white concerns for economic security stand any hope for realization except in the same policy context. As long as black demands can continue to be played off against white hopes, neither blacks nor whites will get what they want. Yet there appear to be no reasons in the nature of the economic system why they could not both get what they want. Thus, whereas Myrdal looked to a principle of cumulation to raise blacks gradually from their condition of subordination through the pursuit of issues that whites did not care too much about, we look to a convergence of black and white interests in full employment to provide the conditions necessary to challenge black subordination, especially in the economy.

Myrdal looked to race improvement groups and their white allies to pursue the politics of democratic social change, but we look to the mobilization of a broad range of voluntary associations and even some business groups to articulate and pursue broad equity goals for the society at large. Of course, we do not expect traditional civil rights groups like the NAACP and the Urban League to put aside their special concerns for blacks. The status of blacks in the economy is and will remain the real test of progress toward equity goals, but effective pressure for common rules for measuring economic justice will have to come from the voluntary sector on a broad scale if it is going to come from anywhere.

Therefore, whereas Myrdal considered the educational process and social planning on a rational basis to lead the way to racial equality, we frankly believe coalition politics is the most viable basis and force for change. Only thus will the pluralism of black voices be released into the public realm. It is one of the damaging fictions of the color line that the black community should speak in only one voice. As long as the color line rules, the black community, as a matter of self-defense, must raise voices of protest, self-affirmation, and redistribution, that is, demands for desegregation, black power, and integration. But these voices can find resonance in the white communities as well because it is not just black history that is at stake in the rule of the color line. The character, the value, and the ultimate meaning of American history are on the line.

We are hopeful that Americans will ultimately choose their own vision of self-respecting citizens in a self-governing community over the separations, the subordinations, the denials of ordinary status, the dynamics of fear and abasement, the political violence, and the rationalizations of the color line. It seems a reasonable hope, but a hope is all it is, or, as King said at the Lincoln Memorial, a dream. We hardly seem to have come to the point that we can say, beyond this is beyond us. If we have, then God have mercy on our souls.

Participants in the

Conference on Open Housing

Aaron, Ely M., Chairman, Chicago Commission on Human Relations
Ayers, Thomas G., President, Commonwealth Edison Company; Chicago Association
   of Commerce and Industry
Baird, John, Baird and Warner Real Estate Company
Ballew, John, Acting Director, Cook County Department of Public Aid
Beatty, Ross, Chairman, Chicago Real Estate Board
Berry, Edwin C., Director, Chicago Urban League
Bevel, Reverend James, Southern Christian Leadership Conference
Brazier, Reverend Arthur, President, The Woodlawn Organization
Callahan, Eugene J., Chicago Conference on Religion and Race
Caples, William G., Vice-President, Inland Steel Company
Cody, Most Reverend John Patrick, Archbishop, Catholic Archdiocese of Chicago
Daley, Richard J., Mayor of Chicago
Dennis, Sam, Community Relations Service, Justice Department
Egan, Reverend Edward, Archdiocesan Commission on Human Relations
Faul, Thomas, Chicago Federation of Labor and Industrial Union Council
Finley, Sydney, Illinois Field Director, national NAACP
Foster, A. L., Cosmopolitan Chamber of Commerce
Foster, Leonard, Garfield Park Chamber of Commerce
Gardiner, John, Church Federation of Greater Chicago
Gray, John, Chicago Association of Commerce and Industry
Griffin, Reverend Arthur, President, West Side Federation
Groebe, Gordon, Chicago Real Estate Board
Hayes, Charles, United Packinghouse Workers
Heineman, Ben W., Chairman, Chicago and Northwestern Railroad
Hill, Lewis, Director, Department of Urban Renewal, City of Chicago
Jackson, Reverend Jesse, Coordinating Council of Community Organizations
Johnson, Robert, Regional Director, United Auto Workers
Jones, George, President, Joe Louis Milk Company; Chicago Conference on Religion
   and Race
Keane, Thomas, Alderman, Thirty-first Ward
Kennedy, David M., President, Continental Illinois National Bank
King, Martin Luther, Jr., Southern Christian Leadership Conference
Kleeman, Jack, Chicago Real Estate Board
Lee, William A., Chicago Federation of Labor

439

Lund, Paul, Assistant to the President, Illinois Bell Telephone Company

Marciniak, Edward, Director, Chicago Commission on Human Relations

Marx, Rabbi Robert, Union of American Hebrew Congregations

McDermott, John, Director, Catholic Interracial Council

McKnight, John, Director, Midwest Field Office, U.S. Commission on Civil Rights

Metcalfe, Ralph, Alderman, Third Ward

Ming, William R., Jr., Attorney; Chicago Commission on Human Relations

Mohl, Arthur F., Chicago Real Estate Board

Montgomery, Right Reverend James, Co-Adjutor Bishop, Episcopal Diocese of Chicago

Nathan, Roger, Illinois Commission on Human Relations

Nolan, Sergeant Samuel, Chicago Police Department, Human Relations Division

Pitcher, W. Alvin, Associate Professor of Ethics and Society, University of Chicago

Purcell, Warren, Cook County Council of Insured Savings Associations

Raby, Albert, Convenor, Coordinating Council of Community Organizations

Ransom, Elbert, American Friends Service Committee

Robinson, William, Republican Ward Committeeman; Treasurer, Coordinating Council of Community Organizations

Schucker, David, Illinois Commission on Human Relations

Simon, Rabbi Mordicai, Chicago Conference on Religion and Race

Siskin, Rabbi Edgar, Chairman, Chicago Board of Rabbis

Spacek, Leonard P., Commercial Club; Chairman, Arthur Anderson Associates

Spike, Reverend Robert, Professor of Christian Ministry, University of Chicago

Stamos, John, Chicago Mortgage Bankers Association

Stayman, Clark, Chicago Mortgage Bankers Association

Swibel, Charles R., Chairman, Chicago Housing Authority

Williams, Kale, American Friends Service Committee

Wormer, John, Metropolitan Housing and Planning Council

Wright, James, United Auto Workers

Young, Reverend Andrew, Southern Christian Leadership Conference

Zimmerman, Reverend Donald, President, Church Federation of Greater Chicago

Adapted from Kathleen Connolly, "The Chicago Open-Housing Conference," 12 January 1967, p. 42.

APPENDIX II

Agreement of the Subcommittee

to the Conference on Fair Housing

Convened by the Chicago Conference

on Religion and Race

This subcommittee has been discussing a problem that exists in every metropolitan area in America. It has been earnestly seeking immediate, practical, and effective steps which can be taken to create a fair housing market in metropolitan Chicago.

In the City of Chicago itself, the policy of fair housing has been established by the clear statement of purpose in the Chicago Fair Housing Ordinance enacted in 1963. It provides:

"1. It is hereby declared the policy of the City of Chicago to assure full and equal opportunity to all residents of the City to obtain fair and adequate housing for themselves and their families in the City of Chicago without discrimination against them because of their race, color, religion, national origin or ancestry.

"2. It is further declared to be the policy of the City of Chicago that no owner, lessee, sub-lessee, assignee, managing agent, or other person, firm or corporation having the right to sell, rent or lease any housing accommodation, within the City of Chicago, or any agent of any of these, should refuse to sell, rent, lease or otherwise deny or withhold from any person or group of persons such housing accommodations because of the race, color, religion, national origin or ancestry of such person or persons or discriminate against any person because of his race, color, religion, national origin or ancestry in the terms, conditions, or privileges of the sale, rental or lease of any housing accommodation or in the furnishing of facilities or services in connection therewith."

The subcommittee has addressed itself to methods of making the Chicago Ordinance work better, the action which can be taken by various governmental groups, the role of the Chicago Real Estate Board, and how to make further progress towards fair housing in the months ahead. It would be too much to expect complete agreement on either the steps to be taken or their timing. Nevertheless, the representatives at the meetings have undertaken specific and affirmative measures to attack the problem of discrimination in housing. Carrying out these commitments will require substantial investments of time and money by both private and public bodies and the wholehearted effort of many Chicagoans of good will, supported by the cooperation of thousands of others.

441

In the light of the commitments made and program here adopted and pledged to achieve open housing in the Chicago metropolitan community, the Chicago Freedom Movement pledges its resources to help carry out the program and agrees to a cessation of neighborhood demonstrations on the issue of open housing so long as the program is being carried out.

The subcommittee believes that the program can be a major step forward. It has confidence that this program, and the more extensive measures bound to flow from it, will achieve the objective of affording every resident "full and equal opportunity to obtain fair and adequate housing without discrimination because of race, color, religion, national origin or ancestry."

The participants in this conference have committed themselves to the following action:

1. The Chicago Commission on Human Relations is already acting to require every real estate broker to post a summary of the City's policy on open housing and the requirements of the Fair Housing Ordinance in a prominent position in his place of business. To obtain full compliance with the Fair Housing Ordinance, the Commission will give special emphasis to multiple complaints and will follow up on pledges of non-discrimination resulting from prior conciliation proceedings. The Commission will increase its enforcement staff and has already requested budgetary increases to support a significantly higher level of effective enforcement activity. This will include year-around inquiry to determine the extent of compliance in all areas of the City, but without placing undue burdens on any broker's business. The Commission will initiate proceedings on its own motion where the facts warrant. It will act on all complaints promptly, ordinarily initiating an investigation within 48 hours, as is now the case. In order to facilitate proceedings on complaints, it has changed its rules to provide for the substitution of attorneys for Commissioners to preside in conciliation and enforcement hearings. Where a formal hearing justifies such action under the ordinance, the license of an offending broker will be suspended or revoked.

The City will continue its consistent support of fair housing legislation at the State level and will urge the adoption of such legislation at the 1967 session of the State Legislature.

2. In a significant departure from its traditional position, the Chicago Real Estate Board announced at the August 17 meeting that its Board of Directors had authorized a statement reading in part as follows:

> "As a leadership organization in Chicago, we state the fundamental principle that freedom of choice in housing is the right of every citizen. We believe all citizens should accept and honor that principle.
>
> "We have reflected carefully and have decided we will—as a Chicago organization—withdraw all opposition to the philosophy of open occupancy legislation at the state level—provided it is applicable to owners as well as to brokers—and we reserve the right to criticize detail as distinguished from philosophy—and we will request the state association of Real Estate Boards to do likewise but we cannot dictate to them."

While not willing to dismiss its appeal from the decision of the Circuit Court of Cook County upholding the validity of the City's Fair Housing Ordinance, the Board has committed itself effectively to remind its members of their duty to obey the ordinance and to circulate to them the interpretation of the ordinance to be furnished by the Chicago Commission on Human Relations. The individual representatives of the Board also committed themselves to join other realtors to participate in, a continuing organization, should one be formed, to promote effective action implementing the principle of freedom of choice in housing.

3. The Chicago Housing Authority will take every action within its power to promote the objectives of fair housing. It recognizes that heavy concentrations of public housing should not again be built in the City of Chicago. Accordingly, the Chicago Housing Authority has begun activities to improve the character of public housing, including the scattering of housing for the elderly across the city, and initiation of a leasing program which places families in the best available housing without regard to the racial character of the neighborhood in which the leased facilities are provided. In the future, it will seek scattered sites for public housing and will limit the height of new public housing structures in high density areas to eight stories, with housing for families with children limited to the first two stories. Wherever possible, smaller units will be built.

In addition, in order to maximize the usefulness of present facilities and to promote the welfare of the families living in them, a concerted effort will be made to improve the opportunities for satisfactory community life in public housing projects. In order to achieve this improvement the participation of all elements in the surrounding communities will be actively enlisted and utilized.

4. The President of the Cook County Board of Commissioners has advised the chairman of the subcommittee by letter that the Cook County Department of Public Aid will make a renewed and persistent effort to search out the best housing for recipients available within the ceilings authorized by the legislature, regardless of location. Each employee of the Department will be reminded that no recipient is to be prohibited or discouraged from moving into any part of Cook County because of his race, color, or national origin. The Department will not be satisfied if recipients live in less satisfactory accommodations than would be available to them were they of a different race, color or national origin.

Department employees will be instructed to report any discriminatory refusal by real estate brokers to show rental listings to any recipient to the Chicago Commission on Human Relations or the State Department of Registration and Education through the Chief of the Bureau of Housing of the Public Aid Department. Department employees will also encourage recipients who encounter discrimination in dealing with brokers to report such experiences to the same agencies. The Chief of the Bureau of Housing will maintain close follow-up on all matters that have been thus reported.

5. The Urban Renewal Program has had some success in achieving stable residential integration in facilities built in renewal developments, with the cooperation of property owners, property managers, community organizations, and neighbors to that end. The Urban Renewal Program will devote itself to producing the same results in its relocation activities and will earnestly solicit the support of all elements of the community in the City, County and metropolitan area in these efforts.

In relocating families, the Department of Urban Renewal will search out the best housing available regardless of location. Each employee of the Department will be reminded that no family is to be prohibited or discouraged from moving into any part

443

of the Chicago metropolitan area because of his race, color, or national origin. Department employees will be instructed to report any discriminatory refusal by a real estate broker to show listings, to the Chicago Commission on Human Relations or the State Department of Registration and Education through the Director of Relocation. They will also encourage families who encounter discrimination in dealing with a broker to report such experiences to the same agencies. The Director of Relocation will maintain a close follow-up on all matters that have been thus reported.

6. The Cook County Council of Insured Savings Associations, by letter and the Chicago Mortgage Bankers Association, at the Committee meeting on August 17, 1966, have affirmed that their policy is to provide equal service and to lend mortgage money to all qualified families, without regard to race, for the purchase of housing anywhere in the metropolitan area.

7. Assistant Attorney General Roger Wilkins, head of the Community Relations Service of the United States Department of Justice, has advised the chairman of the subcommittee that the Service will inquire into the questions raised, under existing law, with respect to service by the Federal Deposit Insurance Corporation and the Federal Savings and Loan Insurance Corporation to financial institutions found guilty of practicing racial discrimination in the provision of financial service to the public. While the matter is a complex one, it will be diligently pursued.

8. The leaders of the organized religious communities in the metropolitan area have already expressed their commitment to the principle of open housing.

The Chicago Conference on Religion and Race, which is co-sponsored by the Catholic Archdiocese of Chicago, the Church Federation of Greater Chicago, the Chicago Board of Rabbis and the Union of American Hebrew Congregations, pledges its support to the program outlined and will enlist the full strength of its constituent bodies and their churches and synagogues in effecting equal access to housing in the metropolitan area for all people. They pledge to:

(1) Educate their membership on the moral necessity of an open and just community.

(2) Urge owners to sell or rent housing without racial restriction.

(3) Support local real estate offices and lending institutions in their cooperation with this program.

(4) Cooperate with and aid in the establishment of responsible community organizations and support them in the implementation of these programs.

(5) Undertake to secure peaceful acceptance and welcome Negro families prior to and at the time of their entrance into any community.

(6) Use their resources to help make housing available without racial discrimination.

(7) Establish, within 30 days, one or more housing centers, with the assistance of the real estate and housing industry and financial institutions, to provide information and help in finding suitable housing for minority families and to urge them to take advantage of new housing opportunities.

9. The representatives of the Chicago Association of Commerce and Industry, the Commercial Club, the Cosmopolitan Chamber of Commerce, Chicago Mortgage Bankers Association, Metropolitan Housing and Planning Council, Chicago Federation of Labor and Industrial Union Council, and other secular groups represented in these discussions recognize that their organizations have a major stake in working out

444

the problems of fair housing. Each such representative welcomes and pledges support to the program outlined in this report. Further, each undertakes to secure the support of his organization and its members, whether individuals, corporations, locals or groups, for the program and their participation in it, including education of their members on the importance to them of fair housing throughout the Chicago metropolitan area.

10. The Chicago Conference on Religion and Race will initiate forthwith the formation of a separate, continuing body, sponsored by major leadership organizations in the Chicago metropolitan area and built on a nucleus of the representatives of the organizations participating here. This body should accept responsibility for the execution and action programs necessary to achieve fair housing. It should be headed by a board consisting of recognized leaders from government, commerce, industry, finance, religion, real estate, labor, the civil rights movement, and the communications media. Its membership should reflect the diverse racial and ethnic composition of the entire Chicago metropolitan community.

The proposed board should have sufficient stature to formulate a strong and effective program and to provide adequate financing and staff to carry out that program. To the extent of available resources, it should carry forward programs such as, but not limited to, the convening of conferences on fair housing in suburban communities to the end that the policy of the City of Chicago on fair housing will be adopted in the whole Chicago metropolitan area. There must be a major effort in the pulpits, in the school systems, and in all other available forums to educate citizens of the metropolitan area in the fundamental principle that freedom of choice in housing is the right of every citizen and in their obligations to abide by the law and recognize the rights of others regardless of race, religion, or nationality. The group should assist in the drafting of fair housing laws and ordinances. It should make clear the stake that commerce, industry, banking, real estate, and labor, indeed all residing in the metropolitan area, have in the peaceful achievement of fair housing. The group should emphasize that the metropolitan housing market is a single market. The vigor and growth of that market is dependent upon an adequate supply of standard housing available without discrimination. The group should promote such practical measures as the development of fair housing centers after the model now being established by the Chicago Conference on Religion and Race. The group should in the immediate future set up specific goals for achievement of fair housing in the Chicago metropolitan area. Finally, the board should regularly review the performance of the program undertaken by governmental and non-governmental groups, take appropriate action thereon, and provide for public reports.

Although all of the metropolitan areas of the country are confronted with the problem of segregated housing, only in Chicago have the top leaders of the religious faiths, commerce, and industry, labor and government sat down together with leaders in the civil rights movement to seek practical solutions. With the start that has been made,

Chicago: Chicago Urban League, 1966; see also Chicago Commission on Human Relations, *Human Relations News of Chicago* 8 (September 1966): 1–4. These two published versions differ in insignificant details from each other and from the orginal document, cited as "Report of the Subcommittee to the Conference on Fair Housing Convened by the Chicago Conference on Religion and Race," 26 August 1966, in chapter 9, note 24.

the subcommittee is confident that the characteristic drive of Chicagoans to achieve their goals, manifest in the Chicago motto of "I Will," will enable the Chicago metropolitan area to lead the rest of the nation in the solution of the problems of fair housing.

Respectfully submitted,
THOMAS G. AYERS,
Chairman

The Color Line

as a Problem of Justice

Theories of justice are perhaps most notable for their differences from each other. They seem not to agree on fundamental definitions and ground rules; neither do they seem to coalesce around common conclusions as to why either general or particular courses of action should be endorsed or undertaken. In view of this thoroughgoing diversity, especially among those who take the problems and concepts of justice most seriously, and even though this apparently unresolvable contentiousness about the "good" has driven many to conclude that only practical complications and infinitely troublesome, counterproductive debates are involved in the use of "justice" language to explicate large social problems, it is surprising and potentially important that there is no major currrently developed theory of justice from whose perspective the rule of the color line could be anything but an injustice. The survey that follows is the briefest possible indication of the reasons for claiming that it is a matter of justice.

A LIBERTARIAN ARGUMENT

Since the color line is a distributive rule, if it is unjust, then any attempt to do justice would necessarily involve public policy aimed at redistribution. Among the serious theorists of justice, perhaps the most outspoken and principled critic of redistributive policies and goals is the libertarian Robert Nozick.[1] According to Nozick, redistributive policies merely for the sake of greater equality have no justification. Inequality per se is not a legitimate political or moral problem. Indeed, from Nozick's standpoint, it is to be desired and expected in a good society. The state does not exist to ensure or to pursue equality. Its raison d'être is liberty for individuals. He advances an "entitlement conception of justice," which entails three principles: acquisition, transfer, and rectification. This latter comes into play only when one or both of the first two have been violated. Unfortunately, this principle of rectification is the least discussed of Nozick's principles, but its sweep is apparently quite wide. "For example," he says,

> Lacking much historical information, and assuming (1) that victims of injustice generally do worse than they otherwise would and (2) that those from the least well-off group in the society have the highest probabilities of being the (descendants of) victims of the most serious injustice who are owed compensation by those who benefited from the injustices (assumed to be those better off, though sometimes the perpetrators will be others in the worst-off group), then a *rough* rule of thumb for rectifying injustices might seem to be the following: organize society

447

so as to maximize the position of whatever group ends up least well-off in the society. This particular example may well be implausible, but an important question for each society will be the following: given *its* particular history, what operable rule of thumb best approximates the results of a detailed application in that society of the principle of rectification? These issues are very complex and are best left to a full treatment of the principle of rectification. In the absence of such a treatment applied to a particular society, one *cannot* use the analysis and theory presented here to condemn any particular scheme of transfer payments, unless it is clear that no consideration of rectification of injustice could apply to justify it. Although to introduce socialism as the punishment for our sins would be to go too far, past injustices might be so great as to make necessary in the short run a more extensive state in order to rectify them.[2]

In the case of the color line, of course, we are not "lacking much historical information," so it seems that libertarians of the Nozick school should be prepared to make a strong case for redistributive "racial justice" based on their entitlement principle of rectification, one of three basic principles. This is potential support from a surprising source for extensive state action in the rectification of the rule of the color line. Support from this quarter, which is generally counted in the "neoconservative" corner, would certainly help in stemming the tide of declining attention to the issues of racial justice in this society and abroad.

A RATIONALIST ARGUMENT

Alan Gewirth's *Reason and Morality* is an argument for a "supreme principle of morality" for both individual and institutional action. His argument drives toward a direct confrontation with the rule of the color line. "Every agent," says Gewirth,

logically must acknowledge certain generic obligations. Negatively, he ought to refrain from coercing and from harming his recipients; positively, he ought to assist them to have freedom and well-being whenever they cannot otherwise have these necessary goods, and he can help them at no comparable cost to himself. The general principle of these rights and obligations may be expressed as the following precept addressed to every agent: *Act in accord with the generic rights of your recipients as well as of yourself.* I shall call this the Principle of Generic Consistency (PGC). . . .

The PGC is an egalitarian universalist moral principle since it requires an equal distribution of the most general rights of action. It says to every agent that just as, in acting, he necessarily manifests or embodies the generic features of action—voluntariness and purposiveness—and necessarily claims the generic goods as his rights, so he ought to accept that his recipients, too, should manifest or embody these same generic features and have these same generic goods as their rights.[3]

Nor does Gewirth's PGC remain an individualistic or merely interpersonal principle. It authorizes both a minimal and a supportive state capable of pursuing both retributive and redistributive justice. "In a broad sense," he says,

both retributive and redistributive justice are corrective and distributive in that both undertake, at least in part, to correct situations that are morally wrong (in that they violate the equality of generic rights) either by distributing penalties to persons who deserve them because of their criminal actions or by redistributing components of well-being. . . . The situation corrected by redistributive justice . . . does not carry a connotation of personal guilt because the situation is a social, dispositional one involving multitudes of persons whose comparative possession of well-being has, at least in part, a much broader historical and institutional base. Redistributive justice, as dynamic, seeks to move toward a previously nonexistent equality.[4]

Gewirth's argument would seem to authorize rather extensive state action on behalf of redistributive policies aimed at correcting the inequalities consequent to the rule of the color line, provided only that persons are not made to pay for crimes which they themselves did not commit and provided that the solution does not consist in imposing deprivations of voluntariness and purposiveness.

AN EGALITARIAN ARGUMENT

In John Rawls's *Theory of Justice,* there are two rules of justice, which in their elementary form are stated as follows:

First: each person is to have an equal right to the most extensive basic liberty compatible with a similar liberty for others.

Second: social and economic inequalities are to be arranged so that they are both (a) reasonably expected to be to everyone's advantage, and (b) attached to positions and offices open to all. . . .

By way of general comment, these principles primarily apply . . . to the basic structure of society. They are to govern the assignment of rights and duties and to regulate the distribution of social and economic advantages.

For the present, it should be observed that the two principles (and this holds for all formulations) are a special case of a more general conception of justice that can be expressed as follows:

All social values—liberty and opportunity, income and wealth, and the bases of self-respect—are to be distributed equally unless an unequal distribution of any, or all, of these values is to everyone's advantage.

Injustice, then, is simply inequalities that are not to the benefit of all.[5]

There have, of course, been sophists in all times who have argued that in some way or other the color line does distribute inequalities which are to the benefit of all.[6] But none of them could meet Rawls's standards for a "well-ordered society." Yet as obvious as that is in general, the case does need to be made much more specifically in relation to the actual dimensions and operations of the color line, which is, in our society at least, part of the "basic structure of society," the very level of reality to which Rawls's theory is addressed.

A UTILITARIAN ARGUMENT

Even the utilitarians, so much out of fashion and favor with these others (but still in command of the intellectual operations of most of our actual institutions, especially of government and business) provide grounds for justice which cannot reasonably be accommodated to the rule of the color line—at least if Dorothy Emmet is to be believed in her creative uncovering of the moral and empirical premises of that tradition.[7] She is aware that the utilitarian tradition, if it is to amount to anything

449

besides the universalization of cultural relativities and collective biases, and if it is to give any sort of moral guidance, must be rooted in something other than either tradition or preference. She claims that the search for such rooting is worthwhile because she finds in utilitarianism a subtle theory of moral judgment. "Although judgment is guided by rules," she observes, "it does not simply apply them automatically. Moral judgment remains problematic; it is indeed possible that skill in making moral judgments can grow through facing the fact that they are problematic."[8]

Consequently, the conditions and the contexts become as important as the judgments themselves. Judgments are problematic because, in part, the nature of the subject making the judgments is problematic in fairly specific and situational ways. In various versions of utilitarianism, the individual has been successively everything and nothing. But for Emmet, "respect for persons as a moral notion is not just awareness of individuals, it expresses a conviction about their status. The romantic notion of the bare subjective 'I' and the behavioristic notion of the incumbent of a role and function can be split off from this as limiting concepts. But in actual fact can we identify the pure subject in action apart from the social and institutional support represented by the notion of the human person?"[9]

The human person is an institutional being whose judgments are institutional judgments with the force arising from that person's institutional roles and functions. "If we look upon the notion of rights and obligations as arising out of the kinds of relations, ascriptive or contractual, in which we stand to people, it is obviously tempting," she says,

> to bring into line the notion of obligation to any other human being as such by talking, as the Stoics did, of the actions proper to a human being. If we do not use the notion of a general human role and function, we can rephrase the question by asking whether, besides particular obligations in particular roles, ethical systems include ideas of what would be right or wrong when done to anyone, whosoever he was. One might imagine an extension of moral relations thus happening logically through the character of moral judgment itself, by which reasons are demanded to justify differential treatment; and in time, in some cases, the reasons getting threadbare.[10]

Surely the rule of the color line could qualify as an institutional case of differential treatment whose reasons are "getting threadbare"; but in Emmet's utilitarianism, this is only the beginning of moral wisdom. It tells us that we face a problem of moral judgment; and of such judgments she counsels: "To face them responsibly is to approach them as *moral* problems, without special pleading, fear or favor. It is also to face them as moral *problems* where the answer is not always given just by looking up the local book of rules." At that point, Emmet's rule of utilitarianism recommends a rational search for a "rational procedural justice" rather than a "universal substantive code."[11]

A LIBERATION ARGUMENT

Finally, in this brief survey of diverse theories of justice, there is the liberationist school, which is generally thought to be set over against these more traditional modes of ethical thinking. According to James Cone, color has become both the literal and the symbolic locus of God's liberating presence in history. "The politics of the resurrection," he says,

> is found in its gift of freedom to the poor and the helpless. Being granted freedom while they are still poor, they can know that their poverty is a contrived phenomenon, traceable to the rich and the powerful of this world. This new knowledge about themselves and the world, as disclosed in and through the resurrection, requires that the poor practice political activity against the social and economic structures that make them poor. . . . If Jesus' presence is real and not docetic, is it not true that Christ *must* be black in order to remain faithful to the divine promise to bear the suffering of the poor? . . . The "blackness of Christ," therefore, is not simply a statement about skin color, but rather the transcendent affirmation that God has not ever, no not ever, left the oppressed alone in the struggle. . . . On the one hand, oppression is the denial of freedom, and therefore the opposite of liberation. But, on the other, in an unredeemed social existence no one can be free who is not oppressed, that is, identified with the struggle of the unfree. . . . It is material reality (social, economic, and political existence with the poor) that makes for the proper understanding of spiritual reality (all oppressed). . . . Because the phrase "all are oppressed" can be understood only from the perspective of the poor, only they are in a position to take seriously the *universal* dimension of the gospel of liberation. This places an awesome responsibility upon them. . . . The criteria of ethical judgment can only be hammered out in the community of the victims of injustice. . . . [Although] being a member of the oppressed community does not grant one immunity from error and sin. . . . White oppressors must be excluded from this black ethical dialogue, because they cannot be trusted. . . . They who are responsible for the dividing walls of hostility, racism and hatred, want to know whether the victims are ready to forgive and forget—without changing the balance of power. . . . There can be no reconciliation with God unless the hungry are fed, the sick are healed, and justice is given to the poor. . . . White people must be made to realize that reconciliation is a costly experience. . . . Separation is a fact of life. . . . We now know that reconciliation must start *first* with black brothers and sisters who have suffered the pain of a broken community.[12]

It is, perhaps, not clear what Cone's notion of ultimate justice through liberation is; but the same could be said of Emmet's natural procedural justice through utilitarianism. It is clear that the destructive rule of the color line stands out as both literally and symbolically indicative of the deepest injustice, an injustice for which Cone will brook no defense whatever, and an injustice which demands a regrouping of forces, new initiatives and demands from the victims, and an ultimate redistribution of power and resources. We did not recount Cone's inconclusive grappling with the complexities of violence as they arise in the rule of the color line or his rejection of nonviolence as an absolute moral principle because, in these respects, he does not differ from the other theorists under consideration. Violence is a moral problem in the rule of the color line, but it is not peculiarly his problem.

CONCLUSION

What this shows, altogether too briefly in this review of diverse justice concepts, is the remarkable unjustifiability of the rule of the color line when viewed from the perspective of these theories which are not otherwise remarkable for

451

their principled agreements. If we have a situation which neither libertarians nor liberationists, neither rationalists, nor egalitarians, nor utilitarians can justify, then it is clear that we have an exceptionally serious justice problem in our common life; judging from the relatively low priority which this issue has on the current national agenda, we have seriously underdeveloped but potentially powerful intellectual and practical resources for generating alternatives to this rule of the color line; and by all accounts, social justice means changing the rules.

Selected Characteristics

of CCCO Delegates

In February 1968, in collaboration with the National Opinion Research Center of the University of Chicago, we conducted a survey of CCCO delegates. Each person listed on the four published rosters of CCCO delegates was mailed a questionnaire with a cover letter explaining its purpose signed by Albert Raby. Fifty-three responses were returned from the total sample of 150 delegates. As the responses to numbers 12, 13, and 14 indicate, however, those delegates who did return the questionnaire were among those most active in CCCO.

The survey was designed to probe the moral and political beliefs of the respondents. Several of the items are interesting because they upset some of the conventional revisionist wisdom about participants in the civil rights movement. For instance, in response to the question, "Would you say you are a person who believes in non-violence?" eighteen said yes and twenty said no. This meant that for more than half of the respondents, including some who answered in the affirmative, the nonviolent discipline of the movement was a tactical rather than a principled commitment. In answer to the question, "Do you approve of the principle of black power?" forty-five said yes and four said no. In addition, forty-eight said yes and one said no when asked, "Should schools be integrated?" This seems to confirm our interpretation that black power and integration were perceived by participants in the civil rights movement as differences of emphasis rather than competing principles.

The information gathered through this survey also enables us to characterize the typical CCCO delegate as well-educated, middle-aged, male, professional, a long-term Chicago resident, and active in a variety of voluntary associations. One delegate in five was female, however.

The following is a summary of some responses to this survey by sex and race.

SURVEY

		Male Black	Male White	Female Black	Female White
1. What is your sex?	Male, 44; Female, 9				
2. What is your race?	White, 31; Black, 22				
3. What is your age?					
Under 20 years		0	0	0	0
20–29 years		0	3	1	0

453

SURVEY—*continued*

	Male Black	Male White	Female Black	Female White
30–39 years	5	11	1	1
40–49 years	8	12	3	0
50–59 years	2	1	0	2
60–69 years	3	1	0	1
70 years or over	0	0	0	0
4. What is your occupation?				
Minister	1	10	0	0
Lawyer	4	4	0	0
Teacher	3	4	0	1
Human Relations	1	3	2	0
Doctor	3	1	0	0
Social Worker	1	1	1	1
Student	0	2	0	0
Homemaker	0	0	1	0
Other	4	3	1	1
5. How much formal education have you had?				
10th grade or less	0	0	0	0
12th grade or less	2	0	1	0
Two years college or less	3	3	2	0
Four years college or less	0	2	0	1
Two years graduate school or less	4	5	2	1
More than two years graduate school	9	16	0	2
6. What is your highest educational degree?				
Grammar school certificate	1	0	1	0
High school diploma	4	2	1	0
College diploma	5	13	1	2
M.A., M.Ed., M.S.	2	6	2	1
Ph.D.	0	1	0	1
M.D., D.D.S., J.D., L.L.B.	6	5	0	0
7. Where were you born?				
Chicago and suburbs	6	13	1	1
Northern city	2	3	0	0
Southern city	4	1	3	0
Northern rural	1	8	0	3
Southern rural	5	0	1	0
Border/West	0	1	0	0
8. In which state or states were you raised?				
Illinois	10	12	3	1
North	1	10	0	3

Selected Characteristics of CCCO Delegates

SURVEY—*continued*

	Male Black	Male White	Female Black	Female White
South	6	1	2	0
Border	0	3	0	0
West	1	0	0	0
9. How many years have you lived in Chicago?				
1–5	0	2	0	1
6–10	1	4	1	0
11–20	5	12	0	0
21–30	4	4	2	0
31–40	2	3	1	2
41–65	5	4	1	1
10. What year did you first become active in civil rights activities?				
1967	0	0	0	0
1966	0	0	0	0
1965	0	0	0	0
1964	1	3	0	0
1963	1	6	1	0
1962	0	3	0	0
1961	2	2	1	0
1956–1960	2	2	2	2
1951–1955	2	5	1	0
1946–1950	1	4	0	0
1941–1945	2	1	0	2
1930–1940	3	1	0	0
1920–1929	3	0	0	0
11. What civil rights organizations have you been active in during the last five years?				
American Civil Liberties Union	0	4	0	0
American Friends Service Committee	0	1	0	0
Catholic Interracial Council	1	0	0	0
Chatham–Avalon Park Community Council	1	0	0	0
Community Organizations	4	12	2	0
Congress of Racial Equality	0	1	1	1
Episcopal Society for Cultural and Racial Unity	1	2	0	1
National Association for the Advancement of Colored People	10	2	1	0

455

SURVEY—*continued*

	Male Black	Male White	Female Black	Female White
National Lawyers Guild	0	1	0	0
Operation Breadbasket	2	0	1	0
Religious Organizations	0	11	1	0
Southern Christian Lead- ership Conference	2	2	1	0
Student Nonviolent Coordi- nating Committee	2	2	2	0
Teachers for Integrated Schools	3	0	0	1
Urban League	4	1	1	0
Other	3	9	3	0
12. During what years were you a delegate or alternate to CCCO?				
1961	2	0	1	0
1962	2	1	2	0
1963	6	8	1	2
1964	9	17	2	3
1965	16	21	3	4
1966	10	17	2	3
1967	8	12	1	2
13. How many years were you a delegate or alternate to CCCO?				
One	3	1	2	0
Two	2	15	1	1
Three	4	4	1	1
Four	2	3	0	1
Five	4	2	1	1
Six	0	1	0	0
Seven	1	0	0	0
14. During what years were you most active in CCCO?				
1961	2	0	1	0
1962	2	1	1	0
1963	5	9	0	1
1964	9	13	1	2
1965	14	17	2	3
1966	9	10	2	3
1967	7	6	0	2
15. What, if any, is your own religious affiliation?				
Baptist	3	1	0	0
Catholic	1	4	2	0
Episcopalian	1	2	0	1
Jewish	0	2	0	0

Selected Characteristics of CCCO Delegates

SURVEY—*continued*

	Male Black	Male White	Female Black	Female White
Methodist	2	5	0	0
Presbyterian	0	1	0	0
Protestant (Other)	5	4	2	1
Quaker	0	2	0	0
Unitarian	2	1	0	0
None	2	4	1	2

Notes

INTRODUCTION

1. This literature is extensive and diverse. Exemplary works include August Meier and Elliott Rudwick, *CORE: A Study in the Civil Rights Movement, 1942–1968* (New York: Oxford University Press, 1973); and Stephen B. Oates, *Let the Trumpet Sound: The Life of Martin Luther King, Jr.* (New York: Harper & Row, 1982). For the local movements see Martin Luther King, Jr., *Stride toward Freedom: The Montgomery Story* (New York: Harper and Brothers, 1958; paperback ed., Ballantine Books, 1958); William H. Chafe, *Civilities and Civil Rights: Greensboro, North Carolina, and the Black Struggle for Freedom* (New York: Oxford University Press, 1980; paperback ed. by the same publisher, 1981); Martin Luther King, Jr., *Why We Can't Wait* (New York: Harper & Row, 1964; paperback ed., Signet Books, 1964); David J. Garrow, *Protest at Selma: Martin Luther King, Jr., and the Voting Rights Act of 1965* (New Haven: Yale University Press, 1978).

2. All of the primary materials now in our possession—Hogan's minutes, John McKnight's account, Alvin Pitcher's notes, and other documents—will be deposited at the Chicago Historical Society. All of these materials are filed by date. To avoid excessive footnotes in this volume, we have included dates of meetings in the text.

   Our files include our notes from interviews with the following CCCO delegates: Timuel D. Black, 23 February 1965; Charles Fischer, 28 February 1965; Herbert Fisher, 21 February 1965; William Hogan, 15 February 1965; James Mack, 22 February 1965; Albert A. Raby, 15 August 1967, 11 September 1967, and 13 June 1985; Don Rose, 15 August 1965; Foster Stockwell, 21 February 1965; Irene Turner, 18 February 1967; and Kale Williams, 26 April 1983.

   An earlier and more detailed version of Chapters 2–6 can be found in the jointly authored appendixes to Alan B. Anderson, "The Issue of the Color Line: Some Methodological Considerations," and George W. Pickering, "The Issue of the Color Line: Some Interpretative Considerations" (both Ph.D. dissertations, University of Chicago, 1975). These appendixes differ only in pagination.

3. Our file of clippings from the five Chicago dailies will be deposited at the Chicago Historical Society.

4. Hannah Arendt emphasizes this intrinsic quality of action and the human significance of stories in *The Human Condition* (Chicago: University of Chicago Press, 1958), pp. 175–247.

5. Alexis de Tocqueville, *Democracy in America*, in two volumes with a critical appraisal of each volume by John Stuart Mill (New York: Schocken Books, 1961).

459

6. W. E. B. DuBois, *The Souls of Black Folk* (Chicago: A. C. McClurg, 1903): rpt. in *Three Negro Classics,* intro. by John Hope Franklin (New York: Avon Books, 1965).

7. Gunnar Myrdal, *An American Dilemma: The Negro Problem and Modern Democracy* (1944; twentieth anniversary ed., New York: Harper & Row, 1962). The quotations are from pp. lxxi and 24.

8. 347 U.S. 483 (1954).

9. For a more detailed examination of alternative interpretations of the civil rights movement, see Alan B. Anderson, "The Issue of the Color Line: Some Methodological Considerations" (Ph.D. dissertation, University of Chicago, 1975), esp. pp. 6–16.

10. In addition to our subsequent references to William James and John Dewey, see James Luther Adams, "The Pragmatic Theory of Meaning," Presidential Address, American Society of Christian Ethics, Washington, D.C., 24 January 1969 (mimeographed); and Richard McKeon, *Freedom and History: The Semantics of Philosophical Controversies and Ideological Conflicts* (New York: Noonday Press, 1952).

11. William James, *The Varieties of Religious Experience: A Study in Human Nature,* Gifford Lectures, 1901–2 (New York: Random House, Modern Library, n.d.), p. 56.

12. For a related argument for the priority of the issue in social ethical inquiry, see Alan B. Anderson, "The Search for Method in Social Ethics," in W. Widick Schroeder and Gibson Winter, eds., *Belief and Ethics: Essays in Ethics, the Human Sciences, and Ministry in Honor of W. Alvin Pitcher* (Chicago: Center for the Scientific Study of Religion, 1978), pp. 107–28.

CHAPTER ONE. THE RACIAL DILEMMAS OF LIBERAL DEMOCRACY

1. John Dewey, *The Public and Its Problems* (Denver: Alan Swallow, n.d.), p. 3.

2. Alexis de Tocqueville, *Democracy in America,* in two volumes with a critical appraisal of each volume by John Stuart Mill (New York: Schocken Books, 1961), 1:452, 427.

3. Ibid., p. 445.

4. Ibid., pp. 451, 426.

5. August Meier and Elliott Rudwick, *From Plantation to Ghetto,* 3d ed. (New York: Hill and Wang, 1976), p. 153.

6. LaWanda Cox and John H. Cox, eds., *Reconstruction, the Negro, and the New South* (New York: Harper & Row, 1973; Harper Torchbook, 1973), pp. 31–34.

7. Ibid., pp. xiv–xv.

8. John Sproat, *"The Best Men": Liberal Reformers in the Gilded Age* (New York: Oxford University Press, 1968), pp. 29–32.

9. John Hope Franklin, *From Slavery to Freedom: A History of Negro Americans,* 3d ed. (New York: Alfred A. Knopf, 1967), pp. 332, 384.

10. Rayford Logan, *The Betrayal of the Negro: From Rutherford B. Hayes to Woodrow Wilson* (New York: Collier Books, 1965).

11. C. Vann Woodward, *The Strange Career of Jim Crow* (New York: Oxford University Press, 1957).
12. 163 U.S. 537 (1896).
13. The definitive biography of Washington is Louis R. Harland, *Booker T. Washington: The Making of a Black Leader, 1856–1901* (New York: Oxford University Press, 1972), and *Booker T. Washington: The Wizard of Tuskegee, 1901–1915* (New York: Oxford University Press, 1983). See Meier and Rudwick, *From Plantation to Ghetto,* pp. 220–31, for a summary of Washington's thought and influence.
14. Booker T. Washington, *Up from Slavery* (New York: Doubleday, Page and Co., 1901); rpt. in *Three Negro Classics,* intro. by John Hope Franklin (New York: Avon Books, 1965), pp. 146–50. The quotations are from pp. 146–47, 148.
15. W. E. B. DuBois, *The Souls of Black Folk,* in *Three Negro Classics,* pp. 221, 247.
16. Ibid., p. 246. For a brief but fair-minded treatment of Washington's complex career, see August Meier, *Negro Thought in America, 1880–1915: Radical Ideologies in the Age of Booker T. Washington* (Ann Arbor: University of Michigan Press, 1963), esp. pp. 100–118.
17. Elliott M. Rudwick, *W. E. B. DuBois: A Study in Minority Group Leadership* (Philadelphia: University of Pennsylvania Press, 1960; rpt. New York: Atheneum, 1969), p. 95.
18. Franklin, *From Slavery to Freedom,* p. 445.
19. Rudwick, *DuBois,* pp. 94–119.
20. Ibid., pp. 110, 115, 116.
21. DuBois, *Souls,* p. 215.
22. For a succinct account of the breakup of the Niagara Movement, see Rudwick, *DuBois,* pp. 99–119.
23. Meier, *Negro Thought;* and Margaret Just Butcher, *The Negro in American Culture, Based on Materials Left by Alain Locke* (New York: Alfred A. Knopf, 1956).
24. Neal R. Peirce, James G. Phillips, and Victoria Velsey, eds., *Revolution in Civil Rights* (Washington, D.C.: Congressional Quarterly Service, 1965), p. 4.
25. Herbert Garfinkel, *When Negroes March: The March on Washington Movement in the Organizational Politics for FEPC,* Studies in American Negro Life, ed. August Meier (New York: Atheneum, 1969), pp. 37–61.

   This victory did not last long. The president's commission lasted hardly a year. Randolph's movement had raised an issue that remained unfinished business on the national agenda even forty years later. Not until 1964 did equality of employment opportunities achieve legal status through Title VII of the Civil Rights Act of 1964. In 1966 the Equal Employment Opportunity Commission came into being under Title VII, twenty years after the final meeting of Randolph's March on Washington Movement (ibid., p. 104).
26. August Meier and Elliott Rudwick, *CORE: A Study in the Civil Rights Movement, 1942–1968* (New York: Oxford University Press, 1973), pp. 3–39.
27. Thurgood Marshall, "The Legal Attack to Secure Civil Rights," an address delivered 13 July 1944 at the NAACP Wartime Conference, reprinted in August Meier, Elliott Rudwick, and Francis Broderick, eds., *Black Protest Thought in the Twen-*

tieth Century, American Heritage Series, 2d ed. (Indianapolis: Bobbs-Merrill, 1971), p. 260.

28. *Smith* v. *Allright,* 321 U.S. 649 (1944).
29. Meier and Rudwick, *From Plantation to Ghetto,* pp. 243–46, 263–64.
30. Gunnar Myrdal, *An American Dilemma: The Negro Problem and Modern Democracy* (1944; Twentieth Anniversary ed., Harper & Row, 1962), p. lv; Ralph J. Bunche, "The Programs of Organizations Devoted to the Improvement of the Status of the American Negro," *Journal of Negro Education* 8 (July 1939):539–50, rpt. in August Meier and Elliott Rudwick, eds., *The Making of Black America: Essays in Negro Life and History,* Studies in American Negro Life, ed. August Meier, 2 vols. (New York: Atheneum, 1969), 2:245–56.
31. Bunche, "Programs of Organizations," p. 245.
32. Ibid., pp. 246–47.
33. Ibid., p. 256.
34. Myrdal, *American Dilemma,* pp. 852–57. The quotations are from pp. 853, 854, and 857. The emphasis on specialization across a broad political spectrum was in keeping with his rank order of discriminations and principle of cumulation, discussed below.
35. Ibid., Appendix 2, "A Methodological Note on Facts and Valuations in Social Science," pp. 1035–64.
36. Ibid., pp. 4–5, 21.
37. Ibid., pp. 23–24.
38. Ibid., p. lxxi. For critiques of Myrdal's central thesis, see Oliver Cox, *Caste, Class and Race* (Garden City, N.Y.: Doubleday, 1948); Robert K. Merton, "Discrimination and the American Creed," in R. M. MacIver, ed., *Discrimination and National Welfare* (New York: Institute for Religious and Social Studies, 1949); and Nathan Z. Medalia, "Assumptions on Race Relations: A Conceptual Commentary," *Social Forces* 40 (March 1962):223–37.
39. Ibid., p. 1031.
40. Ibid., Appendix 1, "A Methodological Note on Valuations and Beliefs," pp. 1027–34. The quotations are from pp. 1030 and 1028.
41. Ibid., pp. 1031, 1032.
42. Ibid., p. 1032.
43. Ibid., pp. 60–61.
44. Ibid., p. 61.
45. Ibid., pp. 75–78; the quotation is from p. 76. See also Appendix 3, "A Methodological Note on the Principle of Cumulation," pp. 1065–72.
46. Ibid., pp. 997–1010. The quotations are from pp. 997, 1003, and 1004.
47. Ibid., pp. 1011–21. The quotations are from pp. 1014 and 1009.
48. Ibid., pp. 1022–24.
49. Ibid., p. 1021.
50. Ibid., p. 24.
51. Ibid., pp. 167–71. The quotations are from pp. 169 and 170. To examine Myrdal's specification of his value premises, the American creed, for the other topics included in his study, see the entries in his Index at "Value premises."
52. Ibid., pp. 209–15. The quotations are from pp. 209 and 212.

53. Ibid. The quotations are from pp. 214 and 218.
54. Ibid., pp. 573–74. The quotations are from p. 573.
55. Ibid., pp. 879–907.
56. St. Clair Drake and Horace Cayton, *Black Metropolis: A Study of Negro Life in a Northern City* (New York: Harcourt, Brace, 1945), pp. 764, 765, 766.
57. Myrdal, *American Dilemma,* p. lxi.
58. DuBois lived until 1963, and he continued to write about racial matters to the end. In discussing his perspective in these pages, we limit our observations simply to the point of view he articulated at the turn of the century in *The Souls of Black Folk* and in the resolutions of the Niagara Movement.

CHAPTER TWO. THE DEVELOPMENT OF THE COLOR LINE IN CHICAGO AND THE EMERGENCE OF THE CIVIC CREDO VIEW

1. For more comprehensive studies of the growth of the color line in Chicago, see Chicago Commission on Race Relations, *The Negro in Chicago: A Study of Race Relations and a Race Riot* (1922; rpt. New York: Arno Press and New York Times, 1968), which was produced by the commission appointed by Governor Frank O. Lowden to investigate the race riot of 1919; St. Clair Drake and Horace Cayton, *Black Metropolis: A Study of Negro Life in a Northern City* (New York: Harcourt, Brace, 1945); Allan H. Spear, *Black Chicago: The Making of a Negro Ghetto, 1890–1920* (Chicago: University of Chicago Press, 1967); Otis Duncan and Beverly Duncan, *The Negro Population of Chicago* (Chicago: University of Chicago Press, 1957); Arnold R. Hirsch, *Making the Second Ghetto: Race and Housing in Chicago* (Cambridge: Cambridge University Press, 1983); Thomas L. Philpott, *The Slum and the Ghetto: Neighborhood Deterioration and Middle Class Reform, Chicago, 1880–1930* (New York: Oxford University Press, 1978); Glen Holt and Dominic Pasyga, *Chicago: A Historical Guide to the Neighborhoods: The Loop and the South Side* (Chicago: Chicago Historical Society, 1979); and the periodic reports by Pierre de Vise, for example, *Chicago's Widening Color Gap,* Inter-University Social Research Committee, Report No. 2 (Chicago, 1967).
2. Mary J. Herrick, *The Chicago Schools: A Social and Political History* (Beverly Hills: Sage, 1971), Appendix B, "Legal Rights to Education of Black Children in Illinois," p. 400.
3. Ibid., pp. 52–53; Spear, *Black Chicago,* p. 6; James Q. Wilson, *Negro Politics: The Search for Leadership* (Glencoe, Ill.: Free Press, 1960), p. 50.
4. Spear, *Black Chicago,* pp. 85, 86, 22–23, 87; see also Elliott M. Rudwick, "The Niagara Movement," *Journal of Negro History* 42 (July 1957):187.
5. Spear, *Black Chicago,* pp. 17, 20.
6. Rose Helper, *Racial Policies and Practices of Real Estate Brokers* (Minneapolis: University of Minnesota Press, 1969), p. 224.
7. *Chicago Real Estate Board Bulletin* 25 (April 1917): 315–17, quoted in Helper, *Racial Policies and Practices,* p. 225.
8. Ibid.

9. *Buchanan* v. *Warley,* 245 U.S. 60 (1917).

10. *Chicago Real Estate Board Bulletin* 25 (November 1917): 623–24, quoted in full in Helper, *Racial Policies and Practices,* p. 226. By 1924, it had become part of the National Association of Real Estate Boards' Code of Ethics, Part III, Article 34: "A Realtor should never be instrumental in introducing into a neighborhood a character of property or occupancy, members of any race or nationality, or any individuals whose presence will be clearly detrimental to property values in that neighborhood." In 1950, this article was amended and became Part I, Article 5: "A Realtor should not be instrumental in introducing into a neighborhood a character of property or use which will clearly be detrimental to property values in that neighborhood." It meant the same thing. See Helper, *Racial Policies and Practices,* p. 201.

11. Harold F. Gosnell, *Negro Politicians: The Rise of Negro Politics in Chicago,* intro. James Q. Wilson (1935; rpt. Chicago: University of Chicago, Phoenix Books, 1967), pp. 73–74.

12. Ibid., pp. 37–62; Appendix, Tables XIX, XX, and XXI, pp. 377–79.

13. *Chicago Tribune,* 3 August 1919, quoted in Spear, *Black Chicago,* p. 217. For a full study of the 1919 Chicago riot, see William M. Tuttle, Jr., *Race Riot: Chicago in the Red Summer of 1919,* Studies in American Negro Life, ed. August Meier (New York: Atheneum, 1970).

14. Chicago Commission on Race Relations, *Negro in Chicago,* pp. 109–10, 48–49.

15. Harold M. Mayer and Richard C. Wade with the assistance of Glen E. Holt, *Chicago: Growth of a Metropolis* (Chicago: University of Chicago Press, 1969), p. 284.

16. Rose Helper, "Racial Policies and Practices of Real Estate Brokers: The Racial Practices of Real Estate Institutions in Selected Areas of Chicago" (Ph.D. dissertation, University of Chicago, 1958), p. 587. Thomas L. Philpott (*Slum and Ghetto,* pp. 189–200) has an excellent account of the marketing of restrictive covenants in Chicago. He also describes the role of William MacChesney, a Chicagoan who was also general counsel to the National Association of Real Estate Boards: "MacChesney drew up Article 34, which the association added to its Code of Ethics in 1924. . . . To give Article 34 credibility, MacChesney drafted a model real estate licensing act, which thirty-two states eventually adopted. The act empowered state commissions to revoke all licenses of agents who violated the National Real Estate Board's Code of Ethics" (p. 190).

17. Herman H. Long and Charles S. Johnson, *People vs. Property?: Race Restrictive Covenants in Housing* (Nashville: Fisk University Press, 1947), pp. 10–55.

18. *Shelly* v. *Kramer,* 334 U.S. 1 (1948).

19. Long and Johnson, *People vs. Property?* p. 12.

20. See Zorita Wise Mikva, "The Neighborhood Improvement Association: A Counterforce to the Expansion of Chicago's Negro Population" (M.A. thesis, University of Chicago, 1951).

21. Drake and Cayton, *Black Metropolis,* p. 176; supported by Robert C. Weaver, *The Negro Ghetto* (New York: Harcourt, Brace, 1948), pp. 15–20, 35–51; Otis Dudley Duncan and Beverly Duncan, *The Negro Population of Chicago: A Study of Residential Succession* (Chicago: University of Chicago Press, 1957), pp. 87–107; and

see Gosnell, *Negro Politicians,* Fig. I, p. 21, for a map showing the concentration and distribution of Chicago's black population in 1930.

22. Mayor's Committee on Race Relations, *City Planning in Race Relations: Proceedings of the Mayor's Conference on Race Relations* (Chicago: Mayor's Committee on Race Relations, 1944), as summarized in Drake and Cayton, *Black Metropolis,* pp. 201–2.

23. Long and Johnson, *People vs. Property?* found that "terroristic attacks on Negro homes during a recent two-year period (1944–46) almost doubled the number of such incidents occurring within the two-year period preceding the 1919 riot" (pp. 73–74).

24. *Chicago Defender,* 17 August 1918, quoted in Spear, *Black Chicago,* pp. 203–4.

25. Affidavit of Benjamin C. Willis, 15 December 1961, *Webb v. Board of Education of Chicago,* U.S. District Court, Northern District of Illinois, Eastern Division, No. 61 C 1569, p. 3.

26. Herrick, *Chicago Schools,* pp. 141–43.

27. Harold F. Gosnell, *Machine Politics: Chicago Model* (1937; 2d ed., Chicago: University of Chicago Press, Phoenix Books, 1968), p. 11.

28. Ibid., p. 7; Martin Levit, "The Chicago Schools Committee: A Study of a Pressure Group" (M.A. thesis, University of Chicago, 1947), p. 11.

29. Mayer, Wade, and Holt, *Chicago,* p. 358; Levit, "Chicago Schools Committee," pp. 12, 13.

30. Gosnell, *Machine Politics,* p. 14.

31. Arthur M. Schlesinger, Jr., *The Age of Roosevelt: The Crisis of the Old Order, 1919–1933* (Boston: Houghton Mifflin, 1954), pp. 464–65.

32. Gosnell, *Machine Politics,* pp. 15–16.

33. Levit, "Chicago Schools Committee," p. 14; Mayor's Committee on Race Relations, *City Planning in Race Relations,* pp. 22, 16, 89.

34. Harold M. Baron, "History of Chicago School Segregation to 1953," *Integrated Education* 1 (January 1963): 18.

35. Drake and Cayton, *Black Metropolis,* pp. 77–97.

36. Gosnell, *Negro Politicians,* pp. 89–92; Wilson, *Negro Politics,* pp. 48–51.

37. Myrdal, *American Dilemma,* p. 494; Wilson, *Negro Politics,* pp. 48–51, 81.

38. Drake and Cayton, *Black Metropolis,* pp. 201–6; Philpott, *Slum and Ghetto,* pp. 113–200.

39. Mayor's Committee on Race Relations, *Human Relations in Chicago: Reports of Commissions and Charter of Human Relations Adopted by Chicago Conference on Home Front Unity, 30 October and 6 November 1945* (Chicago: Mayor's Committee on Race Relations, 1945). According to Edwin R. Embree, "Chicago was the first American city to recognize this official responsibility for the human relations of its citizens. Our lead has been followed by more than fifty somewhat similar agencies in cities and states across the country" (ibid., p. 4).

40. Wilma Dykeman and James Stokely, *Seeds of Southern Change: The Life of Will Alexander* (Chicago: University of Chicago Press, 1962), pp. 283–84, 263–64.

41. See Mayor's Committee on Race Relations, *City Planning in Race Relations.*

42. Ibid., pp. 6–11.

43. Ibid., p. 22.

44. Ibid., pp. 22–24.
45. Ibid., pp. 29–31.
46. Ibid., pp. 63–64.
47. Ibid., p. 17.
48. Mayor's Committee on Race Relations, *Race Relations in Chicago: Report of the Mayor's Committee on Race Relations, December 1944* (Chicago: Mayor's Committee on Race Relations, 1944), p. 12.
49. Ibid., p. 13.
50. Mayor's Committee on Race Relations, *Home Front Unity: Proceedings of the Chicago Conference on Home Front Unity, May–June 1945* (Chicago: Mayor's Committee on Race Relations, 1945), p. 6.
51. Ibid., pp. 23–24.
52. Ibid., p. 28.
53. Mayor's Committee on Race Relations, *Human Relations in Chicago*, 1945, pp. 39–40.
54. Mayor's Commission on Human Relations, *Human Relations in Chicago: Report of the Mayor's Commission on Human Relations in 1946* (Chicago: Mayor's Commission on Human Relations, 1946), p. 34.
55. Mayor's Committee on Race Relations, *Human Relations in Chicago*, 1945, pp. 6–8.
56. Mayor's Commission on Human Relations, *Race Relations in Chicago: Report of the Mayor's Commission on Human Relations for 1945* (Chicago: Mayor's Commission on Human Relations, 1945), p. 18.
57. Ibid., pp. 15, 24.
58. Mayor's Commission on Human Relations, *Human Relations in Chicago, 1946*, pp. 61–62, 72; Appendix I, pp. 116–18; Appendix II, pp. 119–55.
59. Ibid., p. 95.
60. National Education Association, Commission on the Defense of Democracy through Education, "Certain Personnel Practices in Chicago Public Schools: Report of an Investigation" (Washington, D.C.: National Education Association, May 1945), pp. 63–64. See also Levit, "Chicago Schools Committee," pp. 79–81; Joseph Pois, *The School Board Crisis: A Chicago Case Study* (Chicago: Educational Methods, 1964), pp. 10–16; and Kay Hodes Kamin, "A History of the Hunt Administration of the Chicago Public Schools: 1947–1953" (Ph.D. dissertation, University of Chicago, 1970).
61. Herrick, *Chicago Schools*, pp. 274–75.
62. Ibid., pp. 276–77.
63. Ibid., pp. 277–78, 284–85.
64. *Chicago Daily News*, 9 February 1949, quoted in Kamin, "Hunt Administration," p. 142.
65. Baron, "Chicago School Segregation," p. 19; Kamin, "Hunt Administration," pp. 145–47.
66. Herrick, *Chicago Schools*, p. 285.
67. Kamin, "Hunt Administration," p. 144.
68. Mayor's Committee on Race Relations, *City Planning in Race Relations*, pp. 63–64.

69. Mayor's Committee on Race Relations, *Race Relations in Chicago, 1944*, p. 3.

70. Chicago Commission on Human Relations, *The People of Chicago: Five Year Report, 1947–51, of the Chicago Commission on Human Relations* (Chicago: Chicago Commission on Human Relations, 1951), p. 2.

71. Ibid., pp. 43, 48.

72. Ibid., pp. 46–48.

73. Mikva, "Neighborhood Improvement Association," p. 108.

74. Herrick, *Chicago Schools*, p. 311.

75. *Chicago Schools Journal*, March 1954, quoted in ibid., p. 425, n. 11.

76. Anthony Lewis and the New York Times, *Portrait of a Decade: The Second American Revolution* (New York: Random House, Bantam Books, 1965), p. 204.

77. Morton Grodzins, *The Metropolitan Area as a Racial Problem* (Pittsburgh: University of Pittsburgh Press, 1958), p. 11.

CHAPTER THREE. THE EMERGENCE OF THE DE FACTO SEGREGATION VIEW

1. *Brown v. Board of Education* 347 U.S. 483 (1954), note 5.

2. *Plessy v. Ferguson* 163 U.S. 537 (1896).

3. August Meier and Elliott Rudwick, *From Plantation to Ghetto*, 3d ed. (New York: Hill and Wang, 1976), pp. 264–65. For an excellent and detailed study of the *Brown* decision and its historical background, see Richard Kluger, *Simple Justice: The History of Brown v. Board of Education and Black America's Struggle for Equality* (New York: Alfred A. Knopf, 1976; paperback ed., New York: Vintage Books, 1977).

4. *Sweatt v. Painter*, 339 U.S. 629 (1950).

5. For the many important connections of the Myrdal study with *Brown* and the litigation that preceded it, see the index listings for Myrdal in Kluger, *Simple Justice*. Although Myrdal's acceptance of school segregation made it possible for both sides to cite him in the school desegregation cases, it is clear that, on balance, his influence was overwhelmingly positive. See also ibid., pp. 657–99.

6. Ibid., pp. 679–80.

7. *Brown v. Board of Education* 347 U.S. 483 (1954).

8. *Brown v. Board of Education* 349 U.S. 294 (1955).

9. Richard Bardolph, ed., *The Civil Rights Record: Black Americans and the Law, 1849–1970* (New York: Thomas Y. Crowell, 1970), pp. 378–93.

10. Neal R. Peirce, James G. Phillips, and Victoria Velsey, eds., *Revolution in Civil Rights* (Washington, D.C.: Congressional Quarterly Service, 1965), p. 78.

11. See below, Chapter 14, notes 9–15.

12. Martin Meyerson and Edward C. Banfield, *Politics, Planning, and the Public Interest* (Glencoe, Ill.: Free Press, 1955).

13. John Fish, Gordon Nelson, Walter Stuhr, and Lawrence Witmer, *Edge of the Ghetto: A Study of Church Involvement in Community Organization* (Chicago: Church Federation of Greater Chicago and the Divinity School, University of Chicago, 1966). The one exception was Hyde Park–Kenwood, where the vital interests of the University of Chicago called for the full use of its power and

prestige in Washington as well as Chicago in an effort to establish the solid and stable middle-class environment the university seemed to require for continued operation. See Julia Abrahamson, *A Neighborhood Finds Itself* (New York: Harper, 1959); and Peter H. Rossi and Robert A. Dentler, *The Politics of Urban Renewal: The Chicago Findings* (New York: Free Press, 1961).

14. "De Facto Segregation in the Chicago Public Schools," *Crisis* 65 (February 1958): 87–93, 126–27.
15. Meyer Weinberg, "De Facto Segregation: Fact or Artifact?" *Integrated Education* 1, no. 2 (April 1963): 30.
16. "De Facto Segregation in the Chicago Public Schools," p. 88.
17. Ibid., pp. 88, 89, 90, 92.
18. See James Q. Wilson, *Negro Politics: The Search for Leadership* (Glencoe, Ill.: Free Press, 1960), pp. 63–65, for a succinct account and fairly moderate interpretation of that election and subsequent events.
19. "De Facto Segregation in the Chicago Public Schools," p. 90.
20. *Webb* v. *Board of Education of Chicago,* U.S. District Court, Northern District of Illinois, Eastern Division, 61 C 1569, "Affidavit in answer to Affidavit of Paul B. Zuber," 15 December 1961, pp. 15, 18, 19, 20–23. Hereafter references to this case will be cited as *Webb 61 C 1569* together with the title and date of the document.
21. *Webb 61 C 1569,* "Affidavit in answer to Affidavit by Paul B. Zuber," 15 December 1961, pp. 15, 18, 19, 20–23.
22. *Taylor* v. *Board of Education,* summarized in U.S. Commission on Civil Rights, *Racial Isolation in the Public Schools,* 2 vols. (Washington, D.C.: U.S. Government Printing Office, 1967) 1:220–21.
23. *Chicago Daily Defender,* 18 February 1961, 4 March 1961. This group was variously known as the Committee to End Discrimination in the Chicago Schools, the Committee to Integrate Chicago Schools, and Chicago Committee for Equality in Education. Its steering committee included Mrs. Harold Baron, sometime spokesperson; George Reed, research chemist; Faith Rich, former teacher, chair of CORE's school committee, and one of the principal authors of "De Facto Segregation"; James King, president of the Gregory School Block Committee; Joseph Levin, psychologist; Rose Simpson and Ella Pappademos, interested citizens and concerned parents; and John Olson and Harold Baron, teachers. Harold Baron was soon to become a researcher for the Chicago Urban League.
24. *Crisis* 68 (April 1961): 240–41.
25. Ibid. 68 (May 1961): 301–3.
26. *Chicago Daily Defender,* editorial, 13 March 1961.
27. Ibid., 5, 13 April 1961. The major community areas of Chicago are shown on Map 3. A comparison of this map with Map 1 shows that Chatham and Avalon Park underwent major racial transition between 1950 and 1960.
28. *Chicago Sun-Times,* 4 September 1961.
29. *Chicago Daily Defender,* 8 September 1961.
30. Ibid.
31. Interview, Herbert Fisher, 21 February 1965. For the background of TWO see Charles E. Silberman, *Crisis in Black and White* (New York: Random House,

1964), pp. 318–50; and John Hall Fish, *Black Power/White Control: The Struggle of The Woodlawn Organization in Chicago* (Princeton: Princeton University Press, 1973).

32. Interview, Herbert Fisher, 21 February 1965.

33. *McNeese* v. *Board of Education*, Cahokia, Illinois, 373 U.S. 668 (1963).

34. *Chicago Daily News*, 31 August 1963.

35. *Webb 61 C 1569*, "Interrogatories Propounded by Defendants to Plaintiffs," 13 December 1961, pp. 6–9; ibid., "Affidavit in answer to Affidavit by Paul B. Zuber," 15 December 1961, pp. 23–24.

36. Ibid., "Affidavit in answer to Affidavit by Paul B. Zuber," p. 26.

37. Ibid., "Motion to Dismiss," 20 November 1961, p. 2.

38. There were front-page accounts in both the *Chicago Tribune* and the *Chicago Sun-Times*, 17 October 1961.

39. *Chicago Sun-Times*, 20 October 1961; interview, Albert A. Raby, 15 August 1967.

40. *Chicago Sun-Times*, 9 November 1961; see also U.S. Civil Rights Commission, *Civil Rights U.S.A.: Public Schools, Cities in the North and West 1962—Chicago, Staff Report to the United States Commission on Civil Rights*, prepared by John E. Coons (Washington, D.C.: U.S. Government Printing Office, 1962), pp. 199–200.

41. See Arvarh E. Strickland, *History of the Chicago Urban League* (Urbana: University of Illinois Press, 1966), pp. 242–59; *Chicago's American*, 19 December 1961.

42. Mary J. Herrick, *The Chicago Schools: A Social and Political History* (Beverly Hills: Sage, 1971), p. 326; Willis quoted in *Chicago Tribune*, 17 October 1961; *Chicago Sun-Times*, 22, 28 December 1961.

43. *Burroughs* v. *Board of Education*, U.S. District Court, Northern District of Illinois, Eastern Division, 62 C 206. For a discussion of some of the issues presented by this case, see U.S. Civil Rights Commission, *Civil Rights 1962*, pp. 212–15.

44. *Chicago Sun-Times*, 6 June 1962.

45. Ibid., 19 February 1962.

46. Ibid., 25 March 1962.

47. Ibid.

48. Interview, Rev. William Hogan, 15 February 1965.

49. *Chicago Sun-Times*, 24 April 1962.

50. Ibid., 26 April 1962.

51. Ibid., 27 April 1962.

52. Ibid., 12 May 1962.

53. Ibid., 12 September 1962. Other groups and institutions already represented on the nominating commission were DePaul University, Illinois Institute of Technology, Loyola University, University of Chicago, Northwestern University, University of Illinois, Roosevelt University, Chicago Association of Commerce and Industry, Chicago Medical Society, Chicago Technical Societies Council, Civic Federation, Chicago Bar Association, Citizens Schools Committee, American Legion–Cook County Council, Chicago Region–Illinois Congress of Parents and Teachers, Chicago Federation of Labor, and Industrial Union Council.

54. *Chicago Daily News*, 1 May 1962.

55. *Chicago Sun-Times*, 19 May 1962.

56. Quoted in Chicago Urban League, Research Department, "Recent Federal Court Decisions on School Segregation in the North" (1962), p. 3.

57. *Chicago Daily News*, 1 August 1962.

58. Ibid., 9 August 1962.

59. Ibid.

60. *Chicago Daily News*, 23 August 1962.

61. *Chicago Sun-Times*, 14 September 1962.

62. Pierre de Vise, *Chicago's Widening Color Gap*, Report No. 2, Inter-University Social Research Committee (Chicago: Inter-University Social Research Committee, 1967), Appendix A-3, p. 144; Appendix A-4, p. 146.

63. *Chicago Sun-Times*, 14 September 1962.

64. *Chicago Daily News*, 20 September 1962.

65. Ibid.

66. Ibid., also reported in the *Chicago Sun-Times*, 21 September 1962.

67. See *Chicago Sun-Times*, 31 October 1962 and 6 December 1962; *Chicago Daily Defender*, 31 October 1962 and 5 December 1962; *Chicago Daily News*, 30 October 1962 and 5 December 1962.

68. *Chicago Sun-Times*, 6 December 1962.

69. U.S. Civil Rights Commission, *Civil Rights, 1962*, p. 230.

70. Ibid., p. 231.

71. Ibid., pp. 198–204.

72. *Chicago Daily News*, 18 January 1962.

73. U.S. Civil Rights Commission, *Civil Rights, 1962*, p. 204.

74. Ibid., p. 232.

75. *Chicago Daily Defender*, 3 December 1962.

76. *Chicago Daily News*, 28 December 1962.

77. Joseph Pois, *The School Board Crisis: A Chicago Case Study* (Chicago: Educational Methods, 1964), pp. 43–44.

78. Benjamin C. Willis, "The Need for Professionalization in Education Today," *Chicago Schools Journal*, March 1954, pp. 273–80, quoted in Herrick, *Chicago Schools*, p. 425, n. 11.

79. De Vise, *Chicago's Widening Color Gap*, p. 103.

80. *Chicago Sun-Times*, 13 December 1962.

81. Pois, *School Board Crisis*, pp. 46–47.

CHAPTER FOUR. THE ISSUE IS JOINED: 1963.

1. Quoted in Mary J. Herrick, *The Chicago Schools: A Social and Political History* (Beverly Hills: Sage, 1971), p. 309.

2. *Chicago Daily Defender*, 19 June 1963.

3. *Chicago Sun-Times*, 11 January 1963.

4. *Chicago Daily News*, 17 January 1963.

5. Matthew Ahmann, ed., *Race: Challenge to Religion* (Chicago: Henry Regnery, 1963), pp. v, 171.
6. Jeffrey K. Hadden, *The Gathering Storm in the Churches* (Garden City: Doubleday, 1969), esp. pp. 161–207.
7. *Chicago Daily Defender*, 6 February 1963.
8. *Chicago Defender*, 2–8 February 1963.
9. The amendment to Paragraph 10:20–11 and 34:2 was as follows: "In erecting, purchasing, or otherwise acquiring buildings for school purposes, the Board shall not do so in such a manner as to promote segregation or separation of children in public schools because of color, race or nationality." The amendment to Paragraph 10:21–23 read as follows: "As soon as practicable, and from time to time thereafter, the Board shall change or revise existing [attendance] units or create new units in a manner which shall take into consideration the prevention of segregation, and the elimination of the separation of children in public schools because of color, race or nationality. All records pertaining to the creation of attendance units shall be open to the public." This amendment is reprinted in the Report of the Advisory Panel on Integration of the Public Schools, popularly known as the Hauser report. See below, chapter 5, note 6.
10. U.S. Commission on Civil Rights, *Public Education, 1963*, Staff Report Submitted to the Commission, 1963.
11. Interview, Timuel D. Black, 23 February 1965.
12. For a succinct account of the drawn-out crisis in Birmingham during 1963, see Anthony Lewis and the New York Times, *Portrait of a Decade: The Second American Revolution* (New York: Bantam Books, 1965), pp. 153–76.
13. Bayard Rustin, *Down the Line: Collected Writings of Bayard Rustin* (Chicago: Quadrangle Books, 1971), p. 108.
14. *Chicago Sun-Times*, 15 May, 12 May, 28 May 1963.
15. Quoted in Lewis, *Portrait of a Decade*, p. 169.
16. *Chicago Sun-Times*, 13 June 1963; *Chicago Daily Defender*, 13 June 1963.
17. *Chicago Sun-Times*, 13 June 1963.
18. *Chicago Defender*, 15–21 June 1963.
19. *Chicago Sun-Times*, 20 June 1963. The interpretation of this event is also based on interviews with Timuel D. Black, Charles Fischer, and Albert A. Raby.
20. *Chicago Daily Defender*, 27 June 1963.
21. See August Meier, "New Currents in the Civil Rights Movement," *New Politics* 2 (Summer 1963): 7–32, esp. p. 14.
22. *Chicago Daily Defender*, 2 July 1963.
23. *Chicago Sun-Times*, 5, 9 July 1963.
24. Ibid., 3 July 1963, editorial.
25. *Chicago Daily News*, 19 July 1963.
26. *Chicago Sun-Times*, 19 July 1963; *Chicago Daily News*, 19 July 1963.
27. *Chicago Sun-Times*, 19 July 1963.
28. *Chicago Daily Defender*, 17 July 1963.
29. Ibid., 23 July 1963; *Chicago Sun-Times*, 21 July 1963.
30. *Chicago Daily News*, 20 July 1963; see also James Q. Wilson, *Negro Politics: The*

Search for Leadership (Glencoe, Ill.: Free Press, 1960), pp. 63–65, for a general description of the world in which these aldermen moved.

31. *Chicago Sun-Times,* 26 July 1963.

32. For an account of these events in the context of CORE's inner evolution from integration to black power see August Meier and Elliott M. Rudwick, *CORE: A Study in the Civil Rights Movement, 1942–1968* (New York: Oxford University Press, 1973), pp. 213–58, esp. pp. 247–48.

33. *Chicago Sun-Times,* 19 July 1963, editorial.

34. For example, see *Chicago Daily News,* 2 August 1963; *Chicago Sun-Times,* 7 August 1963, in which stories of violence arising from the block-by-block expansion of the color line are indistinguishably mixed with reports of civil rights demonstrations.

35. *Chicago Sun-Times,* 29 August 1963.

36. Ibid., 30 August 1963.

37. Ibid., 11 September 1963.

38. Ibid., 28 September 1963; *Chicago Daily News,* 1, 3 October 1963.

39. *Chicago Sun-Times,* 21 August, 6 October 1963.

40. See Stephen D. London, "Business and the Chicago Public School System, 1890–1968" (Ph.D. dissertation, University of Chicago, 1968), p. 148.

41. *Chicago Daily News,* 7 October 1967.

42. Interviews with Foster Stockwell, 21 February 1965, and Don Rose, 15 August 1965.

43. Herrick, *Chicago Schools,* p. 320.

44. *Chicago Daily Defender,* 20 October 1963.

45. *Chicago Sun-Times,* 21 October 1963.

46. Perhaps unbeknownst to the press, the CCCO, after its public meeting in July, had adopted a policy of not sponsoring demonstrations until negotiations had been attempted and had clearly failed to produce results.

47. These demands were published in full in the *Chicago Daily News,* 21 October 1963.

48. *Chicago Sun-Times,* 23 October 1963.

49. *Chicago Tribune,* 24 October 1963.

50. Willis was not noticeably better at producing an inventory of students than he had been at producing an inventory of classrooms. In analyzing the boycott, he used a base figure of 469,733 as the total enrollment in elementary and high schools. For the racial head count, his base figure was 536,163 even though his percentages were based on 508,521, the number actually present on the day of the head count. Even though there is more than a 14 percent difference between 469,733 and 536,163, the same general picture emerges about racially separate schools. The black schools supported the boycott overwhelmingly.

51. The narrative in the following chapters, reporting the initiatives, reactions, and deliberations of the CCCO, is based on the extensive, remarkably revealing, and colorful minutes of the meetings of the CCCO recorded by Father William E. Hogan during 1964 and 1965. Without the discovery of these minutes, this study would never have occurred to us as a possibility. Nor would the interpretations offered here have occurred to us without these arresting records of deliberation and

expressed sentiment. The value of this study as we have brought it to completion is undoubtedly open to much debate, but the value of Hogan's minutes in making an internal study of the CCCO possible is beyond question. Throughout the work, we have tried to construct a study that might be suggestive of the superb primary materials on which it is based. Hogan's minutes have been supplemented with documents, interviews, newspaper reports, and surveys, and, beginning in April 1964, our own notes on CCCO meetings, but invariably his minutes have provided the primary point of reference for understanding the meaning and context of what was said and done. They are rich in the concreteness of the moments they record; and they are a living testimony to a man who was fully present to the issues, the events, the relationships, the actions, and the persons with whom he was engaged in a common enterprise whose fundamental decency can only be suggested. Unless otherwise attributed, the quotations, descriptions, and narratives in the remainder of Chapter 4 and Chapters 5 and 6 are based on the copy of Hogan's minutes transcribed by the authors and in their possession. Originals or copies of all documents quoted, unless otherwise identified, are also in the possession of the authors. Both minutes and documents are filed by date. Upon completion of this project, these materials and others indicated below will be placed in the custody of the Chicago Historical Society.

52. *Chicago Sun-Times*, 1 November 1963; *Chicago Daily News*, 5 November 1963; *Chicago Tribune*, 4 November 1963.
53. *Chicago Daily Defender*, 14 November 1963.
54. CCCO minutes, 11 November 1963.
55. U.S. Commission on Civil Rights, *Public Education, 1963*, p. 85.

CHAPTER FIVE. THE ACTION IS STALLED: 1964

1. At the beginning of 1964, the following groups were members of CCCO: Catholic Interracial Council, Chatham–Avalon Park Community Council, Chicago Urban League, Committee to End Discrimination in Chicago Medical Institutions, Congress of Racial Equality (Chicago Chapter), Cook County Bar Association, Cook County Physicians Association, Dearborn Real Estate Board, Ecumenical Institute, Englewood Committee for Community Action, Episcopal Society for Cultural and Racial Unity, Fellowship for Racial Justice Now (United Church of Christ), Interracial Council of Methodists, National Association for the Advancement of Colored People (Chicago Branch), Negro American Labor Council, Presbyterian Interracial Council, Roseland Heights Community Association, Student Nonviolent Coordinating Committee (Chicago Area Friends of), Teachers for Integrated Schools, and The Woodlawn Organization.

During 1964, the following groups became members of CCCO: Citizens Housing Committee, United Citizens Committee for Freedom of Residence in Illinois, Altgeld-Murray Parents Council, Lincoln Dental Society, National Lawyers Guild (Chicago Chapter), West Chatham Community Improvement Association, American Friends Service Committee (Chicago Office), and Chicago Area Council of Liberal Churches.

473

2. The Freedom Day Committee included representatives from CORE, Student Nonviolent Coordinating Committee, Negro American Labor Council, Committee to End Discrimination in Chicago Medical Institutions, The Woodlawn Organization, and Teachers for Integrated Schools.

3. See *Chicago Daily News*, 18, 19, 22 February 1964, editorials.

4. A. T. Burch, "Turmoil Cripples Schools," *Chicago Daily News*, 29 February 1964.

5. *Chicago Daily Defender*, 11 March 1964; Albert A. Raby, speech to second intergroup dialogue sponsored by CCCO, 19 March 1964.

6. City of Chicago, Board of Education, Advisory Panel on Integration of the Public Schools, Report, "Integration of the Public Schools: Chicago, 1964," 31 March 1964, Philip M. Hauser, Chairman (Hauser report), pp. 15–23.

7. Ibid., pp. 20, 12, 25–38.

8. "A Guide to the Study of the Report to the Board of Education by the Advisory Panel on Integration in the Public Schools," prepared by Members of the Staff of the Chicago Public Schools, 6 April 1964, pp. 1, 4–5, 7–9.

9. Quoted in Chicago Urban League, Research Department, Harold M. Baron, Co-Director, "An Analysis of the Stalemate in the Implementation of the Hauser Report," 23 July 1964 (mimeo).

10. CCCO meeting, 11 April 1964.

11. *Chicago Daily News*, 13 April 1964.

12. Ibid.

13. CCCO meeting, 25 April 1964.

14. Statement by William Cousins to Chicago City Council School Confirmation Hearing, 8 May 1964.

15. See *Chicago Defender*, 9–15 May 1964; *Chicago Sun-Times*, 19 August 1964.

16. *Chicago Daily News*, 27 May 1964, and personal observation.

17. *Chicago Daily Defender*, 28 May 1964.

18. Raby-Simpson statement, 30 May 1964.

19. *Chicago Daily News*, 15 June 1964.

20. "A Pledge of Action for Civil Rights," Illinois Rally for Civil Rights, 21 June 1964; *Chicago Sun-Times*, 22 June 1964.

21. *Chicago Sun-Times*, 23 June 1964; *Chicago Daily Defender*, 22 June 1964.

22. *Chicago Sun-Times*, 13 August 1964.

23. Edwin C. Berry, "The Need for Community Action," address, 25 July 1964 (Chicago Urban League).

24. *Chicago Daily Defender*, 6 August 1964.

25. *Chicago Defender*, 25–31 July 1964.

26. The text of this appeal is in *Crisis* 71 (August–September 1964): 468–69.

27. *Chicago Sun-Times*, 2 August 1964; editorial comment in *Chicago Tribune*, 31 July 1964.

28. "Freedom Democratic Club Program and Time-Table for Victory at the Polls, November 3, 1964" and *What Are the Freedom Democratic Clubs of Illinois?*; Howard Zinn, *SNCC: The New Abolitionists*, 2d ed. (Boston: Beacon Press, 1965), esp. pp. 242–75; and August Meier and Elliott M. Rudwick, *From Plantation to Ghetto*, 3d ed. (New York: Hill and Wang, 1976), pp. 298–99.

29. *What Are the Freedom Democratic Clubs of Illinois?*
30. *Chicago Daily Defender,* 8 September, 9 September 1964; *Chicago Daily News,* 21 August 1964; *Chicago Defender,* 22–28 August 1964.
31. *Chicago Sun-Times,* 10 October 1964.
32. Ibid., 30 October 1964; *Chicago Daily News,* 29 October 1964.
33. Statement of Albert A. Raby at Chicago Board of Education Public Hearing on Policy, 5 November 1964.
34. *Chicago Sun-Times,* 13 November 1964.
35. Robert J. Havighurst, *The Public Schools of Chicago: A Survey for the Board of Education of the City of Chicago* (Chicago: Board of Education of the City of Chicago, 1964).
36. *Chicago's American,* 28 December 1964.
37. Interview, Albert A. Raby, 11 September 1967.

CHAPTER SIX. THE DEFEAT IS DISGUISED: 1965

1. Quoted in August Meier and Elliott M. Rudwick, *CORE: A Study in the Civil Rights Movement, 1942–1968* (New York: Oxford University Press, 1973), p. 329.
2. *Chicago Sun-Times,* 7 February 1965.
3. *Chicago Daily Defender,* 13 February 1965.
4. Ibid., 8 February 1965. For an illuminating analysis of J. H. Jackson's politics and ethics, see Peter J. Paris, *Black Leaders in Conflict: Joseph M. Jackson, Martin Luther King, Jr., Malcolm X, Adam Clayton Powell* (New York: Pilgrim Press, 1978), pp. 44–69.
5. *Chicago Sun-Times,* 10 October 1964.
6. *Chicago Daily News,* 20 February 1965.
7. *Chicago Daily Defender,* 4 March 1965.
8. For a superb discussion of this significance, see W. Alvin Pitcher, "An American Crisis," *Criterion* 4 (Spring 1965):3–14.
9. CCCO meeting, 12 April 1965.
10. *Chicago Sun-Times,* 17 April 1965.
11. Ibid., 29 April, 7 May, 12 May, 23 May 1965.
12. Ibid., 28 May 1965.
13. Ibid., 2 June 1965.
14. *Chicago Daily News,* 7 and 8 June 1965; *Chicago Sun-Times,* 8 June 1965.
15. *Chicago Tribune,* 9 June 1965.
16. Interview, Albert A. Raby, 11 September 1967. At a mass meeting 31 August 1966, when some of the same militants were threatening to march in Cicero, Raby said: "I know these militants. You remember that in the spring of last year we were enjoined from boycotting the schools. The day of the injunction I was recording an interview with Miss Blair [a local television reporter] at the Conrad Hilton. When I came down, these four militant groups offered to continue organizing the community in violation of the injunction. I went right back up and was recorded violating the injunction. I then went to every TV station in town and

violated the injunction. Exhausted, I hadn't been to bed for three, four nights, and expecting arrest, I took my wife to a motel for the night. When I got up, I read what these groups had done: they had 'placed themselves under the discipline of CCCO and NAACP.' Then they had the nerve to come to a meeting that night and say they wanted to violate the injunction."

17. Ibid.
18. *Chicago Sun-Times*, 11 June 1965; *Chicago Tribune*, 11 June 1965.
19. *Chicago Sun-Times*, 13, 14 June 1965; *Chicago Tribune*, 13 June 1965.
20. CCCO meeting, 20 June 1965.
21. CCCO meeting, 16 June 1965.
22. These were Raby's concerns at CCCO meeting, 20 June 1965.
23. *Chicago Tribune*, 17 June 1965.
24. *Chicago's American*, 24 June 1965; CCCO minutes, 24 June 1965.
25. *Chicago Sun-Times*, 30 June, 1, 4 July 1965.
26. Albert A. Raby to Commissioner Francis Keppel, U.S. Office of Education, letter, and "Complaint of the Coordinating Council of Community Organizations," 4 July 1965.
27. *Chicago Sun-Times*, 7 July 1965.
28. Ibid., 8 July 1965.
29. Ibid., 8, 11, 13 July 1965.
30. Ibid., 27 July 1965; personal observation.
31. Ibid., 28 July 1965.
32. Ibid., 4 August 1965.
33. "Kup's Column," ibid.
34. Ibid., 5 August 1965.
35. *Chicago Daily News*, 11 August 1965. See Map 1.
36. *Chicago Sun-Times*, 18 August 1965.
37. Ibid., 24, 26 August, 2 September 1965.

CHAPTER SEVEN. THE SEARCH FOR A NEW BEGINNING: AUGUST 1965–JULY 1966

1. Mathew Ahmann, ed., *Race: Challenge to Religion* (Chicago: Henry Regnery, 1963), p. 96.
2. See Arthur Schlesinger, Jr., "The Evolution of the National Government as an Instrument for Attaining Social Rights," in David C. Warner, ed., *Toward New Human Rights: The Social Policies of the Kennedy and Johnson Administrations* (Austin: Lyndon B. Johnson School of Public Affairs, University of Texas at Austin, 1977), pp. 13–31.
3. Bayard Rustin, "From Protest to Politics: The Future of the Civil Rights Movement," *Commentary* 39 (February 1965): 25.
4. Lyndon B. Johnson, "Special Message to the Congress Proposing a Nationwide War on the Sources of Poverty, March 16, 1964," *Public Papers of the Presidents of the United States: Lyndon B. Johnson. Containing the Public Messages,*

Speeches and Statements of the President, 1963–64 (Washington, D.C.: U.S. Government Printing Office, 1965), 1:377.

5. U.S. Congress, *Equal Opportunity Act*, Section 2, 88th Cong., 1964.

6. Robert J. Lampmann, "Changing Patterns of Income, 1960–74," in Warner, ed., *Toward New Human Rights*, pp. 110, 112.

7. U.S. Congress, *Equal Opportunity Act*, Title II, Sec. 202a, 88th Cong., 1964.

8. Deton Brooks, "Urban Opportunity in Chicago" (Chicago: Chicago Committee on Urban Opportunity, March 1966).

9. For an account of this early period, see Seymour Mann, *Chicago's War on Poverty* (Chicago: Loyola University Center for Research on Urban Government, n.d.).

10. Lyndon B. Johnson, "To Fulfill These Rights," Commencement Address at Howard University, 4 June 1965, reprinted in Lee Rainwater and William L. Yancey, *The Moynihan Report and the Politics of Controversy* (Cambridge, Mass.: MIT Press, 1967), pp. 125–32. The quotations are from pp. 126–28.

11. Ibid., p. 128.

12. Ibid., p. 130.

13. The Moynihan report is reproduced in Rainwater and Yancey, *Moynihan Report,* pp. 39–124, as are other principal documents of this controversy.

14. Martin Luther King, Jr., Address delivered at Abbott House, Westchester County, New York, 29 October 1965, reprinted in Rainwater and Yancey, pp. 402–9. The quote is found on p. 409.

15. Here and elsewhere, we have avoided excessive footnotes, when possible, by indicating the date of the CCCO meeting in the text. This paragraph, for example, refers to the minutes of the CCCO meeting 10 August 1965. When the date of meeting is not in the text, it will be indicated in a footnote, as in notes 16–18 below.

   These minutes are in our possession; they will be placed on file at the Chicago Historical Society.

16. CCCO Minutes, 13, 20, 21 June, 4 August 1965.

17. CCCO Minutes, 21 August 1965.

18. CCCO Minutes, 6 November 1965.

19. Pitcher was associate professor of ethics and society at the Divinity School of the University of Chicago and a full-time volunteer on the CCCO staff.

20. Bevel and Lafayette had worked together in the past. As SNCC staff in 1962, they shared a house in Jackson, Mississippi. In 1963, SNCC dispatched Lafayette to Selma, Alabama, to begin a voter registration drive; Bevel addressed a mass rally of seven hundred there in mid-June. After changing his affiliation to the SCLC, Bevel joined Lafayette in Selma in January 1965 when King decided to concentrate his own voter registration activities there. See Howard Zinn, *SNCC: The New Abolitionists,* 2d ed. (Boston: Beacon Press, 1965), pp. 79, 149; David J. Garrow, *Protest at Selma: Martin Luther King, Jr., and the Voting Rights Act of 1965* (New Haven: Yale University Press, 1978), pp. 31, 39.

21. All parties to this debate agreed that grass-roots organizing was a high priority. Bevel was having difficulty organizing the entire metropolitan area on this basis, however; meantime, the CCCO was initiating its first direct community organizing efforts.

22. Gary Orfield, *The Reconstruction of Southern Education: The Schools and the 1964 Civil Rights Act* (New York: Wiley, 1969), pp. 47–101.
23. Ibid., p. 173.
24. Charles Nicodemas, "Inside Story of School Fund Thaw," *Chicago Daily News,* 6 October 1965.
25. Orfield, *Reconstruction,* pp. 180–82.
26. "The Keppel-Page Letter," *Integrated Education* 3 (December 1965–January 1966):35.
27. *Chicago Daily News,* 2, 5 October 1965; *Chicago Sun-Times,* 3 October 1965.
28. *Chicago Tribune,* 4 October 1965; *Chicago Daily News,* 5 October 1965.
29. *Chicago Sun-Times,* 3 October 1965; *Chicago Daily News,* 2 October 1965.
30. *Chicago Daily News,* 2 October 1965; Orfield, *Reconstruction,* p. 193.
31. Orfield, *Reconstruction,* pp. 193, 195; *Chicago Daily News,* 6 October 1965; *Chicago Sun-Times,* interview with Wilbur Cohen, 11 October 1965.
32. *Integrated Education* 3 (December 1965–January 1966): 35–36.
33. *Chicago Daily News,* 6 October 1965.
34. *Chicago Daily News,* 6 October 1965; *Chicago Sun-Times,* 10 October 1965.
35. Orfield, *Reconstruction,* pp. 202, 205, 206.
36. Orfield, *Reconstruction,* p. 181.
37. CCCO-SCLC Retreat, Lake Geneva, Wisconsin, 8–10 October 1965, Notes, p. 1.
38. Ibid., pp. 2–9.
39. Ibid., pp. 7–9; *Chicago Sun-Times,* 10 October 1965.
40. Retreat Notes, p. 9.
41. Ibid., pp. 11, 13, 27.
42. Ibid., pp. 11, 13, 28; CCCO Executive Committee Minutes, 6 September 1965, p. 3.
43. Retreat Notes, p. 12.
44. Ibid., pp. 10, 21.
45. Ibid., pp. 9, 10, 12, 24, 27, 31.
46. Ibid., pp. 16–20.
47. Ibid., p. 22.
48. Franklin I. Gamwell, "The West Side Christian Parish: A History of Its Decline" (M.A. paper, University of Chicago, September 1969), pp. 22–23, 27.
49. CCCO Minutes, 11 December 1965.
50. CCCO Newsletter, January 1966.
51. "A Proposal" presented by King to CCCO meeting, 6 January 1966, pp. 1–2.
52. Ibid., pp. 3–6.
53. Ibid., p. 6.
54. Ibid., pp. 6–8.
55. Ibid., p. 9.
56. Ibid., p. 9.
57. *Chicago Sun-Times,* 23 January 1966; CCCO Minutes, 28 January 1966; CCCO Newsletter, February 1966; *Chicago Daily News,* 25 February 1966.
58. CCCO Newsletter, January, February, and March 1966.
59. Ibid., March 1966.
60. Ibid., February and March 1966; *Chicago Daily News,* 25 February 1966.
61. *Chicago Daily News,* 25 February 1966; *Chicago Sun-Times,* 28 April 1966.

62. *Chicago Daily News*, 25 February 1966; *Chicago Sun-Times*, 28 April 1966.

63. *Chicago Daily News*, 18, 19 March, 6 June 1966; Philip Dripps, "The Northern Offensive: King in Chicago," *Christian Advocate*, 2 June 1966.

64. *Chicago Daily News*, 19 March, 18 April 1966; *Chicago Sun-Times*, 25 March 1966.

65. *Chicago Daily News*, 25 February 1966.

66. The steering committee at this time consisted of Rev. Shelvin Hall (WSF), Rev. Lynward Stevenson (TWO), John McDermott (CIC), Edwin C. Berry (CUL), Nate Willis (CAPCC), Robert Lucas (CORE), Mattie Hopkins (TFIS), Bernard Lucas (UPHW), P. Falk (organizational affiliation unknown), William Cousins (CAPCC), Mary Perry (CHC), Kale Williams (AFSC), William Hogan (CIC and CCCO recorder), William Robinson (FOR and CCCO treasurer), and Alvin Pitcher and Don Rose from the CCCO staff.

67. "Statement of CCCO to Chicago Board of Education Policy Hearing," 14–15 April 1966; Citizens Housing Committee, "Can Citizens of Conscience Support the New Bond Issues?" n.d. At the 7 May meeting, the following organizations joined CCCO: Lutheran Human Relations Association, Region 4 of the United Auto Workers, Englewood Civic Organization, Clarence Darrow Community Organization, Kenwood-Oakland Community Organization, and Women's International League for Peace and Freedom.

68. *Chicago Sun-Times*, 25 May, 9 June 1966.

69. Ibid., 28 May 1966.

70. The White House conference is described in Rainwater and Yancey, *Moynihan Report*, pp. 271–91.

71. *Chicago Sun-Times*, 28 May 1966.

72. Martin Luther King, Jr., *Where Do We Go from Here: Chaos or Community* (New York: Harper & Row, 1967; Bantam ed., 1968), pp. 27–37; Benjamin Muse, *The American Negro Revolution: From Nonviolence to Black Power, 1963–67* (Bloomington: Indiana University Press, 1968), pp. 235–41; August Meier and Elliott Rudwick, *CORE: A Study in the Civil Rights Movement, 1942–1968* (New York: Oxford University Press, 1973), p. 412; David L. Lewis, *King: A Biography*, 2d ed. (Urbana: University of Illinois Press, 1978), pp. 321–31; Stephen B. Oates, *Let the Trumpet Sound: The Life of Martin Luther King, Jr.* (New York: Harper & Row, 1982), pp. 395–405.

73. William H. Moyer, "An Analysis of the System of Housing Negroes in Chicago," 18 February 1966. Concerning the Cicero riots, see our discussion in chapter 8, p. 229

74. Ibid., pp. 5, 10, 11.

75. American Friends Service Committee, "Open Communities: A Prospectus for a Non-violent Project to Achieve Open Occupancy throughout the Chicago Area," March 1966, pp. 2, 3; "Negro Families Refused Service Ask Your Help," 21 May 1966.

76. Citizens Housing Committee, "Draft: Housing Program," 17 May 1966.

77. "A Program for Education," 24 May 1966; "CCCO Education Committee Meeting," 12 May 1966.

78. Both are dated 7 June 1966.

79. "Goals and Demands of the Chicago Freedom Movement," 19 June 1966, p. 1.

80. Ibid., pp. 1–17.
81. These and the following quotations are from "Chicago Freedom Movement Steering Committee Meeting," 29 June 1966.
82. "Program of the Chicago Freedom Movement," July 1966, pp. 4, 9.
83. *Chicago Sun-Times*, 2 July 1966.
84. *Chicago Sun-Times*, 5, 6 July 1966.
85. Press release, Archdiocese of Chicago, Office of the Archbishop, 10 July 1966.
86. *Chicago Tribune* and *Chicago Sun-Times*, 11 July 1966.
87. Ibid.

CHAPTER EIGHT. CONFRONTATIONS WITH VIOLENCE: JULY–AUGUST 1966

1. *Chicago Tribune*, 12 July 1966.
2. Ibid.
3. Ibid.; *Chicago Tribune*, 13 July 1966.
4. *Chicago Sun-Times*, 12 July 1966.
5. Ibid.
6. Interview, Kale Williams, 26 April 1983.
7. Bernard O. Brown, *Ideology and Community Action: The West Side Organization of Chicago, 1964–67* (Chicago: Center for the Scientific Study of Religion, 1978), pp. 49–51; *Chicago Sun-Times*, 13 July 1966; *Chicago Tribune*, 13 July 1966.
8. Brown, *Ideology and Community Action*, pp. 50–52; *Chicago Sun-Times*, 17, 19 July 1966.
9. Brown, *Ideology and Community Action*, pp. 52–53; *Chicago Sun-Times*, 17 July 1966.
10. Brown, *Ideology and Community Action*, p. 54; *Chicago Tribune*, 14 July 1966; *Chicago Sun-Times*, 17 July 1966.
11. Brown, *Ideology and Community Action*, p. 54.
12. Ibid., pp. 54–55; *Chicago Sun-Times*, 17 July 1966.
13. *Chicago Tribune*, 14 July 1966; *Chicago Sun-Times*, 17 July 1966.
14. *Chicago Sun-Times*, 15, 17 July 1966.
15. Ibid.
16. Brown, *Ideology and Community Action*, pp. 57–59; *Chicago Sun-Times*, 15 July 1966.
17. *Chicago Sun-Times*, 15, 17 July 1966; *Chicago Tribune*, 15, 16 July 1966.
18. *Chicago Tribune*, 16 July 1966. Daley was referring to workshops on nonviolence which Bevel and other SCLC staff had conducted for youth gang members. In that context, newsreels of the Watts riot had been shown to demonstrate the costs of violence and thus to encourage nonviolence.
19. Mike Royko, *Boss: Richard J. Daley of Chicago* (New York: E. P. Dutton, 1971), pp. 150–51; *Chicago Tribune*, 16 July 1966.
20. Royko, *Boss*, pp. 150–51; *Chicago Tribune*, 16 July 1966.
21. *Chicago Tribune*, 16 July 1966; *Chicago Sun-Times*, 27 July 1966.

22. *Chicago Tribune*, 16 July 1966.
23. Royko, *Boss*, p. 151.
24. This committee was usually known as the agenda committee, but on some occasions it was referred to as the steering committee. Its members included co-chairs of the Chicago Freedom Movement King and Raby, Arthur Brazier (TWO), John McDermott (CIC), Edwin C. Berry (CUL), Kale Williams (AFSC), William Robinson (FOR and CCCO treasurer), Charles Hayes (UPHW), Archie Hargraves (UTC), Arthur Griffin (WSF), Jim Wright (UAW), Clay Evans (a prominent black Baptist minister), and Chester Robinson (WSO); attending as staff members were Andrew Young and James Bevel from the SCLC and Alvin Pitcher and Jesse Jackson from the CCCO.

    Pitcher is reported to be the only person who kept notes at these meetings, and copies of these notes are now in our possession; they will be deposited at the Chicago Historical Society. The length of Pitcher's reports varies from a few words on a mimeographed agenda up to a dozen pages or more, and they are usually recorded in a unique combination of abbreviations and symbols, which do not always lend themselves to unambiguous transcription. We are confident, however, of our translation of the materials included here.

    As with our reference to the CCCO minutes, we have avoided excessive footnotes by indicating the date of the agenda committee meeting in the body of the text.
25. *Chicago Sun-Times*, 18 July 1966. This and subsequent newspaper reports did not always distinguish clearly between Gage Park, to the north of Fifty-ninth Street, and Chicago Lawn, directly to the south.
26. *Chicago Sun-Times*, 17, 19 July 1966.
27. See *Chicago Sun-Times*, 13 July 1966.
28. According to the *New York Times* that week, contributions to a number of civil rights organizations were down. Donations to the SCLC had dropped one-third in 1966 compared to the previous year; contributions to CORE were down by one-half; and SNCC was off 40 to 45 percent. The *Times* said there were three reasons for this decline: concern over "black racist" attitudes, "worry or disgust" about attacks on United States intentions and "morality" in Vietnam, and "a decline of enthusiasm now that the Northerner is being jostled by civil rights militancy in his own backyard" (*New York Times*, 25 July 1966).
29. This case, *Gautreaux v. Chicago Housing Authority*, was decided for the plaintiffs by the U.S. Supreme Court in 1976. By then, Dorothy Gautreaux, a CCCO delegate and staff member, had died of cancer.
30. James Redmond, a former assistant to Chicago school superintendent, Herold C. Hunt, had established a progressive record in race relations during his tenure as New Orleans school superintendent in the late 1950s. At the time of his appointment in Chicago, he was serving as the school superintendent in Syosset, New York.
31. Don Rose, "Open City Background Memo and Action Report," 25 July 1966.
32. Ibid.
33. Ibid.
34. *Chicago Sun-Times*, 24, 27, 28, 30 July 1966; *New York Times*, 31 July 1966.

481

35. *Chicago Sun-Times*, 30 July 1966; CCCO-SCLC press release, "Why Halvorsen Realtors?" 29 July 1966.
36. *Chicago Sun-Times*, 31 July 1966.
37. Ibid., 1 August 1966; Karen Koko, "Chicago's Race March: A Walk on the Wild Side," *National Catholic Reporter*, 10 August 1966.
38. *Chicago Sun-Times*, 1 August 1966; *Chicago Tribune*, 2 August 1966.
39. *Chicago Sun-Times*, 7 August 1966.
40. *Chicago Tribune*, 2 August 1966; *Chicago Sun-Times*, 2 August 1966.
41. *Chicago Daily News*, 2 August 1966.
42. *Chicago Daily Defender*, 3 August 1966.
43. *Chicago Sun-Times*, 2 August 1966.
44. Ibid. The reluctance and/or inability of the police to provide adequate protection for the marchers and the countercharges that the movement leaders were not giving the police sufficient notice of their plans were, like marching itself, the issues that dominated subsequent reports of the demonstrations, thus diverting public attention from the issue the movement was trying to raise, open housing (interview, Kale Williams, 26 April 1983).
45. *Chicago Sun-Times*, 3 August 1966.
46. Ibid.
47. Ibid.; *Chicago Sun-Times*, 4 August 1966.
48. *Chicago Sun-Times*, 5 August 1966.
49. Kathleen Connolly, "The Chicago Open-Housing Conference," 12 January 1967, pp. 20–22; "Mayor Richard J. Daley and Dr. Martin Luther King today issued a joint statement of cooperation," n.d.; *Chicago Sun-Times*, 4 August 1966.
50. *Chicago Sun-Times*, 5 August 1966.
51. *Chicago Tribune*, 5 August 1966.
52. *Chicago Sun-Times*, 5 August 1966.
53. *Chicago Sun-Times*, 6, 7 August 1966; David Levering Lewis, *King: A Biography*, 2d ed. (Urbana: University of Illinois Press, 1978), pp. 338–39; Connolly, "Chicago Open-Housing Conference," p. 15.
54. *Chicago Sun-Times*, 8 August 1966.
55. *Chicago Sun-Times*, 9 August 1966.
56. *Chicago Tribune*, 9 August 1966; *Chicago Sun-Times*, 9 August 1966; *Chicago Daily News*, 10 August 1966.
57. *Chicago Sun-Times*, 9 August 1966; American Friends Service Committee Chicago Regional Office, "Urban Affairs Weekly Report for Week Ending August 14, 1966," p. 2.
58. *Chicago Sun-Times*, 10 August 1966.
59. Chicago Commission on Human Relations, Minutes of Meeting, 9 August 1966; *Chicago Sun-Times*, 10 August 1966.
60. *Chicago Sun-Times*, 11 August 1966.
61. *Chicago Sun-Times*, 11 August 1966; [Kale Williams], "Notes and Comments," 10 August 1966; Maria Pappalardo, "Chicago Logs," 12 August 1966.
62. Chicago Freedom Movement, "Real Estate Brokers Could Stop the Marches in Chicago's Closed Communities," 10 August 1966.
63. *Chicago Sun-Times*, 11 August 1966.

64. Chicago Commission on Human Relations, Minutes, 9 August 1966; Connolly, "Chicago Open-Housing Conference," pp. 18–19.
65. "Statement Issued by His Excellency, The Most Rev. John P. Cody, D.D.," 10 August 1966; *Chicago Sun-Times*, 11 August 1966.
66. "Statement by Albert Raby in Response to Archbishop Cody's Appeal." 10 August 1966; *Chicago Sun-Times*, 11, 12 August 1966.
67. *Chicago Sun-Times*, 12 August 1966.
68. Ibid., 13 August 1966.
69. Ibid., 15 August 1966.
70. Ibid., 17 August 1966.

CHAPTER NINE. THE SEARCH FOR AN AGREEMENT: AUGUST 1966

1. See Appendix I for a list of those present. Unless otherwise noted, this and subsequent descriptions of the conference are taken from the accounts dictated shortly afterward by John McKnight, a participant in his capacity as director of the Midwest Field Office of the U.S. Commission on Civil Rights. The transcript of McKnight's recollections is in the authors' possession and will be deposited at the Chicago Historical Society. To keep the number of footnotes to a minimum, we have not referred to this transcript by page number.
2. *Chicago Sun-Times*, 18 August 1966.
3. [Chicago Freedom Movement], "To Achieve Justice and Make Chicago an Open City," 17 August 1966. In the press of events leading to the summit meeting, the agenda committee formulated a bargaining position only the night before the meeting convened. These nine demands were accepted as a good starting point for discussion but did not represent the full range of concerns the movement's leaders expected ultimately to put before the civic elite (interview, Kale Williams, 26 April 1983). King, for example, had opened the summit conference by asking the civic leaders to address the issues of the "dual school system" and "dual economy" as well as the "dual housing market." As it turned out, the nine specific demands were the only ones considered. The consequences of this limitation are discussed in the beginning of Chapter 10.
4. *Chicago Daily News*, 27 August 1966.
5. *Chicago Sun-Times*, 18 August 1966.
6. Spike had recently joined the University of Chicago Divinity School, coming there from his position as director of the National Council of Churches Commission on Religion and Race.
7. See demand 1 (a) through (f), above note 3 in this chapter.
8. *Chicago's American*, 18 August 1966; *Chicago Sun-Times* and *Chicago Daily News*, 19 August 1966.
9. *Chicago Tribune*, 19 August 1966.
10. *Chicago Sun-Times*, 19 August 1966.
11. *City of Chicago* v. *King*, Circuit Court of Cook County, Illinois, No. 66 CH 1938.
12. *Chicago Sun-Times*, 20 August 1966.
13. *Chicago Sun-Times*, 20, 21 August 1966.

14. Ibid., 21, 25 August 1966.
15. Ibid., 22 August 1966.
16. Ibid., 23 August 1966.
17. *Chicago Sun-Times,* 20, 23 August 1966; *Chicago Daily News,* 20 August 1966; *Chicago's American,* 22 August 1966.
18. *Chicago Sun-Times,* 21, 23, 25 August 1966; *Chicago Daily News,* 24 August 1966.
19. *Chicago Daily News,* 24 August 1966.
20. *New York Times,* 24 August 1966.
21. *Chicago Sun-Times,* 24 August 1966; Kathleen Connolly, "The Chicago Open-Housing Conference," 12 January 1967, p. 35.
22. "Project Open City" (first draft), pp. 1–2. This and the following discussion is based in part on the working documents of this committee.
23. "Project Open City" (second draft), p. 2. The first draft set 1 September 1967 as the initial target date.
24. "Report of the Subcommittee to the Conference on Fair Housing Convened by the Chicago Conference on Religion and Race," 26 August 1966. See Appendix II for the full text as it was subsequently published under the title "Agreement of the Subcommittee. . . ."
25. "Report of the Subcommittee," pp. 3–4; *Chicago Sun-Times,* 28 August 1966.
26. "Project Open City" (first draft), p. 1; "Draft," 24 August 1966, pp. 7–8; *Chicago Sun-Times,* 20, 25 August 1966; "Report of the Subcommittee," p. 11.
27. Interview, Kale Williams, 26 April 1983; see note 3 above.
28. *Chicago Daily News,* 29 August 1966; *Chicago Sun-Times,* 25 August 1966; "Report of the Subcommittee," p. 11.
29. Thus the agenda committee had never submitted its original nine demands to the CFM assembly or the CCCO delegates. Neither the summit demands nor the summit agreement was formally discussed outside the agenda committee until 16 September. According to one of the participants in the negotiating process, "During the week of the subcommittee negotiations, there were two or three meetings with the agenda committee. Due to the pressure of time, however, they could not refer the negotiations to any larger body, though some wanted to do so. The time pressures were enormous: the subcommittee itself met for about sixty hours; Swibel was attempting to make some private negotiations; the marches were continuing; the subcommittee needed to keep touching base with the Chicago Freedom Movement's representatives, etc." (interview, Kale Williams, 26 April 1983).

CHAPTER TEN. CONFRONTATIONS WITH FUTILITY: AUGUST–DECEMBER 1966

1. *Chicago Sun-Times,* 18 September 1966.
2. *Chicago Daily News,* 26 August 1966.
3. *Chicago Sun-Times,* 27 August 1966; *Chicago Daily News,* 27 August 1966.

4. *Chicago Daily Defender,* 27 August 1966.

5. *Chicago Daily News,* 26 August 1966.

6. Ibid., 27 August 1966.

7. Ibid.

8. *Chicago Sun-Times,* 30 August 1966. (The quotation is from the demonstrators' handbill, not from a *Tribune* editorial.)

9. Ibid., 28 August 1966.

10. The report of these deliberations is from Chicago Freedom Movement, Action Committee minutes, 30 August 1966.

11. Dr. Martin Luther King, Jr., and Albert A. Raby, "Open Letter to All Marchers," 30 August 1966.

12. *Chicago Tribune,* 31 August 1966.

13. Ibid.

14. *Chicago Sun-Times,* 1 September 1966; also personal observation.

15. *Chicago Sun-Times,* 1 September 1966, editorial.

16. Ibid., 11 September 1966.

17. Ibid., 3 September 1966.

18. Ibid., 5, 11 September 1966. Robert Lucas's first-person account of the Cicero march as well as his other recollections of the Chicago movement are found in Dempsey J. Travis, *An Autobiography of Black Chicago* (Chicago: Urban Research Institute, 1981), pp. 243–55.

19. For a brief history of the Leadership Conference on Civil Rights, see Neal R. Peirce, James G. Phillips, and Victoria Velsey, eds., *Revolution in Civil Rights* (Washington, D.C.: Congressional Quarterly Service, 1965), p. 40.

20. "Proposal for Participation in Project Open Housing for the Chicago Commission on Human Relations from Chicago Freedom Movement," 12 September 1966.

21. *Chicago Sun-Times,* 18 September 1966.

22. Ibid., 23 September 1966.

23. Memoranda, Follow-up Committee to Agenda Committee, 28, 30 September 1966.

24. Chicago Urban League, Research Department, "Racial Segregation in the Chicago Public Schools, 1965–1966," p. 9.

25. Timuel D. Black to Edwin C. Berry, "An Open Letter," 7 September 1966.

26. "Actions for Quality and Equality for All Public School Children in Chicago: Demands Adopted by CCCO for Presentation to James Redmond and the Chicago Board of Education," 18 October 1966.

27. *Chicago's American,* 28 October 1966; *New York Times,* 28 October 1966.

28. "Report of the Follow-up Committee of Summit Agreement," 23 October 1966.

29. *Chicago Daily News,* 2 November 1966.

30. *Chicago Sun-Times,* 4 November 1966.

31. Albert Raby, "The Movement: Divide and Conquer," *Hyde Park–Kenwood Voices,* October 1966, p. 6.

32. *Chicago Daily News,* 3 November 1966.

33. See Mike Royko, *Boss: Richard J. Daley of Chicago* (New York: E. P. Dutton, 1971), pp. 146–47. According to Royko's sources, early in 1966 Daley had called

King "a dirty sonofabitch, a bastard, a prick. . . . [King] came here to hurt Douglas [Sen. Paul Douglas] because Rockefeller gave him dough, that's why he came
here, to try to get Douglas beaten. He's a rabble-rouser, a trouble-maker."
34. *Chicago Daily News,* 3 November 1966.
35. Rt. Rev. James W. Montgomery to James W. Cook, letter, 14 November 1966.
36. Ely M. Aaron to James W. Cook, letter, 15 November 1966.
37. The following sheet was circulated at the meeting:

Englewood Fact Sheet

CENTRAL ENGLEWOOD URBAN RENEWAL PLAN (Ill. R-47):
Area—86.3 acres (appr. 14 blocks), around 63rd & Halsted retail concentration
    bounded roughly by 61st Pl. 65th, Union-Morgan
Clearance—297 buildings (233 residential)
    600 dwellings units (525 family occupied)
Rehabilitation—132 non-residential buildings (7 to be "rehabilitated" to non-
    residential use)
Re-use—"revitalized business area"
    Parking lots enlarged (from 1,200 spaces to 3,200), free
    By-pass routes for thru-traffic, curving north to 61st Pl., east to Union
    "Pedestrian mall" on Halsted, 63rd Sts.—but busses and cabs will continue to
    use both.
    Four small sites (total 3.2 acres) outside by by-pass routes, designated for resi-
    dential re-use. Maximum 48 units per acre (or 144 units), rents, unit sizes not
    specified. These sites added after publicized community opposition to "clear-
    ance for parking."
CONDITION OF AREA:
Over 80% of housing meets Chicago's definition of "standard condition"
85% of housing is Negro owned and/or occupied
Seven existing public parking lots (1,200 spaces), built by city in 1955, are 1/2 to
    1/3 empty during busy shopping days and peak periods (City survey—1962).
    Same survey shows 367 metered street parking spaces would be lost if meters
    eliminated within the Plan boundaries. (p. 26—map of metered parking)
Retail sales volume has declined since 1954, but remains second largest within
    Chicago and third largest in metropolitan area. (Nobbert Engles, pres., Chicago
    City Bank & Trust, cited 100% increase in combined earnings of 12 of the retail
    stores during period 1962 through 1964. Also stated bank showed 35% profit
    increase for 1965 over 1964; had resources of 129.5 million, highest in history:
    and made $64 million in loans, primarily for business. (CHICAGO DEFENDER, p.
    9, Jan. 11, 1966)
Central Englewood (like all of Englewood) lacks needed community facilities—
    youth, health, recreation, education, libraries, etc.

GREEN STREET ALTERNATIVES TO PLAN (proposed in 1963, '64):
Double-decking of existing parking lots (estimated cost for three lots—$800,000
    to provide over 500 additional spaces)

Conservation of housing—rehabilitation where necessary. Much housing already rehabilitated.

Creation of needed community facilities—community center with youth recreation facilities, library and study center, health center, etc.

LEGAL ACTION:

Feb., 1964—Circuit Court suit to obtain release of full plan (obtained in April through negotiation with Mayor). Suit followed year's effort to obtain plan from Chicago Department of Urban Renewal.

Appearances & testimony before all official bodies—Englewood Conservation Community Council; Dept. of Urban Renewal; Plan Commission; City Council; federal regional Urban Renewal Administration. (Washington conference with Weaver and Slayton requested Dec., 1964—not granted—federal approval announced January, 1965.)

Oct. 5, 1965—suit filed U.S. District Court, by Green Street Assn. & over 100 individual plaintiffs.

Feb. 10, 1966—suit dismissed

May 19, 1966—two count complaint filed in Circuit Court (oral argument set for October 29, 1966)

August 4, 1966—three counts appealed in U.S. Circuit Court of Appeals (no date yet for oral argument)

LEGAL ISSUES:

Alleged violations: Civil Rights Act of 1866 (property rights); Civil Rights Act of 1964 (Title VI—federally assisted programs—Chicago relocated by race); Housing Act of 1949 (no relocation plan, no true public hearing); Illinois Urban Renewal Consolidation Act of 1961 (plan fails to meet definition of "conservation area"); Amendments V, XIV, U.S. Constitution.

New Legal Issue—U.S. District Court opinion held that Civil Rights Act of 1964 was intended to protect direct "recipients" of federal grants, e.g., Chi. Dept. of Urban Renewal. Because Green St. Assn. and individual plaintiffs not such "recipients" have no standing to sue. This issue of right to sue under Title VI affects whole Freedom Movement.

38. *Chicago Daily News,* 29 November 1966.
39. For the previous five years, Holmgren had worked in Baltimore on projects aimed at expanding minority opportunities in housing, but he was well acquainted with both the personalities and institutions in Chicago. From 1946 to 1954 he had worked for the Chicago Housing Authority, which had dismissed him because of his advocacy of open housing. From 1955 to 1958, he had directed open housing projects for the American Friends Service Committee; and from 1958 to 1961 he was on the housing staff of the Chicago Urban League.
40. *Chicago Daily News,* 6 December 1966.
41. *Chicago's American,* 8 December 1966, editorial.
42. The reference is to incidents that began in 1953.
43. *Chicago's American,* 17 December 1966.

44. "Statement of Coordinating Council of Community Organizations on the Tentative 1967 Budget of the Chicago Board of Education," presented by Albert A. Raby, Convenor, CCCO, 7 December 1966.
45. *Chicago Daily News*, 21 December 1966.
46. Ibid., 23 December 1966.
47. Ibid., 19 December 1966.

CHAPTER ELEVEN. THE POLITICS OF FAILURE: JANUARY–APRIL 1967

1. *Chicago Daily News*, 10 January 1967.
2. *Chicago Sun-Times*, 12 January 1967.
3. *Chicago Daily News*, 28 February 1967.
4. Ibid., 2 March 1967.
5. Ibid., 15 March 1967.
6. Ibid., 22 March 1967.
7. Ibid., 24 March 1967.
8. Ibid.
9. Stephen B. Oates, *Let the Trumpet Sound: The Life of Martin Luther King, Jr.* (New York: Harper & Row, 1982), pp. 431–32. The sponsoring organizations of the March 25 Peace Parade and Rally were Chicago Area Committee for a SANE Nuclear Policy; Chicago Trade Union Division of SANE; Chicago Area Women for Peace; Veterans for Peace in Vietnam; Women's International League for Peace and Freedom, Chicago and Suburbs; Midwest Faculty Committee on Vietnam; Students for a Democratic Society (SDS) Midwest Regional Conference; and Chicago Area Fellowship of Reconciliation.
10. *Chicago Daily News*, 25 March 1967.
11. Martin Luther King, Jr., 14 March 1967.
12. "A Personal Letter from Al Raby," 16 March 1967.
13. *Chicago Daily News*, 27, 28 March 1967.
14. Meeting announcement and agenda for 1 April 1967 meeting of CCCO.
15. Interview, Albert A. Raby, 11 September 1967.
16. Dr. Martin Luther King, "Beyond Vietnam," 4 April 1967, Riverside Church, New York, published in *Dr. Martin Luther King, Jr., Dr. John C. Bennett, Dr. Henry Steele Commager, Rabbi Abraham Heschel Speak on the War in Vietnam* (New York: Committee of Clergy and Laymen Concerned about Vietnam, 1967), pp. 10–16.
17. *Chicago Daily News*, 10 April 1967.
18. *Chicago Sun-Times*, 13 April 1967.
19. Pitcher's notes of this meeting are not dated. From internal evidence, it took place sometime between late March and early May.
20. McDermott had published an article critical of the Chicago Catholic Archdiocese and Archbishop Cody a few months earlier. See John A. McDermott, "Chicago Catholic Asks: Where Does My Church Stand on Racial Justice?" *Look* 30 (1 November 1966): 82ff. Then on 4 March 1967, the *Chicago Sun-Times* reported

that the Chicago archdiocese no longer recognized the Catholic Interracial Council, which McDermott headed, as an official agency of the church.

21. *Chicago Sun-Times*, 9 April 1967.
22. Ibid.

CHAPTER TWELVE. THE COLLAPSE OF THE MOVEMENT: APRIL–SEPTEMBER 1967

1. *Chicago Sun-Times*, 13 April 1967.
2. CCCO, "Statement on the Permissive Transfer Plan," 12 April 1967.
3. *Chicago Daily News*, 21 April 1967.
4. Ibid., 25 April 1967.
5. Ibid., 3 May 1967; and "School of Community Organization: A Program of Education, Research and Publication for Improving Techniques of Community Organizing and Strengthening Organizations of the Poor."
6. *Chicago Daily News*, 8 May 1967.
7. Ibid., 9 May 1967.
8. Ibid.
9. Robert S. Ingersoll, letter to civic leaders announcing Project: Good Neighbor, 16 May 1967.
10. *Chicago Daily News*, 24 May 1967.
11. Ibid., 26 May 1967; 27 May 1967 and editorial.
12. Ibid., 5 June 1967.
13. Ibid., 6 June 1967.
14. Ibid., 16 June 1967; *Chicago Sun-Times*, 15 June 1967.
15. Ibid., 23 June 1967.
16. Ibid. The decision settled the *Tometz* case, which had arisen in Waukegan, Illinois, where four out of five high schools were all white and the fifth was 76 percent black. A lower court had found the Waukegan Board of Education culpable under the Armstrong Act. The Illinois Supreme Court reversed that finding and held the Armstrong Act to be unconstitutional because it was "arbitrary and unreasonable" and therefore in violation of the Fourteenth Amendment's equal protection clause. *Integrated Education* gave the following brief account of the case: "In the absence of a legislative definition of racial balance, the lower court had improperly provided its own definition. Also criticized by the high court was the fact that the Armstrong Law cited only racial considerations and omitted to consider the educational impact of enforcement on the neighborhood school system" (5 [August–September 1967]:7). This logic was too tortured for the Illinois Supreme Court to live with. About a year later, the court reversed itself, an almost unheard-of event. In reinstating the Armstrong Act, the court decided that "the issue here is whether the Constitution permits, rather than prohibits, voluntary state action aimed at reducing and eventually eliminating de facto segregation." On second thought, the Illinois Supreme Court decided the question in the affirmative. See *Integrated Education* 6 (July–August 1968):5.

489

17. *Chicago Daily News,* 29 June 1967.
18. Ibid., 8 May 1967.
19. Ibid., 8 July 1967.
20. Ibid., 12, 13 July 1967.
21. Ibid., 16 June 1967.
22. See National Advisory Commission on Civil Disorders (Kerner commission), *Report of the National Advisory Committee on Civil Disorders* (Kerner report) (New York: Bantam Books, 1968), pp. 114–15.
23. Ibid., pp. 538–39. For an unsympathetic account of the recurrent creation of commissions to study the outbreaks of violence along the color line, see Michael Lipsky and David J. Olsen, *Commission Politics: The Processing of Racial Crisis in America* (New Brunswick, N.J.: Transaction Books, 1977).
24. *Chicago Daily News,* 17 August 1967.
25. Inter-University Social Research Committee–Chicago Metropolitan Area, "Militancy for and against Civil Rights and Integration in Chicago: Summer 1967," Report 1 (Chicago: Community and Family Studies Center, University of Chicago, 1967).
26. "White and Negro Attitudes towards Race Related Issues and Activities" (Princeton, N.J.: Opinion Research Corporation, 1968).
27. City of Chicago, Board of Education, "Increasing Desgregation of Faculties, Students, and Vocational Educational Programs," 23 August 1967.
28. *Chicago Sun-Times,* 25 August 1967; *Chicago Daily News,* 25 August 1967.
29. "The Redmond Report and Its Implications," CCCO Education Committee, 8 September 1967, p. 10. One of the authors of this CCCO critique, Faith Rich, had also been an author of "De Facto Segregation in the Chicago Public Schools" ten years earlier.
30. Ibid., p. 17.
31. *Chicago Sun-Times,* 12 September 1967; *Chicago Daily News,* 12 September 1967.
32. See statement of Margaret Bush Wilson, chairman of the National Board of Directors, NAACP, 30 March 1978.
33. *Chicago Daily News,* 19, 20 September 1967.
34. Ibid., 22 September 1967.

CHAPTER THIRTEEN. THE TRIUMPH OF THE CIVIC CREDO

1. Gunnar Myrdal, *An American Dilemma: The Negro Problem and Modern Democracy* (1944; Twentieth Anniversary ed., Harper & Row, 1962), p. 1021.
2. Ibid., p. lxxv.
3. "De Facto Segregation in the Chicago Public Schools," *Crisis* 65 (February 1958): 90.
4. See Chicago Commission on Human Relations, *The People of Chicago: Five Year Report, 1947–51, of the Chicago Commission on Human Relations* (Chicago: Chicago Commission on Human Relations, 1951), pp. 43, 46, 48.

5. *Webb* v. *Board of Education of Chicago*, U.S. District Court, Northern District of Illinois, Eastern Division, 61 C1569.
6. *Chicago Sun-Times*, 6 December 1962.
7. Ibid., 6 October 1963.
8. *Chicago Tribune*, 24 October 1963; *Chicago Sun-Times*, 21 October 1963.
9. Karl E. Taeuber and Alma F. Taeuber, "Is the Negro an Immigrant Group?" *Integrated Education* 1 (June 1963): 27–28.
10. Mike Royko, *Boss: Richard J. Daley of Chicago* (New York: E. P. Dutton, 1971), p. 135.
11. Leon Festinger, *A Theory of Cognitive Dissonance* (Stanford: Stanford University Press, 1957).
12. *Chicago Daily Defender*, 3 August 1966.
13. "Project Open City" (second draft), p. 2.
14. *Chicago Daily News*, 22 September 1967.
15. It was also the beginning of the end of the Cook County Central Democratic Committee as a "biracial coalition." For an account of the "black demobilization, 1968–1976," see Paul Kleppner, *Chicago Divided: The Making of a Black Mayor* (DeKalb: Northern Illinois University Press, 1985), pp. 74–90.
16. In his *Civilities and Civil Rights: Greensboro, North Carolina, and the Black Struggle for Freedom* (New York: Oxford University Press, 1980; paperback ed., 1981), William H. Chafe describes a civic ideology in Greensboro, North Carolina, that resembles the civic credo in Chicago.

According to Chafe, "civilities" or the "progressive mystique" shared by Greensboro's white leaders was characterized by four interrelated dimensions: the affirmation of consensus rather than conflict as the key to civic progress, the willingness to discuss ideas as a substitute for implementing the changes they implied, a sense of personal responsibility for and paternalism toward blacks, and an emphasis on good manners to the extent that they were more important than more substantial actions (pp. 7–8).

Each of these ideological characteristics of civic leaders in Greensboro has its analogue in Chicago. As we have seen, the civic credo also made nonpartisan, majoritarian, consensual strategies central to the political process. Its adherents were willing to discuss criticism because they thought their democratic values required them to do so, but, as we have seen, they frequently substituted hearings for changes in policy. Chicago civic leaders emphasized the deficiencies of blacks as set forth in the civic creed's interpretation of the Negro problem and the immigrant analogy, and this led to both attitudinal and behavioral paternalism in Chicago. And because they were convinced that the civic credo was the sensible, rational perspective on race, they perceived those who disagreed as disorderly and irrational, that is, as having a severe case of bad manners. Thus, in both Greensboro and Chicago, civil rights goals were ignored because they challenged civic consensus, and civil rights methods were rejected because they were uncivil or irrational.

The independent recognition of these two similar civic ideologies in different regions of the country provides some confirmation of both, not only in relationship to these two locales but as a more general phenomenon in modern American life. Chafe suggests this more general application of civilities in a brief but provocative discussion (pp. 234–47). He anchors his notion of civilities so firmly in the local culture, however, that it is perhaps unclear what the broader institutional reasons for its power may be. To clarify this question, we have addressed the problem of American institutions in Chapter 14 before taking up the problem of American ideologies in Chapter 15.

CHAPTER FOURTEEN. THE RULE OF THE COLOR LINE

1. Dorothy Emmet, *Rules, Roles and Relations* (New York: St. Martin's Press, 1966), pp. 11–13.
2. Donald R. Matthews, "Rules of the Game," in David L. Sills, ed., *International Encyclopedia of the Social Sciences* ([New York]: Macmillan and Free Press, 1968), 13:571–76.
3. *Oxford English Dictionary,* 1933 ed., s.v. "rule."
4. Roy Wilkins, "The State of the NAACP, 1968" (New York: NAACP, 1969); excerpts published in August Meier, Elliott Rudwick, and Francis Broderick, eds., *Black Protest Thought in the Twentieth Century,* 2d ed. (Indianapolis: Bobbs-Merrill, 1971), pp. 607–10.
5. CCCO debates, fall 1966.
6. Bayard Rustin, "From Protest to Politics: The Future of the Civil Rights Movement," *Commentary* 39 (February 1965): 25–31.
7. Alan B. Anderson, "The Movement Moves North—Or Does It?" mimeo (Chicago, 1966).
8. National Advisory Commission on Civil Disorders (Kerner commission), *Report of the National Advisory Commission on Civil Disorders* (Kerner report) (New York: Bantam Books, 1968), p. 2.
9. See Herbert Wechsler, *Principles, Politics, and Fundamental Law* (Cambridge, Mass.: Harvard University Press, 1961); Raoul Berger, *Government by Judiciary* (Cambridge, Mass.: Harvard University Press, 1977); and Alexander M. Bickel, *The Supreme Court and the Idea of Progress* (New York: Harper & Row, 1970).
10. See Archibald Cox, *The Role of the Supreme Court in American Government* (New York: Oxford University Press, 1976); Ronald Dworkin, *Taking Rights Seriously* (Cambridge, Mass.: Harvard University Press, 1978).
11. *Green v. County School Board of New Kent County,* 391 U.S. 430 (1968).
12. *Swann v. Charlotte-Mecklenburg Board of Education,* 402 U.S. 130 (1971); see J. Harvie Wilkinson III, *From Brown to Bakke: The Supreme Court and School Integration, 1954–1978* (New York: Oxford University Press, 1979), p. 161. Wilkinson's interpretation appears to reflect his experience as a clerk for Justice Powell.
13. *Desegregation of the Nation's Public Schools: A Status Report* (Washington, D.C.: U.S. Commission on Civil Rights, 1979), p. 20; see also George R. Metcalf, *From Little Rock to Boston: The History of School Desegregation,* Contributions to the Study of Education, 8 (Westport, Conn.: Greenwood Press, 1983).
14. *Milliken v. Bradley,* 418 U.S. 717 (1974).

15. See Eleanor P. Wolf, *Trial and Error: The Detroit School Segregation Case* (Detroit: Wayne State University Press, 1981), for a different view of the matter.
16. Malcolm X, *The Autobiography of Malcolm X,* with the assistance of and Epilogue by Alex Haley (New York: Grove Press, 1965; paperback ed. 1966), p. 246.
17. Daniel P. Moynihan, "Memorandum for the President," 16 January 1970, in *New York Times,* 1 March 1970. He argued that blacks were making remarkable progress, further attention to them would only stir the anger of both black and white militants, and other ethnic groups needed more attention—Mexican-Americans, Puerto Ricans, American Indians, and others.
18. Malcolm X, *Autobiography,* p. 275.
19. Gunnar Myrdal, *An American Dilemma: The Negro Problem and Modern Democracy,* (1944; twentieth anniversary ed., New York: Harper & Row, 1962), pp. 53–54; italics added.
20. Karl E. Taeuber and Alma F. Taeuber, *Negroes in Cities: Residential Segregation and Neighborhood Change* (1965; rpt. New York: Atheneum, 1969), Table 4, pp. 39–41; *Chicago Tribune,* 15 May 1983.
21. Karl E. Taeuber and Alma F. Taeuber, "Is the Negro an Immigrant Group?" *Integrated Education* 1 (June 1963): 25–28.
22. William Julius Wilson, *The Declining Significance of Race: Blacks and Changing American Institutions* (Chicago: University of Chicago Press, 1978).
23. *Milliken v. Bradley,* 418 U.S. 717 (1974).
24. U.S. Commission on Civil Rights, *Racism in America and How to Combat It,* Clearinghouse Publication, Urban Series No. 1. (Washington, D.C.: U.S. Commission on Civil Rights, 1970), p. 19.
25. Lester Thurow, *The Zero-Sum Society: Distribution and the Possibilities of Economic Change* (New York: Basic Books, 1980), p. 185.
26. *A "Freedom Budget" for All Americans: Budgeting Our Resources, 1966–1975, to Achieve "Freedom from Want"* (New York: A. Philip Randolph Institute, 1966). See Thurow's discussion in *Zero-Sum Society.* An earlier effort to measure the social costs of the color line is found in R. M. MacIver, ed., *Discrimination and National Welfare* (New York: Institute for Religious and Social Studies, 1949).

CHAPTER FIFTEEN. AMERICAN CREEDS IN COMPETITION: A PROBLEM OF FAITH AND JUSTICE

Portions of Chapters 15 and 16 appeared in an earlier draft form in George W. Pickering, "The Problems of Faith and Justice," *Journal of the Interdenominational Theological Center* 11, nos. 1 and 2 (Fall 1983–Spring 1984): 57–94.
1. It is significant that critical reappraisals of the history of our religious traditions were occasioned by the course and fate of the civil rights movement. See, for example, Winthrop D. Jordan, *White over Black: American Attitudes toward the Negro, 1550–1812* (Baltimore: Penguin, Pelican Books, 1969), esp. pp. 179–215; H. Shelton Smith, *In His Image, But . . . : Racism in Southern Religion, 1780–*

1910 (Durham, N.C.: Duke University Press, 1972); and David M. Reimers, *White Protestantism and the Negro* (New York: Oxford University Press, 1965).

As Roger D. Hatch has pointed out, the issue of race has always posed a major hermeneutical problem for telling the story of religion in America. See his "Integrating the Issue of Race into the History of Christianity in America: An Essay-Review of Sydney E. Ahlstrom, *A Religious History of the American People;* Martin E. Marty, *Righteous Empire: The Protestant Experience in America;* and Robert T. Handy, *A Christian America: Protestant Hopes and Historical Realities,*" *Journal of the American Academy of Religion* 46 (December 1978): 545–70.

2. This loss of thematic unity is especially evident in the explicitly religious literature that grew up both to support and to explain the civil rights movement. Down through 1966 or 1967, this literature was decisively shaped by the desegregationist emphasis and generally looked to integration as the long-term direction for racial justice. See, for example, John O. LaFarge, *The Catholic Viewpoint on Race Relations* (Garden City, N.Y.: Hanover House, 1956); Benjamin E. Mays, *Seeking to Be Christian in Race Relations* (New York: Friendship Press, 1957; rev. ed. 1964); Everett Tilson, *Segregation and the Bible* (Nashville: Abingdon Press, 1958); Kyle Haselden, *The Racial Problem in Christian Perspective* (New York: Harper & Bros., 1959; Torchbook ed., 1964); Paul Ramsey, *Christian Ethics and the Sit-Ins* (New York: Association Press, 1961); Will D. Campbell, *Race and the Renewal of the Church* (Philadelphia: Westminster Press, 1962); James E. Sellers, *The South and Christian Ethics* (New York: Association Press, 1962); Martin Luther King, Jr., *Strength to Love* (New York: Harper & Row, 1963); Joseph T. Leonard, *Theology and Race Relations* (Milwaukee: Bruce, 1963); Martin Luther King, Jr., *Why We Can't Wait* (New York: Harper & Row, 1964); Daisuke Kitagawa, *Race Relations and Christian Mission* (New York: Friendship Press, 1964); Benjamin L. Muse, *Justice for All* (Milwaukee: Bruce, 1964); Joseph R. Washington, Jr., *Black Religion: The Negro and Christianity in the United States* (Boston: Beacon Press, 1964); George D. Kelsey, *Racism and the Christian Understanding of Man* (New York: Charles Scribner's Sons, 1965); Ralph Moellering, *Christian Conscience and Negro Emancipation* (Philadelphia: Fortress Press, 1965); Robert W. Spike, *The Freedom Revolution and the Churches* (New York: Association Press, 1965); William Osborne, *The Segregated Covenant: Race Relations and American Catholics* (New York: Herder & Herder, 1967).

The directions recommended by this body of theological interpretation, however, were in some tension with the sensibilities and activities of the membership of the churches. See Thomas F. Pettigrew and Ernest Q. Campbell, *Christians in Racial Crisis: A Study of Little Rock's Ministry* (Washington, D.C.: Public Affairs Press, 1959), including statements on desegregation and race relations by the leading religious denominations of the United States; Gerhard Lenski, *The Religious Factor: A Sociological Study of Religion's Impact on Politics, Economics, and Family Life* (Garden City, N.Y.: Doubleday, 1961), esp. pp. 120–91; Charles Y. Glock and Rodney Stark, *Religion and Society in Tension* (Chicago: Rand McNally, 1965); N. J. Demarath III, *Social Class in American Protestantism* (Chicago: Rand McNally, 1965); Jeffrey K. Hadden, *The Gathering Storm in the Churches* (Garden City, N.Y.: Doubleday, 1969).

Beginning with the black power statement by the National Committee of Negro Churchmen, 31 July 1966, the weight of religious interpretation began to shift. See Vincent Harding, "Black Power and the American Christ," *Christian Century*, 4 January 1967, pp. 10–13; Nathan Wright, Jr., *Black Power and Urban Unrest: Creative Possibilities* (New York: Hawthorn Books, 1967), which includes an appendix, "Black Power," a statement by the National Committee of Negro Churchmen, 31 July 1966; Vincent Harding, "The Religion of Black Power," in Donald R. Cutler, ed., *The Religious Situation* (Boston: Beacon Press, 1968); Joseph C. Hough, *Black Power and White Protestants: A Christian Response to the New Negro Pluralism* (New York: Oxford University Press, 1968); Albert B. Cleage, Jr., *The Black Messiah* (New York: Sheed & Ward, 1968); Charles H. Long, "The Black Reality: Toward a Theology of Freedom," *Criterion* 8 (Spring–Summer 1969): 2–7; James H. Cone, *Black Theology and Black Power* (New York: Seabury Press, 1969); Robert S. Lecky and H. Elliott Wright, *Black Manifesto: Religion, Racism, and Reparations* (New York: Sheed & Ward, 1969); C. Freeman Sleeper, *Black Power and Christian Responsibility: Some Biblical Foundations for Social Ethics* (Nashville: Abingdon Press, 1969); James H. Cone, *A Black Theology of Liberation* (Philadelphia: J. B. Lippincott, 1970); Robert W. Terry, *For Whites Only* (Grand Rapids: Eerdmans, 1970); Gayraud S. Wilmore, *Black Religion and Black Radicalism: An Examination of the Black Experience in Religion* (Garden City, N.Y.: Doubleday, 1972); Albert B. Cleage, Jr., *Black Christian Nationalism: New Directions for the Black Church* (New York: William Morrow, 1972).

3. This conflict was expressed by Benjamin Mays, who contributed to the desegregation-integration body of advice with his *Seeking to Be Christian in Race Relations*. Yet when he came to write his autobiography in 1971, the integrationist direction had lost its earlier religious self-evidence for him. "The central question confronting every black man," he wrote, "is what he can do to enlarge his freedom, to create in himself a sense of his inherent worth and dignity, and to develop his mind, body, and spirit without the imposition of artificial barriers. Are these more likely to be achieved in a separate or nationalistic society than in a so-called integrated society? There is no easy way; there are no certain answers" (*Born to Rebel: An Autobiography of Benjamin E. Mays* [New York: Charles Scribner's Sons, 1971], pp. 308–9).

4. Thomas Luckmann, *The Invisible Religion: The Problem of Religion and Modern Society* (New York: Macmillan, 1967).

5. Even within the civil rights movement, "liberal" was a derogatory term. Ever since 1962, at least, the theme had been "farewell to liberals," and it had been enunciated by a vice-president of the NAACP. See Loren Miller, "Farewell to Liberals: A Negro View," *Nation* 20 (October 1962): 235–38. By the late 1960s, there seemed to be only what were patronizingly called "old liberals." Martin Duberman, "Black Power in America," *Partisan Review* 35 (Winter 1968): 34–68, is a fine analysis, from a left-leaning perspective, that shows how left and

right began to sound more and more like each other as the civil rights movement collapsed. There were no more liberals left to define a middle that could hold left and right apart.

6. Tom Wolfe, *Radical Chic and Mau-Mauing the Flak Catchers* (New York: Farrar, Straus and Giroux, 1970; Bantam ed., 1971).

7. See Larry D. Shinn, *Two Sacred Worlds: Experience and Structure in the World's Religions* (Nashville: Abingdon, 1977).

8. See Thomas Sowell, *Race and Economics* (New York: McKay, 1976).

9. J. Harvie Wilkinson III, now a member of the federal appellate bench, provided a transparent version of the cry "whites have rights, too" in his account of judicial decisions from *Brown* to *Bakke*. Notice, in the following selection, how he is able to move from "legitimate competing ideals" to the basic affirmation of racist realism, in saying the problem "eludes the American capacity to reshape": "Both busing and affirmative action goals suffered practical drawbacks. More important, each clashed with legitimate competing ideals: the desire for neighborhood schools and color-blind admissions. Against such opposing values, the drive for racial equality began to stall. The single-mindedness of national purpose gave way to a decade of accommodation and compromise. First the Court in *Milliken* v. *Bradley* served notice that the aspirations of the majority counted constitutionally too. Then, in *Bakke,* that competing moral claims must be brokered and negotiated.

"The long voyage from *Brown* to *Bakke* has been one from optimism and confidence to confusion and doubt. School integration has entered a period of seeming contradiction: productive in one setting, disappointing somewhere else. Harmony in one school, tension in another. White flight in one city, stability elsewhere. Black academic progress here, but not there. To generalize nationwide now seems foolish. Rather, one must work to understand the particulars that explain diverse results.

"From *Brown* to *Bakke* has been a maturing journey also. Findings in the education cases laid bare the depth of American prejudice and made clear the true dimensions of our difficulties. We now seem to be many sad and wise days away from those happy forecasts of playground bliss. What we better understand is our own lack of understanding. School integration has taught us at home what Vietnam did abroad: how much eludes the American capacity to reshape. That is hardly surprising" (*From Brown to Bakke: The Supreme Court and School Integration: 1954–1978* [New York: Oxford University Press, 1979], p. 308).

10. This was the argument in *Bakke.*

11. William Bradford Reynolds, "Legitimizing Race as a Decision-Making Criterion: Where Are We Going?" (an address at Amherst College, published in *New York Times,* 30 April 1983), argues against such policies; Daniel C. Maguire, *A New American Justice* (Garden City, N.Y.: Doubleday, 1980), argues for them. See also an excellent review of Maguire by Derek A. Bell, Jr., "Preferential Affirmative Action," *Harvard Civil Rights–Civil Liberties Law Review* 16 (1982): 855–73.

12. An earlier version of this argument appeared in George W. Pickering, "The Task of Social Ethics," in W. Widick Schroeder and Gibson Winter, eds., *Belief and*

Ethics: Essays in Ethics, the Human Sciences, and Ministry in Honor of W. Alvin Pitcher (Chicago: Center for the Scientific Study of Religion, 1978), pp. 217–35.

13. Franklin I. Gamwell has pointed out that this aspect of religious pluralism generates a demand for "religious stability" on the participants: "The first common affirmation required is that all public purposes are finally to be assessed in light of some religious purpose, some all-inclusive requirement or ideal. This does not mean a common agreement regarding the substance or character of that requirement; such agreement would leave no need for debate. The constitutive conviction is simply that this body politic is judged by *some* ideal given in 'the most general context of human existence' rather than none at all. Surely debate about civil religion is defeated unless the participants agree that there is some truth to be pursued. . . .

"The second aspect of religious stability is related—namely, all participants are required to affirm that the religious demands upon public policy are to be discerned by reason and persuasion. There can be no genuine debate among religious perspectives without the common conviction that, as the Enlightenment had it, the essential truths of religion and their claims upon the civil order may be discovered by human reason" ("Religion and the Public Purpose," *Journal of Religion* 63 [July 1982]: 284–85, 286).

14. John Dewey, *The Public and Its Problems* (Denver: Alan Swallow, n.d.), p. 3.

15. Alan Gewirth, *Reason and Morality* (Chicago: University of Chicago Press, 1978), p. 140.

16. See Appendix III, "The Color Line as a Problem of Justice."

17. This same problem is posed in somewhat similar terms in Warren R. Copeland, "The Politics of Welfare Reform: An Inquiry into the Possible Moral, Political, and Religious Importance of Welfare Policy in the United States" (Ph.D. dissertation, University of Chicago, 1977), pp. 172–77; and his "The Economic Policy Debate and Sturm's 'Prism of Justice' " (paper presented to the Annual Meeting of Society of Christian Ethics, Indianapolis, 14–16 January 1983), pp. 20–24.

CHAPTER SIXTEEN. BREAKING THE RULE OF THE COLOR LINE: A PROBLEM OF DEMOCRATIC SOCIAL CHANGE

1. C. Eric Lincoln, "Beyond *Bakke, Weber,* and *Fullilove:* Peace from Our Sins, A Commentary on Affirmative Action" *Soundings* 43 (Winter 1980): 361–80.

2. William Julius Wilson, *The Declining Significance of Race: Blacks and Changing American Institutions* (Chicago: University of Chicago Press, 1978).

3. See David C. Warner, ed., *Toward New Human Rights: The Social Policies of the Kennedy and Johnson Administrations* (Austin: Lyndon B. Johnson School of Public Affairs, University of Texas at Austin, 1977); Martin Luther King, Jr., *Where Do We Go from Here: Chaos or Community?* (New York: Harper & Row, 1967; Bantam ed., 1968); "Showdown for Non-Violence," *Look* 32 (16 April 1968): 23–25, reprinted in August Meier, Elliott Rudwick, and Francis Broderick, eds., *Black Protest Thought in the Twentieth Century* (Indianapolis: Bobbs-Merrill, 1971), pp. 584–95.

4. Benjamin E. Mays, *Born to Rebel: An Autobiography of Benjamin E. Mays* (New York: Charles Scribner's Sons, 1971), pp. 320–21.

5. See Robert Eisner and Paul J. Pieper, "How to Make Sense of the Deficit," *Public Interest,* no. 78 (Winter 1985), pp. 101–18. Determining the role of federal deficits and surpluses in economic growth and full employment is far from a settled matter. Eisner and Pieper have made a strong case against the idea that it was the expansive stimulus of federal spending that fueled inflation and lowered economic growth during the 1970s. They recalculated the federal budget surpluses and deficits from 1955 to 1981, using the concept of a high-employment budget. As they explain: "to measure *the effect of the budget on the economy* rather than *the effect of the economy on the budget,* we want to look at what the budget would be at some fixed level of economic activity, or, more precisely, at some fixed level of employment or unemployment" (p. 111). Economists have used this concept of the high-employment budget for some time, but they have not generally introduced adjustments for changes in interest rates or for changes in the general price level. Eisner and Pieper did make such adjustments, and the results were surprising for the period 1955–81.

They found that "the officially reported deficit of $61 billion in 1980, for example, is converted to a $7 billion surplus when price and interest effects are considered. . . . *The entire perceived trend in the direction of fiscal ease or expansion is eliminated or reversed.* The fully adjusted high-employment budget surplus, as a percent of GNP, for every year from 1977 through 1981, was higher than the surplus of any single year going back to 1965, except for the tax surcharge year of 1969 and the oil-price-shock-year of 1974" (pp. 110, 112).

Thus, although the official budgets appeared to be in deficit, President Carter looked for ways to trim his domestic program to reduce those deficits. With both inflation and unemployment on the rise and the rate of economic growth in decline, it seemed that federal deficits no longer had the power to stimulate the economy. It was not difficult in those circumstances to sell the idea that it was time for less costly government, that the deficits were stagnating the economy.

Yet Eisner and Pieper found exactly the opposite situation in reality: "As late as 1981 we had a roughly balanced official high-employment budget . . . while that budget, adjusted for inflation effects, was substantially in surplus, by about 2 percent of GNP. And each percentage point of surplus in the inflation-adjusted high-employment budget was associated with about 2.4 percentage points *reduction* in the rate of growth of real GNP and .95 percentage points increase in unemployment. It is these inflation-adjusted surpluses, the statistical relation indicates strongly, that largely accounted for the 1981–82 recession" (p. 114).

From this analysis, it would appear that Reagan's deficit was the major cause of the recovery of 1983. "With the sharp decline in inflation and interest rates in 1982 [as a function of the recession], the high-employment budget (adjusted for price and interest effects) moved from a surplus equal to 1.97 percent of GNP in the previous year to a deficit equal to 1.77 percent of GNP . . . —the greatest such swing to expansion on record" (p. 116). This was, of course, not the point Reagan or his supply-side economists wanted to make, but their policies seemed to give new life to the Keynesian analysis after more than a decade during which even the Democrats had given up on it.

According to the Eisner and Pieper calculations, the national debt had actually been declining: "While the federal government reported budget deficits totalling $336 billion from 1947 to 1980, the market value of net federal debt grew by only $222 billion from the end of 1946 to the end of 1980. And over that period, the *real* market value of that debt (in constant 1972 dollars) *declined* by $231 billion" (p. 108).

Counting the mounting debt has been a national pastime since World War II. It is surprising to find, therefore, that even though obsessive attention has been given to the national debt, no attention has been paid to the national assets, without which there is no accurate account of the national net worth. Yet Eisner and Pieper found that "by 1980, the government's total assets far outweighed its debts, and its positive net worth was growing" (p. 102).

It is the clear implication of this analysis that the pursuit of a more inclusive structure of economic opportunity through policies to stimulate economic growth is not unrealistic on economic grounds.

6. Arthur Okun, *Equality and Efficiency: The Big Tradeoff* (Washington, D.C.: Brookings Institution, 1975).

7. See Appendix IV, "Selected Characteristics of CCCO Delegates."

8. See, for instance, Joseph Boskin, ed., *Urban Racial Violence in the Twentieth Century,* 2d ed. (Beverly Hills: Glencoe Press, 1976); and James W. Button, *Black Violence: Political Impact of the 1960s Riots* (Princeton: Princeton University Press, 1978).

9. Gene Sharp, *The Politics of Nonviolent Action* (Boston: Porter Sargent Publishers, 1973), and *Social Power and Political Freedom* (Boston: Porter Sargent Publishers, 1980).

10. Lester Thurow, *Zero-Sum Society: Distribution and the Possibilities of Economic Change* (New York: Basic Books, 1980), p. 185.

11. Ibid., Tables 7-1 and 7-2, pp. 156–57, 158.

12. *A "Freedom Budget" for All Americans: Budgeting Our Resources, 1966–1975, to Achieve "Freedom from Want"* (New York: A. Philip Randolph Institute, 1966).

13. Thurow, *Zero-Sum Society,* p. 194.

14. See, for example, J. Harvie Wilkinson III, *From Brown to Bakke: The Supreme Court and School Integration, 1954–73* (New York: Oxford University Press, 1979), p. 161; William Bradford Reynolds, "Legitimizing Race as a Decision-Making Criterion: Where Are We Going?" *New York Times,* 30 April 1983.

15. Robin Warren Lovin, "The Constitution as Covenant: The Moral Foundations of Democracy and the Practice of Desegregation" (Thesis presented to the Committee on the Study of Religion, Harvard University, March 1978). See pp. 162–80, esp. pp. 162, 168, 171, 175, and 189 (from which the quotation is taken).

16. Jonathan S. Leonard, "What Promises Are Worth: The Impact of Affirmative Action Goals," *Journal of Human Resources* 20 (Winter 1985): 3–20, shows that when affirmative action goals have actually been pursued, and not just complained

about, the results have been both beneficial and measurable even though they consistently fall short of the goal. This leads him to conclude that goals have some validity as an alternative to rigid quotas.

17. Thurow, *Zero-Sum Society,* pp. 200–201.

18. The relation between growth and equity may be advantageous to firms as well as to individuals. This argument is presented in Richard A. Fear and James F. Ross, *Jobs, Dollars, and EEO: How to Hire More Productive Entry-Level Workers* (New York: McGraw-Hill, 1983).

19. For related arguments concerning sexism, see Mary D. Pellauer, "Understanding Sexism," in Roger D. Hatch and Warren R, Copeland, eds., *Issues of Justice: Social Ethics as Practical Inquiry* (Macon, Ga.: Mercer University Press, forthcoming); and Mary D. Pellauer, "The Religious Social Thought of Three U.S. Women Suffrage Leaders: Toward a Tradition of Feminist Theology" (Ph.D. dissertation, University of Chicago, 1980).

For an inquiry concerning the color line and a religious institution, see Randolph A. Nelson, "Racism and the Lutheran Church in America: A Study of an Institutional Response to the Problem of Race in the United States" (Ph.D. dissertation, University of Chicago, 1978).

APPENDIX III. THE COLOR LINE AS A PROBLEM OF JUSTICE

1. Robert Nozick, *Anarchy, State, and Utopia* (New York: Basic Books, 1974).
2. Ibid., p. 231.
3. Alan Gewirth, *Reason and Morality* (Chicago: University of Chicago Press, 1978), pp. 135, 140.
4. Ibid., p. 294.
5. John Rawls, *A Theory of Justice* (Cambridge, Mass.: Belknap Press of Harvard University Press, 1971), pp. 60–62.
6. See, for instance, recurring arguments in David M. Reimers, *White Protestantism and the Negro* (New York: Oxford University Press, 1965).
7. Dorothy Emmet, *Rules, Roles and Relations* (New York: St. Martin's Press, 1966), pp. 11–13.
8. Ibid., p. 108.
9. Ibid., p. 178.
10. Ibid., pp. 179–80.
11. Ibid., p. 108.
12. James H. Cone, *God of the Oppressed* (New York: Seabury Press, Crossroads Books, 1975), pp. 125, 135, 137, 147, 149, 150, 207, 208, 216.

Index

501

Index

Index

511

Index

Marie
Lavigne